Dress in Anglo-Saxon England

For my son David

Dress in Anglo-Saxon England

Revised and enlarged edition

Gale R. Owen-Crocker

with drawings by Christine Wetherell and Rosalyn Smith

The Boydell Press

First published 1986
Manchester University Press
Revised edition 2004
The Boydell Press, Woodbridge

ISBN 1 84383 081 7

The Boydell Press is an imprint of Boydell & Brewer Ltd
PO Box 9, Woodbridge, Suffolk IP12 3DF, UK
and of Boydell & Brewer Inc.
668 Mt Hope Avenue, Rochester, NY 14620, USA

website: www.boydellandbrewer.com

A CIP catalogue record for this book is available from the British Library

Library of Congress Cataloging-in-Publication Data

Owen-Crocker, Gale R.
 Dress in Anglo-Saxon England / Gale R. Owen-Crocker.— Rev. and enl. ed.
  p. cm.
 Includes bibliographical references and index.
 ISBN 1-84383-081-7 (hardback : alk. paper)
 1. Clothing and dress—England—History—Medieval, 500-1500. 2. Clothing and dress—History—Medieval, 500-1500. 3. Anglo-Saxons. I. Title.

 GT732.O94 2004
 391'.00942'0902—dc22

                    2004016862

Edited, designed and typeset by
Freelance Publishing Services, Brinscall, Lancashire
Printed in Great Britain by
the University Press, Cambridge

Contents

List of illustrations

Figures

Chapter III

Chapter IV

Chapter V

Chapter VI

Chapter VII

Acknowledgements

Photographs

The photographs are reproduced by kind permission of Win Stephens; Alison Taylor; *Antikvarisk-topografiska arkivet*, The National Heritage Board, Stockholm, Sweden; The Ashmolean Musuem, Oxford, England; The British Library, London, England; Cambridge University Museum of Archaeology and Anthropology, England; Canterbury Museum, England; Corpus Christi College, Cambridge, England; The Dean and Chapter Library, The College, Durham, England; Museum of National Antiquities, Stockholm, Sweden; Museum of St Albans, Hertfordshire and Hertfordshire Archaeological Trust, England: *Nationalmuseet*, Copenhagen, Denmark; The National Museum of Wales, Cardiff, Wales; *Schleswig-Holsteinisches Landesmuseum für Vor- und Frühgeschischte-Christian-Albrechts-Universität, Schleswig/Schloss Gottorf*, Germany; Southend Museums, England; The York Archaeological Trust, York, England.

Figures

Figures i and ii are reproduced by kind permission of Manchester University Press.

Paintings and drawings

The author acknowledges with gratitude the enormous contributions of Christine Wetherell, principal illustrator of the first edition and Rosalyn Smith, principal illustrator of the revised edition. She also wishes to thank the colleagues and friends who have contributed illustrations, and who are individually acknowledged.

Colour plates D, F and G are from original watercolours by Rosalyn Smith;

Figs 121–2 were drawn by John Hines;

Fig. 238 was drawn by Robin Netherton;

Figs 147 and 214 were drawn by Patricia Reid;

Figs 3, 8, 9, 16–17, 19, 35, 40, 44, 50–52, 57, 60–61, 70–73, 87, 89, 92, 94–6, 101–2, 109, 112–14, 116, 120, 132, 136–7, 151–6, 158, 162, 164, 179–80, 195–6, 200, 206–7, 210, 212, 215–19 and 222–3 were drawn by Rosalyn Smith;

Figs 1–2, 4–7, 10–15, 18, 20–28, 34, 36–9, 41–3, 45–9, 53–9, 62–4, 66–9, 74–80, 82–6, 88, 90, 93, 97–100, 103–8, 110–11, 115, 123–9, 133–5, 138–40, 142, 144, 148–50, 157, 159–61, 163, 165–78, 181–4, 197–9, 201–5, 208–9, 211, 220–1 and 224 were drawn by Christine Wetherell;

Fig. 29 was drawn by John-Peter Wild;

Figs 117–9 were drawn by Kathleen Wood;

Figs 65, 81, 130–1, 141, 213 and 225–37 were drawn by the author;

Fig. 91 was drawn by Christine Wetherell and the author;

Fig. 143 was drawn by Christine Wetherell and Rosalyn Smith;

Figs 32, 33 were originally drawn by Christine Wetherell and adapted by Maria FitzGerald and the author.

The author also wishes to thank the following:

The British Academy, London for a grant towards new plates and drawings for the revised and enlarged edition;

Win Stephens who photographed the Faversham disc brooch;

Elisabeth Crowfoot and the late Sonia Hawkes for the lasting contributions they made to the original version of this book;

Elizabeth Coatsworth, founder and co-Director of the Manchester Medieval Textiles Project, who read part of the book in typescript, and the Project's successive Research Assistants, Maria FitzGerald and Christina Lee;

the numerous museum curators, librarians and archaeologists who have patiently answered my questions;

the many re-enactors who have asked me different and stimulating questions, some of which I have been able to answer;

Joan Horton who read both the original and the revised version in typescript;

John Hines who read part of the book in typescript;

Penelope Walton Rogers who read part of the book in typescript and supplied several helpful references;

The University of Manchester for its financial and academic support;

Richard, David and Peter Crocker for their loyal encouragement.

Note on terminology

I have used British rather than American terminology throughout this book. Thus a dress clasp with a front plate and a fastener consisting of a straight pin on a spring, secured by a catch, is called a 'brooch'. I have reserved the term 'pin' for the fastening device of a brooch ('brooch-pin'), and for the individual straight or hipped pins which do not have front plates. I use the term 'braid' for non-woven narrow wares such as tablet-woven bands. For braided hair I use the term 'plait'.

Introduction to the revised edition

My work on Anglo-Saxon dress began as doctoral research in the Department of English at the University of Newcastle upon Tyne. Deeply interested in Old English literature and enthusiastic about the material culture of the Anglo-Saxon period, I originally planned a thesis on 'Anglo-Saxon secular, non-military costume: a correlation of the literary and archaeological evidence'. It took approximately one week to discover that there was no correlation between the literary and the archaeological evidence for Anglo-Saxon dress, partly because of the time difference – the vast majority of the archaeological evidence came from furnished graves of the pagan period (fifth to early-seventh centuries) while the extant literature in Old English was written down from the ninth century onwards, most of the poetry surviving in manuscripts of the late-tenth century; and also because there was effectively no 'literary evidence' in Old English. Clothing, unless it was battle dress, was hardly mentioned, let alone described, and even armour, though lovingly mentioned by poets, was usually evoked in vague and idealised terms.

Far from being deterred, I became increasingly intrigued by the fact that while I could physically touch the mortal remains of Anglo-Saxon people by excavating their graves, and metaphorically touch their minds by appreciating their artefacts, my conception of their living presence was limited because I did not know how to dress them in my imagination. I embarked on a study of all the evidence available for Anglo-Saxon dress. Many books had been published in the nineteenth and twentieth centuries on the history of costume, yet the dress of England in the Anglo-Saxon period lacked a full treatment distinguishing it from the costume of the later Middle Ages and from medieval dress elsewhere in Europe. Some of the attempts to cover Anglo-Saxon England telescoped time and the inevitable changes which must have taken place over an era of six centuries, a distance as great as that between the present day and the Renaissance. Most information, naturally enough, had been drawn from surviving illuminated manuscripts, but it is

necessary to take into account the fact that most of these were executed in the last century-and-a-half of the Anglo-Saxon era. In
general the early centuries of the period had been treated sketchily,
by reference to (foreign) literary evidence and by very limited acknowledgement of archaeological evidence. Most of the better books
had been published so long before, that the explosion in archaeological research in the later years of the twentieth century postdated them.[1]

Archaeologists had long been aware that in excavating the cemeteries of the early (pagan) Anglo-Saxons they were revealing evidence of costume. James Douglas, a pioneer in the field, noted as
early as 1793 that 'the dead not only had a funereal garment to cover
them entirely, but that they were also entombed with their customary apparel when alive'.[2] The reports of archaeologists had usually
appeared in learned journals and by their very nature dealt with
facts: the dimensions of an object; its relationship to neighbouring
objects; its place in the established typology.[3] This context had not,
at that time, been the place for imaginative leaps and speculations
about dress, how it was made and what it signified: 'Popular Archaeology' was still in the future. However, archaeological evidence
for clothing had been a subject of postgraduate research[4] and from
the 1960s some excavators were making deductions about dress.[5]
Hayo Vierck's important work on the subject was rather obscurely
published in German[6] and not readily available in England, though
it continues to be respectfully cited in academic publications. The

[1] The student will still find the following older works useful: J. Strutt, *Horda
Angelcynnan*, 3 vols (London, 1775–6); J. Strutt, *A Complete View of the Dress and
Habits of the People of England*, 2 vols (London, 1796–9); J. R. Planché, *History of
British Costume* (London, 1847); F. W. Fairholt, *Costume in England*, 4th ed. en-
larged and revised by H. A. Dillon, 2 vols (London, 1896); G. Clinch, *English
Costume* (London, 1909).

[2] J. Douglas, *Nenia Britannica* (London, 1793), p. 56, note.

[3] Pagan Anglo-Saxon burial sites are listed, with bibliography, in A. L. Meaney,
A Gazetteer of Anglo-Saxon Burial Sites (London, 1964). There is a detailed discussion of relevant sites in G. R. Owen, 'Anglo-Saxon Costume', unpublished PhD
thesis, 3 vols (University of Newcastle upon Tyne, 1976), 1, pp. 25–407. Information on subsequent discoveries may be found in annual notes and bibliographies
in *Medieval Archaeology*, *Anglo-Saxon England* and the *Old English Newsletter*.

[4] A. M. Cook, 'The Evidence for the Reconstruction of Female Costume in the
Early Anglo-Saxon Period in the South of England', unpublished MA thesis (University of Birmingham, 1974).

[5] Notably S. C. Hawkes, review of D. M. Wilson, *The Anglo-Saxons*, Ancient
People and Places, 16 (London, 1960), in *Antiquaries Journal*, 41 (1961), pp. 106–8;
E. Crowfoot and S. C. Hawkes, 'Early Anglo-Saxon gold braids', *Medieval Archaeology*, 11 (1967), pp. 42–86; A. M. Cook, *The Anglo-Saxon Cemetery at Fonaby, Lincolnshire*, Occasional Papers in Lincolnshire History and Archaeology, 6 (1981); A.
M. Cook and M. W. Dacre, *Excavations at Portway, Andover, 1974–5*, Oxford University Committee for Medieval Archaeology Monograph, 4 (1985).

[6] H. Vierck, 'Trachtenkunde und trachtengeschichte in der Sachsen-Forschung,
ihre Quellen, Ziele und Methoden'; 'Die anglische Frauentracht'; 'Zur
angelsachsischen Frauentracht'; 'Zur seegermanischen Mannertracht'; 'Religion,
Rang und Herrschaft im Spiegel der Tracht'; and 'Von der Trachtenprovinz zur
bevolkerungs-geschichtlichen Ausage', in C. Ahrens (ed.), *Sachsen und Angelsachsen*
(Hamburg, 1979), pp. 231–43; 245–53; 255–62; 263–70; 271–83; 285–93.

tragically early death of this energetic scholar precluded any wider dissemination.

Linguistic evidence had been examined by L. L. Stroebe in a German dissertation of 1904 which is still largely valid, but only known to language specialists.[7] This academic work listed the Old English garment-names and briefly discussed the functions of the identifiable garments. The introduction to the dissertation included some evidence of costume in Latin texts and some reference to continental archaeology, but did not take into account the considerable amount of excavation which had already taken place in England nor attempt any other correlation with evidence from art. Costume historians had sometimes assigned supposedly contemporary names to the garments they described and illustrated, but no attempt to relate lexis to graphic image conveyed the enormous range of Anglo-Saxon dress vocabulary,[8] or the complexities of the subject: firstly that Old English was rich in synonyms, therefore the number of documented garment-names may exceed the number of garments in use; and secondly, that language, and fashion, are subject to change, so that a garment-name recorded in the eleventh century may have had different connotations when it was originally employed, several hundred years earlier.

When I undertook to remedy the situation and to produce a chronological survey of Anglo-Saxon dress from the full range of available sources I had to learn many new skills. Medieval studies were less interdisciplinary then than they are today, and the bibliographies of the different disciplines were quite independent. I discovered that though there were no literary descriptions in Old English there was textual evidence, particularly in the esoteric area of bilingual glosses; though (at that time) no complete secular garments were known to survive from the Anglo-Saxon period, numerous fragments of textile, often mineralised and very small, had been recorded from archaeological contexts. I read every word of Bosworth and Toller's *Anglo-Saxon Dictionary*[9] and sent for aged editions of obscure texts on inter-library loan. I pored over every figure in the illuminated manuscripts of the period in the British Library, the Bodleian Library and various Cambridge libraries. In museums I examined brooches, buckles and clasps which had secured the clothing, and learned to recognise textile and leather on them; and, like almost every other graduate student of my generation interested in the Anglo-Saxon period, it seems, I dug at Mucking.

[7] L. L. Stroebe, *Die altenglischen Kleidernamen – eine kulturgeschichtlich-etymologische Untersuchung* (Heidelberg, 1904).

[8] Useful and valid correspondences were made, notably in Planché, *British Costume*, but some other writers misleadingly ignored context or juxtaposed English with Latin terms.

[9] J. Bosworth and T. N. Toller, *An Anglo-Saxon Dictionary* (Oxford, 1898, reprinted 1976) and T. N. Toller, *Supplement* (Oxford, 1921) with Enlarged Addenda and Corrigenda by A. Campbell (Oxford, 1972, reprinted 1973).

Photocopying was hardly heard of in the Britain of the early 1970s and computing a rare skill. I used neither. In retrospect I am glad that I copied every detail by hand and considered each case individually, and repeatedly, rather than immediately seeking to categorise the material and create a database. This made me appreciate, particularly with regard to the archaeological evidence, the idiosyncratic and the recurrent. Under University regulations which set no word limit or time limit for a doctoral thesis, there was no reason why I should not be encyclopaedic; the final thesis ran to three volumes, the result of seven years' work.

The book which was written from this research (*Dress in Anglo-Saxon England*, Manchester University Press, 1986; paperback 1990) was, necessarily, a synthesis. The material was arranged in chronological chunks ('fifth- to sixth-century' etc.) because these corresponded with perceived developments in dress; they also reflected changes in the nature of the evidence. The chronological chapters were arranged in pairs, 'female dress' and 'male dress', since gender distinction in the matter of clothing was apparent at every point in the study, though some revisiting of evidence was inevitable in chapters focused round the same dates. The greater amount of evidence for female dress in the earliest chronological period dictated the order: female dress; male dress. A chapter on textiles and textile production linked the chronological chapters. The linguistic evidence was made available in two ways, compressed to a wordlist in the appendix with flags to indicate factors such as common Germanic origin and restricted, scholarly usage; and in the body of the book, as indications of the words which might have been in use in each chronological period.

The book proved useful to social and economic historians, costume historians, local historians, archaeologists, sculptors and illustrators, museum and gallery curators, language specialists and literature scholars, and even, I am told, an academic bride who devised her wedding dress from it. I had hoped that the book would have some practical application for theatrical designers and reconstructors, but this aspect of its usefulness proved much greater than anticipated. I had previously been impressed with Scandinavian museums' interactive, educational exhibits for children, with touchable copies of artefacts, at a time when reconstruction was widely considered unacademic and undesirably populist in Britain. In the 1980s and 1990s debate about the legitimacy of reconstruction was reflected in a change of attitude which saw British museums and media eager to present Anglo-Saxon dress with maximum authenticity. Institutions approached me with a view to dedicated dress reconstruction from their own regional evidence, resulting in a number of new displays. Meanwhile, numerous re-enactment groups, of which the best known are *Regia Anglorum* in England and the Society for Creative Anachronism in the USA, tirelessly continued to make, wear and thus experience, medieval costume, using *Dress in Anglo-Saxon England* and feeding back their practical application of it.

It was the constant queries I received about Anglo-Saxon clothing and requests for the book (by then out of print) from people both within and outside the academic community which prompted me to produce this completely revised and augmented version. Much of the original material has been retained, though often re-expressed, and most of the original drawings are reproduced; however the text has doubled in size and new illustrations have been added. The changes were dictated both by a large amount of new published material, by my own recent research experience and by the theoretical developments which had dominated scholarly thinking in the last decades of the twentieth century. Much of my original evidence for the pagan and conversion period had been gathered from reports in regional and national archaeological journals published throughout the nineteenth and twentieth centuries. However, the recognition of the desirability of commissioning properly funded, comprehensive, illustrated studies with reports by experts in appropriate fields (an idealistic but complex undertaking) had resulted in a backlog of typescript material, some of which was lodged with English Heritage for as long as twenty years, and was not generally available when *Dress in Anglo-Saxon England* was written. This has now appeared in print; indeed the millennium saw the publication of many archaeological sites relevant to costume study, some of them in substantial monographs. Meanwhile, some of the older archaeological material had been reassessed in the light of recent scholarship.[10] My own interest in textiles had been refocused in the 1990s in relation to a joint project, conceived by my colleague Elizabeth Coatsworth of Manchester Metropolitan University, to produce a database of all the medieval textiles of the British Isles. Much of the Anglo-Saxon material was already known to me, unpublished reports having been supplied by the generosity of textile expert Elisabeth Crowfoot, but the appearance of the recent comprehensive archaeological publications made it possible to view those textiles in context, as well as revealing important new material. Lise Bender Jørgensen's research project on north European textiles in the first millennium[11] related regional differences in early Anglo-Saxon textiles to wider geographical and cultural context, provoking debate as to the relative importance of regional or chronological criteria.[12]

---

[10] See for example, E. Southworth (ed.), *Anglo-Saxon Cemeteries: a reappraisal* (Stroud, 1990).

[11] See L. Bender Jørgensen, *Forhistoriske Textiler i Skandinavien. Prehistoric Scandinavian Textiles* (Copenhagen, 1986); 'The textiles of the Saxons, Anglo-Saxons and Franks', *Studien zur Sachsenferschung*, 7 (1991), pp. 11–23; *North European Textiles until AD 1000* (Aarhus, 1992).

[12] See P. Walton Rogers, 'Textiles and clothing', in G. Drinkall and M. Foreman, *The Anglo-Saxon Cemetery at Castledyke South, Barton-on-Humber*, Sheffield Excavation Reports 6 (Sheffield, 1998), pp. 274–9 and microfiche Mf. 2.B13-C12.

Early Anglo-Saxon archaeology had been slow to catch up with other 'New Archaeology', in that it remained tied to historical sources, especially Bede's *Ecclesiastical History*, and continued to concentrate on the typology of decoration on artefacts. In the 1980s the traditional approaches were giving way to 'Processualist' archaeology, where, with the emphasis on 'explicitness and quantification' provided by computerised data, theorists examined the ecological, economic and social causes for the processes that formed and changed culture.[13] The 1980s and 1990s saw the advent of 'Post-processualist theory' which encouraged archaeologists to read the evidence (in this case, of furnished graves) as constructs potentially representative of cultural aspects such as gender, ethnicity and status. The symbolism of grave-goods was discussed by Ellen-Jane Pader,[14] and Karen Brush considered the significance of dress fasteners and accessories in early Anglo-Saxon graves.[15] The pagan and conversion period grave-finds, particularly women's, were also the subject of important studies by Nick Stoodley[16] and Helen Geake.[17] I had, from the beginning of my research, always been conscious that the furnished grave consisted of what the mourners desired should be seen; and that as regards clothing, that desired effect might not be exactly as the dead person would have appeared in everyday life: it could be, for example, 'best clothes', or costume symbolising status or a role in the community. Yet to reject the evidence of archaeology on these grounds would be unnecessarily negative. Those who deposited the dead wished to convey a particular image in each case, and that is what I accepted. In the present reworking of existing material and incorporation of new, however, I have paid particular attention to post-processualist-type 'reading' of cemetery evidence, especially the concept of gendered grave-goods. The fact that there appears to be a 'male kit' and a 'female kit' with regard to pagan grave-goods is an obvious but nonetheless fascinating aspect of early Anglo-Saxon archaeology which has given rise to much research on questions such as: Which artefacts are gendered and which not? How are graves which are not obviously gendered to be 'read'? What is the relationship of 'gendered grave-goods' to biological sex? I had pondered the possibility of cross-

---

[13] See K. M. Wickham-Crowley, 'Looking forward, looking back: excavating the field of Anglo-Saxon archaeology', in C. E. Karkov (ed.), *The Archaeology of Anglo-Saxon England: basic readings*, Basic Readings in Anglo-Saxon England, 7 (New York and London), pp. 1–23.

[14] E.-J. Pader, *Symbolism, Social Relations and the Interpretation of Mortuary Remains*, British Archaeological Reports, International Series, 130 (1982).

[15] K. A. Brush, 'Adorning the Dead; the Social Significance of Early Anglo-Saxon Funerary Costumes in England (5th–6thc. AD)', unpublished PhD thesis (University of Cambridge, 1993).

[16] N. Stoodley, *The Spindle and the Spear: a critical enquiry into the construction and meaning of gender in the early Anglo-Saxon burial rite*, British Archaeological Reports, British Series, 288 (1999).

[17] H. Geake, *The Use of Grave-Goods in Conversion-Period England, c. 600-c. 850*, British Archaeological Reports, British Series 261 (1997).

dressing when devising my original structure of pairs of chapters for the book, and had concluded that if the mourners had dressed a dead person in 'male kit' or 'female kit' the result was 'men's costume' or 'women's costume' in the terms of my definitions. Nick Stoodley's recent study, which includes re-sexing of some skeletons, shows that there are some apparently female skeletons with weapons and some male with brooches and clasps, though the positions of the objects are not always typical of female burials. The number of such cases is statistically small, however, and I felt confident in retaining my chapter headings.

Although there have been some attempts to distinguish Celts from Saxons anatomically[18] we still lack biological criteria for the ethnicity of the persons buried in Anglo-Saxon cemeteries. Regional characteristics are mostly exhibited through women's grave-goods, but we do not know how a woman's regional affiliation was established: through birth, marriage, place of habitation of a mixture of these. I have contented myself with pointing out regional trends, and noting some unusual cases. Computer databasing makes it possible to formalise the ranking of grave-goods, certain objects counting as high status and precious metals obviously indicating wealth, but I have felt it important to consider examples in context – that a grave might be wealthy within a particular cemetery but not in relation to national standards – and have remained aware that simple quantity of excavated grave-goods may be misleading as an indicator of status, since organic objects may have disappeared completely.[19]

The Middle Saxon period (eighth and ninth centuries) has always been the most obscure part of the era for modern historians. As a source of costume history this period produces a small number of unique, major, pieces of evidence: it gives rise to our only description of dress in Anglo-Saxon England by an Anglo-Saxon (Aldhelm) and one of our very few recognisable garments (the recently-discovered 'shirt' from Llan-gors, near Brecon, Wales). There is also evidence from the excavation of occupation sites at Brandon, Suffolk and Flixborough, North Lincolnshire; finds from Barking Abbey, Greater London, and jewellery buried in a container in the eighth-century grave at Boss Hall, Ipswich, Suffolk. These archaeological finds have increased our evidence for clothing in the period since the first publication of *Dress in Anglo-Saxon England*. In terms of a 'wider picture', however, the Middle Saxon remains more elusive than other periods.

Dress research has been made considerably easier by the appearance of a number of comprehensively illustrated books which

---

[18] See p. 35 n.1.

[19] I have explored this topic in a forthcoming article: G. R. Owen-Crocker, 'Gold in the ground or just rust in the dust: measuring wealth by metalwork in Anglo-Saxon graves', in R. Bork (ed.), *De Re Metallica: studies in medieval metals and metallurgy*, (forthcoming, 2004).

were not available when the first edition of *Dress in Anglo-Saxon England* was in preparation. These include the catalogues of two major British Museum Anglo-Saxon exhibitions,[20] David Wilson's colour facsimile of The Bayeux 'Tapestry',[21] Thomas Ohlgren's *Anglo-Saxon Textual Illustration*,[22] particularly valuable for its publication of the illustrated psalter, London, British Library, MS Harley 603, and the most recent volumes of the Early English Manuscripts in Facsimile series and the British Academy Corpus of Anglo-Saxon Stone Sculpture series.

Old English lexis has become much more accessible in recent years, with major research projects in Toronto and Helsinki. The Toronto Old English Dictionary originally on microfiche, now CD ROM, still in progress,[23] is much more user-friendly than Bosworth/Toller, though it will be some time before the whole alphabet has been covered and Bosworth/Toller remains an essential research tool. Since Bosworth/Toller's citations were compiled there have been many improved and more readable editions of Old English texts, including a computerised corpus[24] and computerised editions of individual texts, though they have added little to the corpus of garment names I published in 1986.[25] Concordances on microfiche[26] and computer[27] are valuable new resources, though the scholar needs good knowledge of Old English to exploit them.[28] The innovative University of London *Thesaurus*[29] has made it possible for the first time to search for Old English words under subject headings and with its judicious use of flags, guides the reader with regard to frequency of usage, though dress terms are not easily found in the book.[30]

[20] J. Backhouse, D. H. Turner and L. Webster (ed.), *The Golden Age of Anglo-Saxon Art* (London, 1984); L. Webster and J. Backhouse (ed.), *The Making of England: Anglo-Saxon art and culture AD 600–900* (London, 1991).

[21] D. M. Wilson, *The Bayeux Tapestry* (London, 1985).

[22] T. H. Ohlgren, *Anglo-Saxon Textual Illustration: photographs of sixteen manuscripts with descriptions and index* (Kalamazoo, MI, 1992).

[23] A. C. Amos, A. Di Paolo Healey, J. Holland, C. Franzen, D. McDougall, I. McDougall, N. Spiers, P. Thompson, *Dictionary of Old English* (Toronto, 1986–).

[24] *The Complete Corpus of Old English on Machine Readable Form*, Dictionary of Old English Project, Centre for Medieval Studies, University of Toronto, 1994 edition, indexed and concorded with WordCruncher for DOS 4.50.

[25] In compiling the *Thesaurus* (below, nn. 29, 30), according to a personal communication from Jane Roberts, editor, the only addition to my own findings appears to be a refinement of our knowledge of fur clothing from a post-Conquest entry in the D version of the *Anglo-Saxon Chronicle*: in the eleventh century there were garments of grey squirrel and ermine and garments which combined fur with fine cloth (see p. 244).

[26] A. diPaolo Healy and R. Venezky, *A Microfiche Concordance to Old English*, Publications of the Dictionary of Old English, University of Delaware (1980).

[27] WordCruncher, see note 24.

[28] Non-specialists may sample Old English on labyrinth (www.georgetown.edu/labyrinth link to Old English pages) and sourcebook (www.fordham.edu/halsall/sbook.html).

[29] J. Roberts and C. Kay, with L. Grundy, *A Thesaurus of Old English,* King's College London Medieval Studies, 11, 2 vols (London, 1995).

[30] The relevant section is 4, Material needs, 04.04–04.04.10. The key word which appears in the list of contents is 'Weaving' but the section covers clothing and jewellery, listing useful associated terms such as 'to fix the weft' and 'poorly clad' .

Potential research material on Anglo-Saxon dress is therefore more accessible than it used to be. Interdisciplinarity has become the norm in Anglo-Saxon studies, and though the student may need to seek out a specialised publication, the reference to that source is made available through multi-subject bibliographies.[31] Web-sites are an obvious starting point for many researchers, but they vary in reliability and the scholar must be careful to discriminate, and to question the sources and chronology of any material used. It may be more economical of time to go straight to a scholarly bibliography. The reader might take warning from a serious-minded research assistant's recent attempt to investigate medieval leather garments through the world wide web, which was rewarded with some dazzling pornography!

---

[31] See note 2.

I

A historical framework

The Migration Age

The Anglo-Saxon era began in the fifth century. The traditional date (AD 449) is established by the English historian Bede,[1] and the fact that a cultural change occurred in the east and south of mainland Britain at this time is confirmed by archaeological evidence, especially the characteristic dress accessories which were deposited in graves. The newcomers were Germanic peoples, who crossed the North Sea from their overcrowded homelands to occupy areas of the country which had been the Roman province *Britannia*.[2] This resettlement was just part of a regrouping and shifting of populations which took place in north-west Europe as the Roman Empire disintegrated.[3]

It is now recognised that 'germanism' is something of a modern construct. Inevitably scholars reflect the culture of their own age, and nineteenth-century research on Germanic folklore and language, influenced by contemporary movements of patriotism and unification, created a picture which is being increasingly questioned today. We now acknowledge that cultural ethnicity is not the same as biological identity, also that the membership of an 'ethnically' named group may be different at different historical periods. Migration Age tribes disappear and reappear in history; some of

[1] *Historia Ecclesiastica*, I, 15; B. Colgrave and R. A. B. Mynors (ed.), *Bede's Ecclesiastical History of the English People* (Oxford, 1969), pp. 48–9. Bede locates the arrival of Germanic mercenaries in the year of accession of the Roman emperor Marcian. That the migration was neither single, nor of coherent culture, nor confined to the middle of the fifth century will be demonstrated in the following chapter.

[2] For a detailed study of the settlement the reader is referred to J. N. L. Myres, *The English Settlements*, The Oxford History of England, 1B (Oxford, 1986) and for an authoritative history of the Anglo-Saxon period as a whole to F. M. Stenton, *Anglo-Saxon England*, The Oxford History of England, 2 (Oxford, 3rd ed., 1971). For a useful reference work on Anglo-Saxon persons, places and culture see M. Lapidge, J. Blair, S. Keynes and D. Scragg (ed.), *The Blackwell Encyclopaedia of Anglo-Saxon England* (Oxford, 1999).

[3] H. Ament, 'The Germanic tribes in Europe', in D. M. Wilson (ed.), *The Northern World: the history and heritage of northern Europe AD 400–1100* (London, 1980), pp. 47–70.

them apparently maintained their group identity and blood, others may not have done.[4] 'Ethnicity' may be political, even class-related.[5] As Ian Wood reminds us, the artefacts which signify 'ethnicity' to archaeologists are not mentioned in contemporary texts.[6] These artefacts are often from women's graves, and the 'ethnicity' of women, whether hereditary or acquired through marriage is another area of obscurity.

Despite these reservations, it is clear that the so-called Germanic peoples, who, in the days of the Roman Empire, had occupied territory stretching north–south from Scandinavia to the Danube, east–west from Gaul to beyond the Vistula, shared, to some extent, a common cultural heritage. For example, they spoke various dialects of a language which was Germanic (unlike the Celtic speech of the Britons or the Latin of the Romans) and acknowledged the Northern, rather than the Roman, pantheon of gods. It seems reasonable to suppose, that since they retained and nourished their barbarian culture in spite of the proximity of the Roman Empire, the Germanic tribes might have resembled one another in matters of dress, though (again projecting backwards from a modern mainland Europe in which large areas have only recently emerged from folk- and national costumes) strong regional variations in matter of detail might be expected. In fact, although extremes of appearance, such as extravagant hairstyles, were noted by contemporary observers, modern research points to a lack of national identity with regard to costume and appearance in general.[7]

Many of the Germanic peoples will be mentioned in this book as influences upon or comparisons to the Anglo-Saxons so a brief outline of their geographical distribution here will help to set the scene. An East Germanic group, the Goths, had made a long and indirect migration from the Baltic; in the fifth century the Visigoths established their powerful kingdom in the Iberian peninsula and southern Gaul, and the Ostrogoths theirs in Italy. Some of the techniques and decorative motifs which appear in Anglo-Saxon jewellery of the sixth and seventh centuries have been attributed to Gothic influence.[8] Within what had been Roman *Germania*, small tribes of obscure origin were coalescing into larger political units and

[4] P. J. Heather, 'Disappearing and reappearing tribes', in W. Pohl with H. Reimitz (ed.), *Strategies of Distinction: the construction of ethnic communities, 300–800*, The Transformation of the Roman World, 2 (Leiden, 1998), pp. 95–111.

[5] I. Wood, 'Conclusion: strategies of distinction', in Pohl with Reimitz, *Strategies of Distinction*, pp. 297–303.

[6] Wood, 'Conclusion: strategies of distinction', pp. 299–300.

[7] W. Pohl, 'Telling the difference: signs of ethnic identity', in Pohl with Reimitz, *Strategies of Distinction*, pp. 17–69.

[8] Cloisonné jewellery, probably transmitted to England by the Franks, may have come from the east via the 'Sarmato-Gothic' culture of the Black Sea region; G. Speake, *Anglo-Saxon Animal Art and its Germanic Background* (Oxford, 1980), p. 29; the predatory bird heads which are a feature of the largely seventh-century art style Salin Style II may also be eastern ('Scythian-Sarmatian') and may also have been carried westward by the Goths; Speake, pp. 14–15. Speake discusses the regional/historical background of early Anglo-Saxon art styles (pp. 5–37), which being largely manifested on personal jewellery, are not irrelevant to costume history.

gradually occupying territories formerly within the boundaries of
the Roman Empire. The Alamanni, the first to establish themselves
in this way, had already moved from the Elbe to the Rhine-Danube
region by the mid-third century, although it was only towards the
end of the fifth that power became centralised and the Alamannic
peoples a kingdom. The Alamanni could be claimed the earliest
Germanic inhabitants of Britain, as the Romans had forcibly settled a group of them in northern England in the second century,
but their chief interest for costume historians lies in *Reihengräber*
('row-graves') of the Continental Alamannic cemeteries, which have
been very productive of dress fasteners and accessories,[9] as well as
textile remains.[10] The Burgundians, who had also migrated south-
westwards, were, in the mid-fifth century, settled around Lake
Geneva in a state of reduced numbers and power after defeat by
the Romans. The Langobards, or Lombards, migrated from territory north of the Danube to Pannonia (now western Hungary)
before settling in northern Italy in the mid-fifth century. The
movement of tribes from central Germany made way for a new
formation, which, in the fifth century, was being called by the
new name of Thuringia; the federates probably included the Angles of Denmark, significant contributors to the population of
Anglo-Saxon England. In the course of the fifth century, Thuringia
was to extend south to the Alamannic region and north towards
the North Sea Coast, probably even taking over territories once
held by the Franks and Saxons, two tribes of major importance
for our present purpose.

The Franks, whose origins probably lay in the area between
the Weser and the Rhine, had moved in considerable numbers into
Gaul in the fourth century and, by the middle of the fifth, were
ruling in what is now northern France and north-west Germany.
By the end of that century Childeric had established the powerful
Merovingian kingdom. Frankish influence is an important factor
in the development of Anglo-Saxon culture in general and dress
fashions in particular. Franks may have been among the earliest
settlers, and later Frankish immigrants to Kent brought innova-
tions in jewellery and women's dress fashions. In the sixth century
the marriage of Bertha, the daughter of the king of Paris, to King
Æthelbert of Kent must have brought further Frankish fashions,
though it is the fact that this alliance led to the conversion of the
Anglo-Saxons to Christianity which has gone down in history. The
conversion in itself, however, influenced dress fashions, both in
terms of Christian emblems on dress accessories and in terms of
morality. There were repeated Frankish contacts of various kinds.
In the eighth century, King Offa of Mercia traded with the Franks,

[9] R. Christlein, *Die Alamannen* (Stuttgart, 1978).
[10] The textile evidence from graves of the Migration and Merovingian periods
in Germany and the Netherlands is summarised in Bender Jørgensen, *Prehistoric
Scandinavian Textiles*, pp. 336–8.

and cloaks were among the merchandise exchanged. In the ninth, King Æthelwulf of Wessex took a Frankish bride as his second wife; the attraction of Frankish culture to his son, King Alfred, was to have long-term effects on English scholarship and art, which also affected dress in the late Anglo-Saxon period.

In the centuries immediately before the migration and settlement of England, to the north of the Franks, in the coastal regions round the Elbe and Weser and along the lower reaches of those rivers, the Saxon peoples were living. Like the other great Germanic tribes, the Saxons had probably emerged from an amalgamation of smaller groups. By the fourth century they seem to have been expanding westward along the coast of Frisia. The Saxons' proximity to the sea made them natural voyagers and raiders; they had been making attacks on Roman Britain and northern Gaul since at least the third century. Conversely, some of their number had been employed as mercenaries by the Romans to guard against barbarian attacks on eastern England, which was known as 'The Saxon Shore', their presence demonstrated for us by cremation urns of typically Germanic taste. Through raiding and defence, the English coastline must have been well known among the Saxons before the decision to migrate was taken.

It was the Saxons, together with two peoples from the Danish peninsula, whom Bede named as the original English settlers, in a well-known passage from his *Historia Ecclesiastica*:[11] the Jutes (from Jutland, mainland Denmark) were said to have settled Kent, the Isle of Wight and the area of the south coast which is opposite the Isle of Wight; from Old Saxony came the settlers of areas which became known as the East, South and West Saxon kingdoms; and from Angeln came the settlers who occupied Mid-Anglia, Mercia, Northumbria and other Anglian areas. This is now acknowledged to be an over-simplification, both in terms of the rigid distinctions between the three groups and their areas of settlement, and also in its omission of other Germanic peoples. Bede was clearly rationalising the regional divisions of his own day (the early-eighth century). The heterogeneity of early archaeological finds suggests that the tribes had already mingled on the Continent before the migration to Britain and that the invaders were of mixed stock: objects typical of the Continental Saxon area have been found in 'so-called' Anglian areas of England, and vice-versa. There were, however, certain regional variations which became more marked in the century following the invasion, which justify the subdivision and the labels 'Angle' and 'Saxon'; women's dress is one of the most distinctive of these features. Bede's differentiation of the peoples of Kent and the Isle of Wight from the Angles and Saxons is certainly justified, but historians and archaeologists agree that the Jutes of Denmark did not provide the only, or the most striking source of the distinctive 'Kentish' culture. Again it is in dress

[11] *Historia Ecclesiastica*, I, 15; Colgrave and Mynors, p. 50.

fashions, especially women's dress, that these ethnic characteristics, in this case more heterogeneous ones, appear.

Almost certainly there were other Germanic people among the immigrants. Bede himself, in a lesser-known passage of his *Historia*, mentions Frisians, *Rugini*, Danes, Huns, Old Saxons and the *Boructari* as ancestors of the Anglo-Saxons.[12] The Frisian element is fairly certain: Procopius, a Byzantine scholar, identified Anglo-Saxon settlers as Anglian and Frisian,[13] and the resemblances between the Old English language and Old Frisian[14] suggest that there had been a mingling with the Frisian people in the course of a prolonged south-westerly migration. Archaeological evidence confirms this contact, but also suggests that there might have been a hasty movement of groups of people from Frisia and north Germany in the fifth century when the encroachment of the sea on their homeland forced their removal.[15] (The *terpen* or artificial mounds along the North Sea coast on which the remaining Frisian population continued to live, have been a rich source of archaeological evidence, especially comparative textile material.)[16]

Other Germanic groups came a little later. A Frankish element in the archaeology of Kent, which is not present in the early sites, suggests that there was an influx of wealthy Frankish people from about the year 500, for two generations.[17] Settlers from western Norway seem to have come to eastern England in the late-fifth to early-sixth centuries.[18] The Wuffing dynasty who ruled East Anglia may have migrated from Sweden in the sixth century.[19] Other contributors to the Anglo-Saxon population might have included some 'Swabians' a generic name for a number of tribes originally in north and east Germany, suggested by the survival of the place-name Swaffham in both Norfolk and Cambridgeshire.[20] There may also have been descendants of the Alamannic people who had settled in the country three centuries before.

[12] *Historia Ecclesiastica*, V, 9; Colgrave and Mynors, p. 476.

[13] Procopius *History of the Wars*, VIII, xx, 7; H. B. Dewing, trans., *Procopius*, 7 vols, Loeb Classical Library (London, 1914–40), 5, pp. 254–5.

[14] W. H. Bennett, 'The southern English development of Germanic initial [f s þ]', *Language*, 31 (1955), pp. 367–71; D. De Camp, 'The genesis of the Old English dialects', *Language*, 34 (1958), pp. 232–44; M. L. Samuels, 'Kent and the Low Countries: some linguistic evidence', in A. J. Aitken, A. McIntosh and H. Pálsson (ed.), *Edinburgh Studies in English and Scots* (London, 1971), pp. 3–19.

[15] S. C. Hawkes, 'Anglo-Saxon Kent *c.* 425–725', in P. E. Leach (ed.), *Archaeology in Kent to AD 1500 in memory of Stuart Eborall Rigold*, Council for British Archaeology Research Report, No. 48 (London, 1982), pp. 64–78, at p. 65.

[16] Summarized in Bender Jørgensen, *Prehistoric Scandinavian Textiles*, pp. 335–6.

[17] Hawkes, 'Anglo-Saxon Kent', p. 72.

[18] J. Hines, *The Scandinavian Character of Anglian England in the Pre-Viking Period*, British Archaeological Reports, British Series, 124 (Oxford, 1984), pp. 108–9.

[19] R. Bruce-Mitford, *Aspects of Anglo-Saxon Archaeology: Sutton Hoo and other discoveries* (London, 1974), pp. 55–60. Hines questions this; *Scandinavian character*, p. 289.

[20] C. Hills, 'The archaeology of Anglo-Saxon England in the pagan period', *Anglo-Saxon England*, 8 (1979), pp. 297–329, at p. 297, citing E. Ekwall, *Dictionary of English Place-names* (Oxford, 4th ed., 1960), p. 455; C. Hills, 'The Anglo-Saxon settlement of England', in D. M. Wilson (ed.), *The Northern World* (London, 1980), pp. 71–94, at p. 84.

The Anglo-Saxon settlement of England was not decided by a single battle and a resolution of rivalry between candidates for kingship, as the Norman Conquest would be in 1066. Clearly the Anglo-Saxon settlers consisted of different types of migrants, coming from and to different areas and with variable degrees of organization. Some were apparently *foederati*, Germanic soldiers who had served with the Romans: as early as *c.* 420 men wearing Roman-style belt equipment and women wearing Germanic dress and brooches were settled in southern England. Small groups of them were buried at Dorchester-on-Thames, Oxfordshire,[21] and at Mucking, Thurrock.[22] Tradition, according to the contemporary Welsh historian Gildas, followed by Bede, asserts that the first settlers came as a mercenary force (evidently to Kent) to defend the Britons against the northern peoples (the Picts).[23] There may have been other organized invading forces, such as the alliance of Franks and Saxons whom Vera Evison has identified south of the Thames in the mid-fifth century.[24] At the opposite extreme were the refugees from Frisia escaping the encroaching sea and impossible living conditions at home. There were probably many parties of adventurers, optimists and misfits seeking a new land but bringing their cultural identity with them, Germanic rather than Roman, but already, in some cases, a mixture of customs from different places within the Germanic area.

The Germanic tradition

The Anglo-Saxons retained a consciousness of where they had come from[25] and continued to celebrate traditional features of the war-orientated, Teutonic lifestyle recorded by the first-century Roman historian Tacitus, long after the disappearance of tribal society. Though not entirely immune to Roman influence, there is no doubt that on their arrival in England their dress, like other aspects of their culture, was northern Germanic rather than Roman, and that subsequent changes were the consequence of political, economic and religious developments. At several points in this study,

[21] J. R. Kirk and E. T. Leeds, 'Three early Saxon graves from Dorchester, Oxon.', *Oxoniensia*, 17–18 (1954), pp. 63–76. Nine bronze bars found among the ribs of the male skeleton, originally interpreted as part of a sporran-like leather apron, were later reconstructed as the stiffening of a belt; V. I. Evison, 'Quoit brooch Style buckles', *Antiquaries Journal*, 48 (1968), pp. 231–46, at pp. 238–40. The 'Germanic mercenary' question is discussed, with reference to Continental grave-finds, in S. C. Hawkes, 'Soldiers and settlers in Britain, fourth to fifth century', *Medieval Archaeology*, 5 (1961), pp. 1–70 and in Hills, 'The archaeology of Anglo-Saxon England in the pagan period', pp. 279–308.

[22] Evison, 'Quoit brooch Style buckles', pp. 231–4.

[23] *De Excidio*, 23; M. Winterbottom (ed. and trans.), *Gildas The Ruin of Britain and Other Works* (London and Chichester, 1978), pp. 26 (English) 97 (Latin); *Historia Ecclesiastica*, I, 15; Colgrave and Mynors, pp. 48–53.

[24] V. I. Evison, *The Fifth-century Invasions South of the Thames* (London, 1965).

[25] See N. Howe, *Migration and Myth-Making in Anglo-Saxon England* (New Haven, 1989).

therefore, a parallel from Continental *Germania* may be used to shed light on the more obscure evidence from Anglo-Saxon England. We will find, for example, a very similar gown for women attested in Iron Age Denmark, in the Rhineland in the first and second centuries AD and in Viking Scandinavia, which helps to identify that women in England in the fifth and sixth centuries wore a characteristic Germanic costume which apparently went out of fashion among the Anglo-Saxons by the seventh century.

The illiteracy of the Anglo-Saxons for the century-and-a-half after the settlement inevitably leaves a gap for the historian. Fortunately Roman authors wrote about their barbarian neighbours, and it has become customary for students of the Anglo-Saxon period to seek parallels to and explanations of Anglo-Saxon traditions in Roman observations of the Continental Germans. Their comments are particularly interesting when we are considering the first generations of Anglo-Saxons, since they were closest to the Germanic family.

Classical observers naturally noted the differences between the Romans and the barbarians; points in common may have been ignored. Several Roman authors mention the appearance of the Germanic peoples, often focusing on their Nordic colouring, exotic hairstyles and some unfamiliar dress fashions which were found rather shocking. The evidence of Julius Caesar (from about the middle of the first century BC) stressing as it does the habitual nakedness of the barbarians,[26] is admittedly negative; it does, however, pinpoint the importance of furs, which were undoubtedly a vital part of the clothing of the northern people throughout antiquity and the Middle Ages, though they are rarely depicted or mentioned in Anglo-Saxon sources.[27] Stephen Glosecki suggests that the wearing of animal skins may have been to some extent talismanic, in that the act invoked the powers of the animal.[28]

Regarding the physical hardiness of the Germans, Caesar writes:

… se consuetudinem adduxerunt ut locis figidissimis neque vestitus praeter pelles haberent quidquam, quarum propter exiguitatem magna est corporis pars aperta …

---

[26] Neolithic man had worn garments of flax, and the selective breeding of sheep for wool probably began in the Iron Age; M. L. Ryder, 'European wool types from the Iron Age to the Middle Ages', in L. Bender Jørgensen and K. Tidow (ed.), *Textilsymposium Neumünster: Archäologische textilfunde: 6.5–7.5. 1981 (NESAT I)* (Neumünster, 1982), pp. 224–38, at pp. 224–5. Wool was certainly worn in Denmark, for instance, before Caesar's time; so Caesar's barbarians need not have gone naked unless they were extremely uncivilized, or nomadic and so without resources or, as he says, hardy.

[27] G. R. Owen-Crocker, 'The search for Anglo-Saxon skin garments and the documentary evidence', in E. A. Cameron (ed.), *Leather and Fur: aspects of early medieval trade and technology* (London, 1998), pp. 27–43.

[28] S. O. Glosecki, *Shamanism and Old English Poetry* (New York and London, 1989), p. 182 (with specific reference to the quotation from Tacitus given below).

They have regularly trained themselves to wear nothing, even in the coldest localities, except skins, the scantiness of which leaves a great part of the body bare.[29]

The point is repeated when Caesar praises the chastity of these people in the face of their openness and immodesty about their bodies:

... cuius rei nulla est occultatio, quod et promiscue in fluminibus perluuntur et pellibus aut parvis renonum tegimentis utuntur magna corporis parte nuda.[30]

... and there is no secrecy in the matter, for both sexes bathe in the rivers and wear skins or small cloaks of reindeer [or other] hide,[31] leaving great part of the body bare.

The *Germania* of Tacitus, a tract written in AD 98, is generally considered a reliable description of Germanic customs, although its purpose was not just anthropological; the author had an ethical agenda in that he intended to highlight Roman decadence by pointing out the morality of the Germans. Tacitus mentions that the German people in general were blue-eyed, reddish-haired and tall,[32] and he describes the costume habitually worn by both sexes:

tegumen omnibus sagum fibula aut, si desit, spina consertum: cetera intecti totos dies iuxta focum atque ignem agunt. locuplectissimi veste distinguuntur, no fluitante, sicut Sarmatae ac Parthi, sed stricta et singulos artus exprimente, gerunt et ferarum pelles, proximi ripae neglegenter, ulteriores exquisitius, ut quibus nullus per commercia cultus. eligunt feras et detracta velamina spargunt maculis pellibusque beluarum, quas exterior Oceanus atque ignotum mare gignit, nec alius feminis quam viris habitus, nisi quod feminae saepius lineis amictibus velantur eosque purpura variant, partemque vestitus superioris in manicas non extendunt, nudae brachia ac lacertos; sed et proxima pars pectoris patet.

For clothing all wear a cloak, fastened with a brooch, or, in its absence, a thorn: they spend whole days on the hearth round the fire with no other covering. The richest men are distinguished by the wearing of underclothes; not loose, like those of Parthians and Sarmatians, but drawn tight, throwing each limb into relief. They wear also the skins of wild beasts, the tribes adjoining the riverbank in casual fashion, the further tribes with more attention since they cannot depend on traders for clothing. The beasts for this purpose are selected, and the hides so taken are chequered with the pied skins of the creatures native to the outer ocean and its unknown waters. The women have the same dress as the men, except that very often trailing linen garments, striped with purple, are in use for

---

[29] *Gallic War*, IV, 1; H. J. Edwards (trans.), *Caesar The Gallic War*, Loeb Classical Library (London, 1917), pp. 182–3.

[30] *Gallic War*, VI, 21; Edwards, *Caesar*, pp. 346–7.

[31] Reindeer would have been unknown to Caesar. Two citations explain *reno* as *agnitis*, 'of lambskin', in C. D. F. Du Cange, *Glossarium Mediae et Infimae Latinatis*, with supplements, ed. and revised by L. Faure (Niort, 1883–87); see Owen-Crocker, 'Anglo-Saxon skin garments', pp. 27–9.

[32] *Germania* 4; W. Peterson and M. Hutton, *Tacitus Dialogues, Agricola, Germania*, Loeb Classical Library (London, 1914), p. 268.

women: the upper part of this costume does not widen into sleeves: their arms and shoulders are therefore bare, as is the adjoining portion of the chest.[33]

The description of tailored skin garments is partly corroborated by skin capes found in Danish peat bogs which were made of several pieces of skin,[34] though the information that they could be made from sea creatures, perhaps seals, is unique. The description on the whole is ambiguous for the modern reader. What were those features of women's costumes that resembled men's? Did the women wear the 'underclothes'? Were their bare arms covered by cloaks or skins? Crucially, what was the exact nature of the mens' *veste* (trouser-like or tunic-like)? The wearing of trousers had originally distinguished the barbarian people from the Greeks and Romans, and the classical world regarded these garments with some contempt, although the Romans themselves adopted them from the third century. The exiled poet Ovid noted the 'stitched breeches' (*sutis ... bracis*), which, along with skin garments, kept out the cold for the barbarians of Tomis (now Constanţa, Romania), his reluctant dwelling-place,[35] and as we will see (p. 115; Fig.1) Germanic men were sometimes depicted in trousers on Roman sculptures. Moreover, a seated female figure personifying *Germania* humiliated by Rome is depicted on coins of the Roman Emperor Domitian as naked to the waist and wearing breeches which are clearly visible over her thighs.[36]

It seems that men's hairstyles differed from tribe to tribe.[37] Some fashions were undoubtedly militaristic. Tacitus tells us that the Chatti, a western tribe, allowed their hair and beard to grow until they killed an enemy.[38] The Swabians fastened their hair up in a knot at the side of the head,[39] a style well attested from Roman sculptures (Fig. 1) and a macabre archaeological find (Fig. 2). Tacitus tells us that this style was the mark of a freeman. He observed that young men who were not Swabians were copying the style in his day. The fifth-century poet Sidonius confirms and adds to Tacitus's observations. His comment on Frankish servants with 'oily top-knots'[40] suggests that by his time the Swabian knot hairstyle had spread to lower classes as well as other tribes. He notes that Saxon

Fig. 1 Swabian knot hairstyle on Roman sculpture, Adamklissi Monument, Romania

[33] I have slightly modernised the translation.

[34] E. Munksgaard, *Oldtidsdragter* (Copenhagen, 1974), Fig. 91; M. Hald, *Ancient Danish Textiles from Bogs and Burials*, trans. J. Olsen, English edition, Publications of the National Museum of Denmark, Archaeological-Historical Series, 21 (Copenhagen, 1980), Figs 359–73.

[35] *Tristia*, 3.10.19; also see 5.7.49; A. L. Wheeler, *Ovid in six volumes VI Tristia; Ex Ponto*, second ed., revised G. P. Goold, Loeb Classical Library (Cambridge, MA and London, 1938), pp. 136–7, also pp. 238–9.

[36] See, for example A. S. Robertson, *Roman Imperial Coins in the Hunter Coin Cabinet*, 1 (London, 1962), pp. 287, 288, 293, 296, Plates 50, no. 27 and 51, no. 70

[37] For further details of Germanic hair colour and hair styles see Pohl, 'Telling the difference'.

[38] *Germania* 31; Peterson and Hutton, *Tacitus*, p. 309.

[39] *Germania* 38; Peterson and Hutton, *Tacitus*, p. 317.

seamen were blue-eyed and adds the fact that they shaved their hair round the hair-line, making their faces seem enlarged.

Istic Saxona caerulum videmus
assuetum ante salo solum timere;
cuius verticis extimas per oras
non contenta suos tenere morsus
artat lammina marginem comarum,
et sic crinibus ad cutem recisis
decrescit caput additurque vultus.

Here in Bordeaux we see the blue-eyed Saxon afraid of the land, accustomed as he is to the sea; along the extreme edges of his pate the razor, refusing to restrain its bite, pushes back the frontier of his hair and, with the growth thus clipped to the skin, his head is reduced and his face enlarged.[41]

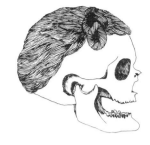

Fig. 2 Swabian knot hairstyle on a skull, Osterby, Denmark

Sidonius also observes the appearance of the Franks, which is of interest to us since Franks were almost certainly among the settlers of south-east England and since the Continental Franks remained in communication with the Anglo-Saxons in the centuries following the migration. Again he focuses on a striking hairstyle, but also mentions facial hair and clothing:

… rutili quibus arce cerebri
ad frontem coma tracta iacet nudataque cervix
saetarum per damna nitet, tum lumine glauco
albet aquosa acies ac vultibus undique rasis
pro barba tenues perarantur pectine cristae.
strictius assutae vestes procera cohercent
membra virum, patet his altato tegmine poples,
latus et angustam suspendit balteus alvum.

… on the crown of whose red pates lies the hair that has been drawn towards the front, while the neck, exposed by the loss of its covering, shows bright. Their eyes are faint and pale, with a glimmer of greyish blue. Their faces are shaven all round, and instead of beards they have thin moustaches which they run through with a comb. Close-fitting garments confine the tall limbs of the men; they are drawn up high so as to expose the knees, and a broad belt supports their narrow middle.[42]

We find then, a short garment, either a tunic or short trousers for men, quite unlike the long looser garments which the Roman tradition dictated for adult males. As we shall see, the fashion of a short, girdled tunic for men, and a long, sleeveless robe for women, accompanied in both cases by a cloak, seems to have been carried from Continental Germany and Scandinavia to Anglo-Saxon England.

[40] *Poems*, V, line 226; W. B. Anderson (trans.), *Sidonius Letters and Poems*, Loeb Classical Library, 2 vols (London, 1936–65), 1, p. 80.
[41] *Letters*, Book VIII, ix, 5, lines 21–7; Anderson, *Sidonius*, 2, pp. 446–7.
[42] *Poems*, V, lines 238–45; Anderson, *Sidonius*, 1, pp. 80–3.

Fig. 3 Piled-up hair on Anglo-Saxon Pot Lid 3324, Spong Hill, Norfolk

Fig. 4 Moustached face on early Anglo-Saxon button brooch, Alfriston, East Sussex

Evidence of early Anglo-Saxon hairstyles being extremely rare, the observations of the Roman authors on this matter are interesting. An androgynous figure on a pot lid from a pagan Anglo-Saxon cemetery at Spong Hill, Norfolk (Fig. 3), has what might be described as a 'top knot', which, while different from the asymmetrical Swabian knot hairstyle, suggests a continuation of the custom of coiling up the hair. The fondness of the Germanic people for shaving is confirmed by (rare) finds of razors and is consistent with late Anglo-Saxon art, where beards are in the minority and are used to indicate age and authority. The moustache without beard is a feature of faces on early Anglo-Saxon button brooches (Fig. 4) and it recurs in the eleventh-century Bayeux 'Tapestry' where it initially distinguishes the English from the Normans. The curious Frankish hairstyle which left the neck exposed may have derived from the ritual of a militaristic nation, for Sidonius mentions elsewhere the Frankish practice of cropping the back of the head after defeat.[43] This hairstyle seems to have survived as a fashion, rather than a militaristic ritual, in eleventh-century Normandy, since the Norman men in the Bayeux 'Tapestry' generally wear their hair this way (Figs 5, 6); in some cases the 'Tapestry' artist exploits it to contribute to the menacing appearance of the Normans.

Anglo-Saxon poets constantly evoked aspects of the Germanic tradition, particularly the heroic ethos of men loyal to a conquering lord, and we might have hoped for the preservation of costume evidence in this literature, especially the long heroic poem *Beowulf*. In fact, unlike the authors of later medieval romances, Old English poets had no interest in describing clothing. In *Beowulf* we learn that a garment might be a precious possession, since clothing is among the gifts presented by Wealhtheow, the queen of Denmark, to the hero as his reward for carrying out a magnificent deed. The poet may have thought a garment a particularly appropriate gift for a lady to give, since textile production was traditionally women's work; but the poet refers to the gift as *hrægl*,[44] one of the commonest and most non-specific of Old English garment-names. Adding to the ambiguity, *hrægl* is a neuter noun which requires no inflexion to make it plural. Possibly the hero was being rewarded with a single magnificent garment; possibly he was being heaped with rewards, including (plural) 'garments and rings'. In general the authors of Old English heroic poetry were only interested in garments which were war-gear. The mail corselet (*byrne*) shone brightly[45] and it also *sang* (the Old English word), the iron rings chinking as its owner moved,[46] or clanking as weapons struck it in battle.[47] The *Beowulf*-poet is fond of referring to helmets, traditionally decorated

---

[43] *Letters*, Book VIII, ix, lines 28–30; Anderson, *Sidonius*, 2, pp. 446–7.

[44] *Beowulf*, line 1195; G. P. Krapp and E. V. K. Dobbie (ed.), *The Anglo-Saxon Poetic Records: a collective edition*, 6 vols (*ASPR*) (London and New York, 1931–42), 4, *Beowulf and Judith*, ed. E. V. K. Dobbie (1953), p. 37. The Modern English, now archaic, 'rail' (as in 'night-rail') derived from *hrægl*.

[45] *Beowulf*, lines 321–2; Dobbie, *Beowulf and Judith*, p. 12.

with figures of boars, gilded and shining, which were supposed to protect the wearer from harm.[48] However, of the garments worn underneath the mailcoat, the everyday costume of lords and servants, and of the women who are mentioned only occasionally in this heroic world, we are told nothing.

There is one form of personal adornment frequently mentioned by Anglo-Saxon poets: the ring (*beag, hring*). From *Beowulf* we learn of arm-rings (*earmbeagas*)[49] and neck-rings.[50] Neck-rings were owned by both men and women, and the Queen possibly wore a ring on her head since she is described as *under gyldnum beage*,[51] 'under a golden ring'. Rings are not generally well represented in Anglo-Saxon archaeology, with the exception of finger-rings, and though they are occasionally shown in Anglo-Saxon art, they are depicted as isolated valuable objects, not being worn (Figs 158, 223). The Continental evidence therefore is valuable in confirming that the objects mentioned in literature certainly existed. Hoards of rings have been discovered from earlier Scandinavian contexts as well as from the Viking Age and an engraved silver plate now in the *Real Academia de la Historia*, Madrid, depicts Germanic soldiers in neck rings (Fig. 7) attending Emperor Theodosius I.

Figs 5, 6 The Norman hairstyle in the Bayeux 'Tapestry' on a standing figure, on a horseman

The settlement

The Anglo-Saxon settlers seem to have arrived in England in relatively small groups. Most either landed on the coast and settled nearby, or travelled up a river, building their village and beginning to farm near its banks. Some journeyed along existing Roman roads to penetrate their new country but generally they did not occupy Roman towns. By the middle of the fifth century immigrants were arriving in such numbers that their language and culture came to dominate large areas of the country, which accordingly became known as *Englaland* ('land of the Angles'). The exact fate of the Celts who were the previous inhabitants of these areas is not clear. Left to their own devices after the withdrawal of responsibility by the Roman Empire *c*. 410, the Britons had enjoyed some short-term prosperity before plague and attacks by Saxon pirates, the Picts and the Scots weakened them. Gildas wrote bitterly of bloodshed, exile and slavery at the hands of the Germanic invaders[52] but modern scholars believe that peaceful co-existence and inter-marriage must have taken place in some areas; it may be significant that some

Fig. 7 Germanic soldier in neck ring attending Emperor Theodosius I; on a silver plate, *Real Academia de la Historia*, Madrid

[46] *Beowulf*, lines 322–3; Dobbie, *Beowulf and Judith*, p. 12.
[47] *The Battle of Maldon*, lines 284–5; E. V. K. Dobbie (ed.), *The Anglo-Saxon Minor Poems*, ASPR, 6 (1942), p. 15.
[48] *Beowulf*, lines 303–5; Dobbie, *Beowulf and Judith*, p. 11.
[49] *Beowulf*, line 2763; Dobbie, *Beowulf and Judith*, p. 85.
[50] *Dyde him of healse hring gyldenne*, 'He took from his neck the golden ring'; *Beowulf*, line 2809; Dobbie, *Beowulf and Judith*, p. 87.
[51] *Beowulf*, line 1163; Dobbie, *Beowulf and Judith*, p. 36.
[52] *De Excidio*, 24–5, 1; Winterbottom, *Gildas*, pp. 27–8, 97–8.

early Anglo-Saxon kings descended from Germanic immigrants had Celtic names, suggesting that their mothers might have been Britons.[53] It was probably from Roman-Celtic tradition that inhabitants of some areas learned the technique of weaving 2 x 1 twill on a two-beam loom and the art of finishing cloth by a form of fulling; but continuity of this kind seems to have been the exception rather than the rule, just as the transmission of the Celtic language and Celtic art to the Anglo-Saxons was intermittent and unusual.[54]

The immigrants' crafts were almost totally Germanic, equipment of *foederati* apart, owing little to the culture of the Romans and practically nothing to the native Celts. The Anglo-Saxons built their homes, for example, of wood, not stone or brick. Their pottery was hand- not wheel-made and their jewellery was shaped and decorated according to barbaric taste, although, as the Germanic people had lived close to the Roman Empire for a long time, they had absorbed and adapted some classical motifs. The migrants must have brought with them the necessities of life including tools, livestock and personal possessions. Some of the earliest jewellery, including equal-armed brooches and saucer-shaped brooches decorated with a running scroll, may well have come to England with the immigrants, either clasping their clothing or safely packed as treasured possessions. When the settlers' garments wore out they had to make new from the resources around them, and they did so using the warp-weighted wooden loom as they had done in their homeland. The basic techniques of spinning and weaving they employed were the traditional methods learned at home on the Continent but the mixing of the migrating peoples resulted in a greater variety of cloth being produced in Anglo-Saxon England than in either mainland Europe or Scandinavia. Lise Bender Jørgensen's comparative study suggests that at the Migration period Scandinavian textiles were predominantly Z/Z-spun 2 x 2 twill wool, and that tablet weaving also originated from this area; whereas Z/S-spun twills including diamond twill and tabby-woven linen were to be found further south in mainland Europe, in the area of Frankish culture.[55] All these varieties can be found in early Anglo-Saxon graves. The archaeological evidence suggests the costumes made from these various textiles were of a traditional Germanic kind, but no doubt there were many distinctions that have been lost to us.

No contemporary historian has given us an account of how the Anglo-Saxon settlers dressed, and they themselves, being illiterate

---

[53] C. Clark, 'Onomastics', in R. M. Hogg (ed.), *The Cambridge History of the English Language I: the beginnings to 1066* (Cambridge, 1992), pp. 452–89, at p. 463.

[54] Exceptionally, the art of Northumbria was strongly influenced by the traditions of Ireland and Iona because of the Celtic mission of St Aidan.

[55] Bender Jørgensen, *Prehistoric Scandinavian Textiles*, pp. 253–4; Z/S spinning and diamond twill had been known earlier in Scandinavia (probably imported from the Roman Empire), but had ceased by the Migration period; Bender Jørgensen, 'The textiles of the Saxons, Anglo-Saxons and Franks'.

at this point, have left no documentary evidence. They were accomplished artists, as their decorated metalwork and pottery shows, but they preferred abstraction to naturalism, zoomorphic and geometric designs to humanistic; the rare representations of human beings from the migration and settlement period – mostly faces only – show almost nothing about dress.

Yet there is tangible evidence of costume. The Anglo-Saxons had not, at this time, been converted to Christianity and it was their pagan custom to supply the dead with grave-goods – possessions necessary for some future existence apparently envisaged as not unlike life in this world. Thus, before cremation or burial, the dead might be equipped with such items as food, tools and personal property, and were evidently dressed in clothing which was fastened and ornamented with jewellery. The grave-goods they wore or took with them to their funeral may have expressed their status and place in the culture of the community. Hundreds of pagan Anglo-Saxon burial grounds, dating from the fifth to the seventh centuries, have been found and excavated in modern times. Although a cemetery may not represent an entire community,[56] and there are unfurnished graves in most burial grounds, thousands of furnished burials have been examined and grave-goods recovered intact. In excavating inhumation cemeteries, archaeologists have found metal fasteners and ornaments associated with the clothing, positioned as they were when the corpse was buried: brooches, for example, at the shoulders, buckles at the waist. In some instances, fragments of textile or leather have survived, attached to the metalwork. From evidence such as this, with the help of comparative material from the Continent, particularly Germanic persons depicted on (naturalistic) Roman sculptures, we can attempt to reconstruct the appearance of the Anglo-Saxons in the first centuries after their arrival.

The emergence of kingdoms

About the year 500, vigorous resistance by the Britons temporarily halted the Germanic intrusion and for a generation the invaders failed to advance further into the country; some re-migrated. By the later part of the sixth century, however, the Anglo-Saxons were firmly established in England, which was divided into kingdoms ruled by dynasties of diverse origin. In the early stages of separation into kingdoms there were the 'Anglian' realms of Bernicia, Deira, Mercia, Lindsey, Middle Anglia and East Anglia; 'Saxon' regions of Essex, Middlesex, Wessex and Sussex; the Jutish/Frankish areas of Kent and the Isle of Wight; and minor kingdoms in the west: the Hwicce, Magonsætan, Tomsætan and Wrocensætan. There

[56] The relative scarcity of children has been noted. The poor or enslaved may not have been included.

is no evidence that costume varied much from kingdom to kingdom except in Kent and the Isle of Wight. The observable differences seem to relate more to the traditionally Anglian, Saxon and
Kentish regions than to the individual kingdoms: different regions
exhibit different tastes in jewellery and Anglian women's costume
has some extra features.

The kingdoms did not enjoy equal prosperity or longevity; kingdoms expanded, contracted and disappeared. The late-sixth and
seventh centuries are often called 'The Period of the Heptarchy'
reflecting the emergence of the seven strongest kingdoms, many of
which had absorbed smaller units. Usually one or other of the kingdoms was dominating all or most of the others, a factor which may
have limited the development of regional tastes. Bede lists seven
rulers whose kingdoms, in turn, held sway south of the Humber.[57]
The *Anglo-Saxon Chronicle* supplies the information that the title
held by these pre-eminent kings was *Bretwalda*, or *Brytenwalda*,
'Ruler of Britain'.[58] The reign of the first *Bretwalda*, Ælle of Sussex
(*c*. 477–*c*. 514) encompassed the years of settlement and defeat by
the Britons at the battle of *Mons Badonicus*. The years before the
recovery are marked by the absence of a *Bretwalda* until Ceawlin of
Wessex, who succeeded in 560 and probably reigned until 591,
though his overlordship may have ended with a British victory in
584. He was succeeded as *Bretwalda* by two major figures, the first
being Æthelbert of Kent, whose Frankish marriage and long domination of southern England were of great importance to the political, religious and cultural development of the nation, including
among its effects the establishment and dissemination of Frankish
dress fashions among the élite in and beyond Kent. Æthelbert died
in 616, when the already powerful King Rædwald of East Anglia
was acknowledged *Bretwalda*. It was probably for Rædwald, who
died in 625, that the famous ship burial at Sutton Hoo was created,
which included in its grave-goods a unique collection of masculine
jewellery and items of clothing.[59]

After Rædwald's reign the southern kingdoms experienced a
temporary domination by the northern, under a series of Northumbrian *Bretwaldas*. (Northumbria was composed of Bernicia and
Deira, originally separate kingdoms.) Edwin of Northumbria, who
married Æthelberg, the daughter of Æthelbert of Kent, acquired
his throne with the help of Rædwald of East Anglia, whom he succeeded as *Bretwalda*. Both men seem to have shared a consciousness
of Roman heritage and an appreciation of Roman style, which in

[57] *Historia Ecclesiastica* II, 5; Colgrave and Mynors, *Bede*, pp. 148, 150.
[58] *Chronicle* for 827; J. M. Bately (ed.), *MS A*, D. Dumville and S. Keynes (ed.),
The Anglo-Saxon Chronicle, a collaborative edition, (1995-), 3 (1986), p. 42, also see p.
cxii.
[59] The definitive publication of the ship burial is R. L. S. Bruce-Mitford (ed.),
The Sutton Hoo Ship Burial, 3 vols (London, 1975–83). For a recent evaluation see
M. Carver, *Sutton Hoo: burial ground of kings?* (London, 1998).

the case of Rædwald at least, was reflected in his choice of dress.[60] Edwin was killed in 632 and was eventually succeeded by his nephew Oswald, king and saint, then by Oswald's brother Oswiu, the last *Bretwalda* mentioned by Bede, who reigned until 670. This was a period of cultural supremacy for Northumbria, an age of church-building, book production and sculpture, but one which has, unfortunately, left us only a little evidence of native dress (pp. 133–4, 169–70).

There followed a long period of domination of the other kingdoms by Mercia, peaking in the reign of Offa (757–96), a king of national power and international connections. Overlord of all the kingdoms south of the Humber, and influential in Northumbria, he corresponded on equal terms with the Frankish emperor and traded with the Empire. Cloaks were among the merchandise exchanged. The resurgence of Wessex in 792, under Egbert, marked the beginning of a West Saxon pre-eminence which resulted, in 886, in the acknowledgement of King Alfred, Egbert's grandson, as leader of all the English peoples who had not then been conquered by the Vikings.

Christianity

During the 'Period of the Heptarchy' the conversion to Christianity had taken place. This event was to affect the Anglo-Saxon people materially as well as spiritually, transforming their culture, and, in the cases of women at least, influencing their choice of dress. Augustine's mission arrived in England from Rome in 597, landing in Kent where the *Bretwalda* Æthelbert, having married into a Christian Frankish family, was receptive. The king was soon converted and allowed the missionaries to establish themselves in Canterbury, which became England's first archbishopric. (The Archbishop of Canterbury remains the leader of the Anglican Church to this day). The example of Æthelbert of Kent encouraged the conversion of other kings, who were linked by dynastic marriages and family relationships, to which was now added the spiritual bond of baptismal sponsorship (godparenthood). The conversion of the populace, though slower than that of the rulers, followed, and by the end of the seventh century all the Anglo-Saxon kingdoms had received Christianity. The people who had come as barbarians from Northern Europe were now subject to the civilising influences of more southern areas of the Continent. Constant traffic through Gaul to England brought scholars, many from Rome, some from as far as the Eastern Mediterranean. In the other direction, missionaries and scholars came from Iona and Ireland to Northumbria and English scholars crossed the Irish Sea to study. It is doubtful if this exchange in itself affected secular dress, since the participants were monks, but it is likely that trade followed the traffic.

---

[60] The Sutton Hoo ship burial included a pair of shoulder clasps which must have been made for a Roman-style cuirass.

In archaeological terms, a transitional period can be observed at the time of the conversion, during which many of the old pagan 'folk cemeteries' were abandoned for new (but fairly short-lived) burial grounds where the deposition of grave-goods was greatly reduced. Although the Church did not expressly forbid grave-goods, and, indeed endorsed them in cases like the burial of the seventh-century Northumbrian saint, Cuthbert, who was accompanied by his pectoral cross, portable altar, clothing and other artefacts, the religious teaching which emphasised spiritual resurrection clearly discouraged the old custom. Political and economic change in England, including the development of kingship and hence centralisation of resources, no doubt contributed to the decline of a practice in which wealth was abandoned to the earth. However, enough grave-goods were deposited during the conversion period to demonstrate that changes were taking place in costume, at least in women's costume, some probably as a result of foreign and Christian influences. Some types of dress fastener seem to have gone out of fashion by the seventh century and there seems to have been more standardization with regard to the shape and decoration of the jewellery worn. Roman and Byzantine influences can be detected in the fashions of some of those who still wore jewellery to the grave, but many did not wear it. After a short period of compromise, funerals with grave-goods were discontinued apart from a few isolated cases from the eighth century, cutting off an important source of evidence about costume. The corpses of later Anglo-Saxon Christians, buried without grave-goods and hence the characteristic artefacts of their era, have become anonymous skeletons lost under successive burials in consecrated ground.

With Christianity came literacy. Education was a major concern of the missionaries, for the training of native clergy was essential if the infant Anglo-Saxon Church was to flourish. The language of the Anglo-Saxons, Old English, was now given a written form, in a Celtic version of the Latin alphabet. Although it is recorded that early scholars composed in Old English and translated into it, very little vernacular material survives from the first two centuries after the conversion. Latin was the language of the Bible and of international scholarship. The Anglo-Saxons achieved mastery of it with remarkable speed; but written Old English was an available tool which could, and would, be drawn upon later.

Literacy was so much a prerogative of the Church that written information about English secular life in general during these early centuries of Christianity is limited, and evidence of dress, secular or otherwise, fragmentary. The great Northumbrian historian, Bede, who completed his Latin *Historia Ecclesiastica Gentis Anglorum* (*History of the English Church and People*) in 731, had no interest in describing dress, but occasionally mentions it. Our only description of Anglo-Saxon clothing by an Anglo-Saxon comes from

Aldhelm, Bishop of Sherborne, who flourished at the turn of the seventh/eighth centuries, writing Latin in a convoluted ('hermeneutic') style greatly admired in his own day and much imitated. His treatise *De Laude Virginitate* ('In Praise of Virginity') includes a condemnation of elaborate dressing by persons dedicated to the Church. The text was extremely popular and was much glossed by later scholars, who thus provided for us Old English names for the garments Aldhelm had described in Latin.

During the eighth century many Anglo-Saxon scholars travelled abroad as missionaries and teachers. Alcuin of York was invited to the Continent by Charlemagne in 782. He became head of the palace school and developed the monastery of Tours into a great centre of learning. The personal influence of the Anglo-Saxon Alcuin may have affected the Emperor's political and commercial relationships with England. Charlemagne's own patriotic taste in clothing is well documented by his biographers, whose detailed picture of aristocratic Frankish dress is particularly relevant since it was evidently compatible with English cloaks. The classically-inspired Carolingian renaissance was later to influence the arts in Anglo-Saxon England, providing inspiration for more Mediterranean tastes.

Other English scholars visited the more northern lands of mainland Europe, returning to the still pagan territories from which their ancestors had migrated. Missionaries such as Boniface, who became Bishop of Old Saxony, and Lull, Bishop of Frisia and Old Saxony, were enthusiastic correspondents. From their (Latin) letters we find that items of clothing passed, as gifts, in both directions, so taking Anglo-Saxon fashions to the Continent and importing foreign styles to England, albeit within limited, mainly ecclesiastical, circles.

The Christian works of art imported from the Continent at the time of the conversion, and after it, infused new humanistic concepts into native art. We have an example of the kind of material introduced in a fragmentary gospel book, Cambridge, Corpus Christi College MS 286, imported with, or soon after, Augustine's mission. It contains a 'portrait' of St Luke and scenes from the life of Christ. Other scholars are known to have imported books and pictures, an outstanding figure in this respect being Benedict Biscop, founder of the Northumbrian monasteries at Wearmouth and Jarrow, who made four journeys to Rome during which he collected such treasures. It does not appear that Anglo-Saxon male clothing fashions were influenced by the Mediterranean dress seen in imported pictures; women's, however, may have drawn towards the depiction of the Virgin Mary in religious art. The major importance of the new art for the costume historian lies in the fact that under its influence Anglo-Saxon artists began to depict human figures naturalistically. The earliest surviving examples, however, show us nothing of native dress. Stylised figures in, for example, the early Northumbrian manuscripts the *Lindisfarne Gospels* and the *Codex Amiatinus* wear obviously foreign costume and most of the clothing that can be distinguished on the finest, and apparently earliest, stone sculptures, the Ruthwell and Bewcastle crosses, is equally indebted to foreign models. There may be less dependence on Mediterranean models in some of the carvings on an early-eighth-century whale-bone box, The Franks Casket; on another ivory carving, the Genoels-Elderen Diptych, which may be Northumbrian or Northumbrian-influenced; on a stone sculpture from Jarrow and in illuminated initials in the *Vespasian Psalter*, an eighth-century manuscript probably executed in Canterbury during the period of Mercian domination.

The Viking Age

The successive cultural achievements of Northumbria and Mercia were outstanding but shortlived. If we are to believe King Alfred of Wessex,[61] the wave of enthusiasm for scholarship had already lost its impetus when Viking invasions disrupted monastic life and destroyed libraries. Vikings, piratical pagans from Scandinavia, attacked the Northumbrian monasteries of Lindisfarne and Jarrow in 793 and 794, and continued to raid English territory during the following half-century. Since those who recorded this history were clerics, it is naturally the disruption to religious life that is chiefly deplored, but the impact of the Viking menace on the secular inhabitants must have been just as great. The Scandinavians became a permanent threat in the 850s when they adopted the tactic of wintering in England rather than returning home. In 865 a very large Viking army landed in East Anglia and a prolonged struggle ensued. King Edmund of East Anglia was killed in 869, and the kings of Northumbria and Mercia were replaced by Viking nominees in 867 and 873. Although the Northumbrian puppet was thrown off after about three years, the Scandinavians shared out land and began to settle in southern Northumbria in 876 and in Mercia the following year. Of the Anglo-Saxon kingdoms only Wessex remained independent and was gradually falling to the Vikings when Alfred of Wessex (reigned 871–99) defeated and made a treaty with the Viking leader Guthrum in 878, regaining control of London in 886. The result was a political and cultural division between the territory controlled by Wessex and Guthrum's kingdom. The political division lasted late into the Anglo-Saxon period; the cultural dichotomy between North and South even longer. It still lingers.

The treaty with Guthrum left Alfred master of an area roughly south of a diagonal line from the Thames to Staffordshire. Mercia was divided between the Anglo-Saxons and the Vikings and, under

[61] H. Sweet (ed.), *King Alfred's Version of Gregory's Pastoral Care*, Early English Text Society, original series 45, 50 (London, 1871–2), pp. 2, 4.

Alfred, English Mercia remained independent, ruled by Ealdorman Æthelred, his son-in-law. North of Guthrum's territory there was a Danish kingdom in York; beyond that, northern Northumbria remained independent, but under ealdormen, not kings. The new settlers made unreliable compatriates: when a Viking army attacked England in 892, the Scandianavian settlers helped them. The Danes of Northumbria and East Anglia were mostly heathen. Their customs and their appearance made them foreign to the Anglo-Saxons, whose antagonism had developed over years of costly strife. For many generations there must have been Scandinavians living side by side with Anglo-Saxons, people whose speech and clothing differed. While their language can be traced through place-name and dialect studies, their dress is much more obscure. Occasional archaeological finds and Viking influenced stone sculptures, less stylised than earlier Northumbrian and later southern art, give us just a little information about dress in the Anglo-Viking regions during this rather obscure period. In the early-tenth century, Vikings of Norwegian origin who had been living in Ireland began settling in north-west England, and a Norse kingdom was established in York. Both Viking Dublin and Viking York have been the subject of archaeological excavation, and in both cases the soil conditions have preserved an unusual number of organic finds. The excavation of York, Viking *Jorvik*, has revealed details of everyday life in this English city during its Scandinavian era, including the making and repairing of clothes and shoes, crafts in which the Vikings and Anglo-Saxons no doubt had something in common, although jewellery- and garment-types may have differed. From Viking York, Lincoln, London and Dublin we have surviving caps or hoods and from Dublin cloth head-bands.

The rise of Wessex, and Christian culture

The history of the south of England, meanwhile, is a story of the increasing dominance of Wessex and of achievement in Christian scholarship and art. King Alfred had stabilized the Anglo-Viking conflict. His son, Edward the Elder, in alliance with his sister Æthelflæd, who ruled Mercia after the death of her husband, Ealdorman Æthelred, fortified towns and extended English influence against the Welsh. It is as a result of the English–Welsh conflict that our only (presumed) Anglo-Saxon surviving garment was preserved, a charred shirt from Llan-gors, near Brecon, Powys, Wales (Plates 10, 11), possibly a casualty of Æthelflæd's destruction of the stronghold in 916. After Æthelflæd's death, Edward annexed Mercia. He extended his influence into Wales and he and his sons attempted to annex Northumbria, which was eventually united to Wessex in the reign of Eadred in 954.

King Alfred, who deplored the way in which scholarship had been neglected and interrupted in England, to the point where the ability to translate Latin into English had been completely lost south of the Humber, instituted an educational programme. All free-born boys whose families could afford it were to be taught to read English and at the same time a number of important books were translated from Latin into English. A team of scholars from outside Wessex helped Alfred; they came from Mercia, Wales, Old Saxony and Frankia. The books which were translated into English were Gregory's *Dialogues* and *Pastoral Care*, Boethius's *Consolation of Philosophy*, Bede's *Historia Ecclesiastica*, Augustine's *Soliloquies* and Orosius's *History*. Also during Alfred's reign the *Anglo-Saxon Chronicle* was compiled and distributed to monasteries for continuation and an Old English *Martyrology* was written. The surviving manuscripts of these 'Alfredian texts' do not give us graphic depictions of clothing, since they are not illuminated, but the texts themselves do contain some useful evidence of dress, in that they enable us to document the use and meaning of certain garment-names in the late-ninth century. Alfred's literary programme, however, had other long-term, if indirect, results for costume historians. His choice of English, rather than Latin, set a precedent for English scholars, and in the following century those who wrote in Old English and glossed Latin texts in the vernacular were to record many garment-names.

Alfred, who had visited Rome and Frankia with his father as a child, and experienced the Frankish culture of his stepmother's court circle, was inspired by Christian Europe. The continued influence from this direction, especially from the Frankish Carolingian Empire, distinguishes Wessex from the North. Relations between England and the Continent seem to have flourished particularly during the reign of Athelstan, who succeeded in 924. Foreign scholars were entertained at Athelstan's court and international alliances were cemented by the sending of royal brides (the king's half-sisters) to Flanders, Carolingian Frankia and Ottonian Germany and by the reception of Alan of Brittany and Hakon of Norway as the king's foster-sons. Thus, in the early-tenth century England was in a position to receive fashions from and to transmit ideas to many foreign lands. Costume, like other aspects of life, may have been affected by this international association.[62] King Athelstan himself is depicted as benefactor to the Church in an illumination commemorating a visit to St Cuthbert's shrine in about 934 (Colour Plate J). Although the style of his garments is unpretentious, a short tunic and simple cloak over close-fitting hose, there is decoration at shoulder and cuffs and if the rich colours of the painting are to be taken at face value, they suggest expensively dyed fabric.

---

[62] The sources and manifestations of Carolingian and Ottonian dress are discussed in a recent publication, M. Müller, *Die Kleidung nach Quellen des frühen Mittelalters; Textilen und Mode von Karl dem Grossen bis Heinrich III*, Ergänzungsbände zum Reallexikon der Germanischen Altertumskunde, 33 (Berlin and New York, 2003).

During the reign of Edgar (959–75), Anglo-Saxon England moved towards another peak of achievement in the arts. In the peaceful years between the Viking wars, leading churchmen appointed by Edgar – Æthelwold, bishop of Winchester, Dunstan, archbishop of Canterbury and Oswald, archishop of York – established the Benedictine Reform in England. Influenced ultimately by the Frankish monastery of Cluny, the reformers founded new, more disciplined religious houses and regularised the practices of others. The reform movement stimulated a great scholarly revival which continued through the reigns of Edgar's sons Edward the Martyr (975–8) and Æthelred II 'The Unready' (978–1016). Latin gospel books, psalters and other religious texts were copied. A Latin grammar and an Anglo-Latin glossary were composed by Ælfric, abbot of Eynsham. Latin texts were glossed in the margins and between the lines. Anglo-Latin glossary lists were compiled from sources like this, and earlier glossaries were copied and conflated, sometimes with the entries arranged in order of subject (such as 'bedclothes' or 'clothing'), sometimes according to simple alphabetical principles. Glossed texts and glossaries are a major source of Old English garment and textile terminology. There was also a great increase in the production of texts in English. The Benedictine Rule was translated from Latin; so were parts of the Old Testament. The gospels were translated in both Anglian and West Saxon dialects. Vernacular prose works of this period include homilies, lives of saints, ecclesiastical laws, scientific treatises and versions of classical stories. In Æthelred's reign there were copied the four books which contain most of our surviving Anglo-Saxon poetry, some of which may have been composed much earlier. In this era of revived enthusiasm for literacy, many bequests and other legal transactions were committed to writing, significantly in English. Clothing is casually mentioned in homilies, laws and other texts. Occasionally, and more informatively, it is specified in a will.

Many books were illuminated, mostly Latin texts. King Edgar himself appears in two illustrations, in very different costumes (Colour Plate K and Fig. 187). Southern English artists, producing work in the Winchester Style, were strongly influenced by Carolingian art, which was itself inspired by classical models. Many of the male figures in English drawings of this period wear a costume probably Roman in origin, which would instantly identify them as holy figures: angels, male evangelists/saints and occasionally God himself. This dress would not have been worn by Anglo-Saxon men. Contrasting with this we find the short tunics and cloaks of ordinary secular men and the vestments of ecclesiastics. Presumably these costumes reflect everyday life. Female figures wear a costume with long, figure-concealing garments and voluminous headdresses, without jewellery, a style which probably owed its popularity to the dissemination of Byzantine depictions of the Virgin Mary through western Europe. As far as we can tell, Anglo-Saxon women did copy this style.

Many Winchester Style figures are formally posed, for example in the *Benedictional of St Æthelwold* (Fig. 170). In other manuscripts, such as the *Harley Psalter* (Colour Plate H) individuals and groups are less rigidly presented, though Carolingian influences are betrayed by stylised posture and swirling clothing. It is important to recognise that medieval artists generally shunned innovation, preferring to copy from an authoritative source; and that, even when we do not know precisely the model the artist used, we can recognise in the fall of a garment or placing of a limb that the artist was working within the convention of his day. Of major importance in terms of innovation are the illustrations to the Old English version of the *Hexateuch* (London, British Library, MS Cotton Claudius B iv), made about the year 1000, in which the artist, while familiar with established conventions, appears to have enjoyed the freedom to create from everyday life.

Anglo-Scandianavian and Anglo-Norman kings

The reign of Æthelred II was less successful politically than culturally. Renewed Viking attacks culminated in the conquest of England by King Swein of Denmark and Æthelred's exile in 1014. When Swein died, the English king returned, promising reform, but was harassed both by Danish forces under Swein's son Cnut and by his own son, Edmund Ironside. When Æthelred died in 1016 these two continued to struggle for power, eventually partitioning the country with Edmund receiving Wessex; but when he died only a few months after his father, the Viking Cnut took possession of this Anglo-Saxon heartland also and eliminated other contenders to the throne. Æthelred's sons and daughter by his second marriage were brought up in their mother's country, Normandy.

The change in dynasty did not transform England, either culturally or administratively, into a Viking province. Archbishop Wulfstan, formerly advisor to Æthelred and Edmund, maintained his influence under Cnut. The Viking king married Æthelred's widow, who was the daughter of a Norman father and a Scandinavian mother, and was known both by her Norman name, Emma, and her English one, Ælfgifu. Cnut became a zealous Christian. It is likely that the Viking king and Norman-Scandinavian queen brought their own tastes in clothing and influenced their own immediate circle – small Scandinavian details are noticeable in the costume of Cnut, who is pictured in London, British Library, MS Stowe 944 (Fig. 188) – but a factor probably of wider importance for costume development was the increase in international trade, keenly pursued by the king, which must have expanded the availability of furs and fabrics. Under Cnut, who succeeded his brother as king of Denmark in 1019 and was acknowledged king of Norway in 1028, England became part of a great northern empire. The king also developed diplomatic, religious and commercial associations with the more southern European states, consolidating all three links in 1027 when he travelled to Rome for the coronation of Conrad II as Holy Roman Emperor.

Cnut died in 1035. His dynasty and northern empire did not long survive him: his sons Kings Harold I and Harthacnut were short lived, both Denmark and Norway were soon lost. By this time, however, England's population must have included very many persons of Scandinavian origin, both descendants of the earlier settlers and the newer arrivals. The most powerful family, headed by Earl Godwine, was part-Scandinavian.

Harthacnut had brought his half-brother Edward, son of Æthelred and Emma, from exile in Normandy in 1041, and was succeeded by him. Edward's arrival probably introduced Norman fashions to the English court, while his marriage to Edith, the daughter of Earl Godwine and his Scandinavian wife Gytha, probably reinforced the tastes of the wealthy Anglo-Scandinavian élite. We see Edward depicted in the Bayeux 'Tapestry' dressed in dignified long robes (Fig. 189) and finds from his tomb demonstrate that he owned imported silks. When he died childless in January 1066, his brother-in-law Harold Godwinesson succeeded him as Harold II. Harold was threatened by three enemies: his own brother Tostig, who had been driven out of his northern earldom the previous year; by King Harold Hardrada of Norway, who was laying claim to England; and by Duke William of Normandy who claimed the throne through his kinship to Edward, reinforced by the allegation that Harold had sworn allegiance to him during a visit to Normandy in 1064.

Tostig and Harold Hardrada were killed in battle against Harold II at Stamfordbridge on 25 September 1066, but three days later William of Normandy landed in England. On 14 October the English army was defeated at Hastings, and Harold, the last Anglo-Saxon, or Anglo-Scandinavian, king was killed. The battle, events leading up to it including Harold's visit to Normandy, and the principal characters involved, are depicted in the Bayeux 'Tapestry', an embroidered hanging almost certainly designed and made in England for a Norman patron, Duke William's half-brother, Bishop Odo of Bayeux, within twenty years of the Conquest. The 'Tapestry' (Figs 5–6, 161, 163, 172, 189–93, 206) presents the dress of various ranks, secular and ecclesiastical, engaged in different activities, as they appeared in the late-eleventh century, and it is a testament to the spinning, dying, weaving and embroidery skills of the age.

This time the change of dynasty was followed by great social changes. The families who had been powerful under the Anglo-Saxon and Viking kings were superseded by Norman barons. Almost all the bishops were replaced by Norman nominees. The introduction of feudalism based on military service drastically changed the social structure of England. The French and Latin languages came to be used for aristocratic and ecclesiastical writings where Old English had been used before. English styles in art and architecture gave way to Norman. Within a few years of the passing of the last Anglo-Saxon king, an era had come to an end; and since the ruling classes, the fashion-conscious classes, were now Norman, we can say that costume, too, passed into the Norman period.

II

Women's costume in the fifth and sixth centuries

Archaeological evidence

The richest source of information on the pagan period in general, and on women's dress in particular, is the furnished inhumation grave. Organic materials like wood, leather and textile will normally have decayed away, except for tiny remnants, but grave-goods of metal, glass and pottery usually survive, and sometimes, dependent on the soil conditions, articles of bone. The characteristic methods of burial, together with the distinctive shape and decoration of the grave-goods, particularly metalwork, demonstrate to the archaeologist that a cemetery is 'Anglo-Saxon' rather than belonging to any earlier era (such as Bronze Age or Romano-British). The population of an Anglo-Saxon village may in fact have included persons who were not ethnically Anglo-Saxon, since Romano-Britons may have lived in the community, and their tastes and costumes may occasionally surface in the choice of brooch type or technical details of textile, but clearly the predominant culture was the Germanic Anglo-Saxon one.[1]

Grave-goods, and in particular, articles which were worn on the body when it was buried, provide our primary source of information about dress in the pagan Anglo-Saxon period. A very large

[1] Detailed anatomical analysis has sometimes shown up genetic features which may indicate ethnicity: a distinctive skull formation of supposed Romano-British women at Stretton-on-Fosse (W. J. Ford, *The Romano-British and Anglo-Saxon Settlement and Cemeteries at Stretton-on-Fosse, Warwickshire*, forthcoming). Phyllis Jackson's research on foot bones (based on her work in chiropody in isolated areas) has led her to identify a characteristic 'Celtic foot' and 'Saxon foot' and to suggest Romano-British descendants among the population buried in the Saxon cemetery at Lechlade, and mixed ancestry of one inhabitant of Anglian Oakington (P. Jackson, 'Footloose in archaeology', *The Journal of British Podiatric Medicine*, 51.5 (1996), pp. 67–70; A. Taylor, C. Duhig and J. Hines, 'An Anglo-Saxon cemetery at Oakington, Cambridgeshire', *Proceedings of the Cambridge Antiquarian Society*, 86 (1997), pp. 57–90, at p. 66). DNA investigation also offers a promising line of research in this matter. Use of a Roman artefact may be explained by the proximity of an old Roman site rather than heritage; R. White, 'Scrap or substitute: Roman material in Anglo-Saxon graves', in Southworth, *Anglo-Saxon Cemeteries: a reappraisal*, pp. 125–52.

number of Anglo-Saxon inhumations have survived undisturbed. The material presented in this chapter and in Chapters III–VI is based largely upon a study of the grave-goods and their positions in relation to skeletons at over eleven hundred sites. (There have been many more sites discovered, but not all have been excavated with sufficient expertise or recorded in enough detail to provide reliable evidence. Some sites are awaiting publication.)

The majority of grave-goods utilised in this study can be categorised as jewellery. We must immediately dissociate ourselves from the modern conceptions that jewellery is almost purely ornamental, and that the way it is worn is a matter of personal choice. In the Dark Ages, jewellery, though decorated, was primarily functional. Buckles secured belts and other straps. Brooches were also fasteners: a brooch pin could secure clothing, either by fastening a garment to itself, or by hooking an outer garment to an inner.

Despite Tacitus's assertion that Germanic women's costume was similar to men's (pp. 17–18, above), the cumulative evidence of grave-goods suggests that the appearance of male and female in early Anglo-Saxon England was very different. The sex of most well-preserved skeletons can be established on anatomical grounds, and following on from that identification it is clear that many grave-goods are 'gendered': weapons (swords, shields, spears, scramasaxes) are found exclusively with men; certain items of jewellery (brooches, beads, wrist-clasps) are normally associated with women and are not regularly found with men.

There is extensive evidence about the costume of Anglo-Saxon women in the fifth and sixth centuries (Colour Plates D, F). It is distinct from the clothing of later periods and this costume, more than any other form of Anglo-Saxon dress, lends itself to illustration and reconstruction. We should not, however, be blind to the many uncertainties about it, and these will be noted as we proceed.

A study of all the furnished, female Anglo-Saxon graves of the fifth and sixth centuries clearly reveals a recurrent pattern in the positioning of grave-goods. The diagnostic feature is that two brooches, either identical or very similar in shape or decoration, are placed at the shoulders. The presence of a pair of brooches positioned in this way indicates that the owner wore a garment of the Greek *peplos* type, a tubular, sleeveless gown which was clasped together, front to back, by the fasteners at the shoulders. Most women had some beads, and there is usually some indication that a belt or girdle was worn. There is sometimes a buckle at waist or hip, but more often the evidence is provided by objects found near the pelvis or thighs of the skeleton, which had almost certainly been attached to a belt. Certain women were equipped with 'optional extras'. Some of these, such as a third, central brooch, wrist clasps and certain girdle attachments, were regional variations; some may have reflected wealth, rank and status. Other women had less than the standard 'paired' brooches and we must seek to explain what their costume might have consisted of.

Despite the frequency of 'paired' brooches, central brooches and wrist clasps, surprisingly few graves have every item, and reconstruction has in the past been dependent on making a composite picture from many burials.[2] Occasionally, however, individual graves suggest modification of established ideas and special studies are given of some of these in this chapter. New reconstructions of costume are based on these.

Brooches

The brooch is the most significant of feminine grave-goods for reconstructing the costume from non-perishable remains. A brooch is nothing more than an ornamented fastener of the safety-pin type. Its functional part is a flexible pin on a spring. This pin passes through the clothing and is secured by a catch to prevent it unfastening. The pin, catch and spring are concealed by the plate, which in early Anglo-Saxon times might take the form of a plain disc, but more often was decorated and could take various shapes. The pin was normally iron, the plate iron or copper alloy ('bronze'), and the latter was sometimes gilded on the decorated face. More rare, but particularly noticeable in the archaeology of Kent, are brooches of precious metals, silver and gold. The fronts of brooches were ornamented by various techniques; casting, engraving or inlaying. Casting seems to have been the commonest method, and since more than one brooch could be made from the same mould,

Fig. 8 Square-headed brooch, Little Wilbraham, Cambridgeshire

[2] Thus my reconstructions in *Dress in Anglo-Saxon England* (Manchester, 1986), p. 33, Fig. 30 and in Lapidge, Blair, Keynes and Scragg, *The Blackwell Encyclopaedia of Anglo-Saxon England*, 'Clothing', p. 107, Fig. 4.

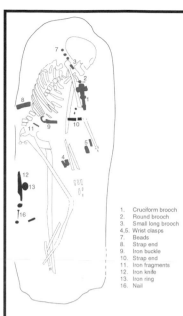

1. Cruciform brooch
2. Round brooch
3. Small long brooch
4,5. Wrist clasps
7. Beads
8. Strap end
9. Iron buckle
10. Strap end
11. Iron fragments
12. Iron knife
13. Iron ring
16. Nail

Fig. 9 Grave 74, Wakerley, Northamptonshire

Fig. 10 Reconstruction of Grave 74, Wakerley, experimenting with short *peplos*

WAKERLEY GRAVE 74 (Figs. 9, 10), which belonged to the last quarter of the sixth century or the beginning of the seventh,[3] contained the remains of a woman aged between thirty-five and forty-five. There are complications in the fact that the skeleton was on its left side rather than the usual supine position, and in discrepancies between the textile report and the grave catalogue/diagram.[4] A large cruciform brooch was found centrally at the upper chest. The brooch was probably damaged when buried and the knobs had been fastened on by thread. The back of the brooch preserved Z-spun threads of a fairly coarse 2 x 2 twill, probably from a cloak. Beneath this textile were Z-spun tabby threads, of a textile of similar quality, probably linen, which Elisabeth Crowfoot thought might have come from a head-covering, veil or hood.[5] A small-long brooch at the right shoulder preserved Z-spun threads of a finer 2 x 2 twill, probably from a *peplos*-type gown, and coarse Z-spun, S-plied threads, with a knot, which had perhaps been a bead string attached to the shoulder brooches. Unusually, but not uniquely, it seems that the shoulder brooches were not matched: at the left shoulder near the jaw there was an applied saucer brooch which had been gilded. The applied brooch would have been unusual at this predominantly Anglian site and was probably treasured for that reason as well as for its rich-looking, gold appearance. It seems to have been worn in the usual way, but had to be matched with a commoner type of fastener. Along the pin of this brooch were Z- and S-spun threads of a different twill textile, probably the same one as that found inside the bronze clasps which were at the wrists and on two strap ends, and on an iron buckle, iron ring and iron fragments, which were found in a horizontal line at the waist area. These probably all came from the long-sleeved under-gown or tunic, and since the warp and weft were spun in different directions, this textile might have been a patterned twill.[6] It is surprising to find evidence of what may be a rather luxurious fabric used for the undergown, which would be, partially at least, covered up by the *peplos*-type gown, and it suggests that the appearance of the undergown may have been important in itself: the *peplos* may only have covered it on formal occasions, or the *peplos* may have been short enough to expose quite a lot of the undergown. A stud on one of the strap ends preserved four twists of tablet-woven braid, and a stud on the other a fragment of leather strap, which itself preserved some of the Z-spun threads which probably belonged to the *peplos*-type gown. The implication is that the belt equipment was carried between the Z/S-spun twill and the Z-spun *peplos*. Possibly the undergown was girdled with the tablet-woven braid, and a buckled leather belt held a pouch or objects now lost. Z-spun threads on a knife and a nail, found behind the legs of the skeleton, may have come from a bag or from the skirts of either garment, though an iron ring found with them preserved the Z- and S-spun threads characteristic of the undergown, suggesting that garment extended at least to below the knees.

[3] B. Adams and D. Jackson, ed. L. Badenoch, 'The Anglo-Saxon Cemetery at Wakerley, Northamptonshire: excavations by Mr D. Jackson 1968–9', *Northamptonshire Archaeology*, 22 (1988–9), pp. 69–183 and microfiche, at p. 175.

[4] Both with regard to the numbering of finds and about the number of small-long brooches in the grave (Crowfoot assumes a 'pair of small-long brooches ... on the shoulders'; other information suggests only one); E. Crowfoot, 'The textiles', in Adams, Jackson and Badenoch, 'Wakerley', p. 172.

[5] *Ibid*.

[6] As on the spearhead in Grave 34 at the same site, where Z/S threads from a broken diamond or chevron twill were identified; Crowfoot, 'Wakerley', p. 170.

brooches which were genuine pairs could be manufactured. By the middle of the sixth century, cast settings were being filled with garnet, a semi-precious stone, and by the end of that century there had appeared individually constructed brooches decorated with gold cells, or *cloisons*, painstakingly built in elaborate shapes and filled with garnets.

The shape and decoration of brooches varies considerably, although most correspond with recognised types fashionable in particular regions or periods. They can be categorised as 'long' ('bow') or 'circular' according to the shape of the front plate. Long types include the so-called **'square-headed'** (Fig. 8 and Colour Plate A; the title is something of a misnomer: long brooches seem to have been often worn with the 'head' pointing downwards or sideways and the 'head' is usually rectangular rather than square);[7] the **cruciform** (also a misleading name – the knobs which give the brooch head its cruciform shape were originally functional – these brooches have nothing to do with Christianity), which vary from simple specimens to elaborate versions over 17 cm long (Figs 11, 12); **radiate-headed** brooches (Fig. 13); and the modest **'small-long'** (Fig. 14, Colour Plate B), which, because of its lack of distinctive decoration and many different manifestations, has not yet been the subject of extensive study.[8] On the more showy brooches, practical details were turned into decorative: the square 'head' concealed functional parts; the cruciform and radiate 'heads' incorporated the two knobs which had originally been attached to the spring, and made an ornamental feature of them, the cruciform adding a third knob, the radiate several. In the latest development of cruciform brooches ('florid cruciform brooches') the knobs were flattened into wings. Cruciform brooches often have a stylised horse head at the narrow end and the fronts of the larger and more opulent variety of square-headed brooches ('great square-headed brooches') are covered with geometric or zoomorphic ornament. The decoration on brooches is generally used today to establish a classification and chronology. Its significance for the maker and the wearer – religious, magical, ethnic, social or otherwise – is lost to us. Possibly future study of ornament in context may recover some of this 'language' of decorative ornament.[9]

Modern excavation, where graves are numbered in sequence as they are discovered, does not always reveal the chronological

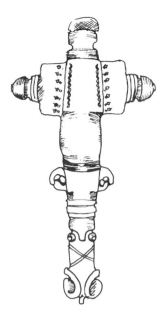

Fig. 11 Simple cruciform brooch, St John's, Cambridge

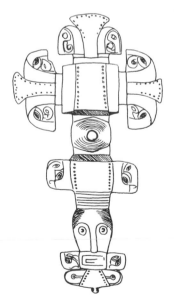

Fig. 12 Florid cruciform brooch, one of a pair, Newnham Croft, Cambridgeshire

[7] I understand that re-enactors have found that brooches fastened with the spring (the 'head') uppermost are inclined to come unfastened, whereas if the pin catch and pin end are at the top a brooch stays fastened. I am grateful to Ben Levick of *Angelcynn* for this information.

[8] I understand that research is being undertaken at the University of York under the supervision of Dr Tania Dickinson.

[9] As the interpretation of the symbols on cremation urns is today being considered; J. D. Richards, *The Significance of Form and Decoration of Anglo-Saxon Cremation Urns*, British Archaeological Reports, British Series, 166 (1987).

Fig. 13 Radiate-headed brooch, Little Wilbraham, Cambridgeshire

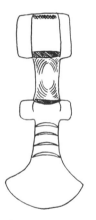

Fig. 14 Small-long brooch, Newnham Croft, Cambridgeshire

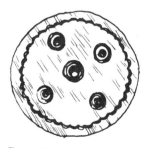

Fig. 15 Simple disc brooch, one of a pair, St John's, Cambridge

relationship of burials. Obviously the establishment of a chronology would be important evidence for the development of dress. In a study based on selected sites, Mette Palm and John Pind have suggested that cruciform brooches went out of fashion between 525 and 600 and have considered whether the great square-headed brooch replaced the florid cruciform brooch as a dress fastener.[10] John Hines, while agreeing to the lack of associations between square-headed and cruciform brooches in grave-groups, argues for the contemporaneity of some florid cruciforms and some great square-headed on grounds of size, materials, technique and decoration,[11] and suggests that what is indicated is not a change in dress fashion but alternative and concurrent fashions. The question remains open; Palm and Pind's arguments are stimulating but their grounds for assigning grave groups to different dates is ultimately subjective and their observations were based on a limited number of sites, mostly in Norfolk. The situation may differ elsewhere.

The simplest circular brooches had a plate consisting of a copper alloy **disc**, either plain or ornamented with a simple pattern such as a series of rings enclosing dots (Fig. 15). More elaborate were **Kentish disc brooches**, which were often made of silver and inlaid with **garnet** or coloured glass. The simpler ones had three or four keystone-shaped garnets alternating with animal ornament, and more complex examples had garnets in cloisons alternating with geometric filigree gold ornament (Figs 64, 67 and Colour Plate Ca). The **saucer brooch** consisted of a decorated plate surrounded by an angled rim (Fig. 16). There is a great range of decoration on surviving examples, mostly geometric, and though they were probably mass-produced, some, with gilding on the front, must have looked quite opulent. The **applied brooch** (Colour Plate Cb) was of similar appearance to the saucer brooch, but was constructed differently, being made in separate parts rather than cast as a whole. Many excavated applied brooches have fallen apart and their fragile rims and rimless front-plates are unimpressive now; but they must once have been bright and attractive, with their shining ornament which often incorporated abstract animal designs. The **button brooch** was like a miniature saucer brooch in shape. It was often decorated with a stylised face (Figs 4, 17). The front plate of a button brooch is sometimes found as an additional ornament on the bow of an elaborate square-headed brooch. The **annular** brooch consisted of a circle of wire or flattened metal with a pin lying across it (Fig. 18), and the rarer **penannular** of an incomplete circle (Fig. 19).

[10] M. Palm and J. Pind, 'Anglian English women's graves in the fifth to seventh centuries A. D. – a chronological analysis', in L. Jørgensen (ed.), *Chronological Studies of Anglo-Saxon England, Lombard Italy and Vendel Period Sweden*, University of Copenhagen Institute of Prehistoric and Classical Archaeology, Arkæologiske Skrifter, 5 (1992), pp. 50–80, at pp. 58–67.

[11] J. Hines, 'The seriation and chronology of Anglian English women's graves: a critical assessment', in Jørgensen, *Chronological Studies*, pp. 81–93, at pp. 85–6.

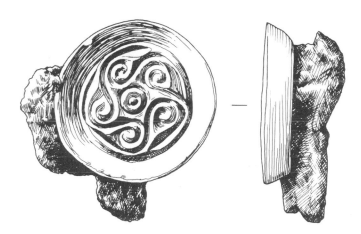

Fig. 16 Saucer brooch, Butler's Field, Lechlade, Gloucestershire

Both types, as they occur in Anglo-Saxon cemeteries, are simply decorated, for example with a few parallel lines, or, in the case of the flat annular, with a ring of simple stamps, though the penannular, which may testify to the survival of Romano-British tastes and inhabitants, has much grander relatives in Celtic context. **Quoit brooches** combined the penannular and annular shapes in a double ring, and were elaborately decorated with animal ornament in an imitation of appliqué technique (Fig. 20).[12]

A few brooches from early Anglo-Saxon context do not fit into the broad categories of 'long' and 'circular'. These include the **equal-armed brooch** (Fig. 21), a type which was only current in the Migration period and possibly not manufactured in England. Small **bird-shaped** brooches (Fig. 66) were mostly confined to Kent. Apparently Anglo-Saxon women also sometimes acquired old Roman brooches and brooches of overseas manufacture which they wore to secure their native dress at each shoulder, pairing the unusual 'foreign' brooch with a with more familiar Anglo-Saxon one.

Some of these brooch types were of limited distribution. The quoit brooch, rather an opulent style, has been found only south of the Thames, and like equal-armed brooches, only in the earlier part of the pagan Anglo-Saxon period, though its distinctive art style may have continued into the sixth, decorating flat penannular brooches.[13] Saucer brooches were most popular in Saxon areas. Tania Dickinson has suggested that simple disc brooches were originally a fashion of the Saxon settlers of the Thames Valley in the fifth

Fig. 17 Button brooch, Buckland, Dover, Kent

Fig. 18 Annular brooch, one of a pair, Newnham Croft, Cambridgeshire

[12] S. Suzuki, *The Quoit Brooch Style and Anglo-Saxon Settlement: a casting and recasting of cultural identity symbols* (Woodbridge, 2000).

[13] It is possible that the (two) such brooches found in sixth-century context were heirlooms; J. Hines, *A New Corpus of Anglo-Saxon Great Square-Headed Brooches* (Woodbridge, 1997), p. 248.

Fig. 19 Artist's reconstruction of a penannular brooch based on an example from Sewerby, East Yorkshire

century, spreading north and east at a later stage.[14] Distribution of the less common applied brooches is concentrated in the Upper Thames valley. Cruciform brooches were particularly popular in Anglian areas, and annular especially favoured by Northumbrian Angles. Annular brooches probably became more popular in relation to long brooches as the sixth century progressed. Small square- or rectangular-headed brooches with a distinctive-shaped foot are found in Kent from the earliest period, probably a heritage of the 'Jutish' connections of the earlier settlers, but square-headed brooches are also common in Anglian areas, and often occur in Saxon cemeteries too. Radiate-headed brooches and inlaid brooches in general were largely characteristic of Kent and feature in sixth-century context, probably the result of Frankish settlement at that time.

It is possible that the pagan Anglo-Saxon vocabulary differentiated between different categories of brooch, but if so, the words, like the brooches themselves, were short-lived. Several words meaning 'clasp' are documented from later Anglo-Saxon times, and of these, *dalc* and *spennels* are the most likely to have been in use in the pagan period.

The *peplos*-type gown

Fig. 20 Quoit brooch, Sarre, Kent

Brooches are most often found in pairs at either side of the upper part of the body of female skeletons, and all the types listed above, except the rare quoit brooches, have been found in pairs. In the overwhelming majority of cases, excavators describe these as being found 'at the shoulders' or 'at the clavicles', though there are variations in the terminology used by excavators and evidently the precise arrangement of the brooches differed at individual sites and in individual graves. At Fairford, Gloucestershire, Wylie found brooches which he described in 1852 as being 'in pairs one on either breast',[15] which, if understood literally, indicates an unusually low position; while at Mucking, brooches observed when the site was under excavation had been placed high on the shoulders or on either side of the neck of the skeleton.[16] The wearer, or the person who dressed her for the grave, seems, in most cases, to have aimed for a symmetrical effect, pairing at the shoulders brooches which matched, or were at least of similar size and shape. The fashion of

Fig. 21 Equal-armed brooch, Mucking, Thurrock

[14] T. M. Dickinson, 'On the origin and chronology of the early Anglo-Saxon disc brooch', in S. C. Hawkes, D. Brown and J. Campbell (ed.), *Anglo-Saxon Studies in Archaeology and History*, British Archaeological Reports, British Series, 1, 72 (1979), pp. 39–80.

[15] W. M. Wylie, *Fairford Graves* (Oxford, 1852), p. 23.

[16] Thanks to the kindness of Margaret Jones and W. T. Jones, the author was able to observe some of these *in situ* in the 1960s. The publication of this major site is now in progress under the editorship of Helena Hamerow.

wearing a pair of brooches at or near the shoulders appears consistently in a large proportion of female graves in all regions where fifth- and sixth-century burials occur. This distribution suggests that there was a common garment worn by women of all the Germanic tribes who settled Britain.

Indications of what this garment looked like are fortunately provided by the art, archaeology and anthropology of other countries. It is apparent that women of various civilisations have used pairs of brooches at the shoulders to clasp together the front and back of a tubular, untailored garment. The *peplos* of classical Greece was clasped this way (Fig. 22), so was an Algerian costume observed as recently as the nineteenth century (Fig. 23).[17] There is considerable evidence that a garment of this kind was for many centuries a traditional part of Germanic costume. An early Scandinavian example survives and is displayed in the National Museum of Denmark in Copenhagen (Plates 1, 2). This garment, which was recovered from the peat bog of Huldremose, probably dates from the first centuries AD.[18] It consists of a tube of fabric 1.68 m long and 2.64 m in circumference and has been displayed as a gown long enough to be pouched over a belt or arranged with a cape effect at the shoulders. As it has been reconstructed, this cape is shorter than on the Greek *peplos*, but resembles the modern example from Algeria. The Germanic female costume described by Tacitus, a trailing, sleeveless garment which left the arms and shoulders exposed (pp. 17–18, above), may have been a gown of this kind. Captive German women shown on Roman sculptures wear this dress. They are clearly depicted on the second-century Column of Marcus Aurelius in Rome, wearing cylindrical garments clasped at the shoulders by small, round brooches (Figs 24, 25). In Scandinavia a related garment of this kind seems to have been the norm from about the eighth century AD[19] and remained characteristic of women's dress in the Viking period both in Scandinavia itself and in migrant Viking communities. It is attested by twelfth- and thirteenth-century graves in Finland.[20] In the twelfth century an Arab named Ibn Fadlan, who was travelling in the Volga region, observed and recorded the customs of a group of Swedish Vikings (the *Rus*) whom he encountered. His description of Rus women begins: 'Each

Fig. 22 The Doric *peplos* from a Greek vase-painting

Fig. 23 Algerian costume observed in the nineteenth century

[17] J. R. Allen, 'The Celtic brooch and how it was worn', *Illustrated Archaeologist* (December 1892), pp. 162–75.

[18] Hald, *Ancient Danish Textiles*, pp. 53–4, 361–3. The garment is illustrated in colour in Hald, Fig. 443. It probably belongs to the earlier part of the Roman Iron Age, which extends approximately 0–400 AD.

[19] Munksgaard, *Oldtidsdragter*, p. 206. The Huldremose *peplos* is unique among early Iron Age costumes. The usual costume for women in Denmark in this period seems to have been a blouse, skirt and shawl or scarf. For the origin of the *peplos* and a suggestion that it may have been known in the Bronze Age, see I. Hägg, 'Some notes on the origin of the peplos-type dress in Scandinavia', *Tor*, 1 (1967–8), pp. 81–127.

[20] Exhibited in Helsinki Museum.

Figs 24, 25 Germanic costume (sleeveless, sleeved), Column of Marcus Aurelius, Rome.

Plate 1 Iron Age garment from Huldremose, Denmark, unbelted

Plate 2 Iron Age garment from Huldremose, Denmark, belted

Figs 26, 27 The Scandinavian *Hängerock*

woman wears on either breast a box of iron, silver, copper or gold; the value of the box indicates the wealth of the husband'.[21] Ibn Fadlan's 'boxes' are a recognisable description of the convex, oval fasteners which appear in the graves of Viking women and which are sometimes, today, called 'tortoise brooches' because of their shape. To Ibn Fadlan they appeared to be 'on either breast'. As a woman lay in her grave the brooches would be on or near the clavicles like the brooches of Anglo-Saxon women. Textile remains on brooch-pins from the tenth-century archaeological site of Birka, Sweden, enabled Agnes Geijer to reconstruct the garment which they had fastened. She concluded that the garment, which she called *Hängerock*, 'suspended skirt', consisted of a rectangular length of fabric which was wrapped round the body and attached to the tortoise brooches by loops stitched to the front and back (Figs. 26, 27).[22] The loops, though characteristic of Birka, may not have been typical of the Viking world in general; Charlotte Blindheim, for example, found that the brooches which had secured a similar costume at Vernes in Norway, a tenth- to twelfth-century site, had been attached directly to the fabric of the gown.[23] It was probably a

[21] H. M. Smyser, 'Ibn Fadlān's account of the Rūs with some commentary and some allusions to Beowulf', in J. B. Bessinger Jr. and R. P. Creed (ed.), *Medieval and Linguistic Studies in Honour of Francis Peabody Magoun, Jr* (London, 1965), pp. 92–119, at p. 96.

[22] A. Geijer, *Birka, III: die Textilfunde aus den Gräbern* (Uppsala, 1938), pp. 152–5.

[23] C. Blindheim, 'Vernesfunnene og Kvinnedrakten i Norden i Vikingtiden', *Viking*, 9 (1945), pp. 143–62.

Hängerock that was fastened by the oddly named 'dwarf-pins' at the shoulders in the costume characteristic of a middle-class woman in the tenth- or eleventh-century Norse poem *Rígsþula*:

> ... smokkr var á bringu
> dúkr var á hálsi
> dvergar á oxlum.

a blouse on her bosom, a kerchief at her neck, dwarf-pins at her shoulders.[24]

Fig. 28 Menimane's costume from her funerary monument, Mainz, Germany

The most important comparative material comes from the investigation made by John-Peter Wild into the costume of women depicted on funerary sculptures of the first and early-second centuries in the Rhine Valley. The costume is exemplified on the figure of a woman whose name is given on her monument as Menimane (Fig. 28). Menimane wears a tubular gown clasped front to back by brooches. The brooch which secures the gown on her left side is clearly visible, part-way down her upper arm. The right-hand fastening is obscured by her cloak. Menimane was able to arrange her gown off the left shoulder because it was secured to an undergarment by a brooch at the centre of her chest. The collar and cuff of the undergarment are clearly indicated. Unlike the bare-armed Germanic women on several Roman works of art[25] and as described by Tacitus and Ibn Fadlan, the Rhineland women depicted on this group of monuments are consistently shown wearing a sleeved garment beneath the gown, a fashion which also appears as a variant of the bare-armed costume on the Marcus Aurelius Column. What we might consider the 'normal' position for the Rhineland gown involved a fastening at each shoulder (see Wild's reconstruction of a sculpture from Ingelheim, Fig. 29), but some of the Rhineland carvings demonstrate that, given the undergarment for modesty and as a secure base to which the gown could be pinned, the gown itself need not be arranged symmetrically: Menimane's gown was draped off the left shoulder; on the sculpture of a girl, from Mainz, the gown has been fastened in the usual way at the left shoulder, but at the right side it has been arranged *under* the arm, so exposing the undergarment at the chest and over the right breast (Fig. 30).

Fig. 29 Costume of a woman on a sculpture, Ingelheim, Germany, Drawn by J.-P. Wild

The costume identified by Wild bears a resemblance to the reconstruction of the dress of a richly-equipped young woman who was buried in the early-fifth century at Zweelloo, Drenthe, Netherlands. The wooden coffin had survived, making it possible to transfer the entire burial to the archaeological laboratory at Amersfoort

---

[24] *Rígsþula* 16; U. Dronke (ed. and trans.), *The Poetic Edda*, II, Mythological Poems (Oxford, 1997), p. 166.

[25] Cook, 'The Evidence for the Reconstruction of Female Costume', lists, in addition to sources mentioned in the present book: the *Gemma Augustea* for 12 A. D.; the *Gemma Tiberiana*; and the fifth-century Arcadius Column, formerly in Constantinople.

Fig. 30 Costume of a girl on a sculpture, Mainz, Germany

Fig. 31 The costume of the 'princess' of Zweeloo, Drenthe, Netherlands, as reconstructed and drawn by J. Ypey

where the positions and relationships of the grave-goods were observed and measured in unusual detail.[26] (Inhumations are normally excavated from above, sometimes rapidly, to avoid theft or destruction.) Jaap Ypey's resulting reconstruction of the costume included a tubular gown, clasped by brooches at the shoulders (Fig. 31), which was probably similar to the costume being worn by the Anglo-Saxon settlers across the North Sea (Figs 32, 33).

Having reconstructed the Germanic version of the *peplos* from the typical arrangement of brooches (Figs 34 a–c, where the garment is a long gown like Menimane's), we can see that the brooches themselves were not essential. Fasteners of perishable material might have been used instead of metal brooches. A skeleton, probably that of a young girl, in Wakerley Grave 61, had two bone pins, dissimilar in size but similar in style, which might have been brooch-substitutes.[27] The girl herself might not have acquired the status or wealth to own metal brooches. Similar pins, again slightly different in size but without ornament, were found with a girl aged about eleven in Grave 22 at Oakington, Cambridgeshire. In this case, however, the girl also had a silver-plated great square-headed brooch, the most opulent item found in the cemetery, so we cannot assume bone pins were a mark of low status.[28] Other organic fasteners such as horn rings which functioned as annular brooches, from several Anglian sites,[29] a bone button from Chessel Down, Isle of Wight[30] and a wooden wedge from Stapenhill, Staffordshire[31] are perhaps rare survivals of types which may have been in common use. Metal pins and buckles might sometimes have fulfilled the role of brooches, and could, perhaps, have fastened the gown, though no regular pattern emerges. In Cambridgeshire graves there are several cases of buckles being found at the upper part of women's bodies, including, from Barrington B, an instance of a pair of buckles

Fig. 32 Reconstruction of the dress of an Anglian woman of the sixth century

[26] W. A. Van Es and J. Ypey, 'Das grab der "prinzessin" von Zweeloo und seine bedeutung im Rahmen des Gräberfeldes', in H.-J. Hässler (ed.), *Studien zur Sachsenforschung (Festschrift A. Genrich)* (Hildesheim, 1977), pp. 97–126.

[27] Adams, Jackson and Badenoch, 'Wakerley', p. 158 and p. 124, Fig. 58.

[28] Taylor, Duhig and Hines, 'Oakington', pp. 22 and (Fig.) 87.

[29] Sleaford, Lincolnshire, Grave 50 (G. W. Thomas, 'On excavations in an Anglo-Saxon cemetery at Sleaford in Lincolnshire', *Archaeologia*, 50 (1887), pp. 383–406, at p. 391); Nassington, Northamptonshire, Grave 10 (E. T. Leeds and R. J. C. Atkinson, 'An Anglo-Saxon cemetery at Nassington, Northants', *Antiquaries Journal*, 24 (1944), pp. 100–28, at p. 105); Newnham, Northamptonshire (A. Meaney, *A Gazetteer of Anglo-Saxon Burial Sites* (London, 1964), p. 193); Londesborough, E. Yorkshire, Grave 9 (M. J. Swanton, 'An Anglian cemetery at Londesborough in East Yorkshire', *Yorkshire Archaeological Journal*, 41 (1963–6), pp. 262–86, at p. 279); Market Weighton, E. Yorkshire (T. Sheppard, 'An Anglo-Saxon grave in East Yorkshire and its contents', *The Antiquary*, 42 (1906), pp. 333–8, at p. 336.) The two last-mentioned rings were of the bone from the base of deers' horns; separate iron pins accompanied them; the Market Weighton example was found at the waist.

[30] T. Wright, 'Discoveries of Anglo-Saxon antiquities', *Journal of the British Archaeological Association*, 1st series, 2 (1847), pp. 50–9, at p. 54.

[31] Grave 7. J. Heron, 'Report on the Stapenhill explorations', *Transactions of the Burton-on-Trent Natural History and Archaeological Society*, 1 (1889), pp. 156–93, at p. 163.

in the positions normally occupied by brooches.[32] Possibly the gown in this case was secured by buckled shoulder straps. Simple pins are not uncommon finds. Although we might imagine a straight pin would easily fall out, if the shaft was hipped, as many were, it was less likely to slide through the material. Many pins have perforated heads and ring-heads, and these may have been attached to strings or thongs which would hold them in place, even if they were worn point upwards.[33] The perforation or ring was not essential; any pin which had a head might have had string tied round it to secure it in this way (Fig. 35). A pin might have been paired with a single brooch to make a set of shoulder fastenings, or it might have secured a gown to the under-bodice if it was held by only one brooch.

The evidence from Continental sculptures that the gown need be clasped only at one shoulder offers another explanation for the fact that some female skeletons have only one brooch. This is a variation found in Anglian, Saxon and Jutish regions. At Long Wittenham, Berkshire, only young women were limited to a single brooch,[34] and in Wiltshire the fashion is particularly associated with children,[35] though this is not a national pattern. Possibly this was a

Fig. 33 Sixth-century Anglian dress with cloak

Figs 34 a–c Reconstruction of the cylindrical gown

[32] Grave 93. Possibly also Grave 90; W. K. Foster, 'Account of the excavation of an Anglo-Saxon cemetery at Barrington, Cambridgeshire', *Cambridge Antiquarian Society Communications*, 5 (1880–4), pp. 5–32, at p. 27.

[33] S. Ross, 'Dress Pins from Anglo-Saxon England: their production and typo-chronological development', unpublished D. Phil thesis (University of Oxford, 1991), p. 397.

[34] J. Y. Akerman, 'Report on researches in an Anglo-Saxon cemetery at Long Wittenham, Berkshire, in 1859', *Archaeologia*, 38 (1860), pp. 327–52 at pp. 337–48.

[35] Harnham Hill (J. Y. Akerman, 'An account of excavations in an Anglo-Saxon burial ground at Harnham Hill, nr. Salisbury' and 'Notes on some further discoveries', *Archaeologia*, 35 (1853), pp. 259–78, 475–9, at p. 261); Petersfinger, Grave 46 (a single brooch in Grave 48 was Roman not Anglo-Saxon; E. T. Leeds and H. de S. Shortt, *An Anglo-Saxon Cemetery at Petersfinger, near Salisbury, Wilts* (Salisbury, 1953), p. 30); Winterbourne Gunner, Grave 7 (J. Musty and J. E. D. Stratton, 'A Saxon cemetery at Winterbourne Gunner, near Salisbury', *Wiltshire Archaeological Magazine*, 59 (1964), pp. 86–109 at p. 91).

Fig. 35 Reconstruction of how a pin can be fastened with string

matter of status, but perhaps a simpler form of dress was a matter of convenience.[36] At a very few sites, for example, Wheatley, Oxfordshire, single brooches were more popular than pairs, but this was never typical of the region in general. If a brooch was worn at one shoulder only, women appear to have preferred the left. Cruciform, annular and saucer brooches appear most often in this role, but the rarer penannular occurs in at least four cases.

We must also consider the cases such as some graves at Sleaford, Lincolnshire, in which women who were evidently buried in their clothing since they had grave-goods such as buckles, clasps, and usually, beads, were without brooches or any other obvious fastener at the shoulder.[37] Apart from the explanation that organic fasteners might have been used, there is also the possibility that the gown could have been stitched. We cannot, then, state categorically that these women were *not* wearing the *peplos*-type gown, though this is possible. The quality and quantity of jewellery found in women's graves demonstrates that the garment was worn by the wealthy and the not-so-wealthy. We do not know, however, if it was worn by the lowest strata of society – the very poor and slaves. As has been demonstrated, the gown could be secured without metal fasteners, and possibly the poor wore it this way, as a folk-costume common to all; but perhaps the gown was a mark of rank, status, or even of ethnicity, and there were some women who did not wear it, including both poor and more prosperous women.

How much farther can we go in reconstructing the Anglo-Saxon *peplos*? It probably appeared to be tubular but we do not know if it was made of a rectangular or a cylindrical piece of cloth. It was possible to weave a cylinder of cloth on a two-beam loom, a type which may have survived in England from Roman times (see p. 295), but overwhelming evidence both in the form of loom weights and in the nature of Anglo-Saxon textile remains suggest that the loom in general use in the pagan period was the warp-weighted (see pp. 287–90). On this a square or rectangle of cloth would be produced, which could be turned into a cylinder by stitching two edges together; alternatively the cloth could simply be wrapped round the woman – there would be no need for cutting or shaping – and secured at the shoulders by brooches and at the waist by a belt or girdle, but leaving one side open. As far as I am aware, none of the textile fragments which have been found on Anglo-Saxon shoulder brooches preserves either a corner of cloth (which would imply that the gown was open) or a seam (which might indicate that it was stitched into a cylinder). Perhaps we have failed to recognise evidence (see p. 74, Worthy Park). This is obviously a detail which archaeological textile experts may yet clarify.

Figs 36, 37 Seated woman, nursing mother on an ivory diptych, Halberstadt, Germany

[36] Re-enactor Melanie Wilson of *Wulfingas 450 AD* reports that the *peplos* is conveniently adapted for a child using one brooch. This method of fastening is preferable when the child is out-growing the garment.

[37] For example Graves 4, 48, 51, 71, 90, 207; Thomas, 'Sleaford', pp. 389, 391, 393–4, 402.

The gown could certainly be girdled or belted, but it is versatile in this respect and could accommodate a woman's changing figure and needs. On the fifth-century Halberstadt Diptych, an ivory carving, women wear the gown pulled in just below the breasts, then hanging loose below (Fig. 36). This might have been a comfortable arrangement during early pregnancy. Ungirdled, the garment was probably full enough to be worn through to the birth of a child. The shoulder fastening was of course convenient for breast feeding, as shown on the same carving (Fig. 37),[38] though women who did not need or wish to slip the *peplos* down could have put the garment on and off without unfastening the brooches.[39] With one brooch unfastened, the upper part of the *peplos* could help support and cradle a baby.

Most Continental depictions of the *peplos* show it girdled at the waist. In the costumes of some figures on the Marcus Aurelius Column and on a Mainz sculpture (Fig. 30) the material has been pouched to conceal the belt. A Roman sculpture of a woman believed to represent the province of *Germania* (Fig. 38) shows the costume pouched, presumably over a concealed girdle, while a second belt is visible. Ypey's reconstruction of the Zweelloo costume, with the beaded belt visible (Fig. 31), assumed such an arrangement.[40] Pouching the material over the belt would take some of the weight off the shoulders, and off the fabric at the points where it was attached to the brooches. It would be a quick and practical way of shortening the garment in wet or dirty conditions[41] or if it was to be worn by a woman who was smaller than the original owner, having been recycled through inheritance or the age-old practice of 'passing down' clothes to younger or socially inferior members of the community. It has generally been assumed that the tools and indicators of status which hung at a woman's belt were suspended *outside* the peplos. Evidence from Grave 74 at Wakerley (p. 38 above) suggests that in this case at least objects hung *between* the peplos and the undergarment, and therefore from a belt round the tunic, not the *peplos*. If the *peplos* were open down one side, or relatively short, it would be easy to reach the tools.

We have, in the past, lacked evidence about the length of the Anglo-Saxon *peplos*-type gown. The garments on Roman sculptures were floor length. The North African garment was also long, and the surviving Huldremose garment is certainly long enough to reach to the wearer's feet. However, a shorter version of it, probably calf-

Fig. 38 Sculpted figure, probably representing *Germania*, collection in the Villa Pamfili-Doria, Rome

[38] This does not take account of an undergarment.

[39] 'It has been observed of some small-long brooches, typically shoulder brooches, that their catch-plates appear to have been bent over so that the brooch is effectively clenched shut, and could not easily be opened (pers. comm. M. D. Howe)'; Hines, *Great Square-Headed Brooches*, p. 281.

[40] Van Es and Ypey, 'Das grab der "prinzessin" von Zweeloo'.

[41] This is confirmed by members of the re-enactment groups *Regia Anglorum* and *Theod*, particularly as a result of working at 'Bede's World' (Jarrow, Co. Durham) and West Stow Anglo-Saxon village (Suffolk). I am grateful to Hazel Uzzell for discussing this point with her fellow-members on my behalf.

Fig. 39 Figure on an altar, Klagenfurt, Austria

length, was apparently worn by women and girls in the first and second centuries AD in the provinces of Noricum and Pannonia (the areas of present-day Austria and Hungary) as typified by a relief carving on an altar found at Klagenfurt, Austria (Fig. 39).[42] The Viking equivalent of our gown is usually illustrated by modern artists as a calf-length over-garment worn with an ankle-length dress beneath it,[43] but this seems to be a convention, and I know of no firm evidence for these dimensions. It would probably be wise, though, to rid ourselves of the assumption that women's dress, until the twentieth century, was always long. Certainly it has rarely been shorter than the ankle since late Saxon times, if we are to believe pictures, but in the Dark Ages matters may have been different. Continental examples contemporary to our period provide precedents. Grave finds in Alamannia demonstrate that (unlike in England) garters with decorated strap ends were popular in the first half of the sixth century; if, as seems likely, they were intended to be displayed, the accompanying skirts must have reached only to just below the knee.[44] Royal Frankish costume in the second half of the sixth century, as exemplified in the dress of a richly equipped woman found in the Cathedral of Saint-Denis, Paris, who wore a ring engraved with the name 'Arnegundis', similarly included a tunic short enough to reveal leather garters with metal buckles and strap ends, though a longer robe like a coat which opened down the front was worn over it (see p. 99).[45]

Our uncertainty about the nature of the early Anglo-Saxon undergarment only adds to the problem about the length of the *peplos*. A gown worn without an undergarment (and in non-Anglian areas there is little or no evidence of the latter) might well be long, for warmth; but if it covered a long undergown, it might conceivably be shorter, like the example on the Klagenfurt relief. In Grave 74 at Wakerley, textile on grave-goods suggests that the undergarment hung at least to well down the legs. If we reconstruct the Wakerley costume making the *peplos* much shorter than the undergown, namely about hip length, it bears a remarkable resemblance to garments shown on Greek sculptures (Fig. 22), which have a frill round the hips, perhaps indicating a short garment worn over a longer one.

Our surviving textile material (see Chapter VIII) is initially unimpressive in comparison with that from Scandinavia and other

[42] J. Garbsch, *Die norisch-pannonische Frauentracht im 1 und 2 Jahrhundert* (Munich, 1965).

[43] This seems to be the norm in popular books, for example F. Birkebæk, *Norden i Vikingtiden* (Göteborg, 1975), and in the catalogues of major Viking exhibitions such as J. Graham-Campbell and D. Kidd, *The Vikings* (London, 1980).

[44] R. Christlein, *Die Alamannen* (Stuttgart, 1978), p. 81.

[45] J. Werner, 'Frankish royal tombs in the Cathedrals of Cologne and Saint-Denis', *Antiquity*, 38 (1964), pp. 201–16. The ring was inscribed *Arnegundis* with a representation of the word *Regina*. The personal name has been identified as that of the wife of the Merovingian king Chlothar I. However, the lady in the grave may not have been Arnegund herself, but someone who received the ring as a gift from the Queen; see D. M. Wilson, 'A ring of Queen Arnegund', *Germania*, 42 (1964), pp. 265–8.

Germanic areas of the Continent. The peat bogs of Scandinavia and northern Germany have been richly productive of ancient textiles which include complete garments; early churches in Frankia have yielded richly-dressed corpses; and Alamannic *Reihengräber* have provided much textile and other evidence of dress. Nevertheless, the Anglo-Saxon pagan period offers a rich source of information, for many metal grave-goods preserve fragments of the cloth to which they were fastened, or against which they rested. Sometimes the textile survives in its natural state, more often it is mineralised, replaced by rust, or simply exists as an impression of woven cloth in rust. From such remains it is possible to make deductions about the fibre, spin and weaving of the cloth. Pioneered by Grace M. Crowfoot and continued and expanded by Elisabeth Crowfoot, such textile study has now become a recognised part of Anglo-Saxon cemetery archaeology. Although the majority of these fragments are tiny, rarely measuring more than a few centimetres across, painstaking analysis and the sheer quantity of examples[46] mean that there is a considerable amount of evidence about clothing, though it is very selective, since the vast majority of material comes from female graves and from brooches at the shoulders. Textile finds suggest that the *peplos*-type gown was often made of a light wool textile, usually 2 x 2 twill, but that it could also be made of the rarer broken diamond twill and 2 x 1 twill (see pp. 293–5). In some cases it seems to have been made of linen, which was usually, but not always, tabby woven. Penelope Walton Rogers has noted that at Castledyke South, Barton-on-Humber, North Lincolnshire, the seven women wearing linen gowns were particularly well-equipped with grave-goods;[47] at this site at least, linen may have been a status symbol. There is, as yet, no scientific evidence that the main body of the gown was dyed, though the Anglo-Saxons certainly appreciated bright colours and it may be that there was once pigmentation, lost during over a thousand years in the earth. As colour occasionally survives in tablet-woven braids, however, it might have been preserved in other textiles, had it been present. Perhaps Anglo-Saxon women at this period contented themselves with naturally pigmented wool and plain linen, apart from their brightly coloured braids. Even without artificial dye they could have created patterned fabric by combining variation in spin direction with appropriate weaving techniques: the diamond-patterned twills seem to have exploited the use of Z-spun threads for warp and S- for weft, and stripes or checks could be created entirely from such 'spin-patterns' or 'shadow patterns', though it may be that an occasional S-spun thread in cloth with predominantly Z-spun warp and weft was

---

[46] One cemetery alone has yielded about 280 fragments of mineral replaced textile; E. Crowfoot, 'The textiles', in B. Green, A. Rogerson and S. G. White, *The Anglo-Saxon Cemetery at Morning Thorpe, Norfolk'*, East Anglian Archaeological Report, 36.1, 1987, pp. 171–88.

[47] Walton Rogers, 'Textiles and clothing', in Drinkall and Foreman, *Castledyke*, pp. 274–9 and microfiche Mf. 2.B13-C12, at p. 276.

also originally differently pigmented as well as differently spun.[48]

Evidently the gown often had a decorative edging at the neck, since fragments of tablet-woven braids (pp. 283–5, Plate 6 and Figs 228–30) are frequently found on the backs and pins of shoulder brooches. The warp-weighted loom as used in Scandinavia up to modern times could characteristically employ a starting border which was tablet-woven[49] and Anglo-Saxon weavers evidently also used this method of setting up the warp on some occasions. Analysis of tablet-weave on two matching brooches from Blewburton Hill, Berkshire, demonstrated that here the wearer had exploited the functional border created in preparation for weaving the twill fabric of which the gown was made.[50] The shoulder brooches had been attached to the starting border, which ornamented the neckline with its chevron pattern. There was no raw edge requiring hemming, and the strong braid provided firm attachment-points for the brooches and would not be ripped by them as the thinner fabric of the gown might have been. Not all tablet-woven edgings necessarily came from starting borders, however. Elisabeth Crowfoot has suggested that some of the more elaborate braids at the necks of garments, which had perhaps been decorated with embroidery, were woven separately and attached by stitching.[51] Fragments of plaits and fringes have also have been found occasionally on brooches and these may also be the remains of decorative edgings. We do not know if these were functional as well as ornamental. (If any of these edgings were stitched into loops, like the examples from Birka, there has been no evidence of it.) There is visible proof that tablet-woven braids were brightly coloured though the evidence comes from a possible girdle and wrist bands rather than neck-edging.[52] Tablet-weaving is a domestic and versatile craft, and merely by varying the details of colour, threading direction and turning of the tablets, an exponent could produce a unique pattern. Doubtless it was in

[48] There is a possible S-spun stripe in textile on one of a pair of saucer brooches from Grave 79 at Barrington A, a high-status grave at that site; E. Crowfoot, 'Textiles associated with metalwork', in T. Malim and J. Hines with C. Duhig, *The Anglo-Saxon Cemetery at Edix Hill (Barrington A), Cambridgeshire*, Council for British Archaeology Research Report, 112 (1998), pp. 235–46, at pp. 239, 244.

[49] M. Hoffmann, *The Warp-weighted Loom: studies in the history and technology of an ancient implement*, Studia Norvegica 14 (Oslo, 1964), pp. 151–83. There are historic textiles woven on the warp-weighted loom without a starting border and there are borders woven by methods other than tablet weaving, but Hoffmann refers to a tablet-woven starting border as 'normal' for the warp-weighted loom. [50] A. S. Henshall, Appendix to A. E. P. Collins and F. J. Collins, 'Excavations on Blewburton Hill, 1953', *Berkshire Archaeological Journal*, 57 (1959), pp. 68–71.

[51] E. Crowfoot, in A. M. Cook and M. W. Dacre, *Excavations at Portway, Andover, 1974–5*, Oxford University Committee for Medieval Archaeology Monograph, 4 (1985), p. 99, cites Finglesham Grave 203 and Mucking Grave 814.

[52] For example, the fragment of a possible belt from St John's Cricket Field, Cambridge, G. M. Crowfoot, 'Textiles of the Saxon period in the Museum of Archaeology and Ethnology', *Proceedings of the Cambridge Antiquarian Society*, 44, 1951, pp. 26–32 at 28–30. A new photograph of it is reproduced here (Plate 6). More recently the remains of braids patterned in contrasting colours have been identified from Morning Thorpe, Norfolk (below, note 75).

features like this that a woman expressed her individuality or her affiliation to a family with its inherited tradition, while wearing a 'folk' costume common to a much wider group.

The *peplos* with its brooches and accompanying beads is a potential indicator of social features such as wealth, status, tribal affiliation, kinship group and age (see Chapter IX). As such, it is possible that it was worn only on formal occasions and that the everyday working dress of women was a simple garment of tunic type (see below, pp. 54–62). Against this possibility we must count the great quantity of manifestations of the *peplos* in Anglo-Saxon cemeteries. It is also worth noting that re-enactors who wear it universally praise its comfort and practicality. In hot weather they choose to dispense with the tunic worn under the *peplos* rather than the *peplos* itself. The Anglo-Saxon *peplos* has been assumed to be long. If it was short, as in the experiment suggested by the Wakerley textiles (p. 38), its functionality would diminish.

We cannot be sure what the Anglo-Saxons called this important garment. Indeed its name may have disappeared in the late-sixth to early-seventh centuries when the garment went out of use in England. None of the clothing-names applied to women's gowns in late Anglo-Saxon texts (tenth- and eleventh-century documents) can be readily identified with this early garment. The words *tunece* and *cyrtel* were used regularly for women's gowns in the tenth century, but *tunece*, since it derives from the Latin word *tunica*, probably did not enter the English language until after the conversion to Christianity. *Cyrtel*, related to the Old English verb *cyrtan*, 'to shorten' (itself loaned from Latin *curtus*, 'short') may have been used in pagan times, but originally, at least, was probably used for a garment of which the distinctive feature was its shortness. As we have seen, we do not know the length of the Anglo-Saxon *peplos*, but depictions of the Germanic costume on Roman monuments generally (with the exception of the Noricum/Pannonia variation) show it as long. If, in some (Anglian) areas at least, it was worn short, it could have been called *cyrtel*. The word *wealca*, related to the verb *wealcan*, 'to roll, toss', was evidently used of a loose garment wrapped round a woman, a description which could apply to the garment in question; but we must not put too much stress on this apparent similarity, for the word is only documented once from an early-eleventh-century Old Testament translation, and there is no proof that it was in use earlier. There remains the word *slop*, which is only documented from Old English texts as a compound element (for example *ofer-slop*, 'an over-garment, ecclesiastical vestment'), though it almost certainly existed independently in the spoken language since *sloppes* were worn in England in the fourteenth century.[53] The Icelandic cognate *sloppr* signifies 'a loose

---

[53] See Geoffrey Chaucer, *The Canterbury Tales: The Parson's Tale*, subdivision 420; L. D. Benson (ed.), *The Riverside Chaucer* (Oxford, third edition, 1990), p. 300. The citation refers to men's garments, shamefully short.

gown', and probably the Old English word meant something similar. There is no positive evidence that the *slop* was worn by women, but this word seems the most likely candidate for the name of the gown among the garment-names documented.

This seems the appropriate context to correct the common misapprehension that the English name for the Anglo-Saxon woman's dress was *gunna* and that the modern English word 'gown' descended directly from it. The word *gunna* was certainly known to the Anglo-Saxons but it is Latin not English. It occurs only in eighth-century Latin correspondence in contexts which demonstrate that it was the name of a long garment worn by monks. It was probably fur.[54] 'Gown' is not recorded in English until the fourteenth century.[55] It probably *is* related to *gunna*, but through the Old French *goune*, rather than in the close relationship that has been implied.

The tunic and undergarment

Tacitus and Ibn Fadlan record that German women were bare-armed, and some appear this way in Roman art, but it is improbable that Anglo-Saxon women faced an English winter without some clothing over their arms, even allowing for some variation in climate from our own day. It is more likely that they wore, like some figures on the Marcus Aurelius Column and the women on the Rhine valley group of sculptures (Figs 25, 28, 29, 30), a sleeved tunic, over which the *peplos*-type gown functioned like a modern pinafore-dress. The undergarment is depicted on the Rhineland sculptures only as a tight-sleeved bodice with an aperture at the front, where it is clasped together by a brooch, or by several brooches in a vertical row. The gown is secured to this bodice by a central brooch pinned horizontally, which is sometimes different in shape from the shoulder brooches. Indeed, the Germanic costume represented by the Rhineland sculptures, as Wild has reconstructed it, characteristically includes three brooches: a pair to fasten the gown on the shoulders and a third, worn centrally, securing the gown to the under-bodice.

In England, the three-brooch arrangement is very common in traditionally Anglian areas (Figs 32, 33), particularly modern Cambridgeshire, Lincolnshire, Northamptonshire and Suffolk. 'Third' brooches do occur in traditionally Saxon areas, but mostly as isolated cases, rather than a regular feature of a cemetery. Some of the

---

[54] The word is used by the ecclesiastics Cuthbert of Wearmouth and Boniface (M. Tangl (ed.), *S. Bonifatii et Lulli epistolae*, Monumenta Germaniae Historica, Epistolae 4, Epistolae Selectae, 1 (Berlin, 1916), No. 116, p. 251, lines 14–15; No. 114, p. 247, lines 21–2). It is glossed by the Old English word *heden* in the Corpus Glossary; W. M. Lindsay (ed.), *The Corpus Glossary* (Cambridge, 1921), p. 87, line 185.

[55] See J. A. H. Murray, H. Bradley, W. A. Craigie and C. T. Onions (ed.), *The Oxford English Dictionary*, 12 vols (Oxford, corrected edition with supplement, 1933); *Supplement* (1972): gunna.

'Jutish' graves of Hampshire and Kent contain more than two brooches, but in number and position these differ from the simple arrangement of a pair of shoulder brooches with a third between, and usually below them, which is so noticeable in Anglian cemeteries. It is of course, impossible for the modern reconstructor to decide whether a third brooch fastened the gown to the undergarment, or whether it clasped a cloak or shawl over the gown, unless there is clear evidence from textile remains. Where a third brooch is noticeably larger and heavier than the shoulder brooches, or where there are remains of coarse textile (about 9 x 9 threads per cm) it is reasonable to suppose that there was a cloak or other, heavier garment; but where the brooch is of similar size to the shoulder brooches, and there is evidence of an undergarment from wrist clasps and/or textile, we may have a costume like the Rhineland one. However, sometimes the implications of brooch size and of textile quality conflict: a female buried in Grave 80 at Wakerley offers an example. She wore a pair of annular shoulder brooches, one of which preserved on the back the remains of fine diamond-patterned twill, probably from the *peplos*-type gown. A large square-headed brooch was on the chest between the shoulders, but the textile on the back of it was not the coarse weave of a cloak (cf. Grave 74 at the same site, Fig. 10), but a fine twill, Z-spun in both warp and weft, a textile also found on an iron key at the left of the pelvis. This fine twill, then, probably derived from an undergown, the presence of which was confirmed by the presence of wrist clasps. At Castledyke, however, it was clear from the textile evidence in four cases that cruciform brooches at the throats had fastened thick textile, evidently from cloaks, and that at this site long pins (one bone, probably from a pig, one metal) rather than brooches had fastened gowns to undergarments.[56] It is always possible, of course, that for some women a central brooch fulfilled both functions, clasping a cloak and also securing the gown to the undergarment, especially in the grave, where the arrangement of clothing was both iconic and final.

The Anglian women who wore a third brooch at the centre of the chest normally chose one unlike the shoulder brooches. Even in Anglian areas where paired long brooches (usually cruciform) are often associated with a third brooch of the same type, this central one usually differs in size and/or decoration. Square-headed and cruciform brooches were worn in central position more often than round brooches, although in a few cases saucer or applied brooches were used in this way and there are rarer instances of annular, disc, swastika-shaped and also of equal-armed brooches in this role. In some cases only a single, centrally-placed brooch has

[56] Cruciform brooches with coarse textile were found in Graves 29, 74, 137 and 163. In Grave 29 the coarse tabby weave 'also covered the belt which fastened the tubular gown at the waist'. Central pins were found in Graves 137 and 158; Walton Rogers, 'Textiles and clothing', in Drinkall and Foreman, *Castledyke*, p. 278; see also Drinkall and Foreman, p. 75.

been found in a woman's grave. In these instances the woman's gown was perhaps stitched at the shoulders, and the single brooch could either have attached the gown to the undergarment or fastened the central aperture of the bodice.

Since the undergarment is the only item of female clothing from this date known to have sleeves,[57] the little metal fasteners known to Anglo-Saxon archaeologists as **wrist clasps** were probably attached to this garment. Although they have been found at Kempston, Bedfordshire, where the Saxon culture of Essex and Wessex overlapped with Anglian,[58] and as far west as Warwickshire,[59] it is clear that wrist clasps were predominantly an Anglian fashion. Interestingly, clasps do not seem to have been popular in the Anglian homeland on the Continent (the Schleswig-Holstein area); rather, they are found in Norway, eastern Sweden and the Swedish island of Gotland, and in Denmark.[60] They seem to have arrived in England *c.* 475, perhaps with immigrants from western Norway.[61] The earliest Anglo-Saxon manifestations of clasps are in eastern England, in the Lincolnshire and Norfolk areas, but the fashion evidently spread rapidly, and examples have been found as far north as North Yorkshire (Anglo-Saxon Northumbria) and in the Midland counties of Leicestershire and Northamptonshire. At Barrington A, Cambridgeshire, a meeting point of East Anglian, Mercian and Saxon (Thames Valley) culture, several women wore wrist clasps in conjunction with (typically Saxon) saucer brooches paired at the shoulders, though it may be significant that the excavators found that clasps were commoner with cruciform and annular brooch 'costume sets' (Anglian styles) at Barrington and neighbouring South Cambridgeshire cemeteries.[62] Wrist clasps seem to have gone out of use about a century after their introduction.[63]

The use of clasps was much more restricted in England than in Scandinavia: in Norway men had worn clasps of the rectangular type at wrists and ankles (presumably securing the trouser-bottoms) and women had worn them at the bosom as well as the wrist, and in

---

[57] Hines's suggestion that wrist clasps were attached to 'a development of the *peplos*-type dress with sleeves added to the body' (*Great Square-Headed Brooches*, p. 281), is hardly practical: the under-arm area with its extra material and the separable shoulder would not provide an appropriate fixing point for a sleeve.

[58] Grave found 3 June 1863; S. E. Fitch, 'Discovery of Saxon remains at Kempston', *Reports of the Associated Architectural Societies*, 7 (1863–4), pp. 269–99, at pp. 270, 285.

[59] At Alveston Manor, Baginton, Bidford-on-Avon and Churchover; J. Hines, *Clasps, Hektespenner, Agraffen. Anglo-Scandinavian Clasps of Classes A–C of the 3rd to 6th Centuries A.D. Typology, diffusion and function* (Stockholm, 1993), pp. 110, 122–5.

[60] Palm and Pind, 'Chronological analysis', in Jørgensen, *Chronological Studies*, p. 68.

[61] Hines, *Scandinavian Character*, pp. 35–109, where the distribution and typology of clasps, both English and Scandinavian, is discussed in detail. I am grateful to Professor Hines for replying to my individual queries.

[62] Graves 29, 79, 95; Malim and Hines, *Edix Hill (Barrington A)*, p. 316. The archaeoethnographic potential of dress study is discussed in Chapter IX.

[63] Palm and Pind, ' Chronological analysis', p. 69 (based on a study of five sites).

greater quantity than in England. In England only women appear to have worn clasps;[64] they wore them at the wrist and never more than one pair at each wrist. There are very few occurrences of clasps being found in other positions: at Bifrons, Kent, a pair of clasps evidently replaced brooches;[65] a pair found between the legs of a female skeleton at Barrington A, associated with a purse group,[66] had probably either been contained in the purse or had fastened it; a pair found under the pelvis of a Castledyke skeleton and an 'extra' hook on the chest of another may have had unusual uses or been carried as spares.[67] Two examples of what were described as '?ankle clasps' were found in a female grave with brooches and wrist clasps at Empingam II, Rutland, but they seem to have been associated with the chatelaine complex, which was quite extensive.[68] No consistent pattern emerges and these were evidently idiosyncratic cases. In Scandinavia, clasps were attached to garments by various means, including buttons and rivets. In England they appear to have been stitched in most cases, which may represent a change in the gender of dress construction. In Scandinavia, where clasps were often riveted onto the garment, the fixing would perhaps have been carried out by the men who were the metalworkers. In England, attachment may have been carried out by the women who wore the clasps. Scandinavia and England share three basic types of clasp, those of spiral wire (Fig. 40), cast clasps with spiral or stylised zoomorphic ornament (Fig. 41) and cast rectangles (particularly popular in England; Fig. 42). Each pair of clasps consists of two pieces designed to hook together, sometimes with a third triangular portion, the 'gusset plate' (largely confined to East Anglia and Cambridgeshire),[69] which was designed to conceal the slit where the sleeve opened (Fig. 41). A full set of clasps as worn in England would consist of identical pairs at each wrist, although in practice sets were often made up of pieces which did not match, and sometimes the sets of clasps supplied as grave-goods were incomplete. Where only one pair was worn it was usually at the left wrist. Sometimes there is evidence of an attempt to supply a substitute for a missing clasp. In a grave at Linton Heath, Cambridgeshire, the clasps at one wrist

Fig. 40 Spiral wire wrist clasps, Barrington A, Cambridgeshire

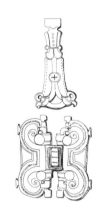

Fig. 41 A pair of cast wrist clasps with gusset plate, one of a set, Lakenheath, Suffolk.

[64] Although Stilborg includes clasps from six graves at Morning Thorpe in his survey of male grave-goods (O. Stilborg, 'A chronological analysis of Anglo-Saxon men's graves in England', in Jørgensen, *Chronological Studies*, pp. 35–45), in all these but Grave 126 there had probably been either a disturbed female grave or a double burial. In Grave 126 the clasp was incomplete and not in a position consistent with being worn; see Green, Rogerson and White, *Morning Thorpe*.

[65] Hines, *Scandinavian Character*, p. 108.

[66] Grave 10. This was an extra pair. The woman had a pair of clasps at each wrist; Malim and Hines, *Edix Hill (Barrington A)*, p. 44.

[67] Drinkall and Foreman, *Castledyke*, p. 271.

[68] Grave 83. There were girdle hangers, keys, an ivory ring, two lace tags, strap fittings and other metal fragments; J. R. Timby, *The Anglo-Saxon Cemetery at Empingham II, Rutland*, Oxbow Monograph 70 (Oxford, 1996), p. 117.

[69] Hines, *Clasps*, p. 74.

were balanced by studs at another,[70] and at Woodstone, Peterborough, beads were found at the right wrist of a skeleton with clasps at the left.[71] One can only speculate why so many sets of clasps were buried incomplete: being thin, they may have cracked easily, especially the popular rectangular type. If they had been supplied by a travelling merchant they might have been impossible to match; perhaps, though many look unimpressive to the modern eye, they were an expensive luxury, too costly to replace.

Their function has not always been obvious; the excavator of Sleaford, Lincolnshire, where thirty-seven of the ninety female graves contained clasps, many of them embedded in leather, considered that the clasps had fastened leather wrist-bands or bracelets.[72] The conclusion that wrist-clasps fastened sleeves was reached by Grace M. Crowfoot when she was able to analyse textile preserved on clasps from two Suffolk sites, Mildenhall[73] and Mitchell's Hill[74] and this explanation is now generally accepted for English clasps. As Crowfoot reconstructed it (Fig. 42), the sleeve had been close-fitting, with a slit at the wrist to enable the hand to pass through. The sleeve was edged with a cuff which had been stitched to the clasps. The slit in the sleeve was closed by hooking together the two halves of the clasp. The remainder of the aperture could be closed by the addition of a triangular gusset plate. The fragments of cuff examined by Grace M. Crowfoot were woollen, braided by the technique of tablet-weaving (below, pp. 283–5) and, since they were the same width as the clasps, could have been woven specially for them. More recent research by Elisabeth Crowfoot confirms the association of tablet-woven cuffs with wrist clasps, and has demonstrated that the cuffs could be braided in several colours[75] or decorated with brocading or embroidery. At least one of the tablet-woven wrist bands from Barrington A had been brocaded in horsehair, creating diagonal patterns of soumak (wrapped) weave on untwisted

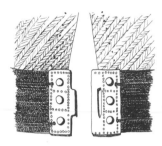

Fig. 42 Reconstruction of how clasps fastened the sleeve cuff from a rectangular wrist clasps with textile remains, Mildenhall, Suffolk. After G. M. Crowfoot

[70] Grave 9; R. C. Neville, 'Anglo-Saxon cemetery excavated January 1853', *Archaeological Journal*, 11 (1854). pp. 95–115, at pp. 96–7; the two studs were at the right wrist. The clasps were said to be found at the waist but presumably had been worn at the left wrist. It is common for the find-position of clasps to be described in relation to the waist or pelvis since the arms were often laid over the body.

[71] Grave 7; G. W. Abbott, 'Further discoveries in Anglo-Saxon cemeteries at Woodston [*sic*] Hunts', *Peterborough Natural History, Scientific and Archaeological Society Report*, 49 (1920), pp. 34–9, at p. 36.

[72] Thomas, 'Sleaford', p. 387. I have deduced that the burials were female from the typically gendered grave-goods.

[73] G. M. Crowfoot, 'Textiles of the Saxon period'.

[74] G. M. Crowfoot, ' Anglo-Saxon tablet weaving', *Antiquaries Journal*, 32 (1952), pp. 189–91. Dr Blindheim had reached this conclusion in analysing Scandinavian material; C. Blindheim, 'Drakt og smykker', *Viking*, 11 (1947), pp. 1–139, at pp. 79–82.

[75] The remains of patterned braids with blue, white and red-purple threads were observed in wrist clasps from two different graves (358 and 360) at Morning Thorpe, Norfolk (E. Crowfoot, 'The textiles', in Green, Rogerson and White, *Morning Thorpe*, pp. 172, 182–3). The weft of a sample was probably dyed with a red mordant dye, madder or kermes, and the warp with a different red or purple dye; P. Walton, 'Appendix: tests for dyes on a braid from wrist-clasp J (Grave 360)', appendix to Crowfoot, in Green, Rogerson and White, *Morning Thorpe*, p. 174.

cords within the tablet braid.[76] The leather cuff seems to have been a local variation of the Lincolnshire area. There are examples from Welbeck Hill[77] in addition to the well-known Sleaford cases. In most cases the position of the clasps suggests that sleeves reached to the wrist. However, a female skeleton in Grave 1 at Oakington, Cambridgeshire, had pairs of clasps about half way along the bones of each forearm, suggesting her sleeves were considerably shorter than usual.[78]

Although clasps have been found in many cemeteries over a wide area, they were only worn by a minority of women at these sites, evidently being an optional extra rather than a necessity. It may be relevant to note that some re-enactors, who find the *peplos* comfortable to work in, report that both the sleeves and the wrist clasps of the undergown are inconvenient.[79] It is possible, then, that sleeves were pushed up or folded back for work[80] and were worn tightly clasped at the wrist only by women who did not have to perform physical labour. Clasps have been found with women equipped with many and various grave-goods, which would suggest the status of someone who might have servants or slaves; but they have also been found in graves with relatively few grave-goods. In these cases they may have been worn by working women when they had completed their labour and were able to appear leisured. The mourners preparing a body for the grave may have aimed to display maximum status, even if this meant using unmatching clasps to complete the appropriate costume.

The fashion for wearing clasps may have been imported from Norway in the 470s, but this need not mean that the garment they fastened came at the same time and by the same route, though tablet-weaving might have owed some of its popularity to this influence. As we have seen, a sleeved undergarment already accompanied the *peplos*-type gown on some Continental sculptures of Germanic women. Nor does the prevalence of the third brooch and wrist clasps in Anglian areas mean that their absence in other areas should be interpreted as the absence of the undergown. As John Hines notes, clasps were common in Jutland and might have been expected to travel with Jutish migrants to Kent, but there is as yet no evidence

[76] Grave 10. Grave 106 may have been another example. There is also evidence of this from Snape, Suffolk; Crowfoot in Malim and Hines, *Edix Hill (Barrington A)*, pp. 235–46 at p. 239, Fig. vii and p. 246.

[77] Information on this site was kindly provided by the excavator, G. Taylor, including a textiles report by Elisabeth Crowfoot.

[78] I take this point from the illustration of the grave in Taylor, Duhig and Hines, 'Oakington', p. 72. This very detailed figure shows that the clasp on the right arm hooked left over right and that on the left arm right over left, but the clasps did not appear to be hooked together when excavated, though they were close and parallel.

[79] Hazel Uzzell reports that the tight sleeves have been found uncomfortable for working in, and Ben Levick notes that metal wrist clasps, which have been known to sever the warp threads on a vertical loom, have had to be removed for weaving.

[80] Ian Uzzell has demonstrated to me that tight sleeves, even with a slit, can not be folded back very far.

of it; and he concludes that in Kent 'this area of material culture rapidly failed';[81] we cannot know if the garment, or only the metal fastener, was abandoned. An isolated piece of evidence from Petersfinger, Wiltshire, warns against too ready dismissal of the sleeved garment in Saxon regions: two identical button brooches attached to leather and woollen textile were found at the wrists of a female skeleton.[82] Where there was no fastener for the sleeves they could have been tidied up by turning them back, as on a sculpture from Mainz (Fig. 30) or they could have been secured by pins or sewing stitches. It was common practice to pin or stitch the clothing at least up to the seventeenth century, and more recent costumes than this have been made for the wearer to be stitched in.[83] Any of these possibilities could have been available to the Anglo-Saxon woman who wished to wear her sleeves fastened at the wrist for any length of time.

Surviving textile fragments on clasps suggest that the undergown could be made of various materials and weaves. The Mildenhall and Mitchell's Hill sleeves were of twill-woven wool (the Mildenhall at least being the common 2 x 2 weave) and material attached to clasps at Woodstone, Huntingdonshire, was also twill.[84] Textile on clasps from a Lakenheath, Suffolk, grave was tabby-woven although other fabrics in the grave, probably from cloak and gown, were twill. In this case the undergarment may have been bordered by a simple tablet-woven braid, while a more complex braid edged the gown.[85] The button brooches from Petersfinger preserved two woollen textiles, one twill, the other tabby. In some cases shoulder brooches preserve more than one textile on their undersides, which provides evidence for an undergown as well as a *peplos*. The brooches from Blewburton Hill preserved three layers of textile. The coarsest of these was the twill material edged with tablet-woven braid which probably derived from the gown. Under this the woman had worn two layers of finely-woven textile, of which the outer, and finer, was a 2 x 2 twill. Textiles on a brooch from Welbeck Hill suggest that the owner dressed in a twill gown with tablet-woven border, over a twill-woven garment of linen. The distribution of different textiles in Grave 74 at Wakerley (Fig. 10) seems

---

[81] Hines, *Clasps*, p. 89.

[82] Leeds and Shortt, *Petersfinger*, pp. 21, 45–6. The skeleton did not have the usual paired brooches at the shoulders. Instead there was a semi-circular-headed brooch of Frankish type at the neck and a third button brooch (which like the others had a stylised face) at the breast. The woman was perhaps influenced by both Kentish and Anglian dress fashions though in a Saxon area.

[83] This was certainly a feature of later medieval and Renaissance dress. It probably continued as an *ad hoc* custom until machine-made clothes became the norm and reduced the practice of hand sewing. We may note that Mark Twain's fictional hero Tom Sawyer was stitched into his shirt by his Aunt Polly every morning. When he went swimming illicitly he had to sew himself up afterwards!

[84] Grave 9; Abbott, 'Woodston', p. 36.

[85] E. Crowfoot, 'The textiles', Appendix III in P. Hutchinson, 'The Anglo-Saxon cemetery at Little Eriswell, Suffolk', *Proceedings of the Cambridge Antiquarian Society*, 69 (1966), pp. 29–32, at p. 32.

to suggest a 2 x 2 twill *peplos* over a diamond-twill undergown, while Grave 80 at the same site suggests the opposite, a diamond-twill *peplos* over a 2 x 2 twill undergown. At Sewerby, East Yorkshire, in Grave 57 (Figs 51, 52), the *peplos* was probably of chevron twill wool and the undergown of three-shed twill (2 x 1 or 1 x 2).

In its general shape, this sleeved undergarment with a central aperture at the neck must have resembled the tunic worn by men. There are different ways of making such a tunic: it is possible to weave in one piece a garment with both sleeves and a neck aperture: there is a north European example in the man's 'Gallic coat' found at Reepsholt (East Friesland), Germany.[86] Alternatively, sleeves can be sewn on separately after weaving as were the close-fitting sleeves on a man's tunic from Thorsbjerg (Schleswig), Germany (Fig. 79 and Plate 4).[87] Both these garments are bog finds and date from the Roman Iron Age.

It may have been such a tunic that Tacitus was observing when he noted the similarity between the dress of men and women in Germania, a point apparently contradicted by the strongly gendered distribution of grave-goods in Anglo-Saxon cemeteries. Representations on the Marcus Aurelius Column and the Menimane *stele* give no clue to the length of the woman's tunic – because the skirts of the overgown are ankle-length, the undergarment could be as short as a modern blouse or as long as the overgown. On the Klagenfurt relief (Fig. 39) the undergarment is longer than the gown. Although the appendages which hung from Anglo-Saxon women's belts have been less fruitful sources of textile than shoulder brooches, there is now some evidence from this area of a grave to suggest the skirts of a garment, and, as in the case of Wakerley Grave 74, to imply that the undergarment hung beneath the girdle attachments.

Inge Hägg's investigation of the textile on Viking Age brooches from Birka, Sweden, shows a triple layer of garments: women wore a pleated shirt, covered by a tunic, over which they wore the *Hängerock*, 'suspended skirt', with brooches.[88] It seems very likely that Anglo-Saxon and other Germanic women also wore some kind of underwear beneath the sleeved tunic and the *peplos*-type gown (though by its very nature it would not show and would not appear on any of the Continental sculptures). Very possibly a woman who had access to linen would prefer to wear this fibre rather than wool next to her skin (see Bede's comment on this, p. 133), but evidence is limited and is likely to remain so, because textile is usually preserved by contact with metal, and an inner garment might not lie

[86] Hald, *Ancient Danish Textiles*, pp. 336–8. Dr Hald considered that, although the wool of this particular garment indicated local manufacture, the style was too loose for northern climates and was probably imported from the East.

[87] Hald, *Ancient Danish Textiles*, p. 339.

[88] I. Hägg, 'Viking women's dress at Birka: a reconstruction by archaeological methods', in N. B. Harte and K. G. Ponting (ed.), *Cloth and Clothing in Medieval Europe: essays in memory of Professor E. M. Carus-Wilson* (London, 1983), pp. 316–50.

in contact with a brooch or buckle. The iron on which much Anglo-Saxon textile has been preserved, is, in any case, more likely to preserve wool than linen.[89] At Castledyke, however, there was evidence for linen undergowns in four graves, and at both this site and West Heslerton, North Yorkshire, there was evidence that undergarments were cinched by buckled belts.[90]

Several of the documented Old English words for undergarments could have been in use at this time, though we have no evidence as to which, if any, applied to women's costume. The words are *cemes*, *ham*, *hemeþe*, *scyrte*, *serc* and *smoc*, of which the first three could probably be used of a garment worn next to the skin. *Smoc* may have been borrowed into Old Norse as *smokkr*, which in *Rigsþula* is associated with the 'dwarf-pins' at the shoulders (Ursula Dronke translates it 'blouse' and interprets it as the undergarment).[91] It is related to the (later) Middle High German verb *smüchen*, 'to adorn',[92] which may imply that the *smoc* was decorated in some way, as the Birka tunics were (in those cases with appliqué and embroidery). *Scyrte*, related to the Old English verb *scyrtan*, 'to shorten', might have been applied to a garment which was shorter than others, perhaps a tunic that was shorter than the outer gown or an undergarment shorter than the tunic. (Old English *sc* was pronounced [ʃ] or 'sh'.) *Cyrtel* (see above) had a similar meaning. It is possible that the sleeved tunic was originally shorter than the *peplos* and was called *cyrtel*. This may have evolved into a longer garment, and, when the outer gown became obsolete, virtually replaced it. This would explain why the word *cyrtel* came to be the major name for a lady's garment in later Anglo-Saxon times. (Note that Modern English 'kirtle' may mean a tunic or an outer petticoat.)

The belt or girdle

The costume of Anglo-Saxon women in pagan times could certainly include a girdle or belt, from which various items might be suspended. It has usually been supposed that this belt was worn over the *peplos*, where the belt equipment would be conveniently positioned in life and displayed as an indication of status in death. Recent association of girdle attachments with textile, however, leads me to suggest that the tool-bearing belt may, at least sometimes,

[89] R. C. Janaway, 'Corrosion preserved textile evidence: mechanism, bias and interpretation', *Evidence Preserved in Corrosion Products: new fields in artefact studies*, United Kingdom Institute for Conservation of Historic and Artistic Works, Occasional papers, 8 (1989), pp. 21–9, esp. p. 27.

[90] Linen undergarments in Castledyke Graves 112, 115, 134, 163; belted undergarments in Castledyke Grave 134, West Heslerton Grave 2B58; Walton Rogers, 'Textiles and clothing', in Drinkall and Foreman, *Castledyke*, p. 276.

[91] '*smokkr* is hap. leg. in ON; probably borrowed from OE smocc'; Dronke, *Edda*, p. 223.

[92] F. Holthausen, *Altenglisches etymologisches Wörterbuch* (Heidelburg, 1934) p. 303.

have been worn over the tunic and under the *peplos* (see Wakerley Grave 74, above) an arrangement which would keep the tools from getting in the way when a woman was working.[93] This would also keep them hidden, which would be counter to the usual assumption that grave-goods were arranged for conspicuous display. (This is a matter which should be kept open. It is always possible that a second textile found with girdle attachments may derive from a pouch.) A second belt or girdle might, in such a case, have been worn over the *peplos*, simply cinching it at the waist or having the cloth pouched over it.

Belts are attested by the survival of buckles *in situ* and by the regular discovery, in numerous graves, of objects at the waist or hip area of skeletons which had obviously been attached to belts. The dark outline of a leather belt has sometimes been visible to an excavator on opening a grave, including at least one woman's burial (at Burwell, Cambridgeshire).[94] Leather sometimes survives attached to strap ends and to objects originally fastened to belts and there are numerous fragments of leather preserved inside buckles. Though some of those from older excavations are undocumented, they can be observed in museum collections. Detailed attention to leather remains is a relatively recent feature in archaeological reports, and even now, it is not always possible if specimens are too deteriorated. The thickness of leather straps may, however, be deduced by measuring the distance between the front and back plates of a buckle. At Lyminge, Kent, belts were between about 2 mm and 4.5 mm thick,[95] while at Barrington A they varied between about 2 mm and 6 mm.[96] Leather thicker than 4 mm is usually from cattle; thinner leather may be from split cattle skin or from a thinner-skinned animal such as a calf, deer, goat, pig or sheep.[97] The woman in Grave 3 at Barrington A had a belt that was probably pigskin, fastened by a buckle with a counterplate.[98] There is less surviving evidence of textile belts, although the tablet-weave which was in use for wrist clasps and neck bands would have made attractive girdles if they were woven in contrasting colours as in Plate 6. Since wool is inclined to stretch it would be less practical than linen or leather for weight-bearing. Tablet-weave is sometimes preserved on girdle attachments, for example on a key from Ipswich, Suffolk[99] and possibly on girdle hangers at Barrington A.[100] It may have derived from

[93] A problem, particularly with latch lifters, which tend to catch in things! Information from Hazel Uzzell.

[94] Grave 2B; T. C. Lethbridge, *Recent Excavations in Anglo-Saxon Cemeteries in Cambridgeshire and Suffolk*, Cambridge Antiquarian Society Quarto Publications, 2nd series, 3 (1931), p. 48.

[95] A. Warhurst, 'The Jutish cemetery at Lyminge', *Archaeologia Cantiana*, 69 (1955), pp. 1–40, at pp. 7, 12, 15–16, 18, 25.

[96] J. Watson, 'Organic material associated with the metalwork', in Malim and Hines, *Edix Hill (Barrington A)*, pp. 230–5 at p. 235.

[97] Watson, 'Organic material', p. 234.

[98] Watson, 'Organic material', p. 234. Grave 10 is described in Malim and Hines, p. 44.

[99] Grave 106; G. M. Crowfoot, ' Anglo-Saxon tablet weaving', p. 191.

[100] Grave 106; E. Crowfoot in Malim and Hines, *Edix Hill (Barrington A)*, p. 245.

the girdle itself or from a band which suspended the objects. Textile found on the underside of buckle tabs with a skeleton of indeterminate sex from Alfriston, East Sussex, was faintly patterned in a way that suggested embroidery.[101]

Buckles have been found with female skeletons in all areas with significant numbers of burials. Yet they are less common than brooches and relatively rare in some areas rich in other grave-goods (for example Gloucestershire, Lincolnshire, Norfolk and Rutland). They occur slightly less often with women than with men.[102] Pagan-period buckles are usually small and simple. Zoomorphic examples are generally dated to the fifth century, and buckles with plates of various rounded designs – circular, heart- or kidney-shaped – to the fifth or early-sixth. In the sixth century buckle loops were usually round, oval or D-shaped, sometimes with a decorative 'shield' on the tongue.[103] Women's belts were evidently not usually elaborate, even where other grave-goods suggest that a person was relatively affluent, though metal studs and belt plates are occasionally found with women. Elaborate belt equipment is more prevalent in Kent than in other areas. Where a buckle is present it may indicate the position of the belt. There appears to have been considerable variation in the way it was worn. It could be round the waist or at the hip. (There does not seem to be any Anglo-Saxon evidence for a belt immediately below the breasts, as on the Halberstadt Diptych, but an unbuckled girdle could, of course, disappear without trace.) Some buckles were worn centrally at the front of the body, a few at the back and some at the left or right side. There seem to have been some local preferences: for instance at Abingdon, Oxfordshire, buckles were found predominantly at the right[104] and at Barrington B, Cambridgeshire, the left was chosen; but no consistent pattern emerges.

Metal strap ends (which would prevent the ends of belts or girdles from fraying) occur in a few pagan graves distributed over a wide area. (They were to become much more popular in the Middle Saxon period.) They are not always associated with buckles and may testify to the presence of a strap or belt where there is no other evidence. It is often the case that a female skeleton without buckle, strap end or any other direct evidence of a belt is accompanied by grave-goods clustered at the hips which had evidently been suspended from a belt or girdle. In these cases the belt must have been fastened by some means other than a buckle. Many women no doubt secured their girdles by knotting them. Others may have utilised the rings or large beads which excavators have found in the waist

---

[101] Grave 20; A. F. Griffith and L. F. Salzman, 'An Anglo-Saxon cemetery at Alfriston, Sussex', *Sussex Archaeological Collections*, 56 (1914), pp. 16–53, pp. 33–4.

[102] Stoodley, *The Spindle and the Spear*, p. 34, gives the proportions as 44% of males, 34% of females.

[103] Stoodley, *The Spindle and the Spear*, p. 20.

[104] E. T. Leeds and D. B. Harden, *The Anglo-Saxon Cemetery at Abingdon, Berkshire* (Oxford, 1936). The county boundaries have changed since this publication.

areas of skeletons. Rings, which are frequent finds in many areas of Anglian and Saxon settlement, have generally been interpreted as suspension rings for keys and other hanging objects. Most, especially when associated with belt buckles, probably did function this way; but in graves where no other belt fastener has been found, it is possible that a ring was stitched to the girdle and the other end knotted through it. The large, single beads found near the waists of women in many cemeteries in Anglian and Saxon areas could have been ornamental, or, as often suggested, they might have functioned as spindle whorls (p. 68, below). It is possible, though, that some were attached as toggles to girdles which were secured by means of a loop, or a 'button hole' in the girdle. Groups of beads have been found at the belt area of female skeletons in a few areas of Saxon settlement. Unless they hung from the neck or the shoulder brooches by unusually long strings, these could have been attached to the girdle, or to a pouch; or they could have been contained in the pouch.

There are various ways in which objects could be attached to the belt, varying in complexity: they could be simply stuck through it; threaded on to it, if they had a perforation; tied to it with thread or a length of braid or thong; or attached by strapwork which might include an additional buckle and strap end. The commonest of girdle adjuncts is the knife. Indeed this is the commonest of grave-goods, many skeletons being accompanied by nothing else. The Anglo-Saxon knife as excavated consists of a metal blade and a tang which originally fitted into a handle of perishable material, especially horn, but also wood (willow or poplar and hazel have been identified) or bone.[105] Knives vary in size and shape but it is clear that they were essentially domestic utensils, not weapons. Both size and shape may have been social indicators: in a survey carried out by Heinrich Härke, women's knife blades were never longer than 128 mm, longer than children's but not so large as the largest knives carried by adult men;[106] at Castledyke, angle-backed knives with straight or curved cutting edges were associated with persons whose dress was identifiably Anglian (such as women with paired annular brooches).[107] They were usually carried at the belt, sometimes in leather sheaths, which at Castledyke were identified as calf- and sheep- or goatskin.[108] They have been found at the back of the belt and centrally at the front, but mostly were worn at the hip. A majority of people seem to have carried the knife at the left hip, which was probably convenient for a right-handed person. The

---

[105] A. MacGregor, 'Hides, horn and bones: animals and interdependent industries in the early urban context', in Cameron, *Leather and Fur*, pp. 12–13; G. Edwards and J. Watson, 'Organic remains', in Drinkall and Foreman, *Castledyke*, pp. 241–2, 283–4 (taking account of Norton and Sewerby as well as Castledyke).
[106] H. Härke, 'Knives in early Saxon burials: blade length and age at death', *Medieval Archaeology*, 33 (1989), pp. 144–8. Forty-seven cemeteries were analysed.
[107] Drinkall and Foreman, *Castledyke*, p. 283.
[108] Edwards and Watson, 'Organic remains', in Drinkall and Foreman, *Castledyke*, p. 242.

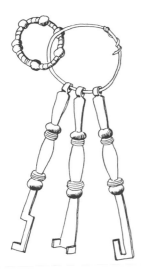

Fig. 43 Keys, Ozengell, Kent.
After A. L. Meaney

positions of surviving knives suggest that they were stuck through the belt and, surprisingly, were often carried point upwards. Occasionally a knife may have hung from the belt on a strap, sometimes in addition to another carried in the usual way. Three women at Castledyke had knives which might have been attached to the leg.[109]

The choice of other girdle attachments seems to have been more dependent on region, date and sex of the wearer. Women wore a greater number and variety of appendages than men. Keys, or latchlifters (Fig. 43), have been found at the hips of women in most regions at this early period. They consist of hooked rods, designed not to turn in a lock but to lift the latch of a door, a gate or a chest. They have been found attached to rings and evidently they sometimes dangled from the belt, although in other cases they may have been carried in pouches which were themselves attached to the belt. They are sometimes found singly and sometimes in groups. It is interesting to note that archaeologists in the north of the Netherlands generally associate keys in their area with Christian influence;[110] but the keys carried by Frisian women were of Roman type, often bearing a Christian symbol on the handles, quite unlike the Anglo-Saxon latchlifters. Possibly the Anglo-Saxon custom of carrying keys derived from contact with a Romanised Christian community. It seems more likely, though, that in our area and period keys were primarily functional and secondarily indicative of woman's status as housekeeper. We may question exactly what rank might be indicated by this: the chief domestic servant, or the 'lady of the house'? If the latter, did the category include any woman who was head of a household, or only those of certain rank (not necessarily the highest rank)? Was it confined to the middle-class lady or did it extend to any lady of middle-class or above? A number of excavators have considered this question but the evidence is inconsistent: at Polhill, Kent, the graves with jewellery were not the graves with keys,[111] while at Sewerby the richest female grave did not have keys though it did have girdle hangers.[112] At Barrington A, on the other hand, keys accompanied the richest female burials.[113] In *Rígsþula*, hanging keys (*hanginluklu*) characterise the bride of the class of carl, a family who own their own home, farm the land, eat well and dress neatly and distinctively.[114] Keys are not, in this text, mentioned in connection with the lower class of thrall or

[109] Drinkall and Foreman, *Castledyke*, p. 282. Martin Foreman suggests this was for ease of access when working in a squatting position.

[110] I am grateful to Mr de Leeuw of the Provinciaal Museum van Drenthe, Assen, the Netherlands, for this information.

[111] S. C. Hawkes, 'The dating and social significance of the burials in the Polhill cemetery', in B. Philp, *Excavations in West Kent 1960–1970*, Kent Archaeological Rescue Unit (Dover Castle, 1973), pp. 186–201 at p. 195.

[112] S. M. Hirst, *An Anglo-Saxon Inhumation Cemetery at Sewerby, East Yorkshire*, York University Archaeological Publications 4 (York, 1985), p. 88.

[113] A. Meaney, 'Girdle groups: reconstruction and comparative study', in Malim and Hines, *Edix Hill (Barrington A)*, pp. 268–75, at p. 274.

[114] Dronke, *Edda*, p. 167, stanza 23; also pp. 165–7, stanzas 15–16, 18, 22.

the higher one of earl. Although we cannot assume that the rigid social divisions implied in an Icelandic literary text from several centuries later are direct correlation of the situation in pagan Anglo-Saxon England, the detail corroborates the suggestion of archaeologists that the keys were diagnostic of status.[115] It would seem likely that certain items, such as clothing, soft furnishings, food and drink, as well as jewellery, drinking vessels and other luxuries were effectively owned by the lady of the house, and distributed by her as required. In Old English poetry, ladies (including those of highest rank) are depicted as dispensers of drink to their husbands, warrior-retainers and guests,[116] and it is the wife who provides a change of clothing for her husband, presumably from her chests of textiles.[117] Although fifth- and sixth-century keys are not so individual as modern keys and might not prevent theft by someone else equipped with latch lifters, they would deter a casual thief and a pilfering child or servant, and could keep wandering animals out of the house. They served to distinguish between public property and private. Anyone in possession of something normally kept under lock and key was either an honoured recipient of a gift, or a thief!

The belt accessories known to archaeologists as 'girdle-hangers' (Fig. 44) are rather enigmatic: they bear some resemblance to keys, and perhaps derive from Roman keys, but no convincing function has been suggested for them other than that of suspending small objects from their squared, openwork ends. Audrey Meaney suggests 'they must have been far more symbolic than useful' and, citing two obscene Old English riddles, points out the phallic symbolism of keys, concluding: 'The girdle-hangers symbolised not only a woman's care for her husband's property, but also that she had the key to his manhood'.[118] Often found in pairs, sometimes joined at the top, girdle-hangers were exclusively feminine accessories and are characteristically Anglian, though examples have been found outside the Anglian region, for example in Oxfordshire (a Saxon region) and in Kent.

Crystal balls, sometimes framed in silver, and spoons with perforated bowls, are often associated together (Fig. 68) and were probably worn as girdle attachments, usually by women with an elaborate costume which included a headdress and an unusually large quantity of brooches, in sixth-century Kent and Kentish-influenced

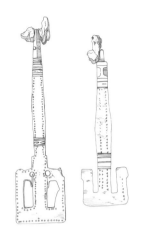

Fig. 44 Girdle-hangers, Sewerby, East Yorkshire

Fig. 45 Toilet implements, East Shefford, West Berkshire

[115] I owe this point to Hines, *Great Square-Headed Brooches*, p. 263.

[116] For example *Beowulf*, lines 612–29; Dobbie, *Beowulf and Judith*, pp. 20–21; *Maxims* I, ii, line 90; G. P. Krapp and E. V. K. Dobbie (ed.), *The Exeter Book*, The Anglo-Saxon Poetic Records, 3 (New York, 1936), p. 159. Old English poetry may have been written down as late as the tenth century (the date of the surviving manuscripts) but frequently depicts an earlier, idealised, heroic age.

[117] *Maxims* I, ii, line 98; Krapp and Dobbie, *The Exeter Book*, p. 160. Audrey Meaney cites the Laws of King Cnut to demonstrate that the wife was keeper of the keys to store-room, chest and cupboard (citing A. J. Robertson, *The Laws of the Kings of England from Edmund to Henry I*, (Cambridge, 1925), pp. 212–14); A. L. Meaney, *Anglo-Saxon Amulets and Curing Stones*, British Archaeological Reports, British Series 96 (1981), p. 178 and note 55.

[118] Meaney, *Amulets*, pp. 179–81.

Fig. 46 Cosmetic brush, Cassington, Oxfordshire. After D. Brown

Fig. 47 Tweezers, Saxby, Leicestershire

Fig. 48 Shears, provenance unknown

areas. This dress, and the possible function of the balls and spoons will be discussed below (pp. 93–5).

The chatelaine chain, which was to become very popular in the seventh century, appears in some earlier female graves. The metal chain was attached to the belt and small objects suspended from it. This fashion is not confined to any one region. Rings found grouped in some graves may have been tied together for similar effect. Other rings, found individually, had been used to suspend objects such as keys and toilet articles. Little metal tools for the care of the appearance and personal hygiene were carried by women in this early period: sets of toilet articles (Fig. 45), consisting of one or two pin-like tools for cleaning the nails or picking the teeth, together with a spoon-shaped tool for cleaning the ears, suspended from a ring, would be hung from the belt, carried in a pouch or sometimes hung round the neck in a bag[119] or dangling from a brooch, as was the Viking custom. Little metal tubes once thought to be needle cases are now identified as cosmetic brushes (Fig. 46), on the evidence of examples which retained some bristles.[120] Tweezers (Fig. 47) have been found in some female graves although they are more often associated with male skeletons. We do not know why they were carried; they may have had a variety of uses, such as removing thorns from the skin and plucking out facial hair.

Women probably carried around with them the tools for their constant occupation – spinning. Some of the large beads which have been found in women's graves could have functioned as spindle whorls, and may be all that remains of a distaff and spindle, tucked into a woman's belt or carried in a work-bag at her hip.[121] Other functional articles recovered from early cemeteries include shears (Fig. 48) and fire-steels. The latter were almost certainly mounted on small pouches which contained fire-making materials – tinder and flint – and which could be attached to the belt (Fig. 49). These early examples of fire-steels are often quite elaborate, being inlaid and decorated with stylised birds' heads. Almost all the surviving examples have been found in south-east England on sites where there is a strong Frankish influence, although a very plain example

[119] Personal tools on the chest were a particular feature of the Lechlade cemetery; A. Boyle, D. Jennings, D. Miles and S. Palmer, *The Anglo-Saxon Cemetery at Butler's Field, Lechlade, Gloucestershire* Volume 1: Prehistoric and Roman activity and Anglo-Saxon grave catalogue, Thames Valley Landscapes Monograph No. 10 (Oxford, 1998).

[120] Originally noted on Continental examples (D. Brown, Untitled, *Medieval Archaeology*, 18 (1974), pp. 151–4), the bristles have now been observed in Anglo-Saxon context, e.g. Watchfield, Grave 315; C. Scull, 'Excavation and survey at Watchfield, Oxfordshire, 1983–92, *Archaeological Journal*, 149 (1992), pp. 124–281, at p. 201.

[121] Most spindles and distaffs were probably of wood and have not survived from Anglo-Saxon cemetery context. Possible woods are illustrated by the remains of spindles and distaffs of yew and of distaffs made from ash, hazel, prunus and poplar from seventh- to tenth-century Ireland; J. H. Hedges, 'Textiles and Textile Production in Dark Age Britain', unpublished M.Phil. thesis (University of Southampton, 1980), pp. 284–6.

has been found in Driffield, East Yorkshire.[122]

Key-rings and other girdle adjuncts may have been tied to the belt by thongs or cords. In Grave 10 at Worthy Park, Hampshire, a plait of plied threads had probably been used for this purpose.[123] Many of the clusters of objects found at women's waists or hips may have been carried in leather or cloth bags which have rotted away. Perhaps in some cases these bags were striped or checked: fine textile, with a repeated stripe of S-spun thread in the predominantly Z-spun twill, was found on keys and a purse mount at the left waist and hip in Grave 10 at Worthy Park.[124] Some containers are attested by the survival of ivory rings, cut from the wider parts of elephant tusks.[125] Though once thought to have been suspension rings or bracelets (and indeed, some may have been re-used as such) these are now generally interpreted as pouch frames (Fig. 50). The discovery of an unusual textile with an ivory ring at West Heslerton has suggested that these particular ivory-framed bags may have been imported ready-made,[126] though pouches were used widely over the Germanic area. In some cases, particularly among the Alamanni, bags seem to have been closed by means of bronze openwork discs, but no such plaques are known from Anglo-Saxon context,[127] and are not really necessary as the pouch hangs down like a pocket and effectively closes itself when the hand is removed.[128] Costume historians might assume that, though a wooden pouch frame might be covered by cloth or leather, an ivory one, because of its rarity and attractiveness, would be required to be visible, and pouches have been reconstructed accordingly; but the fact that an ivory ring at West Heslerton had been entirely concealed by the leather of the pouch it framed alters the picture.[129]

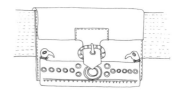

Fig. 49 Fire-steel, Krefeld-Gellep, Germany, on reconstructed pouch and belt. After D. Brown

Fig. 50 Reconstruction of how an ivory ring could have functioned as a pouch frame. After A. L. Meaney

[122] D. Brown ('Fire-steels and pursemounts again', *Bonner Jahrbücher*, 177, (1977), pp. 451–77) argued that objects previously identified as purse mounts were in fact fire-steels, and reconstructed two types, one with stylised birds' heads, the other with horses' heads, which fastened differently. In most cases the sex of the owner is not identified, but there are almost certainly examples from female graves at Holywell Row, Suffolk and Alfriston, Sussex, as well as Driffield. Brown does not suggest what material the pouches were made of, but I note that 'purse mounts' are often recorded in association with decayed leather.

[123] Unpublished. Information from Elisabeth Crowfoot's report on the textiles at Worthy Park, Kingsworthy, Hampshire, Ancient Monuments Laboratory Report 1706 (1974).

[124] The purse itself may have been leather. Leather was also found on the purse mount; E. Crowfoot, Worthy Park.

[125] Meaney, *Amulets*, p. 252.

[126] Drinkall and Foreman, *Castledyke*, pp. 285–6 (citing Penelope Walton Rogers). A possible similar case is recorded at Easington, Co. Durham, where a well made 2 x 1 twill was associated with chatelaine objects and was thought to derive from the pouch; it was noticeable that this was the only 2 x 1 twill recorded at the site; P. Henry, 'The Textiles', in H. Hamerow and J. Pickin, 'An early Anglo-Saxon Cemetery at Andrew's Hill, Easington, Co. Durham', *Durham Archaeological Journal*, 11 (1995), pp. 59–63 at p. 61.

[127] Meaney, *Amulets*, pp. 250–2.

[128] Information from Hazel Uzzell.

[129] Watson, 'Organic material', in Malim and Hines, *Edix Hill (Barrington A)*, pp. 230–5, at p. 234. The West Heslerton Grave 906 purse group is described in J. Watson and G. Edwards, 'Conservation of material from Anglo-Saxon cemeteries', in Southworth, *Anglo-Saxon Cemeteries: a reappraisal*, pp. 97–106 at pp. 100–1, which is cited in the Barrington publication, though the point about the ivory ring being entirely covered by leather is not made there.

Ivory had not yet become prized by the Anglo-Saxons as a medium for sculpture[130] and they were used to utilising natural materials – antler, bone, horn – so although ownership of these large organic rings may have been a mark of status[131] we may be wrong to assume an aesthetic appreciation of them.

Ivory pouch rings are usually found on the left, slung from the girdle, though Meaney considered that in two cases at Barrington A the pouches had been slung from the shoulder, one hanging down parallel to the left side of the body, the other suspended diagonally from the right shoulder.[132] The recurrence of certain items in association with ivory rings suggests that the rings were the frames of 'amulet-bags' and that their owners were 'cunning women', healers or practitioners of magic.[133] Typical contents include cowrie shells (which, with their resemblance to female pudenda, may have been fertility amulets), animals' teeth, Roman coins, pieces of broken glass and rings of iron or bronze. Meaney notes that bag collections characteristically include something old – at least a hundred years at the time of burial.[134] It is worth noticing if women with ivory rings had any of this characteristic equipment elsewhere about their persons; for example a female skeleton with an ivory pouch ring, recently excavated from the Minerva Business Park site at Peterborough, wore a Roman melon bead, broken but repaired with a strip of metal so that it could be strung on her necklace. This was perhaps her 'something old' though it was not carried in the pouch. A woman with a unique amuletic collection from Bidford-on-Avon may also have owned an 'antique' in the shape of an early post-Roman brooch, which had not been made locally, which she wore paired with an Anglo-Saxon one.[135]

Women seem occasionally to have carried individual items at the waist which can only be explained as amulets: a perforated animal tooth on a wire ring at Sleaford;[136] a piece of bone on a wire loop at Nassington;[137] at Catterick a woman dressed with paired annular brooches in the style typical of the pagan period, carried a small (28 mm), simple, metal cross at the left of the waist.[138]

---

[130] The Franks Casket, which is whalebone, is seventh- or eighth-century, and little walrus ivory carvings ninth-, tenth- and eleventh-century.

[131] Meaney, 'Girdle groups', in Malim and Hines, *Edix Hill (Barrington A)*, p. 275. An antler ring, maximum diameter 92 mm, was found with girdle adjuncts including an ivory ring with other feminine grave-goods (though the bone was thought to be male) in Grave 98 at Empingham II, Timby, *Empingham II*, p. 122.

[132] Graves 79 and 83; Meaney, 'Girdle groups', in Malim and Hines, *Edix Hill (Barrington A)*, pp. 269 and 272.

[133] Meaney, *Amulets*, pp. 249–50; T. M. Dickinson, 'An Anglo-Saxon "cunning woman" from Bidford-on-Avon, in M. Carver (ed.), *In Search of Cult: archaeological investigations in honour of Philip Rahtz*, University of York Archaeological Papers (Woodbridge, 1993), pp. 45–54.

[134] Meaney, *Amulets*, p. 250.

[135] Dickinson, 'An Anglo-Saxon "cunning woman"', p. 45.

[136] Grave 191; Thomas, 'Sleaford', p. 401.

[137] Grave 30; Leeds and Atkinson, 'Nassington', p. 110.

[138] P. R. Wilson, P. Cardwell, R. J. Cramp, J. Evans, R. H. Taylor-Wilson, A. Thompson and J. S. Wacher, 'Early Anglian Catterick and *Catraeth*', *Medieval Archaeology*, 40 (1996), pp. 1–61, at pp. 39–40.

It is evident, then, that at least one belt or girdle was a part of the woman's costume, that it was sometimes, but not always, fastened by a buckle, and that it functioned not only to confine the clothing but also to carry tools, amulets and personal items which were often contained in a pouch; but it is not yet clear whether these things would have been visible or if they were worn under the *peplos*. The belt may have been called in Old English *belt* or *fetel*; the related word *fetels*, which in Anglo-Saxon Bible translation is used of a money bag, is a possible name for the pouch which hung at the belt.[139]

Cloaks, capes or shawls

Burial in a cloak or other overgarment may have been dependent on external factors such as the season of death, or it may have been a status indicator, for the evidence of it is intermittent; any fasteners apart from the paired brooches seem to be 'optional extras' which are certainly not found in the majority of graves. As we have seen, it is difficult to determine the functions of the 'third' brooches and pins which are found at the centre chest or at one shoulder in a minority of graves, because there are various possibilities – fastening the opening of a tunic, fastening the *peplos* to the under-tunic or fastening a cloak. Where such a fastener is particularly large (and the florid cruciform and great square-headed types are the most obvious candidates for cloak fasteners) it is reasonable to suppose that it clasped a heavier garment such as a cloak. Yet textile on the four brooches in Grave 12 at Sewerby[140] suggests that there it was the smallest brooch which fastened the cloak: a small-long brooch at the left of the neck preserved napped, fairly coarse (10 x 10) twill and possibly part of a finer, braided border. The fine twill *peplos* was clasped at the other shoulder by a cruciform brooch which had the napped fabric on its front. The *peplos* possibly passed under the left arm while a pair of cruciform brooches secured it to the undergown on either side of the chest. Tabby weave and flax on the upper brooches were thought to be from a headveil, but I would suggest they might have been from this undergown.[141]

Hines notes that great square-headed brooches, which are often assumed to be cloak fasteners, were associated with 'very high wealth and social status'.[142] However, in many cases a large pin may have functioned in the same way as one of these elaborate brooches: a comparison of two similarly-equipped graves from the Minerva Business Park

---

[139] Or, possibly, a saddle bag, Joshua 9:4–5, S. J. Crawford (ed.), *The Old English Version of the Heptateuch, Aelfric's Treatise on the Old and New Testament and his Preface to Genesis*, Early English Text Society, original series, 160 (1922), p. 391.

[140] Hirst, *Sewerby*, p. 47, Fig. 17.12.

[141] Hirst, *Sewerby*, pp. 46–8; (Crowfoot) 54. The two writers disagree about the positioning of the *peplos* in this grave.

[142] Hines, *Great Square-Headed Brooches*, p. 1. Hines analyses the relative richness of women's graves containing great square-headed brooches at pp. 295–301.

site shows that one had a central square-headed brooch, the other a central pin.[143] We must question whether the mere fact of wearing a cloak carried the same status if it was fastened by a pin, or was it the metal fastener rather than the garment which carried prestige? Possibly the difference was chronological, and the women belonged to different generations of fashion.[144] Seamus Ross suggests that most of the fifth- and sixth-century pins in graves were cloak pins, since, in a comparison of their diameter with the diameters of brooch pins, he found little difference, and with the addition of string or a thong, they could have had equal or even greater strength than brooches.[145]

It is only rarely that stratification of grave-goods suggests that a fastener has clasped an outer garment (or wrap): at Barrington B (Grave 72) a large cruciform brooch overlay a smaller cruciform brooch, one of a pair which had evidently fastened a *peplos*-type gown. In Grave 45 at the same site a pin was similarly positioned in relation to paired brooches, while at Mucking a pin was found centrally across the chest and the beads of a woman also equipped with paired brooches. John Hines cites three instances of a great square-headed brooch overlying one of the pair of shoulder brooches (Berinsfield, Oxfordshire 102; Lechlade, Gloucestershire 57 and 'apparently' Spong Hill 24) with, in each case, different textiles on the large brooch and the shoulder brooches.[146] However, this means of diagnosis is apparently contradicted in the finds from Sewerby, where in Graves 49 and 57, although the middle brooch of three overlapped one of the others, the textile evidence suggested that a cloak was worn *outside* that brooch.[147]

Where coarse textile has been found on the back of a third brooch, interpretation as a cloak fastener is probable, as in Grave 74 at Wakerley. We might also expect to find textile from cloaks on the fronts of shoulder brooches which had clasped the *peplos*-type gown, though such cloth could also derive from headdresses or from blankets or shrouds in which corpses might have been wrapped. In fact, much of the textile that has been identified from the fronts of shoulder brooches consists of tabby-woven linen, which suggests either shroud material or headdress fabric. There are, however, some brooches with twill textiles on the fronts[148] including examples from Haslingfield and Mucking with different textiles on the undersides. The textile on the front of the Mucking brooch was coarser than that

---

[143] I am grateful to the Hertfordshire Archaeological Trust and BBC Television for this information.

[144] See Palm and Pind, 'Chronological analysis', in Jørgensen, *Chronological Studies*, pp. 58, 67, where on data from four Norfolk and one Yorkshire site, dress pins were found to have a limited 'life' in the sixth century while great square-headed brooches were thought to continue into the seventh.

[145] Ross, 'Dress Pins', p. 397.

[146] Hines, *Great Square-Headed Brooches*, pp. 285–6.

[147] Hirst, *Sewerby*, p. 48.

[148] There are examples from Barrington (a trefoil-headed brooch, Ashmolean Museum No. 1909 270a); Haslingfield, Cambridgeshire (a square-headed brooch, Ashmolean Museum No. 1909 226); Welbeck Hill (Grave 56, on the pin of an annular brooch, lying over another, tabby textile. Information from Elisabeth Crowfoot. Also Mucking, Grave 341, on the pin of an annular brooch, one of a pair at chest and shoulder; observed by the author shortly after excavation, courtesy of W. T. Jones.

on the back. A coarse woollen twill from Sewerby Grave 57 had yellow-dyed Z-spun threads in both systems, with a stripe of S-spun thread which was dark and naturally pigmented appearing in what was probably the weft. This textile, which was found on the front of a large cruciform brooch at the front of the body and on a wrist clasp, was interpreted as a cloak, which may have been lined with sheepskin.[149]

SEWERBY Grave 57 (Figs 51, 52) The lack of surviving bone and a shift of grave-goods towards the head of the grave complicate interpretation of this burial, but it was very rich in textile remains, and the woman evidently was elaborately dressed. A small-long brooch and an annular were apparently 'paired' together and there was a large cruciform brooch with the annular at the left shoulder. An amber bead was with them. There were also wrist clasps, a 'bracelet' and a buckle. Elisabeth Crowfoot posits a gown of chevron twill (found on the back of the small-long brooch, on the ring of the annular and on the back of the large cruciform) over an undergown of fine three-shed twill (found on the pin catch of the small-long brooch), which had tablet-woven wrist bands with a brocaded step-pattern, secured by wrist clasps. The striped, coarse woollen twill of the cloak was found on the front and on a knob of the cruciform brooch, and what was thought to be sheepskin lay over the textile. This sheepskin, which also may have lain over one of the wrist clasps, could have been a lining for the cloak, or a fleece laid over the body. A coarse, tabby weave on the front of the annular brooch 'could have come from a hood'.[150]

Figs 51, 52 Reconstruction of the clothing in Sewerby, East Yorkshire Grave 57

[149] E. Crowfoot, 'The textiles', in Hirst, *Sewerby*, pp. 52, 54.
[150] Crowfoot in Hirst, *Sewerby*, pp. 52–4. Hirst's diagram p. 167 shows that the annular brooch overlay the cruciform but the cruciform was face down, suggesting displacement. The grave-goods are reversed in Fig. 17 (p. 47) of the Sewerby publication. I have worked to the grave plan, Fig. 80.

At Lakenheath (Little Eriswell), Suffolk, brooches worn under the chins of two females (in addition to 'paired' brooches at the
shoulders) may have clasped outer garments and again the survival
of several textiles in the graves makes it possible to speculate about
the costume.[151] In Grave 28 coarse twill textile was found on girdle
hangers and keys, and layers of a finer twill on a toilet set. Possibly
the coarse twill derived from a cloak fastened under the chin by a
square-headed brooch, and the finer twill from the *peplos* secured
by paired saucer brooches. The woman in this grave had worn a
leather belt (traces of which were found inside a bronze buckle and
strap end). Fur or hair had been in contact with the girdle hangers,
possibly from a pouch, but possibly from a fur garment. The
woman's body, with its clothes, jewellery and other possessions,
may have been wrapped in a shroud, since coarse threads of tabby-
woven textile were found on the outside of a buckle, and on a knife
and piece of iron. There was probably a similar arrangement in
Grave 33 at the same site, where there were three textiles preserved
on a 'third' brooch under the chin (a coarse twill and two different
tablet-woven braids), a fourth (tabby) on wrist clasps and a fifth
(finer twill) on iron fragments and a ring found above the knees. A
reconstruction of the costume would suggest that the finer twill derived from a gown, fastened by paired brooches and perhaps bordered by one tablet braid. The cruciform third brooch may have
clasped a cloak, under the chin. The tabby-woven textile perhaps
derived from the sleeves of a tunic worn under the *peplos*, which may
have been bordered at the neck by the other tablet-woven braid. (The
third brooch may also have clasped the *peplos* to this undergarment.)

A cloak fastened by a large brooch or pin may have taken the
form of a square or rectangle, woven on the warp-weighted loom,
with tablet-woven starting and closing borders, and possibly with
tablet-woven side borders too, which would enclose the body of the
cloth in a firm, possibly colourful, edge. The top and bottom of the
weave might have ended in a fringe. This is largely speculation
from older Scandinavian evidence, but some of the textiles from
Worthy Park may fit this specification: in Grave 77, an annular
brooch at the left clavicle, under the chin, preserved an area of tablet-woven braid which appeared to edge a Z/Z-spun tabby weave.
This was the only brooch in the grave. The same, or very similar,
textiles were found at the waist area, the tablet-weave on a buckle
at the right of the waist and the tabby on an iron key at the right
hip as well as on a bronze object (position unspecified). Elisabeth
Crowfoot notes that the presence of the same tablet-weave at chin
and hip suggests that in this case the braid may have bordered a
cloak. It should be noted though, that the tabby was a closely woven and fairly fine textile (the thread count ranged between 15 x 14

---

[151] P. Hutchinson, 'The Anglo-Saxon Cemetery at Little Eriswell, Suffolk', *Proceedings of the Cambridge Antiquarian Society*, 69 (1966), pp. 10–12; E. Crowfoot, 'The
textiles', Appendix III in Hutchinson, pp. 29–32, at pp. 31–2.

threads per cm to 13 x 13), finer than one might expect for a cloak. A coarser (c. 10 x 10) tabby weave in Grave 10 at the same site, found on a buckle at the right of the waist of a female skeleton had what Crowfoot thought might be fringe associated with it.[152]

A cloak which was clasped centrally could easily be drawn over the head to form a hood. Re-enactors have established that a hood of this kind stays in position better if the portion of the cloak which will cover the shoulders and head is folded double before being pinned by the brooch. This makes for a double thickness over the shoulders and leaves a flap to come up over the head (Fig. 33). I do not know of any supporting evidence in the form of a double thickness of textile on a central brooch or pin but this is obviously something to be looked for.[153] The finds of 'extra' brooches and of pins at the shoulder suggest that alternatively a cloak could be clasped asymmetrically, a style which was evidently common in the Germanic world. A female figure probably representing *Germania capta* on a Roman monument wears a large cloak secured on the right shoulder. It conceals the left shoulder and hangs down the back to the woman's feet (Fig. 53). Menimane's cloak, which, like the captive's, probably consisted of a rectangular piece of material, is clasped at the right shoulder by a clearly depicted brooch, but hangs down the front of the body, partly concealing the *peplos*-type gown, then passes *under* the left arm, leaving arm and shoulder exposed (Fig. 28).

Fig. 53 Sculpted figure, probably representing *Germania capta*, Temple of Hadrian, Rome

Roman sculptures offer other possibilities: the provincial Roman goddess Nehallenia (Fig. 54) is depicted on several third-century altars found near the present-day city of Middelburg (the Netherlands). She wears a neat, symmetrical cape, which is sometimes clasped at the centre of the chest.[154] Another Roman sculpture (Fig. 38) shows a woman simply wrapping a shawl or cloak round her arms without any fastener. Women could have tied together the corners of such a garment, or tucked them into their belts if they needed their arms free. Outer garments like this would have left no trace in the form of a fastener, but they might leave textile on belt equipment.

Linguistic evidence suggests that an early form of cloak consisted of a rectangular piece of cloth which could also be used as a blanket or curtain indoors. The nouns *hwitel*, *loða* and *rift*, which were probably in use at this time, all have a range of meaning including 'cloak', 'blanket', 'curtain', when they are documented in later texts (see pp. 109–10). The *hwitel* was certainly worn by women (although we do not know whether men wore it also). The garment-name survived as 'whittle' in English dialects as late as the nineteenth century, when it signified a woman's fringed shawl.[155]

Fig. 54 The goddess Nehallenia, on an altar found in the East Scheldt estuary, The Netherlands

[152] E. Crowfoot, Worthy Park, Ancient Monuments Laboratory Report 1709.

[153] Information from Ben Levick of *Angelcynn*. The idea was inspired by a fold-crease in a Scandinavian bog cloak.

[154] I am grateful to Miss A. A. van der Poel of the Zeeuws Museum, Middelburg, for information on Nehallenia.

[155] J. Wright (ed.), *The English Dialect Dictionary*, 6 vols (London, 1898–1905), 6 (1905), p. 479.

The cloak called *mentel* was certainly worn by women in the tenth century (when it was secured by a brooch or pin, the *mentel-preon*) so the word may have been used of a woman's garment earlier.

The large number of Old English words apparently meaning 'a cloak', or other outer garment, suggests, even allowing for some synonymy, a greater variety of types than archaeological evidence can demonstrate. The *hwitel* (originally at least) was probably of white (*hwit*), that is, undyed, fabric, and by the early-eighth century was standardised in some way as it could be used as legal tender.[156] It was perhaps of fixed weight or size. The *hacele*, which was worn by women in Christian times, may have been hooded. The words *ofer-slop*, *pad* and *sciccing*, which also signify cloaks, and were probably in use in the fifth and sixth centuries, may have been the names of other distinctive styles.

Furs and skins

The outer garments considered so far have been of woven textile. Another possibility is that animal skins were worn, either in the form of leather or with the fur, hair or wool still attached.[157] Classical writers, as we have seen (pp. 16–18), emphasised the importance of skins and furs in Germanic costume. Ponchos which exploited the natural shape of an animal were worn by northern people from ancient times (Fig. 1) and it is likely that Anglo-Saxon people made fur jerkins out of the fleeces of sheep or the skins of other domestic animals such as goats, as well as using the skins for pouches, belts and other leather products. The traces of sheepskin or leather found on the pin catch of a cruciform brooch from Barrington B, Grave 110, may have come from such a garment. Possible traces of tablet weave and twill were found on the brooch suggesting the usual woven clothing was also worn, though the relationship between the proposed skin garment and the *peplos* is not apparent.[158] Another possibility is that fur was used to line woven garments. This is one possible interpretation of the sheepskin in Grave 57 at Sewerby (p. 73 above). If it was a garment lining, it belonged with the striped yellow twill discussed above,[159] making one of the most elaborate garments identified from

---

[156] Ine's Laws (44,1) include the definition of *gafolhwitel* as the rent of a hide of land; F. Liebermann (ed.), *Die Gesetze der Angelsachsen*, 3 vols (Halle, 1898–1916), 1 (1898), p. 108. This economic use of cloth was not unique in north-west Europe in medieval times: in Iceland, *vaðmál*, a homespun woollen cloth, was used as the standard measure of value from the eleventh century for several hundred years, and in Norway also certain payments could be rendered in cloth; see J. Jochens, *Women in Old Norse Society* (Ithaca, NY and London, 1995), pp. 141, 148–9.

[157] G. R. Owen-Crocker, 'The search for Anglo-Saxon skin garments and the documentary evidence', in Cameron, *Leather and Fur*, pp. 27–43.

[158] From the nineteenth-century excavations at Barrington; E. Crowfoot in Malim and Hines, *Edix Hill (Barrington A)*, p. 237.

[159] E. Crowfoot in Hirst, *Sewerby*, p. 54.

early Anglo-Saxon England. The horn handle of a knife found under the left arm of a skeleton (probably, from the presence of jewellery, female) at Empingham II preserved textile on one side and hair described as 'from a fleece or fur lined garment' on the other.[160] Some of the cases of fur or leather associated with girdle attachments, such as Lakenheath Grave 28 (p. 74 above) offer additional possibilities.

There are many Old English words for fur or skin garments, common to other Germanic languages, which strengthens the possibility that such garments were worn in early Anglo-Saxon times though, as we have seen, the archaeological evidence is slight. *Rocc*, which could apparently be made of goatskin, badgerskin or simply general animal (*deor*) skin is a likely name for the fur or sheepskin jerkin/poncho I have suggested. The *crusene* was also sheepskin, and the *heden* skin or fur; the *sciccels* might sometimes be made of fur. The *loða* was a cloak, perhaps sometimes made of fur or woven with a shaggy effect;[161] perhaps this term might have been applied to the napped fabrics which occasionally occur in Anglo-Saxon graves.

Headgear

The appearance of women's hair and headdress in the pagan period is not easily deduced from archaeological evidence. No metal fasteners appear so regularly as to be considered characteristic and the hair itself does not survive. (A knot of human hair in the Ashmolean Museum, from Greenwich Park, Greater London, which was once believed to come from a woman's grave, is not now acceptable evidence. It is believed to come from a male, Iron Age grave, the 'Swabian knot' of a warrior culture.)[162] This almost complete void presents a problem for anyone reconstructing the costume, or even imagining it, for the head is the most expressive and individual part of the human body. Nowhere are the prejudices of the reconstructor's own era and education more strongly invoked! In the absence of any positive evidence a reconstructor may choose to picture an early Anglo-Saxon woman in the voluminous headdress of late Anglo-Saxon manuscripts; or with a pair of plaits, interlaced with a gold band, which may have been characteristic of the later medieval times or the evocation of them in art of the modern Romantic Period. Small rings have occasionally been identified by excavators as possible fasteners for braids of hair (two rings

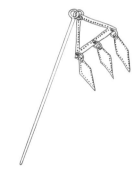

Fig. 55 Pin with *Klapperschmuck*, Newnham Croft, Cambridgeshire

---

[160] Timby, *Empingham II*, p. 106.

[161] The Icelandic cognate *loð-* was used of the pile-woven fabric made into the shaggy coat (*loðkápa*) or shaggy cloak (*loðólpa*), which imitated scarce fur; Jochens, *Women*, p. 114.

[162] The hair was published and (inaccurately) described as a plait in J. Douglas, *Nenia Britannica*. The denial here is based on unpublished information from Elisabeth Crowfoot. I have examined the hair and confirm that it is a twist or knot.

Fig. 56 Pin with bird's head, Faversham, Kent

Fig. 57 Possible female head on stone sceptre, Sutton Hoo, Suffolk

from Lakenheath;[163] one from Bidford, Warwickshire)[164] but these suggestions are so rare and there are so many rings in Anglo-Saxon cemeteries with so many possible uses that this cannot be taken as firm evidence of dangling plaits. In any case, a solid ring seems an impractical fastener for a plait of hair. Nineteenth-century archaeologists, for whom hairpins on the bedroom floor must have been part of everyday life, were inclined to identify as 'hairpins' archaeological pins which had in fact been found far from the head. (Students should be prepared to examine individual grave reports for evidence on this point.) In particular pins with *Klapperschmuck*, free-hanging ornaments which would jingle (Fig. 55), have been identified as hairpins; but it is apparent that no particular type was used exclusively for the hair and that different people might use similar pins in different ways.[165] Pins *have* been found at the skulls of female skeletons, but the occurrences are relatively few, and this positioning is less common than pins lower down the body, for example on the chest. Decorated pins (Fig. 56) are not common and nowhere do 'hairpins' occur in any quantity. They are almost always single finds. It is possible, of course that pins were made of organic material, such as wood, and have disappeared. Bone pins would probably have survived, though, had they been present. Combs, too, were worn in the hair in the nineteenth and early-twentieth centuries, which probably inspired some suggestions of this function for archaeological finds, but there is no evidence that this was an Anglo-Saxon fashion. The later part of the twentieth century has freed us from the assumption that adult women must always wear some kind of headcovering, and that long, loose hair was inappropriate for virtuous matrons. There is a danger, however, that a picture of Dark Age woman with wild, tangled locks is replacing previous prejudices. In fact the many combs found in Anglo-Saxon contexts[166] suggest that care of the hair was important, and practical considerations suggest that women would not bend over an open fire or do dirty jobs with loose hair.

In short, any reconstruction of the hair and headdress for this period is based on guesswork and no reconstruction should be considered authoritative. The best we can do is to compare Continental

---

[163] G. B[riscoe], and W. E. Le Bard, 'An Anglo-Saxon cemetery on Lakenheath airfield', *Proceedings of the Cambridge Antiquarian Society*, 53 (1959), pp. 56–7; information from Lady [G.]Briscoe, Lady [T.] Briscoe, Mrs P. Hutchinson and A. R. Edwardson, Moyse's Hall Museum, Bury St Edmunds.

[164] Meaney, *Gazetteer*, p. 260.

[165] A pin with *Klapperschmuck* in Castledyke Grave 158 was found at the centre of the chest and had evidently, from the textile on it, secured a cloak; Drinkall and Foreman, *Castledyke*, pp. 79–80, Walton Rogers, 'Textiles and clothing', in Drinkall and Foreman, p. 278.

[166] This includes occupation sites, cremation urns and inhumation graves. Burials sometimes suggest that a comb was carried on the person (e.g. Grave 116 at Castledyke where a comb was at the right waist and a knife at the left, or Grave 10 at the same site where a comb under (or in) a woman's hand could have been tied to the belt (Drinkall and Foreman, *Castledyke*, pp. 36–7, 68–9) but often combs seem to have been placed on or beside the body.

and later archaeological finds, and images from art, to suggest some possibilities. The (supposedly) female heads on the sceptre from the Sutton Hoo Ship Burial, which constitute five of the eight human faces carved on this massive stone object, appear to be bareheaded, with hair drawn back off the face (Fig. 57).[167] The unique, androgynous figure on the Spong Hill pot lid (Fig. 3) has a large 'bun' on top of the head; this could represent the hair alone, or more likely the hair confined within a cap, or even a pill-box shaped hat, like one found in a Merovingian or Carolingian level at Raskwerd, the Netherlands.[168] The Spong Hill figure's ears are exposed and there is no suggestion of a fillet, dangling hair or a veil. Women in Viking art (Figs 121–2) wear the hair drawn back into a similar 'bun' or a knotted or plaited 'pony-tail'. Plaiting the hair is a versatile technique and the resulting braids do not need a metal fastener to secure them. The ends could be prevented from unravelling, for example, by the use of a bit of the thread that women were constantly spinning. Plaits could be arranged on the head in various ways, again being tied rather than clipped with anything metal. Germanic women on Roman sculptures sometimes wear the hair unbound, draped by a loose veil (Fig. 58). A veil is prone to slip or be blown about by the wind, unless it is fixed in some way. A woman depicted on a first-century Roman gem, the *Grand Camée de France* (Fig. 59), wears a headband round her veil, antedating a style depicted in the Old English illustrated *Hexateuch* by almost a thousand years. Fillets, attested because they were brocaded with gold, were certainly known in sixth-century Kent (p. 96 below), and there is plenty of linguistic evidence for them from the later Anglo-Saxon period. It is possible that they were worn by early Anglo-Saxon women either alone or to secure a veil. A different kind of fastening, consisting of two small pins at the temples, secured the red satin veil of the royal woman who wore the 'Arnegundis' ring, buried in Saint-Denis. This Merovingian Frankish veil hung down as far as the woman's waist at the back.[169] There is a possible parallel for this in the 'scarf' or veil apparently worn by a woman at Mill Hill, Deal, Kent (p. 96).[170]

Caps were worn by Germanic women in ancient Scandinavia: Bronze and Iron Age examples, woven in the technique known as *sprang*, have been found in Denmark. A well-known example was

Fig. 58 Girl in a 'trouser suit' on a sculpture, Mainz, Germany

Fig. 59 Figure on the *Grand Camée de France*, Paris, *Bibliothèque Nationale*

[167] Bruce-Mitford, *Sutton Hoo*, 2 (1978), p. 315. All four faces at the presumed top and one at the bottom of the sceptre are beardless; see Figs 238–9, pp. 318–19.

[168] Information from Dr Boersma, Groningen Museum voor Stad en Land, the Netherlands; see A. E. Van Giffen, 'Mededeeling omtrent her systematisch onderzoek, verricht in de jaren 1928, 1929 en 1930', *Jaarverslag van de Vereeniging voor Terpenonderzoek*, 13–15 (1929–31), pp. 16–46, at p. 23, Fig. 6.1.

[169] Werner, 'Frankish royal tombs', p. 214 and Fig. 13.

[170] Grave 105C; K. Parfitt and B. Brugmann, *The Anglo-Saxon Cemetery on Mill Hill, Deal, Kent*, The Society for Medieval Archaeology Monograph Series, No. 14 (1997), pp. 31–2, 160, p. 192, Fig. 55, p. 213, Fig. 76.

worn by a girl whose body was recovered from Arden Mose. She wore the network cap over a coiled plait of hair.[171] *Sprang* is attested from slightly later in Norway and from the Viking Age in Sweden,[172] but as far as I know, though *sprang* was apparently known in Britain in the Bronze Age,[173] there is as yet no evidence that the Anglo-Saxons used it. Caps might be made in other techniques, perhaps by weaving, or they might be made of skin. Drawstring caps, fitting closely over braids or rolls of hair, appear on Rhineland sculptures of women wearing Menimane's costume. Vikings (possibly women) in Anglo-Scandinavian towns owned silk caps or hoods which might have been tied under the chin or knotted at the nape of the neck. Wool as well as silk versions of this garment have been found in Viking Dublin (see p. 230). If such things existed in the pagan period they would not have survived in the soil conditions of Anglo-Saxon cemeteries. The woman in the 'dwarf-pin' costume of *Rígsþula* wears 'a curving cap' (*sveigr*), though curving headdresses may be a feature of Icelandic culture rather than of the *peplos*-related costume in general.[174] A woman on the Halberstadt Diptych appears to wear a high hat (Fig. 36).

Possibly some of the unexplained items from Anglo-Saxon graves are the remains of headgear. Bead decorations thought to be 'hair ornaments' were found at the back of the skull of a woman in Grave 18 at Lechlade. They consisted of nine and eight annular beads, respectively, strung on copper rings.[175] Small metal clips, resembling the staples we use to fasten together sheets of paper, have been found with Anglo-Saxon skeletons of both sexes. They may not always have been used for the same purpose, for in one instance clips were associated with wood, in another with a leather pouch. Another possible function for such clips is that they could have secured wooden or leather objects (such as cups) which were laid in the grave and have otherwise disappeared. When clips are found near the skull it is tempting to suggest that they might have secured leather headgear. Most have been found singly, but there are exceptions: nine clips, positioned near the head of a girl at Lyminge, Kent, extended away from the head in diminishing sizes;[176] At Petersfinger, Wiltshire, five clips lay near the head of a girl.[177] Two clips found on either side of the head of a woman at Little Wilbraham, Cambridgeshire,[178] resemble the arrangement of the pins securing the veil of the Frankish woman from Saint-Denis.

---

[171] P. V. Glob, *The Bog People*, trans. R. L. S. Bruce-Mitford (London, 1969), Plates 26–7.

[172] Hald, *Ancient Danish Textiles*, pp. 251–2.

[173] Bender Jørgensen, *North European Textiles until AD 1000*, p. 19.

[174] Dronke, *Edda*, pp. 222–3.

[175] Boyle, Jennings, Miles and Palmer, *Lechlade*, 1, pp. 61–2.

[176] Grave 37; Warhurst, 'Lyminge', pp. 25–6.

[177] Grave 57; Leeds and Shortt, *Petersfinger*, pp. 37, 50.

[178] Lethbridge, *Recent Excavations*, pp. 73, 79.

Many Anglo-Saxon women may not have had individual head-gear. They may have simply drawn the cloak over the head in cold or wet weather and some cloaks may have been made with attached hoods. The middle-class woman in *Rígsþula* has some kind of neck-erchief (*dúkr var á hálsi*) and the sculpture of a woman from Ingelheim seems to show two additional layers of cloth at the neck. Possibly Anglo-Saxon women also would have worn some kind of scarf which could tuck into the neck of the undergown, or be pulled over the head for warmth. Women in Iron Age Denmark habitu-ally wore scarves; a garment of this kind found round the head and neck of a bog burial at Huldremose was approximately 1.37 m long and 49 cm wide, with fringed ends. Anglo-Saxon women might have used a warm piece of cloth in the same way. However, the textile finds considered relevant to this question have tended to be tabby-woven flax, and tentatively identified as 'veils'. They include fragments on the fronts of brooches from Laceby, North East Lin-colnshire[179] and Tallington, Lincolnshire,[180] Grave 80 at Wakerley,[181] Grave 57 at Sewerby[182] and in several graves at Castledyke.[183] (Now that excavators are well aware of the possibility of textile survival these finds from the fronts of brooches are being recorded, but it is likely that evidence was inadvertently lost from older excavations, when material was cleaned off the decorated surfaces in order to identify and categorise the ornament.) Tabby-woven fabric found on the backs of brooches is now also being identified as veil- or hood-material which has been tucked behind a brooch to secure it, for example Grave 74 at Wakerley[184] (p. 38 above) and in Grave 12 and possibly Grave 19 at Sewerby.[185] A caution is necessary: it is possible, of course, that the tabby-woven textiles were not from garments but the remains of cloths laid over the faces of the dead.

The linguistic evidence suggests a considerable range of head-gear. The word *hæt* (Modern English 'hat') was probably already in use in pagan times, also the more specific *cuffie* and *scyfel*. The *cuffie*, at least in late Anglo-Saxon times, was perhaps a loose-fitting hood or scarf, and the *scyfel* originally a hat or cap with some kind of projection. (We might compare the Icelandic *sveigr*.)[186] The *binde*, a

[179] F. H. Thompson, 'Anglo-Saxon sites in Lincolnshire: unpublished material and recent discoveries', *Antiquaries Journal*, 36 (1956), pp. 181–99, at p. 184; G. M. Crowfoot, Appendix to Thompson (1956), pp. 188–9.

[180] Unpublished information from Elisabeth Crowfoot.

[181] E. Crowfoot in Adams, Jackson and Badenoch, 'Wakerley', p. 171.

[182] E. Crowfoot, 'The textiles', in Hirst, *Sewerby*, p. 54.

[183] Walton Rogers, 'Textiles and clothing', in Drinkall and Foreman, *Castledyke*, p. 278. The evidence was found in nine graves, dating both from the sixth century and later.

[184] E. Crowfoot in Adams, Jackson and Badenoch, 'Wakerley', pp. 171–2.

[185] E. Crowfoot in Hirst, *Sewerby*, p. 54.

[186] ' … a head-dress with a curved crown, bending forwards over the forehead', Dronke, *Edda*, p. 222. The Anglo-Viking and Irish Viking hoods discussed in Chap-ter VII were made from rectangles of cloth but stitched in a curve to fit the head, which left a point. It is easy to imagine how this feature might be exaggerated, to make it correspond with the Icelandic description, for example by using more cloth to make the point bigger, pulling it forward, possibly stuffing it to make it firm. The Icelandic headdress might of course have been entirely different in construction.

fillet, was to be considered typical headgear for secular (married) women in late Anglo-Saxon times, and probably it was in use earlier. It is likely that *binde* was the name for the gold-brocaded headband worn by a very few sixth-century Kentish women and possibly for cloth fillets which have left no trace.

Footwear

There is almost no archaeological evidence of shoes from the fifth and sixth centuries. A lace tag containing 'worsted thread' was found in a sixth-century grave at Chessel Down in the Isle of Wight,[187] but the identification of this with footwear is tentative as the position of the object was not recorded, though it was similar to what appear to be shoe-lace tags from the seventh century. Possibly the poorer classes went barefoot, and, as we see from later Anglo-Saxon illustrations of agricultural labour, it may have been practical to do some farm work without shoes as they would get bogged down in mud.[188] The Spong Hill pot-lid figure is barefoot. However, the climate surely demanded some protection for the feet in winter and the making of footwear need not have been a sophisticated matter.[189] In 1964 Dr Calvin Wells suggested from the incidence of leg fractures among the early Anglo-Saxons that these people habitually wore clumsy footwear,[190] but this is a generalisation that has not been supported from more recent evidence.[191] We can guess, from later examples, that shoes would be flat soled (heels are a development of horse-riding peoples, who utilise stirrups). They would be round-toed, and would mostly fit around the ankle, with openings fastened by laces or thongs and leather toggles. The absence of any remains of shoes from the period may mean that people were *buried* barefoot, though they owned shoes in life; or it may be, that in the absence of the metal hobnails which are typical of Roman shoes, or the metal lace tags or buckles which occur occasionally in seventh-century graves, entire shoes may simply have rotted away. Leather finds from Anglo-Saxon excavations are usually preserved in damp conditions or by proximity to metalwork; these conditions may not have applied to shoes in graves.

In contrast, there is much linguistic evidence, suggesting that a variety of types of footwear already existed in the fifth and sixth

---

[187] I. Dennett, 'Isle of Wight', *Transactions of the British Archaeological Association*, Winchester Congress (1845), pp. 148–60, at p. 154.

[188] Alan Baxter, of West Stow Anglo-Saxon village, reports that re-enactors fighting in shoes find they are soon ruined by wet and mud.

[189] See M. Hald, *Primitive Shoes*, trans. I. Nixon, Publications of the National Museum of Denmark, Archaeological-Historical Series, 1. 13 (Copenhagen, 1972).

[190] C. Wells, *Bones, Bodies and Disease* (London, 1964), p. 51.

[191] Leg fractures do not seem common among recently excavated skeletons and the slightly later shoes which survive are not clumsy. Information from Patricia Reid, who has recently completed a doctorate on north European footwear.

centuries: the ordinary shoe, *scoh*, which, to judge from later evidence was probably an ankle-boot; a lower-cut shoe or slipper, *swiftlere*; raw hide shoes, a type of which we have examples from other countries (Fig. 85) called in Old English *hemming* and *rifeling*[192] and the bag-like *socc*. The existence of the word *crinc* suggests a shoe drawn together with thongs. The *hosa* may have been a boot or a legging.[193]

Leggings

We cannot know how Anglo-Saxon women kept their legs warm. They may have simply added extra layers of under-tunics in winter or they could have had some special protection for the legs. Archaeological evidence is lacking on this point so we must rely on linguistic evidence and Continental art for guidance. There are three types of legging which might have been worn: trousers, socks and bindings.

It is possible that Germanic women wore trousers and that these might not require a skirt to cover them. The evidence for this is a controversial sculpture from Mainz, which shows a seated girl, apparently wearing a long veil and diamond-patterned trouser-suit (Fig. 58). The sculpture is, however, unique and it is possible that we have not understood the carver's intention. However, the Spong Hill pot lid (Fig. 3) also clearly shows the legs of a seated figure; they are not concealed by skirts, though marks at wrist and ankle suggest that the person is clothed in tight fitting sleeves and leg coverings rather than naked. There is an Old English word *strapul*, meaning a legging, perhaps the leg of a pair of trousers. The word probably derived from Latin *strebula*,[194] 'the flesh about the haunch'. It is found glossing *tubroces, uel brace*.[195] Latin *tubroces*, or *tubragus*, properly signified a legging or wrapping for the shins (though the Anglo-Saxons seem to have used the word for a humble type of boot made of hide).[196] *Brace*, or *bracae*, signifies 'trousers'. The thirteenth-century text *Ancrene Wisse* demonstrates that women could wear *streapules* (as a penitential garment) and that they were fastened

[192] See p. 123, n. 76.

[193] See p. 256, n. 83.

[194] Holthausen, *Wörterbuch*, p. 325. Holthausen lists Greek and Latin cognates, but not Germanic. The word is not documented in Old English before the tenth century, but since it has evidently undergone the first Germanic consonant shift (Grimm's Law), the voiced stop [b] becoming the voiceless stop [p], it must have been borrowed from Latin into Germanic before the Anglo-Saxon settlement.

[195] T. Wright (ed.), *Anglo-Saxon and Old English Vocabularies*, 2nd edition, ed. and collated by R. P. Wülcker, 2 vols (London, 1884, reprinted Darmstadt, 1968), col. 125, line 2.

[196] The Northumbrian ascetic St Cuthbert, according to Bede's *Life*, was 'shod' (*calciatus*) 'with boots' (*tibracis*), which were made of skin and which covered foot and shin; *Vita Sancti Cuthberti*, XVIII, B. Colgrave (ed.), *Two Lives of St Cuthbert* (Cambridge, 1940), p. 218.

by laces.[197] Another Middle English text, Trevisa's translation of Higden's *Polychronicon*, mentions that *strapeles* extended up to the thighs.[198] The *strapul*, then, in post-Conquest times, covered the whole leg, perhaps being the leg part of a pair of trousers, and was fastened with laces. A version of this garment may well have existed in our period.

The Old English word *brec* is much better documented. Originally the plural of *broc*, the term was usually singular in Middle English ('a breech'). The word is not specifically associated with women in any Old English text but again the thirteenth-century *Ancrene Wisse* indicates that as a penitential garment, women might wear the *brech*. The Old English term appears to have principally signified a short pair of pants or trousers, covering the loins or extending down the thighs, for it glosses *lumbare*[199] ('loin cloth') and *femoralia*[200] ('covering for the thigh', 'breeches') and is described as a thigh-covering in an Old English text.[201]

In the absence of any evidence for knitting or *sprang*, we must assume that any leg coverings the Anglo-Saxons wore were woven or of leather. As such they would lack the elasticity we associate with leg coverings today, and would have required shaping by tailoring or binding to the leg if they were not to hang loose. The words *hosa*, a boot or legging, and *socc*, a loose bag-like foot covering, may have been used of garments worn inside shoes or boots or of the footwear itself (see p. 83 above). Both words were probably in use in pagan times but we have no evidence to associate them with one sex or the other. Both men and women probably wound pieces of cloth or leather (*hose-bendas*, *winingas*) round their shins and feet, either directly against the skin or over stockings or trousers, in which case the bindings both provided warmth and kept the other leg coverings in position.

Jewellery

In addition to the brooches, buckles and pins with which their clothing was fastened, women were also usually adorned with non-

[197] J. R. R. Tolkien (ed.), *Ancrene Wisse*, Early English Text Society, original series, 249 (1962), p. 214, lines 15–17 (f. 113b).

[198] C. Babington and J. R. Lumby (ed.), *Polychronicon Ranulphi Higden*, Rolls Series 41, 9 vols (London, 1865–86), 5 (1874), p. 355.

[199] Lindsay, *Corpus Glossary*, p. 108, line 287; Wright/Wülcker, *Vocabularies*, col. 433, line 12.

[200] *Benedictine Rule*, 55; [M. M.] A. Schröer (ed.), *Die angelsächsischen Prosabearbeitungen der Benedictinerregel*, Bibliothek der angelsächsischen Prosa, ed. C. W. M. Grein, R. P. Wülcker and H. Hecht, 13 vols (Kassel, 1872–1933) 2 (1885–8), p. 91, line 8, glossary p. 240.

[201] The *Indicia Monasterialia*, a handbook of sign language for silent monks, states: *Brecena tancen is þæt þu strice mid þinum twam handum up on þin þeah* ('the sign of *brec* is that you stroke up your thigh with your two hands'); F. Kluge, 'Zur Geschichte der Zeichensprache angelsächsische Indicia Monasterialia', *Internationale Zeitschrift für Allgemeine Sprachwissenschaft*, 2 (1885), pp. 116–37, at p. 127, para 102. There is a more recent edition by D. Banham, *Monasteriales Indicia: the Anglo-Saxon monastic sign language* (Pinner, 1991).

functional jewellery. Beads (Colour Plate E) are considered strongly gendered grave-goods, and are very common in female graves. The most recurrent position in which beads are found is in a festoon between the shoulder brooches, the pins of which sometimes retain the remains of the bead strings, usually mineralised, which had been tied to them. A central brooch could be fastened over the beads, keeping the festoon in position, as in one case at Hunstanton Park, Norfolk.[202] Possibly this festooning of the beads at the front of the body was a device to show off the woman's possessions and status as she lay prepared for the grave. The festoon is found so frequently, however, that it probably reflects actual practice. Beads could also be worn in other ways, in fact there are countless arrangements of beads in graves, but these appear to be idiosyncratic. Some women may have worn a string of beads round the neck (though they are only rarely recovered from under the vertebrae or skull, so this was not very common). A small loop of beads might dangle from one of the shoulder brooches which may also have supported a festoon. Beads may have sometimes been stitched onto girdles or hung from them. They may also have been sewn in clusters to the garments. Beads that have occasionally been found near the skulls of women with average supplies of grave-goods may have been attached to the hair or headdress; they occur more than once near the heads of elaborately dressed Kentish women. Many women wore bead bracelets round one or both arms, although this was not a general habit at any one site. Two amber beads at the right ankle of a skeleton at Petersfinger might have decorated a shoe or garter[203] and nine large beads at the right ankle of a woman at Lyminge may have formed an anklet.[204] There are many scatterings of beads on or beside a skeleton which we cannot explain, which is not surprising if we consider that a bead string might easily swing out of position, twist or even break as a corpse was being lowered into the grave, and that beads would drop as the body beneath them decayed.

The number of beads worn varied greatly, from single beads to two hundred and more. Generally, women well-equipped with brooches and jewellery had the most beads, but this was not a universal rule; I know of no study that has attempted to quantify beads in relation to the supposed status of other grave-goods and would not expect a consistent picture to emerge from such research.[205] At several cemeteries, for example at Mucking, excavators have noted that the corpses of children had single beads or only a few of them.[206]

---

[202] T. McK. Hughes, untitled, in *Proceedings of the Society of Antiquaries*, 2nd series, 18 (1899–1901), pp. 310–21, at p. 319.

[203] Grave 37; Leeds and Shortt, *Petersfinger*, p. 28.

[204] Grave 39; Warhurst, 'Lyminge', p. 27.

[205] If we consider, for example, the grave plans of a selection of graves containing square-headed brooches, supposedly high-status objects, in Hines, *Square-headed Brooches*, pp. 287–92, we see that the number of beads varies from zero to over eighty.

[206] Information from W. T. Jones.

At Long Wittenham, Berkshire, some women had elaborate bead ornaments, including one instance of 280 beads; but none of the elaborate arrangements accompanied young people and several children had only one, two or three beads.[207] This would seem to support the view that simpler bead ornaments were considered suitable for young people. In Sewerby Grave 28, conversely, a child was accompanied by 130 beads, some of which were particularly small.[208] Beads have sometimes been found in association with metal rings. Some of these may have been earrings, notably in Castledyke Grave 160,[209] though at Holywell Row, Suffolk, the festoon of beads had probably been suspended from the rings which were sewn to the garment.[210] Rings were not so popular in this period as they were to become in the seventh century and beads were rarely strung onto rings until then.

The most common beads were glass. These are found in a great variety of colours and shapes. They can be monochrome or decorated with trails of contrasting colour. Margaret Guido's recent study of glass beads from early Anglo-Saxon England illustrates the complexity of this subject.[211] Guido initially categorises beads by colour, subcategorising into monochrome/polychrome and by shape and design. It is not yet clear if glass beads were manufactured in England or if they were all imported. Guido's distribution maps demonstrate the very different locations of different bead types; not all are so simple as the distribution of 'pink' beads, which on the Continent is concentrated in the lower Elbe and Jutland regions, and in England occurs in cemeteries on the east coast, the inhabitants of which may have migrated from exactly those regions.[212] Chronology, too, has proved inconclusive. Though 'terracotta-coloured' glass, for example, appears to have a straightforward time-span, becoming hugely popular in the sixth century and remaining fashionable in the seventh, many of Guido's colour groups appear in early and later pagan graves, and some of them continue into the Middle Saxon period.[213] Custom appears to have differed between sites: at Sewerby, for example, strings of blue beads were in relatively 'poor' graves, at Castledyke they were in relatively rich seventh-century graves.[214] Any re-enactor creating a bead string would be wise to copy a specific example from a single grave,

[207] J. Y. Akerman, 'Report on researches in an Anglo-Saxon cemetery at Long Wittenham, Berkshire, in 1859', *Archaeologia*, 38 (1860), pp. 327–52. The grave with over 200 beads was No. 71, p. 343.

[208] Hirst, *Sewerby*, p. 71.

[209] Grave 160; Drinkall and Foreman, *Castledyke*, p. 80.

[210] Grave 1; Lethbridge, *Recent Excavations*, p. 2.

[211] M. Guido, *The Glass Beads of Anglo-Saxon England c. AD 400–700*, ed. M. Welch (Woodbridge, 1999).

[212] Guido, *Beads*, pp. 55–6. Even here the correlation is more complex than expected. Beads were found in sixth-, not fifth-century graves.

[213] M. Welch, 'Conclusion', in Guido, *Beads*, p. 94.

[214] Drinkall and Foreman, *Castledyke*, p. 265.

and/or to consult Guido's distribution maps for maximum compatability between components.

Amber beads were also extremely common, reaching maximum popularity in the late-sixth century. Although amber probably entered England from the east coast, either as a native find from the shores of eastern England or as an import from north-east Europe, it is as characteristic of graves in the western areas of Saxon England as in the predominantly Anglian eastern counties. Amber, which is a fossil resin with 'magnetic' qualities, was well known in Continental Europe and the Near East for its prophylactic value as well as being appreciated for its rich colour. The supposed curative powers of amber are ancient and manifold. It could be powdered and taken in liquid, blended with honey, burnt like incense or worn as an amulet, especially on a necklace. It was considered a cure for a wide range of ailments, including fever, internal ills and troubles of the skin, ears and eyes. It was believed to be especially efficacious in preventing chills and tonsillitis and against witchcraft.[215] Anglo-Saxon women may therefore have worn amber not only for its visual attractiveness but also for superstitious reasons; it was certainly condemned as 'pagan' by the early-sixth-century archbishop Caesarius of Arles[216] and was to decline sharply in use in the seventh century, though this may have been due to cessation of supply as well as Christian disapproval.[217]

Rarer beads were of crystal, which also perhaps was endowed with 'magical' properties (see pp. 94–5 below), jet, shell and stone. It is evident that some bead groups consisted of several, or many, similarly shaped and coloured beads, for example small annular blue glass beads, or medium-sized amber beads, sometimes with a large central bead of the same material; while other assemblages were made up of beads of different colours, patterns, shapes, and even of different materials, amber, for example, mixing with glass and monochrome mixing with polychrome. Women with more than one bead string may have had two contrasting styles, for example a cluster of monochrome beads of glass or amber plus a heterogeneous festoon. Beads were sometimes graduated according to size, but the overall impression one gets is that often the beads were not arranged according to size, shape or colour, except perhaps for one or more large beads at the centre of a string. A bead string at Warren Hill, Suffolk, where there was a continuous arrangement of three small beads then a large one, is unusual.[218] It is not always possible to translate the scattering of beads in a grave into an ordered row.

[215] Meaney, *Amulets*, p. 70.

[216] Meaney, *Amulets*, pp. 14, 70–1.

[217] If the amber was from the coast of East Anglia it may have been the product of a short-lived native industry. If it was imported, from the Baltic or the other side of the North Sea, supplies may have been affected by the change in trade from northerly to southerly which occurred in the seventh century; Meaney, *Amulets*, pp. 68–70.

[218] H. Prigg, 'The Anglo-Saxon graves, Warren Hill, Mildenhall', *Proceedings of the Suffolk Institute of Archaeology amd Natural History*, 6 (1888), pp. 57–72, at p. 59.

Figs 60, 61 Bracteate pendants, Buckland, Dover, Kent

Pendants were often attached to strings of beads, and, less often, worn alone. At this early period pendants were rarely elaborate. By far the commonest type consisted of a Roman coin, pierced for suspension. Bracteates (Figs 60, 61),[219] gold pendants ultimately copied from Roman coins, but of various designs, were first imported from Scandinavia and then made in both Kent and Anglian districts;[220] so were scutiform (shield-shaped) pendants, usually silver, which appeared at the end of the sixth century or the beginning of the seventh[221] (originally pagan amulets, these were readily adapted to Christian taste when their ornament became cruciform);[222] and simpler ornamented disc pendants. The little bucket-shaped pendants[223] which in England seem to have been a sixth-century Anglian phenomenon, could be strung with beads, worn as a separate festoon, carried at the hip, or in one case, at Bidford-on-Avon, apparently stitched on to (or contained in) a leather 'bib' or satchel slung round the neck. They may, possibly, have reflected the woman's ceremonial role as dispenser of drink, though the fact that in several instances the miniature buckets contained textile suggests some different interpretation; they were probably amuletic.[224] Other pendants were idiosyncratic: individual women wore a Roman intaglio,[225] the lid of an enamelled Roman-British seal-box,[226] the escutcheons of Celtic hanging bowls[227] animals' teeth[228] and an eagle's talon.[229] Some at least of these were probably lucky charms and may be compared with the contents of the ivory-ring pouches which also tended to contain something old and something of animal origin. In an investigation of animals' teeth at Castledyke, Gail Drinkall took into account the dental health of the persons who carried them, which suggested they were amulets against toothache.[230] A woman buried in Grave 42 at Wakerley had a quartz pebble in silver slings like a small version of the crystal balls worn by prosperous Kentish women, and perhaps,

---

[219] S. C. Hawkes and M. Pollard, 'The gold bracteates from sixth-century Anglo-Saxon graves in Kent, in the light of a new find from Finglesham', *Frümittelalterliche Studien*, 15 (1981), pp. 316–70.

[220] Hines (*Scandinavian Character*, pp. 199–220) suggests that Anglian England received Scandinavian influence in this respect both directly and indirectly, through the importation of Kentish bracteates modelled on Scandinavian.

[221] Adams, Jackson and Badenoch, *Wakerley*, pp. 152–3.

[222] V. I. Evison, *Dover: The Buckland Anglo-Saxon Cemetery*, Historic Buildings and Monuments Commission for England, Archaeological Report No. 3 (1987), p. 56.

[223] Hines, *Scandinavian Character*, pp. 221–35.

[224] Dickinson, 'An Anglo-Saxon "cunning woman" ', p. 51.

[225] Sleaford, Grave 227; Thomas, 'Sleaford', p. 404.

[226] Abingdon, Grave 59; Leeds and Harden, *Abingdon*, p. 42.

[227] E.g. Shudy Camps, Cambridgeshire; T. C. Lethbridge, *A Cemetery at Shudy Camps, Cambridgeshire*, Cambridge Antiquarian Society Quarto Publications, 2nd series, 5 (1936), p. 12.

[228] E.g. Abingdon, Grave 76 (dog); Leeds and Harden, *Abingdon*, p. 45; Castledyke Grave 134 (beaver); Drinkall and Foreman, *Castledyke*, pp. 73–4.

[229] Alfriston, Grave 43; Griffith and Salzman, 'Alfriston', pp. 25, 39.

[230] Drinkall and Foreman, *Castledyke*, p. 239.

like them, prophylactic.[231] Occasional clusters of objects suggest that personal tools and amulets might have been carried in a bag slung round the neck, like the Biford-on-Avon woman's satchel, for example a woman in Grave 163 at Castledyke had tweezers, an earscoop and a polished stone at the neck, though no container had survived.[232]

In Old English literature women are depicted as wearing and owning rings, including neck-rings and probably head-bands.[233] In view of the literary tradition, the infrequency and simplicity of archaeological finds of this kind of ornament is striking. A very few decorative metal collars have been found in female or possibly female inhumation graves,[234] and there are torques from a small number of cinerary urns,[235] which may have belonged to either sex. (A necklet has also been found in the grave of a young man, see p. 127.) These objects have mainly been found in eastern England. Metal bracelets (Fig. 62) are more common though they were not worn by many women at any one site. They have beeen found in a number of graves in Kent, but they occur in other areas too. There may have been local fashions in adornments for the limbs: at Sleaford, a large Lincolnshire cemetery, bracelets of metal and beads occurred in a significant minority of the graves;[236] at Lyminge, Kent, anklets were worn by both sexes[237] and armlets of textile, brocaded with gold thread, were found on women at two sites in Kent (see p. 96 below). Apart from native Anglo-Saxon armlets, which are usually simple bands or spirals, women seem to have taken over objects not originally their own or not originally intended as bracelets, and re-used them. A Romano-British armlet made of glass

Fig. 62 Bracelet, one of a pair, Tuddenham, Suffolk

---

[231] This Wakerley woman was prosperous, but not otherwise 'Kentish', with paired applied brooches and a florid cruciform one, unusual silver wrist clasps and two groups of beads, totalling seventy-four; Adams, Jackson and Badenoch, *Wakerley*, p. 152 and microfiche.

[232] Drinkall and Foreman, *Castledyke*, pp. 81–2.

[233] The queen of Denmark, Wealhtheow, is described as *under gyldnum beage* 'under a golden ring' (line 1163) and as giving a *healsbeag*, 'neck ring' to the hero (lines 1195, 2172) which later passes to Hygd, queen of Geatland; Dobbie, *Beowulf and Judith*, pp. 36–7, 67. In *Beowulf* women appear to wear rings in peace-time, men for war. I first suggested this in *The Four Funerals in Beowulf: and the structure of the poem* (Manchester, 2000), p. 231, n.13.

[234] Empingham II, Rutland, Grave 118, a child of about three years, with amber beads (Timby, *Empingham II*, pp. 125–6); Market Overton II, Rutland (V. B. Crowther-Beynon, 'Notes on an Anglian cemetery at Market Overton, Rutland', *Archaeologia*, 62 (1911), pp. 481–6 at pp. 483–4 and Fig.1(b)); Ipswich, Suffolk, Grave 12, sex indeterminate (N. F. Layard, 'An Anglo-Saxon cemetery in Ipswich', *Archaeologia*, 60 (1907), pp. 325–52 at pp. 335–6, 339); Emscote, Warwickshire; P. B. Chatwin, 'Anglo-Saxon finds at Warwick', *Antiquaries Journal*, 5 (1925), pp. 268–72 at pp. 269–70.

[235] From Caistor and Narford; both Norfolk; R. Rainbird Clarke, 'Norfolk in the Dark Ages, 400–800 A. D.', *Norfolk Archaeology*, 27 (1939–41), pp. 163–249 at pp. 217–18, 247.

[236] Three children (Graves 48, 66, 85), six adults (Graves 50, 65, 143, 155, 193, 194). Four were of beads, the others of wire or flat metal; Thomas, 'Sleaford', pp. 391–3, 398–9, 401–2.

[237] Including an anklet of nine large beads on a woman in Grave 39; Warhurst, 'Lyminge', p. 27.

Fig. 63 Garnet-set brooch with rectangular headplate, Chessel Down, Isle of Wight

Fig. 64 'Kentish' disc brooch with keystone-shaped garnets, Chessel Down, Isle of Wight

encircled the wrist of a woman at Malling Hill, Lewes, East Sussex[238] and what may have once been a penannular brooch was found on the arm of a skeleton at Bifrons, Kent.[239] Ivory rings of the kind we now identify as pouch rings may have been recycled to be worn on the arm since they have been more than once identified as bracelets.

Finger rings have often been found on women who also wore armlets, and, like them, occur in only a small proportion of graves. Finger rings have more often been found in graves of unusual richness than in those of average wealth; frequently the women in these well-equipped graves wore more than one ring. The ring is often found on the fourth finger, the one we call 'the ring finger'; possibly it was a token of marriage, but if so it was not common practice to wear a wedding ring. Rings are sometimes found on other fingers too: at Chessel Down, Isle of Wight, one skeleton had dissimilar rings on both forefingers and another skeleton dissimilar rings on both little fingers.[240] The finger rings of this period, like the native armlets, are very simple bands or spirals. Some finger rings are of precious metals but others are copper alloy or iron. They are not set with gems or treated to any of the elaborate decorative techniques noted in other metalwork. On the whole the 'rings' of pagan Anglo-Saxon archaeology lack the aesthetic appeal of other jewellery, only the fragments of gold-embroidered fillets from a few Kentish graves (p. 96 below) offering possible identification with the splendid *beagas* of Anglo-Saxon poetry. Perhaps early Anglo-Saxon rings, unattractive as they are to the modern eye, are unusual finds because they were only worn by a few, high-ranking people. Perhaps, however, our evidence is unrepresentative. Finer examples may have been bequeathed to relatives rather than committed to the grave.

Varieties of costume in Kent

We have been able to establish that a common costume was worn by women in Anglian and Saxon areas in the fifth and sixth centuries. Variations in the position and number of grave-goods can be explained as additions to and rearrangements of this common dress, with the possibility that some women, perhaps including the poor, and slaves, wore a simpler version of it, without the outer gown and its paired brooches.

The position is less clear in Kent. The fifth-century settlers, who seem to have been Jutes with some Frisians among them or, at any rate, Jutes with strong Frisian associations, and possibly some

Fig. 65 Radiate-headed brooch, Mill Hill, Kent

[238] G. B. Brown, *The Arts in Early England*, 6 vols (London, 1903–37), 4 (1915), p. 458.
[239] Thus E. Fowler, 'Celtic metalwork of the fifth and sixth centuries A. D.', *Archaeological Journal*, 120 (1963), pp. 98–150 at p. 118, though Brown (*Arts*, 4, p. 457) thought it had never been a brooch.
[240] Owen, 'Anglo-Saxon Costume', 1, p. 100.

Franks, have not left much evidence of their clothing since they seem to have cremated their dead, and because later ploughing has destroyed cemeteries. Intercourse between Kent and Scandinavia evidently continued at least up to the early-sixth century, bringing silver-gilt brooches with rectangular headplates (Fig. 63) and gold bracteate pendants (Figs 60, 61, 86) as jewellery for wealthy women. The influx, later in the century, of high status Frankish settlers and Frankish merchandise brought brooches decorated with garnets, some circular, with the stones arranged as rosettes or as circles of keystone-shaped gems (Fig. 64), others radiate-headed (Figs 13, 65) or bird-shaped (Fig. 66).[241] Kentish jewellers developed the circular brooch in particular, at first characteristically with three or four keystone-shaped garnets, then with cloisonné and filigree (Colour plate Ca, Fig. 67), reaching artistic heights in the seventh century with large polychrome disc brooches. Kentish buckles of this early period are frequently more decorative than those of Anglian and Saxon areas, with, for example, chip-carved buckle plates, but under Frankish influence there were also introduced buckles attached to inlaid, triangular buckle plates and studded belts. The textiles of Kent, like the jewellery, suggest an interesting blend of culture rather different from that in the 'Anglian' and 'Saxon' areas. Though Kent shares tablet-weave with the rest of Anglo-Saxon England, and with Scandinavia, there appears to be a greater proportion of tabby-woven linen in Kent than elsewhere, suggesting affinity with the cross-channel area and central Germany.[242]

It is noticeable that, though the shoulder brooch fashion is not unknown in Kent, a pair of brooches was often instead placed one above the other, with the pins horizontal, as if they were closing a vertical opening. Clearly in these cases it was not the *peplos*-type gown which displayed the brooches. At Buckland it was evident that even brooches which did not originate in Kent were worn in this distinctively 'Kentish' way. In Grave 13 two similar, but not identical, square-headed brooches were worn in this manner, with beads between them. The brooches themselves were worn, repaired and old when they were buried with an old woman. They may have been manufactured in the late-fifth or early-sixth century. One had probably originated from the Danish islands east of Jutland and the other from Jutland itself.[243] A pair of small, jewelled, Kentish square-headed brooches were worn in a similar way by a girl buried in Grave 20. In Grave 48 two fifth-century Saxon brooches were worn, a button brooch at the neck and a saucer brooch at the middle

Fig. 66 Bird-shaped brooch, Chessel Down, Isle of Wight

Fig. 67 Cloisonné disc brooch, Sibertswold, Kent

[241] R. Avent, *Anglo-Saxon Garnet and Inlaid Composite Brooches*, 2 vols, British Archaeological Reports, British Series, 11 (1975).

[242] Bender Jørgensen, 'The textiles of the Saxons, Anglo-Saxons and Franks', pp. 11–23; *North European Textiles until AD 1000*, p. 37. Lise Bender Jørgensen's conclusions about English textiles were based on the researches of Elisabeth Crowfoot which are presented in tabular form with bibliography at pp. 154–8 of *North European Textiles*.

[243] Evison, *Buckland*, pp. 35–7, 68–9, 134.

of the chest. The two were connected by chain and beads. (Professor Evison noted that the pin on this (Fig. 17) and other button brooches found in Kent was at right angles to the stylised human face on its front, indicating that it fastened a horizontal aperture, whereas in Saxon areas the pins of button brooches (as Fig. 4) are vertical in relation to the face.)[244] A woman in Grave 71 at Bifrons similarly had two circular brooches, arranged vertically, connected by a chain.[245] At Chessel Down, Isle of Wight, women were equipped with two or three brooches arranged in vertical rows on the chests, their pins horizontal.[246] At Mill Hill women wore as many as five brooches in a vertical row down the front of the body, though it was not clear whether they had secured one or more front-fastening garments. In Grave 61, the row of two bird brooches and three small square-headed began at the right of the neck and curved further to the right, by-passing a buckle at the right of the waist.[247] In Grave 16 at Lyminge there was a radiate-headed brooch, head to the left, at the waist of the skeleton, in addition to a button brooch at the chest which was associated with a string of beads. The radiate-headed brooch is unlikely to have clasped a girdle, since there was a buckle at the waist which could have performed this function.[248] There are various possible interpretations of the brooch positions, not mutually exclusive. In the cases of Buckland Graves 13 and 20, the excavator considered that the brooches had fastened cloaks,[249] but in other cases it seems likely that the brooches fastened the vertical opening of a tunic, like the undergown suggested for Anglian areas. In Buckland Grave 92, however, where there was a Kentish garnet disc brooch at the neck and a Frankish garnet disc brooch lower down on the chest (Fig. 71), the excavator thought they might have fastened two different front-opening garments because of their

---

[244] Evison, *Buckland*, p. 48. The horizontal position is also said to be characteristic of 'later' [non-Kentish] button brooches.

[245] T. Godfrey-Faussett, 'The Saxon cemetery at Bifrons', *Archaeologia Cantiana*, 13 (1880), pp. 552–6, at p. 554.

[246] The lady with the gold braid had five brooches (C. Hillier, *The History and Antiquities of The Isle of Wight* (London, 1855), pp. 28–9). Not every grave is described in detail in this report, but Hillier's conclusion is worth recording: 'The position which the fibulae retained on the skeletons, seemed to point to the conclusion that the part of the Anglo-Saxon attire to which they had been attached was either a long dress, open partly down the front, or a tunic, which, being confined round the waist by a belt of leather or some other substance, was closed at the breast and neck by the fibulae. When two were found they were invariably removed from these positions, and when three were exhumed, it was clear that a similar arrangement had prevailed, with less space between them' (p. 32). See also C. J. Arnold, *The Anglo-Saxon Cemeteries of the Isle of Wight* (London, 1982), p. 71, who adds the caution regarding multi-brooch graves: 'Clearly it is dangerous to make too much of the position of brooches as some may have been purely for ornamental display'.

[247] Parfitt and Brugmann, *Mill Hill*, pp. 46–8.

[248] Warhurst, 'Lyminge', pp. 13, 15.

[249] Evison, *Buckland*, p. 69: ' ... in both cases it is clear that the square-headed brooches would be visible on the cloak, but the other brooches [a small-long and an annular, at the left chest in Grave 13], and in Grave 20, the beads, were adorning the undergarment and were covered by the cloak.' Possibly this assertion is based on stratification of finds, though this is not apparent from the diagrams.

entirely separate bead-strings.[250] I would suggest that the brooches, which were both dainty, might have fastened a veil and a tunic (Fig. 72).

A small number of strikingly rich female graves, dating mostly to the middle of the sixth century, occur in Kent and culturally-related areas (Colour Plate F). Despite the fact that they are buried among other inhumations in 'folk' cemeteries[251] these Kentish ladies may have been of high, possibly royal, birth, for many of them are accompanied by grave-goods rare and fine enough for us to recognise them as luxuries: metal weaving swords (implements for beating up the weft on a loom, tools which were usually, we assume, made of wood or bone) at Chessel Down, Isle of Wight,[252] Finglesham, Graves D3[253] and 203[254] and Sarre[255] in Kent and Holywell Row in Suffolk;[256] glass vessels at Bifrons (Grave 41),[257] the Finglesham graves and Sarre. Most of these ladies wore at least one buckle at the waist[258] and were lavishly equipped with the kind of belt adjuncts that occur in less pretentious furnished graves: knives, keys, coins, rings and tools. Several of the ladies (Chessel Down, Bifrons Graves 6, 42, 64, Lyminge[259] and Sarre Grave 4) were accompanied by crystal balls which lay between the thighs, having evidently been suspended at the front of the clothing. Mill Hill Grave 25B had a similarly mounted ball of smoky quartz between the knees and Grave 105C at the same site had a large (2 cm) bead of the same material on the forearm. Crystal balls have been found on the Continent as far south as the Lombard region of northern

---

[250] Evison, *Buckland*, p. 69: 'This seems to indicate two entirely separate strings of beads, which may have been worn one on an outer garment and one on an inner garment'. Again it is not clear if this is speculation or based on stratification.

[251] Burial in large, sometimes isolated, barrows marks 'princely' graves of the late-sixth to seventh century, and is almost entirely a masculine phenomenon.

[252] 1855 discovery, Grave 1 (Hillier, *Isle of Wight*, pp. 29–30). For a discussion of iron weaving beaters see L. Millard, S. Jarman, and S. C. Hawkes, 'Anglo-Saxon burials near the Lord of the Manor, Ramsgate', *Archaeologia Cantiana*, 84 (1969), pp. 9–30, at pp. 17–22.

[253] W. Whiting and W. P. D. Stebbing, 'Jutish cemetery near Finglesham, Kent', *Archaeologia Cantiana*, 41 (1929), pp. 113–25, at p. 121.

[254] Information from Sonia Hawkes.

[255] Grave 4; J. Brent, 'Account of the Society's researches in the Saxon cemetery at Sarr [sic]', *Archaeologia Cantiana*, 5 (1862–3), pp. 305–22, at pp. 310–20.

[256] Grave 11; Lethbridge, *Recent Excavations*, pp. 4–9.

[257] T. Godfrey-Faussett, 'The Saxon cemetery at Bifrons', *Archaeologia Cantiana*, 10 (1876), pp. 298–315, at pp. 313–14.

[258] Sonia Hawkes suggested to me informally that the elaborate buckles worn at the waist by some of these ladies could have fastened substantial leather belts and that the latter might have had some other function than just to cinch the waist of the dress and to suspend trinkets, namely, to hold up skirts. This is an intriguing possibility, especially since the skirt was part of the traditional costume for women in Denmark before the *Hängerock* took over. There is a well-known example from Huldremose, which still has leather cords threaded through the waistband; it was worn with a chequered scarf and two skin capes (Hald, *Ancient Danish Textiles*, pp. 47–51, Figs 29–30, 156). The heyday of the skirt in Denmark was, however, the Bronze Age, and as Hald has observed 'The technical differences between the early Bronze Age … textiles and the Iron Age … textiles are so great that a chasm separates them' (p. 378). Could the skirt have survived such changes in cloth making?

[259] Grave 44; Warhurst, 'Lyminge', pp. 31–2.

Fig. 68 Crystal ball and silver spoon with perforated bowl, lying as found in a grave at Chessel Down, Isle of Wight

Italy and as far east as Hungary; they are not uncommon in Alamannia, nor in England, where they are not confined to the group of wealthy ladies under discussion;[260] but their centre of popularity seems to have been the Rhineland, and the overwhelming majority of finds have been from Germany, with several other examples from Austria, Belgium, France and the Netherlands. They seem, then, to have been a Frankish fashion, and it is no doubt from the Merovingian Franks that the Kentish people took them. They have been found in male burials (the earliest known example was in the tomb of the Merovingian King Childeric, 481 AD), and they were worn in a variety of ways (at the neck, tied to the belt), but in the majority of cases they have accompanied women in unusually rich graves and were worn, normally mounted in silver slings, dangling at the front of the body. Very often, as in Kent, they were accompanied by silver spoons, perforated in the bowl (Fig. 68).

These quartz crystals receive a lot of attention from students of the period, much of it because they are thought to give some insight into pagan practices.[261] Caution is necessary here, however. Though the dipping of balls in water (and perhaps recovering them with spoons perforated for drainage) seems plausible enough, the practice of dipping crystals in water to cure man or beast is only documented as a modern phenomenon. The custom of using crystals for 'scrying', crystal-gazing for divination and other purposes, is not recorded before the Renaissance. The Germanic people probably copied the use of crystals from the Romans, who certainly utilised them as curative amulets, but in ways related to their ice-like appearance rather than supposed magical properties, using them for cooling the hands, and, according to Pliny, for cauterizing. The crystal beads which appear on bead strings in the pagan Anglo-Saxon period may have been similarly amuletic. It seems probable, though, that the popularity of the crystals among the rich and royal of Frankia owed something to their Christian symbolism. Crystal became a symbol of the Virgin Mary and (because it can act as a catalyst to light passing through it) of the Immaculate Conception. Shining a strong light through a crystal can produce 'interference figures' which flash as cross shapes and as rainbows, both of which are significant in Christian doctrine, the cross as symbolic of Christ's crucifixion, and the rainbow as the manifestation of God's promise after the flood. Crystal was to play a notable part in Carolingian and Alfredian Christian art: Charlemagne had an amulet in which

[260] H. Hinz, 'Am langen Band getragene Bergkristallanhänger der Merowingerzeit', *Jahrbuch des Römisch-Germanischen Zentralmuseums Mainz*, 13 (1966), pp. 212–30. Hinz lists additional English examples from Canterbury, Chatham Lines, Chartham Down, Faversham and Harrietsham, Kent and Kempston, Bedfordshire.

[261] The evidence which follows is derived from Meaney, *Anglo-Saxon Amulets*, pp. 92–6 and from personal discussion with Dr Meaney. The firm suggestion that these crystals may have been popularised in the sixth century as Christian objects is my own conclusion from the facts she has presented to me. I would like to express my thanks to Dr Meaney for sharing her expertise on this subject.

holy relics were set between two hemispherical crystals; crystal was used in the construction of the ninth-century, Anglo-Saxon cloisonné Alfred Jewel and Minster Lovell Jewel. The former depicts a figure of moral or religious significance (see p. 171), the latter a cross. Though Christianity was not to be formally reintroduced into England until Augustine's mission at the very end of the sixth century, it was well established on the Continent before that, and knowledge of it may have survived in Kent from Romano-British times and through Frankish contacts. The fashion for wearing crystal balls may have come from the Continent with Frankish brides whose families had come under the influence of Christianity; or the objects may have been part of a luxury trade which appealed to wealthy pre-Augustinian Christians.[262] What they meant to their wearers, in a predominantly pagan Anglo-Saxon England, and to those who prepared them for the grave, we cannot know. Perhaps they were religious objects or perhaps they were believed to have some magical function; possibly they were used to make fire; or perhaps they were just valued for their beauty and rarity and the fascinating colour changes they could display.

Though crystal balls and perforated spoons are often found together they may not share the same cultural origin and may not have been used together. Spoons might have been wine strainers;[263] their distribution in England, chiefly in the Isle of Wight and Kent, is consistent with the known distribution of imported wine as testified by the pottery in which it was contained. Audrey Meaney notes that 'the strainer was a well-known elegant domestic appliance in Greece and Rome' and suggests that although in Rome the task of straining the wine would have been performed by a slave, it may have been part of the ceremonial ritual of dispensing drink associated with the Germanic lady. In the Old English poem *Beowulf*, two queens and a king's daughter are depicted passing round drink at the feast, though servants also attend the drinkers.[264] If so, the straining spoons, though expensive and beautiful objects in their own right, would also have indicated symbolically the status of a woman whose family could afford imported wine. George Speake, however, considers the Anglo-Saxon spoons too shallow and too unlike Roman wine strainers for this interpretation, and apparently interprets them as sprinklers for water made magic by the crystals.[265]

A common feature of the rich ladies' graves is their abundance of jewellery. Elaborate neck ornaments included coins, bracteates

[262] Augustine's mission of 597 is not a fixed point for Christianity in Kent. As Vera Evison points out, pendants with Christian crosses appeared at Buckland before 597 (*Buckland*, p. 143). The Christian influence could have come from the British Church or from Queen Bertha's bishop, Liudhard.

[263] Meaney, *Anglo-Saxon Amulets*, pp. 87–8.

[264] The relevant lines are: 612–629, 1168–70 (Queen Wealhtheow); 1980–3 (Queen Hygd); 2020–1 (Freawaru, the King's daughter); 1159–62 (servants).

[265] G. Speake, *A Saxon Bed Burial on Swallowcliffe Down*, Historic Buildings and Monuments Commission. Archaeological Report No. 10 (London, 1989), p. 40. At p. 43, however, Speake refers to the Kentish spoons as 'strainer spoons'.

and other metal pendants in addition to beads. These graves contained an unusually high incidence of metal finger rings and armlets. Women buried at Chatham Lines[266] and Sarre Grave 4 had worn armlets of textile brocaded with gold thread. The fashion for gold embroidery may have come from the Franks (see p. 97 below). Perhaps the embroidered armband itself was a Frankish import: the woman with the 'Arnegundis' ring buried in Saint-Denis wore a wide-sleeved robe with gold embroidered cuffs. In this case the embroidery work and almost certainly the silk robe it decorated were Byzantine. The closest parallel to the Kentish fabric 'bracelets' is the pair of padded armbands found in a male grave of the Viking period at Mammen, Denmark,[267] but these were probably attached to sleeves. The Kentish examples are less likely to have been sleeve-cuffs since they were worn on one wrist only in each case.

The woman in Grave 105C at Mill Hill had apparently worn a veil or scarf decorated with gold brocading, which seemed to be fastened under her chin with one Kentish disc brooch and secured on top of her head with another. Fragments of the gold were scattered round the skull of the skeleton, across the body and beside the pelvis. They did not form a continuous strip as if they had edged a garment and they did not lie across the forehead. This distribution is very different from that of gold fragments in other Kentish graves. In at least ten of these, ladies had evidently worn gold-brocaded headbands (Bifrons graves 21, 29, 41, 51, 64; Lyminge Grave 44; Sarre Grave 90; Stowting Grave 9,[268] Chessel Down Grave 1; Holywell Row Grave 11) attested by strips of gold found on or near the skull. There are several other possible examples where gold was found in a grave but the position not recorded.[269] The headbands were probably tablet-woven (see pp. 285–6) and possibly, to judge from Continental examples, made of silk. The gold ornament consisted of strips of gold foil which were brocaded into the woven band and then flattened and burnished. The brocading would resemble solid gold in appearance, and the effect of the gold pattern against the coloured braid, perhaps red, would be similar to that of the gold or gilded jewellery inlaid with garnet or coloured glass which was being introduced to Kent from Frankia. The English fillets seem to have been brocaded only at the front; but the largest

[266] Douglas, *Nenia Britannica*, pp. 63–4.

[267] Hald, *Ancient Danish Textiles*, p. 106, Figs 100, 233; E. Munksgaard, 'The embroideries from Bjerrinhøy, Mammen', in M. Hogestol (ed.), *Festskrift til Thorleif Sjovold på 70-årsdagen*, Universitets Oldsaksamlings Skrifter, Ny rekke, 5 (Oslo, 1984), pp. 159–71, at pp. 163, 169.

[268] J. Brent, 'An account of researches in an Anglo-Saxon cemetery at Stowting, in Kent, during the autumn of 1866', *Archaeologia*, 41 (1867), pp. 409–20, at pp. 411–12.

[269] Crowfoot and Hawkes, 'Early Anglo-Saxon gold braids'; Crowfoot, 'Early Anglo-Saxon gold braids: addenda and corrigenda'. The other possible cases are from Faversham (four, possibly five, instances), Howletts (one, possibly two, instances) and Sarre Grave 94. There are two further examples of gold fragments, of unknown provenance, in the British Museum. It has been assumed that these too were headbands, but the Mill Hill discovery offers another possibility.

measurable examples seem to have had a considerable amount of gold ornament (*c.* 25–34 cm). Possibly the hair concealed the undecorated part (Fig. 69), although it is likely that the braided bands themselves were quite luxurious and worth displaying. Fillets of this kind were popular among wealthy ladies on the Continent in the later-sixth and seventh centuries; they are known from Alamannic and Bavarian graves in southern Germany, from Lombard graves in northern Italy and the former Yugoslavia, and (probably) from Visigothic Spain, as well as much farther north, in Sweden.

Fig. 69 Reconstruction of a Kentish fillet, based on the reconstruction by E. Crowfoot of the gold brocading on the band from Grave 94, Sarre, Kent

The Franks may have inherited the craft of brocading gold from their predecessors the Gallo-Romans, who used it to make garment-borders, but the fashion for fillets was probably Byzantine; it can be seen on some mosaics in Ravenna, which was a Byzantine enclave in Italy, for example the processing Virgins in the Church of S. Apollinare Nuovo (early-sixth-century) wear jewelled fillets round their top-knots, from which long veils hang (Fig. 70). The Kentish ladies wearing these headbands in the mid-sixth century probably derived the fashion from the Franks, for it is in Frankia and Frankish Thuringia that the earliest surviving examples – fifth- and early-sixth-century – are centred. Probably the most elaborate is from a Frankish royal grave in Cologne Cathedral: the gold was elaborately brocaded in soumak (wrapped) weave and a gold and garnet jewel was set at the middle of the woman's brow.[270] Fillets remained a striking feature of Frankish royal costume into the Carolingian period and are mentioned several times in Frankish literature, including the poet Angilbert's description of Charlemagne's kinswomen. These fillets seem to have been worn by brides, but ladies must have continued to wear them after marriage, at least on ceremonial occasions.[271]

The Latin name for a fillet of this kind was apparently *vitta*. Anglo-Saxon glossators, writing in the Christian period, render *vitta* variously with the Old English words *nostle*, *snod*[272] and *ðwæle*. *Snod* and *ðwæle* were almost certainly in use in the pre-Christian period.

Since so much of the costume and jewellery of these ladies is demonstrably influenced by Frankish taste, it is worth considering whether they could have been wearing a Frankish garment which was different from that of their Anglo-Saxon neighbours. The obvious candidate is the sleeved, ankle-length robe which the woman with the 'Arnegundis' ring wore over her knee-length tunic. The open front of this robe was clasped together by brooches at neck and waist. However, women in Kent seem to have been wearing front-fastening garments before the mid-sixth-century influx of rich Frankish material and women without the distinguishing fillets

Fig. 70 Jewelled fillets suspending long veils on an early-sixth-century mosaic in the Church of S. Apollinare Nuovo, Ravenna, Italy

[270] See Crowfoot and Hawkes, 'Gold Braids', pp. 78–9 for discussion and bibliography; also K. Böhner, 'Die Zeitstellung der beiden fränkischen Gräber im Kölner Dom', *Kölner Jahrbuch*, 9 (1967–8), pp. 124–35.

[271] This is the conclusion of Crowfoot and Hawkes, 'Gold braids'.

[272] The use of 'snood' for an ornamental hair net is modern. Until recent times *snod* or 'snood' signified a band. A *snod* is used as the equivalent of a piece of string in an Anglo-Saxon anecdote; B. Thorpe (ed.), *The Homilies of the Anglo-Saxon Church*, 2 vols (London, 1844–6), 2 (1846), p. 28, lines 17–18.

and other luxury items seem to have done so after; it is virtually impossible to distinguish, with the archaeological evidence we have, between a Jutish/Anglo-Saxon front-fastening tunic and a Frankish/ Anglo-Saxon open coat. The most obvious difference between them is likely to have been the material: the 'Arnegundis' grave and other Merovingian Frankish finds include silk garments which were certainly the product of Byzantine trade and fashion.[273] We have as yet no evidence of them from this period in England; but perhaps some future find will suggest that Kentish aristocracy also had access to silk clothes.

The existence of the 'Arnegundis'-type robe in Kent is a matter for speculation. Distribution of brooches in some graves might perhaps suggest an open-fronted robe, but some comparative evidence is negative. The rich Kentish graves containing gold brocading and other luxury objects are often remarkable for the quantity and arrangement of their brooches. There does not seem to be a consistent pattern, but often brooches are found near the waist in addition to a brooch or brooches in the shoulder area. Sometimes the upper brooches are a pair; sometimes they are dissimilar. A number of Kentish graves contained pairs of brooches worn lower down the body than was usual for the *peplos*-type gown; they are usually described as being found on either side of the waist, and occur in graves with pairs of brooches (dissimilar from the waist brooches) at shoulders or neck, and in graves with single brooches at the neck. Perhaps these lower brooches were not functional; this manner of fastening them low down on the body may simply have been a way of displaying accumulated wealth and they may have been merely grave-gifts, possessions to be taken into the next life. It is noticeable that where there are pairs of brooches at the waist like this, they are long brooches, a shape which was probably becoming unfashionable in the later-sixth century in Kent as the developed styles of circular brooches became popular. This phenomenon of the pairs of brooches, as it were, moving down the body, also occurred on the Continent. In a study of the change in female costume in Austrasia (the eastern area of the Frankish Empire, which had Cologne as its capital), Gudula Zeller concluded that the bow brooches found near the hips in graves were unlikely to have been worn that way in life, arguing that they would have been uncomfortable, and that their positions, sometimes overlapping, do not suggest that they were functional.[274] In Alamannia, bow brooches seem to have moved down the body in the mid-fifth century; they were worn one above the other with the pins vertical, and were used to suspend amulets.[275] Hinz demonstrated that the lower of two brooches worn this way was used to suspend the crystal ball, citing specifically Grave 46 at Eick, near the Rhine

---

[273] Bender Jørgensen, *North European Textiles*, p. 111 notes several silk textiles from a sixth-century grave at Perrusson (Grave 6).

[274] G. Zeller, 'Zum Wandel der Frauentracht vom 6. zum 7. Jahrhundert in Austrasien', in G. Kossak and G. Ulbert (ed.), *Studien zur vor- und frühgeschichtlichen Archäologie, Festschrift für Joachim Werner zum 65 Geburtstag*, 2 vols (Munich, 1974), 2, pp. 381–5.

[275] Christlein, *Die Alamannen*, p. 78, Abb. 54.

in Germany, where the remains of the leather strap, decorated with eight silver clips, confirmed the association between brooch and crystal, as well as several other Frankish graves.[276] A radiate-headed brooch in Grave 25B at Mill Hill was thought to have suspended the strap from which the quartz ball and spoon hung. Several of the Kentish ladies with pairs of brooches at the waist had crystal balls and silver spoons; several others did not, but all seem to have carried some tools or trinkets, and although the English brooches were not positioned in the same way as the Continental, it is possible that they, too, were used to hang the straps to which these things were attached. Alternatively, the brooches could have been pinned to the two sides of an open robe like that in the 'Arnegundis' grave, to hold it in place while allowing it to fall open and reveal the garment underneath.

This possibility can be extended to some of the brooches found at the upper part of the body, too. The Frankish robe, if worn as an outer garment, is not really compatible with the *peplos*-type gown fastened in the classic way, with shoulder brooches, firstly since the brooches would be concealed by the outer robe; secondly because there would be a danger of the robe catching, and tearing, on the brooches underneath it; thirdly because the fitted sleeves of such a robe are unlikely companions to the underarm bulk of the *peplos*. Many of the ladies with central brooches or brooches on either side of the waist did not have the pair of shoulder brooches which is common elsewhere. In Finglesham Grave 203 (which, admittedly, did not have a fillet or waist brooches, but had two rich necklaces, a square-headed brooch lying centrally across the beads, and other relevant grave-goods) a pair of brooches was found at the upper part of the body, but rather lower down and wider apart than usual. The excavator, Sonia Hawkes, suggested to me that the brooches, which were small square-headed ones, had been used to pin down the two sides of an open robe. Other Kentish brooches may be explained the same way. An open over-gown is more often associated with the Renaissance than with the Dark Ages, but the 'Arnegundis' robe was of this kind, and it is in fact a feature of folk costumes of various nations that one garment is worn over another in such a way that there is only partial overlap. In the context of folk costume, the style may arise from necessity – if skins or the available pieces of woven cloth were not sufficiently large to cover the body it may have been essential to overlap more than one. At a higher social level, the open robe would show off another luxury garment beneath it, it would eliminate the awkward bulk which the straight *peplos*-type gown must have had round the narrower parts of the body, but it would not need elaborate tailoring, like, for example, the later medieval costumes of Greenland with their elaborate gores which widened a garment below the waist.[277]

---

[276] Hinz, 'Am langen Band'.

[277] E. Østergård, 'The medieval everyday costumes of the Norsemen in Greenland', in L. Bender Jørgensen and K. Tidow (ed.), *Textilsymposium Neumünster:Archäolog-ische textilfunde: 6.5–7.5. 1981 (NESAT I)* (Neumünster, 1982), pp. 267–76, at p. 272.

At Mill Hill the brooches found lower down the body were mostly worn horizontally, one above the other, sometimes in line with other brooches at the neck or chest. At this site the brooches appear to have been fastening together a front-opening garment rather than fixing it in an open position. It was noticeable that long brooches were found in this position and circular higher up the body. In Grave 86 at this site a woman had paired annular brooches and a third annular brooch at the side of the neck, and three horizontal radiate-headed brooches in a vertical row near the waist, in a combination of Anglian and Kentish dress styles. The wearing of annular brooches as fasteners is unusual in Kent, though they are often found as girdle rings.

Not all the ladies with fillets and other luxurious equipment wore brooches in the ways described; the Holywell Row girl was dressed for the grave in the usual Anglian costume of her region though she had a gold fillet and a weaving sword. (This is a peculiar case, however, as the jewellery was old and considered by the excavator to be too big for the girl, so was presumably inherited.) The Chessel Down lady had shoulder brooches, but they were dissimilar, and, as we have seen, Anglo-Saxon women seem, more often than not, to have aimed at a symmetrical look.

It is likely that Kentish women wore veils; the gold fragments from Mill Hill Grave 105C, though they have not been precisely interpreted, give the impression of a full headcovering which radiated out round the recumbent body. The remains of tabby cloth found on the front of the button brooch in Grave 48 at Buckland was probably from a veil (the cloth of the tunic in this case was probably a diamond twill, traces of which were found on metal chainwork associated with the brooch). Tabby weave on the backs of disc brooches from Graves 1 and 13 at the same site might also have been from head veils. Veils were fashionable among wealthy Franks: the woman in the 'Arnegundis' grave had a veil of red 'satin' which 'reached to her waist'; gold threads by the feet of the Cologne Cathedral 'princess' may have derived from a long veil attached to the golden fillet at her head. Again, the fashion was ultimately Byzantine: calf-length white veils with fringed hems hang from the jewelled fillets of Ravenna figures (Fig. 70). The Kentish gold-brocaded fillets may also have been attached to veils, so might an ivory bead found at the forehead of the skeleton in Bifrons Grave 6, which was without gold thread, but contained a crystal ball, silver spoon and more than the average amount of jewellery. Many of the dainty, garnet-set, Frankish-influenced brooches may have fastened headdresses, for example a rosette brooch found at the right shoulder of Finglesham skeleton 203, and the bird brooches which were probably worn at the shoulders of the skeleton in Grave D3 at the same site. Women in later phases at Buckland wore single brooches, circular and set with garnets, placed centrally or slightly to one side of the neck, which had perhaps fastened veils; pins in similar positions

BUCKLAND Grave 92 (Figs 71, 72) This burial was of a woman aged between twenty and thirty. At her neck was a silver gilt disc brooch with three keystone shaped garnets. A string of small beads, twenty-seven amber and eight glass, had probably hung from it. There was a Frankish disc brooch with eight keystone garnets set round a circular garnet, all in silver cloisons, at the middle of the chest. From this there had hung a string of large beads, forty-seven amber, one jet, one blue glass and one cylindrical glass polychrome bead which was the centrepiece. The oval loop of a buckle was found at the waist and the remains of three iron rings which preserved mineralised textile, probably broken diamond twill, at the left pelvis.[278]

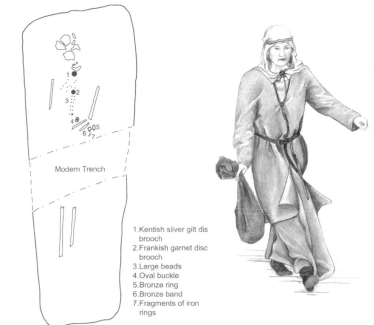

Fig. 71 Buckland, Dover, Kent, Grave 92

Modern Trench

1. Kentish silver gilt disc brooch
2. Frankish garnet disc brooch
3. Large beads
4. Oval buckle
5. Bronze ring
6. Bronze band
7. Fragments of iron rings

Fig. 72 Reconstruction of the clothing from Buckland Grave 92

may have functioned the same way. The gold-adorned veil at Mill Hill was clasped by a brooch under the chin.

It seems likely that Kentish headdresses framed the face more than their Continental counterparts, and that they concealed the ears, for the elaborate earrings which were worn on the Continent were never worn in the ears by Kentish ladies, even when, like the woman in Finglesham Grave 203, they possessed them: this woman

[278] The grave inventory is at Evison, *Buckland*, pp. 237–8 and the brooches and beads are on a grave plan at p. 68. Some of the large beads are drawn and the polychrome one is photographed.

evidently wore a circle of beads at the neck and below it, probably attached to the costume by means of a small silver pin at each end, a festoon of beads and pendants. Two (dissimilar) Frankish earrings hung on each neck ornament, probably as the centre-piece in each case.[279] Frankish earrings, which were probably inspired by Byzantine fashions, consist of a gold hoop suspending a golden cube or polyhedron with jewels set in its sides. They are not uncommon on the Continent and were found in both the 'Arnegundis' grave and the Cologne 'princess' grave. The English headdresses, then, seem to have anticipated the voluminous hood of later fashion rather than following the Frankish pattern, although the custom of wearing a headdress may have come from the Continent, where Christianity was influencing lifestyle.

Though some aspects of their dress may have been Frankish, Kentish ladies seem to have differed from the Frankish in their lack of metal garter- and shoe-fastenings. These items are quite common in both Frankish and Alamannic women's graves from the late-sixth century[280] including the 'Arnegundis' grave. A simple explanation would be that English women wore their skirts longer, or that they did *not* wear their robe open. Clearly there was not a slavish following of Frankish fashion, just a number of Frankish, ultimately Byzantine, trends influencing Kentish women in the upper strata of society. The golden fillet might have been restricted to those of royal blood; but the open-fronted robe, the buckled belt and the headdress may have been adopted separately, or together, by other individuals.

Children's clothing

There is no evidence to suggest that children's garments differed from adults' in anything but size. The same types of brooches and buckles are found with the small skeletons as with the fully grown. The only distinctive point, in fifth- and sixth-century graves, is a neck ornament consisting of a very few beads or a single bead.

In contrast to this fashion, though, is Sewerby Grave 28, with a large quantity of very small beads, unique to that site, accompanying a child. Children were not provided with more than one knife and their knives were smaller than those of adults, though Härke's figures suggest that female juveniles' knives were on average slightly larger than males.[281]

---

[279] I owe these suggestions to discussion with Sonia Hawkes.

[280] I am grateful to Simon Burnell for answering my questions about Frankish and Alamannic dress. There is a detailed reconstruction of how the garter fastenings worked in a seventh-century female grave in G. Clauss, 'Beobachtungen an merowingerzeitlichen Gräbern bei Hockenheim, Rhein-Neckar-Kreis', *Archäologisches Korrespondenzblatt*, 6 (1976), pp. 55–64. See also G. Clauss, 'Strumpfbänder: ein Beitrag zur Frauentracht des 6. und 7. Jahrhunderts n. Chr.', *Jahrbuch des Romisch-germanisches Zentralmuseum zu Mainz*, 23–4 (1976–7), pp. 54–88.

[281] Härke, 'Knives', p. 145, Fig. 1.

Many children's graves have been poor in grave-goods, indicating that the costume was simpler, perhaps stitched or tied together instead of pinned with metal fasteners; or this could indicate a less elaborate funeral. Audrey Meaney concluded from her study of pagan cemeteries that special practices sometimes governed children's funerals[282] and this is confirmed by later excavation reports, and by Sally Crawford's discussion of attitudes to infant mortality[283] though there is no consistent pattern between sites.[284] Conversely, there have been cases where a child's grave was equipped with unusual richness, for example Holywell Row Grave 11 and Finglesham Grave 7. Certainly there seems to have been something symbolic rather than practical about the provision of artefacts for very young children and the same may sometimes have been true of the costume itself. The Holywell Row girl was perhaps dressed for the grave as the woman she should have become, or a symbolic synthesis of fashions, Anglian and Kentish, old and new.

[282] Meaney, *Gazetteer*, p. 20; *Amulets*, p. 245.

[283] S. Crawford, 'Children, death and the afterlife in Anglo-Saxon England', in W. Filmer-Sankey (ed.), *Anglo-Saxon Studies in Archaeology and History*, 6 (1993), pp. 83–91. The majority of Anglo-Saxon cemeteries appear to lack infant burials. The reason may be that the graves of small children were shallow and subject to disturbance; or that infants were not buried there. Our evidence for dress, therefore, is spasmodic and from untypical burials.

[284] Special circumstances may include details such as the lay-out of the body as well costume-related matters such as the absence/type of grave-goods. Amulets are frequently found with children's skeletons and methods of preventing the corpse from 'walking' such as placing stones on the body, though not exclusive to children, are a noticeable feature (Crawford, 'Children, death and the afterlife). Occasionally a child is found with an object it was probably too young to use, for example a cloisonné fire steel with a child of two to six years in Grave 27 at Lyminge; Warhurst, 'Lyminge', p. 20.

III

Men's costume in the fifth and sixth centuries

The evidence

Archaeologists have identified many Anglo-Saxon burials as male, either on anatomical grounds or because weapons were deposited as grave-goods, but the records of graves are far less helpful to us in our attempt to reconstruct men's costume than the cemetery evidence for women's dress. Although males are statistically more likely to be buried with grave-goods than females[1] they are less likely to have dress accessories; weapons, rather than clothing adjuncts, functioned as socio-economic indicators in male burials.[2] The only dress fastener to appear regularly in men's graves is the belt buckle, and even this class of object only accompanies a minority of the male skeletons. No clasps or ornaments are revealed as characteristically masculine fashions. The (relatively few) brooches that are claimed to have been found in male graves are the same types that women wore.[3] Pins have been found with male skeletons, but not regularly enough to be considered a standard part of the costume. Neither the alleged brooches nor the pins indicate how the costume might have been fastened, as they do in women's graves, for they are not positioned consistently. Indeed, Vera Evison suggested that at Buckland some pins might have served to fasten the cloth wrapping round weapons,[4] rather than the dress, and this is a plausible suggestion since some of our most elaborate and unusual textile fragments from Anglo-Saxon graves come from the wrappings of precious grave-goods.

[1] Brush, 'Adorning the Dead', pp. 143, 154.

[2] Heinrich Härke has published several studies of the significance of weapon burials including 'Knives in early Saxon burials'; 'Early Saxon weapon burials: frequencies, distributions and weapon combinations', in S. C. Hawkes (ed.), *Anglo-Saxon Weapons and Warfare*, Oxford University Committee for Archaeology Monograph 21 (1989), pp. 49–61;'Early Anglo-Saxon social structure', in Hines, *The Anglo-Saxons from the Migration Period to the eighth century* (1997), pp. 125–60.

[3] In some of these cases, an unidentified double burial or a disturbed earlier female burial may account for the unusual presence of a brooch or beads in the grave of a male.

[4] Evison, *Buckland*, p. 82.

This lack of metal fasteners means that fewer textile fragments have survived from men's clothing than from women's. Fortunately some of those few remains were well preserved and have been analysed carefully, but, even with the recent increased attention to organic material on the less aesthetically interesting objects in graves, such as knife-blades, the quantity of textile remains very small.

Grave 33 from Abingdon provides a typical example of the way our evidence is limited.[5] On anatomical grounds, the skeleton was identified as a male adult. Above the shoulder, to the right of the head, was a metal spear-head; the wooden shaft of the spear had decayed. Above the right side of the pelvis was a knife-blade about 14.5 cm long; the point lay outermost, towards the right arm. Between the knees were the metal handgrip and boss of a circular shield; the wooden board of the shield had rotted away. The size of the knife (large) was appropriate for the male gender and adulthood of the buried person. The weapons are gendered grave-goods, which may also have reflected ethnicity, age and rank: Heinrich Härke has suggested, controversially, that weapon burials are indicative of those claiming Germanic, rather than Celtic ethnicity. The inclusion of a shield, as well as a spear, in the weapon assemblage suggests elevated status, though the absence of a sword, in a cemetery where two swords were found, implies that the man was not of highest rank. The archaeological evidence, however, reveals nothing about his clothing apart from the position of the knife, which suggests that the man wore a belt.

There is no evidence that the dress of men varied according to status, age or ethnicity, except for the rare suggestion of a baldric and some elaborate metal belt fittings which could only have belonged to wealthy persons. In many male graves there is no evidence of dress at all. It is quite possible that the Abingdon man and many others like him were buried naked, or were naked except for a belt like the little figure in a horned helmet on a buckle from Finglesham (Fig. 73); the similar figure on a metal die for stamping helmet-plaques found at Torslunda, on the island of Öland, Sweden, who wears a prominent belt, is perhaps also naked (Plate 3c).[6] As we have seen (pp. 16–17) both Caesar and Tacitus record the Germanic practice of going without clothes except for a skin cape or a cloak. Indeed, the bodies of men recovered from Danish peat bogs, sacrificed about the time Tacitus was writing, are generally naked. However, the Roman missionaries to England would surely have recorded their horror if they had found their proselytes nude, and other evidence suggests that even before the Anglo-Saxon settlement Germanic men were wearing clothes for everyday life. In Tacitus's day the richest men wore a close-fitting garment which the writer contrasted with the 'long flowing robe' of other peoples. Sidonius, too, describes the Franks as clothed. Only rare discoveries

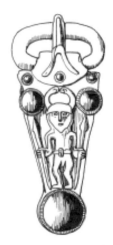

Fig. 73 Male figure with belt and horned helmet on a buckle, Finglesham, Kent

[5] Leeds and Harden, *Abingdon*, p. 37.
[6] The figures may relate to the cult of Woden/Odin.

Plate 3 a–d 'The Torslunda die'. Top left, figure in a ?woven garment fighting beasts; top right, armed men in boar helmets wear long tunics with decorated borders. The right hand figure has either arm rings or short sleeves; bottom left ?Woden cult figure in a horned helmet wears a belt and baldric; bottom right, man with axe wears belted trousers of ?fur. Seventh-century, Torslunda Parish, Björnhovda, Öland, Sweden.

like the belt suite from Mucking, which preserved several different organic materials,[7] suggest that at least some men were buried in their clothes and give a hint of what those garments might have consisted of. Otherwise, to reconstruct male costume in the early Anglo-Saxon period we must rely heavily on older, Continental descriptions and archaeological evidence, especially bog finds; on depictions of Germanic men on Roman sculptures; and upon the linguistic evidence for garment-names which might have been used in these early centuries.

The cloak

Roman writers, Caesar, Ovid and Tacitus, observed the use of fur or skin garments among the northern tribes, which would have seemed strange to them because furs were not necessary in the warmer climate of the Mediterranean and not yet fashionable in southern Europe. Though furs may have no longer been essential in the north

---

[7] Grave 117. Unpublished information from W. T. Jones, including the report on the textiles by Elisabeth Crowfoot (Ancient Monuments Laboratory Report 1589 (1972)).

after the introduction of the warp-weighted loom made for good quality wool fabrics (*c.* 200 AD),[8] they clearly remained an important feature of dress, and one which, for the Roman writers, distinguished the barbarian from the civilised Roman. Caesar and Tacitus identify the fur clothing as a short cloak, mentioning that sometimes this animal-skin garment was the only clothing worn by ancient Germans. Iron Age finds from Danish peat bogs and Roman carvings of barbarians correspond to the observations of the Roman writers. The bog finds are short cloaks or capes which seem to have been worn fur side inward, skin side outward, and were either symmetrical, worn with an opening at the centre front, or asymmetrical, in which case they seem to have been worn in pairs, both fastening on the right.[9] The very small cloaks or capes which appear as the only clothing of German captives on a stone carving found in the foundation of a Roman wall in Mainz (Fig. 74) have been supposed to illustrate Caesar's description of indecently short cloaks of skin or fur (see pp. 16–17).[10] A narrow, poncho-like garment, shown on the figure of a captive man on the Adamklissi Monument, Romania (Fig. 1), corresponds to the skin poncho worn by some primitive northern peoples which exploits the shape of the animal to fit the human with the minimum of adaptation.[11] Isidor of Seville's definition of the (Latin) *reno* as a garment which covers the shoulders and chest and reaches to the navel[12] would seem to correspond to this illustration. A *reno* could probably be made of various skins, including lambskin (though this might be rather small given the size of primitive sheep). This kind of cloak probably survived as a fur or skin jerkin into the Anglo-Saxon period, though it may not always have been worn outermost; in the ninth century Charlemagne would wear a fur jerkin as well as a cloak (see p. 174) and others may have done so too. In Old English the fur or skin garment may have been called *heden* or *rocc*.[13] Fibres which might have come from a fleece, or possibly a pile-woven fabric which would imitate the shaggy appearance of fur or fleece, were found on a spearhead in Grave 22 at Buckland, but it was not clear whether they derived from a garment.[14]

Textile cloaks, short or knee-length, are common on Roman sculptures of German captives (Fig. 75). As far as one can tell, these cloaks were not tailored, but consisted of a square or rectangle of cloth which was clasped on one shoulder, usually the right. The

Fig. 74 Short cloaks worn by Germanic captives on a sculpture, Mainz, Germany

Fig. 75 Cloak and trousers on a prisoner, Arch of Constantine, Rome

[8] Lise Bender Jørgensen argues this on the basis that there are no archaeological finds of skin garments from the later Roman period, see *North European Textiles*, p. 122.

[9] Hald, *Ancient Danish Textiles*, pp. 313–22, Figs 359–78, 380.

[10] Hald, *Ancient Danish Textiles*, p. 320.

[11] Hald, *Ancient Danish Textiles*, pp. 347–54.

[12] *Etymologiae*, 19, 23, 4; W. M. Lindsay (ed.), *Isidori Hispalensis Episcopi Etymologiarum sive Originum*, 2 vols (Oxford, 1911), 2, unpaginated.

[13] The opinions outlined in this paragraph are developed in Owen-Crocker, 'Anglo-Saxon skin garments'.

[14] E. Crowfoot, 'The textiles', in Evison, *Buckland*, p. 195.

Fig. 76 H. Vierck's reconstruction of how the ancient cloak was worn

Fig. 77 Long, fringed cloak on a sarcophagus, Portonaccio, Italy. After H. Vierck

same type of cloak appears regularly on late Anglo-Saxon drawings and paintings of male figures, where it is clasped by a brooch, usually circular. It seems likely, then, that this cloak was an established part of the male Germanic costume before the Anglo-Saxon settlement and remained so throughout our period. (Possibly the garment was first adopted by Germans living close to the border areas, who copied their Roman neighbours; but since a cloak with shoulder fastening is a simple, practical arrangement, it may have developed spontaneously.)

A cloak would consist of a square or rectangle woven in one piece on an upright loom. If the warp-weighted loom was used, a tablet-woven starting border could be employed, and a similar braided border might be added to close the weaving. The side edges of a woven fabric would normally have selvedges, but it was possible to weave in tablet-woven braids at the sides, thus edging the cloak all round with a braided border. We can get some idea of what the cloak of a wealthy man might have been like from fragments of the textiles buried in Grave 5 at Snartemo, Norway, in the sixth century: the red twill cloak had narrow, tablet-woven starting and closing borders and was also decorated with an elaborate tablet-woven band in red, yellow, blue and green, fifty-six tablets wide, with a pattern worked on the forty central tablets; sections of it were embroidered with animal hair.[15]

Hayo Vierk has drawn attention to the large and luxurious cloaks found in the peat bogs of Thorsbjerg, Denmark and Vehnemoor, Germany.[16] Both were of complex weave and dyed with precious dyes in different colours. The edges of the Thorsbjerg garment were braided on more than one hundred tablets, the Vehnemoor on about 146. Both had elaborate fringes. The Thorsbjerg garment was 1.68 m wide and 2.36 m long, the Vehnemoor 1.75 m by about 2.85 m. They were worn by doubling the material lengthwise, and pinning it on the right shoulder (Fig. 76), a manner of dressing shown on a sarcophagus from Portonaccio, Rome (Fig. 77), which depicts noble Germans of the Elbe region. There is a good deal of excess fabric, which would add weight and warmth while demonstrating the wealth of the owner through the conspicuous consumption of cloth. It is probable that the richest Anglo-Saxons wore cloaks of this kind. Less luxurious versions, smaller and with less decoration, could have been common.

Since the cloaks depicted on Germans in Roman art were sometimes clasped by brooches, and since this fashion recurs in tenth- and eleventh-century Anglo-Saxon art, we might expect to find single, round brooches at the shoulders of most male skeletons in pagan graves. Surprisingly, we do not. Brooches in male graves are extremely rare, especially if we deduct from the total those male graves with several typically 'feminine' items which might suggest that there were

[15] B. Hougen, *Snartemofunnene*, Norske Oldfunn, 7 (Oslo, 1935), pp. 69–76, German summary pp. 114–15.

[16] Vierck, 'Zur seegermanischen Mannertracht', in Ahrens, *Sachsen und Angelsachsen*, pp. 266–8.

unidentified female burials also present. Examples occur from different regions of the Anglo-Saxon settlement and are not confined to any brooch type, including long brooches as well as circular, and lacking any consistent positioning. Where male skeletons are accompanied by pins, they are mostly found at the chest, but they are not frequent or regular finds. Otherwise, men in Anglo-Saxon burials do not have the cloak fasteners which we would expect.

Possibly the absence of metal cloak fasteners could be accounted for by the fact that men in the pagan period tied or laced their cloaks, or secured them with clasps made of perishable material; we recall the thorns mentioned by Tacitus (p. 17). The Old English word *dalc*, which later came to signify a brooch, buckle or clasp, may originally have signified a simple fastener of this kind.[17] Bone pins, of the kind found occasionally with female skeletons (p. 46) might have been used. Other candidates include a bone rectangle found at the left shoulder of a male skeleton at Lowbury, Reading,[18] and a circular, perforated bone object which accompanied weapons at Baggrave, Leicestershire.[19] These are both unique, but they give some indication that bone fasteners were used. Wood or horn fasteners might have been employed too.

It is possible, however, that the absence of fasteners in male graves is the result of the cloak being spread over the body as a covering rather than arranged round the body as a garment. Literary and linguistic evidence confirms that the Germanic cloak was a versatile object which could be put to other uses apart from clothing. A biographer of Charlemagne tells us that the emperor was accustomed to employ his cloak as a blanket,[20] and we find the semantic range of several Old English words supports this varied function: Old English *hwitel* could evidently mean 'cloak' or 'blanket',[21] *loða* could signify 'coverlet' although it mostly meant 'cloak', *reowe* meant

---

[17] The word is cognate with, and may derive from, Old Irish *delg*, 'thorn', 'needle'. Holthausen, *Wörterbuch*, p. 70; Bosworth/Toller, *Supplement*, p. 146.

[18] D. Atkinson, *The Romano-British Site on Lowbury Hill in Berkshire* (Reading, 1916), pp. 15–23.

[19] Douglas, *Nenia Britannica*, p. 28.

[20] Notker, *De Carolo Magno*, I, 34; G. H. Pertz, (ed.), *Monumenta Germaniae Historica, Scriptores*, 7, 2 (Berlin, 1829), p. 747, lines 24–5.

[21] In the Old English Bede the word *hwitlas* is applied to bedclothes used in the monastery guesthouse (*Historia Ecclesiastica* IV, 31; J. Schipper (ed.), *Konig Alfreds Übersetzung von Bedas Kirchengeschichte*, Bibliothek der angelsächsischen Prosa, 4, 2 vols (Leipzig, 1898), p. 540, lines 4736–40) where the Latin version has *saga* (Colgrave and Mynors, *Bede's Ecclesiastical History*, p. 444) and *hwitel* appears glossing *sagum* among groups of words concerning bedding (Wright/Wülcker, *Vocabularies*, col. 268, line 2; col. 328, line 2). It is used ambiguously of the cloth with which the biblical Jael covered Sisera (Judges 4:18; Crawford, *Heptateuch*, p. 404) and sometimes, in glossaries, seems to signify a garment, *ruhne hwitel* rendering *amphibalum* ('garment', 'cloak', J. Zupitza, 'Altenglische Glossen zu Abbos Clericorum decus', *Zeitschrift für deutsches Alterthum*, 31 (1887), pp. 1–27 at p. 8, line 140), *hnysce hwitel* rendering *linna* (for *laena*, 'a lined cloak' or *lena*, 'mantle'; Wright/Wülcker, *Vocabularies*, col. 151, line 38) as well as the ambiguous word *sagum* (with garment-words at Wright/Wülcker, *Vocabularies*, col. 268, line 2 although under the heading *Incipit de Lectulo*) and *stragularum* (*hwitla; stragula*, 'a pall'; A. S. Napier, (ed.), *Old English Glosses*, Anecdota Oxoniensia, Medieval and Modern Series, 11 (Oxford, 1900), p. 28, line 1035).

Fig. 78 Gallic coat worn by
Blussus, on his funerary
monument, Mainz, Germany

'cloak'[22] or 'rug',[23] *rift* 'veil' or 'curtain'.[24]

Perhaps the men buried in Anglo-Saxon cemeteries wore some other kind of outer garment, which needed no fastener, such as the poncho-shaped garment with a central hole for the head which Germanic people wore in earlier centuries. I have suggested that the example on the Adamklissi Monument (Fig. 1) was made of skin, but cloth versions may have existed.[25] However, the only corroborative evidence for such a poncho in Anglo-Saxon England is a short garment without arm-slits worn by a beggar depicted in a tenth- to eleventh-century psalter (Colour Plate H). Another possible candidate for Anglo-Saxon male dress is the hooded robe known to modern scholars as a 'Gallic coat'. An example of this may be seen on the figure of Blussus, husband of Menimane, on the couple's funerary monument (Fig. 78). A bulky, 'tunic-form' garment found in a peat bog at Reepsholt (East Friesland), Germany, resembles a Gallic coat in shape although it is not hooded, and others have been identified from Obenaltdorf and Marx-Etzel, also Germany. This garment, however, was probably imported and not native to the North.[26]

If men were buried in cloaks they are likely to have been of fairly coarse-woven wool. Perhaps there was a trace of clothing preserved

---

[22] It glosses *lodix* ('coverlet', 'blanket'; Wright/Wülcker, *Vocabularies*, col. 436, line 28; Lindsay, *Corpus Glossary*, p. 108, line 261) and more than once glosses *colobium* (which can mean 'cloak' though it usually means 'shirt' (e.g. Wright/Wülcker, *Vocabularies*, col. 210, lines 24–6) but mostly glosses lemmata meaning 'cloak', *lacerna* (e.g. in Lindsay, *Corpus Glossary*, p. 102, line 15), *clamidem* (Wright/Wülcker, *Vocabularies*, col. 377, lines 22–3) and *sagulum* (Lindsay, *Corpus Glossary*, p. 157, line 60). In King Alfred's translation of the *Pastoral Care* the word is used of the garment of King Saul (*liniamento* in the Latin version; Sweet, *Pastoral Care*, p. 36, line 6).

[23] There is less evidence for use as a garment-name than in the preceding cases; it glosses *lena* ('mantle', Wright/Wülcker, *Vocabularies*, col. 439, lines 8–9) but this Latin word is obviously being applied to bedding in Bede's anecdote (see note 21 above) where it is rendered *reowe* by the Old English translator (Schipper, *Bedas Kirchengeschichte*, p. 540, lines 4736–40). It is clearly a bedcover in the Laws of Alfred (*Ælfred*, 42, 7; Liebermann, *Gesetze*, 1, p. 76).

[24] 'Cloak' when it glosses *sagum* (Wright/Wülcker, *Vocabularies*, col. 268, line 2), *laena* and *palla* (Lindsay, *Corpus Glossary*, p. 104, line 80, p. 132, line 126) and translates *pallium* and *chlamyde* (e.g. Matthew 5:40, Rushworth Gospels and Matthew 27:31, Lindisfarne Gospels (W. W. Skeat (ed.), *The Holy Gospels in Anglo-Saxon, Northumbrian and Old Mercian Versions* (Cambridge, 1871–87), pp. 51, 235. There is a more recent edition: R. M. Liuzza (ed.), *The Old English Version of the Gospels*, 2 vols, Early English Text Society, original series 314 (Oxford, 1994–2000)), 'veil' when it glosses *cicla* and *biuligo, niger velamen* (Wright/Wülcker, *Vocabularies*, col. 205, line 2, col. 195, line 3) and when *wahrift* translates *uelum* ('the veil of the temple' at Leviticus 4:17; Crawford, *Heptateuch*, p. 290); 'curtain' when *rif* glosses *conopeo* (Napier, *Glosses*, p. 133, line 5276).

[25] We can however, discount the example from Rønbjerg Mose, Denmark, formerly thought to be possibly an ancient garment but now acknowledged as fifteenth-century South American; K.-H. S. Nielsen, 'The notorious Rønbjerg garment – once again', in G. Jaacks and K. Tidow (ed.), *Textilsymposium Neumünster: Archäologische textilfunde – Archaeological textiles: 4.–7.5. 1993 (NESAT V)* (Neumünster, 1994), pp. 236–52.

[26] Hald, *Ancient Danish Textiles*, pp. 336–8; See also E. Munksgaard, 'The Gallic coat from Rønbjerg', in Bender Jørgensen and Tidow, *NESAT 1*, pp. 41–3; K.-H. Nielsen, 'The Rønbjerg garment in tunic-form', in Bender Jørgensen and Tidow, *NESAT 1*, pp. 44–62.

on a throwing axe found at the left shoulder of a male skeleton at Winterbourne Gunner, Wiltshire: an impression of cloth preserved in the rust on the axe showed that the weapon had been in contact with 2 x 2 twill textile, woven with about 9 threads per centimetre in both warp and weft.[27] The textile might of course have been used to wrap the weapon, but the axe could have rested against the corpse's garment.

Unlike the archaeological material, linguistic evidence for outer clothing is extensive and indicates several varieties of garment. The following list of garment-names probably in use in the fifth and sixth centuries is the same as that cited for women's cloaks (pp. 75–6), but there is more evidence that men wore these garments than women, since the contexts in which the words are documented in late Old English texts mostly concern men. In Christian Saxon times both sexes could wear the *hacele* (a cloak which might be hooded), the *mentel* and the *sciccels* (which could be made of fur). Men wore the fur *crusene* and *heden* (which could be hooded) and the *rocc*, a garment which might be made of skin or fur.[28] The *ofer-slop* was worn by men, so was the *loða*, which might be made of shaggy fabric and could be used as a coverlet as well as a cloak. In a ninth-century text *loða* is a synonym of *mentel*. The *hwitel*, originally white (or undyed) was certainly used as a blanket by men, but there is no direct evidence that they wore it as a garment as women did. There is no evidence either as to which sex wore the *rift* (the word could mean a cloak or curtain) and the *sciccing*.

The tunic

The tunic, if this is what Tacitus was referring to (pp. 17–18) was evidently a luxury in the Roman author's time. On Roman monuments, captive Germanic barbarians sometimes appear bare-chested, without a tunic (Figs 1, 74–5), though this could be as a sign of humiliation rather than habitual dress. On other Roman sculptures tunics do appear, and they were regularly worn by the Franks in Sidonius's day (p. 19). We can see from Roman art that these tunics were knee-length or shorter, even as short as hip-length, and that they might have long or short sleeves. They needed no metal fasteners, though they could be worn with a belt or girdle, which might have been buckled, though pouching of the tunic could conceal the fastening. Tunics are worn by three figures on the Torslunda die. Several details of the images on this object parallel Anglo-Saxon art and artefacts, variously found in Kent, Anglian and Saxon regions, but most famously at Sutton Hoo, where the ruling fam-

---

[27] Grave 6; Musty and Stratton, 'A Saxon cemetery at Winterbourne Gunner', pp. 91, 95; E. Crowfoot, 'The textile remains', in Musty and Stratton, p. 108.

[28] *Melotes, uel pera, gæten uel broccen rooc* (Wright/Wülcker, *Vocabularies*, col. 152, line 1; *melote*, 'a sheepskin', 'goatskin garment'), *mastruga, crusene oððe deorfellen roc* (Wright/Wülcker, *Vocabularies*, col. 328, line 18; *mastruga*, 'a sheepskin', 'garment made of skin'), *renones, stiðe and ruge breostrocces* (Wright/Wülcker, *Vocabularies*, col. 151, line 39; *reno*, 'reindeer skin', 'small cloak of skin or fur').

Plate 4 Shirt or tunic from Thorsbjerg Mose, Germany

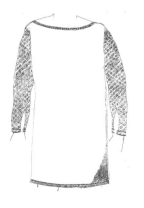

Fig. 79 Tunic, Thorsbjerg Mose, Germany

ily, the Wuffingas, seem to have been Swedish. The figure apparently fighting two beasts with a sword and knife (Plate 3a) wears a short, belted tunic with long sleeves. The texture is of an interwoven pattern which makes a series of diamonds. It is difficult to imagine how a mail coat could be constructed to look like this; more likely the decoration on the garment is a clever and impressionistic representation of a luxury weave, a diamond or lozenge twill. The two figures depicted in profile wearing boar helmets (Plate 3b) wear straight, unbelted garments with prominent decorated borders at the bottom. These could represent tablet-woven braids stitched to, or finishing off, a garment. The tunic of the right hand figure is apparently short-sleeved.

Two long-sleeved tunics have been found in north German peat bogs.[29] One, from Bernuthsfeld Mose, was 105 cm long, and the sleeves were of sufficient length to have been turned back into cuffs, or pushed back in folds. The sleeves were fitted and apparently straight. The better-known, and more sophisticated, garment from Thorsbjerg Mose (Plate 4, Fig. 79) was shorter, 86 cm at the front and 90 cm at the back, which was edged with a tablet-woven band. This tunic was made in four pieces. The separate sleeves were shaped to the shoulder, and narrowed below the elbow, with a decorative edging at the wrist and an opening in the seam to admit the hand. (The aperture could have been secured by clasps.) These sleeves look as if they fitted snugly, although the 'armhole' and inserted sleeve were developments in tailoring which would not take place

[29] Hald, *Ancient Danish Textiles*, p. 339.

until the fourteenth century, and before that, separate sleeves were simply joined to the body of the garment at the top of the side seams. An alternative was to weave the sleeves in one T-shaped piece with the tunic. These north European tunics were apparently put on over the head, but they have no lacing or ties at the neck and the neck opening had to be wide enough to accommodate the head. Tunics depicted in later Anglo-Saxon art are very like these (although they appear more close-fitting at the neck, see p. 246) and it seems likely that men of the fifth and sixth centuries wore similar tunics, which, if they were buried in them, have rotted away in the earth.

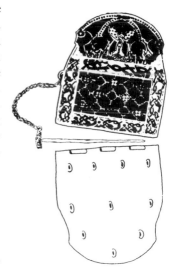

Fig. 80 One of a pair of shoulder clasps, Sutton Hoo, Suffolk

A very few skeletons from pagan-period graves, identified as male, have been equipped with pairs of brooches at the shoulders, a fashion normally associated with females. Possibly some are cases of mistaken identity, possibly there were, as Karen Brush has suggested, cases of transvestism.[30] No contemporary evidence confirms that a garment fastened by this method was a traditional part of men's costume in this period, though an individual might choose to fasten his costume in an unusual manner, or his kin might find it a convenient or significant way of dressing him for the grave. There is a depiction of a man in a cloak fastened by brooches at both shoulders in the early-eleventh-century Old English illustrated *Hexateuch* (British Library MS Cotton Claudius B iv) fol. 54v, but it is unusual among the many drawings of clothed men in this manuscript (see pp. 234–5). There is an ancient Danish example of a shoulder fastening for men: a Bronze Age man buried under a tumulus at Muldbjerg wore a wrap-around garment which was fastened over the shoulders by means of leather straps and discs.[31] The closest comparison in terms of date is the pair of clasps found in a royal ship burial at Sutton Hoo (Fig. 80), deposited *c.* 625, which had evidently secured a leather tunic at the shoulders.[32] There are metal loops on the backs of the clasps, by which they had probably been stitched to the leather garment. Each clasp is made in two parts which are secured together by means of a gold pin. If one part were stitched to the front and the other to the back of a cuirass, the garment could be fastened together at the shoulders by means of these clasps (and was perhaps also fastened at the sides by tapes or buckled straps). This Sutton Hoo costume is, however, unusual in several respects. The clasps are exceptionally fine pieces of jewellery, which probably belonged to a king. The leather cuirass they are believed to have secured would have been a military, or ceremonial garment, probably a manifestation of this king's conscious assumption of Roman culture. The case, then, is not truly comparable with lower-ranking corpses of slightly earlier date buried with pairs of brooches.

[30] Brush, 'Adorning the Dead', p. 156.
[31] P. V. Glob, *The Mound People*, trans. J. Bulman (New York, 1974), Plate 29 and pp. 78, 80.
[32] Bruce-Mitford, *Sutton Hoo*, 2 (1978), pp. 532–4.

It may be useful to consider the textile fragments occasionally found on men's belt equipment, although since we do not know if the belt clasped tunic or trousers we cannot be certain which garment the fabric comes from. The fifth-century buckle and belt plate from Grave 117 at Mucking preserved several layers of organic material. Two textiles, both tabby-woven linen, on the outside of the buckle, have been interpreted as two shrouds. It seems unlikely that such an elaborate buckle suite would be worn in such a way that it would be covered, but this is of course possible, in which case one or both of the linens might derive from clothing. The leather belt, traces of which survived in the buckle, had been worn over a woollen twill garment. At Lakenheath, fine 2 x 2 twill was found on the smaller of two buckles associated with a probable male skeleton.[33] Tabby textiles have been found on the backs of men's buckles at Great Tew, Oxfordshire[34] and Petersfinger.[35]

The north European bog finds and the representations of costume in art confirm that Germanic men (like other Europeans) wore a tunic which was short. This then, may be the garment originally called *cyrtel*, a word associated with the verb *cyrtan*, 'to shorten' and derived from Latin *curtus*, 'short' (see p. 53). Possibly the *pad* was a similar garment. The meaning of the word *pad* has vexed lexicographers and linguists, but it evidently represented a tunic or shirt.[36] We can guess something about its form from the fact that it was incorporated in a compound meaning 'mailcoat', *herepad*,[37] and we know that the Anglo-Saxon mailcoat was tunic-shaped (Fig. 208). Its occurrence in another compound, *hasupada*, literally 'one having a grey garment', a poetic metaphor for 'eagle',[38] suggests that when the *pad* was worn it was visible, that is, it was a tunic rather than an undershirt.

The undergarment

Possibly tunics could be worn one on top of another, the lower one functioning as a shirt. Short-sleeved tunics might fall into this category. Some men, perhaps only the rich, might have worn a linen

---

[33] Grave 12; Hutchinson, 'Little Eriswell', p. 7; E. Crowfoot, in Hutchinson, p. 30. The supposed sex of the skeleton is given in C. Wells, 'Report on the human remains from Little Eriswell', Appendix II to Hutchinson, p. 24.

[34] Information from Elisabeth Crowfoot.

[35] Leeds and Shortt, *Petersfinger*, p. 16; G. M. Crowfoot, 'The textile remains', Appendix II to Leeds and Shortt, p. 61.

[36] Bosworth/Toller, *Dictionary*: 'an outer garment, coat, cloak'; Wülcker: 'a smock-frock or shirt' (Wright/Wülcker *Vocabularies*, col. 42, note); Stroebe (*Die altenglischen Kleidernamen*, p. 11) with some doubt, grouped the word among body garments (*scyrte, smocc*). *Paad* glosses *praetersorium*, (Lindsay, *Corpus Glossary*, p. 144, line 670; p. 147, line 832), probably an error. *Praetersorium* means 'a stray animal'. It may have been confused with *praetexta*, a Roman garment that could take the form of a tunic.

[37] *Beowulf*, line 2258; Dobbie, *Beowulf and Judith*, p. 70.

[38] *hasewanpada*; *The Battle of Brunanburh*, line 62; Dobbie, *Minor Poems*, p. 19.

shirt beneath a woollen tunic. Linguistic evidence suggests that a shirt could be worn beneath the tunic. Several words documented in Anglo-Saxon times[39] seem to signify an undergarment of this kind. The words were common to Old English and other Germanic languages. The *cemes* was certainly worn in conjunction with the tunic in later Anglo-Saxon times. The word *hemeþe*, like *cemes*, was an early loan-word, borrowed into Continental Germanic before the Anglo-Saxon migration. The source of both words, Latin *camisia*, can mean a linen shirt, a man's undergarment or a night-shirt. Evidence from Old English texts confirms that the *serc* was worn by men, implies that it resembled a tunic and suggests that it was unostentatious. Like *pad* (p. 114 above), both *serc* and *ham* appear as compound elements meaning 'armour' or 'mail-coat': *beadu-serc*, *here-syrce*,[40] *fyrd-ham*, *scir-ham*.[41] According to Anglo-Latin glossaries the garment called *smoc* bore some resemblance to the *ham*, *hemeþe* and *serc*[42] though it may have been more ornate.[43]

The trousers

We can be fairly certain that Anglo-Saxon men wore trousers. As we have seen (p. 18, above) the Roman poet Ovid described them as a typical barbarian garment. Trousers appear on Roman sculptures of Germanic men, sometimes beneath a short tunic, sometimes worn only with a small cloak. Where there is no covering tunic, the carvings show that the trousers were fastened round the waist by a belt (Fig. 75). They were apparently rather loose; the slack material was gathered round the waist and it hung in folds round the legs. Most of the trousers on sculptures are ankle-length, but there is some evidence that shorter breeches were also worn in the Germanic area[44] as they were in Gaul, according to the art of the Gundestrup Cauldron.[45]

---

[39] *... he wæs utgangende of hire huse, 7 full oft butan his kemese 7 eac gelomlice butan his tunecan he eft on hire huse cyrde* 'he went out of her house and very often he returned to her house again without his shirt (?) and also often without his tunic', H. Hecht (ed.), *Bishofs Wærferth von Worcester Übersetzung der Dialogue Gregors des Grossen*, Bibliothek der angelsächsischen Prosa, 5 (1900) p. 68, lines 5–8.

[40] *Beowulf*, lines 2755, 1511; Dobbie, *Beowulf and Judith*, pp. 85, 47.

[41] *Beowulf*, lines 1504, 1895; Dobbie, *Beowulf and Judith*, pp. 46, 58.

[42] It is among multiple glosses to Latin *colobium* [in Aldhelm]: *loða, serc, smoc, hemeþe*; Napier, *Old English Glosses*, p. 99, line 3725; and *colobium, dictum quia longum est, et sine manicis* [Isidor's definition] *loþa, hom, uel smoc, mentel*; Wright/Wülcker *Vocabularies*, col. 210, lines 24–5.

[43] See p. 62 and note 92.

[44] The tombstone of the Batavian (a Romanised Rhine German people) horseguard T. Aurelius Scribonius depicts a hunting scene with a horseman in a girdled tunic and, apparently, close-fitting breeches extending to the calf; K. Schumacher, *Germanendarstellungen*, Katalogue des Römisch-Germanischen Zentralmuseums zu Mainz, 1 (Mainz, 1935), Plate 5, 16. Short trousers were being worn by men in Hanover in the fourth century; G. Girke, *Die Tracht der Germanen in der vor- und frühgeschichtlichen Zeit*, 2 vols (Leipzig, 1922), 2, Plate 55A.

[45] Knee-length woven breeches are shown on the cauldron, a Celtic product of Gaul, *c.* 80–50 BC, which was deposited in a Danish peat bog as a votive offering; G. S. Olmsted, *The Gundestrup Cauldron*, Collection Latomus, 162 (Brussels, 1979). pp. 9, 25.

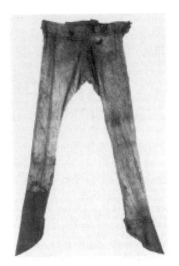

Plates 5a and b Trousers from Thorsbjerg Mose, Germany

Woven trousers, which probably date from the first or second century AD, have been recovered from peat bogs in the Schleswig-Holstein area of Germany.[46] The best-known example (Plate 5 a and b) one of two pairs from Thorsbjerg, was of high quality cloth, woven in broken lozenge twill. The cut of the garment was quite sophisticated, with separate pieces of cloth for each leg, and panels at seat and crotch to shape the trousers to the body. The leg-pieces were ankle-length; woven foot-pieces were attached to them by narrow bands, so that the finished garment was like a pair of tights. The legs themselves were quite narrow, only about 30 cm at the calf, and thus more like the close-fitting leg coverings of later Anglo-Saxon art than the baggy trousers of Roman sculptures. Six loops stitched to the waistband provided attachment points for a belt. These loops were surprisingly clumsy, and the waistband itself inside-out, which suggests that it was worn folded over, concealing the belt. The foot-pieces and belt-loops are unique to the Thorsbjerg trousers,[47] but since only four other pairs have been recovered we cannot be sure that they were really unusual. They may, however, have been characteristic of high quality garments: both features can be seen on a pair of trousers belonging to an important man shown in a tomb wall-painting found at Silistra, Bulgaria.[48] The pair of trousers found at Damendorf was, like the Thorsbjerg garment, of high quality and woven in broken lozenge twill. Since the

[46] Blindheim, 'Drakt og smykker', Fig. 4; Hald, *Ancient Danish Textiles*, pp. 328–30, Figs 391–3, 396–401.

[47] H. Shetelig and H. S. Falk, *Scandinavian Archaeology*, trans. E. V. Gordon (Oxford, 1937), pp. 331–2, considered that the Thorsbjerg garments belonged to a tribe that had migrated from the south, especially demonstrated by the long (rather than short) trousers and the Roman-type footwear.

[48] Vierck, in Ahrens, *Sachsen und Angelsachsen*, Fig. 16.1.a

legs are now torn we cannot know if there were originally foot-pieces. The other surviving pairs of trousers, a second example from Thorsbjerg and others from Daetgen and Marx-Etzel are of inferior weave and cut, made by the economical method of folding over one large piece of cloth to make the leg-pieces, and inserting panels to widen the body part. The Daetgen trousers were slit at the ankle and this was probably common for narrow trousers; as we have seen (p. 56), clasps have been found at the ankles of male skeletons from the Roman Iron Age and the Migration period in parts of Scandinavia where they probably closed a slit in the trousers just as in Anglian England they closed the slit in a tight sleeve.[49]

Recent study of lumps of organic material from the Migration Period chieftain's grave at Evebø, Norway, excavated in 1889, has demonstrated that the man was buried wearing highly-coloured trousers: the background tone was brownish-red, with greenish stripes running in both directions making a pattern of large (c. 15 x 15 cm) checks, and in addition, broad stripes of green and brownish-yellow.[50] The weave (2 x 2 twill) is simpler than the Thorsbjerg and Damendorf examples. The Evebø trousers are the only ones we have with a pattern in colour. Although they were probably unusually elaborate, part of the ceremonial costume of an exceptionally rich man, they are a particularly interesting find since they are so close to the beginning of our period and belong to an area which might have contributed migrants to eastern England.

One of the figures on the die from Torslunda, Sweden, wears trousers without a covering tunic (Plate 3d). The texture of the trousers, which resembles the animal skins on the same object, suggests that the trousers were fur, though of course the craftsman who made the die may have had limited patterns at his disposal and the detail may be misleading. The trousers have a broad belt and fit closely round the legs, with a narrow band at each ankle. The figure, who carries an axe and has roped a large beast (a monster, perhaps) is bare-chested and clearly dressed for action.

This comparative evidence makes it probable that the Anglo-Saxons, too, wore trousers, and some of the textile remains from belt equipment and belt attachments may have derived from them, although we have nothing definite and nothing to rival the Evebø trousers for colour. The Anglo-Saxon trousers would have been belted or girdled at the waist and might have been baggy or narrow, but if they were narrow they were not secured at the ankle by metal clasps as Scandinavian garments were. They were possibly bound

---

[49] Hines, *Scandinavian Character*, pp. 63–5; Hines, *Clasps*.

[50] B. Magnus, 'A chieftain's costume. New light on an old grave find from West Norway', in Bender Jørgensen and Tidow, *NESAT 1*, pp. 63–73, at pp. 69–70; I. R. Pedersen, 'The analyses of the textiles from Evebø-Eide, Gloppen, Norway', in Bender Jørgensen and Tidow, *NESAT 1*, pp. 74–84, at p. 80. I note that in a recent publication the trousers are described as 'checked in red and blue'; L. Bender Jørgensen, 'Scandinavia, AD 400–1000', in D. Jenkins (ed.), *The Cambridge History of Western Textiles*, 2 vols (Cambridge 2003), 1, pp. 132–8, at p. 133.

to the leg by garters or leggings (see next section). The trousers may have been called *brec* and *braccas*. As noted in the previous chapter, *brec* originally signified 'short trousers' and *braccas* 'breeches'.

The leggings

The lower legs of a male corpse found in Daugbjerg Fen, Denmark, were wrapped in leggings which had been bound to the calf by woollen strings. Strips of cloth which might have been knee- or calf-wraps have also been found in German bogs.[51] Early Anglo-Saxon men, according to linguistic evidence, probably wore two types of protection on their legs: firstly a legging proper, or stocking, made of woven fabric or leather; secondly a strip of fabric which could function like the Daugbjerg man's woollen strings, tying on the leggings or confining the loose folds of the trousers, or which could simply be wound round the shin, and probably the foot too, for warmth and protection. Binding strips like these appear very often in late Anglo-Saxon drawings. Later art gives the impression that the leg bindings are made of strips of material, like puttees, though large squares or rectangles can produce a similar effect as demonstrated by later medieval clothing from a burial at Boksten, Sweden (Fig. 210).[52] Re-enactors find that leg bindings give excellent protection against brambles[53] though braided bands are prone to catch in undergrowth. Wool, by its very nature, is liable to snag and stretch;[54] linen or leather has been found more practical. However, wool was certainly used for leg bands in the later Saxon period in towns (see p. 259). While the more prosperous members of society would have had purpose-made leg bindings, no doubt others made use of pieces ripped or cut from old clothes, blankets or bags. Calvin Wells has tentatively suggested, on anatomical grounds, that early Anglo-Saxons habitually wore over-tight bindings round the legs.[55] Certainly if leg bindings of this sort are not tight they will fall down. As any British schoolchild of my own generation will testify, the discomfort of thick woollen kneesocks held up by tight garters is something one soon learns to endure, and the same is probably true of tight leg bindings! Occasionally knives or tools are found in positions which suggest they might have been stuck into a sock or boot, for example a knife was at the left tibia of a man at Eynsham, Oxfordshire[56] but one could not conveniently stick

---

[51] Hald, *Ancient Danish Textiles*, p. 335, Figs 19–20.

[52] The burial is considered mid-fourteenth-century. The clothing is discussed in M. Nockert, 'Some new observations about the Boksten costume', in Bender Jørgensen and Tidow, *NESAT I*, pp. 277–82.

[53] Information from Hazel Uzzell.

[54] Wool fibres have minute 'hooks' which cause them to cling together. Flax is smoother.

[55] Wells, *Bones, Bodies and Disease*, p. 78.

[56] [Anonymous, untitled] *Oxoniensia*, 17 (1952–3), pp. 216–17.

things into a tight leg binding so the rarity of this is not surprising.

The *strapulas* were leggings which (at least later in the medieval period) were laced down to the foot. The interesting origin of this word has already been discussed (p. 83). We know that in the later Middle Ages *strapulas* were worn by men as well as women.[57] Another leg-covering was the *hosa*, which could protect the shin, like a gaiter, or extend to cover the foot, like a boot.[58] The *hosa* could be made of fabric, or of leather, in which case it might be called by the compound name *leþer-hose*. The *hosa* could be fastened by the garter or binding called *hose-bend* or *wining*, and the kind of bindings wound round the leg like puttees could also be called *winingas*.

The belt

Belt equipment is the only part of male costume to be found regularly in pagan graves. The most elaborate belt equipment from the period is generally associated with men rather than women. Leather remains have been found inside many buckles, suggesting that buckled leather belts were common; possibly woven girdles could also be worn by men. Buckles have been found frequently at the waists and hips of male skeletons. Mostly they had been placed centrally, although some have been found at the left and right sides and at the backs of bodies. The fact that buckles accompanied men buried in battlefield cemeteries at Dunstable, Bedfordshire[59] and Old Sarum, Wiltshire[60] where they were the only clothing fasteners recovered from the sites, suggests that the buckled belt was considered a utilitarian item of clothing, rather than a luxury to be plundered.

There are, neverthless, many male graves without buckles. Some of these have belt ornaments and tags, others have objects at the waist or hip, positions consistent with attachment to a belt although no buckle was present. Clearly, many belts, including some with quite heavy equipment hanging from them, could be fastened without buckles. As an alternative, men might have used beads as toggles, but there are only a few archaeological examples to support the possibility; they include a bead found at the waist of an elderly

[57] See pp. 83–4. The English source, the *Ancrene Wisse*, is concerned with women. The *Polychronicon* citation concerns the Langobard people, but suggests that men wore *strapeles*.

[58] See p. 256 note 83.

[59] The buckles were not, however, found in positions consistent with being worn at the belt: the one with skeleton 21 was found near the right foot and the one with skeleton 35 merely described as 'near'; R. C. Dunning and R. E. M. Wheeler, 'A barrow at Dunstable, Beds', *Archaeological Journal*, 88 (1931), pp. 193–217, at pp. 206, 208.

[60] H. P. Blackmore, 'On a barrow near Old Sarum', *Transactions of the Salisbury Field Club*, 1 (1893), pp. 49–51.

Fig. 81 Reconstruction of the
appearance of the Germanic
Roman soldier buried at
Dorchester, Oxfordshire

man buried at Mitcham, Greater London.[61] Perhaps some men se-cured the belt by slotting one end through the other, as on the belt which accompanied the Tollund man, the most famous of the Dan-ish 'bog people'.[62]

Some elaborate belt equipment was military in character. A man buried in the fourth or early-fifth century at Dorchester, Oxford-shire, and believed to be a Germanic Roman soldier, wore an elabo-rate belt which has been reconstructed by Vera Evison. The belt was wide, and it was stiffened by nine bronze bars. The fastening, however, was by means of a narrower strap which was riveted to the broad belt and passed through a buckle which was much narrower than the belt itself. The end of the belt hung down, as seems to have been general in the early medieval period. The Dorchester soldier's belt had metal attachments for a pouch and for a baldric which was buckled at the right shoulder (Fig. 81).[63] Possibly the elaborate belt and diagonal baldric remained semi-military fash-ions into the sixth and seventh centuries. Several, though not all, of the elaborate waist belts found in Anglo-Saxon graves have been associated with swords. The remains of gold decoration from what might have been a baldric survives from a rich, seventh-century barrow burial at Taplow, Buckinghamshire (pp. 195–6, below) and cloisonné jewellery from the Sutton Hoo ship burial, also seventh-century, includes a 'strap-distributer' which probably linked a baldric and a belt; but buckles and other strap fittings have been found at the shoulders and chests of male skeletons in earlier and less splendid graves. This was never a majority fashion, but it oc-curs in Anglian, Saxon and Kentish areas. Knives have sometimes been found on the chests of skeletons, and it is possible that they were attached to such straps.

Some belts, with and without buckles, were ornamented with decorated metal mounts. The buckle suite from Mucking Grave 117, which preserved leather and textile, is an early and particu-larly splendid example (Fig. 82). Many surviving buckles have a decorated plate, and sometimes a matching counter-plate provides a symmetrical effect. Triangular buckle plates are characteristic of Kent. Metal mounts and buckle plates, as well as enhancing the appearance and demonstrating the wealth of the wearer, helped keep the belt rigid and in shape. Less prosperous wearers of belts may have had more economical ways of stiffening the belt. An example from Riseley (Horton Kirby), Kent, had been reinforced with a

[61] No. 223; H. F. Bidder and J. Morris, 'An Anglo-Saxon cemetery at Mitcham', *Surrey Archaeological Collections*, 56 (1959), pp. 51–131, at p. 74. An elderly man, no longer capable of heavy work, might have undertaken spinning, and carried a spindle whorl.

[62] Glob, *The Bog People*, pp. 31–2.

[63] V. I. Evison, 'Quoit brooch Style buckles', pp. 238–40. The buckle was found near the shoulder; metal fragments discarded after excavation may have been the remains of a weapon, or weapons; J. R. Kirk and E. T. Leeds, 'Three early Saxon graves from Dorchester, Oxon.', *Oxoniensia*, 17–18 (1954), pp. 63–76, at p. 65.

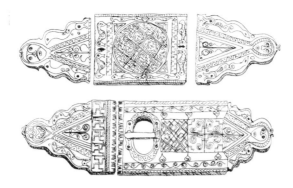

Fig. 82 Belt suite, Mucking, Thurrock

piece of bone.[64] The 'belt' of rib bone found across the waist of a male skeleton in Grave 65 at Lechlade was apparently meant to be seen, since it was decorated with rings and dots. It was attached to iron and associated with a buckle.[65]

The belt may have had various functions. As suggested above, it may have sometimes been the only garment worn: figures on the Finglesham buckle, the Torslunda die and on some later, Viking Age, sculptures seem to show figures naked but for a belt, and sometimes headgear. The Tollund man was, in fact, found naked apart from his leather cap (Fig. 83) and girdle, though it is possible that he once wore garments which have rotted away. Presumably if a man chose to work or fight naked, the belt would be a useful attachment point for the knife and other tools.

Both the trousers as depicted on Roman sculptures, and the tunic as depicted in both Roman and late Anglo-Saxon art, are girdled or belted, though since tunics are usually pouched over the belt itself, the latter is not visible. Where an Anglo-Saxon buckle is particularly elaborate, it is reasonable to suppose that it would be worn where it could be seen, outside the tunic, and that a second belt, girdle or string would have secured the trousers underneath. The presence of two buckles, together with textile evidence, in a (seventh-century) grave at Castledyke, suggests that in this instance one buckle had belted a woollen garment, probably a tunic, and the second buckle, which was underneath this layer of textile, had perhaps fastened the trousers.[66] A second buckle, however, may not always evidence a second belt: at Lyminge, for instance, additional buckles belonged to objects attached to belts. In Grave 12 the

Fig. 83 Leather cap on the head of a man found in a peat bog, Tollund, Denmark

---

[64] Grave lxxv; A. C[umberland], 'Saxon cemetery, "Riseley", Horton Kirby', *Transactions of the Dartford District Antiquarian Society*, 8 (1938), pp. 15–29, at p. 22.

[65] Boyle, Jennings, Miles and Palmer, *Lechlade*, p. 81.

[66] Grave 55; Walton Rogers, 'Textiles and clothing' in Drinkall and Foreman, *Castledyke*, p. 278. For dating of the individual burials in this predominantly sixth- to late-seventh-century cemetery, which also contained some earlier (fifth-century) graves, see pp. 328–30 in the same volume.

position of a small buckle and buckle plate indicated that they had fastened a bag or purse which had been attached to a buckled belt[67] rather like the reconstruction of the Dorchester soldier's costume (Fig. 81), and like the costume of the Alamanni in the fifth and sixth centuries, when a purse was attached to the back of the belt.[68] Such containers might be used to carry fire-making materials and could have a fire-steel attached to the front.[69] (They were not used for coins; England did not have a money economy at this time.)

Men, like women, often carried a knife at the waist, and other tools such as tweezers and shears were sometimes carried at the belt, also amulets, such as a cowrie shell at the waist of a man at Ellesborough, Buckinghamshire.[70] Keys, girdle hangers, toilet articles and suspension rings which are commonly found in women's graves are not usually associated with men, nor are the ivory rings which are thought to be the frames of pouches. Textile evidence on belt accessories does suggest, however, that men also carried pouches of finely woven textile which might be patterned with stripes or checks and decorated with needlework: in Grave 75 at Worthy Park, a knife at the left hip of a male skeleton had a very fine tabby weave both above and below it. A check pattern achieved by alternating blocks of S- and Z-spun threads in both warp and weft was evident in the upper layer, and very fine embroidery was seen on the textile beneath.[71]

Heavier tools, also, might be secured to the belt: two men at Lyminge had axe-heads[72] and hones may have been fastened to the belts of males at Castledyke,[73] while a man at Wakerley had a hone between his knees, which might have hung from his belt.[74] A comb was found among the ribs of the Ellesborough skeleton, and could, perhaps, have been stuck into the belt, though it might have been

---

[67] A bronze buckle and plate, the whole fitting about 5 cm wide, were at the right of the waist, the buckle tongue pointing to the right. The small buckle and plate, about 2 cm wide, were at the pelvis, and the buckle tongue pointed downwards; Warhurst, 'Lyminge', p. 8. Male graves 22 and 30 contained what were identified as purse mounts (Warhurst, pp. 16, 22), but were probably fire-steels mounted on pouches (see note 69).

[68] Christlein, *Die Alamannen*, p. 65.

[69] D. Brown, 'Fire-steels and pursemounts again'. The known examples are all from south of the Thames.

[70] A. H. Cocks, 'Anglo-Saxon burials at Ellesborough', *Records of Buckinghamshire*, 9 (1904–9), pp. 425–9, at pp. 426–7.

[71] There were two layers of textile above the knife. The check pattern was visible on the outermost one. Unpublished, Crowfoot, Worthy Park.

[72] Graves 1, 7; Warhurst, 'Lyminge', pp. 7, 11.

[73] Graves 125, 151; Drinkall and Foreman, *Castledyke*, pp. 70–1, 78, 284.

[74] Grave 23; Adams, Jackson and Badenoch, 'Wakerley', p. 148 and p. 96 Fig. 24.5, also microfiche. Hones are particularly unusual in Anglo-Saxon cemeteries, though more common in Sweden. Martin Foreman notes that where they have been found in England they are normally associated with weapons. They might be status indicators as well as functional tools: hones at Castledyke (which occurred in seventh-century graves as well as those of the earlier period) were thought to have been associated with those who had achieved the legal status of adulthood, though physically still 'boys', while the Wakerley hone accompanied a man equipped as a basic-status warrior with shield and spear; Drinkall and Foreman, *Castledyke*, p. 284.

kept in a container which was placed on the body. Tools are relatively uncommon in male graves, however, and there is no indication that they were deposited other than idiosyncratically. There is no evidence that tools were regularly used as grave-goods to indicate trade or social status.

The belt was probably called by the Old English word *belt* at this time, and the word *fetel* might also be used, perhaps with particular reference to a sword belt.

Footwear

Calvin Wells has suggested that the early Anglo-Saxons did not habitually go barefoot, and that they wore clumsy footwear (see above, p. 82), but no traces of men's shoes have so far been found from fifth- or sixth-century context. People may have been buried barefoot, and might have found it convenient to work without footwear in more situations than modern scholars might suppose. Late Anglo-Saxon manuscripts show men carrying out agricultural work such as ploughing and sowing barefoot, which confirms the experience of some re-enactors that the inconvenience of wearing shoes on churned-up ground outweighs any initial comfort and protection. The early Anglo-Saxons would, however, have been capable of making shoes, and any footwear would presumably have been made of leather and secured with thongs, organic materials unlikely to survive in normal cemetery conditions. A pair of Iron Age shoes, found on the body of a man in Rønbjerg Mose, Denmark, gives us some idea of the kind of workmanship Germanic people were capable of in the Dark Ages (Fig. 84). The shoes were made of ox-hide, each shoe cut from a single piece of hide, and secured by thongs which also strapped them to the foot.[75]

Linguistic evidence suggests that the common name *scoh* and the plurals *gesceo* and *gescy* ('shoes') were in use in pagan times. The vocabulary suggests that there was some variety in shoe types already at the time of the settlement. These include the *swiftlere* ('slipper'); the *hemming* and *rifeling*, raw-hide shoes which perhaps bore some relation to the modern Irish 'pampootie' (Fig. 85) and which may have been worn by agricultural workers;[76] and the *cæles* and

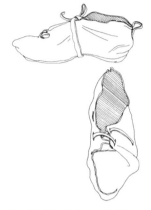

Fig. 84 Pair of shoes, Rønbjerg Mose, Denmark

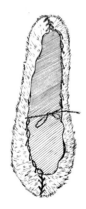

Fig. 85 Modern raw hide shoe ('pampootie'), Aran Islands, Republic of Ireland

[75] Hald, *Primitive Shoes*, pp. 38–9, Figs 29–31.

[76] *Himming* glosses *pero* in the Corpus Glossary; Lindsay, p. 36, line 306. Lindsay gives no source for this lemma, but the glossator may have known Isidor's definition: *perones et (s)culponeae rustica calciamenta sunt* (Lindsay, *Isidori*, XIX, xxxiv, 13). The glossator of the eleventh-century version of this word-list in London, British Library MS Cotton Cleopatra A iii added *i. ruh sco* ('that is rough/hairy/shaggy shoe'; Wright/Wülcker, *Vocabularies*, col. 468, line 31). The *rifeling* was evidently similar. It glosses *obstrigelli* (Wright/Wülcker, *Vocabularies*, col. 125, line 33; *obstrigillus* 'a shoe sole, sandal fastened to the feet by straps') and in the fifteenth century, *pero* (S. H. J. Herrtage, *Catholicon Anglicum*, Early English Text Society, original series 75 (1881), p. 305). 'Rewelynys' and 'Hemmynys' are virtually synonymous in a fifteenth-century poem, except that the former are said to be made 'of Hydis' and the latter 'of Hart' (D. Macpherson, *Ðe Ogygynale Cronykil of Scotland*

Fig. 86 Moustached figure on a bracteate, Faversham, Kent

Fig. 87 Moustached figure from purse lid, Sutton Hoo, Suffolk

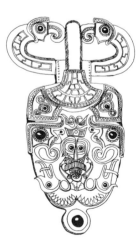

Fig. 88 Moustached face on buckle, Åker i Vang, Norway

socc, bag-like foot coverings. As far as we know, these shoe-types were worn by both sexes.

Hair and headgear

The remains of many combs have been found in Anglo-Saxon context, both on settlement sites and in cremations, where they are common; less often in inhumation graves. Although some of these combs might have been textile tools, others, especially those found with men, who were not traditionally the textile workers, were probably for personal grooming. Some of the shears and tweezers found in male graves may have been used for the same purpose. This suggests that care of the hair and beard was considered important, as it was later in Iceland when neatly trimmed hair and beard and a close-fitting tunic served to distinguish a man of the rank of 'carl' from the lower 'thrall'.[77] Since the settlers of Anglo-Saxon England were intending to devote themselves to agriculture and colonisation, it is probable that the more extravagant hairstyles of their kinsmen were left behind. The uncropped wildness of the Chatti and the knots of the Swabians were after all, as Tacitus tells us, largely designed to frighten the enemy. Although the seated figure on the pot lid from Spong Hill, with its 'bun' of hair or pillbox cap (Fig. 3), could be either male or female, there is no independent evidence to suggest this was a masculine hairstyle in Anglo-Saxon times. Probably Anglo-Saxon men cut their hair short, as the Franks did; by the sixth century long hair for men seems to have been confined to the Merovingian kings in Frankia.[78] The human faces which occur on button brooches (Fig. 4), and occasionally on other Anglo-Saxon metalwork, usually appear to have moustaches, comparable with the luxuriant examples on the Torslunda die (Plate 3a

be *Androw of Wyntown*, 2 vols (London, 1795), 2, p. 189, lines 271–4). In modern times 'rivilin' survived in Scotland as the name of a shoe made of untanned ox- or sealskin (Wright, *English Dialect Dictionary*, 5 (1905), p. 131) and was still in use in the 1970s in the Shetland Isles as a name for 'cowskin moccasins' (A. Leigh, 'Dialect dialling', *The Sunday Times* (Oct 20, 1974), p. 13). This type of shoe is well attested from northern Europe. It is normally made from a single piece of hide cut from the lower part of the hind leg of an animal, the baggy heel of the animal's skin becoming the toe of the shoe. The skin was sewn together at the sides and back. There was no separate sole (Hald, *Primitive Shoes*, p. 179). The hairy side faced outwards. The hair was retained in winter but stripped off for summer (Hald, *Primitive Shoes*, p. 175). A more primitive version was made by wrapping a piece of hide round the foot and securing it with thongs round the ankle (Hald, *Primitive Shoes*, pp. 166–7). In Scandinavia, this type of footwear was worn by peasants, so that the words *hriflingr* and its near-synonym *fitjungr*, originally shoe-names, came to signify persons of this class (Hald, *Primitive Shoes*, p. 176).

[77] *Rigsþula*, 115; Dronke, *Poetic Edda*, p. 165. The carl was married to a wife who wore the 'dwarf-pin costume' (pp. 45, 66) and had a daughter-in-law with dangling keys, the equivalents, perhaps, of many of the women buried in fifth- and sixth-century Anglo-Saxon cemeteries.

[78] J. M. Wallace-Hadrill, *The Long-haired Kings and Other Studies in Frankish History* (London, 1962), pp. 156–7.

and d), on a bracteate pendant from Faversham (Fig. 86), on the purse-lid from the seventh-century ship burial at Sutton Hoo (Fig. 87) and on a buckle of similar date from Åker, Norway (Fig. 88). 'Male' faces on the stone sceptre from Sutton Hoo are bearded, some moustached (Fig. 89), figures on the Sutton Hoo helmet and the human face on the shield are beardless. Beardless faces may represent youths, but since men are depicted more often without beards than with them, it seems likely that it was the custom to shave, particularly among the upper classes. An Anglo-Saxon razor blade, together with a hone and shears, were recently recovered from an early cremation urn at Peterborough, unburnt personal possessions placed with the ashes of the dead man.[79]

Fig. **89** Bearded and moustached face from sceptre, Sutton Hoo, Suffolk

There is little evidence to suggest that men wore hats or caps in the fifth and sixth centuries. A buckle found near the ear bones of a male skeleton at Ipswich, Suffolk,[80] might have been attached to some kind of headgear, and so might other metal remains found near the heads of a few male skeletons elsewhere; but no two finds are similar, and there is no consistent pattern. Clips of the type sometimes found with females (p. 80, above) have been found at the heads of male skeletons, for example at Holywell Row,[81] but similar clips have also been found at the legs, hips and chests of male skeletons, so even if some of them belonged to leather caps, these clips had other uses too. Possibly men wore headgear that has left no trace in English soil. The Tollund man wore a pointed leather cap fastened under the chin by thongs, and the Raskwerd cap (Chapter II, p. 79) is woven, of pillbox shape with a peak, examples of two very different kinds of headgear worn by Germanic people, the former from well before the Anglo-Saxon period, the latter probably slightly later than the fifth and sixth centuries under discussion here. Neither literature nor art, however, suggests that Germanic men wore hats or caps regularly, and perhaps individual need or taste dictated a man's choice, though headgear has been a strong indicator of ethnic identity in modern times. Probably hooded cloaks, or the versatile rectangular cloak which could be pulled over the head, provided protection against bad weather.

Neverthless, the word *hæt*, antecedent to modern English 'hat', was probably in use in the fifth and sixth centuries. There was also the word *hufe*, which in Middle English was applied to men's headgear. *Hod* probably signified 'hood'. The words *cæppe* and *cappa* may have been in use at this time or they may date to after the conversion. Their semantic range seems to extend from 'cap' to 'hood'.

[79] Minerva Business Park site, unpublished. Information from Hertfordshire Archaeological Trust and BBC Television.

[80] Grave 75; Layard, 'Ipswich', p. 344.

[81] Graves 23, 93; Lethbridge, *Recent Excavations*, pp. 17, 42. The clips in the former case were associated with rotten wood. Lethbridge thought they might have belonged to a wooden comb.

Gloves

In view of the popularity of gloves in the Germanic world, and in the light of linguistic evidence, it is likely that gloves and mittens were known in the early Anglo-Saxon period. The term *glof*, which may derive from a word meaning 'the palm of the hand', is probably quite ancient as it has cognates in other Germanic languages.[82] The word *hond-scio*, literally 'hand-shoe' and hence 'mitten', survives only because it was used as a proper noun. It occurs as the name of a warrior in the poem *Beowulf*, where the poet obviously understands and plays upon its literal sense, including making a gratuitous reference to a *glof*;[83] probably it was once a common noun in English as in other Germanic languages.[84] Margarethe Hald has suggested that the structure of these cognate words ('hand' + 'shoe') implies a common development of shoes and mittens, and is able to illustrate examples of woven and skin mittens, which survive respectively from Bronze Age Scandinavia and from the Viking Age. They were made from two pieces of material, one larger than the other, stitched together with a semi-circular seam, like modern mittens.[85] It seems likely that our Old English word and its Germanic cognates were originally applied to hand coverings of this type.

Jewellery

As we have seen, men were buried in less jewellery than women. A large, single bead was sometimes attached to a sword hilt as a mark of distinction,[86] and beads may sometimes have been used as toggles on men's belts, but the occurrence of decorative beads in male graves is rare – there were only two instances in the large cemetery of Barrington A, for example, one of a male with a single bead, the other with a bead and a 'spindle whorl', both in weaponless graves. The rarity of rings is again surprising in view of the Old English literary tradition, and also since the hoards of rings found in Scandinavia would seem to confirm the importance of this kind of ornament in the Germanic North. Arm rings are not normally found

---

[82] Stroebe, *Die altenglische Keidernamen*, pp. 30–1, suggested that the prefix *ge*-had been added to an element cognate with Gothic *lofa* and Old Norse *lofe*, 'palm of the hand'. Cf. T. W. Arnoldson, *Parts of the body in Older Germanic and Scandinavian*, Linguistic Studies in Germanic, 2 (Chicago, 1915), pp. 60–1.

[83] *Beowulf*, line 2076; Dobbie, *Beowulf and Judith*, p. 64; the question is examined in detail in Owen-Crocker, *Four Funerals*, pp. 160–1; for the theme of the hand in the poem see p. 186.

[84] This argument, expressed in *Dress in Anglo-Saxon England* (1986), failed to convince the editors of the *Thesaurus of Old English* and *hondscio* is omitted from that work.

[85] Hald, *Primitive Shoes*, p. 26, Figs 10, 19–20.

[86] V. I. Evison, 'The Dover ring sword and other sword-rings and beads', *Archaeologia*, 51 (1967), 63–118.

in male graves; the few recorded examples belong to early excavations where the sexing of the skeletons cannot be relied upon. Anklets have occasionally been found, for example with a boy at Holywell Row[87] and another in the grave with a five-year-old child who also had a necklet and a spear, at Empingham II.[88] Another anklet was found in a cinerary urn at Caistor-by-Norwich, Norfolk.[89] These are rare in the context of Anglo-Saxon England as a whole, though as noted above (p. 89) ankle ornaments seem to have been a peculiarity of Lyminge, where they were worn by both sexes. A necklet of silver wire, with a flattened front shaped like a crescent moon, was found in what was possibly a boy's grave at Wakerley, again a rare type of ornament for Anglo-Saxon England. The example from Emscote, Warwickshire, was found with typically feminine grave-goods[91] so this type of ornament cannot be said to be typical of one gender or the other. As we have seen (p. 89), neck rings are worn by both sexes in Old English literature, in fact the same neck ring can pass as a gift from one sex to the other. Finger rings are very rare in male graves. A simple wire example was found at Everthorpe, East Yorkshire,[92] and an elaborate example, made of gold and set with a Roman intaglio, was found in a boat burial at Snape, Suffolk, evidently the grave of an important man. The size of the ring suggested it was worn on the thumb or forefinger.[93] A ring of similar dimensions, set with a garnet, was found at Dover, Kent.[94]

The words *dalc* and *spennels* were probably in use in the fifth and sixth centuries. They could signify 'clasp' or 'brooch' and might have been used of some of the buckles which men wore. *Hring* could mean an ornamental ring or a ring-shaped fastener (hence this too might be used of a round or oval buckle) while *beah* signified an armlet or neckring (and could perhaps have been used for an anklet).

---

[87] Grave 23, round the right ankle; Lethbridge, *Recent Excavations*, p. 17.

[88] Timby, *Empingham II*, p. 122.

[89] R. R. Clarke,'Norfolk in the Dark Ages, 400–800 A. D.', *Norfolk Archaeology*, 27 (1939–41), pp. 163–249, at pp. 217–8.

[90] Grave 40; Adams, Jackson and Badenoch, 'Wakerley', pp. 156–7, p. 106, Fig. 38.1.

[91] P. B. Chatwin, 'Anglo-Saxon finds at Warwick'. Another came from Market Overton, Rutland; Brown, *Arts*, 4 (1915), p. 424.

[92] Meaney, *Gazetteer*, p. 288.

[93] R. Bruce-Mitford, *Aspects of Anglo-Saxon Archaeology: Sutton Hoo and other discoveries* (London, 1974), p. 124.

[94] B. Philp, 'Saxon gold ring found at Dover', *Kent Archaeological Review*, Spring 1973, p. 10.

IV

Women's costume from the seventh to the ninth centuries

The seventh century saw a change in female costume, a development which the Anglo-Saxons seem to have shared with all the Germanic and Germanised peoples with the exception of the Scandinavians, and possibly the Visigoths.[1] For the Anglo-Saxons, this was first manifested in Kent in the second half of the sixth century[2] spreading to other regions by the beginning of the seventh. It reflects a discontinuation of links with the North and initially at least, an increasing influence of the Frankish Empire and, through the Empire, the Mediterranean world, especially Byzantium. Helen Geake has recently argued that some of the items from the latest furnished graves indicate 'a classical influence ... which is less Byzantine and more Roman', part of a conscious renaissance of Roman culture in Britain.[3] A further change (or perhaps, one which happened simultaneously, but among the women of the non-ruling classes, only later spreading through the upper strata) seems to have established a simpler costume with little jewellery (Colour Plate G).

Archaeological evidence

The beginning of the seventh century brings changes in funerary practice, with fewer grave-goods in general, many unfurnished graves and a small number of women's graves with a few items of very opulent jewellery. By the eighth century the practice of furnishing a grave seems to have been uncommon. Since this

---

[1] H. Vierck, 'La "Chemise de Sainte-Bathilde" à Chelles et l'influence byzantine sur l'art de cour mérovingien au VIIe siècle', in É. Chirol (ed.), *Actes du Colloque International d'Archéologie, Rouen 3–4–5 Juillet 1975 (Centenaire de l'abbé Cochet)* (Rouen, 1978), pp. 521–64.

[2] H. Geake, *The Use of Grave-goods in Conversion-period England, c. 600–c. 850*, British Archaeological Reports, British Series 261 (1997), p. 129.

[3] Geake, *Grave-goods*, p. 120; see also H. Geake, 'Invisible kingdoms: the use of grave-goods in seventh-century England,' *Anglo-Saxon Studies in Archaeology and History* 10 (1999), pp. 203–15.

development coincides with the conversion to Christianity the change has been attributed to the influence of the new religion which encouraged shroud burial, an abandonment of the material possessions of earthly life and, for the ruling classes immediately and ultimately for the wider population, church- and churchyard-interment, though the new Anglo-Saxon Church does not seem actively to have forbidden grave-goods. Certainly, as Christianity became established, unfurnished burials became the norm in both England and western Frankia, though we may note a contrast with eastern Frankia and Alamannia, where there are many furnished graves and an enviable amount of evidence from which to reconstruct the costume. There may, however, have been reasons other than religious contributing to the transformation in Anglo-Saxon burial practice: economic factors, such as changes in attitude to property and to inheritance;[4] and differences in the perception of cultural identity which left people less anxious to express the gender, ethnicity and social role of their dead than they had been before. Whatever the reasons for the changes in burial practice, there is sufficient evidence to show that women's dress was altering at the same time.

Archaeologists have identified a number of 'conversion period' cemeteries, which were typically used only briefly.[5] The inhabitants, having abandoned their traditional pagan burial places and begun new cemeteries, probably nominally Christian, in which very few grave-goods were deposited, seem nevertheless to have been reluctant to abandon completely the customs of their ancestors, and express nervousness and superstition in practices such as decapitation of the corpse. Perhaps in defiance of Church teaching and contemporary ideologies, they have left sufficient grave-goods to show that the gaudy, clumsy festoons of beads, the barbaric brooches and wrist clasps were no longer fashionable. The sheer quantity of jewellery that was once worn had decreased (or at least less was buried) and it differed in type and decoration from that of the fifth and sixth centuries. The nature and arrangement of the grave-goods suggests that the garments themselves had changed. The relatively small number of cemeteries belonging to the conversion period form a homogeneous group yielding similar grave-goods. Evidently the regional variations in women's dress had disappeared. The recognition of changing burial practices and changes in dress fashions in the conversion period cemeteries has

---

[4] J. Shephard, 'Anglo-Saxon Barrows of the Later Sixth and Seventh Centuries AD', unpublished PhD dissertation (University of Cambridge, 1979).

[5] The concept of the 'conversion period cemetery' was established by a series of investigations published in the 1960s to 1970: A. Ozanne, 'The Peak Dwellers', *Medieval Archaeology*, 6–8 (1962–3), pp. 15–52; M. Hyslop, 'Two Anglo-Saxon cemeteries at Chamberlains Barn, Leighton Buzzard, Bedfordshire', *Archaeological Journal*, 120 (1963), pp. 161–200; and A. L. Meaney and S. C. Hawkes, *Two Anglo-Saxon Cemeteries at Winnall, Winchester, Hampshire*, The Society for Medieval Archaeology Monograph Series, 4 (1970).

made it possible to identify late graves in large 'folk cemeteries' which had been established in the pre-Christian period and which remained in use into the seventh, even the eighth, century.

Graves containing particularly splendid jewellery identify ladies of the rich, presumably the ruling, classes in various localities (although some of the examples from the Peak District are artistically inferior), but Kent has produced the majority of examples, reflecting the relative richness and the strong Frankish connections of that kingdom in the seventh century. It is possible that

Fig. 90 Necklace, Desborough, Northamptonshire

most of this jewellery originated in Kent, and arrived in other regions as gifts.[6] The Desborough necklace with its central cross (Fig. 90) is a testimony of Christian faith. Similarly, a cruciform device on circular brooches, which had begun as a perhaps insignificant development on Kentish disc brooches of the mid-sixth century,[7] becomes very prominent on the composite, polychrome brooches which are the most complex and luxurious manifestation of the inlaid disc brooch type. Perhaps at a time when the practice of providing grave-goods was declining, these brooches were permitted in burials because they displayed the symbol of the new religion so prominently. The decoration of personal possessions with religious emblems can be seen intermittently throughout the rest of the

---

[6] The opinion of my colleague Nick Higham.

[7] Cast disc brooches with garnet inlay probably began with triple designs — three triangular or wedge-shaped garnets, sometimes three subsidiary inlays and corresponding chip-carved ornament. The transformation of the same ingredients — triangular garnets, subsidiary settings and ornament — into a quadruple, symmetrical structure, creates a quincunx design (four round settings and a central boss) which persisted into late Anglo-Saxon jewellery. This quadruple design can be 'read' as cruciform. See Avent, *Anglo-Saxon Garnet and Inlaid Composite Brooches*; R. Bruce-Mitford, 'Late Saxon disc brooches', in R. Bruce-Mitford (ed.), *Aspects of Anglo-Saxon Archaeology* (London, 1974), pp. 303–45.

Anglo-Saxon period.[8]

Among the rare, richly-furnished graves from the eighth century are examples from Winchester, Hampshire[9] and Grave 93 in the (generally earlier) cemetery at Boss Hall, Ipswich, Suffolk, where dress accessories characteristic of the period were buried in a leather pouch at a woman's neck.[10] A few artefacts have been recovered from the Christian graveyard at Whitby, North Yorkshire,[11] which was from 657 to 867 the site of a well-known convent founded under the abbacy of the royal saint, Hild. During this period it is probable that shrouds, which needed no fasteners (apart from, occasionally, a pin or two) replaced clothes as burial attire: there are, for example, no grave-goods from the tenth- and eleventh-century Christian Anglo-Saxon cemetery at Raunds, Northamptonshire. Paganism lingered among the Viking population who were settled in considerable numbers in the north and east of England by the end of the ninth century, though relatively few furnished graves have been found. There is, however, some evidence to suggest that immigrant Viking women wore the traditional costume based on a pair of brooches.

Later archaeological finds are rarely grave-goods. Some have been excavated from dwelling sites, others are stray finds. Archaeology in surviving cities, such as York, Winchester and London, though dependent on external factors, such as building programmes, can offer a narrow but rich slice of urban culture in Anglo-Saxon and Anglo-Viking times. The excavations of Viking York, because of wet conditions, have been particularly productive of organic material, including leather and textile.[12] The debris of industrial workshops, both manufacturing and repair, have yielded discarded and unfinished products which paint a vivid picture of town life.[13]

Abandoned dwelling sites, once identified, may be excavated more freely than those where occupation has continued. Among such discoveries is the Middle Saxon site at Flixborough, possibly an ecclesiastical settlement associated with the royal abbess Etheldreda, who went on to found a convent at Ely;[14] Brandon,

---

[8] It is not a custom confined to jewellery; other metalwork such as the sword hilt may bear religious symbolism.

[9] Grave 23; S. C. Hawkes, 'The Anglo-Saxon necklace from Lower Brook Street', in M. Biddle (ed.), *Winchester Studies*, 7.ii: Object and economy in medieval Winchester, ii (Oxford, 1990), pp. 621–7.

[10] Webster and Backhouse, *Making*, pp. 51–3.

[11] C. R. Peers and C. A. R. Radford, 'The Saxon monastery at Whitby', *Archaeologia*, 89 (1943), pp. 27–88, at pp. 58–9.

[12] P. Walton, *Textiles, Cordage and Raw Fibre from 16–22 Coppergate*, The Archaeology of York, 17.5 (1989); P. Walton Rogers, *Textile Production at 16–22 Coppergate*, The Archaeology of York, 17.11 (1997).

[13] See A. J. Mainman and N. S. H. Rogers, *Craft, Industry and Everyday Life*, The Archaeology of York, 17.14 (2000).

[14] I am grateful to Dr Ben Whitwell and the staff of the former Humberside Archaeological Unit for access to the finds from Flixborough and to unpublished reports. Major finds are discussed briefly and illustrated in Webster and Backhouse, *Making*, pp. 68–101.

which probably also had a monastic element;[15] and the nunnery/
monastery of Barking Abbey.[16] The inhabitants of Middle Saxon
England appear to have been extraordinarily careless about their
possessions, losing pins and strap ends in large quantities; but because these artefacts have not been found on the person we cannot
know if they were clothing fasteners or had some other function.
We can however, identify changes in the style and decoration of
metalwork, particularly the fashion for disc-headed pins, the increase in strap ends and the use of simple safety-pin brooches.

Evidence of art

Our earliest depictions of full-length female figures are on ivory
carvings. The Franks Casket,[17] a whalebone box identified as Northumbrian from its inscription and decorative details, probably made
as a reliquary in the eighth century, is decorated on the top and all
four sides with scenes representing Christian stories, Northern
myths and Roman history. While other early artists depicted mostly
biblical subjects, the Franks Casket carver represented an eclectic
range of *dramatis personae*, apparently dressed in secular costume.
The sculptor's sources are unknown, although he certainly worked
from models; but there are details in his wardrobe which are unlike the costumes of either Late Antique or later Anglo-Saxon work.
Possibly they were taken from life. Several figures are identifiable
as female: the Virgin in the Nativity scene on the right front panel
of the box is too stylised for any deductions about her costume to
be made, but the scene on the left front panel, which represents the
legend of Welund the Smith, well-known from Old English and
Continental literature, clearly depicts Beaduhild, Welund's rape
victim and daughter of his enemy, as well as another female figure.[18] Egil's wife appears in another scene from northern legend on
the casket lid. As I will argue below, there are also female figures on
the right side.

The Genoels-Elderen ivory panels,[19] probably originally book-
covers, dating from the second half of the same century, may also
be Northumbrian work, although this is a contentious issue.[20] The
panels depict religious subjects, the Annunciation of the Angel

[15] Webster and Backhouse, *Making*, pp. 81–8.

[16] Webster and Backhouse, *Making*, pp. 88–94.

[17] J. Beckwith, *Ivory Carvings in Early Medieval England* (London, 1972), pp. 13–18.

[18] The identity of the second figure is uncertain. I assume her to be a servant of
Beaduhild's (she carries a bag like the heroine's servant in the Old English poem
Judith) though she could represent Beaduhild herself approaching Welund's smithy.

[19] Beckwith, *Ivory carvings*, pp. 20–2.

[20] C. L. Neuman de Vegvar, 'The origin of the Genoels-Elderen ivories', *Gesta*,
29 (1990), pp. 8–24 explains the various arguments for the origin of the Diptych: it
has been considered Insular on the grounds of its script, linear style and border
motifs, but Continental affiliations, especially Frankish, have been suggested. The
author argues for a Bavarian origin.

Gabriel to the Virgin Mary, and the Visitation of Mary to her cousin Elisabeth, with attendant figures, possibly servants or other figures from biblical narrative. The costumes of the figures are again not in the classical mould.

There are female figures on early stone sculptures, again mostly Northumbrian, most often representing the Virgin Mary, though other New Testament women are also depicted.[21] Their costume is distinguished from that of male figures and some individual details can be distinguished, though weathering and other damage limit their usefulness as a source.

Literary evidence

The conversion to Christianity brought literacy with it, and, by the end of the seventh century and the beginning of the eighth, men of English birth were recording their history and observations in fluent Latin. Scholars soon began to annotate Latin texts with Old English glosses and to compile Latin–Old English vocabularies from these notes, arranging the material variously, either according to source, to subject matter or to simple alphabetical principles. The oldest extant word-list containing Old English garment names is the Corpus Glossary (Cambridge, Corpus Christi College MS 144), an eighth-century, Mercian text.[22]

The scholars who wrote about clothing, and have thus left us some evidence, only did so secondarily. The primary aim was a scholarly or moral one. We learn from Bede, for example, that it was usual to wear linen, while to wear wool (next to the skin, presumably) was the custom only of the very ascetic, such as the royal abbess St Etheldreda whose sanctity Bede was anxious to demonstrate.[23]

There seems to have been no uniformity about dress for early Anglo-Saxon nuns; many sisters appear to have been far less ascetic than St Etheldreda, failing to appreciate that unworldly clothing should have been a feature of convent life. It seems that many early nuns continued to be over-concerned with clothing, an attitude soon condemned by the Church. At the Council of *Clofeshoh*, held in AD 747, it was decreed that people in Holy Orders should wear simple dress[24] and it was found necessary to state that nuns should undertake occupations more suitable than making fine

---

[21] Sometimes figures are identified by inscriptions, as on the Ruthwell Cross (see the plates in B. Cassidy (ed.), *The Ruthwell Cross: papers from the Colloquium sponsored by the Index of Christian Art, Princeton University 8 December 1989*, Index of Christian Art Occasional Papers 1 (Princeton, 1992)). In other cases identification depends on iconography.

[22] Lindsay, *Corpus Glossary*.

[23] *Historia Ecclesiastica*, IV, 25; Colgrave and Mynors, *Bede*, p. 392.

[24] A. W. Haddan and W. Stubbs (ed.), *Councils and Ecclesiastical Documents relating to Great Britain and Ireland*, 3 vols (Oxford,1869–78), 3 (1878), p. 369.

garments, which was equated with fleshly indulgence.[25] Bede records that the nuns of Coldingham in Northumbria wove and wore elaborate garments, adorning themselves like brides. His witness was a reliable one — a monk who had lived at Coldingham and came to Bede's own monastery after Coldingham was burnt down; a divine retribution, it was thought.[26]

These two criticisms of nuns testify to an interest in clothing and an ability to make it. Nuns' needlework skills were of course in demand for clothing the communities to which they belonged, and some of them must have been trained to embroider and to work with expensive materials for the production of mass vestments. Secular women no doubt had equal or greater interest in clothing, and those employed to make clothes for the rich and royal probably had similar skills, though there is no documentation of it from this period.

Ironically, it was the Church's desire to stamp out sinfully extravagant costume which provoked the only description of women's dress to survive from the Anglo-Saxon period. In the prose version of his *De Virginitate*, a moral work on virginity dedicated to distinguished contemporary nuns,[27] composed towards the end of the seventh century or in the first decade of the eighth, Aldhelm of Malmesbury criticised the elaborate dress of some persons vowed to the religious life:

> subucula bissina, tunica coccinea sive iacintina, capitium et manicae sericis clavatae; galliculae rubricatis pellibus ambiuuntur; antiae frontis et temporum cincinni calamistro crispantur; pulla capitis velamina candidis et coloratis mafortibus cedunt, quae vittarum nexibus assutae talotenus prolixius dependunt.[28]

Aldhelm's Latin is notorious for its convoluted syntax and for the obscurity of its vocabulary, enriched with archaisms, Grecisms and neologisms, features of the much-admired 'hermeneutic style'. Unfortunately this often-quoted passage is ambiguous both in the range of its application and in the meaning of individual words. Students of the Anglo-Saxon period have generally assumed that the entire quotation refers to women's dress; reasonably so, since the entire essay was addressed to women, since the reference to veils seems to point to women and because the passage is the climax of a long peroration against coloured and elaborate clothing for women.

---

[25] Hadden and Stubbs, *Councils*, p. 369.

[26] *Historia Ecclesiastica*, IV, 25; Colgrave and Mynors, *Bede*, pp. 424, 426.

[27] Scott Gwara questions the traditional view that the text was written for the nuns of Barking, Essex, arguing that although the first dedicatee, Hildelith, may have been the abbess of Barking, there is no evidence that the text was designed for such a restricted audience. He suggests that it was directed more widely, to West Saxon and/or Hwiccan abbesses of double (male and female) monasteries; S. Gwara (ed.), *Aldhelmi Malmesbiriensis Prosa de Virginitate*, Corpus Christianorum Series Latina 124, 124A (Turnhout, 2001), 124, pp. 47–55.

[28] *De Virginitate*, LVIII; R. Ehwald (ed.), *Aldhelmi Opera*, Monumenta Germaniae Historica, Auctores Antiquissimi, 15 (Berlin, 1919), p. 318, lines 2–5.

Conversely, in the lines immediately preceding the quotation, Aldhelm has referred to vanity both among persons living the cloistered life and clerics working under a bishop — which must mean men. Logically, then, the description of clothing could include men's as well as women's extravagances, as Michael Lapidge demonstrates in his translation of the prose *De Virginitate*:

> This sort of glamorization for either sex consists in fine linen shirts, in scarlet or blue tunics, in necklines and sleeves embroidered with silk; their shoes are trimmed with red-dyed leather; the hair of their forelocks and the curls at their temples are crimped with a curling-iron; dark-grey veils for the head give way to bright and coloured headdresses, which are sewn with interlacings of ribbons and hang down as far as the ankles.[29]

Presumably men did not wear veils; but the first part of the passage might apply to both sexes, or apply only to men. (The meaning of Latin *subucula* is normally a man's undergarment or shirt.)[30]

Professor Lapidge's readable translation vividly depicts a striking costume; but to accept this as a picture of eighth-century dress without considering other ways of translating Aldhelm's words would be deceptively simplistic. *Capitium* has been translated 'neckline', a use of the word elsewhere confined to ecclesiastical Latin. It can also mean 'a covering for the head'.[31] Lapidge has chosen to translate *rubricatis pellibus* as 'with red-dyed leather' but an interpretation 'red fur(s)' would be equally acceptable. *Vitta* generally means 'a fillet' rather than 'a ribbon'. The interpretations of the colours *iacintinus* and *candidus* are not precisely confined to 'blue' and 'bright' respectively. 'Violet' and 'white' are also possible. Sir David Wilson's interpretation of the same Aldhelm passage is rather different:

> In both sexes this kind of costume consists of an undergarment of the finest cloth, a red or blue tunic, a head-dress and sleeves with silk borders; their shoes are adorned with red-dyed skins; the locks on their temples and foreheads are crimped by the curlers. In the place of dark head coverings they wear white and coloured veils which hang down richly to the feet and are held in place by ribbons sewn on to them.[32]

Both translators have assumed that *galliculae* were some kind of footwear. The word is unusual, but could be an acceptable variant of *caligulae*, 'small boots', or a diminutive of *gallica*, 'a Gallic shoe'.[33]

---

[29] M. Lapidge and M. Herren, trans., *Aldhelm the Prose Works* (Ipswich and Cambridge, 1979), pp. 127–8.

[30] See C. T. Lewis and C. Short (ed.), *A Latin Dictionary* (Oxford, 1897, revised impression 1973): *subucula*.

[31] Lewis and Short, *Latin Dictionary*: *capitium*. Glossators give both interpretations, Latin *mitra* and Old English *hæt*, as well as Old English *heafodsmæl*; Gwara, *Aldhelmi*,124A, p. 734.

[32] D. M. Wilson, *The Anglo-Saxons* (Harmondsworth, revised edition, 1971), p. 94. This rendering is substantially the same as that (by Professor Christopher Hawkes) in Crowfoot and Hawkes, 'Gold braids', pp. 63–74.

[33] See Lewis and Short, *Latin Dictionary*: *gallicula*.

This supposition was made by the late Anglo-Saxon glossator of Aldhelm who rendered *galliculae* with Old English *scos*,[34] as well as the scholars who supplied tenth- and eleventh-century Latin glosses: *calciamenta* and *ficones*.[35] It is possible, however, that Aldhelm, writing some centuries earlier and in a deliberately esoteric style, was not referring to footwear but was employing an obscure word for some kind of garment:[36] a small cloak of Gaulish design suggests itself, for example. If, for the sake of argument, we assume that *galliculae* are not footwear, then *rubricatis pellibus* (which phrase, in any case, is plural) need no longer mean shoe leather or a rather improbable shoe ornament.

If we translate the passage once more, deliberately selecting possible interpretations of the Latin words different from those chosen by Lapidge and Wilson, we could change the picture considerably:

> ... a linen shirt; a scarlet or violet tunic, hooded, and sleeves striped in purple with silks; the [garments] are encircled with dark red furs ... dark-grey veils for the head yield to white and coloured wimples which hang down from the grips of fillets as far as the ankles.

Without wishing in any way to deny the validity of the other translations, aspects of this last picture correspond much better with our evidence than the others. As regards colours, the surviving remains of the clothing worn by the woman with the 'Arnegundis' ring have been described as 'bright red' and 'violet', so we know that the dyes of the Dark Ages produced these effects.[37] We accept that shoes were made of leather, but we have no other evidence that they could be ornamented with fur; yet there are many documented Old English garment-names for clothes made from or trimmed with fur (*basing*, *crusene*, *fel*, *heden*, *loþa*, *pilece*, *rocc*, *sciccels*). *Vittae*, or fillets, are well attested in the Germanic world. Germanic women in Roman and Frankish art wear them, archaeology proves they were aristocratic wear in sixth-century Kent and in sixth- and seventh-century Merovingian Frankia. Literary evidence shows they were worn by Carolingian Franks in the eighth century. Fillets encircling headdresses appear in eleventh-century illuminations and are probably mentioned (as *bindan*) in aristocratic women's wills of the tenth and eleventh centuries. In contrast, the interlacing ribbons of the other translations are unknown, except, possibly, in an eleventh-century picture of Queen Ælfgifu/Emma (Fig. 159). It is fair to say that the wimple, in the later medieval sense of a headdress which concealed the neck as well as the hair, had probably not come into fashion by Aldhelm's lifetime, though the word *wimplum* is used to gloss *mafortibus* more than any other by late

---

[34] Wright/Wülcker, *Vocabularies*, col. 414, line 31.

[35] Gwara, *Aldhelmi*, 124A, p. 734.

[36] Du Cange, *Glossarium mediae et infimae Latinis*: *Gallicula*, gives *calciamenta pastorum* and *signum vestis*.

[37] Werner, 'Frankish royal tombs', p. 212.

Anglo-Saxon glossators of this Alhelm passage,[38] who obviously understood something quite elaborate by the word.

The sleeves which Aldhelm describes probably had coloured borders. This would correspond with the statement of the Langobard historian Paulus Diaconus, that garments with wide, coloured borders were worn (*vestimenta ... hornata institis latioribus vario colore contextis*).[39] The sleeve decoration would have been most luxurious at a time when silk would only have reached England as an import from North Africa or Byzantium. Aldhelm certainly appreciated its exotic nature. He was familiar with silk and its origin; his poems include a riddle on the silk-worm and he mentions silk elsewhere in his writings.[40]

Aldhelm's statement that eighth-century nuns were wearing clothes decorated with silk is supported by evidence that at this time English women were already skilled in the embroidering of ecclesiastical vestments, an art for which the English were later to become internationally famous; three small fragments of gold-thread embroidery from a shrine at Maaseik, Belgium, are now recognised as southern English work of the late-eighth or early-ninth century (see p. 310, below). A piece of silk material now associated with the embroideries, and dated to the same period, is patterned in what has been identified as English taste, with a repeated motif representing King David within a decorated roundel. The nature of the design suggests that Anglo-Saxon women may have been weaving silk at this period (rather than working with imported cloth).[41] If nuns were appropriating the expensive, imported silk threads intended for ecclesiastical vestments, and using their skills as embroideresses or weavers to embellish their own clothes, no wonder Aldhelm raged.

It is clear that the Anglo-Saxons retained their taste for the bright and colourful, which is evidenced from pagan age jewellery; and that this came into conflict with the sobriety of Christian authors, who favoured dark materials and unembellished clothes.

English writers after the event are silent about the change in women's fashions. On the Continent, too, the new style seems taken for granted. Only the comment, in the biography of St Radegund, daughter of the king of Thuringia, that the lady kept her barbaric costume after she had become Queen of the Franks, testifies to the change that had taken place in Frankia by that time (the sixth century).[42]

[38] Variously spelled *Wimplum, wymplum, hwimplum;* Gwara, *Alhelmi*, 124A, p. 736, glosses to lines 13/14. None is earlier than the tenth century. See also p. 220, note 73.

[39] G. Waitz (ed.), *Pauli Historia Langobardorum*, Monumenta Germaniae Historica, Script. Rer. Germ., 48 (Hanover, 1878), p. 155, para 22.

[40] Riddle XII, *Bombix* (Ehwald, *Aldhelmi Opera*, p. 103). Silk is also mentioned in the poetic *De Virginitate*, lines 1146–7 (Ehwald, p. 401) and in Riddles XXXIII, line 4 and C, line 59 (Ehwald, pp. 111, 148).

[41] M. Budny and D. Tweddle, 'The Maaseik embroideries', *Anglo-Saxon England*, 13 (1984), pp. 65–96, at pp. 72–3.

[42] *Vita S. Radegundis*, I, 2; I, 9; B. Krusch (ed.), *De Vita Sanctae Radegundis libri II*, Monumenta Germaniae Historica, Script. rer. Merov., 2 (1888), pp. 358–95, at pp. 365, 368. Cited by Vierck, 'La "Chemise de Sainte-Bathilde"', p. 560, note 71.

Fasteners: brooches, pins and buckles

It is clear that, by the end of the seventh century, the old types of jewellery were no longer being made. Long brooches now gave way to circular. In seventh-century graves we find annular or disc brooches. The annular brooches are of the simpler variety. The majority of our finds have come from cemeteries in the East Midlands, an Anglian area where the annular brooch had been popular in earlier centuries; but examples have been found in other regions too. The seventh-century disc brooches are predominantly a Kentish product, though enough examples have been found in Anglian and Saxon regions to show that the fashion extended outside Kent. The seventh-century brooches, which develop from the simpler Kentish disc brooches of the sixth century, can be extremely opulent. Usually gold, they are of composite construction (made from two or even three discs of metal) and are decorated with garnets set in intricately shaped cloisons (cells) lined with gold foil, arranged in concentric circles round a central boss. Four subsidiary bosses and filigree decoration complete the ornament. The Kingston Brooch (Fig. 91) is our most elaborate example of the type, with more concentric circles than any other, cloisons of great complexity, contrasting colours – two shades of garnet, blue glass and gold – filigree ornament representing serpentine animals and, on the back, a decorated pin catch with an animal- and bird-heads. Some of the brooches also have cruciform designs in cloisonné which, as suggested above (p. 130), may indicate a Christian owner. The 'quincunx' of five bosses can also be 'read' as a Christian cross, or as a representation of the five wounds of Christ. In what is perhaps a fashion of the later examples in the series, cloisonné disc brooches are decorated with more austere arrangements of cells, resembling honeycomb. One effect of this restraint is that the cross design is more prominent.

Fig. 91 Polychrome brooch, Kingston, Kent

The composite gold and garnet cloisonné brooches of the seventh century, unlike their simpler sixth- to early-seventh-century relatives the 'keystone' garnet brooches, do not seem to have been worn in pairs. These elaborate brooches, which were probably all manufactured in the first half of the seventh century,[43] are apparently of individual design and have been found singly, usually at the shoulder, sometimes near the neck, of female skeletons. Many of the annular brooches from this period have also been found singly, although there are a few small pairs (which perhaps had fastened a headdress rather than the old-style gown). Penannular brooches, which are found in a small number of conversion-period graves, may mark a revival of a Romano-British fashion.[44] These too are usually worn singly, though at Winnall, Hampshire, a pair

[43] Geake, *Grave-goods*, p. 33.
[44] Geake, *Grave-goods*, pp. 54, 122.

of small brooches was found at the shoulders of a skeleton and may, again, have fastened a veil.[45] Even these circular brooches seem to have become redundant during the seventh century; some conversion-period cemeteries have yielded no brooches at all. We might be tempted to attribute this decrease entirely to the general decline in the practice of furnishing graves, were it not for the fact that old brooches were being re-used as toys, trinkets and chatelaine rings. A pendant found at Winnall had been made from the central piece of a composite cloisonné brooch.[46] The brooch must either have broken beyond repair, or been considered out of date. A brooch found in a bag with cruciform-decorated pendants in the eighth-century grave at Boss Hall indicates that even where the garnet disc brooch survived there was a loss of artistic finesse; this brooch retains the quincunx/cruciform design, but the sharply defined cloisons and filigree of the earlier period have been replaced with an all-over coverage of indeterminately-shaped cells (Fig. 92).[47]

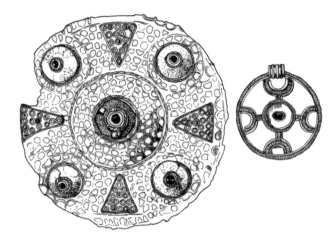

Fig. 92 Brooch and pendant, Boss Hall, Ipswich, Suffolk

Though evidence of circular brooches is sparse for the eighth century, there are a number of examples from the ninth century and later. They retain the basic layout of five bosses forming a cruciform shape,[48] but cloisonné and geometric ornament is replaced by lively animal ornament in the so-called Trewhiddle Style.[49] The finest examples, such as the Fuller Brooch (diameter 11.4 cm; Fig. 133)

---

[45] Grave 8; there were linked pins in the same grave; Meaney and Hawkes, *Winnall*, p. 36.

[46] Grave 5; Meaney and Hawkes, *Winnall*, pp. 39–42. Hawkes considered that the brooch was made in the second quarter of the seventh century, and that the pendant, which was worn alone until it was damaged, was buried 'at a date well on in the second half of the century'.

[47] Webster and Backhouse, *Making*, pp. 51–3.

[48] Bruce-Mitford, 'Late Saxon disc brooches'.

[49] The name is based on the decoration on some of the pieces in a hoard of silver from Trewhiddle, Cornwall. The hoard does not include jewellery.

are of silver, with inlaid niello or openwork providing contrast. The spectacular Strickland Brooch (diameter 11.2 cm) has gold plates and animals with blue glass eyes; and others, such as a brooch from Colchester, Essex, and one from Pentney, Norfolk, have brightly coloured enamelling. There is now a considerable corpus of late Saxon silver disc brooches, thanks to the discovery of a hoard of six in the churchyard at Pentney.[50] The Pentney collection includes two near-pairs of brooches (identical in layout but not in detail) but we have no evidence as to whether they were worn in pairs. All the Pentney brooches have cruciform designs, though the cross is more obvious in some than in others. There are smaller silver brooches without the cruciform design, an eighth-century, gilded example from Flixborough (3.0 cm)[51] and a ninth-century nielloed example from near Barrington (5.3 cm)[52] exhibiting animal and animal-plus-plant ornament, respectively. There are also ninth-century brooches of base metal; a copper alloy example from Leicester has a cruciform design and incised animal ornament;[53] others are plain. Nummular brooches, which incorporated coins, or casts of coins, seem to have been popular. From the late-ninth century the workshops of York were producing dress accessories in pewter and lead.[54] As with all of the brooches which have been found outside the context of burials, we do not know if these circular brooches were worn by men or women, or both. However, two circular ornaments dated to the tenth and eleventh centuries, respectively, on grounds of style, the later one certainly a brooch, are identified by inscriptions as the property of women (see pp. 205, 208), so presumably others were also.

Simple bow brooches which resemble modern safety pins in shape (Fig. 120) seem to have been a seventh-century innovation for the Anglo-Saxons though the bow brooch was an established Roman type. A pair of them, made of silver, were found at Kingston in the same grave as the magnificent Kingston Brooch (Grave 205). They were near the legs of the skeleton and had perhaps been used in this instance to pin the burial wrap over the woman's body; or they might have been contained in a box.[55] Other brooches of this kind have been found, usually singly, in a few other seventh-century graves.[56] Geake questions whether these were actually worn

---

[50] The brooches were discovered in 1977 but it was some years before their significance was recognised. They are described in detail in Webster and Backhouse, *Making*, pp. 229–31.

[51] Webster and Backhouse, *Making*, p. 96.

[52] Webster and Backhouse, *Making*, pp. 232–3.

[53] Webster and Backhouse, *Making*, pp. 228–9.

[54] Mainman and Rogers, *Craft, Industry and Everyday Life*, pp. 2478–9.

[55] Geake, *Grave-goods*, p. 55.

[56] Webster and Backhouse, *Making*, pp. 50–1 mention examples from Shudy Camps, Cambridgeshire, Uncleby, Yorkshire and Whitby, North Yorkshire, citing R. White, *Roman and Celtic Objects from Anglo-Saxon Graves*, British Archaeological Reports, British Series, 191 (1988), pp. 40–1. Geake (*Grave-goods*, p. 55) notes that there were five such brooches contained in the pouch in the bed burial at Swallowcliffe Down, Wiltshire (Speake, *Bed Burial*).

'as brooches' since all the examples from graves were, or might have been, contained in bags or boxes, and since unlike Roman bow brooches, the Anglo-Saxon safety pins are designed to lie flat. She suggests a more utilitarian function.[57]

Straight pins continued to be used in the seventh century, both on the body and on the head, and the many finds of pins from settlement sites from the eighth century onwards suggest that they were in use throughout the period. The seventh century, however, saw developments in technique and artistry which briefly brought the pin into prominence as a luxury decorative item of dress. Some pins were made of silver or gold. Seamus Ross notes that seventh-century pins are often composite, partly cast (as earlier Anglo-Saxon pins had been), but partly the product of the jeweller's art, with filigree work, inlaid garnets and gold foil. There is also a high level of individuality in the pins of the seventh century, which reflects the creativity and eclecticism of the conversion period in general.

In what may have been a continuation of the fashion of the lady in Finglesham Grave 203 (above, p. 102) matching pairs of pins, made of precious metals, appear in a few female graves.[60] Perhaps they were joined together by some organic substance which has now disappeared, for sets of linked pins (Fig. 93) clearly became fashionable in the seventh century and continued in use in the eighth.[61] The seventh-century 'pin suites' normally consisted of two pins, usually of precious metal, their heads usually ornamented with garnets, and linked by a chain. There is a more elaborate triple example from Roundway Down, Wiltshire, in which two garnet-headed pins flank a roundel set with blue glass placed at the centre of the chain. Another triple suite, now incomplete, was found in the nineteenth century in a grave at Little Hampton, near Evesham, Worcestershire. This consisted of triangular-headed pins and a central pendant of gold and garnet.[62] 'Pin suites' are exclusively female jewellery and have been found in the graves of both adults and children. They appear to have been worn at the neck. They are dainty little things; the pins are only about 4 cm long and they could only have fastened light fabrics. When pins which had been originally linked became separated they evidently

Fig. 93 Pin suite, Winnall, Winchester, Hampshire

[57] Geake, *Grave-goods*, p. 55.

[58] Ross, 'Dress Pins', pp. 147–8.

[59] Ross, 'Dress Pins', p. 149. Geake, *Grave-goods*, pp. 66–7, 115 notes the Roman associations of spiral headed pins, a post-conversion 'type', suggesting that some of those in Anglo-Saxon graves may be of Romano-British origin.

[60] Ozanne, 'Peak dwellers', p. 28; Hyslop, 'Chamberlain's Barn', p. 198; Meaney and Hawkes, *Winnall*, p. 47. Geake, *Grave-goods*, p. 112, while noting the precedent of the Finglesham pins, argues that linked pins are unusual in Germanic costume and points to Byzantine and Roman linked pins and Romano-British linked brooches as possible inspiration.

[61] There are examples at Lechlade and Castledyke, cemeteries which continued in use well into the Christian period, and from settlement sites: Southampton and London, late-seventh- to eighth-century, and Flixborough eighth-century.

[62] Ross, 'Dress Pins', pp. 249–50.

Fig. 94 Pin, Brandon, Suffolk

Fig. 95 Pin, Flixborough, North Lincolnshire

continued to be used individually.[63] Single pins with looped heads, which have also been found in conversion-period cemeteries, may once have been fastened to others. The fashion for linked pins was taken up by the non-luxury market, attested by an eighth-century, copper alloy example from Fishergate, York.[64]

Seamus Ross observes that Middle and Late Saxon pins lack the craftsmanship of the seventh-century ones: they are poorly cast, rarely in precious metals, and have been considerably finished and decorated in the post-casting stages of manufacture.[65] Disc-headed pins which sometimes have chip-carved zoomorphic decoration (Fig. 94) and/or cruciform designs, came into fashion in the eighth century, but do not seem to have persisted beyond it. The holes in many of them suggest that they once belonged to linked suites; an example from Flixborough still has a length of chain attached to it[66] and a near-identical pair with a cruciform design from a ninth-century hoard found at Talnotrie, Dumfries and Galloway, Scotland, were 'originally linked'.[67] It may be that they represent a continuation of the seventh-century fashion though the pins are more substantial than in the earlier suites; but as none of the disc-headed pins are cemetery-finds we cannot be sure of their function. There is a unique suite of three disc-headed pins, found in the River Witham in Lincolnshire, which is perhaps a stylistic descendant of the Roundway Down and Little Hampton types, though one of the Witham pins is dissimilar from the others and might have been an addition.[68] There are other flat-headed pins also, in trianglar or subtriangular designs[69] (Fig. 95), other individual shapes, and simple pairs of spirals in a heart shape (Fig. 96). Scholars who handle these flat pins agree that they were almost certainly worn on the body rather than the head. Indeed, the gilded and chip-carved head of the pin from Brandon, which is 3.6 cm in diameter and decorated in a zoomorphic and cruciform design (Fig. 94) would have resembled a disc brooch when fastened in place. Many other pins have small spherical heads, plain or decorated with simple geometric ornament. These are thought to be more suitable for securing

[63] E.g. Castledyke Grave 15; Drinkall and Foreman *Castledyke*, p. 38. See also S. Ross on linked pins in Drinkall and Foreman, pp. 267–70.

[64] Mainman and Rogers, *Craft, Industry and Everyday Life*, p. 2578.

[65] Ross, 'Dress Pins', p. 148.

[66] Webster and Backhouse, *Making*, pp. 97–8.

[67] Webster and Backhouse, *Making*, p. 273. Illustrated on p. 274.

[68] D. M. Wilson, *Anglo-Saxon Ornamental Metalwork 700–1100 in the British Museum*, (London, 1964), pp. 132–4; for single pins see e.g. M. Kitson Clark, 'Late Saxon pin-heads from Roos, East Yorkshire and South Ferriby, Lincolnshire, now in the collections at Hull', *Proceedings of the Leeds Philosophical and Literary Society*, 5 (1942), pp. 333–8; R. J. Cramp, 'An Anglo-Saxon pin from Birdoswald', *Transactions of the Cumberland and Westmorland Antiquarian and Archaeological Society*, 2nd series, 65 (1964), pp. 90–3; R. N. Bailey, 'An Anglo-Saxon pin-head from Pontefract', *Yorkshire Archaeological Journal*, 42 (1967–70), pp. 405–6.

[69] In shape these resemble the styli which were used for writing on wax tablets; the heads were used for erasing. However, styli are usually longer than pins (styli *c.* 14 cm, pins 4.5–8 cm) and their heads generally lack decoration.

the headdress. Seamus Ross notes that four, ball-headed, silver pins from Barking Abbey have gilding which covers the pin-head but only extends a short way down the shaft (about 2 mm) suggesting that the rest of the pin would not have been seen, perhaps being buried in a headdress.[70]

Exacavators of some seventh-century cemeteries have noticed that buckles were particularly small, suggesting that belts were narrower than before. Statistics are limited because of the sharp decline in the practice of furnishing graves at this time, but buckled belts appear to have been less popular with women than with men in some settlements. In contrast, eye-catching belts continued to be worn in some areas of Kent. The triangular buckle popular in both Frankia and Kent continued in use from the sixth to the first half of the seventh century; it was predominantly a male fashion but has been found in a few female graves.[71] A new style with a perforated rectangular plate occurs in the later-seventh and eighth centuries (Fig. 97).[72] The perforations were sometimes designed in such a way that a cruciform pattern was made. A coloured girdle would show through the holes in the metal, giving an effect like polychrome jewellery.

Fig. 96 Pin, Flixborough, North Lincolnshire

Ornamental jewellery

The festoon of beads, which was usually suspended from shoulder brooches of fifth- and sixth-century women, had, like the shoulder brooches themselves, largely disappeared by the seventh century. Beads do not usually occur in large quantities in seventh-century graves. Often a single bead, or a group of three or four only, is found at the neck of a skeleton. The popularity of amber had peaked in the sixth century; possibly the supply had dried up by the seventh, when just one or two amber beads were occasionally worn, not as part of a necklace, perhaps as amulets.[73] Now, on the whole, the simpler beads were of glass. Amethyst had increased in use, appearing mostly as beads. Possibly the barrel- or drop-shaped amethyst stones were recycled Roman ornaments, but if so, Anglo-Saxon women changed their function, wearing them strung lengthwise with other beads, not dangling down, except in rare cases when they were mounted *en cabochon* as pendants. Shell beads, which have been found in Kent, Oxfordshire and Somerset, were a seventh-century innovation. Beads of gold and silver have often been found at conversion-period sites.

[70] Ross, 'Dress Pins', p. 124.
[71] Geake, *Grave-goods*, p. 77.
[72] Dating from Geake, *Grave-goods*, p. 70. Geake suggests Romano-British associations for this buckle type.
[73] Geake, *Grave-goods*, pp. 47, 112.

Fig. 97 Buckle with perforated plate, Sibertswold, Kent

Fig. 98 Elaborate cloak and jewellery worn by the Empress Theodora from a mosaic in the Basilica of S. Vitale, Ravenna, Italy

The most striking feature of seventh- and eighth-century necklaces is the use of pendants. This was a Frankish fashion, copied from Byzantine models, ultimately Roman in origin. The Empress Theodora, on a mosaic in the church of San Vitale, Ravenna (Fig. 98) wears an elaborate jewelled collar round her shoulders, fringed with drop-shaped pendants, as well as a string of jewels above it, round her neck. One of the ladies of her court wears a similar collar (Fig. 99). Jewelled collars with *pendilia* are worn by female figures personifying Constantinople and Rome, as well as by the Empress Ariadne on a sixth-century Byzantine consular diptych which was in use in Italy in the eighth century.[74] The collars were almost certainly a symbol of rank, both in the Byzantine world and the Merovingian, where amber and amethyst drops set in gold frames imitated the Byzantine. They are worn by brides depicted on fourth-century Byzantine ceramics.[75] The jewelled collar and tighter jewelled necklet were imitated in embroidery on the funeral garment still preserved in Chelles, France, and associated with St Bathilde, a seventh-century woman of Anglo-Saxon birth whose career took her from slavery, via marriage with the Merovingian King Clovis II, to the convent at Chelles.[76] The detailed copying of the jewels in embroidery suggests that they represented Bathilde's royal status.

The most sumptuous imitation of the Byzantine style in England took the form of pendant *bullae*, usually consisting of garnet[77] carbuncles (occasionally amethyst) set in metal frames, but also utilising other stones and sometimes discs of metal. The pendants can occur singly, or in simple arrangements, but in their most elaborate form are grouped into necklaces with beads made of gold or silver wire. Outstandingly rich examples of necklaces have been found at Desborough (Fig. 90) and at Cow Lowe, Derbyshire, though Kent, generally, has been the area most productive of *bullae* and may have been the source of supply to other areas.

Wire rings had sometimes been worn in association with beads in the pagan period, but they are recurrent in seventh-century burial sites throughout England and can be considered characteristic of the conversion period. Beads were either threaded on the rings, or, having been found inside the rings, were presumably hung across them on string. The arrangement could vary in number from a single bead strung on one ring to an elaborate festoon of them (Fig. 100). Possibly these arrangements imitated the pendant *bullae* worn by more prosperous women, though wearing *bullae* did not preclude wearing ring-and-bead ornaments as well.

Fig. 99 Elaborate dress and necklace worn by a member of the Empress Theodora's court from a mosaic in the Basilica of S. Vitale, Ravenna, Italy

[74] The Clementinus Diptych; D. Buckton (ed.), *Byzantium: treasures of Byzantine art and culture* (London, 1994), pp. 71–2.

[75] Buckton, *Byzantium*, pp. 31–2.

[76] Vierck, 'La "Chemise de Sainte-Bathilde"'.

[77] The appearance of large garnets for the first time in England suggests a different source: the garnets found in cloisonné jewellery may have come from Central Europe, but the larger garnets may have come from further East, the Black Sea area or Asia, via Mediterranean trade; Geake, *Grave-goods*, p. 110.

Fig. 100 Reconstruction of a ring and bead necklace, based on grave-goods from Winnall, Winchester, Hampshire

A late-seventh-century female burial excavated from Lower Brook Street, Winchester, provided the opportunity for examination of an elaborate necklace that had suffered little disturbance.[78] The young woman wore as many as thirty rings of silver wire, two strung with beads, six assorted *bullae* and a gold ring, which together formed a collar encircling the neck, resting on the clavicles of the skeleton and perhaps originally stitched to the woman's garment. A further dozen tiny beads, found scattered round the neck, had perhaps formed a tight-fitting necklet in the Byzantine style, as worn by two of Theodora's attendants in the Ravenna mosaic.

The cross pendant on the Desborough necklace (Fig. 90) demonstrates conclusively that the collars with *bullae* with or without crosses (and all the other grave-goods associated with them) belong to the Christian period.[79] There was obviously a tradition that this type of neck ornament might be used to suspend a cross: pectoral crosses have been found attached to jewelled collars of the sixth and seventh centuries in Bulgaria and Hungary, and a jewelled cross of Byzantine type is depicted as if suspended from the collar embroidered on the Bathilde garment.[80] In England, however, most *bullae* are not associated with crosses. Conversely, little crosses, generally smaller and simpler than the Continental parallels, have been found in isolation. A gold and garnet example, now known as the Holderness Cross (Fig. 101) finally came to light in 1998, having been kept in a kitchen drawer for thirty years. Its finder, a Yorkshire farmer, had originally spotted it glinting as he walked across his yard after rain.[81] Another magnificent example in gold and garnet cloisonné, found at Ixworth, Suffolk, may have been worn by a woman.[82]

Fig. 101 The Holderness Cross, Ashmolean Museum, Oxford

[78] Hawkes, 'The Anglo-Saxon necklace', in Biddle, *Winchester Studies*, 7.ii, ii, pp. 621–7.

[79] Meaney and Hawkes, *Winnall*, pp. 37, 47, 54.

[80] Vierck, 'La "Chemise de Sainte-Bathilde"', p. 525.

[81] The cross was found at Burton Pidsea, a parish in which an Anglo-Saxon cemetery was identified in the early-nineteenth century. A. MacGregor, 'A seventh-century pectoral cross from Holderness, East Yorkshire', *Medieval Archaeology*, 44 (2000), pp. 217–22.

[82] J. Warren, Untitled, *Journal of the British Archaeological Association*, 1st series, 27 (1871), pp. 258–9. The association with a grave containing a cloisonné brooch cannot be taken as certain.

The bracteate pendants which had been popular in the pagan period continued to be worn, but were often overtly Christian now. Previously, pendants made from Roman coins, or imitations of them, had often borne a human head; now Liudhard, the bishop who was chaplain to Bertha, Queen of Kent, was depicted and named on a gold pendant found in Canterbury.[83] Bracteates now often displayed the Christian cross, depicted in repoussé or filigree, sometimes with a central cloison filled with garnet or glass. This fashion continued into the eighth century: the jewellery buried with the Christian-period woman from Boss Hall included four gold pendants, three of which had cruciform designs (Fig. 92).[84]

Anglo-Saxon women still continued to acquire antiquities and hang them on their necklaces. Roman coins were popular; an enamelled Celtic disc from Camerton, Bath and North East Somerset, may have been treasured for its cross motif.[85] The occasional practice of hanging animals' teeth on the necklace may reflect a continued belief in folk-remedies: they may have been a cure for toothache (see above, p. 88), or an attempt to absorb some of the qualities of the animal the teeth had belonged to. In particular the beaver's tooth, perforated for suspension or mounted in metal, appears in the seventh century.

The jewelled earrings of Byzantine and Merovingian fashion remain absent from England, as do the jewelled bracelets which appear on Ravenna mosaics. Archaeological evidence suggests that bracelets never became really popular with Anglo-Saxon women — only a few metal examples are known from the period — although perhaps more favoured by adult women than in the earlier period, when they are mostly found with children.[86] They often appear in Viking hoards, however. Female figures on the Genoels-Elderen Diptych (Fig. 110) have bands round their arms, some decorated with dots which may represent jewels, some plain, but in every case this could be a braided or embroidered sleeve edging, particularly since the ornamentation is symmetrical, on both arms. It could, of course, be no more than decoration on the carving.

Finger rings do not seem to have been either popular or elaborate in the seventh and eighth centuries but from the ninth century seem to have enjoyed a limited revival. The Winchester excavations have produced a series of rather plain examples which Hinton suggests were the 'normal everyday fashions': of the metal rings there were none of gold, only one silver, the rest copper alloy. There are also examples made of bone, dating from the ninth century onwards.[87] Judging from their size, if they have been identified

---

[83] Webster and Backhouse, *Making*, p. 23, Fig. 5b.
[84] Webster and Backhouse, *Making*, pp. 51–3.
[85] Anon., 'Celtic discs of enamel', *Antiquaries Journal*, 10 (1930), pp. 53–4.
[86] Geake, *Grave-goods*, p. 56.
[87] M. Biddle, 'Unidentified bone objects', in Biddle, *Winchester Studies*, 7.ii, ii, pp. 1129–45, at pp. 1132–3.

correctly, some of the metal rings were so large they could have been worn on the thumb, or over a glove; others were of such small diameter they might have been worn on the end finger joint.[88] In contrast to these unpretentious rings, there are a number of late Anglo-Saxon examples, mostly stray finds, of more precious materials and sophisticated appearance.[89] Usually of gold or of silver, they vary considerably in shape, including hoops and rings with flat bezels. Some have animal decoration in Trewhiddle Style and some of them also have plant ornament of characteristic ninth-century type. Many of these rings have no gender associations, though small size may suggest female ownership and occasional naming inscriptions associate rings with women. Two fairly simple hoops are engraved, respectively *Bvredrvð*[90] and *Eawen mie ah* 'Eawen owns me'.[91] *EAÐELSVIÐ REG[I]NA*, the name and title of Ethelswith (853–88), Queen of Mercia and the sister of Alfred, King of Wessex, is engraved inside a ring (Fig. 102), but we do not know if the queen was the owner or the donor. At 2.6 cm the diameter of the hoop of the ring is rather large for a woman's finger, though it might have been worn on the thumb. Ethelswith, like many Anglo-Saxon royals, was very pious — she died on pilgrimage to Rome — and this ring which she owned, or bestowed, reflects her Christian faith: the niello-inlaid animal which decorates its bezel is the *Agnus Dei*, the 'Lamb of God.'[92]

Fig. 102 a and b Finger ring inscribed with the name of Queen Ethelswith of Mercia, British Museum, London

The 'Byzantine' fashion

The seventh-century polychrome brooches, the jewelled collars, and probably the pin suites, belong to a modified version of Byzantine dress, which may have been transmitted *via* Frankia but which may also have owed something to the religious works of art of Mediterranean origin which were coming to England under the influence of Christianity. The great brooches probably fastened flowing cloaks modelled on the kind of mantle worn by the Empress Theodora on the Ravenna mosaic (Fig. 98) but more usually a garment of men in Byzantine art. The ladies of Theodora's court, in the same scene

[88] D. A. Hinton, 'Metal finger-rings', in Biddle, *Winchester Studies*, 7.ii, ii, pp. 646–52 esp. pp. 646–7.

[89] C. C. Oman, 'Anglo-Saxon finger-rings', *Apollo*, 14 (1931), pp. 104–8; Webster and Backhouse, *Making*, pp. 236–8.

[90] A feminine personal name according to R. I. Page, 'The Inscriptions', Appendix A to Wilson, *Ornamental Metalwork*, pp. 67–90, at p. 83. The ring was found at Swindon, Wiltshire. It has a diameter of 2.1 cm; Wilson, *Ornamental Metalwork* No. 95, p. 178.

[91] A name not otherwise recorded according to Page, 'The Inscriptions' p. 90, but assumed to be a woman's name in C. Fell, *Women in Anglo-Saxon England; and the impact of 1066* by C. Clark and E. Williams (London, 1984), p. 94 and Fig. 32. It also names St Peter in Latin. At 2.8 cm (Wilson, *Ornamental Metalwork*, No. 145, pp. 205–6) it is large for a woman.

[92] Backhouse, Turner and Webster, *Golden Age*, p. 30.

Fig. 103 Beaduhild and another female figure, Franks Casket, British Museum, London

Fig. 104 Hooded figures, Franks Casket

Fig. 105 Centrally fastened cloak on a servant from the ivory Genoels-Elderen Diptych, *Musées Royaux d'Art et d'Histoire*, Brussels, Belgium

(Fig. 99) wear shorter wraps, more like shawls, obviously of rich material, which do not have a brooch fastener. Perhaps the Anglo-Saxon ladies possessing the characteristic necklaces but without brooches were wearing something like this. The Byzantine dress, in each case, has a neckline just below the close-fitting necklet, but the jewelled collar is worn over the outer garment.

The English ladies almost certainly wore a headdress which concealed the ears, and which was open at the throat, revealing the jewellery. It probably took the form of a light veil, and was secured to the shoulders of the the cloak or shawl by the matching pins.[93] We know that very fine material could be woven for veils from the Oseberg, Norway, ship burial, which was deposited in 834:[94] one of the women buried there, probably a queen, had worn a veil of fine linen resembling gauze. Another woman, perhaps her attendant, wore a veil of fine, white wool.[95]

The open-fronted cloak

Aldhelm's omission of brooches in his description of women's dress is surely significant. It may be taken in connection with the fact that though the polychrome brooches of the conversion period are the most magnificent the Anglo-Saxon period has produced, they were relatively rare, and many more female graves of the seventh century have been found without brooches than with them. Yet the disc brooch certainly continued in use in the eighth century and evidently flourished in the ninth and beyond. The explanation for this apparent contradiction may lie in a cloak which opened down the front, and which could, but need not, be clasped by a brooch.

[93] Our strongest indication of the use of these pins comes from the record of the excavation of Grave 39 at Leighton Buzzard, Bedfordshire, which states that the pins were found lying vertically on either side of the skeleton's neck, linked by the chain. The pin suite lay between two layers of textile, which it had fastened together. The outer fabric was the coarser, and was interpreted as the remains of 'either a shroud or a cloak'. An elaborate necklace of rings and beads lay between the layers of textile. The experienced archaeologist E. T. Leeds, considering the evidence of F. G. Gurney, the excavator, suggested that the pins had fastened down a veil (F. G. Gurney, 'A pagan Saxon burial ground at Leighton Buzzard', *Bedfordshire Archaeologist*, 1 (1956), pp. 120–32). The textile from the Leighton Buzzard grave has never been analysed and apparently no longer exists, but the function of the pins was reconsidered when the site was published by Miranda Hyslop, and the suggestion of a veil was rejected: 'it was clear that the pins had been used to fasten a cloak or outer garment to the dress underneath it … no textile remains were found in the region of the skull' (Hyslop, 'Two Anglo-Saxon cemeteries', pp. 161–200). It would be rare, however, to find textile in association with bone unless it were attached to metalwork, and the absence of cloth from this area does not seem sufficient evidence to reject Leeds's suggestion.

[94] Dated by dendrochronology; A. H. Krag, 'Dress and power in prehistoric Scandinavia c.550–1050 A.D.', in L. Bender Jørgensen and C. Rinaldo (ed.), *Textiles in European Archaeology*, *NESAT VI* (Gothenburg, 1998), pp. 125–30, at p. 126.

[95] A. S. Ingstad, 'The functional textiles from the Oseberg ship', in Bender Jørgensen and Tidow, *NESAT I*, pp. 85–96, at p. 94.

The earliest depictions we have of such a garment are on the Franks Casket. On the left-hand side of the casket front are Beaduhild, soon to become Welund's victim, and a second female figure, who wears a voluminous hooded cloak which requires no fastener but is drawn together by her clasped arms, outside which it falls in the many folds characteristic of this carver's work. Beaduhild could be wearing a similar garment (although the hood is not clear) which flows back from her shoulders. Both cloaks are longish (knee- or calf-length), but do not reach down as far as the ankle (Fig. 103).

Fig. 106 Hooded cloak without brooch, Stuttgart Psalter, Germany, *Wuertembergische Landesmuseum* MS Biblia folio 23, fol. 72v

There is a group of three figures on the panel which originally formed the right side of the casket, in a scene which has not been identified. Their costume is neither that of secular males nor the usual 'biblical' costume of Christ and the saints, and resembles the costume of Beaduhild and her attendant closely enough for us to suppose that these figures too are intended to be female;[96] although it seems possible that the sculptor was copying a Roman carving of *Genii Cucullati*, hooded male figures which often appear in groups of three, a motif found in the region of the Roman Hadrian's Wall (which runs through what was Anglo-Saxon Northumbria), perhaps mistaking them for Mother Goddesses which also often appear in groups of three on Roman sculptures.[97] The three figures wear hooded cloaks (Fig. 104), the central one possibly with a brooch, the others without fasteners. The hoods of the two profile figures are pointed, unlike the hoods of figures on the right side and Egil's wife on the casket lid.

Fig. 107 Hooded cloak with brooch, Stuttgart Psalter, fol. 94v

Hayo Vierck recognised a similar cloak, clasped by a circular brooch and without a hood, on an attendant figure on the Genoels-Elderen Diptych (Fig. 105) and noted that the garment is worn by adult and juvenile females in the *Stuttgart Psalter*,[98] an eighth-century manuscript which was produced on the Continent, probably in the monastery of Echternach which was founded by the English missionary Willibrord.[99] There are several depictions of this kind of cloak in the *Psalter*. Sometimes it is drawn over the head into a hood (Figs 106, 107), sometimes it rests on the shoulders, when it is worn with a variety of headdresses: crown (Fig. 108), veil and fillet. It is usually clasped at the centre of the chest by a circular brooch (Figs 107, 108) but sometimes has no fastener (Fig. 106) It is calf- or knee-length, exposing the longer gown beneath it.

[96] It is important to recognise this gender distinction in the costume of the Franks Casket. James E. Anderson (in an unpublished conference paper) considered that the three figures on the right side represent male saints. I note below the resemblance to figures in Northumbrian Roman art; but whatever the significance of the model, I suggest that the Anglo-Saxon artist intended the figures to represent women.

[97] See H. R. Ellis Davidson, *Myths and Symbols in Pagan Europe* (Manchester, 1988), pp. 108–9 and Fig. 3.

[98] H. Vierck, 'Zur angelsachsischen Frauentracht', in Ahrens, *Sachsen und Angelsachsen*, pp. 255–62, at pp. 255, 258. Abb.12. Vierck calls this cloak *palla*, which is a Latin name for a long cloak worn by Roman women.

[99] Webster and Backhouse, *Making*, pp. 159, 162.

Fig. 108 Cloak with central brooch and crown, Stuttgart Psalter, fol. 57v

Fig. 109 The Virgin Mary at the Annunciation, Genoels-Elderen Diptych

This cloak was not the simple rectangle, which, I have suggested, may have been worn in earlier centuries. There was almost certainly some shaping to allow for the shoulders and the fullness that could be pulled over the head, or pushed back like a collar. As regards the name of this cloak, I can only suggest tentatively that it may have been *hacele*.[100]

The chasuble-shaped cloak

The figure of the Virgin Mary, in the Annunciation scene which occupies the upper register of the Genoels-Elderen Diptych, wears a garment which covers her head then hangs down the front of the body like a chasuble or poncho and is lifted by her raised arms (Fig. 109). It is possible that this was taken directly from a Continental model, probably Late Antique, and does not represent Anglo-Saxon dress in any way. It is a style which will reappear on figures of religious women in later Anglo-Saxon art.

The gown

The disappearance of paired brooches and wrist clasps by the seventh century suggests that the tubular *peplos*-type gown, worn over a tight-sleeved blouse or tunic, was replaced by some other costume round about the time of the conversion. Perhaps the tunic, originally an undergarment, replaced the *peplos* as the main garment for women; or perhaps the traditional dress, with its North European, pagan associations, was replaced by a costume of Frankish or even Italian type, since cultural influences from these regions were coming into England with the religious traffic.

Assuming that Aldhelm was including women's dress when he mentioned the *tunica* (above, p. 134) it was probably the new gown that he was describing. It was brightly coloured and probably woven of woollen cloth. However, since Aldhelm mentions silken decoration on the sleeves (the Latin term *clavate* signified a purple stripe), there was perhaps a band of silk, or embroidery worked in silken thread, on the more luxurious robes. The only possible depictions in English or Anglo-Saxon-influenced art are on the Genoels-Elderen Diptych. There the embracing figures of Mary and Elisabeth (Fig. 110) wear girdled gowns with many longitudinal folds or pleats at the front, decoration down both sides and a smooth, unpleated back. It is possible to interpret this costume as an open overdress, with decorated edges, over a pleated underdress. A figure

Fig. 110 Mary and Elisabeth, Genoels-Elderen Diptych

[100] There is an Icelandic cognate *hekla*, 'a hooded garment' (see Bosworth/Toller, *Dictionary*, p. 497), and evidence from an account of the martyrdom of St Pelagia that the *hacele* could be worn by a woman; G. Herzfeld, *An Old English Martyrology*, Early English Text Society, original series 116 (1900), p. 192, line 1.

in the panel above, presumably a servant, wears the girdled garment with similar folds at the front and a smooth back, but lacks the decorative panels. All these gowns may have a short, tight sleeve, edged by a band, over a long, tight sleeve with, in the cases of Mary and Elisabeth, three decorated bands; or there may be a band which is purely decoration at the upper arm of a single, long sleeve. It is not possible to draw any conclusions about the nature of the decoration on the clothing from this depiction. The ivory, even if it was once coloured, is now monochrome, and the style of the decorative panels, a row of pellets, is fairly standard: it is used on Mary's seat, a curtain and the costume of the angel Gabriel elsewhere on the same Diptych, and can be found on other, Continental ivories.

The gown is not visible on the Franks Casket, but gowns are very much in evidence in the *Stuttgart Psalter*, both showing beneath the cloak and at the aperture (Figs 106–8) and being worn without the covering cloak (Fig. 111). They are ankle-length and have fairly wide sleeves, reaching to about the elbow, revealing the tighter sleeves of the undergarment. Wide bands of ornament decorate hem, front and neckline, in a manner that was to be popular in tenth-century Ottonian art on the Continent, though it is not characteristic of Anglo-Saxon work. There are no visible fasteners for these gowns. Presumably they were put on over the head.

It was perhaps in the seventh or eighth centuries that the Old English word *cyrtel*, originally meaning a short garment, came to be applied to a woman's long gown. The semantic change may have come about with the abandonment of the *peplos*-type gown. We might speculate that if the *peplos* originally covered an undergarment that was short, that may have been called *cyrtel*, but that if the former undergarment took over the role of the *peplos* as the main gown, it may have been worn longer and the origin of the name forgotten. Alternatively, if, as the evidence of Wakerley suggests (p. 38) the undergown was long, it may have been the *peplos* itself that was short and was called *cyrtel*. The garment that took its place, either the original undergarment or a new Continental one, may have taken over the established name for a woman's outer gown.

In addition, the Latin loan-word *tunica* was borrowed into English as *tunece* after the conversion to Christianity, and, on the evidence of late Anglo-Saxon wills, was used of a woman's gown as well as a man's tunic. The *cyrtel* and *tunece* seem to have been similar garments although, on available evidence (tenth-century), *tunece* seems to have been applied to gowns of sober colours while *cyrtlas* could be dyed red or blue[101] (below, p. 211).

Fig. 111 Gown without cloak, Stuttgart Psalter, fol. 58r

[101] G. R. Owen,'Wynflæd's wardrobe', *Anglo-Saxon England*, 8 (1979), pp. 195–222, at pp. 203–5.

The belt and girdle

Tastes seem to have diverged in the seventh century, with rather striking belts and buckles in Kent, while in most other areas a tendency towards unobtrusive belts is indicated by smaller buckles (which would have fastened belts generally narrower than earlier ones) and the widespread absence of buckles, which may mean that softer, woven girdles were worn instead of leather belts. The jewelled triangular buckles of Kent probably fastened leather; the rectangular, perforated ones were obviously attached to something coloured, either woven cloth or leather which had been dyed. Organic remains attached to an openwork buckle found in a woman's grave at Burwell, Cambridgeshire, show that the belt was made of a combination of leather and textile.[102] Probably the leather provided the strength, the textile the colour. Fragments of perforated leather have been found at several seventh-century sites, mostly in Kent,[103] including one possible female grave (at Sibertswold). It is not known what this leather came from, but possibly it belonged to ornamented belts.

Fabric girdles would probably be braided on tablets, like the unique fragment from St John's, Cambridge, which has survived through its attachment to a metal strap-end dated to the seventh century (Plate 6). The material was vegetable fibre, linen or hemp, a practical choice since it would not stretch as wool would do. The braid was woven in a simple pattern in white, bluish-green and indigo.

Plate 6 Girdle end with textile, St John's, Cambridge

---

[102] Grave 72; Lethbridge, *Recent Excavations*, p. 60.

[103] B. Faussett, *Inventorium Sepulchrale*, ed. C. R. Smith (London, 1856), pp. 107, 110, 111, 112, 118, 122–3, 125, 132–3; Lethbridge, *Recent Excavations*, p. 57.

Metal strap-ends often occur in graves without buckles. This suggests that a woven girdle was worn which had a metal end to prevent fraying, but which was not fastened by a buckle. (Conversely a leather belt might need a buckle but not a strap end.) The decline in the popularity of the buckled belt which is suggested by the conversion-period and early Christian cemeteries seems to have been permanent. Aldhelm does not mention a belt and there is never a representation of a buckle in late Anglo-Saxon illustrations of women, though their gowns are drawn in at the waist as if girdled. Strap ends, however, become increasingly common finds in the Christian period. Some of them are very simple, consisting of a piece of metal bent over and riveted, undecorated or with the simplest of incised geometric ornament. Many simple examples have been recovered from the eighth-century settlement site at Flixborough. Others are decorated with zoomorphic ornament in characteristic later Anglo-Saxon style, and, by the ninth century, often terminate in a shape imitating an animal's snout (Fig. 112). We cannot be sure that all of these belonged to the costume, as there are many other uses for straps, but almost certainly some of them did.

The word *gyrdels* is first documented in the eighth-century Corpus Glossary[104] and the compound *gyrdels-hringe*, 'buckle', is found in the same word-list.[105] *Gyrdels* is used of a monk's girdle in the Old English version of the Benedictine Rule,[106] but it seems likely that it was applied to secular costume too.

Fig. 112 Ninth-century strap end with animal's snout, Lincoln

Dress accessories

The practice of carrying trinkets and tools at the waist seems to have continued into early Christian times although there were some changes of fashion as regards the objects worn. Girdle hangers are found in some apparently seventh-century burials, but do not appear to have survived long into the conversion period. As far as we can tell, English women did not adopt the type of girdle hangers

---

[104] Lindsay, *Corpus Glossary*, p. 28, line 181, glossing *bra(c)hiale*.

[105] Lindsay, *Corpus Glossary*, p. 105, line 122 glossing *legula* and p. 107, line 237, glossing *lingula*.

[106] *Benedictine Rule*, 55; Schröer, *Benedictinerregel*, p. 92, line 3.

Fig. 113 Satchel from Swallowcliffe Down, Wiltshire. After G. Speake

Fig. 114 Reconstruction of a pouch from tags found in Rome

featuring openwork bronze discs and metal plaques which became popular in Frankish and Alamannic areas of the Continent in the seventh century. The ivory rings which had probably belonged to pouches or amulet bags were no longer current. Amulet-bags as such may no longer have been carried on the person, being replaced as grave furniture by wooden boxes in the seventh century, though bags of different kinds were carried well into the seventh century[107] and possibly beyond, as shown from Castledyke where they were found at the neck as well as at the waist.[108] The woman in the bed burial at Swallowcliffe Down had a satchel (Fig. 113) *c.* 280 mm long and *c.* 200 mm wide. Though it was laid down in the grave, not worn by the dead woman, it was evidently intended for carrying on the person as it was attached to a belt with decorative plates and a double-tongued buckle. The satchel fastened by means of an annular disc and was decorated with a circular mount. George Speake suggests that discs of bone or antler, and mounts, recovered from other sites, also derive from seventh-century satchels.[109] The female figure on the right in the Beaduhild and Welund scene on the Franks Casket (Fig. 103) carries a bag in her hand which may reflect contemporary usage. It was a fashion which evidently continued into the late Anglo-Saxon period (Fig. 171).

Small hooked tags, perforated for stitching to fabric, first appear in seventh-century graves where they are unusual finds which have been associated with men, women and children. They have been found in various positions: below the head, over the skull, at the chest, at the hip, under the knees and over the foot or simply in the fill of a grave.[110] They have been found in the convent cemetery at Whitby and are among the finds of metalwork from the settlement site at Flixborough. The most elaborate versions appear to be

---

[107] Meaney, *Amulets*, p. 249.

[108] Edwards and Watson, 'Organic remains', in Drinkall and Foreman, *Castledyke*, pp. 283–4. A late-seventh-century female grave (Grave 183) had contained a leather bag lined with textile.

[109] Speake, *Bed Burial*, p. 72.

[110] For example at Burwell (Grave 1; Lethbridge, *Recent Excavations*, p. 48) and at Castledyke (Graves 16 and 183; Drinkall and Foreman, *Castledyke*, pp. 38–9, 89–90). See also Webster and Backhouse, *Making*, p. 235.

ninth-century, but as a type they persist into the tenth and eleventh centuries. They are usually found singly, but sometimes occur in pairs, and in one instance, at Shakenoak, Oxfordshire, five were found together. They have sometimes been identified as 'dress hooks'. An unusually elaborate pair, triangular in shape and made of silver, believed from their decoration to be ninth-century, were found under the right knee of a skeleton in Winchester Cathedral,[111] and have been interpreted as 'garter hooks',[112] though it is unclear how they would have worked, and their flimsiness, sharpness, and the fact that the hooks point away from the decorated surfaces (and therefore, by implication, towards the body) make the interpretation improbable. However, a pair of similar tags (Fig. 114) has since been identified as the fastening of a pouch. Found with a hoard of Anglo-Saxon and other coins in Rome, these tags had evidently secured the bag in which the coins were carried; an inscription on the tags has been interpreted as a dedication to Pope Marinus II (942–6).[113] It is clear, therefore, that this particular set of hooked tags belonged to a container rather than the clothing, and also that the hooked part was worn uppermost (opposite to what has usually been assumed) if the inscription was to be read from the front.[114] It is likely that other hooked tags had the same function, being attached to pouches which were carried on the person or laid in the graves of their owners, though there is clearly a reluctance among commentators to part with the conception that they were garment fasteners.[115]

Women seem to have carried toilet articles and tweezers less often in the seventh to ninth centuries than before, although these can still be found in the eighth-century burial at Boss Hall.[116] Nuns as well as seculars seem to have carried these tools, as a toilet set was found at Barking[117] and tweezers at Whitby,[118] both the sites of early convents. Spindle whorls and keys continued to be carried on the person into the seventh century and shears seem to have increased in frequency. Combs are also found in conversion period cemeteries and from Christian period sites. The fact that a comb found near Whitby bears the runic text of part of a prayer in Latin

---

[111] Grave 67; D. A. Hinton, 'Tag-ends', in Biddle, *Winchester Studies*, 7.ii, ii, pp. 547–52, at p. 549.

[112] M. Biddle, 'Excavations at Winchester, 1964', *Antiquaries Journal*, 45 (1965), pp. 230–64, at pp. 263–4.

[113] J. Graham-Campbell and E. Okasha with an introductory note by M. Metcalf, 'A pair of inscribed Anglo-Saxon hooked tags from the Rome (Forum) 1883 hoard', *Anglo-Saxon England*, 20 (1991), pp. 221–9.

[114] Geake, *Grave-goods*, p. 66.

[115] Thus James Graham-Campbell, writing on the Rome pouch fasteners, says 'there is no doubt that [the Winchester tags] will have been in use as fasteners for gartering, as also the pair found at the knees of the skeleton in Birka Grave 905, Sweden … '; Graham-Campbell and Okasha, 'Hooked tags', p. 224.

[116] Webster and Backhouse, *Making*, p. 53.

[117] Webster and Backhouse, *Making*, p. 90.

[118] Peers and Radford, 'Whitby', p. 61, Fig. 13, pp. 62–3.

Fig. 115 Threadbox or reliquary, Burwell, Cambridgeshire

and Old English as well as the beginning of the owner's name, suggests the importance of this particular object.[119]

Women still carried suspension rings at the waist in the conversion period, even utilising for this purpose annular brooches no longer required as ornaments. Long chatelaine chains hanging from the waist were a characteristic fashion of the seventh century, as were the small, cylindrical, bronze containers once thought to be 'workboxes' or threadboxes because fragments of textile were found inside them (Fig. 115). This identification seems improbable. The amounts of textile are probably too small to have been useful and as some of the containers have been found with infants they could not have been used as workboxes by the persons buried with them. These little boxes have been re-interpreted as amulets. They often contain plant remains as well as textile which may be symbolic of the woman's role as healer (with herbs) and textile maker.[120] Another possibility is that the 'workboxes', which are sometimes decorated with crosses, functioned as reliquaries, and the textile fragments inside them, which include our earliest remains of silk, from a baby's grave at Updown, Kent,[121] and a scrap of embroidery, from Kempston, Bedfordshire[122] were holy relics, probably snipped from the vestments of a saint, or potential saint. A woman at Gilton, Kent, had tiny 'Thor's hammers' and 'Woden's spears' among her toilet articles,[123] a surprising pagan touch in the conversion period, which shows that the fashion for displaying religious belief through dress accessories was not confined to Christians.

The undergarment

The undergarment called *subucula bissina*, 'linen shirt', in Aldhelm's Latin diatribe was presumably visible, since he mentions it at all, and probably undyed. (Latin *bissina* is glossed into Old English as *linen* or *hwite*, 'white'.)[124] Aldhelm probably objected to the garment on the grounds that it was linen, which, we know, was considered more luxurious than wool, for Bede records that St Etheldreda chose to wear wool rather than linen as a deliberate mortification of the flesh (above, p. 133). If the outer garment opened

[119] Fell, *Women in Anglo-Saxon England*, p. 122. The comb was not found on the monastery site and the name is only identifiable as *Cy* …

[120] Meaney, *Amulets*, pp. 181–9.

[121] S. C. Hawkes, 'The archaeology of conversion: cemeteries', in J. Campbell (ed.), *The Anglo-Saxons* (Oxford, 1982), pp. 48–9 at p. 49.

[122] E. Crowfoot, 'Textile fragments from "relic boxes" in Anglo-Saxon graves', in P. Walton and J.-P. Wild (ed.), *Textiles in Northern Archaeology*, *NESAT III* (London, 1990), pp. 47–56, at pp. 47–52.

[123] Grave 27; Faussett, *Inventorium*, p. 12; G. R. Owen, *Rites and Religions of the Anglo-Saxons* (Newton Abbot and Totowa, NJ, 1981), Plate 3. A similar miniature spear was found in Grave 13 at Kingston; Faussett p. 45, Plate XII, 6, 7.

[124] Napier, *Glosses*, p. 134, line 5317; p. 163, line 371; L. Goossens (ed.), *The Old English glosses of MS Brussels, Royal Library, 1650, Aldhelm's 'De laudibus virginitatis'* (Brussels, 1974), p. 479, line 5196.

down the front, the linen undergarment would have been visible at the aperture. It might also have been seen at the wrists. There are the wrist-length sleeves of an undergarment protruding from the shorter sleeves of the gown in the *Stuttgart Psalter* (Fig. 111) and close-fitting inner sleeves are a regular feature of women's costume in later Anglo-Saxon art (Figs 159, 174). In painted pictures these sleeves are usually coloured white, as if they were linen.

In an early-eleventh-century manuscript of Aldhelm's text, *subucula* is glossed by the Old English word *ham*, with the slightly later addition *hacele*.[125]

Headgear

We have already seen that dainty pin suites are a feature of the richer female graves of the conversion period, and it has been suggested that these, and also the matching (but not conjoined) pairs of pins found in contemporary graves, were fasteners for veils. The tiny pairs of penannular brooches found at Winnall and Finglesham[126] might have been used in a similar way, so might the suites of disc-headed pins which came into fashion in the eighth century. Single pins have been found near the jaws, at the foreheads and under the skulls of seventh-century female skeletons in more modestly equipped graves. They might have been used to fasten head-cloths on the corpses; alternatively they might have fastened veils and hoods worn as in everyday life, as may the many single pins which have been found at Middle Saxon settlement sites. Neat, round-headed pins from Barking Abbey might have been used to secure head-veils as their partial gilding suggests (above, p. 143).[127] The occasional finds of beads near skulls in furnished graves may be the remains of headdress ornaments.

An enigmatic figure to the right of the Annunciation scene on the Genoels-Elderen ivory appears to have uncovered hair, worn in a neat helmet style, with a narrow headband round the crown. If the figure represents a female servant the style perhaps reflects her social status, though it may be worth noting that narrow diadems are characteristic of angels in late Anglo-Saxon art; but it is likely that headcoverings for women became an established convention after the conversion. Perhaps Christian morality was influential in this respect.[128] From the seventh century onwards, it seems from the evidence of art and literature that it was usual for women and girls to cover their heads. Bede, a Northumbrian, mentions casually

[125] Napier, *Glosses*, p. 134, line 5316; see also Goossens, *Glosses*, line 5195 and note *d*. *Hacele* more often means 'cloak'.

[126] Meaney and Hawkes, *Winnall*, p. 36. The Winnall brooches were found in Grave 8 which also contained a pin suite.

[127] Ross, 'Dress Pins', p. 410.

[128] St Paul taught that women should cover their heads when at prayer, I Corinthians 1:5–6.

that a linen headdress was worn by a girl miraculously cured of paralysis at the site of the saintly King Oswald's death. The miracle occurred soon after Oswald was killed in battle, which happened in 641. If the usual identification of Bede's site of *Matherfelth* with present-day Oswestry is correct, the girl was probably Mercian.[129] Loose hair was almost certainly representative of loose morals, at least in art, its earliest Anglo-Saxon manifestation being the woman drying Christ's feet with her hair on the sandstone cross at Ruthwell, Dumfries and Galloway, Scotland.[130]

Bede's earlier contemporary, Aldhelm, a West Saxon abbot and bishop, condemns, as we have seen, extravagant dress including what may be a hood (*capitium*), possibly striped with silk, and long, white or colourful headdresses (*mafortibus*) attached to fillets or ribbons (*vittarum*). The embracing saints on the Genoels-Elderen Diptych (Fig. 110) may wear long headdresses of this kind, rather than cloaks — the garments hang down the back of the shoulders and swing out as if they are made of light material — though there is no evidence of headbands or silk. The fragments of gold strip from woven braids found at Barking, may, as Leslie Webster suggests, have come from the kind of garment Aldhelm condemns, an elaborate fillet or a sleeve edge, though alternatively they might have derived from ecclesiastical vestments, perhaps even vestments manufactured at the abbey.[131]

We have evidence of an extremely rich headdress from the second half of the ninth century, found in the same grave as the silver hooked tags (above, p. 155), in Winchester Cathedral.[132] The head of the body had probably been wrapped in a veil edged with a gold braid, and there was a second gold braid which may have belonged to a band round the brow supporting a rosette-like ornament made from gold-decorated loops of ribbon, which was found at one side of the head. The sex of the associated skeleton was not identified. A rich Christian grave within the Cathedral might have belonged to an important male ecclesiastic, but if the gold braid was worn at burial (as opposed to the possibility that it was part of a rich textile re-used as a wrap for the head) both veil and headband are more likely to be associated with a woman than a man. We have no evidence from art to suggest that men habitually wore hats, and the simple Phrygian caps occasionally depicted are undecorated (see below, p. 263). The disposition of these gold remains does not suggest an episcopal mitre.

Since Aldhelm condemns artificially curled hair at forehead and temples, we can deduce that the headdresses of the early-eighth century were worn further back than the voluminous coverings

[129] *Historia Ecclesiastica*, III, 10; Colgrave and Mynors, *Bede*, pp. 242, 244.
[130] Luke 7:37–8; Cassidy, *The Ruthwell Cross*, plate 16.
[131] Webster and Backhouse, *Making*, pp. 88–9.
[132] Grave 67; E. Crowfoot, 'Textiles', in Biddle, *Winchester Studies*, 7.ii, ii, pp. 468–88, at pp. 480–1.

shown in later art, which covered forehead, cheeks and neck and concealed the hair. A woman depicted on an eighth-century stone cross from Rothbury, Northumberland, does indeed have hair visible beneath the open veil over her head (Fig. 116);[133] a Mercian sculpture which is perhaps slightly later – eighth- or early-ninth-century, probably depicting the Virgin, at Breedon-on-the Hill, Leicestershire, also shows a woman in an open-fronted headveil, but this time no hair is visible.[134]

Fig. 116 Woman with visible hair and open veil on a sculpture, Rothbury, Northumberland (No. 1 Face C)

Most of the documented Old English words for headgear occur in glosses to Aldhelm's description, so we have good evidence of their meaning, despite the ambiguity of the *De Virginitate* passage. There is not, however, a one-to-one relationship between the Latin vocabulary and the Old English: the Latin words which Aldhelm used are given various English equivalents in the several manuscript of Latin–Old English glosses that record them. *Capitium* was generally, though not exclusively[135] understood to mean a hat or hood. It is glossed by *hod* in several texts, including the early Corpus Glossary,[136] by *hæt*[137] and also by the ambiguous *healsed*.[138] Latin *mafors* is glossed *scyfel* in the Corpus and other glossaries[139] also *wimpel* and *orel*.[140] Latin *vitta* is glossed by *þwæle* in the Corpus Glossary[141] and also by *nostle*[142] and *snod*.[143]

[133] Rothbury 1 Face C; R. J. Cramp (ed.), *British Academy Corpus of Anglo-Saxon Stone Sculpture*, 1, *County Durham and Northumberland* (Oxford, 1984), p. 220, Plate 213, No. 1215, there identified as the woman with an issue of blood, healed by Christ; identified as Martha in a scene depicting the raising of Lazarus in J. Hawkes, 'Sacraments in stone: the mysteries of Christ in Anglo-Saxon sculpture', in M. Carver (ed.), *The Cross goes North: processes of conversion in Northern Europe, AD 300–1300* (York/Woodbridge, 2003), pp. 351–70, at pp. 355–8.

[134] Webster and Backhouse, *Making*, p. 240, Fig. 22.

[135] See p. 135, note 31.

[136] Lindsay, *Corpus Glossary*, p. 32, line 107 (*hood*); see also Wright/Wülcker, *Vocabularies*, col. 199, line 18 and 362, 17.

[137] Wright/Wülcker, *Vocabularies*, col. 313, line 20; Goossens, *Glosses*, p. 479, line 5299.

[138] *Healsed* (Bosworth/Toller, *Dictionary*: 'a cloth for the head') appears to derive from Old English *heals*, 'the neck', so one might expect it to mean a neck cloth or perhaps the neck opening of a tunic. It is used in Old English Gospel translations in reference to a napkin (Luke 19:20) and grave clothes (Lindisfarne John 11:44 and 20:7); Skeat, *Gospels*, pp. 185, 111, 175. *Healsed* glosses *capitium* in a group of Aldhelm glosses in London, British Library MS Cotton Cleopatra A iii; Wright/Wülcker, *Vocabularies*, col. 514, line 1.

[139] Lindsay, *Corpus Glossary*, p. 110, line 9; Wright/Wülcker, *Vocabularies*, col. 442, line 21.

[140] Goossens, *Glosses*, p. 480, line 5210.

[141] Lindsay, *Corpus Glossary*, p. 184, line 176.

[142] Wright/Wülcker, *Vocabularies*, col. 514, line 9; Napier, *Glosses*, p. 219, line 28.

[143] Wright/Wülcker, *Vocabularies*, col. 107, line 35; 125, line 12; Goossens, *Glosses*, p. 480, line 5212. Old English *snod* seems to have meant a cord or fillet; see p. 97, note 272.

Footwear

Fig. 117 Anglo-Viking shoe, on a bone skate, York, drawn by Kathleen Wood

There is definite evidence of footwear for the first time in cemeteries of the conversion period. Shoelace tags have been found in the graves at several seventh- and eighth-century sites, predominantly with the skeletons of women and children. They are sometimes found in pairs, but not always, so perhaps were easily lost and not replaced.[144] The woman buried in Castledyke Grave 206 had a pair of unusual silver tags large enough to accomodate thongs, rather than laces, but their position was not recorded,[145] though a woman in Grave 15 at the same site had a tag under each ankle.[146] A child, probably female, buried at Stanton Harcourt, Oxfordshire, had a bronze lace-tag and shoe leather,[147] but the latter is rare for a grave find. Pairs of buckles, thought to belong to shoes, and suitable for fastening thongs or straps between 6 and 11 mm wide, are an uncommon innovation of the seventh century. Probably a Frankish fashion, they accompanied two women at Finglesham, Kent.[148] Tiny penannular brooches on the shins of the skeleton of a young person at Wakerley may have functioned similarly.[149] Neither buckles nor laces are apparent on later drawings of women's footwear. Possibly both were always unusual, and fashionable only for a short time.

The many finds of shoes from occupation sites, such as Anglo-Saxon London and Winchester[150] and Anglo-Viking York,[151] demonstrate that the footwear in general use was made by the turnshoe method, by which the sole and upper were joined together inside-out, and then turned right-side-out on completion. Anglo-Saxon and Anglo-Viking shoes are stitched together with leather thongs,

Fig. 118 Anglo-Viking boot, York, drawn by Kathleen Wood

Fig. 119 Anglo-Viking slipper, probably a child's, York, drawn by Kathleen Wood

[144] Burwell Grave 83 (Lethbridge, *Recent Excavations*, p. 65); Melbourn, Cambridgeshire, Graves 9, 22 (D. M. Wilson, 'The initial excavation of an Anglo-Saxon cemetery at Melbourn, Cambridgeshire', *Proceedings of the Cambridge Antiquarian Society*, 49 (1956), pp. 29–41, at pp. 33, 36); Winnall, Graves 5, 10 (Meaney and Hawkes, *Winnall*, p. 39); Snell's Corner, Horndean, Hampshire, Grave S18 (G. M. Knocker, 'Early burials and an Anglo-Saxon cemetery at Snell's Corner, near Horndean, Hampshire', *Papers and Proceedings of the Hampshire Field Club and Archaeological Society*, 19 (1958), pp. 117–70, at p. 136); Finglesham, Kent, Graves 20 (with five) and 157 (with two) mentioned in discussion of Castledyke, and Castledyke Grave 15 (with two, under each ankle; Drinkall, in Drinkall and Foreman, *Castledyke*, pp. 38, 75–6, 271).
[145] Drinkall, in Drinkall and Foreman, *Castledyke*, pp. 93–4.
[146] Drinkall, in Drinkall and Foreman, *Castledyke*, p. 271.
[147] Grave 2; D. B. Harden and R. C. Treweeks, 'Excavations at Stanton Harcourt, Oxon, 1949, II', *Oxoniensia*, 10 (1945), pp. 16–41, at p. 35.
[148] Graves 20, 157; Hawkes, 'Polhill', in Philp, p. 194: Geake, *Grave-goods*, p. 65.
[149] Grave 10. Information taken from Geake, *Grave-goods*, p. 65.
[150] J. H. Thornton, 'Shoes, boots and shoe repairs', in Biddle, *Winchester Studies*, 7.ii, ii, pp. 591–621.
[151] J. H. Thornton and A. V. Goodfellow, 'Leather shoes', in I. M. Stead, 'Excavations at the south corner tower of the Roman fortress at York, 1956', *Yorkshire Archaeological Journal*, 39 (1956–8), pp. 515–38, at pp. 525–30; K. M. Richardson, 'Excavations in Hungate, York', *Archaeological Journal*, 116 (1959), pp. 51–114; A. MacGregor (ed.), *Anglo-Scandinavian Finds from Lloyds Bank, Pavement and other sites*, The Archaeology of York, 27.3 (1982), pp. 138–42.

Plate 7 Viking shoe, York

not nailed as Roman shoes were. They have leather soles and are completely flat.

The typical shoe was ankle high (Plate 7 and Fig. 117), often with a wrap-around upper. The shoe was sometimes fastened by mean of a latchet, or with thongs which passed through slits in the leather and round the ankle. Some may have been thonged over the instep.[152] The York excavations have revealed other footwear: a boot, fastened by means of a leather toggle (Fig. 118) and a slipper, the sole of which extended up the back of the heel (Fig. 119). Apparently early medieval shoemakers rarely distinguished between right and left shoes,[153] though footwear would no doubt stretch and mould itself to the wearer. Most of the footwear that has been found is very plain: the shoes do not have exaggerated toes or ornamentation in the form of tooled leather; fancy stitching is rare. If Aldhelm's reference to *galliculae*, however, was describing boots and not some other item of clothing (pp. 134–6), then, apparently footwear could be made elaborate by colouring the leather or adding attractive fur.

The common name for 'shoe' was undoubtedly *scoh*, and there were other names for individual types of footwear. The compound word *stæppe-scoh*, 'slipper', was in use in the eighth century,[154] a synonym of *swiftlere* (which was only documented later)[155] since both words gloss Latin *subtalaris*[156] and signify a footcovering which was certainly lower than the ankle. The Corpus Glossary also contains the term *slebeschoh*[157] which is spelt *slypesco* in a later text,[158]

[152] 'It is not always clear whether the thong samples are for sole attachment or are part of an *instep* tie', Thornton, 'Shoes, boots and shoe repairs', in Biddle, *Winchester* 7.ii, ii, p. 593.

[153] MacGregor, *Anglo-Scandinavian Finds*, p. 138, but cf. p. 144.

[154] Lindsay, *Corpus Glossary*, p. 171, line 708.

[155] Wright/Wülcker, *Vocabularies*, col. 125, line 26. In the Old English gloss to Ælfric's *Colloquy*, *swyftleras* are distinguished from *sceos* (Latin *ficones*); G. N. Garmonsway, *Aelfric's Colloquy* (London, 1939), p. 35, line 171.

[156] *Swiftlere* is a corruption of the Latin *subtalaris*; A. Campbell, *Old English Grammar* (Oxford, 1959), p. 214.

a word which survived until the nineteenth century in Somerset dialect[159] and persists today in the derivative 'slip-shod' — 'having shoes on the feet but no stockings' and hence 'slovenly' or 'careless'. An Anglo-Saxon 'slip-shoe' seems to have been a bag-like foot covering easily slipped on. The word *socc* seems to have signified much the same in the eighth century, when both gloss Latin *soccus*.[160] *Socc* in a later text glosses *callicula* (*caligula*).[161] Perhaps this bag-like boot was what Aldhelm meant when he used the word *gallicula*.

Leggings

Although there are many documented Old English words signifying trousers, loin-cloths, socks and leg bands there is still very little evidence of what women wore on their legs. There is, however, a unique insight from Totternhoe, Bedfordshire, where a cake of mud found at the feet of two female children preserved the impression of linen, perhaps from a stocking.[162] The shoe and garter fittings common in Frankia and Alamannia are largely absent from England and Aldhelm does not mention garters or stockings in his condemnation of elaborate dress. It is reasonable to suppose that the legs were concealed by ankle-length skirts.

There have been various archaeological finds which might have been fasteners for leg coverings, but they are all individual and there is uncertainty about their use. At Kingston, a pair of silver bow brooches (Fig. 120) was found by the left thigh of the female skeleton who wore near her right shoulder the most splendid polychrome brooch ever to have been found in Anglo-Saxon context (Fig. 91).[163] These simple 'safety-pins' were so unostentatious compared with the cloisonné brooch that it has been suggested that they were not meant to be seen, and the distinguished scholar G. Baldwin Brown suggested that they might have fastened hose.[164] Attractive as the suggestion is, the brooches could equally well have had some other use, as suggested above (p. 140), such as securing a garment wrapped round the body (perhaps a very full cloak as suggested by the cloisonné brooch). Though the bow brooches are unpretentious, they are of precious metal (silver) and are beautifully made, with an unobtrusive decoration of parallel lines. They give

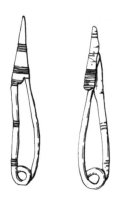

Fig. 120 Silver bow brooches, Kingston, Kent

[157] Glossing Latin *soccus*; Lindsay, *Corpus Glossary*, p. 165, line 394.
[158] Wright/Wülcker, *Vocabularies*, col. 277, line 29.
[159] See 'slipshoe' in Murray, Bradley, Craigie and Onions, *Oxford English Dictionary*.
[160] Lindsay, *Corpus Glossary*, p. 165, line 394.
[161] L. Kindschi, 'The Latin–Old English glosses in Plantin-Moretus MS 32 and BM MS Additional 32,2461', unpublished doctoral dissertation (Stanford University, 1955), p. 88. Junius had read *rocc*, Wright/Wülcker, *Vocabularies*, col. 125, line 18.
[162] C. L. Matthews, 'The Anglo-Saxon cemetery at Marina Drive, Dunstable', *Bedfordshire Archaeological Journal*, 1 (1962), pp. 25–47, at pp. 28–9, 31–2.
[163] Faussett, *Inventorium*, pp. 77–8.
[164] Brown, *Arts*, 4 (1915), p. 722.

us an insight into what the more utilitarian possessions of a wealthy lady were like. At Soham, Cambridgeshire, two annular brooches were found beside the tibia of a woman's skeleton.[165] The excavator thought they might have fastened a skirt, but we have no evidence that Anglo-Saxon women wore a wrap-around skirt like a kilt that would require this kind of fastener. The brooches might have secured garters or stockings, or, as suggested in the case of Kingston, a cloak that was wrapped round the body. This burial was much disturbed so the evidence is not reliable. The woman buried in Castledyke Grave 138 had a single lace tag against the left fibula, rather high for a shoelace and perhaps the remains of a garter fastening; but again, it could have been something else.[166] The ninth-century hooks found at the knees of the Winchester Cathedral skeleton were thought, from their position, to be 'garter hooks', but as discussed (p. 155 above), I have become convinced that they were pouch fasteners.

The costume of the Viking settlers

At least some of the Viking women who were coming to England from the ninth century seem to have continued to wear the traditional Germanic costume supported by pairs of brooches. Archaeological evidence suggests that they wore the typically Scandinavian 'tortoise' brooches at the shoulders, accompanied by a single trefoil brooch worn centrally, which probably fastened the tubular garment to the undergown. This evidence is, however, extremely limited and it does not appear that the immigrants established pagan cemeteries in which they buried their dead in native dress.[167] Even without furnished graves, if the 'tortoise' brooches had been worn by large numbers of immigrant Viking women we might expect to

---

[165] Grave 9; T. C. Lethbridge, 'Anglo-Saxon burials at Soham, Cambridgeshire', *Proceedings of the Cambridge Antiquarian Society*, 33 (1931–2), pp. 152–63, at p. 161.

[166] Drinkall, in Drinkall and Foreman, *Castledyke*, pp. 76, 271.

[167] There were tortoise brooches in a female grave at Bedale, North Yorkshire (W. H. Longstaff, Untitled, *Archaeological Journal*, 5 (1848), pp. 220–1) and there are others from Scottish sites; a trefoil ornament has been found at Kirkoswald, Cumbria (Wilson, *Ornamental Metalwork*, pp. 7, 17, 139–40 and Plate XIX) and there is a trefoil brooch from Lakenheath Warren, Suffolk, in the Cambridge University Museum of Anthropology and Archaeology. A mould for making trefoil brooches has been found in York (R. A. Hall, *Viking Age York* (London, 1994), p. 110). Archaeological evidence suggests the Vikings mostly used Christian burial grounds already established in England (see D. M. Wilson, 'The Vikings' relationship with Christianity in Northern England', *Journal of the British Archaeological Association*, 3rd series, 30 (1967), pp. 37–46; J. Graham-Campbell, 'The Scandinavian Viking-Age burials of England — some problems of interpretation', in Rahtz, Dickinson and Watts, *Anglo-Saxon Cemeteries 1979*, pp. 379–82) and though there is textual evidence to suggest otherwise (E. M. Treharne, 'A unique Old English formula for excommunication from Cambridge, Corpus Christi College 303', *Anglo-Saxon England*, 24, 1995, pp. 185–211, at p. 198), the corpus of furnished pagan graves is small.

Fig. 121 Viking woman in train with hair in a 'bun', silver-gilt figure, Klinta, Köping, Oland, Sweden, drawn by John Hines

Fig. 122 Viking woman in train dress under short pointed cloak, hair in knotted pony tail, on a picture-stone, Alskog, Tjängvide, Gotland, Sweden, drawn by John Hines

have found more of them. It should be noted that much of the pioneering work that was done on Scandinavian women's dress used Swedish material,[168] while the immigrants, traditionally at least, came from Denmark and from Norway. There is a sharp decrease in tortoise brooches in Denmark from the ninth to the tenth centuries, and few graves with such brooches in the south-west of the country by the tenth century.[169] There appears to have been a change of dress fashion in Denmark which may have been reflected to some extent in Anglo-Viking England.

The evidence of decorated metalwork and carved stones from Scandinavia (again mostly Swedish) shows a woman's costume with a 'train' effect at the back, probably made by cutting the garment so that it was longer at the back than at the front (Figs 121, 122). This same effect may be seen on later Anglo-Viking sculpture. It has been generally assumed that the 'train' costume and the 'paired brooch' costume are one and the same, but it must be noted that brooches are not usually visible on the profile figures depicted in the 'train'. It seems likely that this 'train' costume belongs to a higher rank in Scandinavian society than the 'paired brooch' one; the use of extra material, particularly if it is to trail on the ground, is a symptom of that conspicuous consumption that has marked the wealthy classes throughout much of the history of mankind. In the Icelandic poem *Rigsþula* it is the woman of the class of jarl who wears a costume with a train, whereas paired pins and keys belonged to the class of carl (pp. 45, 66 above). The jarl woman has the leisure to sit admiring her own arms,[170] clad in fine linen, and she wears a single nummular brooch:

> ... en húskona
> hugði at ǫrmum,
> straukof ripti,
> sterti ermar.
> Keisti fald,
> kinga var á bringu —
> síðar slœður,
> serk bláfan ...

... while the mistress of the house studied her arms, stroked the fine linen, tightened the sleeves. High curved her head-dress, a coin-brooch was at her bosom, a trailing robe she wore, a bodice blue-dyed ...[171]

In some Scandinavian depictions of the 'train' garment it seems to

---

[168] Geijer, *Birka, III*. However, similar costume existed in Norway; Blindheim, 'Vernesfunnene'.

[169] A. H. Madsen, 'Women's dress in the Viking period in Denmark, based on the tortoise brooches and textile remains', in Walton and Wild, *NESAT III*, pp. 101–6, at pp. 101–3.

[170] In a society with few, if any, mirrors, she could not sit admiring her face.

[171] Dronke, *Edda*, p. 168.

be worn under a short cloak which hangs in a point at the back (Fig. 122).

Though the *Rigsþula* woman wears a headdress, women are bare-headed in Viking art, either wearing their hair in a 'bun' (Fig. 121) or, more commonly, in a knotted pony-tail (Fig. 122). Viking women wore beads, but the great number of rings — for the neck, the arm and the finger — which have been recovered from areas of Viking occupation suggests that these portable forms of bullion were more popular ornaments. Mostly of silver, the circlets were sometimes flattened and stamped with simple decoration or made from several rods which were twisted together like a rope.

V

Men's costume from the seventh to the ninth centuries

The archaeological evidence

As we have seen in Chapter IV, the burial practices of the conversion period resulted in a higher proportion of unfurnished graves or graves with fewer artefacts than found in cemeteries of the fifth and sixth centuries. It is possible to date a few furnished male graves to the conversion period by their association with female graves equipped with the characteristic jewellery of this period, or by the inclusion of some weaponry which appeared only in the seventh century: the 'sugar-loaf' shield boss, a taller boss than its 'mammary' counterpart of the fifth and sixth centuries; and the scramasax, a short, one-edged sword or fighting knife. Since shields and scramasaxes were probably confined to men of relatively high social status or mature years[1] this evidence is socially restricted. A few cemeteries, such as Polhill,[2] which continued to receive furnished burials into the eighth century before the practice of providing grave-goods died out altogether, confirm some developments in dress fashion, but from the material remains we have, it does not appear that the conversion period brought such drastic changes to men's costume as it did to women's.

The early-seventh century, however, also saw the deposition of some of the richest male burials of the Anglo-Saxon era. The most outstanding is the Sutton Hoo Ship Burial, which can be dated, chiefly from the coins contained in a purse, to c. 625. It was almost certainly the burial of a king, probably King Rædwald of East Anglia, and although no remains of the body have survived and there is no evidence of what the corpse was dressed in, many items of regalia were deposited in the burial, which included buckled harnesses, shoes and headgear. Further, the acid soil, wet conditions

---

[1] Härke, 'Early Saxon weapon burials', in Hawkes, *Anglo-Saxon Weapons and Warfare*; H. Härke, ' Changing symbols in a changing society: the Anglo-Saxon weapon burial rite in the seventh century', in M. O. H. Carver (ed.), *The Age of Sutton Hoo* (Woodbridge, 1992), pp. 149–65.

[2] Philp, *Excavations in West Kent*, pp. 164–214; Hawkes, 'Polhill', in Philp, pp. 186–99.

and large quantity of metalwork in the Ship Burial created favourable conditions for the survival of textile. This burial under Mound 1 at Sutton Hoo, therefore, offers a great deal of evidence on costume, though it is unique: on the one hand it is clearly the product of extreme wealth, on the other it exhibits exotic tastes drawing on both the Swedish heritage of the Wuffing dynasty and prestigious fashions of the Franks and Romans.[3] An undisturbed chamber grave, found at Prittlewell, Southend-on-Sea, Essex, in 2003 offers a contemporary (*c.* 630) parallel from the same social stratum. The acid soil had destroyed all bone and (according to information available at time of writing) other organic material, so there is only a small amount of evidence for dress, but that indicates wealth and prestige. The material is at present under excavation and conservation at the Museum of London (see p. 277, note 34).

The 'princely' burial found under a mound at Taplow, Buckinghamshire was also extremely rich, although the absence of most of the skeletal material and other difficulties on excavation were confusing factors and it is impossible to reconstruct the costume with certainty, though clearly there were unusual details here also.[4] Barrows at Benty Grange, Derbyshire[5] and Broomfield, Essex[6] also include interesting material but are without the skeletal remains which might have clarified the finds for the costume historian.

Ninth-century, and later, archaeological evidence comes from stray finds, hoards and artefacts from occupation sites. Apart from the rare exceptions which bear the name of a person on them, it is not possible to assign many of these objects to men, or even to confirm that they are part of the dress. Conversely, organic finds such as shoes (Plate 7) and a unique sock (Plate 8) give first-hand evidence of clothing in later Saxon and Anglo-Viking urban context.

[3] See Bruce-Mitford, *Sutton Hoo*.

[4] The conflicting accounts by contemporary observers are examined critically in Crowfoot and Hawkes, 'Early Anglo-Saxon gold braids', pp. 44–50. The textile from Taplow and other unpublished sites referred to in the discussion of the Sutton Hoo textiles is analysed in Appendix 4 (pp. 468–79) to E. Crowfoot, 'The Textiles', in Bruce-Mitford, *Sutton Hoo*, 3 (1983), ed. A. Care Evans, i, pp. 409–79, the Taplow textile at pp. 475–8.

[5] T. Bateman, *Ten Years Diggings in Celtic and Saxon Grave Hills in the Counties of Derby, Stafford and York 1848–58* (London and Derby, 1861), pp. 28–33.

[6] C. H. Read, Untitled, *Proceedings of the Society of Antiquaries*, 2nd series, 15 (1893–5), pp. 250–5; E. Crowfoot, Notes in S. E. Chadwick, 'The Anglo-Saxon cemetery at Finglesham, Kent, a reconsideration', *Medieval Archaeology*, 2 (1958), pp. 1–71, at pp. 36–7; E. Crowfoot, 'The textiles', in Hutchinson, 'Little Eriswell', pp. 29–30; H. M. Appleyard and A. B. Wildman, 'Fibres of archaeological interest', in D. R. Brothwell and F. S. Higgs, *Science and Archaeology*, 2nd ed., revised and enlarged (London, 1969), pp. 624–34, at p. 631.

Plate 8 Viking sock, York

The evidence of art

Human figures, especially male figures, began to appear regularly in Anglo-Saxon art after the conversion to Christianity, which brought with it humanistic and naturalistic styles unknown in the country since Roman times. The majority of the figures in seventh- and eighth-century manuscript illuminations, and on the finest of the sculptured crosses, those at Ruthwell and at Bewcastle, Cumbria, represent Christ, the four Evangelists and other Christian figures, and are derived from foreign models, generally Late Antique in style. The men are clean-shaven and wear Roman dress: an ankle-length, one-piece garment, the *tunica*, under a cloak, the *pallium*, which has no brooch fastener and which wraps around the body leaving one arm free. This dress, which I will term 'classical costume' remains the dress for the Deity, Christ, angels and saints throughout Anglo-Saxon art.

However, if we exclude as 'classical' the dress of the most elaborate, and central, illuminations in the early manuscripts and consider the costume in minor decorations, we find different evidence. In Insular[7] manuscripts, decoration was not confined to formal, full-page pictures, but included lavish frames and embellishment of the text, with contorted birds and beasts among the letters. In the eighth- or ninth-century *Book of Kells* (Dublin, Trinity College MS A I 6, *Codex Cennanensis*)[8] human figures in secular dress, usually bearded, are added to the zoomorphic scheme. They appear in minor decorations including initial letters and wear tight-fitting knee-breeches and sometimes cloaks, clearly neither the classical costume, which also appears in the manuscript, nor ecclesiastical. *Kells*, if not actually created in Ireland, is heavily influenced by Irish tradition and the dress of these figures is probably Celtic. In other eighth-century art we find male figures in a different kind of secular dress, the short tunic. This is a costume which is found

Fig. 123 Figure in mail, Franks Casket

---

[7] The term 'Insular' covers Northumbria, Ireland and Iona. The exact provenance of many manuscripts is unknown.

[8] See P. Brown, *The Book of Kells* (London, 1980).

on male figures throughout European art in the early Middle Ages, and, given the dependence of artists on earlier models, it is difficult to distinguish what features, if any, are characteristically Anglo-Saxon. For example, the best known of the illuminations in the eighth-century *Vespasian Psalter* (British Library MS Cotton Vespasian A i),[9] a 'Southumbrian' manuscript of the 'Tiberius' group,[10] is the full-page illumination of King David composing, surrounded by figures in secular costume; however, the miniature belongs to a well-established tradition, ultimately Greek, and the appearance and costume of David himself are a symbolic combination of Christological and episcopal. It would be unwise, then, to draw conclusions about Anglo-Saxon costume from this illumination. However, the same manuscript contains a less well-known historiated initial depicting two figures thought to be David and Jonathan, which has no known source. These figures, one in a short tunic, the other in a longer garment, might possibly be drawn from life.

Fig. 124 Figure in helmet, Franks Casket

Men appear on all the carved whalebone panels of the Franks Casket (described on p. 132). The men wear a vernacular, secular costume of cloak, tunic and trousers, and some have mail shirts or helmets (Figs 123–6). Many stone carvings of Northumbria and Mercia bear figures in secular costume. They are not all of the artistic merit of the earlier Ruthwell and Bewcastle Crosses, but may be of more relevance for the study of Anglo-Saxon dress. The craft of stone carving was patronised by Viking settlers, whose taste influenced both the subject matter and the execution of the artists. Some Viking fashions, particularly the wearing of trousers without a covering tunic, may be depicted on some of these carvings.

Fig. 125 Figure in short cloak, Franks Casket

It is not always possible to date stone carvings precisely, but a number of interesting examples fall into the period under consideration in this chapter. They include a unique stone from Repton, Derbyshire, probably eighth-century, with an equestrian figure of a king (perhaps a posthumous 'portrait' of King Æthelbald of Mercia), and two clothed figures disappearing into a serpent's mouth. The equestrian portrait is derived from Late Antique models, so some features of the costume may not be authentically Anglo-Saxon, but there are insular features in the weapons – sword and seax – and the moustached face which suggest some local input to the design.[11] A small figure stands amid vine-scroll, attacking a beast (Fig. 127), on a carving which has been dated to the early-eighth century from Jarrow, Tyne and Wear, the monastery which

[9] See D. H. Wright, *The Vespasian Psalter*, Early English Manuscripts in Facsimile, 14 (Copenhagen, 1967).

[10] I owe the term 'Southumbrian' to Michelle Brown, of the British Library, who prefers to identify this group of manuscripts as 'Tiberius' (after the Tiberius Bede, British Library, MS Cotton Tiberius C ii) rather than the misleading term 'Canterbury' manuscripts which has been used in the past.

[11] M. Biddle and B. Kjølbye-Biddle, 'The Repton Stone', *Anglo-Saxon England*, 14 (1985), pp. 233–92.

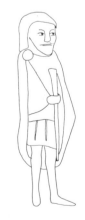

Fig. 126 Figure in long cloak, Franks Casket

Fig. 127 Figure in tunic, on a sculpture, Jarrow, Tyne and Wear

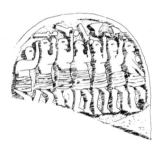

Fig. 128 Warrior figures, on a sculpture, Lindisfarne, Northumberland

Fig. 129 Figure in tunic, cloak and headband, on a sculpture, Codford St Peter, Wiltshire

was the home of the Venerable Bede.[12] The figure has been described both as 'a hunter'[13] and 'of juvenile appearance'.[14] The parallel folds or pleats in his garments are repeated on the skirts of a row of weapon-carrying figures on a grave-slab, probably ninth-century (Fig. 128). The row of warriors is generally interpreted as a depiction of the Vikings who famously raided the island monastery of Lindisfarne in 793.[15] The parallel folds are again found on a figure at Codford St Peter, Wiltshire (Fig. 129) thought to be ninth-century,[16] and a rare example of West Saxon figure sculpture of this date. This attractive carving has aroused considerable discussion regarding exact date, style and interpretation. It has been identified both as 'completely English'[17] and as derived from a Frankish model.[18] The figure is active, reaching up with his right hand and holding some object in his left. Rosemary Cramp has suggested that the man is dancing.[19] T. D. Kendrick thought the figure was holding a musical instrument.[20] K. G. Forbes, who thought the person was cutting alders as part of a ceremony confirming fishing, trapping and cutting rights, considered the object to be a knife.[21] My personal opinion is that the object in the left hand resembles a mallet and that the figure reaching up to the vine scroll above him represents the sculptor.[22] The importance of the carving for the present purpose, is however, that the clothing is shown clearly and it is unique.

Two ninth-century figures from the church of St Mary Bishophill Junior, York (Fig. 130) wear unusual costumes. One of them, who carries a horn, may be a hunter. Several figures of archers appear on stone crosses, perhaps representing the Devil[23] or Egil, the archer figure from Northern legend who appears on the lid of the Franks Casket. As archery was practiced in Anglo-Saxon England, a carver might have drawn on his own knowledge in depicting it, therefore the distinctive clothing of an archer depicted on a mid-ninth-century cross shaft from Sheffield, South Yorkshire (Fig. 131), may be authentic.

[12] Cramp, *Corpus of Anglo-Saxon Sculpture*, 1, p. 115, No. 20.

[13] R. J. Cramp, *Early Northumbrian Sculpture*, Jarrow Lecture (1965), p. 10.

[14] C. C. Hodges, 'Anglo-Saxon remains', in W. Page (ed.), *Victoria County History*, Durham, 1 (London, 1905), pp. 211–40, at p. 233.

[15] Cramp, *Corpus of Anglo-Saxon Sculpture*, 1, pp. 206–7, Plate 201, No. 1133.

[16] R. J. Cramp, 'Tradition and innovation in English stone sculpture of the tenth to the eleventh centuries', in D. Miloĉjić (ed.), *Kolloquium über spätantike und frümittelalterliche Skulptur*, 3 (Mainz, 1972), pp. 139–48.

[17] D. Talbot-Rice, *English Art 871–1100* (Oxford, 1952), p. 90.

[18] T. D. Kendrick, *Anglo-Saxon Art to AD 900* (London, 1938), pp. 180–1.

[19] Cramp, 'Tradition and innovation', in Miloĉjić, *Kolloquium*, p. 140.

[20] Kendrick, *Anglo-Saxon Art*, p. 180.

[21] K. G. Forbes, 'The Codford Saxon carving', *Wiltshire Archaeological Magazine*, 62 (1967), pp. 34–7.

[22] This would not be unparalleled; a sculptor is represented on an early Norman font at Bridekirk, Cumbria; W. S. Calverley, *Notes on the Early Sculptured Crosses, Shrines and Monuments in the Present Diocese of Carlisle*, Cumberland and Westmorland Antiquarian and Archaeological Society Extra Series 11 (1899), plate opposite p. 71.

[23] B. C. Raw, 'The archer, the eagle and the lamb', *Journal of the Warburg and Courtauld Institutes*, 30 (1967), pp. 391–4.

Male figures appear on a few pieces of ninth-century metal-work. The Alfred Jewel, (Fig. 132) a gold terminal (associated by its inscription with Alfred, King of Wessex, who died in 899), may have been part of an *æstel*, a pointer to aid the reader of a precious book. The figure depicted upon it, in enamel, has been plausibly interpreted as the Sense of Sight, though, given the early medieval facility for multiple interpretation it might also represent Christ, King Alfred or Wisdom or more than one of these.[24] We can distinguish some details of the figure's costume. Possibly the cloisonné plate was cut down from something larger, not originally Anglo-Saxon, which would limit its value as costume evidence.

The personified Sense of Sight appears once more, this time with the other four senses, on the ninth-century, silver Fuller Brooch (Fig. 133). The personifications, which are arranged in a quincunx surrounded by a border of roundels, take the form of male figures in attitudes of tasting, smelling, hearing and touching, around the central staring figure of Sight.[25] The stylised subsidiary figures are not unlike those of the *Vespasian Psalter*, which, as we have seen, is derived from a Continental model, but no such source is known for the Fuller Brooch. A figure similar in style, if not in costume, appears on the silver and niello hilt of a sword from Abingdon (Fig. 134), which may be ninth- or early-tenth-century.[26]

Fig. 130 Figures with horn and frilled collar, on a sculpture, St Mary Bishophill Junior, York. After W. G. Collingwood

The literary evidence

We have one, rather indirect, reference to the clothing of the secular Anglo-Saxons in early Christian times from Paulus Diaconus, an eighth-century Italian chronicler. Paulus, in the course of describing the garments of Langobard people shown in seventh-century pictures ornamenting the palace of Queen Theudelinde at Monza, mentioned, in comparison, the garments of the Anglo-Saxons: *vestimenta vero eis erant laxa et maxime linea, qualia Anglisaxones habere solent, hornata institis latioribus vario colore contextis*[27] ('indeed their clothes were roomy and especially linen, as the Anglo-Saxons were accustomed to have, embellished with rather wide borders woven in various colours'). The reference to 'borders' suggests the hems of garments rather than cuffs, but the general idea of having a decorated border corresponds to Aldhelm's description of ornamented sleeves. In the 740s, St Boniface, missionary to the Continental Frisians and Saxons, in a letter to Cuthbert, Archbishop

Fig. 131 Archer, on a sculpture, Sheffield, South Yorkshire. After W. G. Collingwood

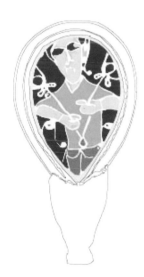

[24] Webster and Backhouse, *Making*, pp. 282–3.
[25] Webster and Backhouse, *Making*, pp. 280–1.
[26] D. A. Hinton, *A Catalogue of the Ornamental Metalwork 700–1100 in the Department of Antiquities, Ashmolean Museum* (Oxford, 1974), p. 1 pl. III, I (f).
[27] Waitz, *Pauli Historia Langobardorum*, IV, para. 19, p. 155. Perhaps by Paulus's time the Langobards had abandoned Germanic costume in favour of Italianate fashions.

Fig. 132 Figure on the Alfred Jewel, Ashmolean Museum, Oxford

Fig. 134 Figure on sword hilt,
Abingdon, Oxfordshire

of Canterbury, expressed his opinion about the degeneracy of such decorations, which he described as *latissimis clavis vermium marginibus clavata*,[28] which has variously been translated as 'ornaments shaped like worms'[29] and 'embroidered purple stripes',[30] depending on whether the reference to 'worms' is interpreted as a decorative motif or the source of expensive insect-dye. Boniface considered such ornaments were sent by anti-Christ and suggested that the wearing of purple-coloured garments denoted homosexual tendencies in men committed to monastic life.[31] Such extravagances of dress must have been available to seculars. If we are to believe the statement of the post-Conquest writer William of Malmesbury, expensively-coloured cloth, as well as opulent accessories, were expressly used as signifiers of rank and status by the ninth century: William records that, at what was evidently a formal investiture, King Alfred gave his grandson, the future King Athelstan, a scarlet cloak (*chlamyde coccinea*), jewelled belt and gold ring.[32]

Paulus's evidence that the Anglo-Saxons wore linen is corroborated by Bede and Aldhelm (above, pp. 133–4) and should be taken in conjunction with the debate about the use of linen and wool as reflected in archaeological textiles (see p. 297). Evidently linen was the preferred fabric of the Anglo-Saxons by the eighth century when the age of migration was well past and they had become a settled community.

Surprising as it may seem today, it appears that many early Anglo-Saxons who chose to enter the Church did not recognise decorous dress as a natural corollary to their vocation. Both nuns and male clerics were accused of wearing worldly and extravagant dress. Most of the references to clothing from Anglo-Saxon writers are moralistic; either, like the quotation from Aldhelm (above, p. 134), condemning fashion-conscious dress, or as in Bede's occasional praises, applauding saintly persons for their unworldly attitude to clothing. The Church had to issue advice to its servants about sobriety in dress and also had to ban military equipment. Boniface described to Cuthbert of Canterbury reforms which had been made in the Continental Church, recommending that similar measures be taken in England: *Interdiximus servis Dei, ut pompato habitu vel sago vel armis utantur*[33] ('We have forbidden the servants of God to possess ostentatious dress or mantle or arms'). The matter was agreed at the Council of *Clofeshoe* in 747: *nec pompaticis, et quae ad inanem gloriam more saecularium pertineant, utantur indumentis, sed*

---

[28] E. Dümmler (ed.), 'S. Bonifatii et Lulli epistolae', *Monumenta Germaniae Historica Epistolae 3*, Merovingici et Karolini Aevi, I (Berlin, 1892), p. 355, line 19.
[29] Speake, *Anglo-Saxon Animal Art*, p. 91.
[30] E. Emerton, *The Letters of Saint Boniface* (New York, 1940), p. 140.
[31] Emerton, *Letters*, p. 140 and n. 2.
[32] *De Gestis*, II, 132; W. Stubbs (ed.), *William of Malmesbury De Gestis Regum Anglorum*, Rolls Series, 40, 2 vols (London, 1887–9), p. 145.
[33] Haddan and Stubbs, *Councils and Ecclesiastical Documents*, 3, p. 378.

simplici, propositioque congruenti eorum vestiantur habitu[34] ('they are not to use ostentatious clothing which pertains to the vain glory of secular custom, but they are to be clothed with habits simple and suitable for their purpose').

Simplicity in clerical dress was still being urged in 798 by the English scholar Alcuin, then living in the Carolingian Empire, in correspondence with the Archbishop of Canterbury;[35] and, according to the later testimony of William of Malmesbury, Alcuin's sensitivity on this point caused him to warn English clerics visiting the Empire, where ecclesiastical habits were worn, to refrain from wearing the brightly-coloured garments which were, apparently, usual among English churchmen.[36] It seems that in England the notion of a 'uniform' dress for persons in religious orders was not established immediately; and it was not until the second half of the ninth century that the lay habit was abandoned, according to a letter of 873 from the Pope to the Archbishops of Canterbury and York[37] (but see p. 326).

We have many references to clothing in seventh- and eighth-century letters, particularly those exchanged between English missionaries to the Continent and their friends and colleagues at home. Even as austerity was being advocated, garments and precious textiles were exchanged both as personal gifts and to enhance the glory of the Church. Clearly many such items were bestowed and received through the activities of the missionaries.[38] Though undocumented, secular travellers, such as diplomats, traders and pilgrims, must have contributed to the import–export of garments and fashions. Undoubtedly by the eighth century there was a regular commercial trade between England and the Continent which included fur and textiles. The correspondence between King Offa of Mercia and the Frankish Emperor Charlemagne (below, p. 179) confirms that cloaks were exported from England to the Empire and suggests that the clothing of eighth-century England was not incompatible with that of Carolingian Frankia. It may, therefore, be worth bearing in mind the descriptions Charlemagne's biographers gave of the Emperor's habitual dress. Einhard stressed that Charlemagne detested any clothing other than his native costume;[39] it is interesting that he felt the need to make this point and to describe the dress in detail.

---

[34] Haddan and Stubbs, *Councils and Ecclesiastical Documents*, 3, p. 369.

[35] Haddan and Stubbs, *Councils and Ecclesiastical Documents*, 3, p. 520.

[36] *De Gestis*, para. 82; Stubbs, *William of Malmesbury*, 1, pp. 82–3.

[37] E. Caspar,'Fragmenta registri Iohannis VIII, papae', *Monumenta Germaniae Historica, Epistolae*, 1, 7 (Berlin, 1928), No. 36, pp. 293–4.

[38] Haddan and Stubbs, *Councils and Ecclesiastical Documents*, 3, p. 434; M. Tangl (ed.), *S. Bonifatii et Lulli Epistolae*, Monumenta Germaniae Historica, Epistolae 4, Epistolae Selectae, 1 (Berlin, 1916), No. 63, p. 131, lines 18–20; No. 76, p. 159, line 18; No. 116, p. 250, lines 25, 32–4, p. 251, lines 14–15; No. 125, p. 263, lines 5–6.

[39] Einhard, who was writing twenty years after the Emperor's death, may have idealised Charlemagne's actions and character (see D. Bullough, *The Age of Charlemagne* (London, 1965), pp. 14–15), but there is no reason to doubt his description of Frankish dress.

This may be because the costume had become, or was becoming, out-of-date:

> Vestitu patrio, id est francisco utebatur. Ad corpus camisam lineam et feminalibus lineis induebatur; deinde tunicam quae limbo serico ambiebatur, et tibialia; tum fasciolis crura, et pedes calciamentis constringebat, et ex pellibus lutrinis et murinis thorace confecto humeros ac pectus hyeme muniebat; sago veneto amictus, et gladio semper accinctus ...[40]

> He wore the national dress of the Franks. Next to his skin he had a linen shirt and linen drawers; and then long hose and a tunic edged with silk. He wore shoes on his feet and bands of cloth wound round his legs. In winter he protected his chest and shoulders with a jerkin made of otter skins or ermine. He wrapped himself in a blue cloak and always had a sword strapped to his side ...[41]

The *tunica* favoured by Charlemagne was almost certainly short since it is recorded that a costume which Popes Hadrian and Leo persuaded the Emperor to wear on exceptional occasions in Rome included a long tunic (*longa tunica et clamide amictus*).[42] On other state occasions his festive dress was probably not different in style from his everyday clothes, only in the richness of its materials: it included a suit of gold cloth, jewelled shoes and a golden cloak-brooch.[43]

The Monk of St Gall's description of Charlemagne's dress is similar to Einhard's, but includes three distinct leg-coverings, among them cross-garters:

> Erat antiquorum ornatus vel paratura Francorum calciamenta forinsecus aurata, corigiis tricubitalibus insignita, fasciolae crurales vermiculatae, et subtus eas tibialia vel coxalia linea, quamvis ex eodem colore, tamen opere artificiosissimo variata. Super quae et fasciolas in crucis modum, intrinsecus et extrinsecus, ante et retro, longissimae illae corrigiae tendebantur. Deinde camisia clizana; post haec balteus spate colligatus ... Ultimum habitus eorum erat pallium canum vel saphirinum quadrangulum duplex, sic formatum, ut cum imponeretur humeris, ante et retro pedes tangeret, de lateribus vero vix genua contegeret.[44]

The dress and equipment of the Old Franks was as follows: their boots were gilded on the outside and decorated with leather laces more than four feet long. The wrappings round their legs were scarlet. Underneath these they wore linen garments on their legs and thighs, of the same colour, but with elaborate embroidery. Long

---

[40] Einhard *Vita*, para. 23; Pertz, *Monumenta Germaniae Historica, Scriptores,* 7, 2, p. 455, lines 32–5.

[41] L. Thorpe, trans., *Einhard and Notker the Stammerer Two Lives of Charlemagne* (Harmondsworth, 1969), p. 77.

[42] Pertz, *Monumenta Germaniae Historica, Scriptores,* 7, 2, p. 456, line 3.

[43] Pertz, *Monumenta Germaniae Historica, Scriptores,* 7, 2, p. 456, lines 4–5.

[44] Notker *Gesta*, I, para 34; Pertz, *MGH, Scriptores,* 7, 2, p. 747, lines 1–11.

leather thongs were cross-gartered over these wrappings and linen garments, in and out, in front and behind. Next came a white linen shirt, round which was buckled a swordbelt ... The last item of their clothing was a cloak, either white or blue, in the shape of a double square. This was so arrranged that, when it was placed over the shoulders, it reached to the feet in front and behind, but hardly came down to the knees at the sides.[45]

As we shall see, the long cloak,[46] a garment Charlemagne was particularly attached to, may have become unfashionable in England during the Emperor's lifetime. The Monk's description of it suggests that its proportions and arrangement resembled the ancient cloaks of Denmark and North Germany as reconstructed by Hayo Vierk (Fig. 76).

Literary evidence suggests that in the late-eighth century the dress and hairstyles of the Northumbrians differed from the fashions adopted elsewhere in England. Alcuin wrote a letter to King Æthelred of Northumbria in 793 which included the cleric's usual warning against extravagance in appearance:

Considerate habitum, tonsuram, et mores principum et populi luxuriosos. Ecce tonsura quam in barbis et in capillis paganis adsimilari voluistis.[47]

Consider the dress, the way of wearing the hair, the luxurious habits of the princes and people. Look at your trimming of beard and hair, in which you have wished to resemble the pagans.[48]

The context from which this quotation is taken makes it clear that by 'pagans' Alcuin refers to the Vikings, whose first, devastating, raid (on Lindisfarne) had taken place earlier that year. It seems that the extravagant fashions of dress and hair to which Alcuin objected resembled Viking fashions rather than Anglo-Saxon or Frankish (Alcuin would have known Frankish fashions well since he had been at Charlemagne's Palace School in Aachen since 782); but it is unlikely that the English were consciously *copying* their enemies the Vikings, since the Scandinavians had not yet begun to settle in England. Indeed the resemblance of Northumbrian fashions to those of 'pagans' had been noticed, four years before the raid on Lindisfarne, by the papal legate who had visited the kingdom in 787. A section of the legate's report entitled *Ut reliquias paganorum rituum quisque abjiciat* ('That the remainder of every one of the pagan customs should be abandoned') included the statement: *Vestimenta etiam vestra, more gentilium, quos, Deo opitulante patres vestri de orbe armis expulerunt, induitis.*[49] ('Also you put on your clothes

---

[45] Thorpe, *Einhard and Notker*, p. 132.

[46] As Sonia Hawkes pointed out to me, the description is consistent with a horseman's cloak, designed to protect the horse's neck and rump.

[47] Haddan and Stubbs, *Councils and Ecclesiastical Documents*, 3, pp. 493–4.

[48] D. Whitelock (ed.), *English Historical Documents c. 500–1042*, (London and Oxford, 1955), p. 776.

[49] Haddan and Stubbs, *Councils and Ecclesiastical Documents*, 3, p. 458.

Fig. 135 Figure in breeches, the *Book of Kells*, Dublin, Trinity College, MS A I 6, fol. 200r

Fig. 136 Figure in pointed cloak, the *Book of Kells*, fol. 89r

Fig. 137 Stylised figure in symmetrical cloak, the *Book of Durrow*, Dublin, Trinity College, *Codex Durmachensis*, fol. 21v

in the manner of gentiles, which, with God's help, your fathers expelled from the world with arms.') People expelled by force from Northumbria by the Germanic Angles would, presumably, have been British, that is, Celtic. It is quite likely that the nominally Anglian population of Northumbria continued to include many people of Celtic stock[50] and that they dressed like Britons rather than like the Anglo-Saxons of other kingdoms. Perhaps the offending costume included the tight knee-breeches, worn without a covering tunic, as depicted in the *Book of Kells* (Fig. 135) which the Roman world would have regarded as barbaric. Possibly it included a distinctive cloak. There were several varieties of Irish cloak, some of which may have been known to the Anglo-Saxons. The tenth-century Old English gloss to the (Latin) *Lindisfarne Gospels*, which is in the Northumbrian dialect, translates the Latin word *pallium* ('cloak') with the noun *bratt*.[51] This word is not Germanic; it is derived from Celtic and, indeed, survived into modern times in Welsh and Gaelic.[52] The term seems, then, to have passed into the Northumbrian dialect of Old English from Celtic speakers. In Irish literature the *bratt* is a traditional feature of Celtic dress, which takes the form of an elaborate cloak, brightly coloured, sometimes fringed and extravagantly large, to the extent that it might be wrapped round the body as many as five times. It is worn in conjunction with an ankle-length, belted tunic called *léine*.[53] Another candidate is the short cloak, pointed at the back and sometimes having a wide collar, depicted in the *Book of Kells* (Fig. 136). It is worn by riders on horseback, including a tonsured figure, and seems to have accompanied knee-breeches without a covering tunic. There is also a symmetrical cloak perhaps worn without a fastening by the symbol of St Matthew in the *Book of Durrow* (Dublin, Trinity College MS 57, *Codex Durmachensis*, fol. 21v; Fig. 137), and worn with a pennanular brooch at the right of the chest by the figure of Christ on the Cross of Muiredach, Monasterboice, Co. Louth (Fig. 138); and a rectangular cloak not unlike the Anglo-Saxon one, but worn over a longer garment, seen on the 'Warrior and Churchman' panel of the cross of the Scriptures, Clonmacnois, Co. Offaly.[54]

Kells figures (Figs 135, 136, 140) also have long hair and long pointed beards; although Alcuin criticised the 'trimming' of the Northumbrians' hair and beards, the aspect distasteful to him was

[50] W. Rees, 'Survivals of ancient Celtic custom in medieval England', *Angles and Britons*, O'Donnell Lectures (Cardiff, 1963), p. 168; G. W. S. Barrow, 'Northern English Society in the early Middle Ages (in the twelfth and thirteenth centuries)', *Northern History*, 4 (1969), pp. 1–28; L. Alcock, 'Quantity or quality: the Anglian graves of Bernicia', in V. I. Evison (ed.), *Angles, Saxons and Jutes: essays presented to J. N. L. Myres* (Oxford, 1981), pp. 168–86 at pp. 177–80.

[51] Matthew 5:40; Skeat, *Gospels*, pp. 50–1.

[52] Campbell, *Old English Grammar*, p. 220; Bosworth/Toller, *Dictionary*, p. 121.

[53] M. A. FitzGerald, 'Insular dress in early medieval Ireland', in G. R. Owen-Crocker (ed.), *Anglo-Saxon Texts and Contexts*, Bulletin of the John Rylands University Library of Manchester, 79.3 (1997), pp. 251–61, at p. 252.

[54] FitzGerald, 'Insular dress', *passim*.

perhaps excessive length of this kind. Very short hair was a Roman fashion and may have been seen as desirable by the Roman-trained clerics.

The papal legate who visited Northumbria was concerned to reform pagan practices. It would have been inaccurate to condemn the Celts as pagan since Christianity had been preached in Celtic England, Ireland and Wales before Augustine's mission, as any reader of Bede's *Ecclesiastical History* (completed in 731) would have known. Further on in his report, however, the legate referred to the Northumbrians' practice of casting lots, a notorious Germanic pagan practice recorded by Tacitus.[55] This suggests that some of the undesirable customs of the Northumbrians derived not so much from enemy peoples as from the pagan past of the Angles themselves. Remote from cross-channel trade and the influence of Frankia, the Northumbrians were, perhaps, affected little by costume changes which followed the conversion in other Anglo-Saxon kingdoms. The Church's criticism of Northumbrian dress suggests that these fashion changes were not entirely spontaneous but strongly encouraged by the Roman party. In Northumbria the more conservative Celtic Church had a strong hold and the Northumbrians of the eighth century were probably still wearing a distinctly Northern costume, which, more by accident than design, left them looking more like their enemies the Vikings than the southern Anglo-Saxons or their neighbours in the Carolingian Empire.

Fig. 138 Figure in symmetrical cloak with pennanular brooch, Cross of Muiredach, Monasterboice, Co. Louth, Republic of Ireland. After J. R. Allen

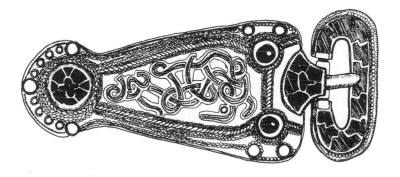

Fig. 139 a and b Buckle and clasp, Taplow, Buckinghamshire

[55] *Germania*, 10; Peterson and Hutton, *Tacitus*, p. 276.

Quite what the changes were that took place at the conversion, and in which ways the Northumbrians lagged behind or diverged from the other Christian peoples of north-west Europe we cannot be certain, and archaeological evidence does not enlighten us. It seems likely that they involved short/long hair, and perhaps some of those unguents which Sidonius had disapproved of; trousers, which classical writers had always seen as barbaric; and an unfamiliar cloak; but in what way this costume was offensively luxurious to the ecclesiastics, remains a mystery. Perhaps the legate saw ecclesiastics in Celtic shoes (Figs 141,147), which may have been more ornate than the plain Anglo-Saxon ankle boots.

The literary evidence considered so far has been written in Latin, with some glossing into Old English. The end of the period, which includes King Alfred's educational programme, brings texts in the vernacular containing a few garment-names.

Fig. 140 Human ornament showing extravagant hairstyles, shoes and sock, the *Book of Kells*, fol. 40v

The cloak

There is some rare material evidence of what may have been a heavy, twill cloak, parts of which were striped, in the mineral-replaced textile on a spear and the hand grip of a shield from what was perhaps a late-pagan burial at Ardale, Essex.[56] The gift of such a garment must have been welcome to an Anglo-Saxon missionary working among the heathen in north-west Europe: the king and queen of Northumbria sent twelve cloaks to Lull in 773. The royal donors, perhaps in modesty, called these 'small gifts'.[57]

The cloaks on the Franks Casket are typical of the garments we are to find in later manuscript illuminations. They are rectangular; that is, they have corners and are held together by a brooch at the right shoulder, rather than being tailored to fit the body. The cloaks on the back face of the Casket (Fig. 126) are longish – about knee-length. Those worn by the Magi on the front of the Casket are shorter, reaching just below the waist (Fig. 125). The differences in the images probably reflect different models, but both cloak styles may have been current.

Ninth-century sculptures show us some different cloaks, rare support for the variety of garments hinted at by the many cloak-names which have survived in documentary evidence. The 'falconer' figure from York (Fig. 130) wears a hooded cloak. His companion appears to be bare-headed but wears a cloak with a frilled collar. The Codford St Peter figure (Fig. 129) appears to wear a cloak arranged symmetrically over both shoulders and confined at the waist

Fig. 141 Figure wearing Irish shoes, the *Book of Kells*, fol. 29r

[56] E. Crowfoot, 'Textiles from Ardale Anglo-Saxon cemetery', in T. J. Wilkinson (ed.), *Archaeology and Environment in South Essex: rescue archaeology along the Grays by-pass, 1979–80*, East Anglian Archaeology, 42 (1988), pp. 54–5.
[57] Haddan and Stubbs, *Councils and Ecclesiastical Documents*, 3, p. 434.

by the same belt which secures the tunic. The cloak, like the rest of this figure's costume, is carved in deep grooves so that it appears to be pleated or folded.

The biographies and correspondence of Charlemagne indicate that a change took place in cloak fashions during the Emperor's lifetime, and that the citizens of the Empire were following their neighbours in changing to a shorter cloak. Both Charlemagne's biographers mention (above, pp. 174–5) that the cloak was a traditional part of Frankish costume, the Monk of St Gall adding that Charlemagne was accustomed to wear, for evening service, a long flowing cloak 'the use and the very name of which are forgotten'.[58] The Emperor disliked the striped Gaulish cloaks which were being imported into his realm by Frisian merchants, because they were short. His acerbic comments on the briefer cloaks is a testament to the versatility of the long cloak which was going out of fashion:

> ... adiciens: Quid prosunt illa pittaciola? in lecto non possum eis cooperiri, caballicans contra ventos et pluvia nequeo defendi, ad necessaria naturae secedens tibiarum congelatione deficio.[59]

> 'What is the use of these little napkins?' he asked. 'I can't cover myself with them in bed. When I am on horseback I can't protect myself from the winds and the rain. When I go off to empty my bowels, I catch cold because my backside is frozen.'[60]

A similar change was evidently taking place in England, as we see in a letter from Charlemagne to King Offa of Mercia. The Empire had been trading regularly with Mercia, receiving cloaks and exporting stone, which exchange Charlemagne exploited to make his point courteously but firmly:

> nostri de prolixitate sagorum deposcunt, ut tales jubeatis fieri, quales antiquis temporibus ad nos venire solebant.[61]

> [but as you have intimated your wishes concerning the length of the stones] so our people make a demand about the size of the cloaks, that you may order them to be such as used to come to us in former times.[62]

We cannot put a name to every variety of cloak current in England during the seventh, eighth and ninth centuries; but we may note that the terms *mentel* and *sciccels* were probably in use for secular garments and that the word *hacele* may sometimes have been used of a hooded cloak.

---

[58] *Gesta*, I, 31; Pertz, *MGH, Scriptores*, 7, 2, p. 745, lines 33–4; Thorpe, *Einhard and Notker*, p. 129.

[59] *Gesta*, I, 34; Pertz, *MGH, Scriptores*, 7, 2, p. 747, lines 24–6.

[60] Thorpe, *Einhard and Notker*, p. 133.

[61] Haddan and Stubbs, *Councils and Ecclesiastical Documents*, 3, p. 497.

[62] Whitelock, *English Historical Documents*, p. 782.

Fig. 142a Reconstruction of helmet, Sutton Hoo, Suffolk

Fig. 142b Reconstruction of plaque from Sutton Hoo helmet showing 'dancing' warriors

Fig. 142c Reconstruction of plaque from Sutton Hoo helmet showing rider and footsoldier

A wrap-over coat

The helmet found in the Sutton Hoo Ship Burial (Fig. 142a) is decorated with stamped bronze plaques bearing geometric, zoomorphic and anthropomorphic decoration.[63] The plaques on the cheek-pieces originally bore a scene of two male figures in horned helmets engaged in a ritual dance (Fig. 142b) and a scene repeated round the helmet and over the top of it shows a combat (Fig. 142c). The male figures in both scenes wear knee-length coats which wrap over at the front and have wide facings, which are decorated with chevrons in the 'dancing' scene, billets in the other. The garments have long sleeves with deep, decorated cuffs, which are mostly straight, but in the case of the fallen warrior in the combat scene, taper to the wrist. The garment of the fallen warrior is patterned to resemble chain mail, but the others are plain, and Rupert Bruce-Mitford insists that the figures on both plaques wear 'coats', not mail shirts, despite the fact that they carry weapons and wear helmets.[64] The Sutton Hoo helmet was old when it was buried, and may date to the sixth century, even the earlier part of the sixth century, though it was deposited in the early-seventh. It is of the Swedish Vendel type, and the 'dancing warriors' plaque is paralleled on a helmet from the boat burial site of Valsgärde, Sweden (no. 7). The coat was probably depicted again on some bronze foil, fragmentary when excavated, from the East Mound at Gamla Uppsala, also Sweden. The 'combat' scene is parallelled on a repoussé gold disc brooch from Pliezhausen, Germany, where, as in the Sutton Hoo scene, the coat of the fallen warrior is patterned to resemble mail, while the coat of his opponent, on horseback, is plain. A fragment of silver foil, which has been recovered from a seventh-century burial mound at Caenby, Lincolnshire, probably depicted a man in a similar costume. Bertil Almgren has argued that the wrap-over coat is a 'kimono' type of garment, of Sassanian Persian origin, which was copied in Sweden on Vendel period helmets;[65] however, the appearance of a similar garment on the fifth-century Halberstadt Diptych suggests that the garment was already established in Germanic costume in the Migration Period.

The 'dancing warriors' and 'combat' scenes are probably associated with the cult of Woden, and the wrap-over garments, like the horned helmets, might be part of the regalia of the Woden cult. The wrap-over garment might be considered iconographic in England, had not Penelope Walton Rogers recognized a fragment of tablet-woven braid running vertically behind a belt buckle in

[63] The helmet is described in detail in Bruce-Mitford, *Sutton Hoo*, 2 (1978), pp. 150–231.

[64] Bruce-Mitford, *Sutton Hoo*, 2, pp. 186–97.

[65] B. Almgren, 'Helmets, crowns and warriors' dress from the Roman Emperors to the chieftains of Uppland', trans. H. Clarke, in J. P. Lamm and H. Å. Nordström, *Vendel Period Studies*, Museum of National Antiquities, Stockholm, Studies, 2 (1983), pp. 11–16, at p. 15.

Castledyke Grave 126, which she identified as part of a wrap-over coat.[66] Possibly there is another example of the garment in the grave of a man accompanied by a lyre, buried in the eighth century in St Severinus, Cologne, Germany. The 'minstrel's' breast and neck bore a loop of silk braid brocaded in spun gold (Fig. 143). This might have been the remains of a decorative facing or collar from a similar coat. Collars are not usual on Anglo-Saxon figures, but a fighting figure on piece of a stone panel or frieze, from Monkwearmouth, Tyne and Wear, perhaps ninth-century, is dressed in a garment 'possibly having a wide collar.'[67]

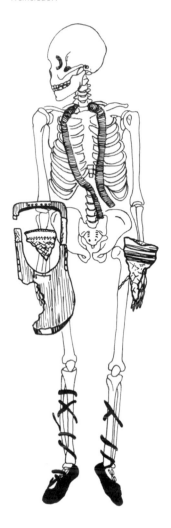

Fig. 143 The 'Minstrel's Grave', St Severinus, Cologne, reconstructed after F. Fremersdorf

The waistcoat or jacket

Charlemagne, we know, wore a *thorax*, a garment (made of fur) to protect the upper part of his body. The Anglo-Saxons may have done so too. The documented word *breost-rocc* may describe such a garment.[68] Three of the satellite figures on the Fuller Brooch (Fig. 133) appear to wear little cloth jackets or boleros which are unique in Anglo-Saxon art. The outstretched left arm of the figure representing the sense of hearing shows a seam running down the arm. A fourth figure (the Sense of Touch) appears to wear a different garment, a waist-length jacket with a broad collar, but it seems quite likely that the artist was forced to do something different here because of the constraint of the position of the arms; the figure is portrayed touching one hand with the other.

Garments of skin and fur or of shaggy appearance

Fur, being organic, has a low survival rate archaeologically, but increased awareness of organic remains among excavators is beginning to bear fruit. A fragment of what was probably mineralised fur survived, detached from an iron necklet in Grave 1661, Bainesse Farm, Catterick, North Yorkshire. It is possible that this was a male grave since metal necklets, though uncommon finds, occur elsewhere with male juveniles. This skeleton was of a young person, with no typically feminine grave-goods, only a small buckle thought to be of seventh-century type.[69] It may have been that the fur lay against the metal, the skin side outside, though there is no evidence whether the necklet was worn over or under the fur. Fur was also

[66] Walton Rogers, in Drinkall and Foreman, *Castledyke*, p. 279 and p. 277 Fig. 135.

[67] Monkwearmouth 7; Cramp, *Corpus of Anglo-Saxon Sculpture*, 1, p. 125, Plate III, no. 610. The sculpture is dated on the basis of the sword type. The collar is not visible in the plate.

[68] Owen-Crocker, 'The search for Anglo-Saxon skin garments', pp. 38–9.

[69] Wilson, Cardwell, Cramp, Evans, Taylor-Wilson, Thompson and Wacher, 'Early Anglian Catterick and *Catraeth*', pp. 36–7.

recorded in another recent archaeological report on Empingham, Rutland.[70]

Literary evidence makes it clear that fur and animal hair were used for luxury clothing. From the eighth century we have written evidence of hair and fur garments crossing the North Sea as gifts. Goat-hair bedclothes and a cloak of silk and goat's hair were among the gifts sent to England by the missionary Boniface;[71] in the other direction, Boniface's colleague Lull was the recipient of an otter-skin robe (called *gunna* in Latin), a gift from the Northumbrians.[72] The furs of native animals, such as otter and marten,[73] were probably being traded to the Continent on a commercial scale at this time by the enterprising Frisians.[74] The literary evidence suggests that cloaks could be made of fur, but not all fur garments were cloaks. The *thorax* which Charlemagne wore, and which was probably a waistcoat or jerkin (certainly distinct from his cloak, which is separately described by Einhard, p. 174 above) was made of fur, specifically otter-skin or ermine, which seem to have been luxury pelts. It seems probable that the Anglo-Saxons too wore jerkins of skin, probably with minimal shaping, as their northern kinsmen had done for centuries. The skins of domesticated animals, sheep and goats, probably provided more utilitarian, but no less warm, protection for lower ranking persons.[75]

A long fur garment might be called *crusene*, *fel*, or *heden*, and the *basing*, *rocc* and *sciccels* could be fur or fabric. The *pilece* was also fur, and a citation in which Adam and Eve are described as making *pylcan* from skins[76] suggests that fur or skin loin cloths or breeches may have been known; the (possible) fur trousers on the Torslunda die provide a precedent (above, p. 117; Plate 3d).

It is possible to create woven cloth with a shaggy effect resembling fur. In our period this might have been achieved by utilising the wool of a double-coated sheep,[77] or by pile-weaving, a technique in which long loops of thread were inserted while the cloth was on the loom. Pile-woven cloth is well attested in the early medieval period in north-west Europe. Eighth- and tenth-century

---

[70] Timby, *Empingham II*.

[71] Tangl, *S. Bonifatii et Lulli Epistolae*, No. 76, p. 159, line 18; No. 63, p. 131, lines 18–20. Perhaps the goat's hair was used for embroidery as in finds from Norway (p. 285); perhaps it was woven; or it may have been hide.

[72] Tangl, *S. Bonifatii et Lulli*, No. 116, p. 251, lines 14–15.

[73] A marten-skin coat is mentioned in a Welsh lullaby, probably ninth-century; K. H. Jackson (ed.), *The Gododdin: the oldest Scottish poem* (Edinburgh, 1969), p. 151.

[74] D. Jellema, 'Frisian trade in the Dark Ages', *Speculum*, 30 (1955), pp. 15–36, at p. 31.

[75] Lull's garment is called, in Latin, *gunna*. *Gunna* is glossed by the Old English word *heden* in the Corpus Glossary (Lindsay, *Corpus Glossary*, p. 87, G. 185) and *heden* elsewhere glosses Latin *melote*, 'an animal skin, particularly sheepskin or goat' (Napier, *Glosses*, 39, line 1471); see Owen-Crocker, 'The search for Anglo-Saxon skin garments', p. 38.

[76] C. W. Bouterwek (ed.), *Screadunga* (Elberfeld, 1858), p. 20, lines 28–9.

[77] Appleyard and Wildman, 'Fibres of archaeological interest', p. 631.

fragments have been recovered from Sweden and late-ninth- to tenth-century examples from the Isle of Eigg (Scotland) and the Isle of Man. Shaggy cloaks were among articles traded by the Frisians, Europe's merchants, from about 600 to 900, and were made in and exported from Ireland at this time.[78]

From Anglo-Saxon England a softer and more luxurious version of pile-woven textile, with 'decorative lines of soft, silky locks' has been identified among finds from the Sutton Hoo Ship Burial, Broomfield Barrow, Essex and Banstead Down, Surrey, also possibly Snape, Suffolk.[79] Other seventh-century male barrow burials are recorded as yielding finds of reddish-brown animal hair, sometimes in contact with textile. They are widely distributed but all belonged to men of high rank; they include Taplow, Benty Grange, and possibly Broome, Norfolk. Possibly these also were pile woven textile or fur-and-cloth garments. They may have been newly fashionable, possibly imported. Cloaks of shaggy appearance might have been called by the Old English garment-name *loða*[80] since the Old Icelandic cognate *loði* is a name for a shaggy, pile-woven mantle.[81]

Fur garments, and shaggy, woven garments that looked like fur may have been luxurious, but conversely, animal skins could form the humblest of garments. The eighth-century hermit St Guthlac is reputed to have eschewed both wool and linen garments in favour of skin, certainly for penitential reasons.[82]

The tunic

In Anglo-Saxon art of the Christian period, the majority of male figures wear girdled tunics, usually cut short enough to reveal the knee. Such tunics are represented in the *Vespasian Psalter*, not only in the Greek-derived miniature which focuses on King David, but also as worn by one of the figures in the 'David and Jonathan' initial. This is the earliest surviving English manuscript to depict figures in tunics rather than long robes. Active figures in the short tunics of secular costume were being depicted on the Continent by the ninth century, in a form which was to influence later Anglo-

---

[78] E. E. Gudjónsson, 'On ancient and medieval pile weaving, with special reference to a recent find in Iceland' (English summary), *Árbók hins íslenzka fornleifafélags* (1962), pp. 65–71.

[79] Sutton Hoo 10; Broomfield B4; E. Crowfoot, 'The Textiles', in Bruce-Mitford, *Sutton Hoo*, 3, ii, p. 443; J. R. Barfoot and B. Price-Williams, *The Saxon Barrow at Gally Hills, Banstead Down, Surrey*, Research Volume of the Surrey Archaeological Society, 3 (1976), pp. 69–71 (Appendix by E. Crowfoot).

[80] The word is documented from this period as a gloss (Lindsay, *Corpus Glossary*, p. 102, line 15 and p. 157, line 60, glossing *lacerna* and *sagulum*) and in Alfredian translation (Sweet, *King Alfred's Version of Gregory's Pastoral Care*, p. 196, line 21, glossing *liniamento*).

[81] Gudjónsson, 'Pile weaving', p. 68.

[82] *Vita Sancti Guthlaci*, XXVIII; B. Colgrave (ed.), *Felix's Life of St Guthlac* (Cambridge, 1956), p. 94.

Saxon art. It seems clear that the short tunic was the typical secular costume for men right across mainland Europe, though Ireland, with its breeches, distinctive cloaks and long tunic, seems to have kept somewhat independent.

A number of tunics appear on carvings of this period. Some of the male figures on the Franks Casket wear tunics with bodices which conceal the girdle, and short skirts hanging in many folds (Figs 124–5). The Repton rider wears a comparable pleated skirt beneath a short mail garment on his upper body. Martin Biddle and Birte Kjølbye-Biddle suggest Antique models lie behind the heavily pleated skirts on both carvings.[83] Other Franks Casket figures wear straighter skirts, their tightness indicated by a line beneath the buttocks. Some of the tunics have plain, close-fitting sleeves. Other sleeves have a corrugated or pleated appearance.

The West Saxon, Codford St Peter figure (Fig. 129) wears a tunic marked in vertical folds to the girdle. The skirt, which ends above the knee, is marked horizontally, perhaps to indicate a contrast of texture – a contrast with the cloak and also, perhaps, with the bodice. The left sleeve is full to the elbow, and closely pleated from elbow to wrist. The right sleeve, which is close-fitting, seems to have fallen back from the raised right arm. The Jarrow figure (Fig. 127) wears a knee-length tunic with long, pleated or wrinkled sleeves. The Sheffield archer (Fig. 131) wears a round-necked tunic, its skirt above the knees. The sleeve of this garment is close-fitting but smooth, flaring slightly at the wrist above a decorative band. (This sleeve is unusual and was possibly peculiar to the costume of the archer, since its closest parallel is the sleeve of another archer figure, this time on an ivory reliquary, probably of eleventh-century date.[84] The archers on the Bayeux 'Tapestry', however, have close-fitting, not flared sleeves.) Many of the cruder sculptures of the Viking Age depict figures in knee-length skirts, which probably represent similar tunics.

Turning to metalwork, we find that the figure on the Alfred Jewel (Fig. 132) wears a vivid green, V-necked garment, which leaves the forearms bare. The green colour does not continue below the waist which could suggest a contrasting skirt. The artistic effect of this piece of cloisonné, however, is so dependent on colour-contrast that it would be unwise to draw firm conclusions from the variations. Four of the figures on the Fuller Brooch (Fig. 133) wear, under their jackets, belted tunics with full, heavy-looking skirts, each with a stylised fold or pleat at the centre front. In three cases this makes the tunic appear to hang lower at the sides than in the middle. This fullness of the skirt may explain the stylised interpretation of dress on a number of sculptures from the ninth century

---

[83] Biddle and Kjølbye-Biddle, 'The Repton stone', pp. 265–6.
[84] Beckwith, *Ivory Carvings*, cat. 45, p. 128; Raw, 'The archer, the eagle and the lamb', p. 394, Plate 45a.

and later, in which the hem of the tunic hangs in an inverted U shape. Most of the extant examples are in areas of Viking influence, for example at Norbury, Derbyshire (Fig. 144) and Alstonfield, Staffordshire,[85] but there is a possible case on one of a group of figures on a southern piece, at Burford, Oxfordshire.[86] Rather different tunics are worn by the figures on the Lindisfarne sculpture (Fig. 128) They are very short, and patterned in wide, horizontal bands. The figures on the stone probably represent Viking raiders, so their costume may have been slightly different from that of the Anglo-Saxons and the later (settled) Anglo-Vikings.

Paulus Diaconus emphasised the wide borders on the tunics of the Anglo-Saxons (above, p. 171). None of the English representations from our period suggest such borders, though they can be found in later art. (Fig. 188 shows a plain border round the bottom of a tunic, Colour Plate I, lower right, a decorated border edging the lower edge and side slits of a tunic.) A border might consist of a strip of cloth in a contrasting colour or fibre, and if it were dyed in a rare and expensive dye or woven in imported silk, this would have been a luxurious touch. Elisabeth Crowfoot and Sonia Hawkes suggest that silk borders such as Aldhelm describes 'would probably have been imported ready-made, like lengths of ribbon'.[87] An unusual fine diamond-twill textile, which was perhaps originally striped or checked, and which might have come from a tunic, preserved in mineralised form at Ardale, had a tablet-woven border.[88] There are patterned borders on the (longish) tunics of the Swedish Torslunda die (Plate 3b) and also on the long tunics on some Irish sculptures, including the Cross of the Scriptures, Clonmacnois, The High Cross of Durrow and the Cross of Muiredach (Fig. 138),[89] and Anglo-Saxon borders may have been similarly ornamental. The Swedish and Irish borders have the appearance of tablet-woven braids, which could, like the Ardale example, have been integral to the weaving, or attached at a later stage. Another method of creating a decorated border would be to embroider it, as the tenth-century Llan-gors garment was embroidered (below, pp. 217–18; Plates 9, 10), or to work embroidery onto a separate piece of cloth, which was subsequently attached to the garment. An embroidered border from Mammen, Denmark, may come from a tunic: the back cloth was an unusual 2 x 1 twill and the embroidery, carried out in stem stitch, depicted human masks and gripping hands in a design related to the Borre Style. Embroidered, padded cuffs and appliqué

Fig. 144 Armed figure on a sculpture, Norbury, Derbyshire

[85] G. Le Blanc Smith, 'Some Norman and pre-Norman remains in the Dovedale district', *The Reliquary*, 3rd series, 10 (1904), pp. 232–47, at pp. 233–4, Fig. 1.

[86] E. M. Guest, 'A sculptured stone in Burford church', *Antiquaries Journal*, 10 (1930), pp. 159–60, Fig. 1.

[87] Crowfoot and Hawkes, 'Gold braids', p. 57.

[88] The tablet weave comprised the side border of the weaving; E. Crowfoot, 'Ardale', pp. 54–5.

[89] FitzGerald, 'Insular dress', Figs 19–22, 24.

strips may have belonged to the same elaborate garment.[90] A fragment of what had once been textile decorated with gold has survived embedded in the tip of a sword from a man's grave at Faversham, Kent. This may derive from a border.[91]

At the other end of the social scale, there survives what might be part of a leather sleeve, one of the many off-cuts from the leatherworking industry, from Anglo-Viking York.[92] This serves as a reminder of the need for more practical and protective garments, for example in battle when a mailcoat was not owned, and for trades such as butchery and working with red hot metal where physical injury was a daily possibility.

The Old English word *cyrtel* was almost certainly applied to the tunic, with the newer Latin loan word *tunece* coming into use as a synonym.

The longer tunic and gown

While the short tunic was apparently the regular wear for men in this period, we find occasional evidence that a longer garment could be worn. Both the figures on the St Mary Bishophill Junior, York, sculpture (Fig. 130) wear tunics cut well below the knee but not reaching to the ankles. Rosemary Cramp has suggested that the figures wear the voluminous lay habit, shorter than the habit which superceded it in the late-ninth century.[93] A few male figures on Viking Age sculptures (which are difficult to date precisely) wear long, straight garments which contrast with the costume of their companion-figures. Some have been interpreted as characters from biblical narrative, such as Isaac on a cross from Bilton, North Yorkshire.[94] It is uncertain whether the sculptors were influenced by the long garments of Christian tradition; possibly they were depicting garments worn in their own day. Long garments had become fashionable for men of high rank by the eleventh century, but we cannot be sure that they were worn any earlier. However, a longer garment appears in the 'David and Jonathan' initial of the eighth-century *Vespasian Psalter*. The artist, presumably, was differentiating between

---

[90] Munksgaard, 'Embroideries', in Hogestol, *Festskrift til Thorleif Sjovold*, pp. 162–3, 169. Magnus Petersen's watercolour sketch is reproduced at p. 160, Fig. 2.

[91] E. Crowfoot, 'Early Anglo-Saxon gold braids: addenda and corrigenda', *Medieval Archaeology*, 13 (1969), pp. 209–10.

[92] Mainman and Rogers, *Craft, Industry and Everyday Life*, p. 255 Fig. 118 and p. 256.

[93] R. J. Cramp, *Anglian and Viking York*, University of York Borthwick Papers, No. 33 (1967), p. 13; J. Lang, *British Academy Corpus of Anglo-Saxon Stone Sculpture*, 3, *York and Eastern Yorkshire* (Oxford, 1991), p. 84.

[94] W. G. Collingwood, 'Anglian and Anglo-Danish sculpture in the West Riding', *Yorkshire Archaeological Journal*, 23 (1914–15), pp. 129–299, at pp. 139–41, p. 140, Fig. d.

the characters by means of this dress, but again, we cannot know if traditional iconography or contemporary fashion dictated his choice.

The undergarments

Aldhelm (above, p. 134) stated that a linen shirt was worn with the tunic. Since such a garment would be covered by the tunic, we do not see it in graphic depictions, unless the pleated sleeves belong to this undergarment rather than the tunic (cf. pp. 250–1, below). There is ample linguistic evidence for such a garment, however. In Old English it could be called *cemes*, *ham* or *scyrte*.

There is some evidence that loin cloths were worn when tunics were not. It is possible that these were normally worn as undergarments concealed beneath the tunic. There are examples on a small metal object found in a pagan grave at Breach Downs, Dover, Kent,[95] on the Abingdon sword hilt (Fig. 134) and on several northern sculptures. In at least one case – a Viking Age fragment from Lythe, North Yorkshire[96] – the figures are wrestling. They seem to be bare-chested but wear short, unbelted skirts. Figures probably representing Adam and Eve on carvings from Pickhill, North Yorkshire[97] and Urswick, Cumbria[98] wear similar garments.

In the Corpus Glossary the words *gyrdels* and *brec* both appear to mean 'loin-cloth'.[99] (*Brec*, ancestor to modern English 'breeches', seems to have principally signified short trousers covering the loins or extending down the thighs.) Later glossaries record the words *underwrædel* and *wæd-brec*, both, apparently, names for loin-cloths.[100]

The trousers

Anglo-Saxon men probably wore trousers beneath their tunics. The figures of the Magi on the Franks Casket wear curious trousers,[101]

---

[95] V. I. Evison, 'The Dover, Breach Downs and Birka men', *Antiquity*, 39 (1965), pp. 214–17, at pp. 214–15, Fig. 2.

[96] W. G. Collingwood, 'Anglian and Anglo-Danish sculpture in the East Riding', *Yorkshire Archaeological Journal*, 21 (1910–11), pp. 254–302, at p. 290, Fig. 1.

[97] W. G. Collingwood, 'Anglian and Anglo-Danish sculpture in the North Riding of Yorkshire', *Yorkshire Archaeological Journal*, 19 (1906–7), pp. 267–413 at pp. 380–1 Fig. d, 385.

[98] Urswick 1; R. N. Bailey and R. Cramp, *The British Academy Corpus of Anglo-Saxon Stone Sculpture*, 2, *Cumberland, Westmorland and Lancashire North-of-the-Sands* (Oxford, 1988), pp. 148–9, Plate 568.

[99] *Gyrdils broec* glosses *lumbare*; Lindsay, *Corpus Glossary*, p. 108, line 287.

[100] *Underwrædel* glosses *subfibulum, uel subligaculum* (Wright/Wulcker, *Vocabularies*, col. 153, lines 1–2); *wædbræc* glosses *perizomata, uel campestria, uel succinctoria* (Wright/Wulcker, *Vocabularies*, col. 125, 3–5) and *perizomata, uel campestria* (col. 328, line 7). This word is used in the Old English prose Genesis, again translating *perizomata*, rendering Adam and Eve's garments made from fig leaves (Genesis 3: 7; Crawford, *Heptateuch*, p. 89).

[101] The Magi were traditionally depicted in rich and exotic costumes, which sometimes included elaborate leggings (for example, the mosaic in the sixth-century

Fig. 145 Figure with possible trousers, on a pendant, Riseley, Horton Kirby, Kent

corrugated like the limbs of a 'Michelin Man' (Fig. 125). Possibly this was a Northumbrian style, as very similar trousers are depicted on a Northumbrian coin.[102] The artist may have been representing very loose trousers, such as we see on Roman sculptures of German captives (Fig. 75), but which were tied at intervals down the legs and pouched over the strings, as gardeners and agricultural workers have sometimes worn them in relatively recent times.

Elsewhere on the Franks Casket, and in other representations of men, it is hard to decide whether the figures wear close-fitting trousers beneath their tunics, or if they are bare-legged. The kneeling archer figure on the Sheffield cross (Fig. 131) evidently wears trousers, indicated by lines at the backs of the legs which suggest folds, and by the double lines at each ankle. A similar double line appears at each ankle of the figures representing Taste, Smell, Hearing and Touch on the Fuller Brooch (Fig. 133). As on the Sheffield archer figure, the lines could mark the end of the trouser-leg or the top of a shoe, or both.

The figures disappearing into the serpent's mouth on the Repton stone wear close-fitting breeches over the thighs, in conjunction with a close-fitting upper garment to the waist. Small figures decorating the text of the *Book of Kells* wear tight breeches which reach down to the top of the calf; these are worn without a covering tunic though on the rare occasions when the cloak is absent it appears that a close-fitting shirt, either tucked into the breeches or ending at the waist, is worn (Fig. 135). So many of the figures are fantastical, however, with naked limbs patterned and naturalistic body parts growing decorative excrescences, that it would be unwise to rely too much on the identification of a shirt. Figures on horseback in the same manuscript wear similar, sometimes even shorter, breeches, with a pointed cloak and some kind of shirt which is only visible at the neck (Fig. 136). As already mentioned, close-fitting leg-coverings of this kind may have been characteristic of Celtic dress. Similar breeches appear on the Gundestrup Cauldron, a Celtic object found in Denmark, and which dates to about the first century BC.[103] The fashion of wearing trousers without a tunic also seems to have been favoured by Scandinavians. The trousers with the appearance of fur on the Torslunda die (Plate 3d) are worn this way. A gold pendant found at Riseley (Horton Kirby), Kent (Grave 56), which though probably made in Kent reflects Scandinavian taste, shows a stylised figure without a tunic, but with lines at the ankles suggesting trousers (Fig. 145). A figure on a bracteate from Grave 29 at Bifrons, Kent, however, has lines at the knees, which suggest short breeches of the *Kells* type (Fig. 146). A number of Viking Age

Fig. 146 Figure with possible knee breeches, on a pendant, Bifrons, Kent

basilica of S. Apollinare Nuovo, Ravenna, Italy and the English *Benedictional of St Æthelwold*, see below, Chapter VII, p. 258). The Franks Casket carver, who has obviously misunderstood a background of palm trees in his model, may have misinterpreted some unfamiliar dress here. I have not, however, found a likely source.
[102] I am indebted to Anna Gannon for this information.
[103] FitzGerald, 'Insular dress', p. 252.

sculptures from the north of England depict figures with belts but without tunics. They include a group surrounding the boss of the cross at Bilton.[104] The figure of Isaac on the same cross wears no belt or tunic, but ornaments at the head and chest suggest the figure was intended to be clothed; perhaps the sculptor thought of him in trousers.

Several Old English words for trousers are documented. The commonest, *brec*, seems to have been used of a loin-cloth in the earliest occurrence, in the Corpus Glossary, but in later texts seems to have signified short trousers. The Corpus Glossary also lists *bræcce*[105] while *braccas*, although only documented later, has cognates in Scandinavian languages, so was probably established early.[106] The term 'trews' is Celtic (Irish *truibhas*).[107]

The leggings

On the Continent, the Merovingian Frankish fashion for fancy gartering, which came into use in the sixth century and became very popular in the seventh, is well evidenced in the Alamannic region,[108] where buckles are regularly found under the knees or ankles of richly-equipped male skeletons. These probably belonged to leggings consisting of bands at the ankle and the top of the calf, linked by a vertical strip. The horizontal bands secured a rectangular piece of cloth round the lower leg.[109] The 'minstrel' buried in St Severinus, Cologne, wore cross-garters, or crossed shoe thongs, over his white linen stockings, as demonstrated by the X-shaped fragments of sheep's leather found over the shins (Fig. 143),[110] and the rider and one of the other figures on the Repton stone appear to wear closely wound gartering which crosses, in the manner of Charlemagne.[111] Lace tags found at the legs of skeletons at Finglesham[112] and Polhill[113] in Kent may be slight evidence that the Frankish fashion reached England. Celtic fashion may have differed from Germanic:

[104] Collingwood, 'Anglian and Anglo-Danish sculpture in the West Riding', p. 140, Fig. b.

[105] *Bra(e)ccae* glosses *sarabar(a)e*; Lindsay, *Corpus Glossary*, p. 158, line 96.

[106] Holthausen, *Wörterbuch*, p. 31.

[107] FitzGerald, 'Insular dress', p. 252.

[108] Christlein, *Die Alamannen*, p. 63.

[109] Clauss, 'Beobachtungen an merowingerzeitlichen', pp. 55–64; Clauss, 'Strumpfbänder', pp. 54–88. I am grateful to Dr Clauss and to Frau Dorit Reimann-Kummer for their detailed answers to my questions.

[110] F. Fremersdorf, 'Zwei wichtige Frankengräber aus Köln', *Jahrbuch für Prähistorische und Ethnografische Kunst*, 15–16 [1941–2] (1943), p. 136.

[111] Biddle and Kjølbye-Biddle ('The Repton stone', pp. 266–7) discuss whether the rider wears high boots, which on Continental equestrian carvings are decorated with 'criss-cross lines', but conclude that garters are represented on the grounds that one of the serpent's victims has the same detail.

[112] Hawkes, 'Polhill', in Philp, *Excavations in West Kent*, p. 194.

[113] Philp, *Excavations in West Kent*, p. 175; Hawkes, 'Polhill', in Philp, p. 194.

woven socks are suggested in both the *Book of Durrow* and the *Book of Kells* (Figs 137, 140).

Footwear

From the seventh century we find more evidence of footwear than before: there is some evidence of shoes in furnished graves, some indication in early Christian period art and the material remains of leather footwear from urban archaeological sites.

A man buried in the seventh century at Banstead Down evidently wore ankle boots of soft leather with eyelets for leather thongs; on the right foot was found part of what may have been a strap to fasten the boot inside the right ankle. This footwear was evidently similar to the later finds from York.[114] A Frankish fashion for buckled shoes may have been transmitted to south-east England in the seventh and eighth centuries, as evident from shoe buckles found in male graves at, again, Finglesham[115] and Polhill,[116] Kent, in the Prittlewell Chamber grave and in the Sutton Hoo Ship Burial (*c.* 625), where the remains of four shoes, made by the turnshoe method, were found. Traces of decorative stitching was found on the vamps of two of the Sutton Hoo shoes. They were light, for indoor wear, and were certainly in the luxury class. They had evidently been fastened by laces, terminating in metal strap ends, and were buckled, since one shoe bore the impression of a square buckle plate. A pair of silver and a pair of bronze buckles, plus several strap ends and some woven tape were also associated with the Sutton Hoo footwear.[117]

The shoes in common use would be either of 'slip-on' type or would be secured by a toggle and thong or a tied thong fastener. Two of the basic shapes established by Viking examples of leather footwear from York, the ankle-shoe or short boot and the slipper (Plate 7, Figs 117–118) are depicted on contemporary or near-contemporary art. The ankle shoe seems to have been common in northwest Europe at this time, featuring in the Carolingian Empire and Scandinavia, though methods of thonging may differ. Both archaeology and art show that footwear at this time was flat-soled and flexible, without exaggerated toes or other ostentatious features. The personified Senses on the Fuller Brooch (Fig. 133) wear high shoes with triangular cut-outs at the ankle for ease in putting on and off. The Codford St Peter figure (Fig. 129) wears slippers with triangular projections up the heels. Similar shoes are worn by the figure on the Abingdon sword hilt (Fig. 134).

---

[114] Barfoot and Price-Williams, *Banstead Down*, p. 69.
[115] Graves 95, 108; Hawkes, 'Polhill', in Philp, *Excavations in West Kent*, p. 194.
[116] Philp, *Excavations in West Kent*, p. 175; Hawkes, 'Polhill', p. 194.
[117] Bruce-Mitford, *Sutton Hoo*, 2 (1978), pp. 442–3; K. East, 'The Shoes' in Bruce-Mitford, *Sutton Hoo*, 3 (1983), ii, pp. 788–812.

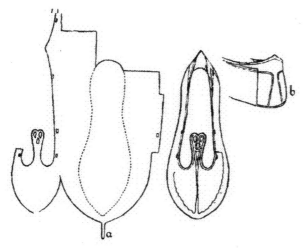

Fig. 147 Irish shoe drawn by Patricia Reid

There is a large corpus of Irish shoes from peat bogs which can be dated to the early Christian period, on the basis of the style of decorative motifs which are incised into the leather, usually on decorative tags at the instep (Fig. 147), but sometimes also at the heel.[118] The instep tag is clearly shown on shoes in the *Book of Kells* (Fig. 141). As already stated, it is quite possible that in Anglo-Saxon Northumbria, where Celtic Christianity flourished and Irish motifs were widely used in manuscript illumination and sculpture, such shoes would also have been known; but there is, so far, no proof of this.

Unusual footwear is worn by an angel depicted on a stone carving from Slaidburn, Lancashire (Fig. 148). The figure wears either high shoes or low boots with a pair of flaps at each ankle. Richard Bailey, noting a parallel to ecclesiastical footwear on a Scottish sculpture, has suggested that ecclesiastical or liturgical shoes are depicted here.[119] Similar footwear, however, is worn by one of the human beings decorating the initial letter 'b' in successive verses of the Beatitudes in the *Book of Kells* (fol. 40v). These stylised human figures, which are entwined with contorted birds and geometric motifs in the Insular manner, have a distinctly secular look with their full heads of hair, dark beards and green or purple stockings (Fig. 140).

St Cuthbert, renowned for his asceticism, habitually wore leather boots, which his biographer Bede, writing in Latin, called *tibracis*. (Bede's anecdote reveals Cuthbert's extreme piety, not through his choice of footwear but by his self-neglect. He removed his *tibracis* only once a year, for the Easter foot-washing ceremony, when it was found that constant friction from the boots when the saint genuflected had caused calluses on his feet.)[120]

Fig. 148 An angel with ankle boots on a sculpture, Slaidburn, Lancashire

[118] Hald, *Primitive Shoes*, Figs 191 a-b.
[119] R. N. Bailey, *Viking Age Sculpture* (London, 1980), pp. 232–3.
[120] *Vita Sancti Cuthberti*, XVIII; Colgrave, *Two Lives of St Cuthbert*, p. 218.

In Viking York, bone 'skates' were attached to the shoes in winter enabling the wearer to slide over the frozen puddles (Fig. 117). Archaeologists have found many of these bones, polished by the friction of 'skating'.

The word *calc*, 'a sandal' entered the Old English language after the conversion[121] but this Roman style of footwear was probably not worn in Anglo-Saxon England: when the artist of the *Lindisfarne Gospels* attempted to depict sandals on the feet of the four Evangelists, he misunderstood them. Other footwear names in use at this time were *scoh*, 'shoe', *hemming* and *rifeling*, 'raw hide boot' or 'raw hide shoe' and *slife-scoh* and *swiftlere*, 'slipper'.

Gloves

Gloves were certainly in use in England by the eighth century since an anecdote in the Old English *Life of St Guthlac*, which derives from Felix's Latin *Life*, concerns the loss of a pair of gloves belonging to a brother named Wilfred.[122] Falconers would have worn gauntlets, and one such glove is depicted on the Bewcastle Cross, which is probably eighth-century.[123] The gauntlet is on the hand of the figure in the bottom panel, which probably represents St John the Evangelist, accompanied by his symbol, the eagle (thus balancing the figure of St John the Baptist in the upper panel), but the fact that the eagle is on some kind of perch and the human figure wears the gauntlet suggests that a secular patron may also be represented here, in a kind of double interpretation which is not unusual in Anglo-Saxon Christian iconography. Surprisingly gloves or gauntlets do not appear to have been worn in battle.[124]

Archaeological evidence from the Continent demonstrates that gloves could be extremely elaborate. The Alamannic cemetery at Oberflacht, Germany, yielded remains of leather gloves lined with soft cloth and laced at the back of the hand,[125] while the Frankish 'minstrel' buried in Cologne (Fig. 143) had on his left hand a glove of cow's leather decorated with closely-placed strips resembling seams and on his right hand a deer-skin glove with ridge-and-groove ornament and a pattern of indentations.[126]

---

[121] It derives from Latin *calceus* (M. Serjeantson, *A History of Foreign Words in English* (London, 1935, p. 282) and is only documented once, in biblical translation, *sandaliis: calcum*; West Saxon version Mark 6:9; Skeat, *Gospels*, p. 42.

[122] *Guthlac*, XI; C. W. Goodwin (ed.), *The Anglo-Saxon Version of the Life of St Guthlac* (London, 1848), pp. 54, 56.

[123] Bewcastle 1; Bailey and Cramp, *Corpus of Anglo-Saxon Sculpture*, 2, pp. 61–72, Plate 96.

[124] Rupert Bruce-Mitford investigated the possibility that the figures in the 'wrap-over coat' costume depicted on the Sutton Hoo helmet and elsewhere wore gauntlets, but concluded that they did not, and that the decoration at the wrists represented cuffs; Bruce-Mitford, *Sutton Hoo*, 2 (1978), pp. 194–5, note 1.

[125] C. R. Smith, *Collectanea Antiqua*, 7 vols (London, 1848–80), 4 (1848), p. 208.

[126] Fremersdorf, 'Zwei wichtige Frankengräber aus Köln', pp. 137–8.

By this period the word *glof* was in common use. *Hand-scio*, 'mitten' may have become an archaism only used as a man's name and in a placename (see above, p. 126).

Breast plates and helmets

The Sutton Hoo Ship Burial contained a pair of gold clasps which have been interpreted as shoulder fasteners for a Roman-style leather cuirass (Fig. 80).[127] The jewelled clasps have loops on their reverse sides which were evidently intended to be stitched on to leather. There was a pair of clasps for each shoulder; the two halves of each pair were made to fit together, secured by a gold pin, and they were curved to fit the body. Probably the leather cuirass was made in two parts – front and back – and held in place by the clasps and by a leather belt or harness. Although the cuirass is depicted on Roman imperial statues, and on consular diptychs, which is perhaps where the Sutton Hoo workshops derived the idea, the clasps are unique.

Despite allusions to mailcoats in the heroic poetry of the Anglo-Saxon period, the general absence of archaeological evidence for them, even in graves equipped with fine weapons, suggests that, at least in the earlier centuries of the Anglo-Saxon era, they were a rare luxury, and it was not unusual to fight without protective clothing – on the Franks Casket some spear-carriers are not equipped with armour. The only archaeological remains we have of a mailcoat are from the Sutton Hoo Ship Burial, our richest Anglo-Saxon find. The Sutton Hoo mailcoat is heavily rusted, but it is evident that it was made of rows of metal rings alternately riveted and soldered together, and that it was probably knee-length.[128] On the Franks Casket (Fig. 123), large circles covering the upper bodies of fighting men probably indicate mail coats, thought they could conceivably represent something else, like a garment of pelts. It is noticable that though both ringed garments and helmets appear on the Casket, they are worn by different figures, rather than together.

There are a few sculptures which may have been intended to show armour. W. G. Collingwood believed that a coat of mail was worn by a figure on a sculpture from Kirklevington, Stockton-on-Tees (Fig. 149)[129] which probably dates to the period in question,

Fig. 149 Figure in mail coat or unusual tunic on a sculpture, Kirklevington, Stockton-on-Tees

[127] Bruce-Mitford, *Sutton Hoo*, 2 (1978), pp. 532–4.
[128] Bruce-Mitford, *Sutton Hoo*, 2, pp. 234, 238.
[129] Collingwood, 'Anglian and Anglo-Danish sculpture in the North Riding of Yorkshire', pp. 344, 352–3; short-sleeved mailcoats, with scalloped lower edges similar to the Kirklevington garment, appear in late Anglo-Saxon manuscripts (e.g. London, British Library, MSS Cotton Cleopatra C viii, fol. 18v and Harley 603, fols 13v, 56v).

but his interpretation has not been accepted by all.[130] Figures on a few sculptures, such as one from Norbury (Fig. 144), wear tunics of which the skirts are divided into panels by horizontal and vertical lines. This may be simply a stylistic trait, but it is possible that the sculptor intended to show protective clothing, such as divided mail skirts.

Only four helmets survive from the Anglo-Saxon period, one of them, the Sutton Hoo example (Fig. 142), possibly imported from Sweden. None bear the horns with birds' head terminals depicted on the 'dancing warriors' plaque on the Sutton Hoo helmet and on a few other objects thought to be associated with the cult of Woden. Both the Sutton Hoo helmet and the slightly later one from Coppergate, York,[131] derive from Roman parade helmets and fit right over the head, providing face protection and a neckguard, a shape also found (more crudely) in depictions on the Franks Casket (Fig. 124) and on the Swedish Torslunda die (Plate 3b). The Sutton Hoo helmet is surmounted by a protective crest which terminates in beasts' heads. A stylised human face which cleverly doubles as a flying dragon decorates the front and protective boars' heads feature on either side of the face, at the ends of the eyebrows. The Coppergate helmet also has beasts' heads at the eyebrows. An interlacing design decorates the nose guard and a Christian invocation is inscribed on its crest. The helmets from Benty Grange (Fig. 150) and Wollaston, Northamptonshire[132] are of a different shape, being designed to protect the top of the head, like caps, though both also have nose-guards and the Wollaston example has cheekguards. On both of them there is the free-standing figure of a boar, a pagan symbol, which is also worn on the Torslunda die (on the other kind of helmet). The Wollaston helmet has so far not revealed any other decoration but the Benty Grange helmet has a silver cross on the nose-piece. Although the Anglo-Saxon helmets fall broadly into two types, each of them is individual and they were clearly precious items. Interestingly they all carry some religious emblem, either pagan or Christian, or, in the case of Benty Grange, both.

Conical headgear appears on several stone sculptures, but it is not clear if this represents helmets or hats. If the Kirklevington man (Fig. 149) wears a mailcoat then it is possible he wears a helmet, though as we have seen from the Franks Casket, the two need not go together. Judging from Anglo-Saxon art, hats do not seem to have been in common use.

Fig. 150 Helmet, Benty Grange, Derbyshire

[130] J. T. Lang, 'Some late pre-Conquest crosses in Ryedale, Yorkshire: a reappraisal', *Journal of the British Archaeological Association*, 3rd series, 36 (1973), pp. 16–25, at p. 19, interpreted the costume as 'civilian dress consisting of a broad sleeved smock and a conical cap'.

[131] D. Tweddle, *The Anglian Helmet from 16–22 Coppergate*, The Archaeology of York, 17.8 The Small Finds (1992), reconstructed pp. 942–45, Fig. 408 a-d.

[132] I. Meadows, 'Wollaston: The "Pioneer" burial', *Current Archaeology*, 154 (1997), pp. 391–5.

Buckles, belts, baldrics and harnesses

Archaeological evidence confirms that the belt, sometimes buckled, continued as part of the male costume. Very often a knife was carried at the belt, and it seems to have become more common in the conversion period to have a leather sheath for this. Pouches of leather or leather-and-fabric seem to have become fashionable during the seventh century, of which the most elaborate is the coin purse from the Sutton Hoo Ship Burial, attested by its intricate cloisonné lid, which was probably slung on a thin belt fastened by a large (13.2 cm) and sumptuously decorated gold buckle. This fastener was apparently not fixed to a single belt and could have been tranferable. The buckle is hollow, which has led to the suggestion that it might have been a reliquary.[133] The majority of buckles worn at this time were small and undecorated, but there is a significant number of bigger, more opulent examples. Large triangular buckles were popular in Kent in the first half of the seventh century. Mostly confined to male graves, they were sometimes elaborately decorated with filigree and garnets, and sometimes accompanied by a matching counterplate. Double-tongued belt buckles were a male fashion of the second half of the seventh century and again, some evidently belonged to wealthy owners.[134] Buckles were sometimes being used as manifestations of religious belief in the seventh century: the openwork buckles which sometimes carry a cross motif are found with men as well as with women; a sub-triangular silver buckle from a man's grave at Crundale Down, Kent, carries a fish, a Christian symbol, on its plate, executed in gold. As this buckle is hollow it could, like the Sutton Hoo buckle, have functioned as a reliquary.[135] The fish emblem is also displayed on a more modest copper alloy buckle, with a tongue-shaped plate, from a man's grave at Eccles, Kent.[136] The place-name, which derives from Latin *ecclesia*, 'church', suggests a strong Christian tradition, perhaps going back to Roman times, in that area.[137] In contrast, a silver buckle from Finglesham bears a dancing figure with spears, wearing a horned helmet, a recognisable Woden-cult talisman (Fig. 73).[138]

The seventh-century barrow at Taplow contained the equipment of a wealthy man including elaborate gold jewellery (Fig. 139) which appears to have been worn in an unusual way. A large triangular buckle was worn at the shoulder. It has zoomorphic ornament and a cross executed in cloisonné. It was found attached to

[133] Bruce-Mitford, *Sutton Hoo*, 2, p. 588.
[134] The only double-tongued buckle known to be associated with a woman was found with the bag in the Swallowcliffe Down bed burial; Geake, *Gravegoods*, p. 78.
[135] Webster and Backhouse, *Making*, pp. 24–5, Fig 6.
[136] Webster and Backhouse, *Making*, p. 25, Fig. 7.
[137] Myres, *The English Settlements*, p. 33.
[138] Webster and Backhouse, *Making*, p. 22.

strips of gold which had been brocaded onto tablet weave, lying diagonally across the body area. The position and interpretation of this gold have been disputed and the gold material has been discussed as the edging of a cloak, but Elisabeth Crowfoot and Sonia Hawkes make a convincing case for a gold-adorned baldric and belt.[139] The man had worn at the left of his waist two pairs of curved gold clasps (four pieces), similar to the buckle in shape and style of the goldwork, but without cloisonné decoration. The clasps were designed to be sewn to a garment, probably a belt. Though in effect they resemble the Kentish triangular buckle and triangular counterplate, they are without the tongue which characterises a buckle. As a type of fastener they are comparable with the Sutton Hoo clasps but differ very much in shape and decoration and, judging from their apparent find-position, in function. The splendour of the masculine jewellery from Taplow, which is only comparable with the finds from the Sutton Hoo Ship Burial, was no doubt an indication of the owner's high rank. Its style was perhaps military – we might compare the regalia of the earlier Germanic-Roman soldier buried at Dorchester which included baldric and belt (Fig. 81). The royal man commemorated by the Sutton Hoo Ship Burial may have had at least one, probably two, harnesses, since there were jewelled buckles and a strap distributor decorated in cloisonné in two different designs, as well as other jewelled buckles of individual style. The leather strapwork seems to have been hung up inside the burial chamber. Since it was not found associated with a body we cannot be certain that it was the regalia of a person (rather than a horse, or a structure, for example) but the probability is that it represents military dress.

Buckles and other remains of strap equipment have occasionally been found at shoulder or breast in less elaborate male graves, both of the pagan period and the conversion. Perhaps these were the remains of baldrics which denoted rank or military status. Alternatively they might have derived from harnesses which carried tools, as we see on the ninth-century sculpture from Codford St Peter (Fig. 129) where the man appears to have a knife at his chest, attached to straps.

Buckles do not appear on male figures in the art of the Christian period, though belts sometimes do. The 'hunter' on the St Mary Bishophill Junior sculpture (Fig. 130) wears a double belt from which a horn is suspended. His companion carrries a knife at the belt. The belt of the Codford St Peter figure (Fig. 129) apparently circles both cloak and tunic, a unique arrangement. Belts do not appear on the Franks Casket and the tunics are pouched in such a way as to conceal them, but the tunics are clearly cinched in at the waist. Belts appear on Viking Age figures without tunics. Probably in some cases the belts were meant to support close-fitting trousers,

---

[139] Crowfoot and Hawkes, 'Early Anglo-Saxon gold braids', pp. 44–50; see also Bruce-Mitford, *Sutton Hoo*, 2 (1978), p. 534.

which are not clearly indicated,[140] but the man on the Finglesham buckle is clearly naked apart from his horned helmet and a belt with a large buckle. The old tradition was to fight naked, but a belt might be useful in such circumstances for holding knives and other extra weapons. We do not know if the custom persisted, which it might have done among the more recently-pagan Vikings, or whether the naked figure with a belt was simply iconographic.

The words *gyrdel*[141] and *gyrdels*,[142] documented in our period and used of monks' girdles, were probably also in use for secular garments. In addition there are the words *belt* and *fetel*, which are only documented from later texts.

Headgear, hair and beard

Representations in art suggest that Anglo-Saxon men wore their hair fairly short, not cropped close to the head in Roman fashion but cut around the neck, or at least above the shoulders. This might have been in obedience to St Paul's dictum that men should have short hair.[143] Celtic fashions may have been different: the *Book of Kells* shows the hair rather long at the front in a fringe or curls on the forehead, sometimes cut short at the back but often hanging down quite long and curling (Figs 135, 140). Men vowed to monasticism would have their hair tonsured, so that even though their dress may not have distinguished them from seculars, their profession was immediately recognisable. The Celtic tonsure, which would have been seen in Anglo-Saxon England at least until the Synod of Whitby (664), involved shaving the front of the head from the forehead, but leaving the crown hair long, like a tiara. This is probably shown on the figure of St Matthew's symbol in the *Book of Durrow* (Fig. 137). The Roman tonsure involved shaving the crown of the head, leaving the hair in a symbolic 'crown of thorns' in the form of a circlet.

As far as one can tell from the art of the seventh, eighth and ninth centuries, Anglo-Saxon men often wore longish, pointed beards with or without moustaches (Fig. 89). The drooping moustaches of two faces on a clasp (for a book or casket) from Dorchester, Oxfordshire, probably seventh- or eighth-century, sweep down to the chin in a way that suggests they joined a

---

[140] For example at Bilton; Collingwood, 'Anglian and Anglo-Danish sculpture in the West Riding', p. 140, Fig. b.

[141] A homilist used the phrase *to his gyrdel* (B. Thorpe (ed.), *The Homilies of the Anglo-Saxon Church*, 2 vols (London, 1844–6), 2, p. 354, line 18) in an account of a holy man standing up to his loins in water, *usque ad lumbos* in the Latin Bede (*Historia Ecclesiastica* V, 12; Colgrave and Mynors, *Bede*, p. 496); however, the homilist may have known the Old English version which has *oð midde sidan* (Schipper, *Bedas Kirchengeschichte*, p. 632, line 1876).

[142] The word glosses *bra(c)hiale*; Lindsay, *Corpus Glossary*, p. 28, line 181.

[143] I Corinthians 11:14.

pointed beard.[144] In the *Barberini Gospels* (Vatican, MS Biblioteca Apostolica Vaticana, Barb. lat. 570; Fig. 151) a naked figure, assailed by snakes, pulls on a splendid beard. Unlike men in Irish art, where beards are occasionally plaited (Fig. 216, The Cross of the Scriptures, Clonmacnoise), Anglo-Saxon men seem to have worn their beards loose. Some men appear clean-shaven (the Fuller Brooch, the Codford St Peter, Sheffield archer and York sculptures, Figs 129–31, 133), though it is possible the artists were portraying youthful figures; others are beardless but moustached. They include the Repton rider and the (secular) figure of the blind man healed by Christ on a carving from Rothbury, Northumberland.[145]

No headdress appears consistently. Fillets, although normally associated with women, and secondarily with angels (see discussion below, Chap VII p. 262) certainly appear occasionally on male figures. The 'crinkly band' over the head of the Repton rider has been interpreted as a diadem signifying rank, as found on Continental models such as coins and consular diptychs.[146] It should, however, be considered in conjunction with other, admittedly rare, evidence of male headbands in non-regal context in Anglo-Saxon art. The Codford St Peter figure (Fig. 129), who is clad in unusual, but distinctly male, secular dress, wears a headband, and a historiated initial in a ninth-century manuscript, Oxford, Bodleian Library, Hatton 20, fol. 34v (Fig. 152) depicts a head with curls of hair, a fillet and a beard. The beard, though it has a functional role as the 'tail' of a letter Q, clearly demonstrates masculinity. Another possibility for the Repton rider's 'crinkly band' is that is represents a plait of hair. It will be suggested in Chapter VII that this Celtic hairstyle was adopted by the Vikings. The Repton stone is believed to be pre-Viking, but it does have some potentially Celtic features, including the short breeches of the serpent's victims.[147]

A little human head in what appears to be green Phrygian cap decorates a letter in the *Tiberius Bede*, an eighth-century manuscript (London, British Library, MS Cotton Tiberius C ii, fol. 5v; Fig. 153); but it may be only the colour contrast that makes this fairly typical example of eighth-/ninth-century 'Southumbrian' ornament appear like a cap. An archer figure on a sculpture from Bradbourne, Derbyshire, may wear a conical cap,[148] and a close-fitting hat may have been worn by a man on a carving at Brailsford, Derbyshire.[149]

Fig. 151 Bearded head, *Barberini Gospels*, Vatican, MS Biblioteca Apostolica Vaticana Barb. lat. 570, fol. 1r

Fig. 152 Bearded head with fillet, Oxford, Bodleian Library MS Hatton 20, fol. 34v

---

[144] D. M. Wilson, 'The Bronze Ornament (Fig. 11 and Plate VI)', Appendix 3 to J. May, 'Romano-British and Saxon sites near Dorchester, Oxon.', *Oxoniensia*, 42 (1977). pp. 73–5; this reference and additional suggestions from Sonia Hawkes.
[145] Rothbury 1, Face C; Cramp, *Corpus of Anglo-Saxon Sculpture*, 1, p. 220, Plate 213, No. 1215.
[146] Biddle and Kjølbye-Biddle, 'The Repton stone', pp. 262–4.
[147] Biddle and Kjølbye-Biddle, 'The Repton stone', pp. 284–6.
[148] T. E. Routh, 'A corpus of pre-Conquest carved stones of Derbyshire', *Derbyshire Archaeological Journal*, 58 (new series 11) (1937), pp. 1–46, at p. 20.
[149] W. G. Collingwood, 'The Brailsford Cross', *Derbyshire Archaeological Journal*, 45 (1923), pp. 1–13, at p. 3, Fig. 4.

The St Mary Bishophill falconer wears a hooded cloak (Fig. 130). Wool and fur, including otter-skin, perhaps from caps, were among the Sutton Hoo finds[150] but hats and caps do not appear, now or later, to have been a regular part of Anglo-Saxon male dress. Matters may have been different in the Viking north of Britain: a woollen hood, found in a peat bog in St Andrews parish, Orkney, Scotland, has been dated to the later-eighth or ninth centuries. It is woven in herringbone twill, with two tablet-woven bands attached to the lower edge, the bottom one ending in a deep fringe which would have hung round the shoulders.[151]

Fig. 153 Head with Phrygian cap, London, British Library MS Cotton Tiberius C. ii fol. 5v

Jewellery

Elaborate buckles and clasps evidently formed part of the regalia of important men in the seventh century, but there is no archaeological evidence that brooches were worn by men. It is very likely that some of the disc-headed and other elaborate pins which have been found at settlement sites, in hoards and as stray finds (above, pp. 141–3) belonged to men, particularly the disc-headed examples which are more obviously suitable for wear against the body. Certainly pins were not female gendered objects, since from about the eighth century it was decreed that the ecclesiastical pallium should be fixed by pins and this was certainly done in later Anglo-Saxon England.[152] An elaborately-decorated silver pin from the Trewhiddle hoard (deposited 872–5) may have been ecclesiastical, since it was found in association with a chalice and a scourge. Possibly secular men wore pins too, as they had done occasionally in the pagan period. It is very probable that some of the strap ends, both decorated and undecorated, which are common finds from the later Anglo-Saxon period, belonged to male costume but there is no definite evidence to associate them with one sex or the other and no indication how they were worn. From the seventh century onwards we have evidence from art that disc brooches fastened men's cloaks, but we cannot know if any of the archaeological finds from the later period (which were not associated with graves) were the property of men.

By the ninth century, it seems, gold was in short supply. Only rarely is gold found on brooches; the finest ninth-century examples

---

[150] Bruce-Mitford, *Sutton Hoo*, 2 (1978), pp. 445, 452.

[151] A. S. Henshall, 'Early textiles found in Scotland', *Proceedings of the Society of Antiquaries of Scotland*, 86 (1951–2), pp. 1–20, at pp. 9–14; P. A. Henry, 'An Analysis of Archaeological Textiles with Special Reference to the Scandinavian Period in Scotland', unpublished BA dissertation (University of Durham, 1992). I have included this garment among men's clothing because of its similarity to later medieval men's hoods.

[152] Ross, 'Dress Pins', p. 411. Ross points out that the graves of Archbishop Wulfstan of York (one pin) and Archbishop Hubert of Canterbury (2 pins) did not conform to the *Ordo* which prescribed three pins.

Fig. 154 Finger ring found in Bologna, Italy

are silver, others are base metal. This century saw a fashion for elaborate finger-rings, a few of which are gold, which suggests they were luxury items. The fourth finger is called *goldfinger* in King Alfred's Laws, which suggests that this finger, called the 'ring-finger' today, was the usual location for a ring; the damages to be paid to a man for the severing of this finger were greater than for other fingers (though less than the thumb).[153] Some of the surviving rings probably belonged to men, for example, one with a massive, rosette-shaped bezel, found near Bologna, Italy, which has a diameter of 3.4 cm (Fig. 154). A 2.7 cm gold and niello ring from Kingsmoor, Cumbria, has an incomprehensible runic inscription, and was probably amuletic. There are similar runic inscriptions on a ring probably from Bramham Moor, West Yorkshire, and an agate ring of unknown provenance. A fashion, perhaps brief, for putting names on finger rings, has left us an example bearing the name of Æthelwulf, king of Wessex from 839 to 858–9 (Fig. 155). Its design, which incorporates two birds, perhaps peacocks, and several four-lobed devices which may be read as crosses, probably has Christian significance. Two figures on a stone sculpture at Urswick wear what may be high-necked garments or rarely-depicted neck rings.[155]

Different ethnic groups within the British Isles would have been distinguishable by the form of their jewellery. A hoard of eighth-century silverware from St Ninian's Isle, Shetland, thought to be Pictish, shows strong influence from Anglo-Saxon decorative art, especially Northumbrian, but characteristically Celtic style is also apparent, especially in the brooches, which are the large penannular type popular in Ireland.[156]

Fig. 155 King Æthelwulf's finger ring, London, British Museum

Dress accessories

Men, as well as women, seem to have carried pouches, including those with hooked tags as fasteners (above, pp. 154–5). Although men never carried personal articles in the same quantity as women, a fragment of a pair of eighth-century silver tweezers from Brandon is engraved with a niello-inlaid runic inscription which gives a man's name: *Aldred*.[157] Men also carried horns at the belt as evidenced from the St Mary Bishophill sculpture (Fig. 130), and they probably continued to carry domestic knives, as well as the larger fighting knife, or scramasax, which came into fashion in the

---

[153] Ælfred 43; Liebermann, *Die Gesetze*, 1, p. 82.

[154] Wilson, *Ornamental Metalwork*, No. 27, p. 137. The comparisons are made by Page, 'The Inscriptions', in Wilson, pp. 23–4.

[155] Urswick 1; Bailey and Cramp, *Corpus of Anglo-Saxon Sculpture*, 2, p. 148, Plate 564. I owe the identification of the torques to Elizabeth Coatsworth.

[156] A. Small, G. Thomas and D. M. Wilson, *St Ninian's Isle and its Treasure*, Aberdeen University Studies No. 152 (Oxford, 1973).

[157] Webster and Backhouse, *Making*, p. 85, Fig. 66l o.

conversion period. Leather sheaths for scramasaxes, and one for a knife, survive from Anglo-Viking York, dating from the ninth century onwards.[158] Elaborately decorated with geometric and zoomorphic devices, they are rare evidence of a flourishing fashion in personal adornment.

[158] Mainman and Rogers, *Craft, Industry and Everyday Life*, pp. 237–42, p. 239, Fig. 107, Plates XI-XIV.

VI

Women's costume in the tenth and eleventh centuries

The literary evidence

The tenth-century Benedictine Reform brought with it an intellectual revival. English scholars were composing in their own language and were also glossing or translating into English some of the numerous Latin texts in circulation. In an enthusiasm for learning, and what seems to have been an urge to conserve material already in existence, texts were copied and recopied. Many manuscripts from the late Anglo-Saxon period survive today and not only give us some specific information about dress in England, but also provide us with a vocabulary of Old English garment names recorded as glosses.

Ælfric, the best-known scholar of his day, has left us evidence that fabrics and jewels were being imported regularly into England. In the *Colloquy*, a Latin work composed about the year 1000 for the instruction of boys in a monastic school, Ælfric creates the character of the *Mercator*, or merchant, who traffics in *Purpurum et sericum, pretiosas gemmas et aurum, uarias uestes et pigmenta* ...[1] ('Purple and silk, precious gems and gold, coloured [or various] garments and dyes ...'). Other literary evidence is more general: among the *Maxims* of the *Exeter Book* a passage about a sailor's wife pictures the woman as the keeper of the household's clothes (she washes her husband's sea-stained garments and gives him fresh ones).[2]

In general the Old English prose and poetry texts best known to scholars of literature are frustratingly unspecific about dress and clothing accessories. In the poem *Beowulf*, which survives in a manuscript of about 1000 AD, a neck-ring (*healsbeag*) passes from woman to man and vice versa as a gift,[3] and the Queen of Denmark

---

[1] Garmonsway, *Aelfric's Colloquy*, (p. 33, lines 159–60.

[2] *... leof wilcuma/ Frysan wife, þonne flota stondeð;/ wæsceð his warig hrægl ond him syleþ wæde niwe ...* 'the dear one is welcome to the Frisian woman when his ship is still; she washes his tired garment and gives him new clothing ...'; *Maxims* I, II, lines 94–5, 98; Krapp and Dobbie, *Exeter Book*, p. 160.

[3] Owen-Crocker, *Four Funerals*, p. 222 and p. 231 n.13.

wears a ring,[4] possibly on her head (as the Virgin Mary is crowned with a ring in the *Prayer Book of Abbot Ælfwine*, London, British Library, MSS Cotton Titus D xxvi and xxvii, fol. 75v; see below, p. 225 and Fig. 156).The same queen rewards the hero with the gift of a garment (*hrægl*), an object particularly within the province of a woman, as armour and weapons were in the province of her husband the king; she also gives him the aforementioned neckring and two arm rings (*earmhreade twa … hringas*).[5] None of these items is described. The tenth-century poem *Judith* paints an idealised and remote portrait of its heroine, *torhtan mægð*, 'bright maiden', *ælfscinu*, literally 'shining like an elf', which we might render as 'ethereally beautiful' and *wundenlocc*, 'with hair wound round', which could mean 'with plaited hair' or 'with curled hair'.[6] More specific evidence can be derived from lesser-known texts, many of them instructive or legal documents. We are fortunate in having copies of the wills of some wealthy Anglo-Saxon ladies who bequeathed clothes, especially Wynflæd[7] and Æthelgifu.[8]

The Anglo-Latin glosses which survive in many manuscripts must be used with caution. They identify many Old English garment-names,[9] but these terms are definable only by the Latin words they gloss. Some of these Old English garment terms do not survive in any other context. (This is why we do not know if some of the garment-names belonged exclusively to women's costume or men's.) Many of the lemmata concerned with dress derive ultimately from glosses to Aldhelm's description of clothing in *De Virginitate* (above, p. 134). Some of the others can be traced back to the *Etymologiae* of Isidor of Seville.[10]

An interesting source of information is the *Indicia Monasterialia*, a catalogue of sign-language by means of which silent monks might communicate.[11] When an item of clothing was required, the explicit instructions given for miming can indicate to us the shape of the garment and where on the body it was worn. Most of the garments referred to in this text are monastic, but there is one revealing reference to a woman's fillet (below, p. 224). Less explicitly, the relatively large numbers of Old English texts and translations surviving from the period contain numerous passing references to clothing, which although not precise descriptions, do contribute to our corpus of information.

Fig. 156 Virgin Mary with the Christ Child and the Dove of the Holy Spirit, *Prayer Book of Abbot Ælfwine of Winchester*, London, British Library MSS Cotton Titus D xxvi and xxvii, fol. 75v

Fig. 157 Weeping Virgin figure, London, British Library, MS Harley 2904, fol. 3v

Fig. 158 Woman presenting a torque to her son, *Harley Psalter*, London, British Library MS Harley 603, fol. 67v

---

[4] Line 1163; Dobbie, *Beowulf and Judith*, p. 36. She is also called *goldhroden*, lines 614, 640 and *beaghroden*, line 623; Dobbie pp. 20–1.

[5] Lines 1194–5; Dobbie, *Beowulf and Judith*, p. 37.

[6] Lines 14, 77; Dobbie, *Beowulf and Judith*, pp. 99, 101.

[7] D. Whitelock, *Anglo-Saxon Wills* (Cambridge, 1930), No. III; I discussed the bequests of clothing in detail in Owen,'Wynflæd's wardrobe'.

[8] D. Whitelock, N. Ker, and Lord Rennell, *The Will of Aethelgifu* (London, 1968).

[9] See Appendix A, p. 332.

[10] Lindsay, *Isidori*. Isidor lists and defines Latin garment-names. Sometimes he gives unusual interpretations of well-known words, for example his definition of *palla* (XIX, 25, 2); cf. A. Souter, *A Glossary of Later Latin to 600 A. D.* (Oxford, 1949), p. 283.

[11] Kluge, 'Indicia'.

Fig. 159 Queen Ælfgifu/
Emma, London, British
Library, MS Stowe 944, fol. 6r

Fig. 160 Queen Ælfgifu/
Emma, London, British Library,
MS Additional 33241, fol 1v

Fig. 161 Queen Edith, Bayeux
'Tapestry'

The evidence of art

With the era of the Benedictine Reform, pictorial representations of women appear with some frequency for the first time in the Anglo-Saxon period. Many of these, it must be stated, are removed from everyday life since they represent mythical, allegorical or biblical subjects. Often, details of attitude or costume are recognizably stylised, in the manner of the Winchester School, as, for example the hunched shoulder and fluttering drapery of the weeping Virgin figure in the late-tenth-century manuscript London, British Library, Harley 2904 (Fig. 157). The *Harley Psalter* (London, British Library, MS Harley 603) contains a large number of lively line drawings with many interesting depictions of clothing (Colour Plate H, Fig. 169) and a rare depiction of a ring, or torque (Fig. 158).[12] It is necessary to remember, when using this manuscript as evidence, that it is an early-eleventh-century copy, made in Canterbury, of the early-ninth-century *Utrecht Psalter* (the Netherlands, Utrecht, *Universiteitsbibliotheek* 32 (Script. eccl. 484)) and that though it may shed light on secular clothing, that costume may not be peculiar to the Anglo-Saxons of the eleventh century. There is reason to believe, however, that at least some artists, particularly the early-eleventh-century illuminators of the Old English *Hexateuch* (Colour Plate I, Figs 165, 171, 175) were influenced by life as well as by other drawings,[13] and from their work we can deduce features of costume. The same is true of the Bayeux 'Tapestry', although only three clothed women appear in it (Figs 161, 163, 172; the technique of the 'Tapestry' is discussed in Chapter VIII).

We have near-contemporary 'portraits' of royal ladies whose costume may be compared with that of figures in other works: Cnut's queen, Ælfgifu (Emma), appears in a drawing probably made in 1031[14] in a Winchester manuscript, London, British Library, Stowe 944 (Fig. 159) and in a Flemish or northern French manuscript, London, British Library, Additional 33241, made the following decade (Fig. 160). Edith, wife of Edward the Confessor, is seen in the Bayeux 'Tapestry' (Fig. 161). In the medium of sculpture, there are some female figures, including the Virgin and a 'midwife' on small ivory carvings. Stone sculptures, usually weathered or damaged to some extent, portray more male figures than female. Stone sculptures are commonest in the Viking-influenced north in

---

[12] The ring is passed from a woman to a boy or man, who carries a staff and is perhaps departing. A coming-of-age may be depicted here. Ohlgren, *Illustration*, p. 38. It (rather oddly) illustrates the text ' … Surely I have behaved and quieted myself as child that is weaned of his mother … ' (Psalm 130 (131):2, quoted from the Authorized Version).

[13] C. R. Dodwell and P. Clemoes, *The Old English Illustrated Hexateuch*, Early Manuscripts in Facsimile, 18 (1974), p. 66.

[14] This being the year of the accompanying text, as shown by internal dating. The dates of English illuminated manuscripts are taken from E. Temple, *Anglo-Saxon Manuscripts 900–1066*, A survey of manuscripts illuminated in the British Isles, 2 (London, 1976).

Plate A Great square-headed brooch, Paglesham, Essex

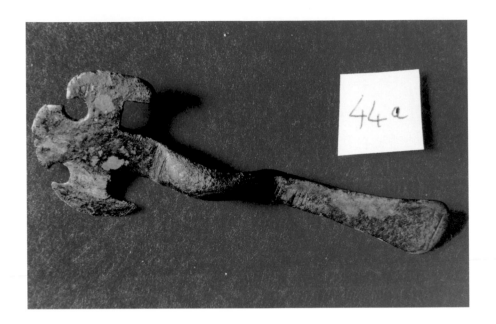

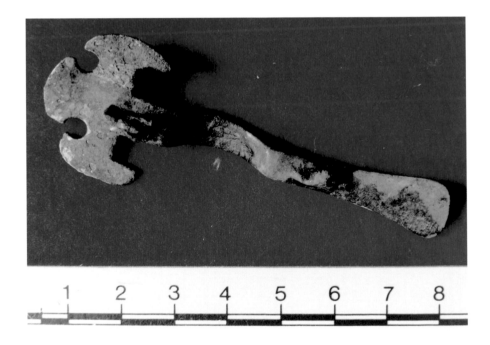

Plate B a and b Small-long
brooch, Barrington A,
Cambridgeshire

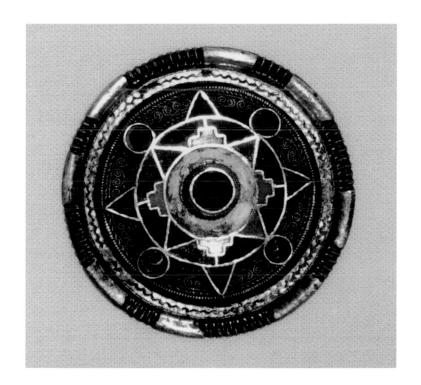

Plate C Circular brooches:
a Disc brooch with garnets and blue glass, Faversham, Kent
b Applied brooch, Minerva Business Park, Peterborough

Plate D Anglian women's dress in the sixth century

Plate E Anglo-Saxon beads, Ashmolean Museum, Oxford

Plate F Kentish women's dress, middle ranking and high ranking

Plate G Male and female dress of the seventh century

N CANTICVM GRADVVM ·CXXVI·

NISI DNS EDIFI
cauerit domum.
inuanum laborant qui
edificant eam
Nisi dns custodierit ciuita
tem. inuanu uigilant
qui custodiunt eam
I nuanum est uobis ante

lucem surgere. surgite
post quam sederitis qui
manducatis panem do
loris
Cum dederit dilectissuis
somnum. hec est heredi
tas dni filii merces fruc
tus uentris

Sicut sagitte inmanu po
tentis. ita & filii excusso
rum
Beatus uir qui impleuit
desiderium suum exipsis.
non confundetur dum lo
quetur inimicis suis in
porta

Plate H London, British Library MS
Harley 603, fol. 66v: Psalm 127
(128):1–3

Plate I London, British Library MS Cotton Claudius B iv fol. 66v; Genesis 46:1–4,5

Plate J Cambridge, Corpus Christi College, MS 183 fol. 1v: King Athelstan presenting a copy of Bede's *Life of St Cuthbert* to the saint.

Plate K London, British Library MS Cotton Vespasian A viii, fol. 2v: King Edgar presenting the New Minster Charter

Plate L London, British Library MS Cotton Tiberius C vi fol. 8v: David kills Goliath

this period. Pagan and secular subjects are sometimes depicted on them, even though the monuments are ostensibly Christian. The most famous, the Gosforth Cross, Cumbria,[15] depicts a woman in the trailing gown of Scandinavian tradition.

Archaeological evidence

The 1990 discovery of pieces of a linen garment, embroidered in silk, at Llan-gors Crannóg, Powys, Wales (Plates 9, 10) adds a new and exciting dimension to the archaeological evidence of dress for this period; and coming from secular context, the needlework contributes new information to the knowledge we already have of late

Plate 9 Embroidered linen garment, Llan-gors, Wales

Anglo-Saxon embroidery from ecclesiastical textiles.

The great silver disc brooches which first appeared in the ninth century continued to be made in the tenth and eleventh, and it is from the latest example in the series that we confirm that such brooches could be worn by women: the brooch from Sutton, Isle of Ely,[16] bears on its reverse an inscription naming the female owner, Ædvwen.[17] The brooch, which is decorated in the Anglo-Scandinavian Ringerike Style, is artistically inferior to the masterpieces of the

[15] Bailey and Cramp, *Corpus of Anglo-Saxon Sculpture*, 2, pp. 100–5, Plate 304.

[16] Wilson, *Ornamental Metalwork*, pp. 174–7 and Plates XXXI, XXXII.

[17] The inscription takes the form of a curse against anyone who steals the brooch, referring to the owner as 'her' (Old English *hyo* and *hire*); R. Page, Appendix A to Wilson, *Ornamental Metalwork*, pp. 86–8.

Plate 10 The Llan-gors garment: computer-generated reconstruction of detail

ninth century. The later brooch from Kings School, Canterbury, is also less impressive[18] suggesting a deterioration in this kind of jewellery, perhaps because the upper classes were no longer wearing such things and what are preserved are the possessions of a lower social stratum.[19] Some of the disc brooches have perforated designs, anticipating perhaps the decline of the solid plate brooch, which seems to have gone out of fashion by the end of the eleventh century, in favour of openwork and annular styles.[20] Most of the superior brooches that survive from this period are made of silver. There is a rare exception in the gold brooch set with pearls circling a stylised enamelled head, from Dowgate Hill, London,[21] but on the whole gold and and even silver are rare finds, and the majority of surviving brooches from late Anglo-Saxon England are of base metal. It has been thought that this reflects a genuine shortage of precious materials in secular hands, especially for use in jewellery. Economic reasons for such a shortage have been suggested;[22] or piety may have decreed that gold and silver were confined to religious pieces.[23] However, C. R. Dodwell has demonstrated from documentary

[18] Wilson, *Ornamental Metalwork*, pp. 124–7.

[19] D. A. Hinton, 'Late Anglo-Saxon metalwork: an assessment', *Anglo-Saxon England*, 4 (1975), pp. 171–80, at p. 179.

[20] D. A. Hinton, 'Disc and rectangular brooches', in Biddle, *Winchester Studies*, 7.ii, ii, pp. 636–39, at p. 637.

[21] D. Buckton, 'Late tenth- and eleventh-century cloisonné enamel brooches', *Medieval Archaeology*, 30 (1986), pp. 8–18, at p. 16, Fig. 59. The brooch is 'not universally accepted as English work', Hinton, *Ornamental Metalwork*, p. 36.

[22] Michael Dolley blames, at least in part, the over-valuation of the silver coinage, preventing ordinary individuals from being able to afford to wear gold and silver; M. Dolley, 'The nummular brooch from Sulgrave', in P. Clemoes and K. Hughes (ed.), *England before the Conquest: studies in primary sources presented to Dorothy Whitelock* (Cambridge, 1971), pp. 333–49, at p. 346.

[23] David Hinton points out that many of the surviving artefacts, even when they have a secular function, have religious emblems upon them. He suggests that even though there was considerable wealth in private hands it was no longer fashionable for the aristocracy to vaunt it by 'rich display'; Hinton, 'Late Anglo-Saxon metalwork', pp. 179–80.

sources that magnificent treasures of gold and silver were in the possession of the Church at the Norman Conquest of 1066,[24] articles which, probably, had been in secular ownership previously. It is apparent, both from the wills of laymen/women and from the records of gifts given by seculars to religious foundations, that costly jewellery was certainly in circulation and that this jewellery was probably gold.[25] We must draw the conclusion that personal ornaments of precious metals existed but have rarely survived. Meanwhile, the growing urban populations of centres such as York and London were probably demanding affordable dress accessories which were accordingly made in base metals.[26]

Circular brooches were the general rule. Nummular (coin) brooches seem to have been very common, sometimes exhibiting rare and exotic connections: a tenth-century, base metal brooch found by a 'mudlarker' beside the River Thames has a 'central motif cast from a Cufic [Babylonian] coin, a dirham of the Ummayyhad dynasty, 696–750 AD'.[27] There are a few disc brooches from this period with animals on them (Fig. 162), a style probably originating

Fig. 162 Animal brooch, Winchester

[24] C. R. Dodwell, *Anglo-Saxon Art: a new perspective* (Manchester, 1982), especially Chapter VII. Dodwell enumerates (p. 215) the following uses of gold and silver: ' ... large-scale effigies ... textile coverings of tombs and altars, on costumes and vestments, in jewellery, weapons, ships, domestic plate, household furnishings, reliquaries, book-bindings, church vessels and altars ...'.

[25] Dodwell, *Anglo-Saxon Art*, pp. 188–9.

[26] Mainman and Rogers, *Craft, Industry and Everyday Life*, pp. 2478–9, note that in York the manufacture of lead and pewter dress accessories, begun in the ninth century, continued into the tenth, and that pewter is found in association with an eleventh-century hoard from Cheapside, London.

[27] Description from the British Museum. I am grateful to my colleague Alan Shelston for this information.

in East Anglia.[28] A small (3.3 cm), openwork, silver disc from Cuxton, Kent, which has been dated to the tenth century, has a central motif of a bird and its prey, and the decorative border inscription *Ælfgivv me ah*, 'Ælfgivu owns me'.[29] Ælfgivu is a female name, popular among the Wessex royal family in the tenth and eleventh centuries. There is a small corpus of polychrome enamelled brooches, including a gilded, copper alloy example from Brasenose College, Oxford, with a cruciform and zoomorphic design in yellow, green, blue and white; from Ixworth, Suffolk, a brooch with a cruciform design in white and two shades of blue; and from Colchester, Essex one with a geometric design in green, white and two shades of blue. Some of these brooches have a series of lobes round the perimeter of the tray which carries the enamelling. These enamelled brooches seem localised largely in the east of England: East Anglia, London and Kent.[30]

There is a rare non-circular brooch from Winchester[31] and another now in the Ashmolean Museum, Oxford.[32] They were probably made in England but copy a type originating in the Rhineland and North Germany. 'Ansate' brooches, equal-armed bow brooches, which are found on the Continent from the seventh to the ninth centuries, appear in England in the tenth, in Anglo-Viking context at York and at Ravensdale, Lincolnshire. There are other examples from London and Norwich.[33]

The disc-headed pins which were popular in the Middle Saxon period seem to have disappeared by the tenth century, although plain, straight pins seem to have continued in use and ring-headed ones were quite common. Seamus Ross observes that late Anglo-Saxon pins were apparently mass-produced in response to increased demand, and had largely lost their decorative role.[34] Strap ends continued in use, and we have many examples of them, both perforated and solid, plain and decorated. The small objects which archaeologists have called 'dress hooks' also continued in use, but as we have seen (above, p. 155), in at least one instance they seem to have secured a money bag, and it is uncertain whether any of these were directly associated with clothing. Finger rings continued in

---

[28] N. Smedley and E. Owles, 'Some Anglo-Saxon "animal" brooches', *Proceedings of the Suffolk Institute of Archaeology and Natural History*, 30 (1965), pp. 166–74; Hinton, 'Disc and rectangular brooches', in Biddle, *Winchester*, 7.ii, ii, p. 636.

[29] Wilson, *Ornamental Metalwork*, No. 14, , Plate XVII.

[30] The Brasenose disc is assumed to derive from a brooch, but no remains of the pin are left. The Brasenose disc is 6.4 cm in diameter, but the other two examples are much smaller, 2.1 cm and 2.6 cm respectively; Backhouse, Turner and Webster, *Golden Age*, pp. 100–1, Figs. 91–3. See also Buckton, 'Late tenth- and eleventh-century cloisonné enamel brooches'.

[31] No. 2009. The brooch is about 28 mm long and is rectangular with trefoil, lobed corners. It is either patterned or keyed for enamel; Hinton, 'Disc and rectangular brooches', in Biddle, *Winchester*, 7.ii, ii, pp. 636–8.

[32] Hinton, *Ornamental Metalwork*, No. 35.

[33] Mainman and Rogers, *Craft, Industry and Everyday Life*, p. 2571.

[34] Ross, 'Dress Pins', p. 149.

popularity and a variety of types are known, including hoops made of plaited wire, or cast and decorated. Some rings have bezels in which Roman jewels are mounted.[35] Simple examples of green glass have been found from this period in Winchester.[36] Part of a ring of jet was found in the cemetery at Sedgeford, Northamptonshire.[37] We do not have surviving rings for the arm or neck decorated in late Anglo-Saxon style, though they are mentioned in literature and attested in association with women in the *Harley Psalter* (Fig. 158) and the *Hexateuch* (Fig. 223). Torques of silver, of various sizes, often twisted or plaited, with a simple hook fastening, are, however, characteristic finds from Viking Age hoards in Scandinavia, and may have been worn by Viking settlers in England.

Still within the realms of archaeological evidence, we may learn something about late Anglo-Saxon textiles from the vestments of St Cuthbert, recovered when the reliquary coffin of the saint was opened in 1827. The fabrics recovered included imported silks and native embroideries. The silks, even in their present fragmentary state, give us some idea of the wares which the merchants known to Ælfric were bringing to England, some of which doubtless were worn by wealthy seculars. The embroideries, with the tablet-woven braids which edged them, demonstrate the kind of techniques which might have decorated the fillets, cuffs and borders of secular garments.

Colour in art and reality

Many of the pictures in Anglo-Saxon manuscripts are line drawings executed in brown or coloured inks (Colour Plates H, L). Others are painted in a gloriously rich variety of shades (Colour Plates I-K). It would be wise, however, not to interpret too literally the colouring of garments shown in late Anglo-Saxon art. The embroiderers of the Bayeux 'Tapestry' might colour a horse green with two terracotta legs! The effect is not incongruous in context, for one responds to the tonal contrast rather than the degree of realism in the shades; but this means that when a woman is depicted in the Bayeux 'Tapestry' wearing a brown robe with hanging sleeves lined in blue (Fig. 163; also see Appendix B) we cannot take it as proven that the Anglo-Saxons literally lined their sleeves with a different colour. The variety of shade conveys the difference between the outer and inner surfaces of the sleeve as it does the outer and inner sides of the horse's legs.

Fig. 163 Woman with hanging sleeves, Bayeux 'Tapestry'

[35] Examples are taken from Backhouse, Turner and Webster, *Golden Age*, pp. 98–9, Figs 87–90.

[36] R. J. Charleston, 'Glass rings', in Biddle, *Winchester Studies*, 7.ii, ii, pp. 652–3.

[37] I am grateful to Sophie Cabot for this information.

Similarly, the painters of Anglo-Saxon illuminations may not have been concerned with literal depictions of dress colours. Manuscript illuminations, to judge by some unfinished scenes from the *Hexateuch*, were executed in outline which was subsequently 'coloured in' rather as a child fills in a colouring book, and with the same disregard for consistency. (Folds and creases were inked in subsequently.)[38] If we consider a scene from the 'Tapestry' in which a cask of wine is carried by waggon (Scene 37),[39] we may note that the barrel hoops, wheels and harness are coloured in a way that is decorative rather than realistic: the spokes, for example, are alternate red and green. How much reliance, therefore, can we place on the contrasting girdles and stockings of the accompanying figures? When the Virgin Mary, depicted in the *New Minster Charter* (London, British Library, MS Cotton Vespasian A viii, fol. 2v; Colour Plate K), a manuscript dating to after 966, wears a red headdress, green cloak, brown gown and blue underdress, the colour contrast is probably there to show the quantity and therefore the richness of her dress, and the variety of the palette of the artist, engaged in a sumptuous production, rather than to depict literally the colours a tenth-century woman might have worn simultaneously (a combination which is, to modern eyes, rather tasteless!)

Sometimes, however, a painter may have used colour significantly. The illustration of King David in the *Vespasian Psalter* is given added symbolism by the fact that the monarch wears a red tunic and purple imperial mantle. The purple altar cloth and deep blue chasuble of St Æthelwold in a miniature in that bishop's own *Benedictional* (London, British Library, MS Additional 49598, fol. 118v) may well be authentic. The brown and cream garments worn by St Æthelthryth (Etheldreda) in the same manuscript, therefore (fol. 90v), given the Church's directives to women about wearing dark garments for religious services, may have been appropriate colours for a famously ascetic nun, though her costume (Fig. 170) is that of tenth-century art, not that of the saint's lifetime, three centuries earlier.

A painter may sometimes have misunderstood the outline (perhaps because it was made for him by another artist, or because he copied it from a model he did not understand) and introduced an unwarranted change of colour. There is an example of this in an illumination in London, British Library, MS Harley 2908, fol. 123v, which led the costume historian J. R. Planché to conclude that women's costume included a single mitten.[40] I feel that the painter

---

[38] I am assuming the opposite for the Bayeux 'Tapestry', that is, that the black or navy blue stem stitch lines were worked before the laid and couched work, since the lines of couching change angle slightly at each stem stitch line; but until a study and photographs of the back of the embroidery are made available, I cannot be certain of the sequence of the work, or if it was consistent.

[39] Wilson, *Bayeux Tapestry*, Plate 38.

[40] Planché, *History of British Costume*, p. 38, Fig. This drawing is probably Continental, see Owen, *Anglo-Saxon Costume*, I, pp. 6–7.

has misunderstood the drawing: the figure makes a traditional gesture in which the upraised hand is covered by the robe. In dividing up the field and colouring the area over the hand blue, the painter has created a false impression of a mitten. Similarly, the areas of decoration on cuffs, hems and sometimes on the skirts and shoulders of women in illustrations may be authentic — we have literary evidence for the first two kinds of ornament — or they could be artistic flourishes.

Provided we avoid the kind of naivety which led one costume historian to believe that Anglo-Saxon men habitually dyed their hair and beards blue because they are painted blue in the *Hexateuch*, the richness of colour in Anglo-Saxon art can tell us much about the taste of the people. The polychrome jewellery of early centuries has testified to their love of bright colour; the dyed threads in the extant embroideries, wool in the case of Bayeux, silk in the case of the Cuthbert vestments, demonstrate something of the range of fabric colours available at the most wealthy level of late Anglo-Saxon society.[41] The Bayeux 'Tapestry' was embroidered in ten colours: two reds, three shades of green, two shades of blue, blue-black, beige and yellow.[42] In the Cuthbert embroideries there are shades of reds, greens and fawns, plus brown, pink, blue and white as well as metallic gold. The richest fabric we know of was called *godweb* in English, *purpura* in Latin. A thick, silken cloth which could be made in various colours as well as the purple suggested by its Latin name (below, p. 302), it was a luxury textile suitable for liturgical use but which could be owned by wealthy seculars. In her late-tenth-century will, Æthelgifu bequeathed *iii godwebbenan cyrtlas* as well as other garments of various shades: *hire rotostan cyrtel* ('her brightest cyrtel'), *minne blæwenan cyrtel* ('my blue kirtle') and *oðera hire dunnan cyrtla* ('others of her brownish kirtles').[43] The *dunnan* ('brownish') garments were perhaps made of undyed wool.[44] Dun-coloured garments were prized, however, for in the same century a woman named Wynflæd saw fit to bequeath *hyre bestan dunnan tunecan* ('her best brownish tunic') as well as *hyre blacena tunecena* ('[one] of her black tunics').[45] As I have suggested elsewhere,[46] the darker garments bequeathed by this lady may have been for religious use. Indeed, it was expected that women should wear sober clothing on religious

[41] The Bayeux 'Tapestry' was supposedly commissioned by Odo, brother of William the Conqueror and Earl of Kent after the Conquest. The Cuthbert embroideries were commissioned by Ælfflæd, Queen of Wessex.

[42] I. Bédat and B. Girault-Kurtzeman, 'The technical study of the Bayeux Tapestry', in P. Bouet, B. Levy and F. Neveux (ed.), *The Bayeux Tapestry: embroidering the facts of history* (Caen, 2004), pp. 83–109, at p. 91. The colours have evidently changed since the earliest coloured copy of the 'Tapestry' was made and continue to deteriorate; R. Greig and D. Hill, 'The Bayeux Tapestry: a dramatic colour change', *Medieval Life*, 15 (2001), p. 15 and rear cover.

[43] Whitelock, Ker and Rennell, *Aethelgifu*, p. 13, lines 47–9.

[44] Whitelock, Ker and Rennell, *Aethelgifu*, p. 82.

[45] Whitelock, *Anglo-Saxon Wills*, No. III, pp. 10–15, at p. 14.

[46] Owen, 'Wynflæd's wardrobe', pp. 203–4.

Fig. 164 The Virgin Mary in a front-fastening cloak, *Athelstan Psalter*, London, British Library, MS Cotton Galba A xviii, fol. 120v

Fig. 165 Woman in an open cloak, Old English *Hexateuch*, London, British Library MS Cotton Claudius B iv, fol. 66v

Fig. 166 *Superbia* in a cloak with central brooch, Prudentius's *Psychomachia*, London, British Library, MS Additional 24199, fol. 12r

occasions: *Wif moton under brunum hrægle to husle gan*[47] ('Women must attend Eucharist in a dark garment').

Cloaks

There are numerous cloak names documented from the late Anglo-Saxon period, of which the most common are *basing, hacele, hwitel, loða, mentel, rift, sciccels* and *wæfels*. In most cases the sources of the words are glosses, but literary evidence proves that the *hacele* and *mentel* could be worn by women (although both words were also applied to men's garments): in an account of the martyrdom of St Pelagia a *hacele* is worn by a woman (apparently as a penitential garment, though this is not a usual association) and in Wynflæd's will a *mentel*, one of two owned by this lady, is bequeathed to the testatrix's granddaughter, and a *mentelpreon* ('cloak-pin' or 'cloak-brooch') to her daughter. The granddaughter, recipient of *hyre beteran mentel*, is also to receive a fastener: *hyre ealdan gewiredan preon* (which might be translated as 'her old wire brooch' or 'pin'; though a more imaginative translation such as 'her antique filigree brooch' gives a more attractive interpretation of the bequest).

The symmetrical cloak which could be draped over the head and which was sometimes fastened by a central brooch continues to be depicted in this period, but only in a minority of illustrations; it was perhaps going out of fashion. It is worn by the central figure of the Virgin Mary in an Ascension scene in the *Athelstan Psalter* (London, British Library, MS Cotton Galba A xviii, fol. 120v; Fig. 164). The drawing is one of a number of Anglo-Saxon illustrations added to this ninth-century Continental manuscript in the first half of the tenth century, though the iconography of the art is Byzantine.[49] A similar cloak, without the closing brooch, can be seen draped over the head of a woman journeying on foot in the *Hexateuch* (Colour Plate I, Fig. 165). There is what appears to be a cloak of the same kind worn by the figure of the Virgin on an ivory carving of the Last Judgement, now in the Cambridge Museum of Archaeology and Anthropology.[50] A garment draped as loosely as this would seem insecure unless it was a very temporary arrrangement, however. There is a dramatic representation of the style in a depiction of the personified vice *Superbia* ('Pride') in illustrated manuscripts of Prudentius' allegorical poem *Psychomachia* (Fig. 166). We must be cautious about using the Prudentius drawings as evidence for Anglo-Saxon dress and customs, because all four

[47] *Confessionale Pseudo-Egberti*; B. Thorpe (ed.), *Ancient Laws and Institutes of England* (London, 1840), p. 162.
[48] Herzfeld, *Martyrology*, p. 192, line 1.
[49] Ohlgren, *Illustration*, p. 1.
[50] The ivory is rather worn; Beckwith, *Ivory Carvings*, Plate 41, cat .18, p. 121.

known cycles of illustrations are based on a fifth-century Continental original.[51] However, it is interesting to find that the costume described in the text as a *palla* (a 'garment' or 'cloak') gathered *a pectore nodum* ('in a knot at the breast')[52] is realised by the artist as a hooded cloak clasped by a round, central brooch, a type of fastener known to have been current in Christian Anglo-Saxon England.

A garment which could be either a small cloak or a shawl or a scarf is wound round the head of the personified *Luna* (the Moon) as illustrated in the early-eleventh-century London, British Library, MS Cotton Tiberius B v (Fig. 167). There is no visible brooch or pin, and the arrangement of the garment, which has one narrow end or corner hanging below the arm, seems improbable, or at best insecure. The swirling garment represents the moon's rays (as the sun's rays are depicted round the head of *Sol* in the same illustration) and the artist may have been as indifferent to reality on this point as he was in the harnessing of the beasts which draw the couples' chariots.

Fig. 167 *Luna* in a swirling garment, London, British Library MS Cotton Tiberius B v, fol. 47r

The sleeveless overgarment, with and without hood

Women are very often depicted in a loose, sleeveless garment which hangs from the shoulders, and which might normally cover the arms. When the arms were raised (the position in most illustrations) the garment hung down between them as far as the knees, in a point or curve. At the back it was more voluminous and longer. This cloak was worn over a longer garment, and in some cases artists seem to depict another, knee-length robe between the two. At the wrists the tight sleeves of another garment are always visible, and sometimes the looser sleeve of a gown may be seen between the cloak and the tight sleeves. The costume can be seen on the allegorical figure of *Philosophia* in Cambridge, Trinity College, MS 0. 3. 7, a Canterbury manuscript of Boethius' *Consolation of Philosophy* dating to *c*. 970 (Fig. 168). Some drawings suggest that this garment was hooded, as for example on fol. 8 of the *Harley Psalter* (Fig. 169). Others suggest that a separate headdress was worn over it. The distinction is not always very clear-cut in ink drawings, which at this time often had numerous 'fussy' lines depicting swirls and folds (and especially in black and white reproductions of them which do not convey different ink colours); but it is more obvious in paintings such as the frontispiece to the *New Minster Charter* (Colour Plate K).

Fig. 168 *Philosophia*, Cambridge, Trinity College, MS 0. 3. 7, fol. 1r

[51] H. Woodruff, *The Illustrated Manuscripts of Prudentius* (Cambridge, MA, 1930), p. 21.

[52] H. J. Thomson, *Prudentius*, Loeb Classical Library, 2 vols (London, 1949–53), 1 (1949), p. 292, line 187.

Fig. 169 Woman with projecting headdress and poncho-shaped cloak, *Harley Psalter*, fol. 8r

Fig. 170 St Æthelthryth/ Etheldreda, *Benedictional of St Æthelwold*, London, British Library MS Additional 49598, fol. 90v

Fig. 171 Woman in poncho-shaped cloak and fillet, carrying a bag, *Hexateuch*, fol. 76r

The shoulders of female figures are normally covered by the headdress, but one must assume that the cloak (if not hooded) was of a rectangular or oval shape, with an aperture for the head which was concealed by the headdress. The draping of the garment would be dependent on the position of the hole. As the garment was longer at the back than the front it seems that the aperture was not central.

Germanic *men* on Roman sculptures are depicted in a short cloak of the poncho type, which was probably made of animal skin, and derived its shape from the natural dimensions of the beast (Fig. 1). Men evidently continued to wear fur jerkins. However there is no evidence of continuity between these and the cloth garment worn by women in late Anglo-Saxon illustrations. Indeed, it seems likely that the feminine garment was introduced and popularised through Christian iconography. In Anglo-Saxon art the Virgin was generally depicted in this costume, and it is also found on allegorical figures such as *Philosophia* (Fig. 168) and in the illustration of St Æthelthryth (Fig. 170) in the *Benedictional of St Æthelwold* (a Winchester manuscript of *c.* 971–84), where it appears to be confined at the waist by a broad sash. The use of the garment in these very stylised and derivative illuminations might lead to the suspicion that this *pallium*-like cloak was simply copied from imported manuscripts and not actually part of an Anglo-Saxon woman's wardrobe. It is *not* worn by Queen Ælfgifu-Emma in the early-eleventh-century 'portrait' of her (Fig. 159). However, there is some evidence that it was actually worn in the eleventh century, for it appears in the *Hexateuch* (Fig. 171) and in the Bayeux 'Tapestry', possibly on the figure of Queen Edith (Fig. 161) and more clearly on a figure labelled 'Ælfgyva' (Fig. 172), who has not been definitively identified, but who was presumably one of the royal or high-ranking ladies known to have borne this or similar names in the early-eleventh century.[53] The garment may have been an aristocratic one.

The sleeved gown

Many female figures appear in long, sleeved gowns. The necklines of these garments are concealed by the headdress, but the gown seems to be tailored, unlike the sleeveless overgarments just discussed which hang loosely from the shoulders. Until the early-eleventh century the sleeves are depicted as either straight or only slightly flared at the lower end and are often turned back to form a cuff (Fig. 173). Sometimes the sleeve only reaches to the forearm (or falls back when the arm is raised) and sometimes leaves exposed the tight sleeve of an undergarment (Fig. 174, left hand). The *Hexateuch* contains several depictions of women in straight

[53] The most famous being Queen Ælfgifu-Emma, and Cnut's mistress Ælfgifu of Northampton.

sleeves, which when hanging down, conceal the hands completely (Colour Plate I, Fig. 175). This, apparently a device for keeping the hands warm, does not seem to be illustrated anywhere else in Anglo-Saxon art. Strips of simple ornament drawn at the sleeve ends by the *Hexateuch* artist suggest that embroidered or braided borders decorated these sleeves.

More elaborate sleeves may have been coming into fashion in the early-eleventh century. Several women in the *Harley Psalter* have extended sleeve-cuffs, including a queen seated at table (Colour Plate H) and a woman giving a ring to her departing son (Fig. 158) in the earliest manifestations of this style in English art.[54] Although Ælfgifu-Emma, Cnut's queen, has only slightly flared cuffs in the drawing in Stowe 944 (Fig. 159) the Virgin placed above her wears fairly wide sleeves (Fig. 176). In a drawing of her executed in the 1040s (in London, British Library, MS Additional 33241) Ælfgifu-Emma, now Cnut's widow, but still in a public and influential position as mother of an unmarried king, is perhaps fashionably dressed with wide, decorated sleeves which hang in points (Fig. 160).[55] The exaggerated sleeve is also found in a drawing of the Crucifixion in the *Gospels* belonging to Judith, Countess of Flanders (New York, Pierpont Morgan Library 709), which is no earlier than the 1050s;[56] both the Virgin Mary standing beside the cross and a small female figure kneeling at its foot[57] wear gowns which have long pointed sleeves with contrasting cuffs (Figs 177, 178). Similar sleeves are worn by the woman who leads her child from a burning building at scene 47 of the Bayeux 'Tapestry' (Fig. 163). Although there is no evidence as to the woman's identity, the house she flees is a substantial two-storey building and she was perhaps the lady of the manor rather than a peasant. This woman's gown has been reconstructed by Robin Netherton, who demonstrates that the cut is quite economical, not, as one might have imagined from the dangling sleeves, an extravagant use of unnecessary material (Fig. 238).

Many of the pictured gowns are ankle-length. Some have a pronounced hem or border of contrasting colour at the bottom of the skirt (Figs 165, 168, 170, 172, 177). In some illustrations an area of fullness suggests that the garment might have trailed on the ground. (Figs 163, 168). The feet, unnaturally tiny, are always visible in

Fig. 172 'Aelfgyva', Bayeux 'Tapestry'

Fig. 173 *Luxuria* dancing with an elaborate scarf, Prudentius's *Psychomachia*, London, British Library, MS Additional 24199, fol. 8r

Fig. 174 *Pompa* with stole and visible inner sleeves, Prudentius's *Psychomachia*, London, British Library, MS Additional 24199, fol. 21v

---

[54] The Harley illustration to Psalm 127 (128):1–3, fol. 66v, is quite different from the version of this Psalm in the Utrecht Psalter (fol. 73v) which does not include the distinctive sleeves; E. T. Dewald, *The Illustrations of the Utrecht Psalter* (Leipzig, 1933), Plate CXII.

[55] The manuscript is not English, so might reflect Continental fashion, though as we see, the sleeves are consistent with those being depicted in English art in the eleventh century.

[56] The manuscript is dated to *post* 1051, but the Crucifixion is considered an addition to the manuscript and may be 'a good deal later'; C. R. Dodwell, *The Pictorial Arts of the West 800–1200* (New Haven, CT and London, 1993), p. 113 including caption to Fig. 103, p. 145 n.101.

[57] Usually, but not universally, interpreted as Judith of Flanders herself (1032–94).

Fig. 175 Woman with hanging sleeves, *Hexateuch*, fol. 66v

Fig. 176 The Virgin Mary, London, British Library MS Stowe 944, fol. 6r

Fig. 177 The Virgin Mary, *Judith Gospels*, New York, Pierpont Morgan Library, MS 709, fol 1v

these drawings, but the hem of the skirt sometimes looks as if it has been kicked up, a stylistic feature. There is considerable fullness, like a frill, at the bottom of the garment of the Virgin on a carved stone from Stepney, London, though in this case the garment does not reach the feet.[58] Decoration is occasionally suggested on the skirts of these gowns, for example that of the weeping Virgin in London, British Library, MS Harley 2904 (Fig. 157) though the majority are left plain. The decoration may indicate embroidery, or pattern in the weave, floral rather than geometric, but it seems randomly placed in comparison to the more precise decoration on cushions or curtains. The ornament on the clothing may be impressionistic, but it could represent rich fabrics that were actually in use. We are aware of the diamond- and lozenge-patterned twills which were the more sophisticated products of the warp-weighted loom, and the patterned silks which were being imported, and possibly also woven in England from imported thread, at this time.[59]

Figures in Carolingian and Ottonian illumination often wear gowns with elaborate strips of ornament down the front, sometimes joining neck bands and borders at the edges of skirts (Figs 107, 111, 160). Depicted colourfully, usually with a series of circles or ovals, these strips perhaps represent applied silk bands, since roundels are characteristic of woven silks. We do not find such flamboyant ornament in Anglo-Saxon art. Bands of ornament are almost always confined to the cuff in depictions of women and the circles on them are modest in size, sometimes mere dots (Fig. 175). One of the recipients of Aldhelm's *De Virginitate* pictured in a late tenth-century manuscript of that text in London, Lambeth Palace Library MS 200 (fol. 68v) has a fairly wide sleeve edged with a pattern of circles, alternating with pairs of dots, between plain, narrow borders. This is probably the most elaborate example. Continental paintings also often show decorative bands at the thigh and the upper arm. Bands at the thigh are only faintly and occasionally suggested in English art, as for example in the figure of the Virgin in London, British Library, MS Arundel 60, fol. 12v (Fig. 179).

In illustrations the arms of female figures are almost always covered. (The mythological figure of *Luna*, Fig. 167, is a rare exception.) In some cases it appears that the wide-sleeved garment was worn beneath the draped one, while close-fitting inner sleeves indicate yet another garment beneath. There are several instances where an artist has drawn a woman with a wide sleeve on one arm and the other arm holding up the material of a *pallium* (e.g. Fig. 174). Possibly the artist, in confusion, has drawn an impossible

---

[58] D. Tweddle, M. Biddle and B. Kjølbye-Biddle, *Corpus of Anglo-Saxon Stone Sculpture*, 4, *South East England* (Oxford, 1995), Fig. 354.

[59] The piece of silk patterned with roundels depicting King David, from Maaseik, Belgium, which is thought to be in English taste and is associated with English embroideries, suggests that an English silk-weaving industry was established by the eighth or ninth century. See p. 137.

hybrid, but perhaps the costume could look like this if one garment were worn over the other.

When one tries to assign a name to the sleeved gown, it is necessary to recognise that this is the garment which seems to have been worn by secular women on most occasions, that it could be brightly coloured and might have decoration at the wrists and elsewhere. If we consider the wills of wealthy Anglo-Saxon ladies in the late Anglo-Saxon period, we find that the garment mentioned most often is the *cyrtel*. The *cyrtel* could be made in various colours, possibly in various fabrics, and it was valuable enough to be bequeathed. Despite the facts that the derivation of *cyrtel* suggests a short garment (see p. 53, above), and that the word continued to be used of the short tunic worn by men, it seems likely that its meaning had become extended and by this time it was used of the woman's gown.

Fig. 178 Woman, probably Judith of Flanders, *Judith Gospels*, New York, Pierpont Morgan Library, MS 709, fol 1v

The girdle and sash

In some illustrations the gown hangs loose, in others it appears to be pouched over the hips, as if over a concealed girdle. Some figures wearing the draped, sleeveless, outer garment appear to have a broad, self-coloured sash at the waist. A diagonal line suggests that the sash may be wrapped round twice or arranged with a twist in it (Fig. 174). A rather different impression is given by a crucifixion painting which includes a kneeling woman, perhaps Judith of Flanders, at the foot of Christ's cross (Fig. 178). The body of the figure, unlike most Anglo-Saxon pictures of women, is in profile. A tight belt is visible at the front of her gown, cinching the fabric to show off her waist, but it does not seem to continue round the back. The only parallel known to this author is on the earlier Genoels-Elderen Diptych (Fig. 110).

There are never, in late Anglo-Saxon art, any pendent girdle ends with or without strap tags, nor are there buckles. No tools or personal ornaments hang from the girdle or sash.

The undergarment

Pieces of a unique garment, of fine-woven linen (*c.* 25 threads per cm) partly embroidered in silk, have been recovered from Llangors, Wales, a place which has been tentatively identified with *Brecenanmere*, a site, probably royal, destroyed by the forces of Æthelflæd of Mercia in 916.[60] The garment (Plate 9) survives only

Fig. 179 The Virgin Mary in decorated gown, London, British Library MS Arundel 60, fol. 12v

[60] According to the Mercian Register inserted into the Anglo-Saxon Chronicle; S. Taylor (ed.), *MS B, The Anglo-Saxon Chronicle*, 4 (1983), p. 50; trans. in D. Whitelock, ed., *The Anglo-Saxon Chronicle* (London, 1961), p. 64.

as charred fragments, now monochrome, but the pieces retain three different embroidery designs: a border with pairs of confronted lions (Plate 10); a geometric design of triangles; and a main design of hexagons composed of vine-scroll and enclosing two different types of bird, all set against an embroidered background. At the time of writing meticulous analysis of the stitching continues and the re-creation of the embroideries achieved so far is not definitive.[61] It is not certain whether the garment was Welsh or English, or even that it belonged to a woman rather than a man, but it gives an entirely different picture from that supplied by art and text, in that it shows that a linen garment could be important enough to be decorated with embroidery and that this embroidery was quite different, in its position and designs, from any decoration graphically depicted.

In manuscript art the sleeves of an undergarment are often visible at the wrist of a female figure. In painted pictures they are coloured white, suggesting linen material. The sleeves usually have a wrinkled appearance, perhaps because they were rather long and were pushed up above the tight band at the wrist, but perhaps because they were deliberately pleated for decorative effect. The undergarments of the Viking women buried at Birka, Sweden, were arranged in fine folds, an effect achieved by the *plissé* technique in which the fabric was drawn together with needle and thread, soaked and stretched, thereby creating tight pleats. They were not permanent and would wash out, though the stitching would continue to hold the material together. The Birka garments are now believed to have been imported into Sweden, probably from Kiev, certainly from a Slavonic area,[62] which makes it less likely that they were known in England, but the parallel is worth noting. Pleats are known to have been worn in England in the later Middle Ages, and it is possible that they had been devised independently at an earlier stage.

The undergarment sleeve usually has tight cuffs, depicted by a band wider than the bands of pleating/wrinkling on the forearm. The Virgin Mary depicted in a Nativity in the *Boulogne Gospels*, Boulogne, *Bibliothèque municipale*, MS 11, fol. 12 (Fig. 180),[63] appears to have some kind of fastening at the cuff, a button or round-headed pin, perhaps, but this may be deceptive; the artist may have begun, but not continued, the kind of ornament we find as a band elsewhere.

Fig. 180 The Virgin Mary with ?buttoned cuff, *Boulogne Gospels*, Boulogne, *Bibliothèque municipale* MS 11, fol. 12r

[61] H. Granger-Taylor and F. Pritchard, 'A fine quality Insular embroidery from Llan-gors Crannóg, near Brecon', in M. Redknap, N. Edwards, S. Youngs, A. Lane and J. Knight (ed.), *Pattern and Purpose in Insular Art*, (Oxford, 1991), pp. 91–9. Further information from Mark Redknap, on whose advice I have included the garment in a chapter on female dress.

[62] A. Geijer, 'The textile finds from Birka', in Harte and Ponting, *Cloth and Clothing*, pp. 80–99, at pp. 87–8.

[63] The illuminations in this Continental manuscript (written at St Bertin) are by an English hand. The manuscript is late-tenth- to early-eleventh-century; Backhouse, Turner and Webster, *Golden Age*, No. 42, pp. 60, 65.

Hair and headgear

Many depictions of women from this period show headdresses which cover the head and neck. These headdresses usually appear more voluminous than a cloak simply pulled over the head would be. In crowd scenes women are usually distinguishable by their covered heads. If we are to believe the illustrations in the *Hexateuch*, which show scenes of childbirth and (extremely circumspect) representations of the begetting of children, women also sometimes wore these headdresses in bed.[64] In a Christian society which followed St Paul's dictum that women should cover their heads (I Corinthians 2:5–6) uncovered hair seems generally to have been an indication of vice, at least in art, as we have seen in the case of the reformed prostitute on the Ruthwell Cross (Chapter IV, p. 158, above). Examples from late Anglo-Saxon art include the personified vice *Avaritia* in the version of Prudentius's *Psychomachia* in London, British Library, MS Cotton Cleopatra C viii, who has an uncovered head and loose hair. In the *Hexateuch* (fol. 33v), Lot's daughters have loose hair in bed which may underline the fact that they are sinning — they are committing incest with their father.[65] The distinguished costume historian James Laver stated that in the Anglo-Saxon period 'young girls wore their hair long and loose over their shoulders, with a band to keep it from being too unruly. In the privacy of their homes women of all classes wore their hair the same way.'[66] These suggestions may seem plausible enough, but they are not substantiated by Anglo-Saxon art. Headbands were certainly worn, but in conjunction with cloth headdresses, not in isolation (see pp. 224–5, below). Manuscript art includes many representations of women in their homes, including intimate situations, and their heads are covered. Artists certainly did not distinguish between maiden and matron; they depicted the astrological sign *Virgo* as a woman wearing the usual headdress (see London, British Library, MSS Arundel 60, fol. 5 and Cotton Tiberius B v, fol. 7), and in the *Hexateuch*, where the artist, who was evidently following the text, must have been aware that he was depicting unmarried girls, likewise pictured them with covered heads (e.g. Fig. 171). Strangely, since nuns above all women were expected to wear a veil,[67] a nun called Godgytha, identified and depicted on an ivory seal, is shown bare-headed. The nun is depicted on the reverse

[64] However, Sarah and Hagar, depicted at fol. 27v, sleep with uncovered heads. At fol. 28r, two women without headdresses wash the infant Ishmael, but they have the block of hair of the standard male head in this manuscript, rather than the individual hairs of Sarah and Hagar.

[65] I owe the observation of Lot's daughters' hair to Seamus Ross, 'Dress Pins', p. 416.

[66] J. Laver, *Costume*, The Arts of Man (London, 1963), p. 26.

[67] The Old English word *rift*, 'veil' is used very often of nuns' clothing, and came to stand for 'the religious life' as we speak of 'taking the veil' today; see Bede, *Historia Ecclesiastica* IV, 19; Schipper, *Bedas Kirchengeschichte*, p. 442, line 2501.

of the seal, however, in an evident addition to the seal of a man, Godwin, on the primary side. Godwin is depicted with distinctive hair, and the carver may simply have copied it.[68]

The headcloth concealed hair, neck and, usually, the shoulders. There is an exception to the last in the depiction of the woman fleeing the burning building in the Bayeux 'Tapestry', where the headdress appears to be tucked into the neckline of the gown. Occasionally the headdress seems to hang lower than the shoulders, combining the functions of headdress and cloak (see 'The sleeveless overgarment', above.) This headdress perhaps owed its existence to the dissemination of Byzantine art through Christian Europe, although its origins lie, probably, further east – a similar headdress is worn by the Virgin on a sixth-century Syrio-Palestinian ivory panel[69] – but it seems to have appeared on Byzantine mosaics as early as the fifth century (at Sta. Maria Maggiore, Rome, on the triumphal arch).[70] It was not, at this stage, the only women's headgear depicted, but it continued to be shown during the period when Byzantine art was at its most spectacular and influential, the ninth to thirteenth centuries.[71]

There is some variation in the way this headdress is depicted by Anglo-Saxon artists. This may be partly a matter of personal style, but it may reflect differences of construction. Some females (often biblical figures) appear to wear very loose headdresses which are depicted in the 'fussy' art style of the time with many little lines suggesting folds and edges; others have a closer-fitting version. Possibly the former represents a long rectangle of cloth wrapped round the head and inconspicuously pinned (see pp. 225–6, below), with the end of the cloth on the outside at one side of the head (usually at the right). Though not so precarious as one might think,[72] since linen clings to itself and pins can secure cloth firmly, a headdress of this kind was probably not suitable for hard physical work. The closer-fitting version could depict a rectangle or oval of cloth with an aperture in it, resembling the garment known as a wimple in later medieval times[73] and which has survived until our own day among some orders of nuns. The extremes of the two styles can be

---

[68] Backhouse, Turner and Webster, *Golden Age*, pp. 113–14, No. 112.

[69] D. Talbot-Rice, *Byzantine Art* (Harmonsworth, revised and expanded edition, 1968), Fig. 12.

[70] Talbot-Rice, *Byzantine Art*, Fig. 108, lower.

[71] See the Virgin Hodeghetria, a tenth-century piece in the Victoria and Albert Museum, London; Talbot-Rice, *Byzantine Art*, Fig. 419.

[72] I am grateful to Robin Netherton for allaying my own doubts on this matter by a practical demonstration.

[73] Chaucer's Prioress wore a 'wympul' which was 'pynched' (probably pleated; *The Canterbury Tales*, *The General Prologue*, line 151; L. D. Benson (ed.), *The Riverside Chaucer* (Oxford, third edition,1990), p. 25). The author of the thirteenth-century *Ancrene Wisse* considered wimples extravagant and worldly, warning anchoresses that they should veil, not wimple, themselves (Tolkien, *Ancrene Wisse*, p. 215, line 25). See Murray, *et al.*, *Oxford English Dictionary*, 'wimple: a garment of linen or silk, formerly worn by women, so folded as to envelop the head, chin, sides of the face and neck.'

seen in Figs 174 and 159. The figure of *Vita* on Lady Gunhild's Cross, an ivory associated with the niece of King Cnut dating to *c.* 1075, now in the *Nationalmuseet*, Copenhagen,[74] is depicted as a woman with a headdress wrapped around her head and hanging down, with a fringed end over her left breast. The costume of this figure, which includes wide sleeves, a belt and apparently a pleated skirt, is unusual. The headgear of the Virgin on an ivory carving of the Nativity now in Liverpool Museum,[75] is also very unusual. It takes the form of a close-fitting cap or turban, which leaves no hair showing. It could be an example of nightwear, since the Virgin is depicted in bed.

There are numerous documented Old English names for head-gear, but when we seek a name for the typical headdress, certain words stand out because of their later associations, one being *wimpel*,[76] another *cuffie*, or *cuffia*, to which the modern English 'coif' is related. Possibly the more voluminous head-wrap was called by this name. The term may also be connected to Old English *cufle* or *cugele* 'a monk's cowl', which would imply that, on the contrary, the *cuffie* was hood-like in form or in appearance. The word cer-tainly referred to a garment of some value, since it appears as a bequest in Wynflæd's will.[77] Alternative headdress names are *hæt*, *hod* and *hufe*.

We may see the headdress unwrapped in some depictions of female figures. The dancing figure of *Luxuria* in the London, Brit-ish Library, Additional 24199 manuscript of Prudentius wears a piece of cloth like a long scarf over her head (Fig. 173). It crosses over her chest, passes under her arms and hands and forward over her right arm. A similar cloth is worn round the head of the Virgin in some ivory carvings (Fig. 181); one end of the garment encircles the neck, falling forward onto the shoulder. The scarf or veil is worn by a woman in a group of female figures addressed by the poet in London, Lambeth Palace Library, MS 200 (Fig. 182a). In this case, as the woman probably represents one of the nuns to whom the text was dedicated, this additional headgear may represent the holy veil.

Possibly the scarf could be worn wrapped round a hat, since a figure in the eleventh-century *Paris Psalter* (France, Paris, *Bibliothèque Nationale*, MS Fonds Latin 8824, fol. 3) wearing what appears to be a round hat, carries what looks like a scarf.[78] There is

Fig. 181 The Virgin Mary with headdress over ?a plait of hair, from an ivory book cover, Paris, *Bibliothèque Nationale* MS lat. 323 D/58/90

---

[74] Beckwith, *Ivory Carvings*, Plate 86, cat. 43, p. 127.

[75] Beckwith, *Ivory Carvings*, Plate 56.

[76] The word is recorded in glosses: to *ricinum* (Wright/Wülcker, *Vocabularies*, col. 107, line 37); *anabola* (Wright/Wülcker, *Vocabularies*, col. 125, line 8); *cyclade* (*veste*) (Goossens, *Glosses*, p. 419, line 4172); and *mafortibus* (W. S. Logeman, 'De Consuetudine Monachorum', *Anglia*, 13 (1891), pp. 365–454, at p. 37 (where the lemma is no longer visible); Goossens, *Glosses*, p. 480, line 5210).

[77] Whitelock, *Wills*, p. 14, line 17.

[78] B. Colgrave (ed.), *The Paris Psalter*, Early English Manuscripts in Facsimile, 8 (Copenhagen, 1958).

a cloth wrapped round such a hat in a ninth-century Carolingian illumination.[79] A group of women in the *Harley Psalter* seem to have projections under their hoods which could belong to some kind of caps or hats (Fig. 169). It is tempting to identify this projection with the *scyfel*, a word found in glosses translating Latin *mafors* ('a woman's veil')[80] and *maforte* ('headdress')[81] for among its cognates is Icelandic *skupla*, *skypill*, 'a woman's hood hiding or shading her face'.[82] The modern 'shovel' as in 'shovel-hat' may be related.

A veil which is squarish, rather than long, is held by an angel over the head of Queen Ælfgifu-Emma in the Stowe 944 miniature (Fig. 159). Queens seem to have worn a distinctive headdress, possibly a veil of this kind, in conjunction with a crown, since the monks' gesture representing 'the King's wife' implies it: *Cyninges wifes tacen is þæt þu strece onbutan heofod, and sete syððan þine hand bufon þin heofod*.[83] ('The sign of the King's wife is that you extend [your hand] about your head, and afterwards set your hand above your head'.) Queens depicted on the Lady Gunhild's Cross[84] and in the *Stuttgart Psalter* (Fig. 108) wear veils under their crowns. The *Stuttgart Psalter* (for example on fol. 58r) also shows the veil being worn by itself, decorated at the front and hanging down at the back, leaving the neck exposed, but the manuscript is of course Carolingian, and neither the form of decoration nor the fashion of the exposed neck are typical of English art.

Evidently Anglo-Saxon women did not use their veils to conceal their faces; in biblical narrative (Genesis 38:14–19) Tamar plays the harlot in order to conceive by her father-in-law, and so that he does not recognise her, she conceals her face. The Anglo-Saxon artist illustrating the *Hexateuch* resorted to the unconvincing device of Tamar spreading a hand across her features (Fig. 223).

Several documented Old English words appear to mean 'veil'. *Rift* is used very often of nun's clothing. Wynflæd, who was apparently a secular, bequeathed a *rift*,[85] but she may have owned it because she was a vowess, one of those pious women, often widows, who chose to live the religious life although they were not professed nuns.[86] To Wynflæd the *rift* differed from the *cuffie*. She seems to have bequeathed the former to a religious and the latter to a secular.[87] Probably the *rift* could be worn in conjunction with a headband (see below), in view of Wynflæd's bequest of *hyre betsð haliryft and hyre betstan bindan*, 'her best holy veil and her best fillet', to

[79] Austria,Vienna, *Nationalbibliothek Cod.* 2687; A. Goldsmidt, *Die deutsche Buchmalerei*, 2 vols (Florence and New York, 1928), 1, Plate 62.
[80] Wright/Wülcker, *Vocabularies*, col. 268, line 6.
[81] Lindsay, *Corpus*, p. 110, line 9; Wright/Wülcker, *Vocabularies*, col. 442, line 21.
[82] Bosworth/Toller, *Dictionary*, p. 846.
[83] Kluge, 'Indicia Monasterialia', p. 128, para. 119.
[84] Beckwith, *Ivory Carvings*, pp. 58–9, Plate 84.
[85] Whitelock, *Wills*, p. 14, line 15.
[86] J. L. André,'Widows and vowesses', *Archaeological Journal*, 49 (1892), pp. 69–82.
[87] Owen, 'Wynflæd's wardrobe', p. 199.

Ceolthryth.[88] The word *wrigels*, sometimes signifying the wrapping of a corpse, could also be used of the holy veil.[89] *Orel*, although it is found mostly in glossaries rather than literary texts, could also have been used with religious significance.[90]

Normally headdresses, both of the 'hood' type and the open veil, are depicted without any decoration, though there are what appear to be patterned headdresses on two female busts in the frame of an illumination (fol. 62r) in the *Bury St Edmunds Psalter* (Italy, Vatican, *Bibliotheca Apostolica Vaticana*, Rg. lat. 12), a Canterbury manuscript from the second quarter of the eleventh century (Fig. 183). This overall patterning suggests a woven silk. There is a dif-

Figs **182a** and **b** Abbesses or nuns in elaborate headdresses, Aldhelm's *De Virginitate*, London, Lambeth Palace Library, MS 200, fol. 68v

ferent kind of decoration on the headdresses of some of the group of female figures in Lambeth Palace Library MS 200, fol. 68v (Fig. 182b). Three of the ladies appear to have embroidered, possibly jewelled, headdresses. In one case, there is just a simple ornament at the forehead; in the others there is a medial line and one has decoration on either side of the line.[91] It may be significant that the dress of this group of women includes decorated headdresses, a decorated sleeve and some unusual shoes, since over-elaborate headdress, sleeve and (arguably) footwear are among the inappropriate garments mentioned by Aldhelm in this well-known text (above, pp. 134–7). The artist is not illustrating Aldhelm's description, which relates to dress in the eighth century; but he may have depicted a tenth-century equivalent of extravagant clothing in direct relation to the text. Elaborate dress among nuns was still an issue

Fig. **183** Figure with decorated headdress, *Bury St Edmunds Psalter*, Rome, Vatican *Bibliotheca Apostolica*, Reg. lat. 12, fol. 62r

---

[88] Whitelock, *Wills*, p. 14, lines 15–16.

[89] R. Morris (ed.), *The Blickling Homilies of the Tenth Century*, Early English Text Society, original series, 58, 63, 73 (1874–80), p. 61, line 16; U. Lindelöf, *Rituale Ecclesiae Dunelmensis*, Surtees Society, 140 (1927), p. 106.

[90] W. W. Skeat, *Aelfric's Lives of Saints*, 3 vols, Early English Text Society, original series, 76, 82, 94, 114 (1881–1900), reprinted as two volumes (Oxford, 1966), 1, p. 172, line 36.

[91] Unfortunately the relevant figures are only minor ones in the group (see Temple, *Anglo-Saxon Manuscripts*, Illustration 132). The most decorated headdress seems to belong to the costume with the decorated sleeve (above, p. 216) and distinctive light-coloured ankle shoes.

in the late Anglo-Saxon period. Christine Fell has pointed out that the late-tenth-century nun, St Edith of Wilton, dressed, according to her post-Conquest biographer, more richly than the Bishop of Winchester considered appropriate and indeed, on her seal she is shown in a headdress set back from the front of the hair, with some kind of decoration on it, as well as decoration (or even a necklace) at the chest.[92]

A fillet was considered a characteristic feature of the secular (married) woman's appearance, as we may deduce from the *Indicia Monasterialia*. The sign-language to be used in indicating a woman gives us some idea of the appearance of the fillet: *Gewylces ungehadodes wifes tacen is þæt þu [strice] mid foreweardum fingrum þin forwearde heafod fram þam anum earan to þon oþrum on bindan tacne.*[93] ('The sign for any unconsecrated woman is that you [indicate] with your forefingers your forehead from one ear to the other in the sign of a *binde*.') Some cloth bands found in Hiberno-Norse levels in Dublin, Ireland, preserve human hair, indicating that they functioned as fillets though the gender of their Viking owners is not known.[94] Evidence from both text and art suggests that the fillet was worn (by women)[95] in conjunction with a headdress of fabric rather than by itself. Wynflæd bequeathed two fillets in her will; one bequest, to a woman who was probably a secular, consisted of *cuffian and bindan*,[96] the other, to Ceolthryth, a woman who seems to have been attached to a convent, consisted, as we have already noted, of *hyre betsð haliryft and hyre betstan bindan* ('her best holy veil and her best fillet'). 'Bands' are the garments (or jewellery) most commonly bequeathed by women. Queen Ælfgifu-Emma left a *bænde* to her sister-in-law in her will of 1012,[97] and she wears a decorated band across her forehead, under her hood (or wimple), in the 'portrait' of her in MS Stowe 944 (Fig. 159) executed more than twenty years later. Two streamers ending in decorated tags emerge from her hood at the back, suggesting that in this case, the fillet consisted of a narrow piece of fabric, embroidered or brocaded at the front and ends, possibly jewelled, and of considerable length. It probably resembled the narrow band worn by the allegorical *Pompa* in Prudentius illustrations (Fig. 174) where it was presumably an indication of worldly vanity. In shape, though not in the manner of wearing, this band may have resembled the ecclesiastical stole.

[92] Fell, *Women in Anglo-Saxon England*, pp. 125–6. The seal is illustrated at Fig. 49.

[93] Kluge, 'Indicia', p. 129, para. 127.

[94] E. Heckett, 'Some Hiberno-Norse headcoverings from Fishamble Street and St John's Lane, Dublin, *Textile History*, 18.2 (1987), pp. 159–74; F. A. Pritchard, 'Silk braids and textiles of the Viking Age from Dublin', in L. Bender Jørgensen, B. Magnus and E. Munksgaard, *Archaeological Textiles*, NESAT II (Copenhagen, 1988), pp. 149–61.

[95] Men (occasionally) and angels also wear fillets in Anglo-Saxon art.

[96] Whitelock, *Wills*, p. 14, line 17.

[97] J. M. Kemble, *Codex Diplomaticus Ævi Saxonici*, 6 vols (London, 1839–48), 3 (1845), No. 721.

Another kind of headband is worn outside the headcloth. It appears to be a continuous ring, like earlier headbands on the *Grand Camée de France* (Fig. 59) and the Halberstadt Diptych (Fig. 37). Such a band could have been of cloth or leather, it could have been richly brocaded or embroidered with gold, on a base of braided textile, or possibly, it could have been have been made of solid metal. There is an example of the latter in a depiction of the Virgin Mary, in the *Prayer Book of Abbot Ælfwine* (Fig. 156) obviously by the artist who drew the Stowe 944 'portrait' of Cnut and Ælfgifu-Emma. The Virgin's band is decorated in a similar way to Emma's band, with narrow borders and a central area of dots, and it projects out over the forehead at the same angle, but it is worn lower over the brow. It has a trefoil at the back indicating that it is to be 'read' as a crown. The artist perhaps restricted himself to one trefoil in order to leave room for the dove of the spirit which is perched on Mary's head.[98]

We have three late Anglo-Saxon wills in which gold bands are bequeathed (they are called *bænd* or *bend*),[99] and although the contexts do not make it certain that these bands are for the head, it seems probable, since the Old English word *bend* is found elsewhere glossing Latin *diadema* and *nimbus*.[100] They were all bequeathed for their bullion value; in each case the testator directed that the bands should be divided up. That precious metal could be reclaimed from gold-brocaded braids is demonstrated by a goldsmith's hoard now in the *Statens Historisk Museum*, Stockholm, Sweden, which included 'gold and silver threads, apparently flat strips unpicked from textiles and rolled up into balls'.[101]

In Anglo-Saxon art, women's hair is usually concealed beneath a headdress, except for occasional suggestions at the forehead. Unusual exceptions are Godgytha, on her seal (above, pp. 219–20), who appears to have long hair, perhaps in a plait, and a depiction of the Virgin on an ivory book-cover (France, Paris, *Bibliothèque Nationale* MS lat. 323 D/58/90; Fig. 181) with what appears to be a plait of hair over the crown, suggesting that women in the late Anglo-Saxon period might wear their hair up. It would be practical, with the very loose-looking headdresses of the age, to have a plait or firm mound of hair to which the wimple, hood or veil could be pinned. Pins are never shown in illustrations, but they are very common

[98] The picture is a rare 'Quinity', i.e. the Trinity plus two additional figures: God the Father is flanked by God the Son and the Virgin Mary. The dove represents the Holy Spirit and the Christ Child is in Mary's arms; see Backhouse, Turner and Webster, *Golden Age*, pp. 75–6.

[99] Byrhtric and Ælfswith bequeathed *healfne bænde gyldene* (Whitelock, *Wills*, p. 28, lines 4–5); Wulfwaru left a *bend*, worth twenty mancuses (Whitelock, *Wills*, p. 64, lines 20–1); Æthelgifu bequeathed to a relative five mancuses [of gold] which were to be cut from her *bend* (Whitelock *et al.*, *Aethelgifu*, p. 13).

[100] Among a group of glosses on the subject of head-coverings and head ornaments, we find *diadema, bend agimmed and gesmiðed* and *nimbus, mid goldgesiwud bend*; Wright/Wülcker, *Vocabularies*, col. 152, lines 25–6.

[101] From a sixth-century grave at Djurgårdsäng, Skara, Vastergotland, Sweden; Crowfoot and Hawkes, 'Gold braids', p. 85.

archaeological finds. Many late Saxon pins have rounded heads, and would have been suitable for securing the ubiquitous head-dress to itself and to the hair beneath it. Several names for pins appear in glossaries. Some of these, readily-comprehensible compounds like *feax-preon*[102] ('hairpin') and *hær-nædl*[103] ('hair-needle'), may have been nonce-words, but we also find *cæfing*,[104] *up-legen*[105] and *þrawing-spinel*,[106] the latter apparently a pin for curling the hair.

The leggings

In Anglo-Saxon art women's legs are normally concealed by the skirts which fall to their feet. However, in the London, British Library, MS Additional 24199 version of Prudentius's *Psychomachia*, the Vice *Superbia* is depicted as a woman on horseback, and enough of her leg is revealed to demonstrate that a strip of cloth is wound round from mid-calf to ankle in parallel bands, with two ends or strings hanging over the bare foot (Fig. 166). Although the evidence is limited, it is possible that these bands were in general use; similar leggings are a very common component of male costume and there is much linguistic evidence of them. Three of the documented words are compounds of obvious meaning: *hosebend*,[107] 'hose band', *sceanc-bend*,[108] 'leg band' and *sceanc-gegirela*[109] 'leg ornament'. *Wining*[110] was evidently a word in common use for a binding round the lower leg, and the word *nostle*, which seems to have been a more general word for a band (including a fillet), could also be used of a leg band.[111]

The footwear

Women in illustrations wear flat-soled ankle shoes, which, in painted pictures, are normally coloured black (Colour Plate I).[112] They are quite plain, except for a contrasting strip running down

---

[102] Wright/Wülcker, *Vocabularies*, col. 107, line 38.

[103] Napier, *Glosses*, p. 33, line 1200; [C. W.] Bouterwek, 'Die ags. Glossen in dem Brüsseler Codex von Aldhelms Schrift De Virginitate', *Zeischrift für deutsches Alterthum*, 9 (1853), pp. 401–530, at p. 435.

[104] F. Kluge, 'Angelsächsische Glossen', *Anglia*, 8 (1885), pp. 448–52, at p. 450; Napier, *Glosses*, p. 124, line 4821, p. 146, line 389; Wright/Wülcker, *Vocabularies*, col. 107, line 28, col. 223, line 16.

[105] Wright/Wülcker, *Vocabularies*, col. 107, line 38, col. 223, line 16.

[106] Napier, *Glosses*, p. 33, line 1200; Goossens, *Glosses*, p. 439, line 4528, p. 479, line 5207.

[107] Napier, *Glosses*, p. 124, line 4822.

[108] Wright/Wülcker, *Vocabularies*, col. 152, line 39.

[109] Wright/Wülcker, *Vocabularies*, col. 467, line 29.

[110] Kluge, 'Indicia', p. 127, para. 103; Wright/Wülcker, *Vocabularies*, col. 125, lines 14, 16, col. 234, line 22.

[111] Wright/Wülcker, *Vocabularies*, col. 153, line 3; F. Holthausen, 'Die Leidener Glossen' *Englische Studien*, 50 (1916–17), pp. 327–40, at p. 330, line 110.

[112] The greenish shoes of the Virgin in Colour Plate K are unusual.

the front of the foot which is sometimes visible on the rare occasions when a foot is not depicted in profile. In many of the illustrations the toes of the shoes are pointed, but not exaggeratedly so. There are hardly any variations in the depiction of women's footwear, apart from the slight stylistic difference between artists. A rare exception is the line drawing in Lambeth Palace Library MS 200 (fol. 68v), where one woman wears ankle shoes which are left uncoloured by the artist. Dots down the front perhaps represent laces or thongs. Two women in the same group wear low shoes or slippers with decorative projections at the instep. Again it is possible that the artist was conscious of Aldhelm's description of elaborate costume. Whatever Aldhelm meant by *galliculae*, at least one later Anglo-Saxon scholar thought it meant 'shoes' (see Chapter IV, pp. 135–6, above). Though the depiction here does not render the *rubricatis pellibus* of Aldhelm's diatribe, it does suggest slightly unusual footwear.

The pictures that we have of women, even when they are illustrating narrative, are formal in pose and stylised in execution; the ankle shoe (*scoh*)[113] was the appropriate footwear in this context. Yet linguistic evidence and archaeological finds show that several different types of footwear were in existence, and some kinds of decoration are known, for example shoe fragments from this period found in Winchester have top bands; others have pointed soles which extend into the upper at the heels.[114] It seems likely that, according to situation, women might also have available to them various designs of ankle-shoe (see Plate 7, Fig. 117), boots (Fig. 118), slippers (*stæppe-scoh*,[115] *slipe-scoh*,[116] *swiftlere*;[117] Fig. 119), raw hide shoes (*hemming, rifeling* (Fig. 85)[118] and possibly, but less likely, sandals (*crinc*,[119] *calc*,[120] *rifeling*).[121] It is very likely that poor women, and those who worked in wet or muddy conditions went barefoot as men did (below, p. 254), but we have no depictions of women in such circumstances. It is only the figures of personified Vices in *Psychomachia* illustrations who go barefoot.

[113] The occurrences of the word in its various forms are numerous. Representative examples are: glossing *calciamentum* (Wright/Wülcker, *Vocabularies*, col. 327, line 31; Luke 3:16, Skeat *Gospels*, p. 41; Garmonsway, *Colloquium*, p. 35, line 171); *calcarium* (Wright/Wülcker, *Vocabularies*, col. 283, line 18); *calceos* (Wright/Wülcker, *Vocabularies*, col. 197, line 13); *caliga* (Wright/Wülcker, *Vocabularies*, col. 362, line 38); *fico* (Wright/Wülcker, *Vocabularies*, col. 125, line 24); and *galliculae* (Wright/Wülcker, *Vocabularies*, col. 414, line 31).

[114] Thornton, 'Shoes, boots and shoe repairs', in Biddle, *Winchester*, 7.ii, ii, pp. 593–4, 596–601, 603, 606, 608.

[115] Lindsay, *Corpus*, p. 171, line 708; Wright/Wülcker, *Vocabularies*, col. 277, line 30.

[116] Wright/Wülcker, *Vocabularies*, col. 277, line 29, earlier *slebescoh*, Lindsay, *Corpus*, p. 165, line 394.

[117] Wright/Wülcker, *Vocabularies*, col. 125, line 26; Garmonsway, *Colloquy*, p. 35, line 171.

[118] See p. 123, note 76.

[119] E. Steinmayer, 'Lateinische und altenenglische Glossen', *Zeitschrift für deutsches Alterthum*, 33 (1889), pp. 242–51, at p. 250, line 2.

[120] Mark 6:9; Skeat, *Gospels*, p. 42.

[121] Glossing *obstrigelli*; Wright/Wülcker, *Vocabularies*, col. 125, line 33.

The 'woman's outfit'

The will of a woman named Wulfwaru includes the bequest to her elder daughter of 'one woman's outfit' (*anes wifscrudes*).[122] Unlike Wynflæd and Æthelgifu, Wulfwaru did not enumerate individual garments in her will, simply leaving to her younger daughter all the remaining female clothing ... *ic geann ealles þæs wifscrudes þe þer to lafe bið*.[123] Nevertheless, the bequest of 'one woman's outfit' suggests that the garments could be conceived as a costume, the individual pieces perhaps matching in fabric or trimming.

Elaborate dress

C. R. Dodwell has shown from documentary sources that sumptuous textiles existed in great numbers in Anglo-Saxon England, textiles which dazzled the Normans who refer to them.[124] These fabrics included imported silks, often patterned; textiles embroidered with gold, not only as an ornament for the edge of a piece of material, but sometimes so heavily decorated with gold as to appear encrusted with it; cloth adorned with pearls and other jewels, and fur-trimmed robes. Most of the evidence for the existence of these textiles concerns their use as religious vestments, but there is every reason to believe that royal and wealthy seculars also possessed such magnificent apparel. As Dodwell points out, the fact that the religious vocation of King Edgar's daughter Edith was said to be tested by jewelled robes and cloaks interwoven with gold is significant: 'there is no reason to think that ... her attire and tastes were different from those of her predecessors or successors'.[125] Mathilda, William the Conqueror's queen, bequeathed one of her own cloaks to be used as a cope. The garment is described as being 'of gold' (*ex auro*).[126] Mathilda is known to have used English embroideresses[127] and if the gold on the cloak was embroidered, it may have been English work.

Anglo-Saxon artists rarely suggest opulent fabrics, particularly for garments. We occasionally find what look like silk, embroidered, or even jewelled, cuffs (Colour Plate I, Fig. 160) and very rarely a suggestion of ornament on a headdress. Pattern on the skirts of a

---

[122] Whitelock, *Wills*, p. 64, line 11.

[123] Whitelock, *Wills*, p. 64, lines 12–13.

[124] Dodwell, *Anglo-Saxon Art*, pp. 170–87.

[125] Dodwell, *Anglo-Saxon Art*, p. 179, citing Goscelin *La Légende de Ste Edith* in A. Wilmart (ed.), 'La légende de Sta Édith en prose et vers par le moine Goscelin', *Analecta Bollandiana*, 56 (1938), pp. 4–101, 265–307, at p. 44.

[126] Dodwell, *Anglo-Saxon Art*, pp. 179–80, citing L. Musset (ed.), *Les Actes de Guillaume le conquérant et de la reine Mathilde pour les abbayes caennaises*, Mémoires de la Societé des Antiquaires de Normandie, 37.16 (1967), at pp. 112–13.

[127] Dodwell, *Anglo-Saxon Art*, pp. 179–80; *Domesday Book*, 1, 74b.

gown is found only occasionally, for instance an exceptionally ornate example on the Virgin figure in a late-tenth-century psalter, London, British Library, MS Harley 2904 (Fig. 157) and, less elaborate, on a Virgin in a psalter dated to *c*. 1060, London, British Library, MS Arundel 60 (Fig. 179).[128] It is equally rare on the cloak. The Virgin from Harley 2904 has a floral motif at the shoulder, and so has the Virgin in an annunciation scene in the *Boulogne Gospels*, fol. 11v, in this case in addition to the suggestion of a border and other ornament.[129] Generally, such decoration is rather unsystematic, highlighting the knees and shoulders of the figures and the edges of the garments, but not giving a clear picture of overall decoration. An artist wishing to suggest elaborate dress was more likely to do so by adding an extra layer to the woman's garments, indicated in painted manuscripts by colour contrast, for example the Virgin figure in the richly decorated *New Minster Charter* (above p. 210, Colour Plate K).

A fragmentary, late-tenth or eleventh-century sculpture of the Madonna from Sutton upon Derwent, East Yorkshire, has what James Lang describes as 'a collar or necklace of five pear-shaped elements'.[130] This is an unusual indication that necklaces of pendants were still being worn and was perhaps characteristic of the Viking north, the neck being concealed in southern art which presumably reflected the dress of the south.

Viking costume

Female figures on Anglo-Viking sculptures are dressed in the Scandinavian iconographical tradition. There are profile figures on the cross at Gosforth and on a hogback tombstone from Sockburn, Darlington,[131] as well as a full-face figure on a Sockburn cross shaft,[132] which show that the unbelted gown trailing in a 'train' and surmounted by a short cloak or shawl, pointed at the back, was the costume which represented women in Anglo-Viking as well as in Swedish art (Figs 121,122). We do not know how far the sculptors were guided by tradition, or to what extent these carvings represent what Viking women were actually wearing in England in the tenth century.

According to the Icelandic text *Rígsþula*, the dress with the 'train' was aristocratic, and co-existed with the middle-class gown supported by paired pins (the *peplos* equivalent). Such co-existence

---

[128] In both scenes the garments of Christ and St John are similarly patterned.
[129] Backhouse, Turner and Webster, *Golden Age*, No. 42, p. 63 scene at bottom right.
[130] Sutton upon Derwent, 1A; Lang, *Corpus of Anglo-Saxon Sculpture*, 3, p. 220, Plate 868.
[131] No. 15; Cramp, *Corpus of Anglo-Saxon Sculpture*,1, p. 141, Plate 138, 741.
[132] No. 3A; Cramp, *Corpus of Anglo-Saxon Sculpture*, 1, p. 136, Plate 130, 710.

is not evidenced from England, where it seems that Viking women changed their style of dress towards the end of the Anglo-Viking period. The traditional 'tortoise' brooches, worn in Scandinavia in pairs at the shoulders as earlier Anglo-Saxon women had worn brooches, are not characteristic of Viking York and were presumably not fashionable there. However, one cannot imagine that women who had to walk about the muddy streets of low-lying York would have worn a dress with a train to do so. To judge from the evidence of the Sutton brooch (above, p. 205), English Viking women may have adopted the single disc brooch which was popular in late Saxon England, though cheap versions in pewter rather than silver may have been the norm among the growing urban population.

Originally an absence of head covering may have distinguished Viking women from Christian Anglo-Saxons. The Gosforth Cross, which, although a Christian monument includes scenes from northern pagan legend, depicts at the foot of the crucified Christ a woman with the traditionally Scandinavian hairstyle of the knotted ponytail. The hair on the Sockburn cross shaft figure is shown drawn back from the face, probably representing the same style. A figure on a hogback tombstone from Lowther, Cumbria, has long curling hair.[133] Covered heads may have become the norm for Viking women, however, since a large number of headdresses have been found in Viking urban sites, though there is no proof that these were worn by women rather than men, and no indication whether they were day wear, or nightcaps. A tenth-century hood or cap made of silk and with linen ties was excavated from the Coppergate site in York (Figs 184, 185). It could have fitted an adult or a child, and might be fastened so that it framed the face or tied at the nape of the neck. Fragments of two others have been found elsewhere in York,[134] and similar ones have been recovered from Lincoln (Fig. 186) and London.[135] Viking level excavations in Dublin have yielded the remains of thirteen headdresses of the same kind, made in both wool and silk.[136] One of the Dublin finds had probably been adapted for a child. The caps were evidently colourful. The second York fragment had been dyed with madder and the remains of what might have been a child's cap from the same city had been dyed with madder and lichen purple. The silk found at all these sites was imported, but the silk headdresses were almost certainly constructed in Viking Britain, probably a luxury version of an established

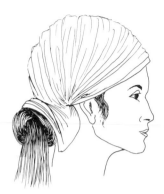

Fig. 184 Silk cap, Coppergate, York, worn tied back, adapted from a reconstruction by Penelope Walton Rogers

Fig. 185 Silk cap, Coppergate, York tied under the chin, adapted from a reconstruction by Penelope Walton Rogers

[133] Lowther 5; Bailey and Cramp, *Corpus of Anglo-Saxon Sculpture*, 2, p. 131, Plate 450.

[134] A. Muthesius, 'The silk fragment from 5 Coppergate', in MacGregor, *Anglo-Saxon Finds*, pp. 132–6; Walton, *Textiles, Cordage and Raw Fibre*, pp. 360–77.

[135] F. Pritchard, 'Textiles from recent excavations in the City of London', in Bender Jørgensen and Tidow, *NESAT I*, pp. 193–203, at p. 197.

[136] E. Heckett, 'Some silk and wool head-coverings from Viking Dublin: uses and origins – an enquiry', in Walton and Wild, *NESAT III* (London, 1990), pp. 85–96.

fashion normally made in native materials, as the Dublin woollen examples testify. The Dublin excavations also yielded the remains of fourteen rectangular scarves with fringed and tasselled ends, which could have been draped over the head and secured by bands. These might have been worn alone, or over caps.

Fig. 186 Silk cap, Lincoln. After Anna Muthesius

VII

Men's costume in the tenth and eleventh centuries

Fig. 187 King Edgar in long robe with sash, London, British Library MS Cotton Tiberius A iii, fol. 2v

Fig. 188 King Cnut in unique costume, London, British Library, MS Stowe 944, fol. 6r

The evidence

The nature of the evidence is the same as that for women's costume in the same period but with the difference that male figures appear much more frequently than female in illuminated manuscripts, sculptures and embroideries. Since the costume of secular men is so clearly distinguished from that of both divine and ecclesiastical figures, one can make deductions from art about medieval dress for men more confidently than one can for women. We have depictions of several monarchs: Athelstan in Cambridge, Corpus Christi College MS 183 (Colour Plate J), Edgar in London, British Library, MSS Cotton Tiberius A iii (Fig. 187) and Vespasian A viii (Colour Plate K), Cnut in London, British Library, MS Stowe 944 (Fig. 188), and from the Bayeux 'Tapestry', Edward the Confessor (Fig. 189), Harold Godwinesson (Figs 190, 191) and the future William the Conqueror, a Norman (Figs 192, 193). Though these are not true 'portraits' in that they have few distinguishing physical characteristics and in some cases were created well after the death of the subject, we can assume that contemporaries would have found their clothing plausible. Furthermore, we have male figures engaged in a great variety of occupations and activities, particularly in the illustrated calendars (London, British Library, MSS Cotton Julius A vi and Tiberius B v), in the *Hexateuch* and in the 'Tapestry'. We are presented, therefore, with a cross-section of society not found in pictures of women, and also a great deal of movement and a variety of angles which are not present in the more static, formal depictions which, with the exception of the illustrated *Psychomachia* manuscripts, characterise the illustrations of women.

Yet, when we try to make deductions about costume from art we must recognise that the depictions are stylised, not just with regard to the posture of the figures and the way that the drapery falls, but also in the details that are omitted and in the lack of variety in costume. The illustrations do not show fasteners, except the ubiquitous circular brooches which secure cloaks. The buckles, pins and strap ends recovered from late Anglo-Saxon levels of excavations are not represented in art. We can assume that some of the archaeological finds of garment fasteners and jewellery belonged to men, but there is no direct proof. Few artefacts from this period are grave-goods and no fasteners have men's names engraved on them. Penannular brooches from the Viking north are more confidently assumed to belong to male costume, both because of their size and because they are male accessories in the Irish tradition.

The literary and linguistic evidence is, like art, more informative on male costume than female. Again, many of the documented garment-names are from glosses, but there are a few textual references that prove certain items were worn by men – anecdotes concerning male characters and instructions in the *Indicia Monasterialia* and the Benedictine Rule. There is particular evidence of rich dress with regard to King Edward the Confessor, though the sources are retrospective, not contemporary. William of Malmesbury records that the clothes the king wore at great feasts 'were interwoven with gold, which the queen had most sumptuously embellished'[1] and (in what may be an interpolated passage) in the *Vita Ædwardi* which Queen Edith herself commissioned, it is recorded that she both decorated the king's garments herself and authorised other work according to her taste:

> … hec a principio sue coniunctionis talibus eum ex suo ipsius opere uel studio redimiuit ornamentis … In quibus ornandis non estimabatur quanto preciosi lapides et rare gemme atque uniones candidi pararentur; in clamidibus et tunicis caligis quoque et calciamentis nulla auri quantitas in uarietate florum multipliciter se effundencium pensabatur.

> Edith, from the very beginning of her marriage [1045] clad him in raiments either embroidered by herself or of her choice … in the ornamentation of these no count was made of the cost of precious stones, rare gems and shining pearls that were used. As regards mantles, tunics, boots and shoes, the amount of gold which flowed in the various complicated floral designs was not weighed.[2]

The implication is that though the king's own taste was austere, corresponding to his (posthumous) saintly image, he indulged the queen's desire to deck him out in elaborate clothes.

Before we begin to consider the garments individually, it should be stated that in dealing with male dress in the late Anglo-Saxon

Fig. 189 King Edward the Confessor in unique costume, Bayeux 'Tapestry'

Fig. 190 King Harold Godwinesson enthroned, Bayeux 'Tapestry'

Fig. 191 Harold Godwinesson captive, Bayeux 'Tapestry'

---

[1] Quoted in Dodwell, *Anglo-Saxon Art*, p. 70.

[2] F. Barlow (ed. and trans.), *The Life of King Edward who Rests at Westminster*, Oxford Medieval Texts (Oxford, 2nd ed., 1992), pp. 22–5. However, Elizabeth Tyler points out the literary artifice of the biography of Edward; E. M. Tyler, '"When wings incarnadine with gold are spread": the *Vita Ædwardi Regis* and the display of treasure at the court of Edward the Confessor', in E. M. Tyler (ed.), *Treasure in the Medieval West*, York, 2000, pp. 83–107, especially pp. 100–1 where she expresses reservations about the inclusion of this passage in discussion of the anonymous *Vita Ædwardi*.

Fig. 192 Duke William of Normandy in short cloak, Bayeux 'Tapestry'

Fig. 193 Duke William and Bishop Odo in long robes, Bayeux 'Tapestry'

period we are not dealing with one costume, but several: the short costume which was the traditional dress of the Germanic people (the sort of clothing the Frankish emperor Charlemagne had felt comfortable in, Chapter V, p. 173); and the long garments (which Charlemagne had resisted) that seem to have been worn by high-ranking English on formal occasions, sporadically at first, but as a general rule by the time of the Norman Conquest. In addition, it seems that different pastimes such as riding, fighting and farming could demand their own variations. Monks and priests celebrating mass wore costumes of a different tradition. Viking settlers may have maintained some differences in dress.

The cloak

Cloaks accompanied both short tunics and long gowns. They seem to have been worn both indoors and out. In the Bayeux 'Tapestry' the cloak seems to be used deliberately to help indicate the important figures in scenes; servants and attendants usually lack cloaks. This device is not used in manuscripts. There, practicality seems to rule: men engaged in energetic labour are usually without cloaks, although the drawings in the *Hexateuch* can be inconsistent, showing a figure wearing a cloak in one scene and the same character in the narrative without it in the following illustration. With the exception of King Edward's dress at the opening of the Bayeux 'Tapestry', the long costume includes a cloak.

Cloaks were squarish or rectangular, not tailored. The cloak was usually secured by means of a single brooch. When worn over the short tunic, it was usually clasped at one shoulder, mostly at the right (Colour Plate J, Figs 195–6, 202, 204) more rarely at the left; the latter may be for artistic effect: for the sake of symmetry in group scenes in the *Hexateuch*[3] and in the Stowe 944 'portrait' of Cnut to enable the king to stretch out his right arm (Fig. 188).[4] The loose material was pushed back, on the brooch side, leaving that arm free. On the other side the cloak might be pushed back or it might be allowed to hang down, covering the arm opposite the brooch. The material at the front could be put to practical use: a man depicted in the *Harley Psalter* (fol. 21r), uses the front of his cloak as a pouch to hold the seed he is sowing. In a scene depicting the martyrdom of St Stephen in the *Benedictional of St Æthelwold* (fol. 17v) two figures hold in the front of their cloaks the stones which they are throwing at the saint. An illustration of a man engaged in physical activity in the Tiberius B v calendar, fol. 7r, shows the surplus material of the cloak turned back, its upper edge tucked

---

[3] I am grateful to my MA student Patricia Cooper for this observation.

[4] See my forthcoming paper 'Pomp, piety and keeping the woman in her place: the dress of Cnut and Ælfgifu/Emma', *Medieval Clothing and Textiles*, 1 (forthcoming, 2005).

into the neck of the man's tunic. The material at the front of a short cloak generally hangs in a curve at about waist height, but occasionally the *Hexateuch* artist depicts it lying straight across the body, so that it has the appearance of a bib.[5] On fol. 54v one such 'bib' has brooches at each shoulder; it was perhaps the careless work of a hasty artist.

It seems that the function of the brooch was not to attach the cloak to the garment beneath, but to hold the cloak together. This is demonstrated in a picture of the biblical David, grappling with a lion, in the *Tiberius Psalter* (London, British Library, MS Cotton Tiberius C vi), fol. 8r: David's cloak has been thrown off, over his head; it falls, the two sides still clasped together, leaving a circular hole for the head. A similar impression is given by the cloak of King Athelstan (Colour Plate J) as he stands, head bowed, in the act of presenting a book. His cloak is clasped high on the shoulder; the neck-band of his tunic is visible lower down the shoulder.

Occasionally the cloak over a tunic is clasped by a central brooch and pushed back over each shoulder in a symmetrical arrangement (for example in Tiberius B v, fol. 7v). A central brooch was common when the cloak was worn over a long robe (Figs 187, 190, 193, 194, left) although the garment could, alternatively, be clasped on the right shoulder as on the king in Fig. 194, right. King Edgar wears a central brooch in the miniature which precedes the text of the *Regularis Concordia* in MS Tiberius A iii (Fig. 187), but this may be iconographic rather than realistic: Robert Deshman suggests that the central fastening of Edgar's cloak imitates an abbot's cope, in a deliberate evocation of 'monastic kingship' which links King Edgar to Saint Benedict.[6]

The brooches depicted as cloak-fasteners are usually round, often represented simply as a circle, or a circle with a central dot. Occasionally brooches of different shapes appear, usually on royal figures with elaborate costume, which includes the long gown and centrally-fastened cloak. There are several squarish brooches shown in the 'Tapestry'. Almost all of the surviving late Anglo-Saxon brooches are circular, but the fact that variations existed is demonstrated by the survival of a rectangular brooch with extended trefoil corners from Winchester.[7] The illuminations do not suggest any decoration on the brooches, whereas archaeological finds from the period are invariably decorated in some way, by casting, engraving or enamelling.

Illustrations occasionally suggest other ways of fastening a cloak. The figure of Longinus, in a crucifixion scene in the *Tiberius Psalter*,

Fig. 194 Pharaoh and one of his councillors in long robes, *Hexateuch*, fol. 59r

Fig. 195 One of the Magi, with brooch and loop cloak-fastening, *Benedictional of St Ethelwold*, fol. 24r

---

[5] I am grateful to my MA student Patricia Cooper for the observation and for the apt term 'bib'.

[6] R. Deshman, 'Benedictus Monarcha et Monarchus: early medieval ruler theology and the Anglo-Saxon reform', *Frümittelalterliche Studien*, 22 (1988), pp. 204–40; *Benedictional*, p. 203.

[7] Number 2009; Hinton, 'Disc and rectangular brooches' in Biddle, *Winchester*, 7.ii, ii, p. 637 and Fig. 170.

fol. 13r, wears a round brooch apparently transfixed by a long pin, which sticks up. It is difficult to conceive how this fastener would have worked, but it has something in common with the large penannular brooches of the Celtic and Anglo-Viking world, which also had pins of exaggerated length. In more than one manuscript the cloak is shown caught up in a small loop which projects behind the brooch (Fig. 195). The cloak of King Cnut in Stowe 944 (Fig. 188) is unusual in several respects. The depiction looks impractical and insecure, but the special decoration of cloak and cloak fastener serve as status indicators. The cloak is drawn through a band and decorated, at the point of fastening, with two ribbons which end in squarish tags. The fastening may be compared to the cloak of a king in the *Bury St Edmunds Psalter*, fol. 22r, which is pulled through a similar band and bunched at the right shoulder. This garment has a vertical band of decoration, which is not a border, arranged so that it falls down the front of the body. Similar decoration borders the back of the cloak at the king's left side (Fig. 196). The ribbon decoration of Cnut's cloak has some resemblance to that on the cloak of Duke William (Fig. 192), which also has an unusual, wide border. William's elaborate cloak in this confrontational scene emphasizes his superiority.[8] There may be another manifestation of the cloak ribbon in the trailing ornament attached to the circular cloak brooch of an armed figure in the *Harley Psalter*, fol. 56v. Both Cnut and William were of Viking descent and it may be significant that Scandinavian archaeology offers a parallel for their cloak ornaments: ribbons made of looped needle netting and tabby weave, edged with tabby and tablet

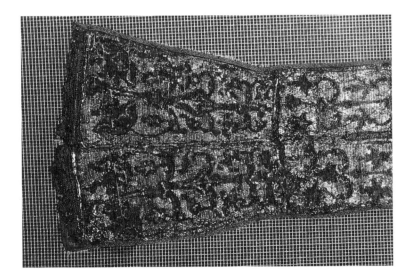

Plates 11 a and b 'Maniple II', perhaps made from a secular ornament, Durham Cathedral

[8] G. R. Owen-Crocker, 'Telling a tale: narrative techniques in the Bayeux Tapestry and the Old English epic *Beowulf*', in G. R. Owen-Crocker and T. Graham (ed.), *Medieval Art: recent perspectives. A memorial tribute to C. R. Dodwell* (Manchester, 1998), pp. 40–59, at pp. 54–5.

weave in gold and silk were found in a male burial at Mammen, Denmark.[9] The so-called Maniple II, from the tomb of St Cuthbert, but perhaps originally a secular ornament, embroidered in silk and gold, offers an English equivalent (see p. 311).

In the painted picture of King Edgar prone before Christ in Vespasian A viii (Colour Plate K) where the king is dressed in a short costume, his cloak has a plain border which the artist has painted gold. This could be merely artist's decoration, or it may reflect the reality of the dress. Gold-edged textiles were certainly in existence; according to a twelfth-century account in the *Liber Eliensis*, Ealdorman Byrhtnoth, a great benefactor of the abbey at Ely, who was killed in 991 fighting against the Vikings at the Battle of Maldon, bequeathed to the church *... duabus laciniis palii sui, pretioso opere auri et gemmarum contextis ...* ('two borders of his cloak, woven with costly work in gold and gems').[10] There are the remains of gold-decorated textiles, some of them probably ecclesiastical, but some possibly from laymen's graves, from Winchester excavations,[11] and there are many examples from contemporary graves in Scandinavia[12] offering parallels to Edgar's gold border. Alternatively, the border to Edgar's cloak might indicate a lining. Vestments in which St Cuthbert's corpse was wrapped seem to have been lined with fawn-coloured silk (p. 299) which would have been extremely luxurious, and it is likely that wealthy seculars also wore lined garments. There may be a survival of such a thing in the piece of red-dyed, diamond-patterned twill, worsted cloth, from York which was associated with a coarse, plain weave textile, that had perhaps provided a warm lining to the worsted garment.[13]

[9] Munksgaard, 'Embroideries', in Hogestol, *Festskrift til Thorleif Sjovold*, p. 163.
[10] A. Kennedy, 'Byrhtnoth's obits and twelfth-century accounts of the Battle of Maldon', in D. Scragg (ed.), *The Battle of Maldon AD 991* (Oxford, 1991), pp. 59–78, at pp. 65, 68.
[11] E. Crowfoot, 'Textiles', in Biddle, *Winchester Studies*, 7.ii, ii, pp. 468–88, at pp. 480–1.
[12] Krag, 'Dress and power'.
[13] 1301/1308, 1330; Walton, *Textiles, Cordage and Raw Fibre*, pp. 435–6.

Depictions of decoration on cloaks are unusual and individual. Generally artists leave cloaks plain. Ornament at the neck and chest of King Edgar's long cloak in the depiction of him in Tiberius A iii is, like the motifs on his gown, suggestive of embroidery; the cloak also has a border (Fig. 187). Edgar's cloak in the Vespasian A viii miniature is deep blue (Colour Plate K) and Athelstan's is a dark purplish tone (Colour Plate J). As already stated in Chapter VI, we cannot assume colour in graphic depictions is representative of real life, but there is perhaps more likelihood of authenticity in a single illumination depicting a real king than in a manuscript or embroidery with narrative scenes illustrating buildings, ships, animals and people with a limited range of colours, where anachronisms such as blue beards and green horses are found.

The size of the cloak could, apparently, vary a great deal. The cloak worn with the long costume was long, probably ankle-length, and full enough to sit on comfortably. (Figures in this costume, which is worn by men in authority, are normally depicted seated.) A cloak of similar dimensions could be worn with the short tunic. It was suspended in such a way as to be short at the front but calf-length at the back. Obviously a large cloak would be more costly than a small one, so, not surprisingly, we find some important personages, King Cnut and the future King Harold II, for example, depicted in long cloaks over tunics. At the other extreme, some cloaks are much shorter, falling to the waist at the back and to the waist or only to mid-chest at the front. The shorter version, sometimes worn by men engaged in agriculture in Anglo-Saxon calendars, would be less expensive and less of an impediment to movement. However, Duke William's elaborate cloak, worn for his confrontation with Guy of Ponthieu, is extremely short but was clearly not seen as undignified. There are some cloaks that are of middle length, falling to the level of the tunic hem at the back. Kings might wear them (Athelstan, for example), also ordinary 'background' figures in pictures.

Linguistic evidence, yet again, points to far greater variety than pictures would indicate. Several words seem to include 'blanket' as well as 'cloak' in their semantic range – *hwitel*, *loða* and *reowe* – and would fit the conception of a cloak as a versatile, rectangular piece of fabric. It was probably this kind of cloak which the Anglo-Saxons imagined when they related the stories of St Martin, who divided his cloak (*sciccels*) with a poor man[14] and *Appolonius of Tyre*, a romance in which a pauper shared his cloak (*sciccels*, *wæfels*) in the same way.[15] The Old English phrases *mid twifealdum mentel* and *mid twifealdum basing* are both found glossing Latin *diploide* ('a double garment'),[16]

---

[14] Morris, *Blickling Homilies*, p. 215, line 6; Herzfeld, *Martyrology*, p. 204, line 9.
[15] P. Goolden, *The Old English Appolonius of Tyre* (London, 1958), p. 20, line 2.
[16] Psalms 108:28 in J. Spelman (ed.), *Psalterium Davidis Latino-Saxonicum Vetus* (London, 1640); Psalms 108:29 in U. Lindelöf (ed.), *Der Lambeth-Psalter*, 2 vols, Acta Societatis Scientiarum Fennicae, 35.1; 43.3 (Helsingfors, 1909–14), 1 (1909), p. 180.

which suggests that the *mentel* and *basing* could be double, either in the sense that they were sometimes lined, or that these names were applied to a type of luxurious cloak which was so large that it was folded double, lengthwise, round the body before being secured by its brooch at the shoulder, like the ancient cloaks described and illustrated in Chapter III (Figs 76–7). It may seem far-fetched to suggest these cloaks were still worn in the tenth century, but men's fashions changed slowly.

The *basing*, *sciccels* and *wæfels*, clearly, could be worn by men, and literary references demonstrate that the *hacele* and *loða* were also male garments.[17] The *hacele* could be hooded[18] and probably reached to the feet.[19] The *heden* might be hooded[20] and of fur or sheepskin.[21] The *hapax legomenon hed-claþ* may have been the name of a similar garment.[22] The *crusene* and *pilece* were garments made of skins; the latter was certainly made of marten skin.[23] The *basing* and *sciccels* could also be fur.[24] The *reowe* was probably rough;[25] the *loða* sometimes shaggy;[26] the *hwitel* probably undyed.[27] The

---

[17] *Hacele* is several times used of a garment belonging to a man: *Orosius* 5, 10, translating Latin *sagum*; J. Bately (ed.), *The Old English Orosius*, Early English Text Society, supplementary series, 6 (Oxford, 1980), p. 124, line 4; Thorpe, *Homilies*, 2, p. 82, line 22; T. O. Cockayne (ed.), *Narratiunculae Anglice conscriptae* (London, 1861), p. 42. *Loða* is used once this way translating Latin *liniamento;* Sweet, *Pastoral Care*, p. 36, line 6.

[18] The Icelandic cognate *hekla* means 'a hooded garment', Bosworth/Toller *Dictionary*, p. 497. An ambiguous occcurrence in the fourteenth-century poem *Sir Gawain and the Green Knight* suggests a *hakel* was a head-covering ('Ich hille had a hatte, a myst-hakel huge', line 2081) but the author could be using *hakel* in another sense, 'a conical cover'; see I. Gollancz (ed.), *Sir Gawain and the Green Knight*, Early English Text Society, original series, 210 (1940), p. 78 and p. 125, note to line 2081.

[19] *hacel vel fotsið (fotsid) sciccel* glosses *lacerna;* Wright/Wülcker, *Vocabularies*, col.153, line 9; F. Kluge, 'Angelsächsische Glossen', *Anglia*, 8 (1885), pp. 448–52 at p. 451.

[20] It translates *cucullum* (Thorpe, *Ancient Laws*, p. 348) and glosses *cocula*; Wright/Wülcker, *Vocabularies*, col. 212, line 24; col. 214, line 36. *Cucullus* can mean a hood fastened to a garment, including a monk's cowl.

[21] The word is cognate with Icelandic *heðinn*, 'fur coat' (Holthausen, *Wörterbuch*, p. 153). In the Corpus Glossary it renders Latin *gunna*, a word which Anglo-Saxon writers used of a fur garment worn by monks (see above p. 182). It also glosses *melote*, 'a sheepskin'; according to Isidor 'a goatskin garment'; Napier, *Glosses*, p. 39, line 1471.

[22] T. O. Cockayne, *Leechdoms, Wortcunning and Starcraft of Early England*, 3 vols, Rolls Series, 35 (London, 1864–6), 1 (1864), p. 346, line 17. The context gives no indication of the nature of the garment, but the *hed-* element is probably related to *heden*.

[23] *Crusene* glosses *cocula* (Wright/Wülcker, *Vocabularies*, col. 212, line 24; 214, line 36). With *deorfellen roc* it glosses *mastruga* ('garment made of skins', 'sheepskin'; Wright/Wülcker, *Vocabularies*, col. 328, line 18). Adam and Eve are said to have worn *pylcan* made from *deadum fellum* (Bouterwek, *Screadunga*, p. 20, lines 28–9). Marten skin examples were among royal gifts in the eleventh century; see p. 244.

[24] They gloss *melote*; Napier, *Glosses*, p. 39, line 147.

[25] The word *reowe* is probably related to the adjective *ruh*, 'rough, shaggy, hairy'.

[26] The Icelandic cognate *loði* is used in the *Elder Edda* of the shaggy, pile-woven mantles which were produced in and exported from Iceland until *c.* 1200 (more commonly called *feldur*); Gudjónsson, 'Pile weaving', p. 68.

[27] The noun *hwitel* probably derives from the adjective *hwit*, 'white'. The Icelandic cognate *hvitill* signifies 'a white bedcover' (Bosworth/Toller *Dictionary*, p. 577). The English word survived as 'whittle' as late as the nineteenth century in dialects, mostly southern, where it was used of a woman's shawl, fringed, and either scarlet or white; Wright, *English Dialect Dictionary*, 6 (1905), p. 479.

hop-pada was possibly wide ('like a hoop').[28] The word could mean 'cope', but might have been in secular use too. The word *stole*, originally a Latin loan word for an ecclesiastical garment, may also have passed into secular use.[29] In addition there are documented the words *ofer-brædels*,[30] *ofer-læg*,[31] *ofer-slop* and *ofer-slype*,[32] all of which stand for outer garments of some kind.

The gown

The English court seems to have lagged behind the other Germanic nations in its acceptance of long dress for men. King Receswinth of the Visigoths had adopted Byzantine costume in the middle of the seventh century, part of a deliberate imitating of Byzantium as regards his court.[33] Charlemagne, Emperor of the Franks, was occasionally wearing such a costume in the late-eighth century, albeit reluctantly, and the fact that his biographers felt obliged to describe his normal, Frankish costume in detail (see Chapter VI, pp. 173–5) suggests that the latter was outmoded by their time.

The influence which led English kings to wear long garments was, almost certainly, ultimately Byzantine, but possibly the direct inspiration came from Italy or France, since merchants, religious travellers and royal envoys were constantly passing through these countries to England. The court of King Athelstan (reigned 924–39) was famously international: at least four of Athelstan's half-sisters became the wives of Continental royals, with all the exchanges of envoys and gifts that the necessary negotiations would have entailed; he fostered boys from royal houses of Frankia, Brittany and Norway, who were unlikely to have arrived empty-handed, as well as scholars from many countries. It is likely that English kings received foreign textiles and garments as gifts, and wore them for state occasions. However, Athelstan is not pictured

---

[28] Wright/Wülcker, *Vocabularies*, col. 188, line 14. *Hop* is related to modern English 'hoop'; Holthausen, *Wörterbuch*, p. 169.

[29] The word appears among a list of vestments (Wright/Wülcker, *Vocabularies*, col. 327, line 23) but it also appears in biblical translations, in Anglian texts: Mark 16:5, Luke 15:22, Luke 20:46: Skeat, *Gospels*, pp. Mark 13–1, Luke 156–7, 198–9. It refers to the scribes' garments.

[30] The word has various meanings including a vestment, but it may have been in secular use too, e.g. Wright/Wülcker, *Vocabularies*, col. 107, line 26.

[31] Thus Bosworth/Toller *Dictionary*, deduced from an entry in the Leiden Glossary: *anfibula oberlagu*; H. Sweet, *The Oldest English Texts*, Early English Text Society, original series, 83 (London, 1885), p. 111, line 1.

[32] Certainly *ofer-slop/slype* could be used of vestments, but may have been in secular use too, e.g. Cockayne, *Leechdoms*, 3 (1866), p. 200, lines 5–7, and Luke 20:46, Skeat, *Gospels*, pp. 198, 199.

[33] F. Lot, *The End of the Ancient World and the Beginning of the Middle Ages* (London and New York, 1931), p. 282; Vierck, 'La "Chemise de Sainte-Bathilde"', p. 550.

in a long gown. If the 'portrait' of King Edgar in Tiberius A iii is at all realistic, the long gown may have been established as a costume for kings by his reign (957–75). However, if we dismiss this portrait as iconographic, evidence for the adoption of the long gown focuses on the eleventh century. A king and his advisers are depicted in long garments in the *Hexateuch* (Fig. 194) which was probably illustrated at the time when Scandinavian kings were ruling, or early in the reign of Edward the Confessor (1042–66). Edward himself wears long garments in the Bayeux 'Tapestry'. He is dressed in a long robe under a long cloak when he receives his brother-in-law on his return from Normandy, and this is the costume of other authority figures in the embroidery (Harold, William, Odo and, on one occasion Guy of Ponthieu).

Earlier Carolingian art had exploited the imperial dignity of long garments[34] and the Ottonian Emperors, with their Byzantine connections, are depicted in long robes.[35] In late Anglo-Saxon art, the long gown is used to indicate rank. In the Bayeux 'Tapestry' it distinguishes rulers (not necessarily kings), and also William's half-brother, Odo of Bayeux, the probable patron of the embroidery (Fig. 193, left) from those of lesser rank, including important courtiers such as Harold before his accession and William's less important half-brother, Robert. In the *Hexateuch*, fol. 59, however, courtiers as well as king wear long gowns as they pass judgement (Fig. 194). The figures represent the biblical Pharaoh and associates who are not included in the biblical account. The man they condemn (Pharoah's chief baker; Genesis 40:22) and his executioner are contrasted by wearing ordinary short tunics. Presumably the *Hexateuch* artist, who drew upon contemporary life for some aspects of his illustrations, would not have chosen to introduce a group of courtiers in long dress if this was not authentic. This manuscript, then, goes against the evidence of the 'Tapestry' and suggests courtiers were wearing long gowns by the early-eleventh century.

The gown is shown as ankle-length and is quite loose-fitting. It has long sleeves, which in some cases appear smooth, in others the sleeves have the wrinkled or pleated appearance which is common in Anglo-Saxon art. At the wrist there is a narrow but pronounced band. The most elaborate gown of this kind is worn

[34] The emperor Charles the Bald is wrapped in a long cloak in the *Vivian Bible* (France, Paris, *Bibliothèque nationale*, MS lat.1, fol. 423 (dated 845/6)) and in the *Codex Aureus* (Germany, Munich, *Bayerische Staatsbibliothek*, Clm. 14000, fol. 5v, dated 870), where, however, the tunic beneath the cloak is short; Dodwell, *Pictorial Arts*, Figs 57, 48.

[35] Otto II married the Byzantine princess Theophanu in 972; the royal couple are depicted in Byzantine robes on an ivory (Paris, *Musée de Cluny*). Otto III wears long gown and cloak in the *Aachen Gospels* (Germany, Aachen, Cathedral Treasury, MS fol. 16); H. Meyr-Harting, *Ottonian Illumination; an historical study* (London, revised one-volume edition, 1999), Part I, Figs 1, 29.

by King Edgar in Tiberius A iii (Fig. 187). The gown falls to mid-calf and has a decorative border and cuffs. The skirts are patterned irregularly with small circles and trefoils, suggesting embroidery or encrusted gems. From hip to chest the king's body is wrapped in close-fitting fabric patterned with rows of small circles. This fabric looks like a girdle or sash wrapped four times around him.

Colour contrast sometimes suggests that the ankle-length garment was worn under a shorter robe, which had long sleeves and was girdled. The outer robe, in these cases, is longer than the tunic usually worn by seculars and clings round the legs, unlike the tunic which flares slightly (although the difference between seated and standing figures could account for the last point). Harold wears this more complex costume at his coronation (Fig. 190) but not subsequently. It is not confined to royalty, for we see some of the king's councillors wearing it in the judgement scene from the *Hexateuch* (Fig. 194). In one scene in the 'Tapestry', William and his half-brother seem to wear short skirts or aprons of a contrasting colour (Fig. 193) which I suggest are a misinterpretation of the dress in the *Hexateuch* judgement scene: the manuscript is an acknowledged source of the 'Tapestry'.[36] Here, as so often in the 'Tapestry', the designers may have been using elaboration of the garments to pinpoint the important characters in the scene, disregarding realism.

No words are readily identifiable as names for the long garment, but some of the words discussed in the last category may have been used, for example *ofer-brædels*, *ofer-læg*, *ofer-slop*, and *ofer-slype*.

King Edward, enthroned with crown and sceptre at the opening of the 'Tapestry' (Fig. 189) wears a different long garment, without a cloak. It either has a gold neck-band or he wears a gold torque. (The 'Tapestry' embroiderers made an error at the neck, as the lines at either side of the central knot or boss are placed inconsistently.) The front of the gown is uniquely embellished with what look like gold buttons or toggles, fastening it over a white shirt. The king wears a broad belt which again appears to be gold, embroidered or brocaded in red, and narrow gold wrist bands; just below each knee is a double band of gold enclosing a row of red and white squares, one adorned with a *fleur-de-lis* matching the motifs on his crown.[37]

---

[36] The relationship was identified in relation to one scene in F. Wormald, 'Style and design', in F. M. Stenton (ed.), *The Bayeux Tapestry*, (London, 2nd ed. 1965), pp. 25–36, at p. 32 and has been developed by several scholars since.

[37] Similar, if simpler, bands occur elsewhere in the 'Tapestry'. Duke William carries plain, self-coloured bands in the same position as King Edward. Guy of Pontieu, Harold's captor, has elaborate ones. Edward himself has a decorated band at his thigh in a later illustration. Nevinson considered that such bands were part of a short, upper tunic, the same colour as the ankle-length gown worn beneath (J. L. Nevinson, 'The costumes', in Stenton, *The Bayeux Tapestry*, pp. 70–5, at p. 71.) Certainly some costumes did include a short upper tunic, as we shall see below; but to me the bands in question do not look like this. Possibly the embroiderers decorated the skirts of garments to show the rank of the wearer, or were depicting fancy garters which, by realistic standards, would not have been visible under the gowns.

It is interesting to compare the details of Edward's dress (which are unlike anything in Anglo-Saxon art)[38] with features of the exotic dress from tenth-century male burials found at Birka, Sweden. These include metal buttons, gold-embellished tablet weave and embroidered trimmings, one of which (from Grave 529) features a repeated *fleur de lis* very like the one on Edward's clothing.[39] Metal buttons also figure in the elaborate funeral costume of a Viking chief noted by the Arab traveller Ibn Fadlan, who like the excavators of Birka, described the garment they decorated as a caftan.[40] The buttons in this case were gold, as Edward's ornaments seem to be. It is reasonable to suppose that Queen Edith, a wealthy Anglo-Scandinavian, whose care for her husband's wardrobe was noted above, might have acquired or commissioned buttons, braids and possaments from Scandinavia, copies or imports from further east, and dressed him in a caftan; and that his elegant dress was remembered twenty years later in the 'Tapestry', as it was in literary accounts.

Edward is said to have received presents via ambassadors from Germany, Frankia and Denmark after his coronation, as well as lavish gifts from his most powerful subject, Earl Godwine.[41] The coronation gifts may have been the source of a figured silk garment in which the king was buried, some of which was recovered when his tomb was damaged in 1685.[42] The undyed silk was patterned with roundels containing pairs of griffins and panthers, arranged in staggered rows, with pairs of doves and falcons between them. Hero Granger-Taylor suggests a Persian origin for the cloth and notes 'the comparatively wide availability' of such silks by the mid-eleventh century.[43]

Undergarments to the gown

Undergarments are occasionally shown beneath the gown; for example, there is a frill of white below the long robe of a king in London, British Library, MS Royal 13 A I, fol. 17v. Such an undergarment would be like a petticoat or long shirt. Among the Old English undergarment names documented, *cemes* seems to be the

[38] Both the first and second sections of the 'Tapestry' begin with some features which are not continued, especially embroidery of small details in contrasting colours, including features of costume, which were perhaps decoration for decoration's sake and were discontinued as too labour-intensive. However, it is possible that these areas show authentic detail.

[39] Geijer, *Birka III*, Plates 27–9, esp. 27.2,3, 28.7.

[40] Quoted in G. R. Owen, *Rites and Religions of the Anglo-Saxons* (Newton Abbot and Totowa, NJ, 1981), p. 99.

[41] Barlow, *Life of King Edward*, pp. 14–19; Tyler, 'Wings incarnadine', pp. 88–9.

[42] Krijnie Cigaar suggests this may have come direct from the east, perhaps as a coronation gift: K. Cigaar, 'England and Byzantium on the eve of the Norman Conquest', *Anglo-Norman Studies*, 5: *Proceedings of the Battle Conference, 1982* (1982), pp. 78–89.

[43] Hero Granger-Taylor, 'Byzantine textiles' (in Buckton, *Byzantium*, pp. 151–3), noting the comparatively inferior quality of this 'group' of textiles, which includes the buskins of Pope Clement II, is not receptive to the suggestion of a diplomatic gift.

most likely name for such a garment, since it is derived from Latin *camisia*, which meant a linen shirt or nightgown and, in Late Latin, a long undergarment for men. *Ham, hemeþe, smoc* and *underserc* are also possible names (see p. 253, below).

In the *Harley Psalter*, fol. 66v, there are figures in long garments (probably meant to be monks, for the garments are cowled, and the figures possibly tonsured), who wear long trousers or underpants beneath their robes (Colour Plate H, bottom left). In these illustrations the feet are bare. It seems very likely that seculars wearing long gowns would wear similar long underpants. Such a garment might have been called *bræce*, 'trousers', *braccas* or *brec*, 'breeches', or perhaps *strapul* (plural *strapulas*), 'a covering for the leg'.

Fur garments

There had probably been a gradual change in the the custom of using fur for garments. Originally worn for practical reasons in the colder regions of northern Europe where fur was readily available, but despised in the Graeco-Roman world, fur seems to have enjoyed a change of status and environment, becoming popular as a luxury item of dress in the Islamic Empire from the eighth century onwards, supplied by Viking merchants. As demand grew, so did the trades of hunting and trapping, and also the areas of forest exploited for these purposes.[44] In turn, the northern areas which had always utilised furs may have begun to use them differently, with more consciousness of fashion and prestige. The high status of fur in the North in our period is reflected in the fact that the rich, pagan grave excavated at Mammen contained a cloak which was either fur or fur-lined. The pelt was long-haired and looked like beaver or marten, although analysis was not possible.[45] Marten skins were certainly being traded and worn in the British Isles in late Anglo-Saxon times. Domesday Book mentions them being imported into Chester[46] and marten skin garments (*on merðerne pyleceon*) were among the lavish gifts of fur and textile given by King Malcolm of Scotland and Margaret his wife to Margaret's brother Edgar Ætheling of England in 1075 along with what may have been garments of (imported) grey squirrel and ermine ([*pyleceon* of] *graschynnene and hearma scynnene*) and fur garments lined with fine cloth or garments of fine cloth lined with fur (*on scynnan mid pælle betogen*).[47] As former exiles in Central Europe, Edgar's branch

[44] J. Howard-Johnston, 'Trading in fur, from classical antiquity to the Middle Ages', in Cameron, *Leather and Fur*, pp. 65–79.

[45] Munksgaard, 'Embroideries', in Hogestol, *Festskrift til Thorleif Sjovold*, pp. 166, 169–70.

[46] W. Beamont, *A Literal Extension and Translation of the Domesday Book relating to Cheshire and Lancashire* (Chester, 1863), p. 4.

[47] G. P. Cubbin (ed.), *MS D, The Anglo-Saxon Chronicle*, 6 (1996), p. 86. The possible meanings of the words are discussed in detail in Owen-Crocker, 'The search for Anglo-Saxon skin garments', in Cameron, *Leather and Fur*, pp. 36–7.

of the royal family and their retinue were perhaps accustomed to wearing furs and may have encouraged the fashion for them on their return to England in 1057. This account of the gifts to Edgar Ætheling is our earliest evidence for the custom of combining good quality cloth and fur to make a lined garment, a feature which was to be of major importance to dress fashions later in the Middle Ages. Though it is entirely possible that earlier garments such as Charlemagne's otter or ermine jerkin were lined with cloth, textile had not been a significant part of the appearance of the garment. Christine Fell has pointed out that according to William of Malmesbury, Edith of Wilton made a disparaging reference to the tenth-century Bishop Æthelwold of Winchester wearing 'ragged furs'.[48] If the story were true, the churchman was perhaps wearing the garment called *fel* in Old English and *gunna* in Latin, which had long been a part of the ecclesiastical wardrobe in England (p. 182, above), but which was comfortable rather than elegant.

The Old English word *rocc* probably signified a fur jerkin and the *heden* and *crusene* were perhaps cloaks. The word *pilece* remains problematic; a reference to Adam and Eve making themselves *pylcan* of skins suggests loincloths rather than cloaks, and the word 'pilch' survived into modern times associated with the loins: meanings include a protective apron and a baby's pants keeping a nappy (a diaper) in place;[49] but the references to Edgar Ætheling's gifts suggest something grander than fur loincloths! Probably the word *pilece* was derived from Latin *pellis*, skin or hide, Late Latin *pellicia*, and described what the garment was made of rather than a specific item of clothing. It perhaps meant a loin cloth in one context and a gown or cloak in another.

The tunic

The tunic, which was almost certainly called *cyrtel* and *tunece* in Old English, is the commonest male garment to appear in Anglo-Saxon art. It could be worn by kings (specifically Athelstan, Edgar in Vespasian A viii, Cnut and some, but not all of the kings in the *Harley Psalter*), by high-ranking men, fighting men, farm workers and servants. Tunics are most often shown as about knee length, but some artists depict them considerably shorter (for example in the *Cædmon Manuscript*, Oxford, Bodleian Library, MS Junius 11); some, notably in the *Hexateuch*, rather longer. The variation of length does not seem to be a chronological development: our latest example, the 'Tapestry', shows tunics to the knee. The tunic was confined at the waist or hip by a belt or girdle. Sometimes the tunic

[48] Fell, *Women in Anglo-Saxon England*, p. 126. The reference may be found at: *De Gestis*, II, 218; Stubbs, *William of Malmesbury*, 11 (1887), pp. 269–70.
[49] Owen-Crocker, 'The search for Anglo-Saxon skin garments', in Cameron, *Leather and Fur*, pp. 36–7.

Fig. 197 Overbalancing figure, *Bury St Edmunds Psalter*, fol. 90v

Fig. 198 Man in a tunic with string at the neck, *Calendar*, London, British Library MS Cotton Tiberius B v, fol. 4r

Fig. 199 Man in a tunic with V-shaped neckband, *Calendar*, London, British Library MS Cotton Tiberius B v, fol. 4r

is drawn pouched over the belt, so that it is concealed; sometimes, as in the 'Tapestry' where colour contrast is used, the belt is clearly visible, with no pouching.

The fullness of the skirt is indicated by stylised lines and a flared shape. The fullness is shown effectively by an overbalancing figure in the *Bury St Edmunds Psalter*, fol. 90v (Fig. 197); the skirt of the tunic cascades in a circular swirl. Sculptors developed their own way of showing this fullness by carving a skirt that was longer at the sides than in the middle, with a curving hem. This style is common on Anglo-Viking carvings (Fig. 144), but it can also be found on a southern piece, from Burford, Oxfordshire.[50]

Anne Hedeager Krag suggests that the red tunic and gold cuffs of King Edgar in Vespasian A viii (Colour Plate K) denote status.[51] If the colouring of royal donor portraits is realistic, the light shade of King Athelstan's tunic (Colour Plate J) suggests linen, and its pale yellow border may indicate silk, or gold brocading, though there is no pattern on it. The skirts and bodice of a tunic are almost always plain, apart from a border which is often but not always included. There are exceptions to this plainness in the *Tiberius Psalter*, where tunic skirts have a floral pattern as well as rows of dots and lines, and dotted cuffs and necklines (Colour Plate L); but this illustrator decorates other textiles, such as curtains and a table cloth, and we may be looking at artistic flourish rather than authentic clothing. Tunics or shirts could be decorated, but our only surviving example of a tenth-century garment from the British mainland, the embroidered linen garment from Llan-gorse (Plates 9, 10), described in the previous chapter (p. 218) has quite different decoration from what the Tiberius artist suggests, having zoomorphic rather than floral and geometric ornament.

A man's tunic was almost certainly seamed down the sides and put on by pulling it over the head, like the Thorsbjerg garment (Plate 4, Fig. 79). The neckline of Athelstan's tunic (Colour Plate J), is marked by a decorated band placed at the top of the shoulder, indicating an aperture wide enough to pass over the head; but many of the tunics illustrated have close-fitting, round necks, and in reality the head could not have passed through a hole of these proportions unless the tunic opened at the neck. There was probably an aperture which was closed by means of a tied string, tape or ribbon, which is clearly indicated on a figure in the Tiberius B v calendar (Fig. 198) but otherwise is not shown in illustrations. Perhaps it was usual to tuck it out of sight, or perhaps an unseen fastener such as a plain pin was used. (There is no indication that buttons were employed.)[52] Alternatively, it is possible that some

---

[50] Guest, 'A sculptured stone in Burford church', pp. 159–60, Fig. 1.

[51] Krag, 'Dress and power', p. 127.

[52] Medieval buttons have been found in Winchester but their exact date and function are not established. The 'heyday' of buttons was to come in the later medieval period with tightly fitting garments.

tunics opened at the back of the neck and were closed completely at the front. In this case the opening would not show in illustrations which almost always depict men frontally, and when they do not, conceal the back of the tunic with the cloak. In many other cases a slit at the front neck of the tunic is obvious, as this and the neckline of the garment are bordered by a band or collar, which is often depicted in a contrasting colour, or, as in the *Tiberius Psalter*, decorated with dots. Often the band tapers to form a V-shape at the front (Fig. 199) although in the 'Tapestry' the band simply edges the neckline without the V-shaped part at the front. Nevinson, in discussing the tunics of the 'Tapestry', thought that the neck-band represented the collar of a shirt worn under the tunic.[53] It does not seem so to me, and the notion of a collar which is turned back seems very modern. There are documented Old English words, *sweor-claþ* and *sweor-sal* meaning 'collar' or 'neck-cloth', but they are *hapax legomena* from Anglo-Latin glossaries[54] so it is possible that they were nonce-words, rather than terms in regular use naming part of the Anglo-Saxon costume. The author who described King Edward's clothing evidently considered decoration at the top of tunics (and cloaks) to be characteristic of English dress, with gold edging normal for kings.[55] The remains of a garment trimmed in this way do in fact survive, though it is ecclesiastical: a dalmatic found among the relics of St Cuthbert had a neckline edged with tablet-woven braid, the two ends of which were stitched together to make a double width at the front (Fig. 200).[56]

In two illustrations (in London, British Library MS Arundel 155, fol. 93r and the *Tiberius Psalter*, fol. 9r, Fig. 201), the biblical Goliath is pictured in a tunic with this type of border at the neck, with the additional feature of two strings, ending in tags, with which the opening is laced or drawn together. This string is absent from the many other illustrations of this neckline, and once more we may speculate that usually the string was a plain piece of cord, not on show, or that a pin or other fastener (such as a hook-and-eye type clasp) was used instead. It is possible, of course, both in the case of the round-necked tunic and the type with the V-shaped border, that the garment was stitched into place every time a man put it on. There does not seem to be any social difference between men wearing round-necked tunics and those with the V-shaped

Fig. 200 Reconstruction of an Anglo-Saxon dalmatic from the coffin of St Cuthbert, braid reconstructed after Hero Granger-Taylor

Fig. 201 Goliath in elaborate tunic and baldric, London, British Library, MS Cotton Tiberius C vi, fol 9r

[53] Nevinson, 'The costumes', in Stenton, *Bayeux Tapestry*, p. 74.

[54] Together, glossing *collarium*; Wright/Wülcker, *Vocabularies*, col. 210, lines 36–7.

[55] *Nam cum priscis Anglorum regibus antea moris non fuerit lauciorum cultibus uestimentorum uti preter sagos auro supra paratos et huismodi uestes secundum morem gentis* ... 'It had not been the custom for earlier English kings in bygone days to wear clothes of great splendour, apart from cloaks and robes adorned at the top with gold in the national style ...', Barlow, *Life of Edward*, pp. 22–3.

[56] H. Granger-Taylor, 'The weft-patterned silks and their braid: the remains of an Anglo-Saxon dalmatic of *c*. 800?', in G. Bonner, D. Rollason and C. Stancliffe (ed.), *St Cuthbert, his Cult and Community to 1200*, Woodbridge (1989), pp. 303–27.

feature, since they are pictured working alongside one another. The neckline of the tunic is not usually visible on figures that wear cloaks, but where tunics are worn without cloaks, the bordered neckline is commoner than a plain, round neck.

The tunic sleeve of an archer, probably representing Ishmael, on an eleventh-century ivory cross,[57] is slightly flared like that of the earlier Sheffield carving (Chapter V, p. 184). Some tunics, such as the one worn by King Athelstan (Colour Plate J) and many of the examples in the 'Tapestry', have smooth, close-fitting sleeves extending to the wrist. Athelstan's sleeves terminate in a decorated cuff or wrist band. Plain cuffs are sometimes indicated in the 'Tapestry' but are more often absent. (Perhaps the difference in medium explains this, and other, differences in the costume of the 'Tapestry'. It would be much more difficult to execute a narrow band on the costume of a small figure in embroidery than in pen-and-ink or paint.)

The sleeves of male figures in manuscripts are usually marked from elbow to wrist in a series of parallel lines (running round the arm, not longitudinally), terminating at the wrists in a band which is sometimes decorated with dots. The artists' technique here is similar to that used for women's sleeves. The meaning of the parallel lines has been disputed by costume historians. Both Strutt[58] and Planché[59] cited the evidence of William of Malmesbury that the English were accustomed to load their arms with bracelets.[60] Planché considered the possibility that the parallel lines might represent bracelets but rejected it in most instances. In fact, line drawings often suggest bracelets more strongly than paintings: the Stowe manuscript drawing of Cnut (Fig. 188) is a good example. However, the colouring of painted manuscripts does not generally suggest that the forearm is covered by metal bands (see Colour plates I, L). The lines, in any case, are too regular, and being without ornament, do not seem to me to represent bracelets. Planché finally suggested that a single bracelet was worn at the wrist to confine a sleeve that was longer than the arm and pushed up into folds. Strutt had also considered that the bands at the wrists represented bracelets. This is particularly worth considering in relation to the *Tiberius Psalter*, where the outline of the cuff is sometimes drawn in a different coloured ink and dotted decoration is prominent (Colour Plate L) and Vespasian A viii, where King Edgar's cuffs are gold (Colour Plate K). The suggestions of metal bracelets at the wrist are more plausible than the suggestions of a forearm full of parallel bracelets, but again, I remain unconvinced. We know that Anglo-Saxon men wore metal bands, for, apart from William of Malmesbury's

[57] Beckwith, *Ivory Carvings*, cat. 45, p. 128.
[58] Strutt, *Horda Angelcynnan*, 1 (1775), p. 47.
[59] Planché, *History of British Costume*, pp. 25–6, note.
[60] *De Gestis*, para. 245; Stubbs, *William of Malmesbury*, 1, p. 305.

information these bands are mentioned in Anglo-Saxon texts: Wynflæd, for example, bequeathed gold to her grandson, which he was to use to enlarge his ring, or armlet (*beah*).[61] Yet the wrist bands in the illustrations, close-fitting, flattish and either plain or simply dotted, do not have much in common with surviving late Anglo-Saxon metalwork and do not have any obvious opening that a metal band would need – they are too close-fitting to be slipped over the hand. We know, however, that tablet-woven bands were a traditional part of Germanic costume and wrist bands have been identified from sixth-century England. They were still worn in Scandinavia in the tenth century: the man buried at Mammen had luxurious tablet-woven wrist bands, silk and gold, lined with silk and padded with wool. The prominent cuffs of Cnut's tunic in the Stowe manuscript might have been padded, woven bands of this kind.[62] The gold wrist bands on King Edgar's tunic could represent gold-brocaded or gold-embroidered textile borders. Cuffs of fabric, or metal-decorated fabric, seem a more plausible explanation of the sleeve borders than metal bracelets. In support of this we might consider an illustration of a woman in the *Hexateuch* (Colour Plate I, Fig. 175), wearing a blue gown with long sleeves hanging down over her hands; her sleeves end in borders drawn in red, which resemble the men's wristbands, and in this case the bands are surely cuffs, not bracelets.

The men's cuffs are close-fitting, and in some cases, so are the sleeves. To enable the wearer to put the garment on, the wrist band and the sleeve must have been open, like the sixth-century example in Fig. 42, but we do not know how it was closed. The metal wrist-clasp had long gone out of use and was never a male accessory in England in any case. In late Saxon times the sleeve was presumably stitched or secured by a fastener that was not visible once the sleeve was closed.

Assuming that the arms marked with parallel bands are, in fact, meant to be covered by sleeves not bracelets, we find that costume historians have disagreed about their nature. Both Planché and Truman[63] suggested that the wrinkled or pleated appearance of the sleeve was caused by extra material which could be rolled down to cover the hands in cold weather. The painting of a woman wearing her sleeves this way proves that it could be done, but in pictures of men in cold weather (warming themselves at the November bonfire in a calendar, for example) the wrinkled sleeves remain on the arms and the hands are bare.

[61] Whitelock, *Wills*, p. 12, lines 19–20.
[62] Munksgaard, 'Embroideries', in Hogestol, *Festskrift til Thorleif Sjovold*, p. 163.
[63] N. Truman, *Historic Costuming* (London, 1936), p. 14.

There are several documented Old English words meaning sleeve: *earmella*, *earm-slife*, *earm-stoc*, *hand-stoc* and *slif*. The last two could, possibly, be used of a sleeve that covered the hand; *hand-stoc* because it literally means 'hand-sleeve' and *slif* because it glosses Latin *manica* which could signify a sleeve of this type. However, the context in which *hand-stoc* is documented is ecclesiastical;[64] we do not know if the word was also in secular use. *Slif* is used in the Laws of Alfred in defining compensation for wounds received on visible parts of the body in a way that suggests the *slif* did not cover the hand.[65] The linguistic evidence, therefore, does not help us reach a conclusion. The sleeves are depicted in a very similar way to those of women's undergarments. As suggested above (p. 218), the wrinkling effect may not represent loose material pushed up, but deliberate and decorative pleating, which would have a semi-permanent or permanent effect.

Planché considered that the tunic had short sleeves, and that the long, wrinkled sleeves belonged to an inner garment, a fashion which Enlart had observed in Carolingian costume, believing that, there, it was an innovation of the ninth century.[66] The length of the Anglo-Saxon tunic sleeve has not gone undisputed, however. Yarwood, for example, was convinced that tunic sleeves were long.[67] It seems probable that both short- and long-sleeved tunics existed; certainly the smooth sleeves of the 'Tapestry' are uninterrupted from shoulder to wrist. The wrinkled sleeve is more problematical. A number of male figures have a decorative band round the upper arm, which might represent a piece of jewellery or a band of decoration stitched on to a long sleeve. Alternatively, the band may have marked the edge of the short sleeve on an outer tunic and the wrinkled material extending to the wrist might have belonged to an inner tunic. Another possibility is that the sleeve of the tunic was in two parts; the shoulder-to-upper-arm piece perhaps shaped on the loom, the forearm piece a separate attachment. There are examples on the garment of King Edgar in Vespasian A viii (Colour Plate K) King David in Cambridge, University Library, MS Ff.1.23 and a figure representing the constellation *Orion* in London, British Library, MS Harley 2506. These are all illuminations in which a rather elaborate costume would be appropriate. A less elaborate version on a less important figure may be seen in the *Benedictional of St Æthelwold*, fol. 17v, where close-fitting sleeves seem to reach to the elbow, while the wrinkled or pleated sleeves which stretch from elbow to wrist seem to emerge from under the short sleeves. In this case, there is no decorative band. In most cases there is no

---

[64] Kluge, 'Indicia', p. 127, line 14.
[65] Ælfred 66, 1; Liebermann, *Die Gesetze*, 1, p. 84.
[66] C. Enlart, *Manuel d'Archéologie française, depuis les temps mérovingiens jusqu'à la renaissance*, 3 vols (Paris, 1902–16), 3 (1916), p. 18.
[67] D. Yarwood, *English Costume* (London, 1952), p. 40.

distinctive line marking off a short sleeve and no colour contrast to reinforce the impression of two different garments or different pieces of material. It seems to me that we are not dealing regularly with a tunic which had short sleeves revealing shirt sleeves beneath it; rather that the tunic in common use had long sleeves, (which might have been made in two parts) and that an outer tunic with short sleeves could be worn over it.

The belt or girdle of the tunic

The waisted shape of all mens' tunics suggests that they were regularly fastened by a girdle or belt (Old English *gyrdel*, *gyrdels* or *belt*). In some illustrations the girdle is not visible, being concealed by pouching of the tunic, although a bulge at the side or the back often indicates the position of the girdle knot (Colour Plate L). Many pictures, both line drawings and paintings, suggest by double lines that a loose girdle was worn low on the hips (Fig. 199). Where the pictures are coloured, the girdle area is painted the same colour as the tunic, and it is impossible to distinguish whether the artist is depicting a self-coloured girdle or a tunic pouched over the girdle, or rolled round it. In the 'Tapestry', however, girdles are often embroidered in contrasting colours and are therefore more obvious. Here, although the loose, hip-level girdle is found, the prevailing style is a rigid-looking belt worn round the waist, sometimes, apparently, double. The lack of buckles or hanging girdle ends in late Anglo-Saxon art contrasts with the many archaeological finds of buckles and metal belt-ends including a rare late-Saxon cemetery find of a small buckle at the right hip of a male skeleton from an execution burial ground at Ashtead, Surrey, a context that suggests that such things were a basic utilitarian part of dress.[68]

The ubiquitous knives of the pagan period are absent from the costume as illustrated, although they are used at table. Have we moved from a society where a knife was a personal appendage to one where a knife was a table setting? This seems unlikely so early in the medieval period. Harold, in the 'Tapestry', when apprehended by Guy of Ponthieu, appears to brandish a knife which he may have been accustomed to wear at his belt, concealed by his cloak; but this is speculation. The 'Tapestry' artist was not concerned with 'continuity' (in the motion-picture sense of the word) and an object can appear from nowhere. People probably did carry things at their belts; they do so in pagan graves and they did so in the later

---

[68] Grave S 537; G. N. Hayman, ' Further excavations at the former Goblin Works, Ashtead (TQ 182 567), *Surrey Archaeological Collections*, 81 (1991–2), pp. 1–18, at p. 17. Presumably a condemned man would have been stripped of anything valuable; executed corpses are normally without artefacts.

Middle Ages; but Anglo-Saxon artists rarely show it. The figure of Ishmael in the *Hexateuch* appears to have an object tucked into his girdle, but this is a rarity. The scramasax, which had appeared in male burials in the seventh century, continued to be used up to the tenth, and individual examples from this later period are elaborate, inlaid with silver decoration and, in some cases writing.[69] Elaborate leather sheaths from York[70] suggest that the scramasax would be carried in a fashionably decorated scabbard and that the weapon and its container were prestigious dress accessories. It is unlikely that they were only carried on the battlefield.

Since sheaths and scabbards do not appear in graphic images, it seems that a kind of 'shorthand' takes place when weapons are being depicted. The 'Tapestry' artist sometimes makes it appear that a sword is stuck directly through a girdle, but a scene in which Harold and his men surrender to Guy of Ponthieu (Fig. 191) makes it clear that swords had their own belts. These can be seen attached to the hilts of the swords which have been taken off. In both cases shown, the sword belt hangs either side of the hilt, and the two ends have, respectively, a buckle and a strap extension for fixing through the buckle. Normans depicted in the following scene wear their sword belts immediately above the waist belts of their culottes. A more elaborate sword belt (at least it is elaborated by being decorated with dots, beloved of this particular artist) may be seen on the figure of Goliath in the *Tiberius Psalter* (Fig. 201). In this case the belt is worn higher, crossing the chest diagonally. It passes under the arm, rather than over the shoulder, like a baldric, but the artist is obviously oversimplifying, as such a belt would inevitably slip down unless held by a strap joining it at right angles and passing over the opposite shoulder. Clearly a sword could be carried by a man in ordinary dress. It did not require a mailcoat.

The sword belt was probably called *fetel* or *fetels*. When a man named Ælfgar made a bequest of *tueye suerde fetelsade*,[71] he probably meant two swords equipped with fittings of this kind but he may have included decorated leather sheaths of the kind attested from York.

Undergarments to the tunic

There is ample linguistic evidence for the wearing of a shirt or other garment next to the skin, and that this was different from the tunic. We are told, for example, in a text of King Alfred's reign, that the child Boniface went ... *butan his kemese and eac*

---

[69] See, as the most elaborate examples, Backhouse, Turner and Webster, *Golden Age*, No. 94, pp. 101–2; No. 95, pp. 102–3.

[70] Mainman and Rogers, *Craft, Industry and Everyday Life*, pp. 237–42, p. 239, fig. 107, Plates XI-XIV.

[71] Whitelock, *Wills*, p. 6, lines 1–2.

butan his cyrtel ...[72] ('without his shirt and also frequently without his tunic') whilst a twelfth-century text in Old English tells us that John the Baptist, in the wilderness, wore *stiue here to shurte and gret sac to curtle*[73] ('stiff hair as a shirt and a great sack as a tunic'). The noun *shurte* (Middle English spelling, *scyrte* in Old English), was related to the verb *scyrtan* 'to shorten', and essentially, signified a garment which did not cover the lower legs. *Cemes* was derived from Latin *camisia*. A word with similar semantic range is *serc*; glossary entries suggest that this term signified a shirt or tunic, yet the Old English version of the Benedictine Rule demonstrates that a monk would sleep in a *serc* or *syric* as well as wearing a garment of this name during the day.[74] (The text suggests that the night shirt was a different garment.) Other names of undergarments are *ham*, *hemeþe*, *smoc* and *underserc*.

It seems likely that the shirt or undergarment was similar to the tunic in shape, although it was probably made of linen rather than wool (except for the penitential hair shirt attributed to John the Baptist). Different scholars have thought that parts of the shirt were visible outside the tunic: Nevinson thought he saw a collar, Planché and Strutt the sleeves; but, as already explained, this author is not convinced by these observations. However, there is a rare example of a white undergarment showing below the skirt of a tunic in Tiberius B v, worn by a figure representing the constellation *Perseus* (Fig. 202).

Linguistic evidence suggests that loin-cloths were familiar to the Anglo-Saxons. The Old English words *gyrdels*, *underwrædel* and *wæd-bræc* all appear in glossaries against Latin words meaning, among other things, 'loin-cloth'.[75] Unless one of the varieties of tunic discussed below could be classified as a loin-cloth, this is a garment for which, so far, we do not have pictorial evidence. Presumably it would always be concealed by the tunic in illustrations.

Fig. 202 The constellation *Perseus*, London, British Library, MS Cotton Tiberius B. v, fol. 34r

---

[72] Gregory's *Dialogues*, I; Hecht, *Bishofs Wærferth von Worcester Übersetzung der Dialogue Gregors des Grossen*, p. 68, lines 5–8.

[73] R. Morris (ed.), *Old English Homilies*, Early English Text Society, original series, 34, 53 (1868–73), 2nd series, p. 139.

[74] *Rule*, LV; Schröer, *Die angelsächsischen Prosabearbeituungen der Benedictinregel*, pp. 91, lines 3–4 and 89, line 10, respectively.

[75] *Gyrdels* glosses *lumbare* (Lindsay, *Corpus*, p. 108, line 287, Wright/Wülcker, *Vocabularies*, col. 433, line 12). *Underwrædel* glosses *subfibulum*, *uel subligaculum* (Wright/Wülcker, *Vocabularies*, col. 153, lines 1–2). *Wædbrec* glosses *perizomata*, *uel campestria*, *uel succinctoria* and *perizomata*, *uel campestria* (Wright/Wülcker, *Vocabularies*, col. 125 lines 3–5; col. 328, line 7). This word is used in Genesis, again translating *perizomata*, for Adam and Eve's garments made of fig leaves (Genesis 3:7; Crawford, *Heptateuch*, p. 89).

Fig. 203 Man in tucked-up tunic, rear view, *Harley Psalter*, fol. 2v

Fig. 204 Man in tucked-up tunic, front view, *Harley Psalter*, fol. 2v

Fig. 205 Man in tunic with ?side slits, *Calendar*, London, British Library MS Cotton Julius A. vi, fol. 8r

Varieties of tunic

Men engaged in manual labour, or other activities in which the skirt would be an encumbrance, are often shown in what could be a loin-cloth, but what seems to me to be the ordinary tunic tucked up into the girdle at each side. The material falls into a V-shape at the front (Colour Plate H, top; Fig. 204) and at the back either makes a similar V or clings round the buttocks (Fig. 203). The thighs are exposed at the sides. Men dressed in this way usually have bare legs and feet. Some observers may think that breeches are being represented here but I do not. The shape made by the tunic skirt is certainly similar to the appearance of the loose breeches which were worn in the later Middle Ages, but the bodice of the garment and the cloak which is often worn over it are exactly the same as those of men with normal skirted tunics. Perhaps the later breeches evolved from an *ad hoc* arrangement in which the skirts were tucked out of the way.

Some indications of active men suggest that the tunic is slit at the sides. This may be careless drawing of the tucked-up tunic, but there are some cases, as, for example, a figure in a calendar in Cotton Julius A vi, where the garment is not arranged in a way that exposes the thighs, yet a double outline suggests that the front of the skirt was divided from the back (Fig. 205). As with the tucked-up tunic, feet may be bare, however wintry the weather and hard the occupation. Strutt considered the slit tunic to be a 'badge of slavery or servitude',[76] a plausible suggestion, especially in view of the absence of shoes, and an attractive one since we would expect some differences in costume between persons of different rank. However, we cannot consider it proved. Men with ordinary tunics work side-by-side with men in slit tunics; indeed, a man in a slit tunic warms his hands at a November bonfire in front of men in cloaks and tunics, which would surely not have been the case if the man in the slit tunic was their slave. It is possible that the garment we have here is some kind of shirt, and that it was normally worn under the tunic. Perhaps the tunic, together with shoes and stockings, was removed for heavy work, leaving the slit garment outermost.

Normans in the Bayeux 'Tapestry' are often depicted in tunics with divided skirts, that is, culottes (Fig. 206). The English Earl Harold appears to wear them on horseback during and after his visit to Normandy,[77] but, except possibly in a few ambiguous cases[78] these are not worn by the English.

---

[76] Strutt, *Dress and Habits*, 1 (1796), p. 5.

[77] Wilson, *Bayeux Tapestry*, Plates 8, 14,16, 27.

[78] Wilson, *Bayeux Tapestry*, Plate 66; the stem-stitch lines are almost identical to those on the tunic of the adjacent figure, Plate 67. The embroiderers have filled in the space between the latter to make the usual 'skirt' effect. The culottes on a moustached Englishman (Plate 66) may be an error. At Plate 51 the man leading William's horse, who wears a hybrid garment, is likely to be a Norman servant, though he could be an Englishman compelled to serve (as in the cooking and banqueting scenes).

Decoration of tunics in art is normally simple, either taking the form of dotted neck- and wrist-bands or a contrasting border to the skirt. Very occasionally, there is ornament on the skirts of tunics, suggestive of embroidery. It may be found, for example, on figures representing *Gemini* in London, British Library, MS Arundel 60, fol. 4r and on several figures in the *Tiberius Psalter*, some of whom also have ornament on the sleeves (Colour Plate L). There are some unusually elaborate skirts in the *Hexateuch*, where the artist employed colour contrast. Unfortunately the intention is not always clear. The artist may have been indicating a border or inner layers of fabric; he may simply have been indicating the most important figure in the scene as in the case of Colour Plate I, bottom right (Jacob), just as the embroiderers of the Bayeux 'Tapestry' indicate Earl Harold in a crowded scene by a uniquely striped tunic (Fig. 207). The *Hexateuch* artist was required to depict the garment which is known today as 'Joseph's coat of many colours' called *polymita* in Latin and in the Old English version *hringfah*. The Latin term (derived from Greek) referred not to colour but to the technicalities of weaving (*polymitos* '[woven] with multiple shafts')[79] and in rendering it *hringfah* the translator was probably imagining the repeated roundel designs of patterned silks, or possibly the more angular repeated designs of the warp-weighted loom; but the artist achieved an effect very like the depictions of mail in contemporary art (Fig. 208).[80] He painted a short tunic, with slit sides and wide sleeves, coloured blue and covered in circles, in a literal depiction of *hringfah*, 'decorated with rings' (Fig. 209).

Leg coverings

Tunic-clad men in late Anglo-Saxon illustrations usually wear a garment which completely covers the legs. Although the leg coverings are so tight-fitting that the natural shape of the limbs is retained, colour contrast in painted manuscripts and the Bayeux 'Tapestry' makes it apparent that the men are not bare-legged. Since the upper parts of these garments are covered by the tunics, and the lower by shoes and often by gartering, it is impossible to say if they took the form of trousers (covering the abdomen and legs, but not the feet), or tights (covering abdomen, legs and feet, like the Thorsbjerg trousers, Plate 5) or if they were separate stockings (covering the legs and feet and suspended in some way at the top). Where there is no gartering – as in some cases in the 'Tapestry' – we can see that the leg coverings go right down to the shoes and it seems likely that they extended to cover the foot. Since these garments predate, as far as we know, the introduction of knitting into England,

Fig. 206 Norman man in culottes, Bayeux 'Tapestry'

Fig. 207 Harold Godwinesson distinguished by a striped skirt, Bayeux 'Tapestry'

Fig. 208 Armed figure, Oxford, Bodleian Library, MS Douce 296, fol. 40v

[79] Granger-Taylor, 'Byzantine textiles', in Buckton, *Byzantium*, p. 16.
[80] The armed figure shown in Fig. 208 may represent St Michael.

the leg coverings were almost certainly of woven cloth, probably with a seam at the back and tapered to fit the leg, and hence without the bagginess of the Germanic trousers shown on Roman sculptures (Fig. 75) and the looseness of the long underpants worn by the monk in the *Harley Psalter* (Colour Plate H).

Old English names for trousers current at this time were *braccas*[81] and *brec*.[82] The garments we have been considering in the illustrations might also have been called *hosa*.[83]

King Cnut is pictured (Fig. 188) in unusual leg-coverings that take the form of smooth, close-fitting socks, which cover the calf and are decorated at the top with a band. These are not unique, but are unusual in art, and were perhaps an idiosyncrasy of the Viking-born king. A possible parallel may be found in a sock, or shoe-liner, excavated from Anglo-Viking York (Plate 8). Made in a simple version of the non-woven technique known as *nalebinding*, or 'looped needle netting', which is well known in Scandinavia but not otherwise in Anglo-Saxon England,[84] this object is shorter than Cnut's socks, and was probably not meant to be seen, though a narrow band at the ankle was dyed red. There are figures in other manuscripts wearing what appear to be loose, wrinkled socks with pronounced bands or turn-overs at the top, but socks as baggy as these, without visible means of suspension, seem improbable; they would not remain in position. It is more likely that we have here some very stylised representation of the gartering which was a popular fashion (below, pp. 257–9).

Old English *meo* seems to have signified a sock,[85] also *socc*. The *socc* seems to have been a loose, bag-like foot-covering.[86] The two Anglo-Saxon translations of the Benedictine Rule demonstrate that monastic brethren were expected to have 'socks' as well as 'hose', that is, both *meon* and *hosa* in one version,[87] and both *soccas* and

[81] Cockayne, *Leechdoms*, 3 (1866), p. 198, lines 26–7.

[82] Wright/Wülcker, *Vocabularies*, col. 433, line 12; Kluge, 'Indicia Monasterialia', p. 127, para. 102: *Brecena tancen is þæt þu strice mid þinum twam handum up on þin þeah.*

[83] This word is rather ambiguous (see also *hose* in Murray *et al.*, *Oxford English Dictionary* and H. Kurath and S. M. Kuhn (ed.), *Middle English Dictionary*, A–Z (Ann Arbor, MI, 1952–2001)). The *Indicia Monasterialia* shows that the *hosa* covered the lower leg, but does not indicate whether the foot was covered too: *Gyf þu hosa habban wille, þonne stric þu uppweard on þinum sceancum mid þinum twam handum* (Kluge, 'Indicia', p. 127, para. 104). Bosworth/Toller *Dictionary* defines *hosa* 'a covering for the leg, hose', but occurrences suggest that the word could signify a leather boot. It is used to translate Latin *ocrea* ('metal greave; eleventh century: 'thigh boot' or 'legging'; Wright/Wülcker, *Vocabularies*, col. 327, line 29; Logeman, 'De Consuetudine Monachorum', p. 443, line 1115). In later medieval times *hose* were woven. The shoemaker of Ælfric's *Colloquy* made *hosa* of leather (Garmonsway, *Colloquy*, p. 35, line 172).

[84] Walton, *Textiles, Cordage and Raw Fibre*, pp. 341–5, 435. The sock fits a modern British shoe size 6½–7½ (26–8 cm) so probably, but not definitely, belonged to a man. 'Looped needle netting' is described in detail in Hald, *Ancient Danish Textiles*, pp. 285–310.

[85] Wright/Wülcker, *Vocabularies*, col. 125, line 9; col. 197, line 37; Holthausen, 'Die Leidener Glossen', p. 330, line 110.

[86] Lindsay, *Corpus*, p. 165, line 394; see also following note.

[87] *Benedictine Rule*, 55; Schröer, *Benedictinerregel*, p. 89, line 14.

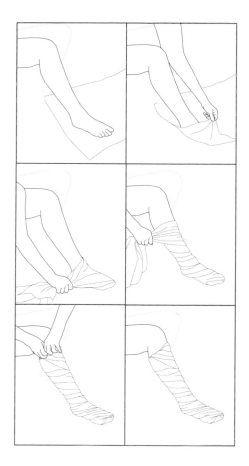

Fig. 210 Lois Swales's demonstration of the leg wraps worn by 'Boksten Man', Sweden

hosan in the other[88] which suggests that *meon* and *soccas* were similar but *hosan* were not synonymous. Presumably the 'socks' and 'hose' were worn simultaneously, not as alternatives.

Much more commonly illustrated than socks are garters or legbindings. They are found in manuscripts, the 'Tapestry' and on a stone sculpture at Barking.[89] The garters appear to have consisted of strips wound round the calf. They may also have covered the foot in some cases, as is apparent from a seated figure in the *Harley Psalter*, fol. 27v; he is without shoes, but his feet, revealed below the hem of a long garment, appear to be wrapped in parallel strips of fabric, like bandages. It should be noted though that a square or rectangle of cloth, closely wrapped round the leg and foot, would produce a similar, if slightly bulkier effect (Fig. 210).

The leg bindings are most often represented by a series of parallel lines, with a diagonal band at the top, either crossing the horizontal bands or lying further up the leg. This type of gartering seems to have been worn at all levels of society from agricultural workers

---

[88] H. Logeman (ed.), *The Rule of St. Benet*, Early English Text Society, original series, 90 (1888), p. 93, line 9.

[89] T. D. Kendrick and C. A. R. Radford, 'Recent discoveries at All Hallows, Barking', *Antiquaries Journal*, 13 (1938), pp. 14–18, at pp. 15–16, Fig. 1, Plate VI.

(pictured in calendars) to King Edgar (in Vespasian A viii, Colour Plate K). Decoration is rare, and kept simple: for example, a figure representing the constellation *Perseus* in Tiberius B v wears garters decorated with a line of dots along the diagonal band (Fig. 202). A figure in the *Harley Psalter*, fol. 72v, wears garters of which the top two strands cross. On the whole, cross-garters according to the modern conception (that is, with a series of X-shaped crosses appearing up the leg) are very rare. They most often appear on representations of the biblical King David or on characters associated with him, such as Saul and Goliath; probably this reflects an iconographical tradition associated with David, rather than current fashion. Nevertheless, garters were probably indeed crossed, for the wearer could put them on by laying the middle of the strip against his leg and, holding the two ends, wrapping the strip round, crossing the ends back and front, the way Charlemagne's biographer described it (Chapter V, pp. 174–5, above). Because the strips were laid closely together, or overlapping, the cross would not be obvious. There is very little variation in the way garters are depicted in manuscript art, and most of the differences can be explained as artists' idiosyncrasies. Some may sketch the gartering with a rapid series of thin lines, which may have the effect of baggy socks, but without any obvious method of suspension. Others draw the parallel lines more firmly, indicating how closely the gartering fitted to the leg. There is slightly more variety in the Bayeux 'Tapestry' where the Normans wear a considerable range of leg bands, sometimes horizontal, sometimes crossed, but always arranged so the leg is exposed between the strands. Duke William wears several different kinds of garters: on one occasion he has two dangling garter-ends with decorative tags at each leg; on another, one at each leg. Englishmen in the 'Tapestry' are usually without garters, indeed, this is one of the features that distinguishes the English Earl Harold from the Normans, although in a scene where he vows an oath to the Norman Duke William, he appears to wear the Norman type of garter, shown as yellow bands over red trousers. A similar effect was achieved by the artist who drew King Edgar in Tiberius A iii (Fig. 187); either the king wore (unique) striped stockings, or his leg bands were wrapped so as to expose the legs at intervals, as they appeared from beneath the long gown.

The fastenings of garters are rarely indicated in art. There is an exception in the *Benedictional of St Æthelwold*, fol. 24r, where the foremost of the three kings wears garters fastened in an elaborate knot, the ends of which dangle and are fastened with squarish tags. Tradition dictated exotic costume for the Magi, however, so these may not be representative of Anglo-Saxon fashion. It is likely, though, that garter ends were finished off with tags, for many of these little ornaments of metal or bone have been excavated (Fig. 211). The garters obviously could be used to bind stockings or trousers closely to the leg, but they were not essential since men in

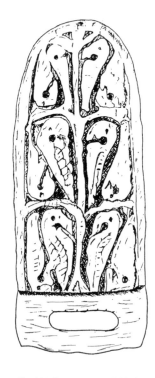

Fig. 211 Bone strap end, York

trousers are often depicted without garters. The garters must have been a useful item in their own right, particularly when wound in close or overlapping strips, for they would keep the legs warm and protect them; Frances Pritchard has suggested that the narrow, woven, wool bands found in late Saxon contexts in London were made for this purpose.[90] Two bands from London are almost identical in every respect from one found in York. All were dyed with lichen purple, which, in Britain, is only found in remote parts of England and Scotland, so they may have been imports, perhaps from Frisia, and as such may have been prestigious.[91] Poorer people may have wrapped their legs in any available rags. Wool would have been the warmest and most readily accessible cloth, and the bands found in London and York are wool. Leather, though less warm, would have been a sturdy alternative. The common name for these leg bands seems to have been *wining*, plural *winingas*.[92] An instruction in the *Indicia Monasterialia* demonstrates how they were worn, also suggesting that monks, as well as seculars, wore *winingas*: *Ðonne þu wynyngas habban wille, þonne do þu mid þinum twam handum onbutan þine sceancan*.[93] ('When you wish to have *winingas*, then gesture with your two hands round your shin.') The word *nostle*, 'band', could evidently be used of a garter, since we find the phrase *mihes nostlun*, 'sock band'.[94] Also documented once each are *hose-bend*,[95] *sceanc-bend*[96] and *sceanc-gegirela*.[97]

Fig. 212 Artist's diagram of a pair of shoes as worn by monks on an ivory box, London, Victoria and Albert Museum

Footwear

Flat, black ankle shoes, with a white strip down the front, are the usual footwear for men in Anglo-Saxon manuscripts, as for women. There are a few variations. Tonsured figures in long, cowled garments depicted on a tenth-century, walrus-ivory box wear shoes with a pronounced band at the ankle and a vertical band down the inner side of the vamp, which was presumably an opening (Fig. 212). More elaborate shoes, decorated at side and toe, and worn with elaborate cross-garters, are shown on King David in Cambridge, Corpus Christi College, MS 391, fol. 24v. Others are worn by a king in the *Bury St Edmunds Psalter* fol. 22r (Fig. 213). Significantly this figure may also represent King David.[98] Generally,

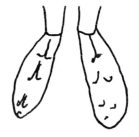

Fig. 213 Elaborate shoes of a king, *Bury St Edmunds Psalter*, fol. 22r

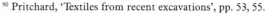

[90] Pritchard, 'Textiles from recent excavations', pp. 53, 55.

[91] Walton, *Textiles, Cordage and Raw Fibre*, p. 340.

[92] Wright/Wülcker, *Vocabularies*, col. 125, lines 14, 16; col. 234, line 22. C.f. Icelandic *vindingr*, 'a strip of cloth wound round the leg instead of hose'; Bosworth/Toller, *Dictionary*, p. 1234.

[93] Kluge, 'Indicia', p. 127, para. 103.

[94] Holthausen, 'Die Leidener Glossen', p. 330, line 110.

[95] Napier, *Glosses*, p. 124, line 4822.

[96] Wright/Wülcker, *Vocabularies*, col. 152, line 39.

[97] Wright/Wülcker, *Vocabularies*, col. 467, line 29.

[98] Ohlgren, *Illustrations*, p. 41, identifies the figure as 'A king (David or Christ as King of Sion?)'.

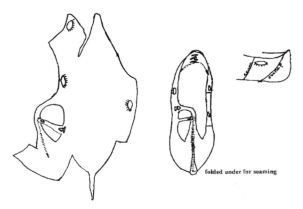

folded under for seaming

Fig. 214 Asymmetric one-piece shoe, Number One Poultry, London, drawn by Patricia Reid

decoration of shoes is limited to the front strip, for example King Edgar's shoes in Tiberius A iii (Fig. 187). It is uncertain whether this is a realistic representation of the way leather was decorated, or simply ornamentation by the artist of a blank space on the shoe, a means of elaborating his picture. Some archaeological finds which do not fit the 'standard' shoe design show that variation was technically possible and actually existed. An asymmetric shoe from Number One, Poultry, London, for example (Fig. 214), bears no resemblance to shoes illustrated.[99] The upper edges of King Cnut's shoes (Fig. 188) are marked by a series of dots, which might be decoration, but which could represent holes through which thongs passed. This may indicate a northern style of footwear favoured by the Viking king, since the detail corresponds to shoes found in north-west Europe and Ireland, also in Viking-period Russia.[100]

The illustrations in the *Cædmon Manuscript* (frontispiece i) seem to depict shoes with long, narrow toes, a style which was to become fashionable in later medieval times. However, long, narrow feet are characteristic of this set of drawings, as we can see by the barefoot figures in the same manuscript (frontispiece ii); the exaggeration of the length of the shoes is probably a stylistic trait. There is little variation in the type of footwear in the manuscripts and 'Tapestry'; such deviations as we can find are in sculpture and metalwork. The Viking Age sculpture at Slaidburn (p. 191) depicts boots, incongruously worn by an angel (Fig. 148). The uppers extend into flaps, projecting on either side of the ankle. There are also flaps on the shoes or slippers worn by a tiny male figure decorating the Abingdon sword hilt (Fig. 134). The latter resembles the footwear of the sculpted figure at Codford St Peter (Fig. 129). We therefore have representations of the *scoh*, 'shoe' and *stæppe-scoh*, *slife-scoh* or

[99] I am grateful to Patricia Reid for unpublished information from her doctoral thesis and permission to reproduce her illustration.

[100] Hald, *Primitive Shoes*, Figs 69–75. 82–3, 174, 176, 188, 223; M. A. Brisbane (ed.), *The Archaeology of Novgorod, Russia: recent results from the town and its hinterland*, trans. K. Judelson, The Society for Medieval Archaeology Monograph Series, 13 (Lincoln, 1992), pp. 183–5, Fig. V.9, 1 and 8. The Russian shoes are called *porshni*. I am grateful to Marc Carlson for these references.

swiftlere, 'slipper'. The boot worn by the Slaidburn figure perhaps corresponds to the Old English word *socc*. We do not have any representations of the raw hide *hemming* or *rifeling*, or the *crinc*, which was perhaps a shoe drawn roughly together, with thongs.[101] The word *calc*, meaning 'sandal', appears in the West Saxon Gospels,[102] but we do not have it in secular context, or any pictures of seculars wearing sandals. Ælfric's *Colloquy* includes among its *dramatis personae* a *sceowyrhta*, 'shoemaker', who produced, among other things, *leþerhose*,[103] 'leather leg-coverings' or 'gaiters'. These garments, which might have taken the form of shin protectors, or of boots, do not appear in art.

Hair and headgear

It has been suggested that English men dyed their hair and beards blue with woad, on the evidence of the dark blue colour often used for hair in the *Hexateuch*; however, the use of colour in Anglo-Saxon art is not realistic (see Chapter VI, pp. 209–10) – green is used effectively for hair in the 'Tapestry' – and there is no need to assume dye was used. Men's hair is generally depicted cut short. The *Hexateuch* is unusual in showing the hair long enough to lie on the neck, mostly with a centre parting. In the Bayeux 'Tapestry', the hair of the English is generally in a fringe at the front, and is cut neatly at the base of the skull without any tapering effect, in contrast to the Normans, who have their hair shaved at the neck, and worn long on the crown, combed forward sometimes with the effect of a peak over the forehead. Harold and some of the other Englishmen in the 'Tapestry' are depicted with long, thin moustaches (Figs 191, 207). Bearded men, sometimes without moustaches, appear in manuscripts, often representing old, respected persons (such as Jacob, Colour Plate I). The beards are often forked. However, most of the illuminated manuscripts and the 'Tapestry', have a high proportion of beardless men including balding, and hence mature, males. One must conclude that Anglo-Saxon men were commonly cleanshaven. The Bayeux 'Tapestry' uses this convention to increase the impact of King Edward the Confessor's death. The priest attending the deathbed of the saintly king has clearly been up all night and has not shaved, as his chin is embroidered with dark stitches lying in different directions, indicating stubble which has not had time to grow into beard.[104] The contrast with other figures in the 'Tapestry' implies that men normally shaved every day.

Viking coiffure may also have been different, featuring longer, 'dressed' hair. A man depicted on a stone fragment from Old Malton,

Fig. 215 Man with plaited hair on a sculpture, Old Malton, near York

---

[101] Murray *et al.*, *Oxford English Dictionary*, 'crank'.
[102] Mark 6:9; Skeat, *Gospels*, p. 42.
[103] Glossing *caligas*; Garmonsway, *Colloquy*, p. 35, line 172.
[104] Wilson, *Bayeux Tapestry*, Plate 30.

Fig. 216 Man with a plaited beard, on a sculpture, Clonmacnois, Republic of Ireland

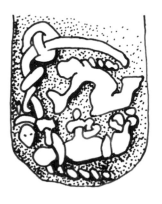

Fig. 217 The god Loki and his wife Sigyn, both with hair in a plaited pony tail, Gosforth Cross, Cumbria

near York, has what appears to be a plait of hair over his head as well as a forked beard (Fig. 215). Plaiting of male hair may have been a Celtic tradition learned by the Vikings in Ireland: figures on the Cross of the Scriptures at Clonmacnoise, Co. Offaly, have long, plaited beards (Fig. 216). The Scots, too, had plaited hair, which distinguished the severed heads of Malcolm II's soldiers when they were were placed on stakes round the walls of Durham, having failed in their seige of the city.[105] On the Gosforth Cross male as well as female figures have the pony-tail hairstyle of Scandinavian tradition (Fig. 217).

Fillets are usually considered characteristic of female dress. Modern costume historians have perhaps been too ready to assume this, by analogy with later medieval and modern clothing fashions. However, though the author of the *Indicia Monasterialia* does suggest that the fillet was characteristic of the appearance of the secular woman (see p. 224 above) it is neither worn by the majority of women in Anglo-Saxon in art, nor exclusively by women. Non-female figures wearing bands over their hair can usually be identified as angels. The fillets in these cases often have a round jewel at the front (Colour Plate K).There are men in headbands in the *Hexateuch*, however (Fig. 218), and the archer figure on an ivory cross now in the Victorian and Albert Museum, London,[106] wears a fillet which is tied at the back of his head. We might see these headbands as a continuation of a minority fashion which appeared occasionally in the ninth century (Fig. 152). Elizabeth Heckett points out that the silk headband was an acceptable part of Viking warrior dress in Old Icelandic literature, and suggests that some of the headbands from Viking Dublin may have been male wear. They included one silk band evidently tied round the head (it was still knotted when found) and other shorter bands which might have been tied on by means of ribbons or braids.[107]

In general, Anglo-Saxon hairstyles/headdress appear to modern eyes to be strongly gendered: that is, men have short hair, women have their hair covered (except in rare examples, usually indicating moral failure, which show it long and loose). Perhaps this is misleading, a kind of artist's 'shorthand' to indicate gender. If Viking men could wear styles which are today normally thought of as feminine, and fillets could appear as items of dress for both male and female characters in the *Hexateuch* cycle, there was perhaps less distinction than has been thought. It is noticeable that the author of the late Old English poem *Judith*, who used the term

[105] Recorded in *De Obsessione Dunelmi*, in T. Arnold (ed.), *Symeonis Monachi Opera Omnia*, Rolls Series, 2 vols (London, 1882–5), 1 (1882), pp. 215–20; the relevant passage is translated in C. F. Battiscombe, *The Relics of St Cuthbert* (Oxford, 1956), pp. 38–9.

[106] Beckwith, *Ivory Carvings*, cat. 45, p. 128.

[107] Heckett, 'Some silk and wool head-coverings', in Walton and Wild, *NESAT III*, pp. 92–3, citing M. Magnusson and H. Palsson (ed.), *Njal's Saga* (Harmondsworth, 1982), p. 248.

Fig. 218 Men in headbands, *Hexateuch*, fol. 140v

wundenlocc, 'with braided hair' or 'with curled hair', to describe his heroine, employed the same word in reference to male soldiers later in the text.[108]

Men mostly appear bare-headed in art, even when depicted in winter. The 'Tapestry' suggests that archers went into battle without headgear although some Norman bowmen appear to wear pointed caps. There is a head in a Phrygian cap in the *Bury St Edmunds Psalter* (Fig. 219). Members of the king's council, depicted in the *Hexateuch* (Fig. 194) wear conical hats. They are passing judgement, the death sentence in fact; like the king, the councillors are depicted as mature, authoritarian figures, in beards and long robes. Possibly the hats relate to their judgemental role. However, although this illustration is a striking one, it should be noted that pointed headgear appears elsewhere in the manuscript, intermittently, on figures in short tunics. What may be a tall hat appears on a badly-preserved, eleventh-century sculpture from Ingleby, Derbyshire. The figure wearing the headgear is apparently engaged in fruit-picking.[109] Hats or caps could have been made of cloth or leather, but their conical shape is similar to that of helmets, which could have been made of metal, or metal and horn. It is sometimes impossible to categorise headgear in manuscripts. The headgear on the figure from Oxford, Bodleian Library, MS Douce 296, fol. 40v (Fig. 208) is tall with its point slightly bent, in the manner of a hat; but the man wears mail and is wielding a sword, so protective headgear would be appropriate, though as we have seen in earlier art, helmet and mail were not necessarily worn together. Two figures on tenth-century sculptures from Middleton, North Yorkshire, represent Viking warriors with their weapons, but they do not wear mailcoats. Their headgear is clearly pointed but no other features of it can be seen.[110] Another figure, on a sculpture from Kirklevington, Stockton-on-Tees, wears an unusual garment which could be a protective coat (Fig. 149) and pointed headgear.

Fig. 219 Head in Phrygian cap, *Bury St Edmunds Psalter*, fol. 87v

---

[108] Line 325; Dobbie, *Beowulf and Judith*, p. 108.
[109] Routh, 'Pre-Conquest carved stones', p. 33, Plate XVI, C.
[110] Lang, 'Late pre-conquest crosses', pp. 16–25.

The Old English word *hæt* appears in several glossaries rendering different Latin words for headgear, and seems to have been a useful general term. More specifically, the *hufe* was a head garment certainly worn by men, including bishops.[111] The verb *hufian*, 'to dress in a *hufe*', is used in biblical contexts, including the consecration of Aaron's sons as priests.[112] The documented occurrences of Old English *hufe*, as a male garment, tend to be in religious context, but the word may have been used more widely, since it is used in secular context in Middle English and was applied to both sexes in the later Middle Ages.[113] Cognates include Greek and Indian words meaning 'hump-backed',[114] so possibly this type of headgear took its name from its tall shape. If so, this would be an appropriate name for the conical hat depicted in Anglo-Saxon art.

A hooded cloak may have been in use for a long time among the Anglo-Saxons, but if not, the cowled habit worn by monks must have accustomed people to the practicalities of such a garment, and it is likely that secular men adopted the style. Itinerants and beggars in the *Harley Psalter* are depicted in hooded garments, both long and short. There appear to be both a cloak and a poncho among the short garments (Colour Plate H).

The cowl worn by monks was called *cugle*. The word *hod*, 'hood', seems to have signified a similar but not identical piece of clothing. The word *cæppe* could also have been used of a hood, but this term seems to have had a wide semantic range, including 'cap', 'cape' and 'cope'.

Kings are depicted in crowns, although the Old English word for crown, *cynehelm*, is a reminder that this insignia was relatively new, and that a helmet, not a circlet, had once distinguished a Germanic monarch.[115] The crowns shown are generally very simple, circular with three vertical projections, which usually terminate in *fleurs-de-lis*. Only Edgar's crown in Tiberius A iii is jewelled (Fig. 187), although we know from documentary evidence that gemstones were exchanging hands as royal gifts at least from Athelstan's time.[116]

Gloves

Byrhtnoth, Ealdorman of Essex and hero of the Old English poem *The Battle of Maldon*, bequeathed, among other things, *binisque*

---

[111] *Biscopes hufe*; Wright/Wülcker, *Vocabularies*, col. 188, line 20.

[112] Leviticus 8:13; Crawford, *Heptateuch*, p. 292.

[113] *Piers Plowman*, A text, Prologue, line 84; Passus III, line 276; G. Kane (ed.), *Piers Plowman, the A Version: Will's Vision of Piers Plowman and Do-well* (London, 1960), pp. 183, 252; Chaucer, *Reeve's Prologue*, line 3911, *Troilus and Criseyde*, III, line 775, V, line 469; Benson, *Riverside Chaucer*, pp. 78, 524, 566.

[114] Holthausen, *Wörterbuch*, p. 177.

[115] W. A. Chaney, *The Cult of Kingship in Anglo-Saxon England* (Manchester, 1970), p. 137.

[116] *De Gestis*, para. 135; Stubbs, *William of Malmesbury*,1, pp. 150–1.

cyrothecis artificiose compositis ('a pair of skilfully made gloves').[117] As we have seen (p. 192 above) gloves had been in use for ecclesiastics for some time; Byrhtnoth's will indicates that they were worn by secular men. Curiously, they are never shown in late Anglo-Saxon art even in circumstances which would seem to demand them. In illustrated calendars and the Bayeux 'Tapestry' men carry birds of prey on their fists without any protection[118] and they fight in the thick of battle with bare hands. This is clearly indicated in the 'Tapestry' where bare linen conveys the flesh tones of faces and hands, while heads and legs are filled in with couched embroidery indicating hair and hose respectively. Not for the first time, we must question whether art is truthful.

Bags and other containers

We may be certain that money bags were fastened to girdles (Old English *fetels* 'a little vessel, bag, belt') but these were probably worn concealed beneath the outer garment so they are not depicted. There is a rare illustration of a bag which would normally be hidden in the *Harley Psalter* (Colour plate H, bottom right), where a beggar raises his arm, and thus his garment, to take alms from a king. Beneath his robe hangs a large container, in this case suspended round his neck. Three 'tails' hang from the bag, indicating that it was made of skins.[119] Another man receiving charity from a king, this time in the *Bury St Edmunds Psalter*, fol. 118r, has a satchel slung on his back.[120]

Men sometimes carried holy relics in containers worn round the neck.[121] The container could take the form of a pouch, like the purple silk example found in York, which was decorated with a cross.[122] Sometimes the shape of the fabric pouch, or *bursa*, was copied in another material, like the silver example from Winchester which has acanthus leaf decoration on one side and a representation of Christ on the other.[123] A surviving ivory cross,[124] and an ivory 'crucifixion group'[125] are both hollow and were probably reliquaries made to be worn.

---

[117] Kennedy, 'Byrhtnoth's obits', pp. 65, 68.

[118] Compare the bottom figure on the earlier Bewcastle Cross, which features a large bird and a man with a gauntlet.

[119] This detail is not in the *Utrecht Psalter* exemplar.

[120] Ohlgren, *Illustration*, p. 294.

[121] D. Tweddle, in Walton, *Textile, Cordage and Raw Fibre*, p. 380, where evidence from Bede (on St Germanus) and Reginald of Durham is cited showing that these were masculine accessories.

[122] 1408; Tweddle, in Walton, *Textile, Cordage and Raw Fibre*, pp. 378.

[123] D. A. Hinton, S. Keene and K. E. Qualmann, 'The Winchester reliquary', *Medieval Archaeology*, 25 (1981), pp. 45–77.

[124] Backhouse, Turner and Webster, *Golden Age*, pp. 122–3, No. 125.

[125] Tweddle in Walton, *Textile, Cordage and Raw Fibre*, pp. 380.

Children's clothing

All the children depicted in Anglo-Saxon illustrations appear to be male. When they are of walking age they are depicted as small-sized adults, usually wearing tunics, although in Stowe 944 a child in a scene depicting a battle for souls wears a long-sleeved gown. This is not a nightgown, since the child wears shoes, and it contrasts with an adult man wearing a tunic in the same picture. This may have been how small children were dressed. Infants, pictured on their mothers' knees, wear long gowns and are either bare-headed or dressed in the type of enveloping headdresses worn by women. Babies in cribs, in depictions of the Nativity, are wrapped from head to foot. Even new-born babies being bathed by nurses while their mothers look on, are depicted as if they wear shirts, with a distinct line at the neck (*Hexateuch*, fols 34r, 75r).[126]

Viking costume

Elizabeth Heckett points out that Irish Vikings had the reputation of wearing expensive clothing, especially hooded cloaks, sometimes adorned with pearls.[127] The many archaeological finds of silk from Dublin and from English Viking cities suggest that Scandinavian settlers who were not necessarily of the topmost class were prepared to spend money on imported luxury cloth. As we have seen, King Cnut may have retained features of Danish dress and King Edward may have worn, among other outfits, an élite Scandinavian costume which was itself an eastern import. It is possible that ethnic Viking dress survived at a lower social level. Many figures on Viking Age carvings wear belted tunics, with flared skirts and sometimes curving hems (see pp. 184–5, above). A few wear longer garments. These include a figure with a horn, hence, perhaps a hunter, on a tenth-century stone from Stavely, North Yorkshire.[128] Other such figures are perhaps biblical, for example Isaac on a stone from Bilton, John the Baptist on one from Sherburn and the Slaidburn angel (Fig. 148). The sculptures are crudely executed and lack detail. It is impossible to know whether the carver was illustrating contemporary costume, or if he had traditional Christian iconography in mind when he depicted long garments.

Many crudely-carved figures on Viking Age sculptures are without tunics, although they wear belts. As suggested above (Chapter

---

[126] Patricia Cooper has suggested to me that the line at the neck is a result of the drawing being constructed in sections.

[127] Heckett, 'Some silk and wool head-coverings', in Walton and Wild, *NESAT III*, p. 95, citing an eleventh-century Spanish Muslim geographer called Al-Udhri, published by D. James, 'Two Medieval Arabic accounts of Ireland', *Journal of the Royal Society of Antiquaries of Ireland*, 108 (1978), pp. 5–9.

[128] Collingwood, 'Sculpture in the West Riding', pp. 241, Fig. c, 242.

V, pp. 196–7) it is possible that the sculptor intended these figures to be naked – although genitals are not shown. The Vikings may have continued the ancient Germanic custom of nakedness when they engaged in activities such as wrestling. On the other hand, the belts, which sometimes hold weapons, could have supported trousers. The figures on the Middleton crosses (above, p. 263) have such belts and also wear hats or helmets, which suggests that they were clothed. We may note, as a precedent, that Germanic barbarians on Roman sculptures are sometimes dressed in trousers without tunics (Figs 1, 75) although probably as indication of captivity and humiliation rather than ethnic dress. It has already been suggested (above, p. 196) that the Scandinavians were in the habit of wearing belted trousers without covering tunics. It may be that they continued to do so and that in this they differed from the Anglo-Saxons.

As shown above, male figures on Anglo-Viking sculptures occasionally have 'dressed' hair as opposed to the loose but cropped hair of the Anglo-Saxons. There is not enough evidence to suggest that a 'Viking hairstyle' (or 'hairstyles'), was a regular feature of the appearance of Anglo-Viking people; the 'dressed' hair may have been iconographic. Undoubtedly, however, the plait and the ponytail would have been recognised as 'foreign' by the southern Anglo-Saxon people, whether on sculptures or in real life.

The taste in jewellery of the Viking settlers seems to have differed from Anglo-Saxon taste, to judge from the contents of hoards. The large cache of silver deposited *c*. 905 at Cuerdale, Lancashire, included arm rings and a hoard from Orton Scar, Cumbria, a silver neck ring and a penannular brooch. A 'thistle' brooch, penannular with thistle-shaped terminals, was found at Newbiggin Moor, Penrith, Cumbria.[129] The penannular brooch suggests Celtic influence transmitted through the Viking presence in Ireland. The neck and arm rings suggest the persistence among the Scandinavians of a common Germanic fashion which the Anglo-Saxons continued to celebrate in their poetry but which is rarely manifested in their archaeology.

Ecclesiastics

Archbishops and bishops are depicted in Anglo-Saxon drawings in ecclesiastical vestments, which belong to the Roman tradition and have only occasional relevance in this book. Vestments stand out clearly from secular clothing in illustrations. Monks wear long habits, with cowls. However, men who were professed monks – and this might include priests, bishops and archbishops – also had the distinctive hairstyle (the tonsure) which imitated Christ's crown

[129] J. D. Richards, *Viking Age England*, English Heritage (London, 1991), pp. 17–18, Plate 5, Colour Plate 2.

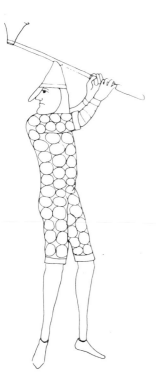

Fig. 220 Figure in mail, Bayeux 'Tapestry'

Fig. 221 Figure in mail from a stone frieze, Winchester, Hampshire

of thorns. From occurrences of the tonsure in art it is clear that ecclesiastics did not wear a distinctive costume at all times. In the Bayeux 'Tapestry' tonsured figures taking part in the funeral procession of King Edward, some of them obviously chanting, wear the normal secular costume of short tunic, trousers and, in one case, a cloak.[130] The same is true of another figure in the 'Tapestry' who is identified in the caption as *clericus*.[131] Bishop Odo of Bayeux, when seated, wears a long costume similar to that of his brother, Duke William.[132] Odo is never pictured in vestments. He appears in military situations, on horseback, in a suit differently coloured and marked with geometric shapes, mostly triangles, rather than the suit of mail depicted by embroidered circles, which is worn by other men.[133] This may reflect the fact that as an ecclesiastic, Odo was not permitted to bear arms; he may have worn a suit of leather to avoid the prohibition. Alternatively, it may be the designer's way of individualising the man who was very probably the patron for whom the 'Tapestry' was made.

Military costume

In the 'Tapestry', horsemen and foot soldiers of both English and Norman armies wear mail garments (Fig. 220) which appear to be all in one piece, with elbow-length sleeves and knee-length legs, and sometimes including a hood. A similar garment with shorter sleeves and legs is worn by a figure (now damaged) on a frieze from Winchester (Fig. 221). The pillaging of fallen warriors, depicted in the lower border of the 'Tapestry', shows mail suits being stripped off, leaving the corpses naked. While a graphic demonstration of the Normans' success, this is hardly realistic. One could not wear mail without some padding, and indeed, the legs and sleeves of conventionally-depicted garments protrude from under the mail suits in the larger pictures which occupy the main register of the 'Tapestry'. The marginal figures are interesting, however, in demonstrating that these mail garments were pulled off over the head. If this detail is authentic, it means that the bottom of the garment could not really enclose the thighs completely in mail as it appears to do. (It would, in any case, be uncomfortable to sit on a horse while enclosed in iron rings, and it would seem an unnecessary expense to protect with mail a part of the body that would be concealed while sitting, though the 'Tapestry' certainly suggests that this was done.) In fact, the mail garment was more likely to have been shaped like a tunic, slit front and back, with a leather or fabric

[130] Wilson, *Bayeux Tapestry*, Plate 30.
[131] Wilson, *Bayeux Tapestry*, Plate 17.
[132] Wilson, *Bayeux Tapestry*, Plate 48.
[133] Wilson, *Bayeux Tapestry*, Plate 67, where he is identified by name; arguably also at Plates 18–19.

border which could be tied round the legs, and perhaps between the legs.

In manuscript art the armour is generally depicted as a mail coat (Fig. 208) with a skirt like a tunic, but sometimes wider, sometimes slit and occasionally with a scalloped edging. In shape these mail coats bear some resemblance to the coat on the Kirklevington sculpture (Fig. 149). The Anglo-Saxons certainly thought of the battle garment as resembling a shirt, for there are many poetic compound words for armour, which literally translated, mean 'battle-shirt', for example *beadu-serce*. The commonest name for a mail coat was, however, *byrne*.

Other kinds of protective clothing may have been worn in battle. Some Norman archers in the 'Tapestry' may wear leather or padded culottes, a costume not shared with the English, although there are several unusual features about this group of soldiers and the embroiderers may give a misleading picture having misunderstood the cartoon they were working from.[134] Armed figures on some Viking sculptures wear tunics of which the skirts are divided into panels by horizontal and vertical lines (above, p. 194). These perhaps represent protective clothing, such as divided mail skirts or leather panelled skirts (?*pilcan*), by analogy with Pictish sculpture, where parallel lines are used to depict armour.[135]

Helmets are generally tall. Some, as in the 'Tapestry', have noseguards. Helmets on a few Viking sculptures have protective pieces over the crown like the earlier helmets from Sutton Hoo and York (above, p. 194). Other armed warriors, for example in the *Hexateuch* and the Cotton Cleopatra C viii Prudentius manuscript wear helmets with a coxcomb effect at the back (Fig. 222). By the time of the Bayeux 'Tapestry', helmets were evidently a standard feature of military dress and they conformed to a standard pattern. This contrasts with the archaeological evidence from the seventh and eighth centuries which suggests that at that time helmets were rare and individual. When did the change take place? The heroic poem *Beowulf*, which survives in a manuscript dating to about 1000 AD, makes frequent mention of helmets which are characterised as being of seventh-century type.[136] However, this is a heroic poem, visualising a world of aristocratic warriors, idealised and hyperbolic. The poem *The Battle of Maldon*, which cannot have been composed before 991 when the battle in question was fought, and might have been considerably later, makes no mention of helmets at all. Many sword-wielding figures appear in skirmishes in tenth-century drawings without any head covering. The 'Tapestry' appears to

Fig. 222 Helmet or hat with coxcomb effect, *Hexateuch*, fol. 25r

[134] Wilson, *Bayeux Tapestry*, Plate 60. I discussed this point in detail in G. R. Owen-Crocker, 'The costume of the Bayeux "Tapestry": culottes, tunics, garters and the construction of the hanging', *Costume*, 28 (1994), pp. 1–9, at pp. 8–9.

[135] J. R. Allen, *The Early Christian Monuments of Scotland* (Edinburgh, 1903), p. 325.

[136] Owen-Crocker, *Four Funerals*, p. 117.

depict a standardisation in military dress which is hardly attested before, though Anglo-Saxon armies had been centrally organized since at least the days of King Alfred and were no doubt highly professional.

Elaborate dress

Fig. 223 Judah's ring and staff are given as a pledge to Tamar (Genesis 38:14–19), *Hexateuch*, fol. 56r

It was not, so far as we can tell, the custom for royalty to wear military dress on ceremonial occasions, and to be portrayed in it, as has been the case in modern times. Of course, the circumstances in which English kings are depicted in manuscripts are usually religious, and armour would have been inappropriate in such situations, though Cnut somewhat incongruously carries his sword as he lays his right hand on an altar cross (Fig. 188). However, the same is true of scenes in the Bayeux 'Tapestry' in which rulers confer, not always in religious circumstances. The ruler may hold a sword, but does not wear armour or helmet. The choice of a long gown, rather than the short tunic, seems to have added to the dignity of late Anglo-Saxon kings. Imported silks and gold embroidery, especially at the borders of garments, made the costume sumptuous, with plant designs playing a major role in this decoration. Men in this period do not seem to have decked themselves out with jewellery, though documentary evidence suggests ownership of it. Edgar, in Vespasian A viii (Colour plate K), may wear a ring, coloured gold, at the upper arm. Edward, resplendent at the opening of the 'Tapestry' possibly wears a neck ring (Fig. 189). Where torques appear otherwise in art, a rare occurrence, they are not being worn. There is the torque being passed from a woman to a young man in the *Harley Psalter* (Fig. 158); and Judah's ring which he leaves with Tamar as a pledge, also depicted as a torque, joined together by a ring and with linear decoration at the narrow part, on either side of the join (Fig. 223). Torques in three sizes are among the temptations the Devil places before Christ in the *Tiberius Psalter*, fol. 10v.[137] Yet the only jewellery to appear regularly in art as part of male costume is the plain, circular, cloak brooch. As so often, we can only conclude that art tells only the partial truth; in reality brooches were ornamented with decoration which is not depicted in art, and other items, especially strap ends and buckles, were certainly in use. The cultural significance of rings is attested in art and in literary and non-literary texts, but the rarity of their appearance as an item of costume leaves us guessing.

When the tomb of Edward the Confessor was opened in 1685, a reliquary cross on a gold chain was found. It was enamelled with religious scenes on both sides, inscribed and tipped with gold and

---

[137] Dodwell, *Anglo-Saxon Art*, p. 28, Fig. 5.

decorated with gems.[138] Beautiful as this jewel must have been, it was placed with the king's body for its Christian significance. It is in keeping with what we know of this very pious era, that this religious piece was worn by a layman while secular jewellery seems to have been relatively unimportant, and was even emblematic of corruption (as in the *Tiberius Psalter*).

---

[138] Cigaar, 'England and Byzantium', p. 91. This cross was apparently worn by James II, but was stolen from him in 1688, and so lost.

VIII

Textiles and textile production

Investigation of textile manufacture is a useful source of economic and social history, particularly, in the Anglo-Saxon period, of women's history. Developments in textiles and manufacturing techniques both indicate and illustrate processes of sociological change. The varieties of fibres, weaves and techniques in the settlement period confirm the evidence of other specialisms (such as pottery study) that the turbulence of the Migration Age provided a melting pot in which geographical and tribal customs and tastes were melded.[1] Changes in cloth and manufacturing equipment mark the distinction between an economy primarily based on the village unit and the urban-centred, commercial structures of later Anglo-Saxon England.[2] As Penelope Walton's study of York demonstrates, a detailed study of the textiles and textile manufacture of one community can attest ethnic change and economic development, in this case from a small commercial and ecclesiastical centre under the Angles to a major Anglo-Scandinavian port.[3]

Archaeological evidence

Excavation has produced two kinds of evidence: fragments of cloth, which on analysis can yield technical details of textile production; and pieces of equipment used in cloth-making.

Over four thousand textile fragments have been identified from Anglo-Saxon context, most of them from pagan graves.[4] The metal grave-goods associated with burials of the pagan and

[1] Bender Jørgensen, 'The textiles of the Saxons, Anglo-Saxons and Franks'
[2] P. A. Henry, 'Development and change in late Saxon textile production: an analysis of the evidence', *Durham Archaeological Journal*, 14–15 (1999), pp. 69–76, at p. 71.
[3] P. Walton, 'Textile production at Coppergate, York: Anglo-Saxon or Viking?', in Walton and Wild, *NESAT III* (London, 1990) pp. 61–72.
[4] The Medieval Textiles Project directed by Dr Elizabeth Coatsworth of Manchester Metropolitan University and Dr Gale Owen-Crocker of Manchester University is creating a data base and annotated bibliography of medieval textiles of

Plate 12 Replaced textile on an annular brooch, Cleatham, North Lincolnshire

conversion period are the chief source of these small fragments of cloth, especially the rusted iron pins of brooches (Plate 12). Many of the fragments are completely mineralised, but sometimes textile survives. Not all surviving textiles are attached to metal: the mere proximity of great quantities of metal, together with favourable soil conditions (acid soil, which had been waterlogged) contributed to the survival of numerous textiles among the king's effects in the Sutton Hoo Ship Burial. Wet conditions, particularly medieval rubbish pits, have often yielded remains of cloth. The excavation of late Saxon urban sites[5] such as the City of London, Winchester and Anglo-Scandinavian York have been productive of organic finds.

The textile remains from burials have the advantage that they are roughly datable from burial practices and associated grave-goods, can usually be assigned to male or female owners, and, from their position, give us some indication of function. (The evidence is limited: since the most frequent source of textiles is the brooch, the majority of surviving fragments have been found with female

the British Isles 450–1500. There is a database of textiles from archaeological sites in the British Isles compiled and held at Textile Research (York, UK). A forthcoming monograph by Penelope Walton Rogers (*Cloth and Clothing in Early Anglo-Saxon England AD 450–700*, Council for British Archaeology English Heritage Report Series) will provide a statistical summary of the data for the fifth to seventh centuries.

[5] Many of which continued in use into the later medieval period.

burials, and usually belonged to the clothing, mostly from the upper body.) Some pieces of cloth from urban sites are considerably
larger than the grave fragments, and are sometimes distinguishable as garments, though they are not gendered; but in many cases
it is often impossible to know if the textiles originally functioned
as dress, furnishing or industrial fabrics, and the whole question of
their use is complex since most textiles probably went through several recycling processes before being thrown away as rags. The
Coppergate, York, finds are securely dated but this is not the case
with all urban textiles, which may derive from cumulative deposits
made over a long period.

With regard to cloth-making tools, again both graves and in-
habited sites give us information. Wool combs, used to prepare wool
for spinning, have survived in fragmentary state from various Saxon
and Viking sites, usually in the form of the iron teeth which were
set into wooden boards. From York, where soil conditions in the
Anglo-Viking period of settlement resulted in organic-rich archaeological deposits, there is a fairly well-preserved wool comb, with a
double row of iron teeth set in an iron-framed wood base.[6] Pagan
women may sometimes have been buried with their spinning equipment: it is common to find large beads in the waist area in women's
graves and it is possible that some of them were whorls, which acted
as fly-wheels on spindles, though the number may have been over-
estimated.[7] Hedges has suggested these were originally accompanied by distaffs that were stuck through the belt, and which, being
made of organic material, have rotted away.[8] Distaffs and spindles
of wood survive from Anglo-Scandinavian York, the distaff tapered
at both ends, with a notch at the top and three corrugations at the
widest part to facilitate the wrapping of the fibre round it.[9] There
have been some finds of bone spindles from late Saxon contexts, a
tenth-century example from York and an eleventh-century one from
Oxford.[10] Iron spindles with bone whorls wedged on them have
been found at a fifth- to sixth-century settlement site at Sutton
Courtenay, Oxfordshire[11] and at Wingham, Kent.[12] Iron spindles
may have been prestige objects: one was found in a casket at a high
status bed-burial dating to the seventh century at Swallowcliffe

[6] Walton Rogers, *Textile Production at 16–22 Coppergate*, pp. 1719–21, Fig. 795;
Hedges, 'Textiles and Textile Production', pp. 280–2.
[7] Personal communication from Penelope Walton Rogers.
[8] Cited in G. Drinkall, M. Foreman and P. Walton Rogers,'Craft and weaving
equipment', in Drinkall and Foreman, *Castledyke*, pp. 292–4 (Foreman, p. 294).
[9] Walton Rogers, *Textile Production at 16–22 Coppergate*, pp. 1731–5, Fig. 804.
[10] Hedges, 'Textiles and Textile Production', p. 283.
[11] Hedges, 'Textiles and Textile Production', p. 283 citing E. T. Leeds, 'A Saxon
village at Sutton Courtenay, Berkshire (third report)', *Archaeologia*, 92 (1947), pp.
79–94 at p. 84, Plate XXII, a, d.
[12] J. Y. Akerman, 'Notes of antiquarian researches in the summer and autumn
of 1854', *Archaeologia*, 36 (1855), pp. 175–86, at p. 178.

Down,[13] two were found with spindle whorls in a casket from Grave 299 at Kingston Down, Kent,[14] again a seventh-century site with some very prestigious artefacts. In the conversion period the fashion for burying with a spindle whorl is more marked than it was in pagan times, with whorls usually made of natural materials: chalk, stone, bone and rarely, amber or quartz.[15]

Excavation of Anglo-Saxon settlement sites, particularly early villages[16] has very often produced finds of large rings, usually of clay though sometimes of stone, which have been identified as 'loom weights', essential accessories of a vertical weaving appliance known as 'the warp-weighted loom' (Colour Plate F, Fig. 224). Loom weights from Grimstone End, Pakenham, Suffolk, were found lying in two rows in the remains of a hut which had been destroyed by fire, and there has been some argument about whether these weights were functional at the time of the destruction, dropped from a loom as it burned, or whether, since the rows are very long, they had been in storage on some kind of rod or rack. Steven Plunkett has recently confirmed that the weights must have been attached to a loom which, measuring about six feet square, is one of the largest examples evidenced from north-west Europe.[17] The warp-weighted loom was used by various peoples including the ancient Greeks, and continued to be utilized until recent times in remote parts of northwest Europe. In Greenland, where wood was precious and constantly re-used, loom parts as old as the twelfth and thirteenth centuries have been preserved.[18] There is a collection of relatively modern warp-weighted looms from Scandinavia in the National Folk Museum in Oslo, Norway, the former curator of which, Marta Hoffmann, has studied the techniques of weaving with this equipment, enabling us to reconstruct exactly how it was used.[19] Study of the warp-weighted loom throughout its history demonstrates that certain tools were associated with it, enabling archaeologists to identify some bone and metal archaeological finds as characteristic weaving tools. At Lechlade, Oxfordshire, a 'thread picker' was identified in Grave 107, where it had been placed on top of a box containing a spindle whorl,[20] and John Hedges lists a number of 'pin beaters',

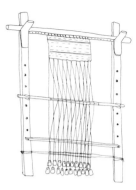

Fig. 224 Warp-weighted loom

[13] Speake, *A Saxon Bed Burial*, p. 52.

[14] Faussett, *Inventorium Sepulchrale*, pp. 66–9.

[15] Geake, *Grave-goods*, p. 58.

[16] There is a general discussion and a gazetteer of sites in P. Rahtz, 'Buildings and rural settlement' and 'Gazetteer of Anglo-Saxon domestic settlement sites', in D. M. Wilson (ed.), *The Archaeology of Anglo-Saxon England* (London, 1976), pp. 49–98; 405–45.

[17] S. J. Plunkett, 'The Anglo-Saxon loom from Pakenham, Suffolk', *Proceedings of the Suffolk Institute of Archaeology and History*, 39 (1999), pp. 277–98.

[18] E. E. Guðjónsson, 'Warp-weighted looms in Iceland and Greenland: comparison of medieval loom parts excavated in Greenland in 1934 and 1990–2 to loom parts from eighteenth and nineteenth century warp-weighted looms in Iceland. Preliminary remarks', in Jaacks and Tidow, *NESAT V*, pp. 178–95.

[19] Hoffmann, *Warp-weighted Loom, passim*.

[20] Boyle, Jennings, Miles and Palmer, *Lechlade*, p. 102.

mostly made of split cattle bone.[21] Larger, sword-shaped beaters were used to 'beat up' the weft on the warp-weighted loom. No doubt most Anglo-Saxon beaters were made of wood, like the example of yew found in Viking Dublin,[22] or of bone. There is a rare, whalebone example which was found in the excavation of a twelfth-century house at Wallingford, Oxfordshire; the Old English owner-formula *Eadbvrg mec ah*, 'Eadburg owns me', is engraved twice on one face of the object, which is thought to be tenth- or eleventh-century.[23] The majority of surviving weaving beaters are earlier, and of metal. Mostly deriving from the graves of wealthy, sixth-century Kentish/Frankish women, these were probably high status objects. They resembled swords in shape, and in at least one instance had been refashioned from a pattern-welded weapon.[24] In recent years beaters resembling, or even perhaps made from, spearheads have also been found.[25] It is interesting to speculate whether their resemblance to weapons had a ritual significance: just as the sword symbolised man's role as a warrior, so the weaving sword might have represented woman's role as peacemaker. Women are several times called 'peaceweavers' in Old English literature.[26]

Discoveries of asymmetrical twill textiles (2 x 1 or 1 x 2) in Anglo-Saxon context have led to the suggestion that another kind of vertical loom, with two beams rather than a single beam and weights, was in use firstly in early Anglo-Saxon England, perhaps a relic from Roman culture, and again from the tenth century when it replaced the warp-weighted loom in urban contexts, perhaps having been reintroduced from France.[27] Since this loom does not leave any trace archaeologically we have no recognisable remains from Anglo-Saxon England to date,[28] though its presence may be deduced by the appearance, in archaeological contexts from the

[21] Hedges, 'Textiles and Textile Production', pp. 305–9.

[22] Hedges, 'Textiles and Textile Production', p. 314.

[23] Eadburg is a feminine name. E. Okasha, *Hand-list of Anglo-Saxon Non-runic Inscriptions* (Cambridge, 1971), p. 119, No. 118; Hedges, 'Textiles and Textile Production', p. 313.

[24] B. Gilmour, Appendix II: 'X-Radiographs of two objects: the weaving batten (24/3) and sword (40/5)', in C. Hills, K. Penn and R. Rickett, *The Anglo-Saxon Cemetery at Spong Hill, North Elmham*, East Anglian Archaeology Report, 21 (Dereham, 1984), pp. 160–3.

[25] Castledyke (Walton Rogers, in Drinkall and Foreman, *Castledyke*, pp. 293–4) and Lechlade (Boyle, Jennings, Miles and Palmer, *Lechlade*, pp. 96–7).

[26] See L. J. Sklute, '*Freoðuwebbe* in Old English poetry', in H. Damico and A. H. Olsen (ed.), *New Readings on Women in Old English Literature* (Bloomington and Indianapolis, IN, 1990), pp. 204–10.

[27] P. Walton Rogers, 'The re-appearance of an old Roman loom in medieval England', in P. Walton Rogers, L. Bender Jørgensen and A. Rast-Eicher (ed.), *The Roman Textile Industry and Its Influence: a birthday tribute to John Peter Wild* (London, 2001), pp. 158–71 at pp. 163–4, 166 suggests the reintroduction from France on the grounds of the distribution of characteristic tools and the use of French loan words in the *Gerefa* list of textile tools (see p. 280).

[28] A small example survives from the Oseberg Ship Burial; Walton Rogers, 'The re-appearance of an old Roman loom', in Walton Rogers, Bender Jørgensen and Rast-Eicher, *The Roman Textile Industry*, p. 163.

beginning of the tenth century, of the single ended pin-beater, a characteristic tool of this loom.[29]

There is a lack of material evidence for finishing processes, such as fulling pits or dyeing vats, though the remains of plants which had probably been used in dyeing have been identified in the excavations of York. Sewing needles of metal and bone have occasionally been found, and even in this humble object there is variation, possibly development in method of manufacture: from York, where the smithy in which iron needles were manufactured has been identified, a type of needle with an elliptical eye (made by welding the ends of a forked shaft) was being overtaken by the needle with a punched, round hole by the end of the Anglo-Viking period. Hedges identifies bone 'bodkins' from both Saxon and Viking contexts,[30] but the function of these larger needle-like objects is not certain. They could have been used for coarser stitching jobs or they might have had some different purpose, such as pinning cloth, including clothing.[31] Glass linen smoothers or 'slick-stones' have been recovered from Viking contexts, but not purely Anglo-Saxon, though a stone example has been found in *Hamwih*, Saxon Southampton.[32] These may have been laundry tools for removing the creases after the linen was washed.[33]

Although women were evidently the principal cloth producers and owners, textiles, which were stored rather than in use, may have been sufficiently valuable to be included as the grave-goods of the wealthy man buried at Prittlewell: the recently-excavated chamber grave contained 'the remains of a large casket that may originally have contained textiles'.[34]

The evidence of art

Although men are depicted carrying out all kinds of activities in Anglo-Saxon art, women, upon whom the making of textile largely depended, are usually pictured in static pose, standing, sitting, or lying down having given birth. There is an exception in the depiction of Sarah on one folio of the *Hexateuch* (fol. 28r). She is unmistakeably spinning: the thread is between her right finger and thumb

---

[29] In urban context they have been found at Beverley, Lincoln, Northampton, Thetford, Winchester and York; they have also been found at the manor site of Goltho; Walton Rogers, 'The re-appearance of an old Roman loom', in Walton Rogers, Bender Jørgensen and Rast-Eicher, *The Roman Textile Industry*, p. 163.

[30] Hedges, 'Textiles and Textile Production', pp. 318–20.

[31] Walton Rogers, *Textile Production at 16–22 Coppergate*, p. 1783.

[32] Hedges, 'Textiles and Textile Production', pp. 318–20.

[33] Personal communication from Penelope Walton Rogers, who believes that the small 'smoothers' of our period have been wrongly associated with the larger marble and glass balls used for calendering linen in post-medieval times.

[34] From an anonymous interim report on the site: 'Prittlewell: treasures of a king of Essex', *Current Archaeology* No. 190, 16.10 (February 2004), pp. 430–6 at p. 430.

Fig. 225 Women working with a skein and 2-beam loom, *Eadwine Psalter*, Cambridge, Trinity College MS R.17.1

and the characteristic shape of the drop spindle wound with thread is apparent. However, there is no distaff in her left hand, which appears to hold a ball. Like many of the *Hexateuch* illustrations, this one is probably incomplete. The scene depicts an encounter between two women as Sarah confronts her rival, Hagar. The inclusion of 'women's work' gives the illustration a very natural appearance.[35] The feminine realm of cloth-making is graphically presented in the twelfth-century *Eadwine Psalter* (Cambridge, Trinity College MS R. 17. 1, fol. 263; Fig. 225).[36] The woman on the left holds the end of a skein of thread on a forked stick, gesturing animatedly to her companion who holds a pair of shears. Two women work at a two-beam vertical loom. They do not appear to be weaving but are perhaps preparing the warp, which only partially fills the loom. The kneeling woman appears to be spreading the warp threads with her fingers; she holds what looks like a comb with an angled handle in her other hand. The woman on the right holds shears.

Apocryphal accounts of the childhood of the Virgin Mary associate her with spinning and assert that she was a weaver of great talent. She is depicted carrying out various textile tasks in medieval art and as Elizabeth Coatsworth has recognised, on some Anglo-Saxon sculptures she is accompanied by spindle, distaff and wool basket.[37] She may hold up the implements rather formally (for

[35] It has been claimed that both Eve and Sarah as depicted in *The Cædmon Manuscript* (pp. 45, 88; see frontispiece ii) carry 'a spindle'(Ohlgren, *Illustration*, pp. 93), but I am unconvinced. The objects held by the female figures are round, and could only be spindle whorls, not spindles, which are rods, not spheres. In Eve's case, the object is surely an apple. In Sarah's, the round object is big for a spindle whorl and lacks the large perforation of a loom weight. I cannot identify it as a textile tool.

[36] The illustration derives from a more impressionistic version in the ninth-century *Utrecht Psalter*, fol. 84r.

[37] E. Coatsworth, 'Cloth-making and the Virgin Mary in Anglo-Saxon literature and art', in Owen-Crocker and Graham, *Medieval Art: recent perspectives*, pp. 8–25, esp. Figs 2 and 3.

example on a stone cross from St Andrew, Auckland and on the Genoels-Elderen ivory) or sit naturally in a chair, spinning, for example in an Annunciation scene on an ivory diptych from Northumbria, now in the *Musée de Cluny*, Paris and on a stone panel from Hovingham, North Yorkshire. These depictions do not teach us anything about Anglo-Saxon spinning. Rather, knowledge of the unchanging tools and technique of hand spinning, which is attested from round the world, enable the iconography to be identified.

Literary evidence

It has been suggested[38] that the warp-weighted loom is referred to in Aldhelm's Latin riddle *De Lorica*, and in the Old English translations of it, the *Leiden Riddle* and the *Exeter Book* Riddle 35. In describing a coat of mail in deliberately oblique terms, the author asserts that although the object he describes is a garment, it was not woven on a loom:

> … Licia nulla trahunt nec garrula fila resultant …
> Nec radiis carpor duro nec pectine pulsor …[39]

translated and augmented in the Old English version:

> … Wundene me ne beoð wefle, ne ic wearp hafu
> ne þurh þreata geþracu þræd me ne hlimmeð
> ne æt me hrutende hrisil scriþeð
> ne mec ohwonan sceal amas cnyssan …[40]

> … Wefts are not interlaced for me, neither have I a warp, nor does thread resound for me through the force of strokes, nor does the whirring shuttle move through me, nor shall weavers' tools beat me from anywhere …[41]

If the warp-weighted loom is indeed referred to here (and this is by no means certain, though the words *þurh þreata geþracu* have been taken to signify the 'shedding' operation of this loom),[42] the poem confirms that this equipment was very familiar to the Anglo-Saxons. At the least it is interesting to find a male scholar, Aldhelm, using

---

[38] E. Von Erhardt-Siebold, 'The Old English "Loom Riddles"', in T. A. Kirby and H. B. Woolf (ed.), *Malone Anniversary Studies, Philologica* (Baltimore, 1949), pp. 9–17; J. Gerritsen, 'Þurh þreata geþræcu', *English Studies*, 35 (1954), pp. 259–62; cf. R. W. Zandvoort, 'The Leiden Riddle', *English and Germanic Studies*, 3 (1949–50), pp. 42–56.

[39] Ehwald, *Aldhelmi Opera*, pp. 111–2.

[40] The *Exeter Book* version. Both texts are printed in A. H. Smith (ed.), *Three Northumbrian Poems* (London, corrected edition, 1968).

[41] Zandvoort's version, which is basically Onion's translation with slight alterations. Gerritsen would render *þreata geþræcu* as 'the crowded many'. I have substituted 'tools' for Zandvoort's 'reeds' since the weaver's reed belonged to the horizontal treadle loom, not the vertical looms.

[42] Elisabeth Crowfoot has observed to me that the riddle as translated here could refer to any pre-treadle loom, not just the warp-weighted.

the technical terms of the woman's craft of weaving. References to looms have also been claimed for Riddles 56 and 70 (identifying their solutions as 'Web in the Loom' and 'Shuttle', respectively)[43] though the riddles are obscure and these solutions are not universally accepted.

Several glossaries contain lists of Latin words relating to textile production, together with their Old English equivalents,[44] and we have a list of the textile equipment necessary for a large eleventh-century estate to own in *Gerefa*, a treatise on the responsibility of a steward.

> he sceal ... habban ... fela towtola: flexlinan, spinl, reol, gearnwindan, stodlan, lorgas, presse, pihten, timplean, wifte, wefle, wulcambe, cip, amb, crancstæf, sceaðele, seamsticcan, scearra, nædle, slic.[45]

> He must ... have ... many textile implements: (?) flaxline (flax fibre),[46] spindle, reel, yarn winder, (?) uprights, beams,[47] (?) presses, (?) some kind of comb, (?) temple [the modern name for a piece of wood used to keep the width of the weaving constant], weft, weft [again; possibly 'warp' intended], wool combs, (?) some mechanism for turning the beam, (?) beater, weaver's stick, (?) picker or beater, or turning handle for the beam, (?) shuttle, seamsticks [ambiguous], shears, needle, (?) linen smoother.'

The translation of several of these words is obviously tentative.[48] Interestingly, though, there is no mention of loom weights, unless this is what is meant by *presse*. Probably the author assumed a two-beam loom (the word *lorgas* which I translate as 'beams' is plural).[49]

Spinning

Spinning was traditionally women's work and women were associated with spinning. In his will, King Alfred distinguished his male

[43] Von Erhardt-Siebold, 'Loom-riddles'.
[44] Wright/Wülcker, *Vocabularies*, col. 186, line 29 (intermittently) – col. 188, line 13; col. 262, lines 5–33; col. 293, line 36–col. 294, line 25; col. 328, lines 19–25.
[45] Liebermann, *Die Gesetze*, 1 (1898), p. 455.
[46] I previously translated this as 'flaxcoil (?distaff)' because of the Bosworth/Toller *Dictionary* reference to an Ælfric gloss of Latin *spirae* as *line* and because a distaff would seem a necessary tool; I now favour the translation 'flax fibre', largely since 'line' still survives as a technical term for raw fibre (Murray *et al.*, *Oxford English Dictionary*, line: 'flax staple that has been separated from the tow by the hackle'); and since Old English *lin(e)* means something thread-like (specifically the wick of a candle), in the *Rushworth Gospels*, *flæx [vel] lin*, Matthew 12:20, Sweet, *Gospels*, Matthew, p. 101). Raw fibre is not a 'tool' in the modern understanding of that word; but neither is weft [thread] which is included in the *Gerefa* list.
[47] Walton Rogers, *Textile Production at 16–22 Coppergate*, p. 1823 translates *lorgas* as 'heddle rods'.
[48] There is a discussion in R. G. Poole, 'The textile inventory in the Old English *Gerefa*', *Review of English Studies*, 40 (1989), pp. 469–78.
[49] Thus Walton Rogers, *Textile Production at 16–22 Coppergate*, p. 1824; Walton Rogers, 'The re-appearance of an old Roman loom', in Walton Rogers, Bender Jørgensen and Rast-Eicher, *The Roman Textile Industry*, pp. 164–6.

and female relatives respectively as 'the spear side' (*spere healfe*)
and 'the spindle side' (*spinl healfe*)[50] and women are still called 'spin-
sters' today. For all but the highest ranking Anglo-Saxon women,
spinning must have been a constant occupation, for the ratio of
hours necessarily spent on spinning before weaving could take place
were probably about 10:1. Spinning was carried out entirely by hand,
for the spinning wheel had not yet been invented, much less the
spinning jenny which would enable several threads to be spun simultaneously and thus bring the process into the industrial age.

The preparation of fibres for weaving was a complex procedure. A fleece (Old English *flæþ*, *flis*), or wool (*wull*) which had
been plucked or sheared from a sheep when required, would be
washed and combed with a wool comb (Old English *camb*, *bannuc-
camb*, *pihtene* or *wull-camb*), and, because wool fibres naturally cling
to one another, could be rolled into a loose 'roving' which was wound
round the distaff (*wull-mod*). This could be carried wherever a
woman went, tucked into her belt to free her hands for other jobs,
and employed whenever her hands were available. The preparation of flax was much more seasonal, and required a settled community with a regular pattern of life to produce it. Flax (*fleax*, *lin*,
linen or *twin*) had to be planted and cultivated, weeded and har-
vested, and subjected to a prolonged and malodorous retting in a
dewy field or a river to rot the woody part of the stem so that the
fibres could be released by beating, prior to combing with a hackle
or flax comb, and winding onto the distaff. Acording to (later medieval) tradition, a flax distaff is very long and would not be tucked
into the belt.

The ends of the fibres on the distaff would be attached to the
stick-like spindle. On the spindle was a whorl (*?hweorfa*), which
acted as a fly-wheel. The spinner rotated the spindle, which continued to revolve. The fibres were pulled from the distaff with the
fingers and thumb, and twisted together into a thread by the rotating spindle. When the spun yarn became so long that the spindle
and whorl touched the ground and ceased to revolve, the spinner
wound the spun thread (*þræd*) onto the spindle and started again.

The spinner could choose the direction of spinning by rotating
the spindle either clockwise or anticlockwise, producing either Z-
spun or S-spun threads (Figs 226, 227).[51] Z-spinning was the more
common in Anglo-Saxon times, but twills in the two types of
threads, Z-spun (warp) and S-spun (weft) are sometimes found in
the same fragment of textile, which is not likely to be random or
accidental. The textiles with mixed spinning are less common than

[50] King Alfred's Will, 27; J. A. Giles (ed.), *Complete Works of Alfred the Great*, 2
vols (1858, reprinted New York, 1969), 1, p. 408 n.9.

[51] Twisting the top of the spindle between finger and thumb, palm downward,
will produce clockwise, Z-spun thread. Using the same movement to twist the
bottom of the spindle, palm up, will produce anticlockwise, S-spun thread. Expanded from J. P. Wild, Introduction to Part I, 'General Introduction', in Jenkins,
The Cambridge History of Western Textiles,1, pp. 9–25, at p. 13.

Fig. 226 Z-spinning

textiles Z-spun in both directions and were probably more luxurious cloths. It is possible for a weaver to produce patterns, including checks, by combining Z- and S-spun threads, effects which the Anglo-Saxons achieved. It is possible that the change in spinning direction enhanced a pattern created by weaving with several heddles or by the use of dyed threads. The fragments of Anglo-Saxon textile surviving are so small, and so frequently mineralised, that they only hint at what the overall effect would have been (see also p. 293).[52] Thread could be spun loosely or tightly. Sometimes more than one thread would be twisted together (plied). The finished threads would be used in weaving on the loom to make fabric for clothing, bedding, hangings and bags; for braiding or plaiting into belts, cuffs and edgings; or for sewing and embroidery thread; and string. Pagan-period spinners often used a large glass bead as a whorl. Excavations of middle and late Saxon settlement sites show that spindle whorls of this period might be made of any convenient substance: Philippa Henry describes them as of 'a variety of materials including bone, antler, wood, ceramic, stone and occasionally lead',[53] and suggests that heavier whorls (over 30 g) were being used for coarse fibre, such as hemp, and the lightest (under 10 g) for flax and high quality wools. The development of the spindle whorl is disputed. Philippa Henry argues that stone spindle whorls from the late-ninth to early-tenth centuries are increasingly lathe-turned and ornamented with incised decoration, a 'change of emphasis and the quality of spindle whorl manufacture' which she relates to increased productivity and professionalism as Anglo-Saxon society became more urbanized and the market economy of the country more developed;[54] finds of stone whorls from York, on the other hand, indicate an evolution in shape, but not in quality of manufacture. Many of the latest York whorls are fairly undeveloped: roughly shaped bone rings chopped from the heads of cattle femora.[55]

Winding

The spindle with thread wound around it could have been used as a bobbin, but this is unlikely; it might have been more convenient

Fig. 227 S-spinning

[52] Hald, *Ancient Danish Textiles*, Figs 68, 73, 74, 76, gives third-century Danish examples of spun patterning. Elisabeth Crowfoot informs me that it is now believed that these fabrics were dyed, though all trace of dye has disappeared.

[53] Henry, 'Development and change', p. 71. Lead whorls from Anglo-Scandinavian York were apparently cast in moulds, and probably made on the site as one was incomplete; Mainman and Rogers, *Craft, Industry and Everyday Life*, p. 2530. There is a discussion of stone spindle whorls from York and a list of the mineral sources of British medieval whorls in P. Walton Rogers, 'Stone spindle whorls', in Mainman and Rogers, *Craft, Industry and Everyday Life*, pp. 2530–1.

[54] Henry, 'Development and change', pp. 69, 72.

[55] Walton Rogers, *Textile Production at 16–22 Coppergate*, pp. 1736–45 and personal communication.

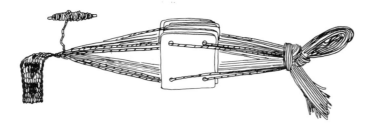

Fig. 228 Tablet weaving

to wind the thread into measurable lengths, in skeins, and from the skeins into convenient balls. It is easy to do this with the hands, but there were specialised tools for the purpose, a skein-winding reel and a swift, examples of which were recovered from the ninth-century ship burial of a woman at Oseberg, Norway.[56] These are possible referents for the Old English words *reol* and *gearnwinde*, which are listed in *Gerefa* as *towtola*, 'textile tools'.

Tablet weaving

The ingenious method of non-loom weaving, or braiding, known to modern exponents as tablet weaving, was used to make girdles, cuffs, ornamental braids to be stitched on to garments and, significantly, for the integral borders of textiles woven on the warp-weighted loom (p. 287). It was a popular technique in Dark Age Scandinavia, and it may have been brought to England by early settlers from that area.[57] It is likely that in Anglo-Saxon England the small (about 4.5 cm) tablets were usually made of organic material such as thin pieces of wood or hide, since very few examples survive from the period.[58] Tablets were usually square with a hole in each of the four corners, although triangular, three-hole, versions existed and circular ones are also known, though not from Anglo-Saxon context.[59] Some tablet weaving used only two holes, either being made on two- rather than four-hole tablets, or on only half the holes of normal square tablets.

[56] Hoffmann, *Warp-weighted Loom*, pp. 291–94, Figs 122, 124. This was, of course, the burial of a wealthy, possibly royal, woman, and these tools might have been rare luxuries.

[57] Bender Jørgensen, 'The textiles of the Saxons, Anglo-Saxons and Franks'. This report focuses on regional distribution of cloth types in the fifth to eighth centuries, with distribution maps and pie charts. The major research project which produced this data, 'North European textile production and trade in the 1st Millennium AD', was later published as Bender Jørgensen, *North European Textiles until AD 1000*.

[58] N. Spies, *Ecclesiastical Pomp and Aristocratic Circumstance: a thousand years of brocaded tabletwoven bands* (Jarettsville, MD, 2000), pp. 94–5, cites a bone example from a grave at Kingston, Kent, a bronze example from the early Anglo-Saxon village site of West Stow, Suffolk, and an antler example from Viking York.

[59] Hedges, 'Textiles and Textile Production', p. 316, cites Pictish and Viking examples. Nancy Spies does not include circular examples though she notes (*Ecclesiastical Pomp*, p. 95) that hexagons and octagons are depicted in late medieval art. These may be fanciful.

In order to weave a braid (Fig. 228), the operator passed a separate warp thread through each hole in each tablet; individual threads entered the holes from either right or left according to the desired pattern. The tablets were placed in a pack and the ends of the warp threads secured. It was simple for the weaver to tie one end to her belt, or she might have secured both ends to posts and sat between them.

The weaver required a bobbin of weft thread and a small beating tool. To make a braid, she would pass the weft through the shed (the gap between the upper and lower warp threads). To change the shed she turned the tablets one quarter, thus altering the relative position of the holes. The weft thread was then passed back through the new shed. (Numerous turns of the tablets can overtwist the warp threads. It is possible to untwist them by reversing the direction of the turning, although this requires care if a pattern is involved. Some modern exponents achieve the desired effect by turning the weaving upside down.)

Fig. 229 Plain tablet twists

Tablet weaving produces a narrow band which is thick and flexible, and which can be patterned on both sides, the weft being concealed except at the edges. Undecorated braids can consist of a series of warp twists lying in the same direction (Fig. 229) or a series of chevrons, consisting of alternate Z and S twists, which gives an effect similar to a plait (Fig. 230). This can be achieved by threading alternate tablets differently, and is a common variation. It is possible to produce geometric patterns, either running continuously or in a series of blocks; two fragmentary braids found at Fonaby, Lincolnshire, had unpatterned chevron borders of unequal width, framing a diagonally-patterned centre area worked partly on two, partly on four, holes of the tablets. There are scraps of similar braids from Mucking,[60] Bergh Apton, Norfolk,[61] and Portway, Hampshire.[62] The most skilled weavers probably produced imaginative designs. This is attested by the tenth-century braids that border the embroidered stole and maniple which were preserved among the relics of St Cuthbert, luxurious work in gold and silk, which are decorated with a series of tiny motifs including animals.[63] There was probably a strong traditional element too, and among the early settlers and the rustic population throughout the period custom may have established patterns which were peculiar to families or regions. Unfortunately the surviving examples recovered so far have been too few and small to test this hypothesis.

Fig. 230 Chevron tablet twists

[60] E. Crowfoot, 'The textiles' in Cook, *Fonaby*, 1981, pp. 98–9.

[61] E. Crowfoot, 'The textiles', in B. Green and A. Rogerson, *The Anglo-Saxon Cemetery at Bergh Apton, Norfolk: Catalogue*, East Anglian Archaeology, 7 (1978), pp. 98–106, at pp. 101, 106.

[62] E. Crowfoot, 'Textiles', in A. M. Cook and M. W. Dacre, *Excavations at Portway, Andover, 1974–5*, Oxford University Committee for Medieval Archaeology Monograph, 4 (1985), pp. 99–102, esp. p. 99.

[63] G. M. Crowfoot, 'The Braids', in Battiscombe, *The Relics of St. Cuthbert*, pp. 433–63.

Braids were certainly made in bright tones, and colour contrast was used to enhance the woven pattern. The narrower braid
from Fonaby, about 2 cm wide, had blue or green in the central
part, bordered by red, with a blue edging to the wider border. A
braid from Mucking had blue, and possibly yellow, threads, bordered by red. The end of a linen braid, found attached to a strap
end from St John's, Cambridge, and probably part of a belt, was
worked in three colours, described in 1951 as white, pale blue-green
and indigo, and still visible today (Plate 6).[64] More recently the
remains of patterned braids with blue, white and red-purple threads
were observed in wrist clasps from two different graves at Morning
Thorpe.[65]

Tablet-woven braids could be embellished further by needlework. Migration Age graves from Norway have produced examples
on which sewn decoration has been worked, in blocks, on untwisted
warp threads at the centre of the braid. This created a swastika
pattern in red, blue and yellow on a braid from Øvre Berg,[66] and a
series of stylised animals worked in hair (probably goat) from
Snartemo (Grave 2)[67] and Evebø.[68] Tablet bands of similar quality
have been found in Sweden and Denmark.[69] The Anglo-Saxons may
also have made use of goat hair.[70] There is now a little evidence of
embroidery or brocading on some of the tablet-woven bands which
probably edged the neck of the *peplos*-type gown in the pagan period; for example in Grave 18 at Dinton, Buckinghamshire, a fifth-
or sixth-century cemetery, there was brocading on a braid found on
the back of a paired disc brooch. Elisabeth Crowfoot suggests that
these more elaborate braids would have been stitched on to the
garment, rather than forming an integral 'starting border' (p. 287).[71]
The most luxurious effect was produced by decorating in gold, which
could be achieved by brocading during the weaving process or
embroidering with a needle on the woven cloth. Gold work was

[64] G. M. Crowfoot, 'Textiles of the Saxon period', pp. 26–32.

[65] E. Crowfoot, 'The textiles', in Green, Rogerson and White, *Morning Thorpe*,
pp. 172, 182–3.

[66] Hougen, *Snartemofunnene*, Plate XVII, pp. 77–9, 115.

[67] Hougen, *Snartemofunnene*, pp. 68–9, 114.

[68] H. Dedekam, 'To tekstilfunde frå folkevandringstiden', *Bergen Museums Årbok*,
1924–5, pp. 1–57, Plates III–IV.

[69] L. Bender Jørgensen, 'Scandinavia, AD 400–1000', in Jenkins, *The Cambridge
History of Western Textiles*, 1, pp. 132–8, at pp. 133–4 notes that thirty-two such brocaded bands have been found in Scandinavia. Fig 3.8 illustrates zoomorphic brocaded bands from Evebø-Eide and Fjordane, Norway and Fig. 3.9 the band brocaded
in geometric design from Snartemo. See also M. Nockert, *The Högom Find and
other Migration Period Textiles and Costumes in Scandinavia*, Archaeology and Environment 9, Högom Find Part II (Umeå, Sweden, 1991).

[70] E. Crowfoot, in Cook, *Fonaby*, p. 96. In a personal communication, Miss
Crowfoot has informed me that the Fonaby examples, which are now lost, were
small and doubtful. They may have been deteriorated silk. The short, coarse hairs
of the goat are not well suited to needlework (except for imported mohair).

[71] E. Crowfoot and G. Edwards, 'The textiles' and 'Fibre identification', in A.
Hunn, J. Lawson and M. Farley, 'The Anglo-Saxon cemetery at Dinton, Buckinghamshire', in *Anglo-Saxon Studies in Archaeology and History*, 7 (1994), pp. 127–8.

probably used for edging garments at wrist, neck or skirt-edge and for decorating the ribbons which adorned the cloaks of eleventh-century kings (Figs 188, 192).[72] It makes rare appearances in high status male graves of the conversion period. Gold from the Taplow barrow, discussed in Chapter IV as a possible cloak edging or baldric decoration, because of its association with a buckle at the shoulder (p. 196, above) might be reconsidered as an early example of the cloak ribbon. The Prittlewell chamber grave preserved a large area of gold 'thread' which, according to a preliminary photograph released by the Museum of London, lay in eight groups at the neck area, six arranged in a semi-circle, with two other diamond-shaped (? zoomorphic) areas immediately below, which looks as though a gold-decorated border might have edged the front of a tunic neckline, or perhaps a cloak tucked round the corpse like a blanket.[73] Gold decoration had earlier been exploited effectively on headbands worn by wealthy, probably royal, ladies in sixth-century Kent (Chapter II, p. 96). Analysis of the remains of these headbands shows that they were decorated in simple geometric patterns, which occasionally incorporated crosses (Fig. 69).[74] In the sixth and seventh centuries the decoration was carried out with strips of solid gold, beaten flat. Later, lamellae (flat metal strips) were wound round a fibre to make filé thread. The most luxurious base fibre was silk, as in the St Cuthbert stole and maniple.[75] The embroideries and tablet-woven braid from Maaseik had a core of cow-tail hair.[76] A tablet-woven braid, part of which is now in Los Angeles Museum, USA, and part in the Abegg Stiftung, Bern, Switzerland (attached to a later episcopal mitre) has been identified by Hero Granger-Taylor as ninth-century insular or insular-influenced work. Decorated in soumak (wrapped) brocading, in two shades of red, two shades of blue, and gold foil wrapped round silk, the braid remains astonishingly bright today.[77]

Weaving

Weaving seems to have been women's work in Anglo-Saxon England as it had been in most cultures throughout history. It continued to be a female task until men began to operate the horizontal

[72] I owe this suggestion to discussion with Elizabeth Coatsworth.

[73] These observations are my own and entirely provisional.

[74] Crowfoot and Hawkes, 'Early Anglo-Saxon gold braids', Figs 13, 14.

[75] E. Plenderleith, 'The stole and maniples: the technique', in Battiscombe, *The Relics of St. Cuthbert*, pp. 375–96. The core of examples from ninth- to tenth-century burials on Cathedral Green, Winchester is now missing, but was so fine it was probably silk; E. Crowfoot, 'Textiles', in Biddle, *Winchester*, 7.ii, ii, p. 469.

[76] Budny and Tweddle, 'The Maaseik embroideries', pp. 65–96, p. 76.

[77] I am grateful to the authorities of both museums for access. Illustrated in Webster and Backhouse, *Making*, pp. 183–4, No. 142.

loom which was introduced into Europe about 1000 AD.[78] Women
may have been thought of as the providers of textiles: in 735 the
missionary Boniface, in a letter, thanks Abbess Eadburh for a gift
of books and also for clothes. It seems possible that Eadburh's monastery had produced the clothing.[79] In the heroic poem *Beowulf*,
the victorious prince is rewarded with weapons, a standard and
horses by the king, but the queen gives him a neck-ring and a garment (*hrægl*); a woman's gift.[80] In the same poem women are mentioned when the hall is decked out with woven textiles (*web*, line
995), the first occasion that women, apart from the queen, have
been seen to take any active part in hall life. The wealthy woman
named Wynflæd, who, in her late Anglo-Saxon will, bequeathed
many items of cloth including garments and hangings, clearly kept
supplies of furnishing textiles in chests.[81]

It is certain that the Anglo-Saxons made use of the warp-
weighted loom (Fig. 224),[82] not just because the non-perishable loom
weights are common archaeological finds, but also because pieces
of cloth from Anglo-Saxon contexts have been found to incorpo-
rate the integral tablet-woven border characteristic of this kind of
loom. The warp-weighted loom consisted of two uprights (?*stodlan*)
and a horizontal beam (*lorh*, *uma* or *web-beam*) across the top. Warp
threads (*wearp*) were attached to the beam, either directly by threading them through holes in the beam, or by means of a tablet-woven
starting border. This was made by setting up the tablets with their
warp threads through the holes, passing a weft thread through the
shed in the usual way, then winding it round a number of pegs set
wide apart before passing it back through the tablets. As this action
was repeated, a tablet-woven braid with a series of long weft loops
at one side would be created. The completed braid would be sewn
through holes in the horizontal beam at the top of the warp-weighted
loom, when the loops, now hanging vertically, would become the
warp for the loom weaving. The ornamental edge could be incorporated into the finished blanket or garment.

The warp-weighted loom normally rested against a wall or a
roof beam, so that the uprights were tilted. A bar (the shed rod) was
fixed between them. Half the warp threads were pulled forward in
front of the shed rod. The rest were allowed to hang straight down
behind it. The lower ends of the warp threads were tied, in bunches,
to the loom weights, in such a way that there was equal weight on
the back and front threads. This division of the warp created a natural shed, that is, the space through which the weft threads (*ab*, *aweb*,

---

[78] Henry, 'Development and change', p. 75.
[79] Suggested by M. Dockray-Miller, *Motherhood and Mothering in Anglo-Saxon England*, (Basingstoke and London, 2000), p. 27; the author also suggests that the monastery was Minster-in-Thanet, Kent.
[80] Owen-Crocker, *Four Funerals*, p. 222.
[81] Owen, 'Wynflæd's wardrobe', pp. 221–2.
[82] Hoffmann, *Warp-weighted Loom*, *passim*.

wefta, or *weft*) passed. This natural shed is characteristic of the warp-weighted loom; a shed must be created mechanically on other looms. The use of thicker warp thread at each end would strengthen the sides of the weaving, particularly important if the finished article was to be a square or rectangular piece, such as a cloak or blanket. Sometimes tablets might be threaded on the warp threads at each end so that a braided side edge could be created during the weaving process.

Attached to the uprights were brackets supporting the heddle rod. This was the movable part of the loom. The warp threads which were hanging free at the back of the loom were attached by threads, or leashes (*?hefeld*) to the heddle rod. By moving this rod away from the loom, the weaver could pull the back threads forward, thus 'changing the shed'. A plain weave (tabby) would require one heddle rod; a simple 2 x 2 twill and more complex twills, three (pp. 293–4).

Weaving by this method was a strenuous task. The weaver had to stand up, rather than sit, as exponents of the later horizontal loom would do. She might climb on a bench to reach the top, which was where the weaving started. Rather than crouch uncomfortably at the bottom, she might wind completed cloth onto the beam at the top of the loom. This would be relatively simple if the beam was made to revolve by means of a handle. This was a sophistication known to the Romans; the Anglo-Saxons may have used it too (*?crancstæf*). The alternative was to lift the heavy beam down, and laboriously wind the cloth on to it. If this winding was not done, the length of the cloth was limited to the height of the loom. Certainly the warp-weighted loom was not capable of weaving bales of cloth which could be cut up, and since spinning and weaving were such labour-intensive procedures, it is likely that waste was minimised. No doubt a weaver would set out to make a garment- or blanket-length and measured her warp threads accordingly.

A single weaver would have been constantly on the move, and weaving was probably carried out more often by two workers. Judging by the size of modern warp-weighted looms and the surviving evidence of medieval ones, the heddle rod was too wide and heavy to be lifted easily by one woman; she would have to lift one side of the rod into its new position then walk to the other side of the loom to repeat the operation with the other end of the rod. The movement of passing the weft through the shed was similarly awkward for one weaver alone. She might have used a shuttle (*hrisl, ?sceaðel*), but this was not the 'flying shuttle' of modern times, for the warp-weighted loom had no conveniently placed bar for the shuttle to run along. Anglo-Saxon weavers, like modern Scandinavian exponents, may have used a loose bobbin of threads which could be thrown into the shed and plucked out the other side. Two weavers could pass the bobbin to each other.

The threads of a web might cling together and could be straightened by means of bone or wooden pickers, which, for the warp-weighted loom, were characteristically pointed at each end ('double-ended pin-beaters'). After the weft had been passed through the warp several times the fabric would still resemble loose netting, and the weft would be deliberately made wavy, to prevent it pulling too tight and narrowing the cloth. The threads had to be compressed by beating with a sword-shaped implement (p. 276), an awkward task with the warp-weighted loom since the threads must be beaten upwards. A braided closing border could be added to the end of the cloth. This was done by attaching tablets to the last threads in the weft direction. The warp threads of the large loom passed through the shed of the tablets before being cut off. A piece of cloth woven on the warp-weighted loom could therefore have an integral, decorative border on all four sides. We have only fragments of tablet-weave from Anglo-Saxon context, but sometimes they hint at grandeur. Elisabeth Crowfoot compared a fragmentary, patterned braid in Grave 8 at Dinton to 'the wide borders of northern cloaks'.[83] An alternative method of closure was to knot the warp threads into a decorative fringe.

Probably most women could weave, obviously with different degrees of skill and specialisation, and in the early centuries of our period utilitarian cloth was probably produced by the women of a community as needed. In recent times in Scandinavia, the warp-weighted loom, which is easily dismantled, was stored in a barn; when a blanket or garment was needed, the loom could be set up against the kitchen wall for the time required to weave it, perhaps a few days. The collapsible nature of the equipment is emphasised by the fact that in the languages of Northern Europe the loom was not referred to as a unit, but in terms of its parts: uprights, beams, rods. The Anglo-Saxons, however, did not have the cosy, all-purpose farmhouse kitchen or the small family unit of modern Scandinavia. Excavation of Anglo-Saxon villages shows that the main hall provided a nucleus, while *grubenhäuser* (small huts with sunken floors or hollows under the floors), housed crafts and industry. As far as we can tell, each *grubenhaus* catered for only one occupation, and where evidence of looms has been found, we seem to have vestiges of buildings catering specially for weaving. Loom weights have been found within *grubenhäuser* on many sites. One, at Old Erringham Farm, Shoreham-by-Sea, West Sussex,[84] and a more substantial building at Upton, Northamptonshire,[85] each had evidence of two looms and were probably designated weaving sheds. The

---

[83] Crowfoot, 'Dinton', pp. 127–8. and at p. 108 of the report. Possible patterned tablet-woven braid was found on both back and front of a large square-headed brooch worn by the woman in Grave 8. A saucer brooch lay beneath the square-headed, and the woman had nearly one hundred beads.

[84] Anon., 'Sussex: Old Erringham', *Medieval Archaeology*, 9 (1965), p. 175.

[85] D. A. Jackson, D. W. Harding and J. N. L. Myres, 'The Iron Age and Anglo-Saxon site at Upton, Northants', *Antiquaries Journal*, 49 (1969), pp. 202–21, at pp. 206–10.

settlement at West Stow, Suffolk,[86] where archaeologists found loom weights in three *grubenhäuser*, as well as other weaving equipment such as combs, may have been a wool centre producing enough cloth to supply other settlements. As Anglo-Saxon society changed, and large estates, both secular and ecclesiastical, arose, weaving certainly became more organised and a specialised task. In some households, the skilled workers were slaves: Wynflæd mentioned two such women in her will, *ane crencestran and ane semestran*, 'a woman weaver and a seamstress'.[87]

The warp-weighted loom continued in use throughout the Anglo-Saxon period – there are loom weights from eleventh-century habitation sites – but in urban contexts finds of the characteristic loom weights and double-ended pin-beaters decline from the mid-ninth century.[88] A proportionate increase in single-ended pin beaters, tools characteristic of the two-beam loom, indicate that this loom took over entirely at some urban sites such as York and also at some rural locations, such as the manorial estate of Goltho, Lincolnshire.[89] The presence of a vertical two-beam loom (Fig. 225) in the earlier Anglo-Saxon period is suggested by 2 x 1, or 'three-shed', twill fabrics from pre-eighth century burials. These uncommon fabrics *could* have been woven on the warp-weighted loom, but are unlikely to have been, since the 'over two, under one' progression (Figs 236–7) does not utilise that loom's natural shed. It is possible that the early examples, or some of them, were imports but not improbable that there was a survival of Romano-British culture, specifically feminine culture, in the use of a different weaving technique and a different loom. In pursuit of this suggestion, which has been made by Elisabeth Crowfoot, I have looked for other evidence of Roman-British survival whenever 2 x 1 twill has appeared in recent publications, and have usually found it. Occasionally this evidence also concerns textiles: finds from Sewerby, for example, included both three-shed twill and napped or teaselled fabrics.[90] In other cases the evidence is in the form of artefacts, remains of pre-Anglo-Saxon pottery or metalwork. The latter in itself is not conclusive evidence that the Romano-British and Germanic cultures co-existed; the Anglo-Saxons seem to have been acquisitive with regard to Roman coins and old Roman brooches, for example. Such objects quite frequently appear in Anglo-Saxon graves and they were old, as much as hundreds of years old, when buried. They may testify to Roman taste, but are not a guide to ethnicity.[91]

---

[86] S. E. West, 'The Anglo-Saxon village of West Stow', *Medieval Archaeology*, 13 (1969), pp. 1–20, at p. 5.

[87] Whitelock, *Wills*, p. 10, line 30.

[88] Henry, 'Development and change', pp. 72, 74.

[89] Walton Rogers, *Textile Production at 16–22 Coppergate*, pp. 1753, 1824.

[90] E. Crowfoot, 'The Textiles from Sewerby, Yorkshire', unpublished Ancient Monuments Laboratory Report, 2127.

[91] White, 'Scrap or substitute: Roman material in Anglo-Saxon graves', in Southworth, *Anglo-Saxon Cemeteries: a reappraisal*, pp. 125–52.

However, a two-beam loom may have continued to co-exist with the warp-weighted, leaving no archaeological trace, until it increased in popularity when tools were specially developed for it; alternatively the loom, and its characteristic tools, may have been reintroduced to England in the late Anglo-Saxon period.

A two-beam loom[92] consists, basically, of uprights and two parallel beams at top and bottom. The loom is vertical, not tilted like the warp-weighted loom. It can be set up by winding the warp thread in a continuous spiral round the two beams. The weaving is compacted with a toothed beater (?*pihten*)[93] rather than a sword-shaped one. After weaving, the cloth is removed by cutting the warp threads or sliding them off the beams. Thus, the finished product is a flat piece of cloth with cut or looped warp threads at top and bottom rather than braided borders. Alternatively, it is possible to weave a cylindrical piece of cloth, by winding the warp threads both around the beams and around a stick or cord laid parallel to them. If, at the end of the weaving, the stick or cord is left in place, the result is a cylinder of cloth; if it is removed, the cloth can be laid out flat. This cylindrical weaving was known in Iron Age Denmark, and the Huldremose gown (Plates 1, 2) was woven this way.[94] 2 x 1 twill has been found on the 'paired' brooches which are characteristic of the *peplos*; but tablet weave has been found so often on these brooches, tablet weave which in some cases has been identified as starting border, that clearly the Anglo-Saxon version of the *peplos* was usually woven as a flat piece of cloth on the warp-weighted loom.

Ultimately both vertical looms gave way to the horizontal, treadle-operated loom, which was already, it seems, in use in York by the eleventh century.[95] A man's tool, it heralded a cultural change: faster weaving, the beginning of mass production and industrialisation. The size of the cloth produced was no longer dependent on the height of the loom. The nine, long, linen strips which make up the Bayeux 'Tapestry', the largest of which measure 13.70 m and 13.90 m, must have been woven on a horizontal loom.

Fig. 231 Tabby

Types of weave

The simplest weave is tabby, or plain weave (Fig. 231) in which the weft threads pass over one, under one, of the warps (Fig. 232). Finds vary from coarse quality, like sacking, to very fine fabrics which

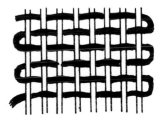

Fig. 232 Tabby

---

[92] Hald, *Ancient Danish Textiles*, pp. 203–18.

[93] Walton Rogers, *Textile Production at 16–22 Coppergate*, p. 1824.

[94] The cylindrical method was not exploited in the making of the garment: the cylinder was opened out and the flat cloth turned sideways to make the gown.

[95] A well-worn piece of equipment, believed to be a heddle cradle, testifies to this; Walton Rogers, *Textile Production at 16–22 Coppergate*, p. 1815.

belonged to garments. Tabby fabric is relatively straightforward to
weave, particularly on the warp-weighted loom, with its natural
shed. Although tabby was sometimes used for wool, it is most often
found in linen and the most popular weave for linen is tabby; it is
no coincidence that an old name for tabby weave in German is
Leinenbindung, literally 'linen weave'. Lise Bender Jørgensen, in
examining Anglo-Saxon textiles chiefly of the pre-Christian period, has noted that the quantity of linen tabby in England (esti-
mating this as about one quarter of examples in Anglian and north
Saxon areas, rising to one third in south-west Saxon areas and one
half in Kent) marks a major difference between the textiles of the
Anglo-Saxons and Scandinavia, and that its chief geographical distribution on the Continent is in Frankish areas, along the English
Channel and in southern and central Germany.[96] While this apparent affinity with the Frankish areas is interesting, and would appear to corroborate the well-documented Frankish element in the
culture of Kent in early Anglo-Saxon times,[97] the assumption that
the presence of tabby linen is a geographical/ethnic phenomenon
has not gone unquestioned. Penelope Walton Rogers argues that
the increase of both tabby and flax in Anglo-Saxon context is a
chronological development rather than just regional distribution.[98]
As she indicates, many of the Kentish sites which have yielded
tabby linen are, indeed, seventh-century and belong to the 'conversion period' rather than the pagan. As we have seen above, the
cultivation of flax and transformation of it into thread is a labori-
ous process which takes several months, and requires a settled community and a seasonal routine. The village at Castledyke, in
discussion of which Penelope Walton Rogers made her chronological point, was a settled community for centuries, which had ample
time to develop an established seasonal economy suitable for flax
production. However, we must also take into account the variations in soil conditions and corrosion products which may have
skewed our data, since some of the cemetery contexts in which early
Anglo-Saxon textiles have survived are more likely to favour wool
than linen (see below); in other words, we may have lost more linen,
and hence tabby, textile, than wool. As we have seen (Chapters IV
and V, pp. 133–4 and 171), eighth-century writers suggest that linen
was both common and preferred. The fine-woven, tenth-century
Llan-gors garment and the professional, regular weave of the

[96] Bender Jørgensen, 'The textiles of the Saxons, Anglo-Saxons and Franks'.
[97] Classically stated in E. T. Leeds, *The Archaeology of the Anglo-Saxon Settlements* (Oxford, 1913) and *Early Anglo-Saxon Art and Archaeology* (Oxford, 1936).
[98] In Grave 94 at Castledyke, which was in the northern kingdom of Lindsey,
there was a belted linen tunic (or undertunic) worn under a fine woollen garment
which was not belted (hence probably a cloak, though possibly a loose or girdled
tunic) indicated by linen found on the underside of the belt buckle and on the
underside of knives on the chest of the skeleton; and by fine wool twill found on
the upper surface of the buckle; Walton Rogers, 'Dress and Textiles', in Drinkall
and Foreman, *Castledyke*, p. 278.

eleventh-century Bayeux 'Tapestry' demonstrate the high quality of linen weaving in the later Anglo-Saxon period.[99]

The most common weave to have survived from the pagan and conversion periods is simple 2 x 2 twill (Fig. 233), a typical product of the warp-weighted loom. This cloth has a pattern of diagonal lines (Fig. 234), and has been found in various textures, usually in wool, but sometimes linen. It was commonly used for the *peplos* and for other garments also. Bender Jørgensen identifies plain twills of this kind as typical of Scandinavia, like the tablet weaves with which they are often associated.[99]

Patterned twills are rarer and were certainly luxury fabrics. These twills probably evolved for the warp-weighted loom and some Scandinavian examples had clearly been woven on it. Their geometric patterns were the result of skilled weaving, using three heddle rods and the shed rod in a complex sequence. The characteristic appearance of the fabric is a series of asymmetrical diamonds or lozenges (Fig. 235). In English, modern experts call these 'broken diamond' or 'lozenge' twills; the Norwegian name *ringvend*, 'ring-weave' is equally descriptive.[100] In England these textiles appear in all areas where there are early Anglo-Saxon graves, though they are relatively uncommon.[101] It is now becoming apparent, however, that the minuteness of the surviving fragments may have kept the figures deceptively low: Elisabeth Crowfoot has several times noted textile fragments with mixed spinning (Z in one direction, S in the other). Though the fragments are too small for a patterned weave to be identified, they may derive from complex twills of this kind in which contrasting spinning direction would enhance the geometric woven pattern. The early Anglo-Saxon examples include some exceptionally rich deposits, including the Sutton Hoo Ship Burial and the Broomfield barrow. There are later examples from urban sites, including York and London.

The English patterned twills belong to a considerable corpus of similar, high quality fabrics known from north-west Europe. The earliest example is a Bronze Age 'mantle' from Gerum, Sweden; a piece of chequered cloth from Karlby, Denmark, belongs to the same era.[102] There are a number of examples from the western

Fig. 233 2 x 2 twill

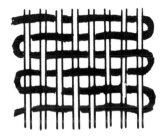
Fig. 234 2 x 2 twill

Fig. 235 Diamond twill.
Advisor Penelope Walton Rogers

[99] Bender Jørgensen, 'The textiles of the Saxons, Anglo-Saxons and Franks'.

[100] Personal communication from Marta Hoffmann, formerly of the *Norske Folkemuseum*, Oslo. This resemblance to rings, and hence to mail, may have given rise to the name *haberget*, well-documented from England and France in the twelfth and thirteenth centuries; c.f. the word *hauberk*, 'a mailcoat' (E. M. Carus-Wilson, 'Haberget: a medieval textile conundrum', *Medieval Archaeology*, 13 (1969), pp. 148–66). Diamond twills of the later period are much coarser than our examples and were probably woven on a horizontal treadle loom; Geijer, 'The textile finds from Birka', in Harte and Ponting, *Cloth and Clothing*, pp. 85–6.

[101] Bender Jørgensen, 'The textiles of the Saxons, Anglo-Saxons and Franks'.

[102] J. P. Wild, *Textile Manufacture in the Northern Roman Provinces* (Cambridge, 1970), p. 48; Hald, *Ancient Danish Textiles*, pp. 44–7.

territories of the Roman Empire, including Roman Britain,[103] and the weave may be depicted on some pieces of Roman provincial artwork: there are incised diamond patterns on the clothing of two women depicted on sculptures from Mainz (Figs 30, 58) and there is a similar effect on the trousers of a male figure ('a Parthian prisoner') depicted on a clay lamp found in Corfu, Greece.[104] Many of the surviving examples come from Viking Age Scandinavia and Iceland. They include the ninth-century Oseberg Ship Burial, the grave of a queen who had the wealth and taste to command the most prestigious goods available, and the tenth-century Viking cemetery of Birka, where patterned twills were found in more than forty graves.[105] Lise Bender Jørgensen's recent survey demonstrates that the centre of distribution appears to be the northern Netherlands and Frisia. This interestingly supports the suggestion made by Agnes Geijer in the 1930s when analysing the Birka textiles: that these luxury patterned twills should be identified with the *pallium fresonicum* or 'Frisian cloth' well-known to historians.[106] According to Charlemagne's biographer the Monk of St Gall, the Frankish Emperor sent some of this cloth to Haroun-al-Rashid in the ninth century.[107] There has been considerable discussion as to whether the patterned twills were native, northern European products, or whether they were imports, and if so, from where. (It is generally accepted that the role of the Frisians who gave their name to the cloth was that of traders rather than manufacturers.) Probably the answer is that some of them were native and some were imports. The Birka twills were of such consistently high quality that it was thought they were the work of skilled professional weavers[108] whose expertise was greater and more standardised than could be found locally. The Viking Age Scandinavian locations are consistent with the probability that this luxury cloth was traded on the international market: Birka was a busy trading port, so was Kaupang in Norway. The various other find spots in Norway are mostly coastal and suggest trading. Various possible non-Frisian sources have been discussed,[109] Agnes Geijer making the well-supported suggestion that the cloth was made in Syria and exported to the West.[110] Some

[103] Wild, *Textile Manufacture*, pp. 48–9, 98–100, 116.

[104] H. B. Walters, *Catalogue of the Greek and Roman lamps in the British Museum* (London, 1914), p. 74, No. 497.

[105] Geijer, *Birka, III*; Geijer, 'Textile finds from Birka' in Harte and Ponting, *Cloth and Clothing*; Hägg, 'Viking women's dress at Birka', in Harte and Ponting, *Cloth and Clothing*, pp. 316–50.

[106] Geijer, *Birka, III*, pp. 41–3.

[107] *Gesta*, II, para 9; Pertz, *Monumenta Germaniae Historica, Scriptores*, 7, 2, p. 752, line 41.

[108] Hoffmann, *Warp-weighted Loom*, pp. 229, 235.

[109] Notably H. Pirenne, 'Draps de frise ou draps de Flandre?' *Vierteljahrschrift für Social- und Wirtschaftgeschichte*, 7 (1909), pp. 308–15.

[110] A. Geijer, 'Var järnålderns "friska kläde" tillverkat i Syrien?' ['The *pallium fresonicum* of the Viking Age, was it manufactured in Syria?'] *Fornvannen*, 60 (1965), pp. 112–32 [English summary pp. 130–2].

of the best-quality Anglo-Saxon examples, such as the remains of a fine, linen pillowcase from Sutton Hoo, may have come from such a source, and it is possible that all the Anglo-Saxon patterned twills were imported through trade with Frisia. On the other hand, as we have seen, the weave was already known in pre-Anglo-Saxon times in north-west Europe, and the Anglo-Saxon examples make up a considerable corpus. It is quite possible that in this English material we have evidence of professional weaving among the Anglo-Saxons, and that it was from England that textiles were exported to Scandinavia and elsewhere. The complexity of the question is illustrated by the Oseberg textiles. Anne Stine Ingstad found three qualities of patterned twill among the fabrics in the Oseberg Ship Burial: one of mohair and such fine quality that she believed it to be Syrian; another typical of finds from burials in north-west Europe, possibly imported from the British Isles; and a third probably woven in the queen's own workshops, professional therefore, but Scandinavian.[111]

Three end twill (Figs 236, 237) which has a 2 x 1 pattern on one side and 1 x 2 on the other, is much less common than diamond or lozenge twill, but sometimes occurs in the same places. This weave, too, was found in the rich Sutton Hoo and Broomfield deposits, and at least one other example (from Lakenheath) is of very high quality. Since, as we have seen, this cloth is unlikely to have been woven on the warp-weighted loom as it does not take advantage of the natural shed, it has been considered that it was imported with (again) Syria as the suggested place of origin.[112] John-Peter Wild, however, has pointed out the relatively large numbers of these textiles from the Roman era which have been found in Germanic areas – Denmark, north and south Germany – and also in Britain,[113] which may imply that the barbarians of western Europe were making the cloth themselves. It is entirely possible therefore, that the Anglo-Saxons learned the art from their Continental kin; or from their Roman predecessors, and neighbours in Britain, with whom they probably intermarried and from whom they probably acquired the two-beam loom.

These weaves, tabby, 2 x 2 twill and the rarer diamond/lozenge twills and 2 x 1 twill, are those which have been found on clothing fasteners in furnished graves, and which no doubt derived from the garments of the people buried there. Pile-weaving, in which loops are inserted in the cloth during the weaving process, does not seem to have been popular among the pagan Anglo-Saxons, although I have pointed out a few possible remains of 'shaggy cloaks' from

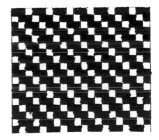

Fig. 236 2 x 1 twill

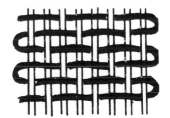

Fig. 237 2 x 1 twill

[111] A. S. Ingstad, 'The functional textiles from the Oseberg ship', in Bender Jørgensen and Tidow, *NESAT I*, pp. 85–96, at pp. 88–91.

[112] Hoffmann, *Warp-weighted Loom*, pp. 251–2.

[113] J. P. Wild, 'Some new light on Roman textiles', in Bender Jørgensen and Tidow, *NESAT I*, pp.10–22, at pp. 12–13.

rich, male graves (Chapter V, pp. 182–3). The technique of pile-weaving is well known from Viking context, however, and the Irish Vikings of York were probably dressing in pile-woven cloaks in the tenth and eleventh centuries.[114]

There is a little evidence for more elaborate weaves, but they do not seem to derive from clothing; sometimes these more unusual cloths seem to have wrapped grave-goods, especially weapons, even weapons which may not seem to us to be rare or precious. For example in Grave 105 at Lechlade, the metal of a spearhead preserved what appeared to be basket weave, a type of extended tabby,[115] and another spearhead at Buckland, Kent (Grave 4) had upon it the remains of what appeared to be Z-spun, S-ply tabby weave enhanced with either embroidery or soumak (wrapped) weave.[116] The helmet recently found at Wollaston, Northamptonshire, preserved some rare cloth in 'summer and winter' weave, which would have had a different appearance on each side.[117] This was perhaps from a bedcover or other ornamental textile. The Sutton Hoo Ship Burial included furnishing fabrics, particularly bedding, one of them (SH 14) a combination of soumak and tapestry weave in a geometric pattern, perhaps from a coverlet,[118] which gives some hints of the luxurious textiles with which wealthy Anglo-Saxons surrounded themselves.

Fibres

The majority of textiles surviving from Anglo-Saxon contexts are too mineralised for the fibre to be identified. Of those which have been identified, rather more are of sheep's wool (*wull*) than of vegetable fibre. The fleece type is, on the whole, what Michael Ryder categorises as 'generalised medium' and this was doubtless produced in England.[119] Very fine wool, such as is found in the Sutton Hoo Ship Burial,[120] may have been imported or it may testify to the survival of fine-woolled animals from the Roman period.[121] Finds of

---

[114] Pile weaving is found in Viking contexts in Scotland, the Isle of Man and Dublin as well as in Sweden, Poland and Iceland. T. Gabra-Sanders, 'A review of Viking-Age textiles and fibres from Scotland: an interim report', in Bender Jørgensen and Rinaldo, *NESAT VI*, pp. 177–85, at pp. 181–2.

[115] Hedges, in Boyle, Jennings, Miles and Palmer, *Lechlade*, p. 101.

[116] Crowfoot in Evison, *Buckland*, p. 190.

[117] P. Walton Rogers, unpublished.

[118] E. Crowfoot, 'The Textiles' in Bruce-Mitford, *Sutton Hoo*, 3 (1983), i, pp. 428–33.

[119] M. L. Ryder, 'European wool types from the Iron Age to the Middle Ages', in Bender Jørgensen and Tidow, *NESAT I*, pp. 224–38, at pp. 226–7.

[120] E. Crowfoot, 'The Textiles', in Bruce-Mitford, *Sutton Hoo*, 3 (1983), i, pp. 440–2, 456–7.

[121] I owe the suggestion of the survival of Romano-British sheep to Penelope Walton Rogers.

vegetable fibre are slightly less common.[122] This may reflect the rather more luxurious role of linen (*lin*, *linen*, or *twin*), something we can deduce from Bede's anecdote about St Etheldreda, who chose to wear wool rather than linen to mortify the flesh (Chapter IV, p. 133); but is also likely to result from various accidents of survival: that the woollen garments were more likely to be in contact with metal, which preserved them, than linen ones, which were perhaps used for underwear; that iron is kinder to wool than to linen[123] (and most brooch pins are iron); and that while wool may survive in waterlogged deposits, linen may not. (The Llan-gors linen garment was exceptional in that it was carbonised before being deposited in water.)[124] The finds may reflect geographical or cultural conditions too, wool being fairly quickly turned into garments, given a supply of pasture and sheep, whereas linen production takes several months and considerable organisation. As most of our textile evidence comes from furnished graves, and there are very few of these from later than the seventh century, we have no means of measuring the relative popularity of linen and wool in the later period.

Woollen fibres have been found in the various twill weaves, and less commonly, tabby. Linen is more usually associated with tabby.[125] The vast majority of our textile finds come from the backs of brooches, and it is clear from these that the woman's *peplos* and cloak were usually made of wool, though the *peplos* could also be of linen, perhaps for summer wear. The sleeved undergarment, to judge from the textiles attached to wrist clasps, was also wool. Textile on the fronts of brooches is much rarer, probably because the mourners who positioned the grave-goods would want jewellery to be displayed, and would not deliberately cover it; and also because, in accordance with archaeological practice before the significance of organic material was generally recognised, substances might be cleaned off the front of a brooch in order to reveal the ornament.

Where the textile on the front of a brooch is found to be linen, it is possible that we have the remains of a shroud, or a bedsheet wrapped round as a shroud (there is no evidence for the exclusive use of material as shrouds) or it may derive from a linen headdress, something which archaeologists are now positively looking for, as we have so little evidence about head-coverings from the early Anglo-Saxon period. An example is the richly-equipped Wakerley

---

[122] Penelope Walton Rogers will discuss the question of wool and linen survivals in her forthcoming monograph *Cloth and Clothing in Early Anglo-Saxon England, AD 450–700*. According to statistics from Textile Research, York, the total quantities are not so far apart as Lise Bender Jørgensen's figures suggest.

[123] Janaway, 'Corrosion preserved textile evidence: mechanism, bias and interpretation', pp. 21–9.

[124] Granger-Taylor and Pritchard, 'A fine quality Insular embroidery', in Redknap, Edwards, Youngs, Lane and Knight, *Pattern and Purpose*, p. 91.

[125] There are cases of linen in more complicated weaves, for example the broken diamond twill used for pillows at Sutton Hoo.

Grave 74, where the front of the square-headed brooch preserved tabby-woven flax.[126]

Finds from Finglesham, Kent[127] of linen threads on the backs of buckles from male graves, suggest that there, in the seventh century, men were wearing linen shirts or tunics which were belted; but usually fibres from the backs of buckles have been found to be wool. This tells only part of the story, as we can see from an elaborate, fifth-century buckle suite found in Mucking Grave 117 (Fig. 82), which was probably worn by a man, one in a position of authority. The buckle suite preserved an unusual 'sandwich' of organic material: linen, leather belt and woollen garment.[128]

Silk, which must always have been expensive and luxurious, seems to have been imported into England from almost the earliest days of Anglo-Saxon Christianity. Both silk thread and woven silks were destined for use in ecclesiastical vestments and hangings and were exchanged as prestige secular gifts. Our earliest authenticated example of silk (thread on a fragment of tabby-woven flax, perhaps a silk stripe or decoration on the linen) was found inside a small seventh-century box, which may have been a reliquary, in a child's grave at Updown, Kent. The textile fragment may have been a holy relic, snipped from an ecclesiastical vestment and perhaps associated with one of the first missionaries, such as St Augustine of Canterbury.[129] Bede tells us that a shirt ornamented with gold and a garment from Ancyra (*camisia cum ornatura in auro una et lena Anciriana una*) were given to the Christian convert King Edwin of Northumbria by Pope Boniface V in the early-seventh century.[130] The 'garment from Ancyra' was probably Byzantine silk.[131] Just a few years later another famous Northumbrian king, Oswald, was able to bestow silk and gold hangings on his religious foundations[132] and the archbishop of York also.[133] Some silks may have been imported into England only to be exported again with the eighth-century Anglo-Saxon missions to the Continent: two crudely patterned examples have survived in the Low Countries: an Asian silk associated with the relics of St Lebwin, now in Utrecht, the

---

[126] Crowfoot in Adams, Jackson and Badenoch, 'Wakerley', pp. 152–3.[127] Unpublished information from E. Crowfoot and S. Hawkes.

[128] The buckle suite is described in Suzuki, *The Quoit Brooch Style*, pp. 124–7. Fig. 3 and Plate 3. Unpublished information on the textiles from E. Crowfoot and W. T. Jones.

[129] Hawkes, 'The archaeology of conversion: cemeteries', in Campbell, *The Anglo-Saxons*, p. 49; E. Crowfoot, 'Textile fragments from "relic-boxes"', in Walton and Wild, *NESAT III*, p. 54.

[130] *Historia Ecclesiastica* II, 10; Colgrave and Mynors, *Bede*, p. 170.

[131] E. Crowfoot, F. Pritchard and K. Staniland, *Textiles and Clothing c.1150–c.1450: medieval finds from excavations in London* (London, 1992), p. 82.

[132] Dodwell, *Anglo-Saxon Art*, p. 129, citing Alcuini *De Pontificibus et Sanctis ecclesiae Eboracensis carmen*, lines 278–9; and J. Raine, *The Historians of the Church of York and its Archbishops*, (London, 1879).

[133] ... *serica suspendens peregrinis vela figuris* ... Alcuini *De Pontificibus*, line 1267; reference from Dodwell, *Anglo-Saxon Art*, p. 129.

Netherlands, and the European 'David silk' associated with Saints Harlindis and Relindis in Maaseik, Belgium.[134]

We can learn something about the nature of imported silks from the remains of precious cloths presented at various times to the shrine of the Northumbrian saint, Cuthbert, and preserved in his reliquary coffin. The tenth- or eleventh-century 'Rider' silk, a cloth probably of Persian origin, and named from the falconer figure incorporated in its design, was printed in gold.[135] The seventh-century 'Nature Goddess' silk, and the eighth- or ninth-century 'Earth and Ocean' silk, had their multicoloured designs woven in.[136] These magnificent textiles may have been used as wraps, rather than made up into vestments,[137] though a weft-patterned silk edged at the neck with a tablet-woven braid (reconstructed at Fig. 200) had been used to make a garment, tentatively identified by Hero Granger-Taylor as an eighth-century dalmatic.[138] Fawn-coloured tissued taffetas had probably been used as linings. These taffetas had probably been woven as early as the seventh century, although we do not know when they were imported.

Fragments from the grave of King Edward the Confessor, who died in 1066, show that the body was shrouded in a golden-coloured silk with a self-coloured pattern woven in a 'damask' technique. The design, of roundels with confronting creatures and conventional plants, is typically Byzantine.[139] The silk was not, probably, made as a shroud; it may have been a garment which the king wore in his lifetime (Chapter VII, p. 243). It must have been unusually opulent for an insular context, and we are fortunate to have first-hand evidence of the most luxurious fabrics in England at the close of the Anglo-Saxon era.

The importation of silk by personal gift was the rule rather than the exception in the seventh, eighth and ninth centuries. We have documentary evidence of silks being presented to English churches as early as the seventh and eighth centuries.[140] Individual pilgrims were able to purchase silks abroad for their churches at home (where they were used as altar cloths and hangings) or for their own use. Theodred, a tenth-century Bishop of London, bequeathed in his will *þere gewele massehakele þe ic on Pauie bouhte* 'the yellow cope which I bought in Pavia'.[141] Pavia, capital of Lombardy

---

[134] Crowfoot, Pritchard and Staniland, *Textiles and Clothing*, pp. 83–4.

[135] G. Brett, 'The "Rider" silk', in Battiscombe, *Relics of St. Cuthbert*, pp. 470–83.

[136] J. F. Flanagan, 'The Figured-Silks', in Battiscombe, *Relics of St. Cuthbert*, pp. 484–525.

[137] Elisabeth Crowfoot has pointed out to me that there is no sign of sewing on the three large silks.

[138] Granger-Taylor, 'The weft-patterned silks', in Bonner, Rollason and Stancliffe, *St Cuthbert, his Cult and Community*, pp. 303–27.

[139] Granger-Taylor, 'Byzantine textiles', in Buckton, *Byzantium*, pp. 16–17.

[140] Lull to York (Tangl, *S. Bonifatii et Lulli Epistolae*, No. 125, p. 263, lines 5–6); Wilfrid to Ripon (B. Colgrave (ed.), *Eddius Life of St Wilfrid — The Life of Bishop Wilfrid by Eddius Stephanus* (Cambridge, 1927), p. 120). See also p. 298, nn. 132, 133.

[141] Whitelock, *Wills*, p. 4, lines 25–9.

in northern Italy, and on the pilgrims' route from England to Rome, was an important trading centre for eastern fabrics.[142]

The motifs of the Llan-gors needlework suggest that designs from imported woven silk were copied in fine embroidery. Innovatory motifs in manuscript illumination from the eighth century onwards are also thought to have been copied from silks; clearly these exotic textiles were influential.

Silk garments had been available to royalty since the seventh century, as we have seen, but silk gradually became accessible to wider, and lower, social circles: the Monk of St Gall records that Carolingian courtiers wore silk (from Pavia) in the ninth century.[143] The earliest example from Anglo-Saxon secular context (apart from the Updown grave) is a double layer of plain silk cut in a circle and gathered to cover a round piece of copper alloy, associated with a mid-seventh-century grave and smith's hoard found at Tattersall Thorpe, Lincolnshire. The object has the appearance of a silk-covered button, but with no visible means of attachment it may have been an amulet.[144] The earliest evidence of secular wearing of silk (as opposed to amuletic use) may come from brocading on a tablet-woven braid from a woman's grave at Norton.[145] Urban excavation demonstrates that by the late Anglo-Saxon period silk was not uncommon. As discussed in Chapter VI, complete and frgamentary silk caps have been recoved from several Viking cities both in England and Ireland (Figs 184–6). From Milk Street, London, there are the remains of a silk ribbon, 9 mm wide, dyed red and blue, and two silken cords, one probably yellow, the other red.[146] A royal present of silk was still significant enough to be documented – as was King Edgar's gift to Kenneth, King of the Scots, in 975[147] – but by the tenth and eleventh centuries the importation of luxury textiles was no longer primarily a personal matter, since professional merchants had established regular trade, as attested by Ælfric (Chapter VI, p. 202). Certainly the imported silk found a ready market. It was still much in demand for ecclesiastical purposes, and wealthy seculars too were probably using silk for hangings and cushions as well as clothing.[148]

[142] Dodwell, *Anglo-Saxon Art*, p. 151.

[143] Pertz, *Monumenta Germaniae Historica, Scriptores*, 7, 2, p. 760, line 41.

[144] E. Crowfoot, 'Textiles', in D. A. Hinton, *A Smith in Lindsey: the Anglo-Saxon grave at Tattersall Thorpe, Lincolnshire*, The Society for Medieval Archaeology Monograph Series, 16 (Leeds, 2000), pp. 94–6. Hinton (p. 116) dates the burial to between *c.* 640 and *c.* 670.

[145] The example is included by Elisabeth Crowfoot in her account of silk in early secular burials in 'Textiles' in Hinton, *A Smith*, p. 95. The suggested identification is made on the grounds of fineness and lack of spin, in P. Walton Rogers, 'Textile remains', in S. J. Sherlock and M. G. Welch, *An Anglo-Saxon Cemetery at Norton, Cleveland* (London, 1992), pp. 57–61.

[146] Pritchard, 'Textiles from recent excavations', p. 197. Most of the Milk Street finds were from pits.

[147] According to the thirteenth-century chronicler, Roger of Wendover; H. O. Coxe (ed.), *Rogeri de Wendover Chronica sive Flores Historiarum*, 4 vols (London, 1841–2), I, p. 416.

[148] Hangings and cushions in ecclesiastical context are illustrated in Dodwell, *Anglo-Saxon Art*, plates 19–20 and hangings in secular context plates 33–5. Dodwell discusses textiles as wall hangings and room dividers in secular context at p. 132.

Although there is documentary and archaeological evidence of many silk textiles in late Anglo-Saxon England, we should not underestimate the value of these fabrics. C. R. Dodwell interpreted a remark of Bede's about the value of some textiles to imply that the price of one silk 'would have kept one and a half families for life'.[149] Against this, is the evidence that Londoners of the tenth century could afford to throw away silk ribbons. There is of course, a difference in scale: a silken robe, elaborately patterned and perhaps encrusted with embroidery, would be a luxury for the highest in the land, and it might be recycled from secular use to ecclesiastical and would be carefully stored when not required. A cord or ribbon was a utilitarian thing, perhaps in constant use; but both had been laboriously extracted from the silk worm cocoon, dyed, woven and imported from the East, with all the dangers and expenses that the journey entailed. If prosperous urban dwellers could be so blasé about silk cords and ribbons, these things must have become fairly commonplace.

The silks discussed so far were imported already woven. It is evident that silk thread was also imported and a significant quantity of silk embroidery survives. It is certain that this work is English, not imported, for there is documentary evidence about English embroideresses as well as the indisputably English embroideries preserved among the relics of St Cuthbert, which anticipate the southern English Winchester Style in their decoration as well as carrying an 'inscription' in Latin (which utilises the Old English letters ash (Æ) and eth (Ð)) stating that they were made to the orders of an English queen for an English bishop (p. 311).[150] The Llan-gors needlework, which may be Anglo-Saxon or Welsh but is certainly Insular, is carried out in two different qualities of silk thread, 2-ply for the motifs and a shiny, unplied thread for the background. The fact that the needlework is used to create a background as well as the primary motifs shows no desire to economise on either time or materials (as in the making of the Bayeux 'Tapestry' where the woollen embroidery was set against the plain background of the linen weave), though the fact that the garment was apparently only embroidered on visible areas suggests practical husbandry of resources. This 'shirt' was also trimmed with silk: a double cord covered the seams and edged the hem and there was also a belt loop of silk ribbon, made in a warp-faced tabby weave.[151] Silk threads for sewing and embroidery might be marketed in relatively small quantities, but silk was apparently being woven in western Europe by the eighth or ninth century and if the English were involved in

---

[149] Dodwell, *Anglo-Saxon Art*, p. 145.

[150] R. Freyhan, 'The place of the stole and maniples in Anglo-Saxon art of the tenth century', in Battiscombe, *The Relics of St Cuthbert*, pp. 409–32.

[151] Granger-Taylor and Pritchard, 'A fine quality Insular embroidery', in Redknap, Edwards, Youngs, Lane and Knight, *Pattern and Purpose*, pp. 92, 97.

this industry considerable amounts of silken thread must have been coming into the country.[152]

The Anglo-Saxons used the words *seoluc* and *side* for silk, but they also used the word *godweb* for very luxurious cloth. The meaning behind this compound word is not simply 'good cloth' but 'a godly or divine cloth'. The term was used to translate Latin *purpura*, which literally means 'purple' or 'purple cloth'. Dodwell, however, has suggested that the Anglo-Saxons did not use the terms *godweb* and *purpura* for the purple-dyed silk which was a not uncommon luxury at the time, but reserved them for some very special material. English churches owned vestments of red, white, green and black *purpura*. Some descriptions imply that there was more than one colour in it. Essentially *godweb/purpura* was thick and irridescent. Dodwell argues convincingly that this material was shot-silk taffeta.[153] Patricia Cooper has suggested to me that the painting of the Evangelists' garments in the seventh-century *Lindisfarne Gospels*, which combine starkly contrasting colours such as red and green, is depicting shot silk.[154]

The finishing processes

The processes by which linen and woollen fabrics were 'finished' were to become major industries in the later Middle Ages: as early as the twelfth century the Lower Brook Street area of Winchester had become a centre for fulling and dyeing,[155] and there were no doubt similar urban concentrations in other towns. The finishing processes for wool included fulling – scouring, beating and bleaching the cloth – teasing, in which the nap of the cloth was raised with teasels, and shearing the raised surface, a procedure which might be repeated several times.[156] We do not know how early these processes became popular. The verb *tæsan*, 'to tease wool' and the noun *fullere* 'a fuller' are Old English words; but the fact is, that of the many fragments of textile from the Anglo-Saxon period, there

---

[152] An English provenance has been suggested for the 'David silk' now in Maaseik, Belgium (Budny and Tweddle, 'The Maaseik embroideries', pp. 72–3) but this is not universally accepted; cf. Crowfoot, Pritchard and Staniland, *Textiles and Clothing*, p. 84.

[153] Dodwell, *Anglo-Saxon Art*, pp. 145–50. Interestingly, the term 'scarlet', which appeared in European languages in the eleventh century, was also originally applied to a kind of cloth and also only later confined to the bright red colour; J. H. Munro, 'The medieval scarlet and the economics of sartorial splendour', in Harte and Ponting, *Cloth and Clothing*, pp. 13–70.

[154] In an unpublished MA essay. I am grateful to Patricia Cooper for this exciting insight. The Evangelists' portraits may be found in colour in T. D. Kendrick *et al.*, *The Lindisfarne Gospels (Codex Lindisfarnensis)*, 2 vols (London, 1956).

[155] D. Keene, 'The textile industry', in Biddle, *Winchester*, 7.i, pp. 200–14 at p. 201.

[156] R. Patterson, 'Spinning and weaving' in C. Singer, E. J. Holmyard, A. R. Hall and T. F. Williams, *A History of Technology*, 7 vols (Oxford, 1956–78), 2 (1956), pp. 191–220, at pp. 214–17.

are very few examples, early or late, which have been teaselled. The rare examples from Anglo-Saxon graves are mostly from sites where there had been continuity of occupation since Roman times and where the Anglo-Saxons almost certainly learned the process from the Romano-Britons.[157] Whether the art was otherwise lost, or whether it continued to be used in some areas is, so far, uncertain. No tubs or other vessels for fulling have so far been identified. However, these finishing processes would produce a thick, felted cloth, the luxury feature of which was the soft finished surface. Such processes would have been inappropriate for the diamond- or lozenge-patterned twills which were the most luxurious product of the warp-weighted loom, for the woven geometric pattern which had taken great skill to achieve would have been obscured by the finishing. This fact does not completely rule out fulling – there is a Romano-British diamond twill from Verulamium which had been finished in this way[158] – but the weave and the finishing are not obviously compatible.

Almost certainly the conception of a luxury woollen fabric changed over the Anglo-Saxon period, and this may have been associated with a change of loom. It seems likely that, together with absorbing other southern European influences, the Anglo-Saxons came to demote the warp-weighted loom to the more mundane purposes, while another kind of loom and elaborate finishing processes came to be the rule for fine clothes. Yet patterned twills continued to be made in late Saxon times (and beyond). They have been found, for example, in eleventh-century context in the City of London.[159] This type of cloth, and the loom on which it was originally woven, continued to be popular among the Scandinavian peoples. Broken diamond twill, as already stated, has been found in Viking Age Scandinavia and it has also been found in Anglo-Scandinavian York.[160]

Linen, too, was subject to finishing processes such as bleaching and smoothing. Glass linen smoothers, which could be heated to carry out this 'ironing' process, have been found in women's graves in Scandinavia and were evidently high-status possessions. Heated stones might have served the same purpose for lower-ranking women. Small examples of glass 'smoothers' from urban

---

[157] E. Crowfoot 'Textiles' in Cook, *Fonaby*, pp. 96, 108 n.10; The unpublished examples are from Mucking (three cases; one Roman, two Anglo-Saxon) and Stretton-on-Fosse (four cases). There have been two possible cases from Fonaby. Penelope Walton Rogers has identified a small number of napped (teaselled) fabrics from Anglo-Saxon cemeteries, such as West Heslerton. They probably derive from cloaks and belonged to prosperous individuals; Walton Rogers, *Textile Production at 16–22 Coppergate*, p. 1774.

[158] Wild, *Textile Manufacture*, p. 84.

[159] Pritchard, 'Textiles from recent excavations', p. 195.

[160] J. Hedges, 'Textiles', in MacGregor, *Anglo-Scandinavian finds from Lloyds Bank, Pavement and other sites*, pp. 102–27.

context in late Anglo-Saxon and Anglo-Scandinavian towns may have been used in laundering linen.[161] Carved whalebone plaques have been found associated with some linen smoothers and have been thought to relate to the operation of 'finishing' linen. They are elaborately carved, however, and may have had cult status. They are not generally found in Viking Britain, but there is an isolated example from a boat burial at Scar, Orkney, Scotland, which may have been brought from Norway by its owner, and another, apparently from eastern England.[162] Perhaps boards of wood, which have not survived, were also used in ironing or pressing operations.

Colour

Most archaeological textiles are brown, having been rendered this colour by the process of deterioration. This consistent dark shade is at odds with the evident enjoyment of bright colours the Anglo-Saxons exhibit in their polychrome jewellery and bright paintings. There are sufficient coloured tablet-woven braids (from St John's, Cambridge (Plate 6), and two cases from Morning Thorpe)[163] to suggest that these edges and decorations to garments were dyed, but visible colour in dress fabrics is rare, and the majority of the textiles from our period which have been scientifically examined have not yielded evidence of dye. Exceptionally, a twill fabric from the rich male burial in Broomfield Barrow (B. 3) had light and dark stripes and another in Grave 23 at Fonaby appeared to be striped.[164] A tabby weave from Mucking (Grave 123, unpublished) had a dark check pattern. There are rather more examples of mixed spinning, in which S-spun threads form stripes or checks in predominantly Z-spun cloth. These have been noted at Finglesham, Mucking and Worthy Park, while at Ardale, Essex, a weft stripe may have been woven into a broken diamond twill weave, unusual 'since it breaks up rather than enhances the woven pattern'.[165] It is possible that many other textiles which only survive in tiny fragments would have revealed a systematic pattern if enough of them had survived. As no colour distinction is visible in these examples, it is possible that the checks and stripes in these, and similar textiles from Iron Age Danish sites, were 'shadow patterns' produced entirely by

[161] Thetford, London, Winchester and York; Walton Rogers, *Textile Production at 16–22 Coppergate*, pp. 1777–8.

[162] O. Owen, 'The carved whalebone plaque', in O. Owen and M. Dolland, *Scar: a Viking boat burial on Sanday, Orkney* (East Lothian, 1999), pp. 73–86. Olwen Owen associated the plaques, and the weaving of flax, with the goddess Freyja. Linen smoothers are also discussed here.

[163] See p. 58, note 75.

[164] E. Crowfoot, 'Textiles' in Cook, *Fonaby*, pp. 91, 96.

[165] E. Crowfoot, 'Textiles from Ardale Anglo-Saxon cemetery', in Wilkinson, *Archaeology and Environment in South Essex*, p. 55.

changes in spinning direction. However, analysis of a Danish example and one from Mucking Grave 975 suggests that there was originally a colour contrast which has now been lost. In the Mucking example there was evidence of a difference in natural pigmentation as well as additional dyeing. It is entirely possible that early Anglo-Saxon cloth was much brighter and more varied than hitherto imagined. Some of the finely-woven checked and striped fabric may have been used for pouches, since it was found at the waist/hip area, but what was possibly striped textile was found on a saucer brooch (one of a pair) from Barrington A (Grave 79, female) and on a pin or nail found with a skeleton at Worthy Park (Grave 63, female), so it may also have been used for garments.[166]

It is likely that there was always a social distinction between those who possessed expensively (and permanently) dyed clothes and those who did not, but this does not mean that the costume of the peasant was monochrome. There was great variety in the natural colour of fleeces, with brown, black, white and grey sheep,[167] and it would have been possible to achieve striped or checked effects by using contrasting wools.[168] Dyestuffs may have been made from native vegetation, such as woad and lichens, which have not survived in the textile remains. It is a fact that modern craft workers can create a wide variety of colours, in many shades, from plants which are believed to have been available to the Anglo-Saxons; but we lack contemporary evidence for the earlier part of the period. We do not know if ordinary people had the knowledge, or the desire, to steep cloth in dyestuffs for a considerable length of time, to produce colour that might rapidly diminish in the rain. Traces of madder have been found in sherds of domestic-sized (c. 2 litre) pots, some of which have sooting indicating that they were heated on a fire. The earliest example is Middle Saxon, from Canterbury. There are late Saxon examples from Thetford and London and late-Saxon to early-Norman from Winchester. These may attest small-scale dyeing activity, reddening a small quantity of yarn, perhaps, though madder could be put to various uses (for example as a medicine) and we cannot be certain the pots were for dyeing fibre.[169] Dyeing cloth on a commercial scale probably took place in Anglo-Scandinavian York for, though no vats for dyeing and mordanting have been found, the concentrations of dye-stuff remains found

---

[166] Elisabeth Crowfoot discusses the evidence of striped and checked textiles in Europe, especially in relation to the Worthy Park finds, in unpublished Ancient Monuments Laboratory Report 1709.

[167] Ryder, 'European wool types', p. 229.

[168] Cf. Broomfield Barrow; E. Crowfoot, 'Textiles', in Bruce-Mitford, *Sutton Hoo*, 3 (1983), i, pp. 468, 470–1.

[169] Walton Rogers, *Textile Production at 16–22 Coppergate*, p. 1769; P. Walton Rogers, 'Identification of dye on Middle Saxon pottery from Christ Church College', *Canterbury's Archaeology 1996–7* (21st annual report) 1999, p. 36. There are earlier (seventh-century) examples from Northern Ireland and western Scotland. I am grateful to Penelope Walton Rogers for this reference.

there were sometimes on such as scale that they 'must represent disposal of waste from a dye-bath'.[170] The dye plants madder, woad, dyer's greenweed and weld were found in York, all of which could have been grown locally. They would yield, respectively, blue, red, yellow and again yellow. A clubmoss, probably imported from Scandinavia, had perhaps been used as a mordant to fix in the cloth the colours from the madder, dyer's greenweed and weld.[171]

A wealthy person might own clothes in a variety of colours. The textiles deposited at Sutton Hoo in the early-seventh century were dyed blue with woad, yellow with weld and possibly red with madder.[172] Æthelgifu's will (Chapter VI, p. 211), with its mention of her blue kirtle as well as her brightest and her brownish kirtles, gives a glimpse of the range of colour in a wealthy woman's wardrobe towards the end of the Anglo-Saxon period. Scraps of silk from late Anglo-Saxon London (p. 300) were coloured red, blue and yellow. A few Continental examples, far better preserved than anything from England, widen the picture: the sixth-century Frankish lady wearing a ring inscribed 'Arnegundis', with her violet-coloured tunic under a red gown;[173] the Norwegian Oseberg queen in a gown of red, with a red dress over it, dyed with madder which was probably imported from the east; and her attendant in a gown of blue, dyed with woad; the high-ranking Danish Viking man at Mammen, in red and blue clothing, enhanced with red and purple silks and red and blue embroidery. The colours were produced by madder and lichen purple, which were probably imported, as well as indigotin.[174]

Aldhelm wrote of clothes being brightly coloured (Chapter IV, p. 134) using the Latin terms *coccinea* and *iacintina* to describe the shades, which later Anglo-Saxons glossed *wealræd* (or *weolcræd*) and *hæwen* or *wæden*, respectively. Bede confirms that the Anglo-Saxons made a dye from shellfish[175] (Old English *wealc*, 'a whelk', 'cockle'). As Ælfric's *Mercator* testifies, dyestuffs were regularly imported (Chapter VI, p. 202). In ancient (Classical) times, it seems to have been normal to dye an entire fleece or hank of linen.[176] In the medieval period textile workers might dye an entire garment after weaving (as was the case with the Oseberg queen's costume) or they could dye some of the spun yarn before weaving. The latter method would have been used if a coloured pattern was to be woven in, as, for

[170] A. R. Hall, Untitled, in Walton Rogers, *Textile Production at 16–22 Coppergate*, p. 1767.

[171] Walton Rogers, *Textile Production at 16–22 Coppergate*, pp. 1766–71.

[172] M. C. Whiting, Appendix to E. Crowfoot, 'Textiles', in Bruce-Mitford, *Sutton Hoo*, 3 (1983), i, p. 465.

[173] Werner, 'Frankish royal tombs', p. 212.

[174] P. Walton, 'Dyes and wools in textiles from Mammen (Bjerringhøj), Denmark', in M. Iversen (ed.), *Mammen: grav, kunst og samfund i vikingetid*, Jysk Arkæologisk Selkskabs Skrifter 28 (Aarhus, 1991), pp. 139–43.

[175] *Historia Ecclesiastica* I, i; Colgrave and Mynors, p. 14.

[176] Wild, *Textile Manufacture*, p. 80.

example, in a striped cloth like that from Broomfield, or for a multicoloured tablet-woven braid. Embroidery threads, silk from the St Cuthbert vestments and wool from the Bayeux 'Tapestry', still bright after a thousand years, demonstrate the impressive range of colours and shades available in the tenth and eleventh centuries. On the Llan-gors garment, the device of changing the direction of blocks of background needlework added to the variety of surface effect in addition to the original colour-contrast.

Sewing

This is a subject about which we know relatively little. There is hardly any sewing preserved on the many textile fragments from Anglo-Saxon graves of the pagan period. Occasionally there survives the remains of the thread with which a pair of wrist clasps was stitched to a braided wrist band, for example Wakerley Grave 80 had one such thread. A stitched seam was preserved on keys in the grave of a woman or girl, dating to the late-seventh century, at Buckland; Elisabeth Crowfoot suggests it could either be the seam of a skirt or the seam of a bag,[177] but unfortunately there was very little in the grave to clarify what the dress might have been like.[178] There are fragments of many tablet-woven braids preserved on brooches, and a few selvedges preserved on grave-goods, and we can see that, while it was the custom to make clothing from whole pieces of cloth, which were edged with starting/closing borders and selvedge, there would be no raw, cut edges, and no necessity for hemming.

Many of the more sophisticated tailoring techniques, such as varieties of seam, facings, gores and buttonholing have been thought to have been introduced in the later Middle Ages when dress fashions changed to more fitted, body-revealing styles,[179] but the middle and late Anglo-Saxon periods were already displaying skilled and detailed tailoring. The Llan-gors garment has both small triangles worked in buttonhole stitch to reinforce points where seams come together, and a triangular gore, the function of which is not clear.[180] Robin Netherton's reconstruction of the gown with hanging sleeves from the Bayeux 'Tapestry' reveals unexpectedly economical and clever cutting (Fig. 238). Tailoring was already a

---

[177] E. Crowfoot, 'The textiles', in Evison, *Buckland*, pp. 190–5, at p. 195.

[178] There were no brooches, only a buckle and belt mount, the remains of keys, a knife and possibly a bone or antler comb which might have been attached to a belt, and a lace tag at the right foot; Evison, *Buckland*, p. 242.

[179] See Kay Staniland's discussion in Crowfoot, Pritchard and Staniland, *Textiles and Clothing*, pp. 150–98.

[180] Granger-Taylor and Pritchard, 'A fine quality Insular embroidery', in Redknap, Edwards, Youngs, Lane and Knight, *Pattern and Purpose*, pp. 97–8.

recognised occupation in the tenth century when Ælfric included in his Latin/Anglo-Saxon *Glossary* the items *sartor:seamere*; *sartrix: seamestre*[181] and Wynflæd bequeathed a slave who was *ane semestran*. We have more evidence of Anglo-Saxon sewing skills from soft furnishings than from dress: the seams joining the sections of linen which make up the Bayeux 'Tapestry' are so neat as to be almost invisible, while the seams on luxurious cushion- or pillow-covers in the Sutton Hoo Ship Burial and at Welbeck Hill had been concealed by decorative sewing or plaits.[182] Hero Granger-Taylor and Frances Pritchard describe the constructional sewing of the Llangors garment as 'high quality ... carefully planned and executed'.[183] The garment had a narrow hem and silk cords, probably made by finger-looping, to conceal the seams which were stitched from the outside. Surviving examples of embroidery, which is an ornamental use of basic sewing stitches, show the competence of the exponents. They must have had good, fine needles, a reliable supply of raw materials and much experience. The Mammen needlework demonstrates a sophisticated use of resources, with long-fibred wool used for embroidery and braiding (and sewing, it is implied but not stated) and shorter, softer, crimpier wools used, on the whole, for larger textiles.[184] Lower social classes of England may not have had access to such a range of wools, but we can assume they could sort the fibre available to them and use it accordingly.

Embroidery and other decoration

Embroidery is decorative sewing; it is closely related to the functional stitching and to ornamental sewing used for practical purposes. The Viking Orkney hood (p. 199), demonstrates the interrelationship. Unpretentious but intricate embroidery covered the sewing which attached a tablet-woven border. The hood had been darned and patched. The darning stitches were chain stitch, a form of sewing which would later evolve into a decorative, embroidery technique. English embroidery was to become famous in the later Middle Ages, when it was known as *opus anglicanum*. It was particularly exploited for the making of orphreys, the embroidered ornaments on ecclesiastical vestments, usually incorporating gold thread.[185] The traditions of embroidery, however, were clearly established in England long before the Norman Conquest. The Anglo-

[181] J. Zupitza (ed.), *Ælfrics Grammatik und Glossar* (Berlin, 1880), p. 190, line 6.
[182] E. Crowfoot 'The Textiles' in Bruce Mitford, *Sutton Hoo* 3 (1983), i, p. 422.
[183] Granger-Taylor and Pritchard, 'A fine quality Insular embroidery', in Redknap, Edwards, Youngs, Lane and Knight, *Pattern and Purpose*, p. 97.
[184] Walton, 'Mammen'.
[185] See A. G. L. Christie, *English Medieval Embroidery* (Oxford, 1938); D. King, *Opus Anglicanum: English medieval embroidery* (London, 1963).

Saxon embroiderers who are named are female, and seem to include both noblewomen and slaves.[186] Embroidery was probably
practised as a domestic craft and the finest work, involving gold,
was considered suitable for great ladies. Post-Conquest encomiasts
flattered Queen Edith by praising her creative talents,[187] and her
elaborate decoration of garments is specifically mentioned.[188] The
association of women with embroidery and embroidery with women
may have been proverbial in Anglo-Saxon times[189] and is certainly
the predominant impression that has been transmitted. However,
as Kay Staniland has shown, professional male embroiderers were
commonplace in the later Middle Ages,[190] and the possibility of
workshops employing male as well as female workers before the
Norman Conquest is something that should be considered, though
such an occupation is contrary to both the heroic and the ascetic
self-images of Anglo-Saxon masculinity which were traditionally
projected. The enormous Bayeux 'Tapestry' is clearly not an ama-
teur, domestic product but the output of (several) professional workshops with standardised techniques,[191] working fast and
economically, using linen and wool which are quite harsh materials in comparison to silk, which was often left to women's softer
hands.[192] Both male and female embroiderers are entirely possible.

From the pagan period there survive only a few fragments of
what were probably fairly unpretentious pieces of embroidery in
wool. From Alfriston, Sussex, there is evidence of a belt which may
have been embroidered in a geometric design. The textile was found
on the inner sides of iron tabs which were found with the belt equipment and was described as being of a delicate quadrangular pattern.[193] There is an oxidized scrap of what may have been a leaf
scroll design worked in stem and satin stitches on a piece of checked

[186] Dodwell, *Anglo-Saxon Art*, pp. 70, 72.

[187] Dodwell, *Anglo-Saxon Art*, p. 28 and p. 258, note 39 interprets the equation
of Edith to Minerva by the twelfth-century Osbert of Clare as a reference to her
skill at embroidery. See also p. 233.

[188] *De Gestis*, II, 220; Stubbs, *William of Malmesbury*, 1 (1887), p. 271. I take this
point from Dodwell, *Medieval Art*, p. 70 and p. 267, note 195. William of Malmesbury
is also a twelfth-century writer.

[189] *Fæmne æt hyre bordan geriseð*, 'It is fitting that a woman should be at her
embroidery' (or possibly '... at her table'. Cf. Bosworth/Toller *Dictionary*, p. 116
borde and *Supplement*, p. 101 *borda* II); Krapp and Dobbie, *The Exeter Book*, p.
159, line 63.

[190] K. Staniland, *Medieval Craftsmen: embroiderers* (London, 1991).

[191] I discuss the different lengths of linen and some of the variations between
the workshops in Owen-Crocker, 'The costume of the Bayeux "Tapestry"'.

[192] I am grateful to Joan Evans for discussing this with me. The association of
silk with women extended to the London silk trade being organised by women in
the later Middle Ages; M. K. Dale, 'The London silkwomen of the fifteenth century', *The Economic History Review*, 4 (1932–4), pp. 324–35.

[193] Grave 20; Griffith and Salzman, 'An Anglo-Saxon cemetery at Alfriston,
Sussex', pp. 34–5, 39–40, 44–5, and information from Lewes Museum.

cloth from Worthy Park, Hampshire,[194] and from Kempston, Bedfordshire, the remains of an interlace design in red, blue and yellow worked on a lozenge twill fabric which may have been dark brown.[195]

The fragmentary garment from Llan-gors (Plates 9, 10), which is probably early-tenth-century, has fine silk embroidery in thread-counted stem stitch, passing over three and back under one thread of the base linen textile. The technique is closely related to soumak brocading (or 'wrapped weave') but unlike the latter is worked at right angles to the weft as well as parallel to it.[196] Since this recent discovery is our only example of (presumably) secular embroidered clothing from the later Saxon period, it is worth considering three other major examples of late Anglo-Saxon embroidery to illustrate its range and technique. There are two groups of embroidered vestments which are generally accepted as late Anglo-Saxon work,[197] the Maaseik and the St Cuthbert (Durham), embroideries; and the eleventh-century Bayeux 'Tapestry', which is a wall-hanging, probably secular. The earliest, but least well preserved of the three, is a group of embroideries now stitched into the composite vestments known as the *casula* of Saints Harlindis and Relindis, kept at Maaseik, Belgium. The attribution to the saints (who seem to have flourished in the early-eighth century) is false, but recent research has demonstrated, on stylistic grounds, that the embroideries are southern English work of the late-eighth or early-ninth centuries. They seem to have been taken to the Continent soon after manufacture. The embroidery is worked on a linen background in silk threads of red, beige, green, yellow, light blue, dark blue and 'spun gold' threads. The designs were outlined in silk, then filled in with gold threads which were attached by surface couching. A polychrome background worked in split stitch and stem stitch, in silk, completely covered the backcloth. Three designs are extant: continuous arcading which contains and encloses areas of densely-packed ornament of zoomorphic, geometric, stem and foliate kinds; roundels containing birds and animals in profile; and four monograms, two with geometric, two with stem and leaf ornament. Large pearls, or beads, were once attached to the embroideries, edging the arcades and roundels, but these were not original and may have been added after the embroideries reached the Frankish Empire, though the work may have been carried out as early as the ninth

[194] Grave 75, found on the blade of a knife; a male grave. Unpublished information from E. Crowfoot and S. Hawkes.

[195] E. Crowfoot, 'Textile fragments from "relic-boxes"', in Walton and Wild, *NESAT III*, pp. 49–52.

[196] Granger-Taylor and Pritchard, 'A fine quality Insular embroidery', in Redknap, Edwards, Youngs, Lane and Knight, *Pattern and Purpose*, p. 94.

[197] Budney and Tweddle, 'Maaseik embroideries', pp. 86–7 also identify two minor pieces: some fragments of gold embroidery, perhaps ninth-century, among the relics of St Ambrose in Milan; and the simply-embroidered pouch from York, dating to the second half of the tenth century.

century.

The St Cuthbert vestments were among the treasures found in
the saint's coffin when it was opened in 1827. The needlework can
be dated by the embroidered words on a stole and maniple, recording that they were made on the orders of Ælfflæd, for Bishop
Frithestan: *ÆLFFLÆD FIERI PRECEPIT ... PIO EPISCOPO
FRIÐESTANO*. Ælfflæd was wife to King Edward the Elder,
Frithestan Bishop of Winchester. This set of vestments must have
been made in southern England about the second decade of the
tenth century and was probably presented to the saint's shrine by
Ælfflæd's step-son, King Athelstan, on his visit in 934. The embroidery, carried out on a background of woven silk, consists of
figures of prophets (stole) and ecclesiastics (maniple), together with
decorative motifs, all outlined in split stitch, in dark brown or green.
Hands, faces, costume and other items are filled in with a variety of
other colours. Spun gold is used for haloes and other details. Tablet-woven braids which edge these and other vestments in the collection, also a tablet-woven *cingulum*, are brocaded with tiny plant,
animal and geometric motifs.[198] The iconography of the embroideries is biblical and ecclesiastical, but the techniques and materials could equally well have been worn by wealthy seculars, and
Elizabeth Coatsworth has suggested that a third embroidery among
the Cuthbert relics may originally have been an item of secular
dress. Though known as 'Maniple II', this piece is generally accepted as the 'girdle' which King Athelstan presented to St
Cuthbert's shrine along with the more famous stole and maniple.
The supposed girdle is decorated in the same materials and techniques as the stole and maniple, but differently ornamented, with
plant and animal motifs (Plate 11). It bears the remains of a fringe
and, unlike the stole and maniple, was originally reversible, so that
if it hung free a pattern would be visible on either side.[199] Dodwell
seems to suggest that the golden bands mentioned in the wills of
various seculars were gold embroideries of this kind, designed to
be worn as fillets, and that the headband worn by Cnut's queen
(Fig. 159) and the stole flaunted by the allegorical *Pompa* (Fig. 174)
were bejewelled, golden embroideries of this kind.[200]

The Bayeux 'Tapestry' is not, technically, a tapestry but an
embroidery, since its decoration is worked with the needle after
weaving, not during the weaving process. This narrative frieze was
probably made for Bishop Odo of Bayeux, half-brother of William
the Conqueror, in the decade following the Norman Conquest. While

[198] Conveniently catalogued in Spies, *Ecclesiastical Pomp*, pp. 219–21.
[199] E. Coatsworth, 'The embroideries in the tomb of St Cuthbert', in N. I. Higham
and D. Hill (ed.), *Edward the Elder* (London, 2001), pp. 292–306. The embroidery
consists of two parallel strips which have been stitched together lengthwise, hence
its resemblance to a maniple.
[200] Dodwell, *Anglo-Saxon Art*, p. 175. In the subsequent paragraph gold hems,
cuffs and other gold embroideries are discussed.

conceived on a grand scale (the surviving hanging is 68.38 m long), it is not executed in a grand manner – it does not have the silk and gold of the Cuthbert and Maaseik pieces. Instead the embroidery is in wool on a linen background, and this linen background is left bare of needlework. Sometimes the white colour of the linen is used in a functional way as colour contrast to the embroidery, for example in a row of differently coloured shields. This exploitation of the linen background is a labour-saving technique. Outlines are worked in stem stitch, usually in a dark colour, though paler shades are sometimes used to convey skin tones. Stem stitch is also used for the letters of the Latin commentary, for narrow items like spears and to suggest folds in costume. Figures, animals and objects are filled in with laid-and-couched work; a range of shades of blues, yellows, reds, pinks and greens are used. Apart from its main, narrative panel, the 'Tapestry' has upper and lower borders, the content of which consists in part of illustrated fables and other episodes but mainly of plant and animal ornament. Though the style is sometimes informal, even frivolous, which shows a lighter-than-usual side of late Anglo-Saxon/early Norman taste, much of the borders is occupied by orderly pairings of birds and beasts in a variety of poses. The arrangement bears some resemblance to the lion border on the Llan-gors garment and gives an indication of designs that might have been used on other secular clothing, or on cushions and other soft furnishings. The St Cuthbert embroideries, too, contain supplementary ornament, including the acanthus leaf which was to become a major feature of Winchester Style art, and which was translated into ornament for clothing. As Dodwell points out, the acanthus leaf is depicted on the vestments of ecclesiastics shown in illuminated manuscripts, and he cites many documented references to plants, beasts and religious scenes being portrayed on vestments. Seed pearls or other jewels were stitched on to provide additional splendour.[201] It is reasonable to suppose that at least some of this ornament documented in ecclesiastical context also adorned the dress of rich seculars.

    Scandinavian survivals offer concrete evidence: the ninth-century garments of the Oseberg queen and her attendant were decorated with needlework. The queen's fine, tabby-woven undergown, which was made of wool, was embellished with appliqué work in wool, silk embroidery in rings and embroidered seams. Her attendant's gown also had appliqué work in a tabby-woven wool. The appliquéd shapes represented, among other things, animal heads.

---

[201] Dodwell, *Anglo-Saxon Art*, pp. 183, 185. The acanthus leaf is illustrated in plates 49 and 50 and colour plate D.

Appliqué and embroidery have also been found on the fronts of women's undergowns at Birka.[202] Perhaps most significant is the stem-stitch embroidery on the man's garment from Mammen, for there was clearly English influence on the decorative elements in this rich, tenth-century deposit, evident both from the Anglo-Scandinavian Jellinge Style ornament on an axe, and in the embroidered motifs themselves. The embroidered motifs at Mammen included stems and acanthus leaves, stylised beasts (lion or deer), facing one another, a leopard and human masks.[203] The woollen embroidery survives as isolated motifs and border, but Elisabeth Munksgaard has noted that needle holes which were not visible on the original photographs of the find indicate that the whole of the backcloth was covered with embroidery, probably in linen, which has not survived,[204] suggesting a dense covering of embroidery could be found on luxurious secular clothing (as confirmed by the recent find from Llan-gors), as well as ecclesiastical textiles such as those from Maaseik and Durham. The Mammen grave also contained a garment, possibly a cape, made of 2 x 1 twill, which was said to have been decorated with gold attachments in the shape of bees when it was found,[205] although these are now lost. This is reminiscent of the gold insects which were said to have decorated the costume of the Frankish King Childeric, excavated at Tournai, Belgium, in 1653.[206] The newly-discovered grave at Prittlewell offers evidence of Anglo-Saxon appliqué in the form of two small

[202] Ingstad, 'The functional textiles from the Oseberg ship', in Bender Jørgensen and Tidow, *NESAT I*, pp. 92, 94. Ingstad refers to the reconstruction of the Birka costume in I. Hägg, *'Kvinnodräkten i Birka. Livplaggens rekonstruktion pa grundval av det arkeologiska materialet'*, *Aun*, 2 (1974), which I have not seen. However, in Hägg, 'Viking women's dress at Birka', in Harte and Ponting, *Cloth and Clothing*, pp. 328, 334, part of the Birka costume is described as a tunic ornamented at the front with tablet-woven bands decorated with silver, mounted on silk. This tunic was worn over the shirt and under the *peplos*-type garment (called 'skirt' by Hägg, following Geijer, *Birka III*).

[203] Hald, *Ancient Danish Textiles*, pp. 103–4, 281–2, Figs 90–2, 294; Munksgaard, 'Embroideries', in Hogestol, *Festskrift til Thorleif Sjovold*. A striking replica of the Mammen clothing has been made, but it should be noted that while this is authentic as regards yarn types, weaving techniques and the vivid red and blue colouring, the style of the costume is unknown. The reconstruction is based on the image of Cnut in BL MS Stowe 944; E. Munksgaard,'Kopien af dragten fra Mammengraven', in Iversen, *Mammen*, pp. 151–54.

[204] Munksgaard, 'Embroideries', in Hogestol, *Festskrift til Thorleif Sjovold*, pp. 166–7.

[205] Munksgaard, 'Embroideries', in Hogestol, *Festskrift til Thorleif Sjovold*, p. 166, notes that the plate-gold bees were said to have been placed on the front of the costume in the shape of a cross, but dismisses this as 'hardly creditable, though there may be just a grain of truth in this statement'. She suggests that 'the bees were originally sequins placed here and there to give highlight to the embroideries' in comparison with metal or mica ornaments at Birka, Sweden; Ladby, Denmark; and Stengade II, Denmark, Grave 3.

[206] Werner, 'Frankish royal tombs', p. 202. Most of the treasure has since been stolen, but two surviving insects of the original three hundred, now identified as cicadas, are shown in Werner, Plate XXIX (b).

(30 mm) crosses, made of gold foil. It is thought that these had been placed upon or attached to the shroud, and indeed there is precedent for this in Lombard graves.[207]

If we want some idea of the kind of motifs that would be used to decorate English clothing we can clearly derive it from the surviving embroideries and the Scandinavian evidence, but we might also look to other manifestations of Anglo-Saxon art for inspiration. In particular, the Trewhiddle Style, which features lively, attractive little animals, normally very secular in their friskiness, yet effectively adapted into an *Agnus Dei* on Ethelswith's ring, would have translated well into needlework and is, indeed, reflected in the Maaseik embroideries. The Bayeux 'Tapestry' borders contain many animals, both realistic and fantastic, demonstrating competence both in translating living things into naturalistic embroidery and in depicting creatures in the characteristic art style (Jellinge) of the eleventh century.[208] The Llan-gors garment, embroidered with animals, and the Mammen textiles, with human and animal motifs reminiscent of both Borre and Jellinge Styles, confirm the interrelationship of designs found on metalwork, sculpture and embroidered clothing. Plant motifs were certainly worked in embroidery. The Bayeux 'Tapestry' border has numerous variations on a few basic designs, including the acanthus leaf and lighter tendrils, as well as a dumpy *fleur de lis*. As Dodwell noted, there is an acanthus leaf device on the shoulder of St Æthelwold's vestments as depicted in the *Benedictional*; acanthus plant ornament unites with humanistic in the St Cuthbert stole and maniple, and the so-called Maniple II, perhaps originally a secular item (p. 311), is entirely decorated in plant ornament. Scraps of gold embroidery from a grave in Winchester suggest plant scroll ornament on a stole or girdle.[209] The geometric designs which have been attested from gold-brocaded bands both from seventh-century graves[210] and from later (Winchester) context were enduring decorative resources.

It is disappointing that the artists depicting secular figures in manuscripts give us so little indication of this kind of decoration. There are only very stylised suggestions of ornament at the cuffs, usually dots or circles, and less often at the hems of garments and rare, faint suggestions of simple floral devices on the bodies of the garments. The flourishes on the garments in Tiberius C vi (Colour plate L), the decoration on the clothing of the Virgin in Harley

---

[207] S. Fuchs, *Die Langobardischen Goldblattkreuze aus der Zone Südwärts der Alpen* (Berlin, 1938), including p. 11 Abb. 1 (map of Italian finds) and p. 24 Abb. 7, an example of a cross from Schwabmünchen, Germany.

[208] See G. R. Owen-Crocker, 'Embroidered wood: animal-headed posts in The Bayeux "Tapestry"', in H. Damico and C. Karkov (ed.), *Aedificia Nova: papers in honour of Rosemary Cramp*, (Kalamazoo, MI, forthcoming, 2005).

[209] No. 1015; E. Crowfoot, 'Textiles' in Biddle, *Winchester*, p. 481.

[210] E. Crowfoot and Hawkes, 'Gold braids'; E. Crowfoot, 'Gold braids: addenda'; E. Crowfoot, 'Textiles' in Biddle, *Winchester*, 7.ii, ii, pp. 480–1.

2904 (Fig. 157), bands round King Edward's shins in the 'Tapestry' (Fig. 189) and the triple circles on King Edgar's costume in Tiberius A iii (Fig. 187) suggest more elaborate ornament, but are surely just a modest indication of what was actually worn.

IX

The significance of dress

What dress meant to the Anglo-Saxons

The naked and the clothed

Nudity has little place in Anglo-Saxon literature or art. The Anglo-Saxons did not celebrate the beauty of the human body and, unlike the convention of our own time, rarely indicated sexual activity by depicting a naked couple; instead procreation was signalled by pictures of well-wrapped partners lying decorously side by side. Since it was the norm for figures to be clothed, naked ones are particularly striking. They include the awkward and embarrassed Adam and Eve, before their exclusion from the Garden of Eden, which they quit dressed in Anglo-Saxon clothes (frontispieces i and ii); devils and monsters whose lack of civilized clothing demonstrates their 'otherness'; and unfortunate souls tumbling towards Hell, exposed and unprotected from the eternal punishment that awaits. The small naked figures in the borders of the Bayeux 'Tapestry', once dismissed as gratuitous pornography, are now being recognised as possible symbols or hints relating to the events portrayed in the main register of the frieze. The scene of a couple about to have sexual intercourse[1] may mean that, like the naked woman, Harold of England is about to be overcome by force; or, more poignantly, that this is the last time an English husband and wife will come together – he and his fellows are soon to die in the Battle of Hastings. Naked men beneath the ambiguous Ælfgiva scene[2] probably suggest that the sexual reputation of the historical Ælfgiva is questionable;[3] and naked corpses being stripped of mail coats beneath the death of King Harold at the Battle of Hastings[4] warn that

[1] Wilson, *Bayeux Tapestry*, Plates 52, 53. Interpretation may vary according to how one reads the woman's gestures: defensive or welcoming.
[2] Wilson, *Bayeux Tapestry*, Plate 17.
[3] J. B. McNulty, 'The Lady Aelfgiva in the Bayeux Tapestry', *Speculum*, 55 (1980), pp. 659–68; see also J. B. McNulty, *The Narrative Art of the Bayeux Tapestry* (New York, 1989).
[4] Wilson, *Bayeux Tapestry*, Plate 71.

the English people, like their dead soldiers, are now unprotected and will be despoiled by the Normans.

Beyond these instances, it is the clothed body that is seen in Anglo-Saxon art. Occasionally, in the line drawings of the Winchester School, one is conscious of an elegant human form beneath the drapery; but in most instances the person is represented by the dress; the clothes *are* the body.

Gender difference

Despite Tacitus's claim that the garments of the different sexes were similar in *Germania*, and the fact that some Old English garment-names were used of both men's and women's clothing, it is clear that gender difference was expressed through dress at all stages of the Anglo-Saxon period, and that the clothing of the two sexes did not evolve simultaneously.

Women's dress: identity and change

Women's clothing went through some major changes during the period, which interestingly reflect the greater cultural influences to which Anglo-Saxon England was subject. English women of the fifth and sixth centuries evidently dressed in a common Germanic costume, the presentation of which was important to the Anglo-Saxon people. The cultural and social identity of a woman was expressed through her costume: wealth, status and ethnicity (of family, perhaps as well as of the individual) were demonstrated through the appearance of the female. Prominent social messaging,[5] such as ethnicity and public rank, was provided by the choice of jewellery at neck and shoulders, while objects hanging at the waist (less public, more intimate in their range of visibility) such as girdle hangers and keys, perhaps reflected domestic function and status. Women's dress constantly evolved in response to foreign influences. In the sixth century the Scandinavian fashion of wrist clasps was transmitted to Anglian areas; and Frankish costume fashions, including brocaded fillets and front-fastening gowns, evidently appeared in Kent. By the seventh century, when the Anglo-Saxon kingdoms were deserting paganism for Christianity, women in all regions appear to have abandoned the *peplos*-type gown and paired brooches in favour of a sleeved robe and a front-fastening cloak which could be pulled up over the head. Long brooches gave way to circular. For the wealthy, a single polychrome disc brooch clasped a cloak at shoulder or chest, and pairs of pins sometimes clasped a garment (probably a veil) at the neck. The glass and amber beads of the pagan period disappeared, and necklaces of pendant bullae, amethyst drops and beads of gold and silver came to be worn by

[5] H. M. Wobst, 'Stylistic behaviour and information exchange', *Anthropological Papers* (University of Michigan), 61 (1977), pp. 317–42, esp. pp. 329–35.

high status women, with necklaces of beads strung across rings providing a less opulent imitation. The tenets and iconography of the new faith contributed to the change of costume: Christian modesty demanded that the head be covered; Byzantine art, imported by the Church, inspired the new necklaces and possibly the cloak and veil. A consciousness of Roman 'heritage' may have contributed to a revival of annular and penannular brooches. Often an Anglo-Saxon woman's jewellery proclaimed her piety: a cross pendant might adorn her necklace, or a cruciform perforation her belt buckle. By the tenth century a bulky headdress concealing hair and neck was the universal fashion for respectable Anglo-Saxon women, though it might be manifested in different forms: a scarf wrapped round the head or a wimple-type hood. A wide-sleeved gown or a robe shaped like a chasuble was worn over other layers of clothing and girdled with a soft sash. Tailoring techniques were given wider application in the late Anglo-Saxon period. Instead of making a *peplos* fit by wrapping the cloth round the body then pinning it into place, a woman wore a pre-shaped, sleeved garment. If a cloak needed clasping it would be fastened at the centre of the chest with a round brooch. Though jewellery is rarely displayed in art, archaeological evidence proves its existence and wills confirm that it was treasured and bequeathed. Golden bands (fillets or rings), were status symbols.

Though Viking women in Scandinavia wore a variant of the *peplos* and paired brooches costume into the tenth century and beyond, this dress-style does not seem to have lingered among the Viking settlers of England. The appearance of Anglo-Viking women, however, at least in the north and west of England, probably differed from that of Anglo-Saxon, especially in regard to the hair and headdress, with women of Scandinavian origin possibly wearing their hair uncovered, in a 'bun' or plait, or wearing a close-fitting cap which could be tied beneath the chin or under the hair at the back like a scarf, while Anglo-Saxon women were influenced by Carolingian and ultimately Byzantine styles of headdress.

Men's dress: conservatism and the manly image

Secular male dress seems to have changed little over the Anglo-Saxon period, though we must rely heavily on Continental evidence for the earlier centuries since male grave-goods generally reveal little or nothing about dress. The characteristic Germanic costume of short woollen tunic, trousers and a rectangular cloak fastened by a circular brooch seems to have remained in use throughout the period although other garments such as fur jerkins, ponchos, 'shaggy' cloaks and a hooded or unhooded coat may also have been known. Probably in the earlier centuries of our period trousers were rather loose, and perhaps bound to the legs at intervals, but by the tenth century they became more close-fitting, like tights, and were often bound by textile or leather garters wound repeatedly round the shins. In the pagan period, belts could be quite elaborate, with buckles and sometimes with ornamental plates, but by the tenth century they seem to have become less conspicuous; it appears that a girdle, rather than a rigid belt, often secured the tunic at this time. In the pagan period men, like women, had carried tools at the belt but there is little evidence of this in later centuries. From the seventh century at least men wore shoes, though they often carried out manual labour barefoot.

A major innovation in male costume comes towards the end of the period in the form of an ankle-length gown, confined at the waist by a sash, and sometimes worn with a long cloak fastened at the centre of the chest or at one shoulder by a brooch. This costume seems to have been confined to men of high rank, who might also own the short costume. Wealthy men would have had access to silk, and royalty and other influential persons would have been the recipients of gifts which introduced foreign styles to a limited circle. There may have been a lingering perception, as expressed by Charlemagne, that foreign styles were effete and traditional Germanic garments more manly. However, the late Anglo-Saxon period seems to have brought a taste, indeed a need, for ostentatious display in the clothing of monarchs, which required careful balancing by their biographers and portraitists. Kings with imperial pretentions must dress accordingly, yet in their role as patrons of the Church must favour simplicity; in particular, Edward the Confessor's public image of sanctity required that his personal tastes be ascetic. We find this conflict resolved in the very selective luxury shown in the portrait of Cnut[6] and the assertion by Edward's biographer that the kings' clothing was chosen by his wife.[7] In general, however, men seem to have been astonishingly conservative about clothing over the centuries. There have, of course, been fashions and experiments, but the outline of a twenty-first-century man, in a longish sweater and trousers, is little different from the stock Anglo-Saxon shape in tunic and trousers.

At all stages in Anglo-Saxon history men were called upon to fight, the less prosperous with spears, the richer with swords, and from the seventh century, scramasaxes. The sword was probably in most cases suspended from a diagonal baldric, though in the eleventh century there is evidence of a sword belt as distinct from the tunic belt. In the early period helmets and mailcoats were rare and must have been status symbols of major importance; by the Norman Conquest they seem to have become more common and standardised.

---

[6] See my forthcoming paper, 'Pomp, piety and keeping the woman in her place'.
[7] See Tyler, 'Wings incarnadine', *passim*.

Dress and status

Social differences would have been instantly visible. Simply woven cloth would have been distinguishable from sophisticated patterned weaves and rare imported fabrics, particularly to women, who constantly worked cloth with their hands. The differences largely lost to us (because of deterioration through time) between textiles which were undyed, home dyed and dyed with expensive materials would have been obvious to the Anglo-Saxons themselves. Silk garments, silk edging to wool or linen garments and decoration with embroidery, especially gold, would have distinguished expensive clothes, silk becoming increasingly available to the prosperous urban dweller by the end of the period. Wealthy men and women of the late Anglo-Saxon period could own many garments and might thus appear in different colours and styles for different occasions, religious or secular. Inferior ranks in society would have been recipients of the recycling process, with the poorest no doubt appearing in the same clothing day in, day out, until it was reduced to rags.

Variant appearance would have been very obvious. 'Foreigners' in Anglo-Saxon context, such as Celtic and Viking men wearing large penannular brooches, with plaited hair and beards, dressed in trousers without the covering tunic or wearing woven socks rather than gartering, would have stood out from the crowd just as much as silk-clad aristocrats in long gowns. Although a variety of colours was available for clothing, at least at the end of our period, there were evidently ethnic preferences. Analysis of archaeological textiles indicates that the English, and the Anglo-Scandinavians of York, particularly favoured madder-dyed red; the Vikings of Dublin and Greenland lichen purple; the Vikings of Scandinavia blue; and the Frisians and north Saxons natural fleece colours including black. An eleventh-century Continental poem mentions the green of Flanders, the black dye of the Rhineland and the natural tawny-red of Suevia.[8]

What does Anglo-Saxon dress signify for the twenty-first century observer?

The selectivity of the evidence

The majority of our evidence is derived from what Roland Barthes calls 'image-clothing':[9] the dress depicted in art is iconic, the dress

---

[8] Walton Rogers, *Textile Production at 16–22 Coppergate*, p. 1769. The text is Winric of Trèves, *Conflictus Ovis et Lini*.

[9] R. Barthes, *The Fashion System*, trans. M. Ward and W. Howard (Berkeley and Los Angeles, 1990), pp. 3–4. Of Barthes' other two categories, 'written clothing' is a very limited form of evidence for us since dress is rarely described in texts of our period; and 'real clothing' only survives as partial evidence in the form of fragmentary and damaged textile remains and dress fasteners/accessories.

supplied as grave furniture was evidently semiotic to some extent. Though both bear some relation to 'real clothing' that relation is not the same in every grave or art work. Our study has attempted to establish, for each period and each sex, a series of constants and to examine examples of dissidence.

Reading, and questioning, the evidence of graves

It is inevitable that grave-goods of the pagan period, and especially women's grave-goods, should contribute to current archaeoethnological discussions, since these artefacts make up such a large proportion of the material culture surviving from the time, but current archaeologists are introducing notes of caution. Christopher Scull warns:

> While it is easy to accept that the practice of furnished burial, and therefore the selection of grave goods, has an ideological component, it does not follow that every element of a grave assemblage is exclusively or primarily intended as a signal of some single or simple ideological affiliation: different items may hold a different ideological or social charge, and this may vary in intensity or meaning with context, and may relate to more than one axis of identity or belief.[10]

Ian Wood points out 'A type of object might signify status in one generation, ethnicity in the next and fashion at some other place or point in time'.[11] The ethnicity, status, religious belief and other individual characteristics of the patron who commissioned a brooch might well be reflected in its decoration though we cannot fully 'read' it; but many surviving brooches, which were old and worn when deposited, may have passed through several owners before they were buried, and so may end up in grave-groups which give mixed and conflicting 'messages'.

A critical assessment of the evidence of ethnicity and social status provided by dress accessories inevitably raises questions. Brooches and other metalwork would drop out of use as a result of loss, damage and wear, while the custom of depositing artefacts with the dead must have steadily used up the supply. When there were no longer any brooches of a particular type available, would a woman be able to obtain more, or would she adapt her costume? If a metalworker was accustomed to making, say, 'Anglian' annular brooches, would he, indeed could he, produce a saucer brooch for a woman of Saxon ancestry?

[10] C. Scull, review of H. Geake, *The Use of Grave-Goods in Conversion-Period England, c.600-c. 850*, British Archaeological Reports, British Series, 261 (1997) in *Archaeological Journal*, 156 (1999), pp. 432–3 at p. 432.

[11] Wood, 'Conclusion: strategies of distinction', in Pohl with Reimitz, *Strategies of Distinction*, pp. 297–303, at p. 300.

What exactly constituted wealth?[12] As John Hines reminds us[13] it is questionable whether it is the mere presence of an object that indicates wealth/status or its quantity. Although many archaeologists have taken great care to enumerate and describe individual beads in a grave, others, including myself, have been inclined to skim over them because they are so numerous, merely noting whether they were few or many, glass or amber or other, and where they were worn. Margaret Guido's recent catalogue[14] opens the door to more meaningful interpretations. If we consider that every glass bead was skilfully made in a complex process, probably overseas, and may have travelled a long distance before being deposited in an Anglo-Saxon grave, we should consider valuing each one individually. In examining grave-goods, we are inclined to rank gold very high, but we must estimate its value in context; in an area or in a period where gold was not available something of copper alloy might be highly prized.

What was status? Was it the same as what we call wealth, that is, prosperity measured in terms of material possessions, or did it involve other factors, such as age and ethnicity, an interpretation Heinrich Härke has suggested in relation to knives and weapons?[15] Was a woman's status dependent on her husband's,[16] or did she bring rank from her own family and if so did her husband share it? Could a woman achieve prestige by her own actions? Was special status indicated by amulets and crystal balls, and if so, was this a hereditary matter or something reflecting a woman's individual qualities? Did an artefact carry prestige because it was new, or, conversely, because it was old?

What was ethnicity? Patrick Geary's criteria for ethnicity are: origins, customs, language, law and religion; thus a 'man might speak a Romance language, dress as a Frank and claim Burgundian law'.[17] One may inherit ethnicity from one parent or the other; one may have 'double' nationality; a wife might adopt her identity from her husband. The status of 'different' ethnicity can vary considerably. At one extreme it can be a social handicap and consequently a person may be embarrassed by it and may even try to conceal it. Conversely a person might be proud of this 'otherness', exhibiting and perpetuating it, for example by naming children in the minority

---

[12] See my essay, 'Gold in the ground or just rust in the dust: measuring wealth by metalwork in Anglo-Saxon graves' in R. Bork (ed.), *De Re Metallica: studies in medieval metals and metallurgy*, Avista Annual Series (forthcoming, 2004).

[13] Hines, *Great Square-Headed Brooches*, p. 235.

[14] Guido, *Glass Beads*.

[15] Härke,'Knives in early Saxon burials'; 'Early Saxon weapon burials', in Hawkes, *Anglo-Saxon weapons and warfare*.

[16] See C. Arnold, 'Wealth and social structure: a matter of life and death,' in Rahtz, Dickinson, and Watts, *Anglo-Saxon Cemeteries 1979*, pp. 81–142, at p. 132.

[17] P. J. Geary, 'Ethnic identity as a situational construct in the Middle Ages', *Mitteilungen der Anthropologischen Gesellschaft in Wien*, 113 (1983), pp. 15–26, at p. 21.

language (see pp. 21–2). Between the two poles are various degrees of integration and indifference. With regard to Anglo-Saxon dress the questions of ethnicity concern the relationship of the Anglo-Saxon settlers to the Romano-Britons; the tribal differences between different groups of settlers; and the integration of later immigrants, including brides, courtiers, settler-farmers and conquerors. If there was a Romano-British element in the population of early Anglo-Saxon England it does not show in the dress styles of pagan graves. It may be, of course, that Celtic ethnicity, rather than low status, is the explanation for the unfurnished graves which are found in almost every 'Anglo-Saxon' cemetery; or that corpses of the Celtic dead were disposed of in some way which has left no trace, and their possessions dispersed by inheritance. There are not great differences between the costumes of 'Angle' and 'Saxon' apart from the wrist clasps, girdle hangers and certain ornaments perhaps originally introduced by immigrant brides. The shape and ornamentation of brooches may differ to some extent, but the costume they clasped apparently did not. Even if a woman wears a 'foreign' brooch, a Roman survival or a Continental piece, there is no suggestion that she wore a 'foreign' costume: the odd brooch is often 'paired' with one of a native type. The Frankish element in Kentish costume is certainly distinctive, but the variation may be result from a combination of factors: ethnicity, status and fashion.

Ironically, the somewhat neglected areas of spinning and weaving may be more valuable indictators of cultural affiliation than the more noticeable grave-goods of metal to which textile fragments are attached. These domestic crafts would have been learned in childhood and, although any person is capable of development or invention, it is most likely that techniques were normally passed down from mother to daughter. Spinning was almost certainly a continuous occupation, dependent only on the supply of vegetable fibre or wool. The latter, before seasonal shearing became the norm, was available all the time where sheep were raised, so the craft could be practised without interruption. Lise Bender Jørgensen has pointed out that Z/Z spinning, simple 2 x 2 twill and tablet-weave are characteristic of Scandinavia; Z/S spinning and diamond twill of the Netherlands and Germany; and tabby weaves of the English Channel area.[18] In England, where there is a much more heterogeneous distribution of textile types than on the Continent, it is possible that variations in spinning and weaving testify to the tribal origins of the women who made them. Diamond twills have sometimes been considered native products, sometimes imports, candidates for the role of the famous *pallium fresonicum*, or 'Frisian cloth', but wherever they were made, is it not possible that their presence reflects a Frisian or central German element in the population? 2 x 1

---

[18] Bender Jørgensen, 'The textiles of the Saxons, Anglo-Saxons and Franks'.

weaving may be the product of Romano-British technology and so testify to a limited Celtic survival.

The interpretation of appearance

Since Anglo-Saxon humanistic art is mostly Christian art, we have no depictions of the dress of the settlement and conversion periods and most of our representations of women belong to the tenth or eleventh centuries. There is little to distinguish the depictions of the Virgin Mary from secular women and the main costume variation – the sleeved robe as opposed to the poncho- or chasuble-like cloak – is not used consistently as an indicator of status. With the exception of Queen Ælfgifu-Emma, importance is generally conveyed by the addition of layers, not by different costume. In contrast, there are certain clear differences in male dress which can be used to 'read' a depiction. This book has been chiefly concerned with the dress of secular people in Anglo-Saxon times, but it is necessary to recognise that in the depiction of men in Anglo-Saxon art, secular medieval dress is only one possibility. 'Classical' dress, an adaptation of a middle- and upper-class costume worn throughout the Roman Empire, is used for depictions of God, Christ, angels and the four Evangelists, who are often shown writing their Gospels.[19] The costume consists of a long-sleeved, ankle-length robe, the *tunica*, which, in the Christian tradition, was normally made of white linen, though it might be painted a different colour for more splendid effect (as in the portrait of Christ in Colour Plate K). Over this is worn the *pallium*, a simple, rectangular cloak (originally white but often depicted in medieval art by a different colour), worn asymmetrically over the robe, covering the left shoulder and passing under the right arm, usually exposing the loose sleeve of the *tunica*. It is either tucked into a self-coloured girdle or wrapped tightly round the waist and is shorter than the robe beneath it. This classical cloak is not fastened by a brooch.[20] Those who wear this costume in Anglo-Saxon art are barefoot (Colour plates H, K). Angels, who often have curly hair (for example on the Genoels-Elderen ivory, and a sculpture from St Andrew, Auckland) sometimes wear, high on the head, a fillet with a small central jewel. Such details can be useful in identifying figures on incomplete or obscure art works; for example the curling hair of the unidentified figure who peeps round a curtain at the Evangelist Matthew in the *Lindisfarne Gospels* (London, British Library, MS Cotton Nero D iv, fol. 25v) might be an angelic indicator.

A second long costume is ecclesiastical dress, which usually takes the form of a symmetrical chasuble over a longer robe (a *tunica alba* or alb, and sometimes a decorated outer tunic, the dalmatic). The chasuble, which had evolved from the Roman

[19] J. Mayo, *A History of Ecclesiastical Dress* (London, 1984), pp. 12–13, 30–2.
[20] In practice it could be fastened by a pin or left loose.

paenula, a heavy, protective, outer garment, covers the shoulders and hangs down in points at centre front and back, with a central hole for the head. The chasuble may be decorated with an embroidered orphrey. An archbishop will wear an archiepiscopal pallium, a Y-shaped decorative woollen strip. An amice, a linen square, may be indicated at the neck and the ends of a stole usually show beneath the chasuble. A maniple is often carried over the arm. The cope, popularised by the Cluniac movement, was being introduced at the end of the Anglo-Saxon period. It was a foot-length, front-opening garment with an attached hood.[21] The mitre was not yet in general use and is not shown in Anglo-Saxon art.[22] The hair of ecclesiastical men is normally tonsured in the 'crown of thorns' style. There were other tonsures: the Celtic version with the hair shaved above the forehead, described by Bede, may be shown on the symbol of St Matthew in the *Book of Durrow* (fol. 21v; Fig. 137); Sarah Keefer has suggested to me that it also worn by St Dunstan as he is depicted enthroned (in Tiberius A iii, fol. 2v).[23] I had previously assumed that the man was known to be balding. Either interpretation suggests a personal knowledge of Archbishop Dunstan and an attempt at portraiture which is unusual in Anglo-Saxon art.

Plate 13 Secular, ecclesiastical, saintly and angelic figures, British Library MS Stowe 944, fol. 6v

[21] Mayo, *Ecclesiastical Dress*, pp. 38–9.

[22] However, Janet Mayo notes that 'St Cuthbert was buried wearing one'; *Ecclesiastical Dress*, p. 32; but vestments were added to and removed from the coffin.

[23] Backhouse, Turner and Webster, *Golden Age*, No. 28, p. 49

Another religious costume is the monk's habit with a cowl which may be worn over the head or pushed back fully or partially, revealing the tonsure. The cowl is essentially attached to a garment, not independent.[24] There are many examples of monks in ankle-length habits of this kind in late Anglo-Saxon art and this dress was obviously a familiar indicator of monasticism and the asceticism of those committed to that way of life. It is significant that St Dunstan, archbishop of Canterbury, and architect of the Benedictine Reform, chose to have himself portrayed in this costume as a simple monk in a position of humility at the feet of Christ, rather than in elaborate vestments (Oxford, Bodleian Library MS Auct., F. 4.32, fol. 1). The cowl, one of the garments decreed for monks by the Benedictine Rule, like the tonsure, is diagnostic of monasticism, and can help us to identify a figure even if only the head is present. The contrast between secular and ecclesiastical figures in art is immediate and obvious (Colour plate H, Plate 13), though the representation of mass vestments must sometimes have been iconic.

The fourth male costume, the one which has chiefly concerned us in this book, is short, consisting of a tunic and optional cloak over it. The short costume may be enhanced by decoration at the cuffs, the neck or the hem of the skirt. This is usually very stylised, with no more ornament than a row of dots or small circles, but even minimal enhancement may signify wealth or the wearer's special status in the narrative context. From the use of the tonsure with the short costume in the depiction of King Edward's funeral in the Bayeux 'Tapestry',[25] we can see that this secular dress was worn by men in holy orders, and therefore that not all male religious men wore monastic habits or ecclesiastical vestments, even in the eleventh century.

There is also the long secular costume, worn by kings and other men in authority, which is distinguished from the 'classical' costume by such features as colour, decoration and the brooch which fastens a cloak, either symmetrically at the chest or asymmetrically on the right shoulder, over a long robe. The choice of long rather than short garments is clearly related to the iconography of rulership. Men in tunics are rarely depicted seated, and when they are, it is generally at a three-quarter angle, and on a bench or folding chair rather than a throne. The full frontal seated position, which so effectively conveys authority, involves splayed knees which, for the sake of dignity, require covering. Thus the unusual calf-length garments of King Edgar in Cotton Tiberius A iii (Fig. 187) and Guy of Pontieu in the 'Tapestry'[26] may owe more to artistic ingenuity than sartorial authenticity.

[24] Mayo, *Ecclesiastical Dress*, p. 33.
[25] Wilson, *Bayeux Tapestry*, Plate 30.
[26] Wilson, *Bayeux Tapestry*, Plate 10.

Finally we must mention military dress, which varies from the mere addition of a helmet to the normal short secular dress, through the rarely depicted mail coat, to the full suits of mail worn with helmets in the Bayeux 'Tapestry'. Again, the depictions are surely in many cases iconic, short-hand indications of a man's role in a particular context: helmets are not tied on, mail is implausible placed between rider and saddle, and no-one, even in pitched battle, appears to protect his weapon hand with a glove or gauntlet.

Semiotic dress

The differences in male costume enable us to distinguish the status of different men in the same picture. BL MS Stowe 944, fol. 6v (Plate 13), for example, shows winged, barefoot angels in classical costume leading men to the Last Judgement: they include barefoot, haloed saints in classical costume, ecclesiastics in two different varieties of vestments and a secular, with an ornamented border on his tunic and a long cloak. In an illustration of the building of the Tower of Babel in the *Hexateuch* (fol. 19r) it is clear that the figure on the left is a spiritual, not a terrestrial, being since he is bearded, barefoot and wearing the classical costume, even though he is perched on a ladder like the tunic-clad workman on the opposite side of the picture; God descends by ladder, man ascends by it. In the *Benedictional of St Æthelwold* (fol. 17v), the martyred saints Stephen and Paul are distinguished from their torturers by their dress: the apostles wear long classical costume, their adversaries short tunics. This is purely semiotic. The saints were martyred by their contemporaries (though Paul died in Rome). There is no reason to suppose that SS Paul and Stephen habitually dressed in Roman costume and their killers in medieval tunics. Occasionally there are inconsistencies: Adam, who in the *Cædmon Manuscript* appears with a short tunic and shoes at his expulsion from the Garden of Eden, wears classical dress immediately after, at the birth of Cain and Abel, though he reverts to the tunic subsequently. The drawing certainly represents Adam, not an angelic or other divine figure, for he wears shoes. The explanation may lie in a change of artist[27] but I would guess that a more likely reason is the fact that an indoor location has been drawn in for the birth scene and Adam is depicted seated, a position consistent, in art, with a long garment. Possibly the only secular long dress known to the artist was the classical; the long gown for kings and nobles may have postdated the prototypes of the *Cædmon Manuscript* drawings.[28] Another innovation of the birth scene is Adam's beard, which is retained in subsequent illustrations. Is this to be explained simply by a change of hand, or is it significant, marking Adam's fatherhood and

[27] The drawings are very similar but there are differences of detail. Compare the bulbous noses of p. 46 with the pointed noses of p. 47, also the hands and hair.
[28] B. Raw, 'The probable derivation of most of the illustrations in Junius 11 from an illustrated Old Saxon *Genesis*', *Anglo-Saxon England*, 5 (1976), pp. 133–49.

maturity? It certainly functions to distinguish him subsequently from his adult sons. The beard is in general a useful identifier, along with costume. Angels are not bearded, but God, Christ, prophets and Evangelists may be. In secular context beards are often used to mark age, hence the ranked busts of ancestors of Christ in the *Boulogne Gospels* (fol. 11)[29] who all wear variations of secular dress, mostly with cloak-brooches, are all bearded. The majority of figures in the *Hexateuch* are beardless, but important patriarchs such as Abraham and Jacob are bearded. In the 'Tapestry' the advanced age of King Edward is clearly indicated by his beard, but most of the other characters are beardless. When bearded figures suddenly appear among Duke William's shipbuilders we may wonder if the artist is indicating the maturity and experience of the craftsmen, but as I have suggested elsewhere, the unusual beards as well as other slight differences in clothing and posture suggest that these ship-wrights were copied from a Noah illustration in the *Hexateuch*.[30] There could be no more successful ship-builder than Noah, of course, and those who recognised the image would appreciate this subtlety.

Anglo-Saxon artists sometimes used dress – together with other indicators like haloes and hair – in symbolic or emblematic ways. The seventh-century 'portrait' of a man writing in the Northumbrian *Codex Amiatinus* (Italy, Florence, *Biblioteca Medicea-Laurenziana*, Amiatinus I, fol. Vr) represents both the Old Testament prophet Ezra and the medieval scholar Cassiodorus. Wearing a version of classical dress, with Hebrew breast plate and headdress, the figure is identified by an inscription as Ezra, who, when the tablets recording the Law were destroyed, recovered it by reciting the material from memory. With his halo, his surrounding scriptorium and books, the figure simultaneously represents Cassiodorus, who maintained the tradition of Christian scholarship by his establishment of a monastery, and who was responsible for translating the Bible into the vernacular.[31] In the *Benedictional of St Æthelwold*, the abbot and monk St Benedict is depicted in both episcopal and papal dress which does not reflect historical fact but rather the emphasis on monastic bishops in the tenth-century Benedictine Reform which was taking place in Anglo-Saxon England.[32] There is even more complexity in the central figure of a full-page miniature in the eighth-century *Vespasian Psalter*.[33] Ostensibly this is a portrait of King David, in the act of composing a psalm, but the dress and attributes of the figure indicate multiple associations. He wears a red tunic and purple mantle and sits on an imperial throne, holding a Germanic lyre. He has distinctive shoes and white stockings which have been thought to be episcopal, the

[29] Backhouse, Turner and Webster, *Golden Age*, p. 62.
[30] Cited in P. Lasko, 'The Bayeux Tapestry and the representation of space', in Owen-Crocker and Graham, *Medieval Art*, pp. 26–39, at p. 38, note 5.
[31] R. L. S. Bruce-Mitford, *The Art of the Codex Amiatinus* (Jarrow, 1967).
[32] R. Deshman, *The Benedictional of Æthelwold*, Studies in Manuscript Illumination, 9 (Princeton, NJ, 1995), pp. 172–3.
[33] Wright, *The Vespasian Psalter*.

halo of a saint, and the hair and beardless face of the youthful Christ. He is simultaneously Old Testament figure, saint and Christ, emperor and bishop, psalmist and Anglo-Saxon *scop*. It is not beyond the bounds of possibility that the artist also flattered the Mercian king with this picture of a monarch enthroned.[34] David, as the composer of many of the psalms which had a central place in Anglo-Saxon worship, is depicted in several other Anglo-Saxon manuscripts. In the seventh- or eighth-century *Durham Cassiodorus* (Durham, Cathedral Library, MS B II 30, fols 81v, 172v), he is represented in both musical and military guises in classical costume (not in armour); in the eleventh-century *Winchcombe Psalter* (Cambridge, University Library, MS Ff 1.23, fol. 4v) his clothing is mostly concealed by a large triangular harp, but it is long, with some ornament at the upper arm and includes a cloak pulled through a shoulder brooch into an elaborate loop; in the *Portiforium Sancti Wulfstani* (Cambridge, Corpus Christi College, MS 391, fol. 24v), which is dated to 1064, he wears a knee-length tunic and coloured stockings, decorated cross garters with a protruding *fleur de lis*, shoes and a centrally fastened cloak. In these later depictions he is crowned. King David's costume is generally quite elaborate but not consistent or diagnostic. If any of these illuminations were to be divorced from its manuscript context, it would not be by his costume that we would recognise David. The recurrent features are his harp, his throne and his attendants.

Decoration on dress may mark out the most significant character in a scene. Thus, the Bayeux 'Tapestry' shows Earl Harold once in a striped skirt (Fig. 207) and Duke William once in a decorated cloak (Fig. 192) without concern for consistency. In the *Benedictional of St Æthelwold*, scenes of apostles including SS Peter and Paul (fols 3v and 4r) include painted ornament on the costume of these two figures, which would perhaps have suggested patterned silk to contemporaries. However, the ornament functions together with the fact that these figures stand slightly in front of the flanking apostles, as an indicator of their relative importance.[35] (They are *identified* by other, well-established characteristics: St Peter has keys and a tonsure; St Paul an exceptionally large book and a bald patch.) In the other two apostle illuminations in this manuscript, the central figures are less prominent in position and undistinguished by dress ornament. In the *Boulogne Gospels*, fol. 11v, the decoration on the cloak of one figure, together with her slightly greater height, identifies her as the Virgin Mary, the more important of the two women in the scene. Conversely, however, the drawings in the *Tiberius Psalter* include ornament on the costumes of servants, as well as on curtains and a table cloth, testifying to nothing but the artist's enjoyment of decoration.

---

[34] Anna Gannon has pointed out to me that the hairstyle of the Vespasian David is shared by portrait busts on coins of King Offa of Mercia.

[35] The figure to the left of St Peter also has some ornament but it is less obtrusive.

As we know from textual evidence that sober colours were preferred for religious observance, we may question whether the predominantly brown tones of St Etheldreda's clothing in the *Benedictional of St Æthelwold* (fol. 90v), together with the (rather implausible) veil which hangs down her back, are references to Etheldreda's reputation as a nun of ascetic tastes (see above, p. 210; Fig. 170); but this possibility has to be set against the apparent lack of consistent use of colour for clothing in the manuscript as a whole and a stylisation that owes everything to the tenth-century Winchester School and nothing to the historical facts that Etheldreda lived in Northumbria and East Anglia in the seventh century.

The general medieval 'rule' that the most important figure in a scene is foregrounded generally works in conjunction with decorative costume, but in one scene in the Bayeux 'Tapestry',[36] where, I suggest, there are two important figures (the Duke of Normandy, future King of England, identified in the inscription above, and, unnamed, his half-brother Odo, bishop of Bayeux, who probably commissioned the 'Tapestry'), the features are used independently: one of a row of riders wears a garment or garments the same shape as the mail suits of the other riders, but marked in multicoloured chequers, rather than the rings which represent chain mail. He carries a club. Although this figure has generally been identified as Duke William,[37] it must surely be his brother Odo (who as a bishop would not have been permitted to carry conventional weapons and who appears at the Battle of Hastings dressed in a similar chequered garment and again carrying a club, where he is identified by the Latin caption).[38] The Duke can be identified either as the figure to the left who is also elaborately dressed, though in mail, and who holds a standard, or the figure under the identifying caption VVILLEM DVX, neither of whom is overlapped.[39]

Knowledge of costume and associated features such as hair and beard, can sometimes show us what a figure is not but may not always help us in a positive identification. There is a profile bust in a roundel in the *Cædmon Manuscript* (p. 2) labelled in Old English letters *Ælfwine*, a man's name. The figure has short curly hair, without a tonsure or beard. He wears a garment draped asymmetrically, with several folds at the left shoulder, but the garment neither exposes the right shoulder as the classical costume would, nor does it fasten at the right shoulder with a round brooch in the manner of Anglo-Saxon secular costume. It simply covers the right shoulder smoothly without folds. The V-shaped lines at the front are suggestive of the Anglo-Saxon cloak, but in the absence of a shoulder fastener this cannot be positively identified. The V-shaped folds are different from the straight lines of the classical garment, while the

---

[36] Wilson, *Bayeux Tapestry*, Plates 18–20.

[37] McNulty, *Narrative Art*, p. 100; Wilson, *Bayeux Tapestry*, p. 179.

[38] Wilson, *Bayeux Tapestry*, Plate 67.

[39] See my forthcoming paper 'Brothers, rivals and the geometry of the Bayeux Tapestry', in G. R. Owen-Crocker (ed.), *King Harold II and The Bayeux Tapestry*.

asymmetrical nature of the folds at the shoulder would suggest this is not a chasuble or other vestment. It could be some kind of hood. It is unlikely to be a cowl, for the neckline of the garment is unlike that of a monk's cowled robe depicted elsewhere, and the lack of tonsure suggests the man is not a monk. Perhaps we have a secular hood here. The only similar thing is worn by a figure representing the Sense of Touch on the Fuller Brooch; but perhaps the Junius drawing is incomplete or careless and does not represent real clothing.

Whenever the evidence of art has been considered in this book, we have been aware of the dependence on models which renders almost all of our material subject to reservations. When the very line of a garment can be shown to be stylised, its closest parallel found in a different medium, made in a different country, is it valid to draw any conclusions with regard to contemporary costume? For example, Robert Deshman has demonstrated the relationship between the hang of the cloaks of King Edgar and the Virgin in Vespasian A viii and those of soldiers and *Ecclesia*, repectively, on the Carolingian Brunswick Casket.[40] Are we therefore entitled to draw conclusions about Anglo-Saxon dress from the length and decoration of Edgar's garments, or even to go further and suggest the colours are significant as Anne Hedeager Krag has done? If we identify specific borrowings, as when the Bayeux 'Tapestry' copies from various surviving Canterbury manuscripts,[41] are we to assume that the significance, as well as the design, has been absorbed? The answer to these questions has to be, sometimes yes, sometimes no. Each instance must be considered individually.

We must beware of stereotypes and modern prejudices, recognising that men and angels, as well as women, can wear fillets; that Viking male hairstyles include plaits and ponytails; that the word *wundenlocc* is used of men as well as a woman in the poem *Judith*; and that though women's association with textile production is implicit in the epithet 'peaceweaver', the term is also applied to an angel, when it can have no such gender association. Equally we must beware of assuming that a unique garment reflects real life: the demand that King Edgar be seated between his archbishops in the Tiberius A iii depiction, and the requirement of expressing the Five Senses as human figures in silver and niello may have been sufficient to produce garments that were entirely imaginative. The important issue is that while bearing all these reservations in mind, we must not take dress for granted; our awareness of the design and decoration of clothing should be as sharp as our perception of all the other features of a graphic image.

[40] Deshman, *Benedictional*, p. 228.

[41] It is recognised that the 'Tapestry' borrows from the *Gospels of St Augustine*, the *Harley Psalter*, the *Hexateuch* and a copy of Prudentius's *Psychomachia*. 'Quotation' by the 'Tapestry' artist is discussed in D. J. Bernstein, *The Mystery of the Bayeux Tapestry* (London, 1986). I consider the borrowing of the Ælfgyva figure in a forthcoming paper, 'Embroidered wood: animal headed posts in the Bayeux "Tapestry"', in Damico and Karkov, *Aedificia Nova*.

Appendix A

Old English garment-names

The only full and scholarly lexicon of Old English is still the nineteenth- to early-twentieth-century Bosworth/Toller *Old English Dictionary*.[1] The excellent new Toronto *Dictionary*, originally on microfiche, now on CD-ROM, is in progress.[2] There are concordances of Old English words, without translation or cross reference to alternative spellings on microfiche[3] and the computer program WordCruncher.[4] The innovative *Thesaurus of Old English* (1995) assembles material thematically.[5]

The names of Anglo-Saxon garments may be derived from three types of text:

1 Works in Old English

These include very limited evidence from poetry[6] and a wide range of literary and non-literary prose texts: wills,[7] laws,[8] the Anglo-Saxon *Chronicle*,[9] sermons[10] and lives of saints[11] and the *Indicia Monasterialia*, a catalogue of sign-language for silent monks.[12]

---

[1] Bosworth/Toller, *Dictionary* and Toller, *Supplement*.
[2] Amos, Di Paolo Healey, Holland, Franzen, McDougall, McDougall, Spiers, Thompson, *Dictionary of Old English*.
[3] *Old English Concordance* microfiche (University of Delaware, 1980).
[4] *The Complete Corpus of Old English on Machine Readable Form*.
[5] Roberts, Kay and Grundy, *Thesaurus*.
[6] Krapp and Dobbie, *The Anglo-Saxon Poetic Records: a collective edition*.
[7] Whitelock, *Wills*.
[8] Liebermann, *Die Gesetze*.
[9] Dumville and Keynes, *The Anglo-Saxon Chronicle: a collaborative edition*.
[10] Thorpe, *Homilies*.
[11] Goodwin, *Guthlac;* Herzfeld, *Martyrology*; Skeat, *Aelfric's Lives of Saints*.
[12] Kluge, 'Indicia' (also Banham, *Monasteriales Indicia*).

2 Works translated from Latin into English or with interlinear gloss in English

These include parts of the Old Testament[13] and the Gospels,[14] monastic rules,[15] the historical, philosophical and religious works translated under the direction of King Alfred,[16] medical treatises,[17] Ælfric's *Colloquy*[18] and the romance *Appolonius of Tyre*.[19]

3 Latin–Old English glossaries[20]

These vocabularies consist of lists of words, sometimes miscellaneous, sometimes arranged according to simple alphabetical principles, or grouped according to sources or subject. The subject-order glossaries are particularly useful for the present purpose, since they include lists of Latin garment-names with their Old English equivalents beside them. Such vocabularies are found in many manuscripts, but often texts are not totally independent of one another, being copied from common exemplars. Many of the lemmata (glossed Latin words) which represent garments derive ultimately from the chapters on dress in Isidor of Seville's *Etymologiae*[21] and from Aldhelm's attack on elaborate clothing in his *De Virginitate* (quoted on p. 134).[22]

Most of the texts from which evidence has been derived are written in the West Saxon dialect. The only examples of Anglian dialect are the Corpus Glossary, which may be Mercian, and the Northumbrian and Mercian glosses to the Gospels (Lindisfarne and Rushworth texts) and the Old English *Martyrology*. The Corpus Glossary is eighth-century, the Alfredian translations and *Martyrology* ninth-century. The rest of the texts are later (tenth- and eleventh-century).

All our written texts are, by definition, post-conversion and some of the vocabulary in them includes Latin loan words which entered English through the medium of Christianity. If, however, a

---

[13] Crawford, *Heptateuch*; Lindelöf, *Der Lambeth-Psalter*; Spelman, *Psalterium*.

[14] Skeat, *Gospels* (also Liuzza, *Old English Version of the Gospels*).

[15] Logeman, *Rule*; Schröer, *Benedictinerregel*.

[16] Bately, *Orosius*; Hecht, *Dialogue Gregors des Grossen*; Schipper, *Bedas Kirchengeschichte*; Sweet, *Pastoral Care*.

[17] Cockayne, *Leechdoms*.

[18] Garmonsway, *Colloquy*.

[19] Goolden, *Appolonius*.

[20] Goossens, *Glosses*; Gwara, *Aldhelmi*; Kindschi, 'Latin–Old English glosses'; Lindsay, *Corpus Glossary*; Napier, *Glosses*; Wright/Wülcker, *Vocabularies*; Zupitza, *Aelfrics Grammatik und Glossar.*

[21] XIX, xxi–xxvi. Also influential are Isidor's sections on fibres (XIX, xxvii), colours of garments (xxviii) and textile equipment (xxix); Lindsay, *Isidori*.

[22] Ehwald, *Aldhelmi Opera*, p. 318, lines 2–5; Gwara, *Aldhelmi*, 1, pp. 734–7.

given Old English word has cognates in other Germanic languages,[23] it is probable that that word already existed in Old English before the conversion, and therefore that it originally referred to a garment worn in pagan times. Such words are marked (c) in the following list.

The glossaries may have preserved archaisms and academic translations which never appeared in everyday speech. Words which are recorded only from glossaries are therefore marked + in the following list, to distinguish them from terms which may have been in popular use.

Many of our surviving texts are religious, and some garment-names have been found only in these. The words have been included in the following list with qualifications such as 'worn by monks', but this does not exclude the possibility that seculars could also wear garments thus named. Garment-names known to be confined to ecclesiastical vestments and monastic habits have not been listed here.

The amount of evidence available about the use of each word is various; an Old English word found translating a recognised Latin word should, itself, be capable of definition; but in practice, the same Old English word may translate more than one Latin term, or may gloss a Latin word with more than one accepted meaning. As a result, some of the Old English words listed are ambiguous. Sometimes a garment-name occurs in a datable Old English text such as a will, the context showing that the garment was worn by a secular, and was valuable enough to be bequeathed, but not how it was worn or what it looked like. In several instances citations prove that a garment was worn by men but there is no evidence that it was worn by women. Yet there is no proof that most of the listed names could *not* apply to the garments of either sex.

Old English was rich in synonyms and the vocabulary of clothing reflects this characteristic. The reader should not be surprised, therefore, to find many words apparently meaning, for example, 'cloak', although every attempt has been made here to distinguish between shades of meaning.

General

claþ (c)	a garment, of both sexes
claþes (c)	clothes, of both sexes
(ge)gerela	a garment, clothes, especialy finery, of both sexes
gerif +	a garment
ge-scirpla	clothes, worn by men
godweb (c)	something made of precious cloth, frequently purple, normally of silk; probably shot-silk taffeta

---

[23] See Holthausen, *Wörterbuch*.

hætera	clothes, particularly those belonging to the poor, often in ragged condition, worn by men
hrægel, hræglung (c)	a garment, clothes, of both sexes; *hrægel* is the commonest Old English garment term
reaf	a garment, clothes, of both sexes; a very common word
scrud (c)	a garment, clothes of both sexes; the word *scrud* is used in formal arrangements to provide clothing for monks and nuns
swæpels (c)	a garment, cloak
(ge)wæd (c)	a garment, clothing; worn by men
-waru (c)	-wear (compound element only, as in *nihtwaru* 'nightwear'); worn by men

claþ, (ge)gerela, hrægel, reaf, scrud and *(ge)wæd* often occur in compounds, for example *bearm-claþ, cildclað*.

Outer garments

basing	cloak, probably rectangular shape, could be made of fur, worn by men
bratt	cloak (Northumbrian dialect, the only garment-name known to be a Celtic loan); by the fourteenth century the word signified an unpretentious garment
casul	cloak, chasuble, possibly restricted to ecclesiastical use (probably post-conversion innovation)
crusene (c)	fur or skin garment, worn by men, valued sufficiently to be bequeathed in tenth century
fel	skin or leather garment reaching to the feet, worn by monks
godweb-cynn	cloak of splendid material, only occurs in a description of St Michael
hacele (c)	full-length cloak, possibly hooded, worn by both sexes
hed-claþ	probably similar to *heden*
heden (c)	leather, fur or sheepskin garment, possibly hooded, worn by monks
hop-pada +	a wide ('hoop-shaped') outer garment, cope, possibly ecclesiastical only
hwitel (c)	piece of material, probably rectangular, which could be used as a cloak or blanket; originally of undyed

	fabric ('white') and possibly of a fixed weight or size; worn by both sexes
loða (c)	cloak which could be used as a coverlet; possibly shaggy; worn by men
mentel	cloak, worn by both sexes; women could fasten it by a brooch or pin; an early loan from Latin *mantellum* which became integrated into the vernacular
ofer-brædels	outer garment, often ecclesiastical
oferlæg, oferlagu +	a garment, cloak
ofer-slop, ofer-slype (c)	overgarment, sometimes ecclesiastical
pad (c)	outer garment, probably taking the form of a coat or tunic rather than a cloak
pilece (c)	a skin or fur garment, worn by both sexes; in the eleventh century made of marten skin
reowe	piece of material which could be used as a coverlet or rug, and possibly as a cloak; perhaps of shaggy or rough texture
rift (c)	piece of material which could be used as a cloak, curtain or veil (popular in Anglian dialects)
rocc (c)	a garment, probably a jerkin or poncho-shaped cloak, sometimes made of fur, sometimes ecclesiastical
sciccels (c)	cloak, probably rectangular, sometimes fur; worn by men
sciccing (c) +	cloak; related to *sciccels*
stole	long outer garment (post-conversion, probably remaining a scholarly word)
wæfels	a covering, which could be used as a cloak

Body garments

These covered all or part of the trunk; if they covered the legs it was in the form of a skirt rather than trousers. The body garment might in practice be worn outermost, for instance indoors or in summer, but could be covered by a cloak or other outer garment.

bearm-claþ	an apron
bearm-rægl +	as *bearm-claþ*
breost-lin +	a linen band for the breast, perhaps a garment, possibly something else,

	such as a wrap for a corpse
breost-rocc (c) +	a garment covering the chest
cemes	a shirt, worn by a male child; an early loan from Latin *camisia* which became integrated into the vernacular
cyrtel (c)	a man's tunic, a woman's gown; originally short, sometimes wool, sometimes fur; valued sufficiently to be bequeathed by women in the tenth century
ham (c)	a shirt
hemeþe (c)	a shirt with sleeves, worn by monks
pad (c)	a tunic or coat
scyrte (c)	a tunic, originally short, worn by men simultaneously with *cyrtel*, probably under it
serc	a shirt, tunic, worn by men; monks wore it both during the day and as nightwear; an unostentatious garment
slop, slype	probably used in Anglo-Saxon times of a loose gown or tunic
smoc (c)	a shirt, undergarment, possibly embellished
tunece	man's tunic, woman's gown of dark colour, possibly worn by women on religious occasions; worn as night wear by monks; sufficiently valuable to be bequeathed by a woman in the tenth century (a post-conversion innovation)
under-serc +	literally 'under-shirt'
wealca	a billowing garment, wrapped round the body; worn by a woman in biblical context

Slop and *slype* are listed in Bosworth/Toller *Anglo-Saxon Dictionary* and defined respectively as 'a loose upper garment, slop, smock-frock, any kind of outer garment made of linen' and 'a garment, slip'. They do not, however, occur in Old English except as compound elements, being documented individually only from later texts.

Hacele, loða and *mentel* appear in glossaries in contexts suggesting the meaning 'shirt', as well as having the primary function 'cloak', but this scholarly use may not reflect normal vernacular usage.

Loin and leg coverings

bræcce +	trousers
braccas (c)	trousers
brec-hrægl	probably trousers
broc, plural *brec*	short trousers, worn by men; by the thirteenth century applied to a woman's garments
cæles (c)	probably a sock
gyrdels	a girdle or loin-cloth
hosa (c)	covering for the lower leg and possibly the foot; probably a leather boot; worn by monks
hose-bend (c)	band worn round the leg, probably to secure the *hosa*; similar to *socc*
leþerhose (c)	leather boot
meo	a sock, worn by monks in addition to *hosa*; similar to *socc*
nostle	a band, which could be secured round the leg, fastening the *meo*
sceanc-bend +	a band worn round the shin
sceanc-gegirela +	a decorative band worn round the shin
socc (c)	a bag-like foot covering, easily slipped on; similar to *meo*
strapul	a legging, fastened by laces, perhaps the leg-part of a pair of long trousers; worn by both sexes, at least after the Norman Conquest (perhaps derived from Latin *strebula*, the flesh about the haunch)
underwrædel	possibly a loin-cloth
wæd-brec	loin-cloth
wining (c)	a band worn round the shins; worn by monks

Shoes

calc	a sandal, probably humble; worn by men (the word is a post-conversion innovation)
crinc	a shoe, possibly not fitted to the foot but drawn together by thongs
fotgewæd	footwear (applied to shoes of monks)
hemming (c)	a raw hide shoe or boot (the name signifies the skin of the hind legs of a deer)
rifeling (c)	a raw hide sandal or boot, similar to *hemming*, probably worn by country people
scoh, gesceo, gescy (c)	a shoe, shoes; *scoh* is the commonest Old

	English word for footwear
slife-scoh, slipe-scoh	a bag-like footcovering, easily slipped on
stæppe-scoh +	a slipper
swiftlere	a low slipper, worn by monks but almost certainly by seculars too (an early loan from Latin *subtalaris*)

Headgear

bænde	a band, possibly worn on the head, metal or gold-embroidered; sufficiently valuable to be bequeathed in the late-tenth century
bend	a headband
binde (c)	a headband, typical headgear of secular married women; valuable enough to be bequeathed in the late-tenth century
cæfing +	a hair pin or ornament for the head; probably worn by women
cæppe (c) +	a cap, hood, hooded cloak; possibly ecclesiastical only
cappa (c) +	a cap; possibly ecclesiastical only
cuffia, cuffie (c)	a headdress worn by women in the late-tenth century, valuable enough to be bequeathed (perhaps derived from medieval Latin *cuphia*); speculatively, it may have wrapped round the head, framing the face, in contrast to the *wimpel*
feax-clað +	a cloth or band for the hair
feax-net +	a hair net
feax-preon +	a hair pin
hær-nædl +	a hair pin
hæt	a cap or hat (related to Latin *cassis*, a helmet)
heafod-clað	a cloth for the head; certainly headgear of this name was worn by religious women by the thirteenth century, but in Anglo-Saxon times the word may only have applied to grave-clothes
heafod-gewæde	a headdress, probably a veil, worn by women
healsed	a cloth for the head or neck, but used of wrappings for holy relics; only one possible occurrence as 'hood'
hod (c)	a hood, similar to monk's cowl
hufe (c)	a hat, possibly domed (headgear of this name was worn by men in the four-teenth century and by women in the

	sixteenth)
nostle	a band, sometimes used as a fillet
orel (c)	a veil, characteristically worn by nuns though probably worn by secular women also
rift	a veil
scyfel (c)	a woman's hat or hood, probably with a projection which shaded the face
snod (c)	a thin band or cord worn on the head
þrawing-spinel +	a hair pin
ðwæle (c) +	a band, fillet
up-legen +	a pin or ornament for the hair
wealca	a garment wrapped round a person, perhaps as a veil
wimpel (c)	a headdress; development in later medieval and modern times suggests it took the form of a headcovering with an aperture for the face; worn by seculars at this time
wræd	a band which could be used as a fillet
wrigels	a veil, certainly worn by nuns, but possibly by seculars also

Gloves

glof	a glove
hand-scio (c)	a mitten (the word only survives as a proper noun in written Old English, but was evidently common Germanic)

Belts

belt (c)	a belt or girdle
fetel (c)	a belt or girdle, especially a sword belt
fetels (c)	a belt; a bag, possibly a purse suspended from the belt
gyrdel	a girdle, belt, worn by monks
gyrdels	girdle worn round hips, monk's girdle, sword-belt

Clasps and ornaments

beag, beah (c)	a ring for finger, arm, neck or head
bul	an ornament worn by women in the early-eleventh century, perhaps a brooch or more likely, a pendant or amulet for the neck
cnæp +	a fastener, perhaps a brooch or button

dalc (c)	a clasp, perhaps a brooch, buckle or pin
fifele +	a buckle or brooch
gyrdel-hring,	
gyrdels-hring +	a girdle-buckle
heafodfrætennes	a head ornament
hring (c)	a ring, brooch or neck-ring
mentel-preon	a brooch or pin for fastening the cloak, worn by women in the tenth century
ofer-feng +	a clasp, latchet of a shoe
preon	a brooch or pin worn by women in the tenth century
sigle	a clasp, perhaps a brooch
spennels (c)	a clasp, perhaps a brooch

Appendix B

A possible cutting plan for an eleventh-century gown

Robin Netherton

Without surviving garments to examine, we cannot know exactly how Anglo-Saxon clothing was cut; however, we can make educated guesses based on the available evidence. Surviving examples of medieval European garments are in general cut from cloth narrow enough to be woven on a one-person loom. Pieces are mostly based on geometric shapes, though they may be modified. Body pieces are typically cut in a single length, with gores to increase skirt width and underarm gussets for flexibility. Shapes suggest that cutting plans were designed to minimise waste of fabric.

The gown worn by the woman fleeing the burning building in the Bayeux 'Tapestry' (Fig. 163) might have been made using a cutting plan as in Fig. 238. This supposes front and back pieces cut to the width of the fabric, sleeves made from a straight tube for the upper arm plus a lower-arm piece that flares to form a hanging cuff, side-seam gores to add skirt fullness, and two triangular gussets under each arm. The fact that the cuff is shown in a different colour from the sleeve suggests a different fabric surface; the construction here assumes a sleeve that flares steeply to form the cuff, which is worn turned back to reveal either a lining or the inner side of the fabric. In Anglo-Saxon art the neckline of women's garments is invariably hidden, but based on men's tunics, scoop or keyhole openings are reasonable guesses. Variations on the basic layout are possible, dependent on the individual's preferences and skill, the wearer's needs and the amount of fabric available. With careful placement of a fold at the top of each repeated section, the front and back pieces can be cut as one, as can the upper-arm and forearm/cuff pieces. The skirt gores can be cut as two large wedges or four narrow ones, depending on whether a vertical fold is used; with four gores one may choose to inset two of them into slits in the front and back pieces and place only one in each side seam. With more fabric, longer cuffs or a wider skirt (with more gores) are possible.

The only equipment needed would be shears and needle and thread. The size of each piece can be determined by holding the

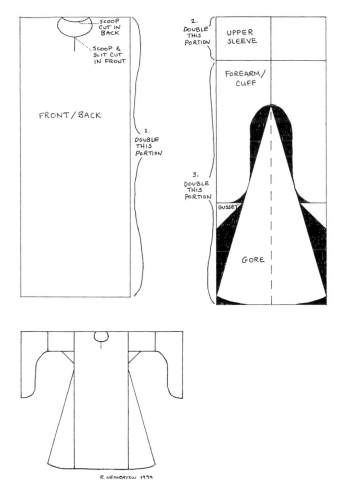

Fig. 238 Possible construction of the gown with hanging sleeves, Bayeux 'Tapestry'. Drawn by Robin Netherton

fabric to the body, or by holding a thread to the body and transferring the distance to the fabric. Pieces are cut in sequence, so that successive shapes reflect cuts already made. Horizontal and vertical cuts follow the fabric grain; diagonals can be found by folding or by using a fabric edge or stretched thread. Use of a straight-edge and chalk make the process slightly easier, but there is no requirement for numeracy or literacy. The cut yields very little waste. Other layouts that are even more economical are possible, but these generally require some sort of template or measuring system to map out the pieces before cutting.

Construction notes

The proportions shown reflect a reconstruction made for a woman 165 cm (5 ft 5 in) tall, American size 14, British size 16. It requires about 5.9 m (6.5 yards) of fabric 57 cm (22.5 in) wide. This is consistent with the width of a woollen fabric woven on a one-person loom, and with extent medieval garments that suggest a typical fabric width of 56–64 cm (22–25 in).

1. *Front and back:* May be separate or cut as one with fold at the top. Determine length as the distance from the top of the shoulder to the desired hem, plus seam and hem allowances. Place neckhole so most is cut from the front piece.

2. *Upper sleeve:* May be cut in four pieces or in two pairs joined at the top fold. Determine length from measurement around widest part of biceps plus ease. Use full measurement if cutting in one piece on fold, or half if cutting in two pieces, plus seam allowance. Selvedge edge of upper sleeve joins front/back pieces with top seam or fold matching, so that half-width of fabric becomes length of upper sleeve on body.

3. This section includes these pieces:

Forearm/cuff: May be cut in four pieces or in two pairs joined at top fold.

Gore: May be cut as four narrow wedges or as two wide ones on fold (dashed line).

Gusset: Four right-angle triangles.

Determine length of this unit as the selvedge length of previously cut upper sleeve (half of folded piece) plus gore length. For gore length, hold front/back piece up to the body and use the distance along selvedge from waist level to the bottom edge of front/back piece. Lay upper sleeve piece on fabric to mask off length needed for top of forearm/cuff. Cut gore(s) from remaining area. From the large piece that is left, cut off enough from bottom of points to form gussets. Shape forearm/cuff from remainder. When attaching forearm/cuff to upper sleeve, top seams or folds need not match; forearm/cuff may be rotated so that cuff hangs in desired position.[1]

---

[1] For a more detailed discussion see Robin Netherton, 'When cut drives fashion: the Norman woman's sleeve shape', *Costume Research Journal*, 12, no. 4 (2001), pp. 4–11.

Bibliography

ABBOTT, G. W., 'Further discoveries in Anglo-Saxon cemeteries at Woodston [*sic*] Hunts', *Peterborough Natural History, Scientific and Archaeological Society Report*, 49 (1920), pp. 34–9.

ADAMS, B. and JACKSON, D., ed. L. BADENOCH, with contributions by J. Bayley, D. Brothwell, E. Crowfoot, H. Härke and T. Pearson, 'The Anglo-Saxon Cemetery at Wakerley, Northamptonshire: excavations by Mr D. Jackson 1968–9', *Northamptonshire Archaeology*, 22 (1988–9), pp. 69–183 and microfiche.

ADDYMAN, P. V. (gen. ed.), *The Archaeology of York*, 20 vols (London, 1976–).

AGER, B. M., 'The smaller variants of the Anglo-Saxon quoit brooch', *Anglo-Saxon Studies in Archaeology and History*, 4 (1985), pp. 1–58.

AHRENS, C. (ed.), *Sachsen und Angelsachsen* (Hamburg, 1979).

AITKEN, A. J., MCINTOSH, A. and PÁLSSON, H. (ed.), *Edinburgh Studies in English and Scots* (London, 1971).

AKERMAN, J. Y., 'An account of excavations in an Anglo-Saxon burial ground at Harnham Hill, nr. Salisbury' and 'Notes on some further discoveries', *Archaeologia*, 35 (1853), pp. 259–78, 475–9.

AKERMAN, J. Y., 'Notes of antiquarian researches in the summer and autumn of 1854', *Archaeologia*, 36 (1855), pp. 175–86.

AKERMAN, J. Y., 'Report on researches in an Anglo-Saxon cemetery at Long Wittenham, Berkshire, in 1859', *Archaeologia*, 38 (1860), pp. 327–52.

ALCOCK, L., 'Quantity or quality: the Anglian graves of Bernicia', in V. I. Evison (ed.), *Angles, Saxons and Jutes: essays presented to J. N. L. Myres* (Oxford, 1981), pp. 168–86.

ALEXANDER, J. J. G. (gen. ed.), *A Survey of Manuscripts Illuminated in the British Isles*, 6 vols (London, 1976–96).

ALEXANDER, J. J. G., *Insular manuscripts 6th to the 9th century*, Insular Manuscripts of the British Isles, 1 (London, 1978).

ALLEN, J. R., 'The Celtic brooch and how it was worn', *Illustrated Archaeologist* (December 1892), pp. 162–75.

ALLEN, J. R., *The Early Christian Monuments of Scotland* (Edinburgh, 1903).

ALMGREN, B., 'Helmets, crowns and warriors' dress from the Roman Empire to the chieftains of Uppland', trans. H. Clarke, in J. P. Lamm and H. A. Nordström, *Vendel Period Studies*, Museum of National Antiquities, Stockholm, Studies, 2 (1983), pp. 11–16.

AMENT, H., 'The Germanic tribes in Europe', in D. M. Wilson (ed.), *The Northern World: the history and heritage of northern Europe AD 400–1100* (London, 1980), pp. 47–70.

AMOS, A. C., DI PAOLO HEALEY, A., HOLLAND, J., FRANZEN, C., MCDOUGALL, D., MCDOUGALL, I., SPIERS, N. and THOMPSON, P., *Dictionary of Old English* (Toronto, 1986–).

ANDRÉ, J. L., 'Widows and vowesses', *Archaeological Journal*, 49 (1892), pp. 69–82.

ANDERSON, W. B. (trans.), *Sidonius Letters and Poems*, Loeb Classical Library, 2 vols (London, 1936–65).

ANON, 'Celtic discs of enamel', *Antiquaries Journal*, 10 (1930), pp. 53–5.

ANON., Untitled, *Oxoniensia*, 17 (1952–3), pp. 216–7.

ANON., Untitled, *Sussex Notes and Queries*, 15 (1958), p. 69.

ANON., 'Sussex: Old Erringham', *Medieval Archaeology*, 9 (1965), p. 175.

ANON., 'Prittlewell: treasures of a king of Essex', *Current Archaeology*, 190, 16.10 (February 2004), pp. 430–6.

APPLEYARD, H. M. and WILDMAN, A. B., 'Fibres of archaeological interest', in D. R. Brothwell and F. S. Higgs (ed.), *Science and Archaeology* (London, 2nd ed., revised and enlarged, 1969), pp. 624–34.

ARNEBORG, J. and ØSTERGÅRD, E., 'Notes on archaeological finds of textiles and textile equipment from the Norse western settlement in Greenland (a preliminary report)', in G. Jaacks and K. Tidow (ed.), *Textilsymposium Neumünster: Archäologische textilfunde – Archaeological textiles: 4.–7.5. 1993 (NESAT V)* (Neumünster, 1994), pp. 162–77.

ARNOLD, C., 'Wealth and social structure: a matter of life and death,' in P. Rahtz, T. Dickinson, and L. Watts (ed.), *Anglo-Saxon Cemeteries 1979: the fourth Anglo-Saxon symposium at Oxford*, British Archaeological Reports, British Series, 82 (1980), pp. 81–142.

ARNOLD, C. J., *The Anglo-Saxon Cemeteries of the Isle of Wight* (London, 1982).

ARNOLD, T. (ed). *Symeonis Monachi Opera Omnia*, Rolls Series, 2 vols (London, 1882–5).

ARNOLDSON, T. W., *Parts of the Body in Older Germanic and Scandinavian*, Linguistic Studies in Germanic, 2 (Chicago, IL, 1915).

ATKINSON, D., *The Romano-British Site on Lowbury Hill in Berkshire* (Reading, 1916).

AVENT, R., *Anglo-Saxon Garnet and Inlaid Composite Brooches*, 2 vols, British Archaeological Reports, British Series, 11 (1975).

BABINGTON, C. and LUMBY, J. R. (ed.), *Polychronicon Ranulphi Higden*, Rolls Series 41, 9 vols (London, 1865–86).

BACKHOUSE, J., TURNER, D. H. and WEBSTER, L. (ed.), *The Golden Age of Anglo-Saxon Art*, British Museum Exhibition Catalogue (London, 1984).

BAILEY, R. N., 'An Anglo-Saxon pin-head from Pontefract', *Yorkshire Archaeological Journal*, 42 (1967–70), pp. 405–6.

BAILEY, R. N., *Viking Age Sculpture* (London, 1980).

BAILEY R. N. and CRAMP, R., *The British Academy Corpus of Anglo-Saxon Stone Sculpture*, 2, *Cumberland, Westmorland and Lancashire North-of-the-Sands* (Oxford, 1988).

BALDWIN BROWN , G., *see* BROWN , G. B.

BANHAM, D., *Monasteriales Indicia: the Anglo-Saxon monastic sign language* (Pinner, 1991).

BARFOOT, J. R. and PRICE-WILLIAMS, B., *The Saxon Barrow at Gally*

Hills, Banstead Down, Surrey, Research Volume of the Surrey Archaeological Society, 3 (1976).

BARLOW, F. (ed. and trans.), *The Life of King Edward who Rests at Westminster*, Oxford Medieval Texts (Oxford, 2nd ed., 1992).

BARROW, G. W. S., 'Northern English Society in the early Middle Ages (in the twelfth and thirteenth centuries)', *Northern History*, 4 (1969), pp. 1–28.

BARTHES, R., *The Fashion System*, trans. M. Ward and W. Howard (Berkeley and Los Angeles, 1990).

BATELY, J. (ed.), *The Old English Orosius*, Early English Text Society, supplementary series 6 (Oxford, 1980).

BATELY, J. M. (ed.), *MS A*, The Anglo-Saxon Chronicle, a collaborative edition, 3 (1986).

BATEMAN, T., *Ten Years Diggings in Celtic and Saxon Grave Hills in the Counties of Derby, Stafford and York 1848–58* (London and Derby, 1861).

BATTISCOMBE, C. F., (ed.), *The Relics of St. Cuthbert* (Oxford, 1956).

BEAMONT, W., *A Literal Extension and Translation of the Domesday Book relating to Cheshire and Lancashire* (Chester, 1863).

BECKWITH, J., *Ivory Carvings in Early Medieval England* (London, 1972).

BÉDAT, I. and GIRAULT-KURTZEMAN, 'The technical study of the Bayeux Tapestry', in P. Bouet, B. Levy and F. Neveux (ed.), *The Bayeux Tapestry: embroidering the facts of history* (Caen, 2004), pp. 83–109.

BENDER JØRGENSEN, L., *Forhistoriske textiler i Skandinavien. Prehistoric Scandinavian Textiles* (Copenhagen, 1986).

BENDER JØRGENSEN, L., 'The textiles of the Saxons, Anglo-Saxons and Franks', *Studien zur Sachsenferschung*, 7 (1991), pp. 11–23.

BENDER JØRGENSEN, L., *North European Textiles until AD 1000* (Aarhus, 1992).

BENDER JØRGENSEN, L., 'Scandinavia, AD 400–1000', in D. Jenkins (ed.), *The Cambridge History of Western Textiles*, 2 vols (Cambridge, 2003), 1, pp. 132–8.

BENDER JØRGENSEN, L. and RINALDO, C. (ed.), *Textiles in European Archaeology*, Report from the 6th NESAT Symposium, 7–11th May 1996 in Borås (*NESAT VI*) (Gothenburg, 1998).

BENDER JØRGENSEN, L. and TIDOW, K. (ed.), *Textilsymposium Neumünster:Archäologische Textilfunde 6.5.–7.5. 1981 (NESAT I)* (Neumünster, 1982).

BENNETT, W. H., 'The southern English development of Germanic initial [f s þ]', *Language*, 31 (1955), pp. 367–71.

BENSON, L. D. (ed.), *The Riverside Chaucer* (Oxford, third ed., 1990).

BERNSTEIN, D. J., *The Mystery of the Bayeux Tapestry* (London, 1986).

BERTELSEN, R., LILLEHAMMER, A. and NÆSS, J.-R. (ed.), *Were they all men? An examination of sex roles in prehistoric society*, Acts from a workshop held at Utstein Kloster, Rogalan 2.–4. November 1979 (NAM Forskningsseminar nr. 1), (Stavanger, 1987).

BERTRAND, S., *La Tapisserie de Bayeux et la manière de vivre au onzième siècle*, Glossaire Bayeux; introductions à la nuit de temps, 2 (La Pierre-qui-Vire, 1966).

BESSINGER, J. B., Jr. and CREED, R. P. (ed.), *Medieval and Linguistic Studies in Honour of Francis Peabody Magoun, Jr* (London, 1965).

BETHURUM, D., *The Homilies of Wulfstan* (Oxford, 1957).

BIDDER, H. F. and MORRIS, J., 'An Anglo-Saxon cemetery at Mitcham', *Surrey Archaeological Collections*, 56 (1959), pp. 51–131.

BIDDLE, M., 'Excavations at Winchester, 1964', *Antiquaries Journal*, 45 (1965), pp. 230–64.

BIDDLE, M. (ed.), *Winchester Studies*, 7.ii: Artefacts from Medieval Winchester, ii: Object and Economy in Medieval Winchester (Oxford, 1990).

BIDDLE, M., 'Unidentified bone objects', in M. Biddle, *Winchester Studies*, 7.ii, Artefacts from Medieval Winchester, ii: Object and Economy in Medieval Winchester (Oxford, 1990), pp.1129–45.

BIDDLE, M. and KJØLBYE-BIDDLE, B., 'The Repton Stone', *Anglo-Saxon England*, 14 (1985), pp. 233–92.

BIRKEBÆK, F., *Norden i Vikingtiden* (Gothenburg, 1975).

BLACKMORE, H. P., 'On a barrow near Old Sarum', *Transactions of the Salisbury Field Club*, 1 (1893), pp. 49–51.

BLINDHEIM, C., 'Vernesfunnene og Kvinnedrakten i Norden i Vikingtiden', *Viking*, 9 (1945), pp. 143–62.

BLINDHEIM, C., 'Drakt og smykker', *Viking*, 11 (1947), pp. 1–139.

BÖHNER, K, 'Die Zeitstellung der beiden fränkischen Gräber im Kölner Dom', *Kölner Jahrbuch*, 9 (1967–8), pp. 124–35.

BONNER, G., ROLLASON, D. and STANCLIFFE, C. (ed.), *St Cuthbert, his Cult and Community to 1200* (Woodbridge, 1989).

BORK, R. (ed.), *De Re Metallica: studies in medieval metals and metallurgy*, Avista Annual Series (forthcoming, 2004).

BOSWORTH, J. and TOLLER, T. N., *An Anglo-Saxon Dictionary* (Oxford, 1898, reprinted 1976) and TOLLER, T. N., *Supplement* (Oxford, 1921) with Enlarged Addenda and Corrigenda by A. Campbell (Oxford, 1972, reprinted 1973).

BOUET, P., LEVY, B. and NEVEUX, F. (ed.), *The Bayeux Tapestry: embroidering the facts of history* (Caen, 2004).

BOUTERWEK [C. W.], 'Die ags. Glossen in dem Brüsseler Codex von Aldhelms Schrift De Virginitate', *Zeischrift für deutsches Alterthum*, 9 (1853), pp. 401–530.

BOUTERWEK, C. W. (ed.), *Screadunga* (Elberfeld, 1858).

BOYLE, A., JENNINGS, D., MILES, D. and PALMER, S., *The Anglo-Saxon Cemetery at Butler's Field, Lechlade, Gloucestershire* Volume 1: Prehistoric and Roman activity and Anglo-Saxon grave catalogue, Thames Valley Landscapes Monograph No. 10 (Oxford, 1998).

BRENT, J., 'Account of the Society's researches in the Saxon cemetery at Sarr [*sic*]', *Archaeologia Cantiana*, 5 (1862–3), pp. 305–22.

BRENT, J., 'An account of researches in an Anglo-Saxon cemetery at Stowting, in Kent, during the autumn of 1866', *Archaeologia*, 41 (1867), pp. 409–20.

BRETT, G., 'The "Rider" silk', in C. F. Battiscombe (ed.), *The Relics of St. Cuthbert* (Oxford, 1956), pp. 470–83.

BRISBANE, M. A. (ed.), *The Archaeology of Novgorod, Russia: recent results from the town and its hinterland*, trans. K. Judelson, The Society for Medieval Archaeology Monograph Series, 13 (Lincoln, 1992).

B[RISCOE], G. and LE BARD, W. E., 'An Anglo-Saxon cemetery on Lakenheath airfield', *Proceedings of the Cambridgeshire Antiquarian Society*, 53 (1959), pp. 56–7.

BROTHWELL, D. R. and HIGGS, F. S. (ed.), *Science and Archaeology* (London, 2nd ed., revised and enlarged, 1969).

BROWN, D., Untitled, *Medieval Archaeology*, 18 (1974), pp. 151–4.

BROWN, D., 'Fire-steels and pursemounts again', *Bonner Jahrbücher*, 177,

(1977), pp. 451–77.

BROWN, G. B., *The Arts in Early England*, 6 vols (London, 1903–37).

BROWN, P., *The Book of Kells* (London, 1980).

BRUCE-MITFORD, R. L. S., 'Iconography of the Fuller Brooch', Appendix B in D. M. Wilson, *Anglo-Saxon Ornamental Metalwork 700–1000 in the British Museum* (London, 1964).

BRUCE-MITFORD, R. L. S., *The Art of the Codex Amiatinus* (Jarrow, 1967).

BRUCE-MITFORD, R. [L. S.], *Aspects of Anglo-Saxon Archaeology: Sutton Hoo and other discoveries* (London, 1974).

BRUCE-MITFORD, R. L. S. (ed.), *The Sutton Hoo Ship Burial*, 3 vols (London, 1975–83).

BRUSH, K. A., 'Adorning the Dead; the social significance of early Anglo-Saxon funerary costumes in England (5th–6th c. AD)', unpublished PhD thesis (University of Cambridge, 1993).

BUCKTON, D., 'Late tenth- and eleventh-century cloisonné enamel brooches', *Medieval Archaeology*, 30 (1986), pp. 8–18.

BUCKTON, D., *Byzantium: treasures of Byzantine art and culture* (London, 1994).

BUDNY, M. and TWEDDLE, D., 'De vroeg-middeleeuwse stoffen te Maaseik', *Overdruk uit het oude Land van loon Jaargang*, 38 (1983), pp. 231–71.

BUDNY, M. and TWEDDLE, D., 'The Maaseik embroideries', *Anglo-Saxon England*, 13 (1984), pp. 65–96.

BULLOUGH, D., *The Age of Charlemagne* (London, 1965).

CALVERLEY, W. S., *Notes on the Early Sculptured Crosses, Shrines and Monuments in the Present Diocese of Carlisle*, Cumberland and Westmorland Antiquarian and Archaeological Society Extra Series 11 (1899).

CAMERON, E. A. (ed), *Leather and Fur: aspects of early medieval trade and technology* (London, 1998).

CAMPBELL, A., *Old English Grammar* (Oxford, 1959).

CAMPBELL, J. (ed.), *The Anglo-Saxons* (Oxford, 1982).

CARUS-WILSON, E. M., 'Haberget: a medieval textile conundrum', *Medieval Archaeology*, 13 (1969), pp. 148–66.

CARVER, M. O. H. (ed.), *The Age of Sutton Hoo* (Woodbridge, 1992).

CARVER, M., 'The Anglo-Saxon cemetery at Sutton Hoo: an interim report', in M. O. H. Carver, (ed.), *The Age of Sutton Hoo* (Woodbridge, 1992), pp. 343–71.

CARVER, M. (ed.), *In Search of Cult: archaeological investigations in honour of Philip Rahtz*, University of York Archaeological Papers (Woodbridge, 1993).

CARVER, M., *Sutton Hoo: burial ground of kings?* (London, 1998).

CARVER, M. (ed.), *The Cross goes North: processes of conversion in Northern Europe, AD 300–1300* (York/Woodbridge, 2003).

CASPAR, E., 'Fragmenta registri Iohannis VIII, papae', *Monumenta Germaniae Historica, Epistolae*, 1, VII (Berlin, 1928).

CASSIDY, B. (ed.), *The Ruthwell Cross: papers from the Colloquium sponsored by the Index of Christian Art, Princeton University 8 December 1989*, Index of Christian Art Occasional Papers 1 (Princeton, NJ, 1992).

CHADWICK, S. E. [later HAWKES], 'The Anglo-Saxon cemetery at Finglesham, Kent, a reconsideration', *Medieval Archaeology*, 2 (1958), pp. 1–71.

CHANEY, W. A., *The Cult of Kingship in Anglo-Saxon England* (Manchester, 1970).

CHARLESTON, R. J., 'Glass rings', in M. Biddle (ed.), *Winchester Studies*,7.ii: Artefacts from Medieval Winchester, ii: Object and Economy in Medieval Winchester (Oxford, 1990), pp. 652–3.

CHATWIN, P. B., 'Anglo-Saxon finds at Warwick', *Antiquaries Journal*, 5 (1925), pp. 268–72.

CHIROL, É. (ed.), *Actes du Colloque international d'Archéologie, Rouen 3–4–5 Juillet 1975 (Centenaire de l'abbé Cochet)* (Rouen, 1978).

CHRISTIE, A. G. L., *English Medieval Embroidery* (Oxford, 1938).

CHRISTLEIN, R., *Die Alamannen* (Stuttgart, 1978).

CIGAAR, K., 'England and Byzantium on the eve of the Norman Conquest', *Anglo-Norman Studies*, 5: *Proceedings of the Battle Conference, 1982* (1982), pp. 78–89.

CLARK, C., 'Onomastics', in R. M. Hogg (ed.),*The Cambridge History of the English Language I: the beginnings to 1066* (Cambridge, 1992), pp. 452–89.

CLARKE, R. R., 'Norfolk in the Dark Ages, 400–800 A. D.', *Norfolk Archaeology*, 27 (1939–41), pp. 163–249.

CLAUSS, G., 'Beobachtungen an merowingerzeitlichen Gräbern bei Hockenheim, Rhein-Neckar-Kreis',*Archäologisches Korrespondenzblatt*, 6 (1976), pp. 55–64.

CLAUSS, G., 'Strumpfbänder: ein beitrag zur Frauentracht des 6. und 7. jahrhunderts n. Chr.',*Jahrbuch des Romisch-germanisches Zentralmuseum zu Mainz*, 23–4 (1976–7), pp. 54–88.

CLEASBY, R. and VIGFUSSON, G., *An Icelandic-English Dictionary*, 2nd ed. with supplement by W. A. Craigie (Oxford, 1957, reprint 1975).

CLEMOES, P. and HUGHES, K. (ed.), *England Before the Conquest: studies in primary sources presented to Dorothy Whitelock* (Cambridge, 1971).

CLINCH, G., *English Costume* (London,1909).

COATSWORTH, E., 'Cloth-making and the Virgin Mary in Anglo-Saxon literature and art', in G. R. Owen-Crocker and T. Graham (ed.),*Medieval Art: Recent Perspectives. A memorial tribute to C. R. Dodwell* (Manchester, 1998), pp. 8–25.

COATSWORTH, E., 'The embroideries from the tomb of St Cuthbert', in N. I. Higham and D. Hill (ed.), *Edward the Elder 899–924* (London, 2001), pp. 292–306.

COATSWORTH, E., FITZGERALD, M., LEAHY, K. and OWEN-CROCKER, G. R., 'Anglo-Saxon Textiles from Cleatham, Humberside', *Textile History*, 27.1 (1996), pp. 1–37.

COCKAYNE, T. O. (ed.),*Narratiunculae Anglice conscriptae* (London, 1861).

COCKAYNE, T. O., *Leechdoms, Wortcunning and Starcraft of Early England*, 3 vols, Rolls Series, 35 (London, 1864–6).

COCKS, A. H., 'Anglo-Saxon burials at Ellesborough', *Records of Buckinghamshire*, 9 (1904–9), pp. 425–9.

COLGRAVE, B. (ed.), *Eddius Life of St Wilfrid – The Life of Bishop Wilfrid by Eddius Stephanus* (Cambridge, 1927).

COLGRAVE, B. (ed.), *Two Lives of St Cuthbert* (Cambridge, 1940).

COLGRAVE, B. (ed.), *Felix's Life of St Guthlac* (Cambridge, 1956).

COLGRAVE, B. (ed.), *The Paris Psalter*, Early English Manuscripts in Facsimile, 8 (Copenhagen, 1958).

COLGRAVE, B. and MYNORS, R. A. B. (ed.),*Bede's Ecclesiastical History of the English People* (Oxford, 1969).

COLLINGWOOD, W. G., 'Anglian and Anglo-Danish sculpture in the

North Riding of Yorkshire', *Yorkshire Archaeological Journal*, 19 (1906–7), pp. 267–413.

COLLINGWOOD, W. G., 'The Lowther hogbacks', *Transactions of the Cumberland and Westmorland Antiquarian and Archaeological Society* (2nd series), 7 (1907), pp. 152–64.

COLLINGWOOD, W. G., 'Anglian and Anglo-Danish sculpture in the East Riding', *Yorkshire Archaeological Journal*, 21 (1910–11), pp. 254–302.

COLLINGWOOD, W. G., 'A rune-inscribed Anglian cross-shaft in Urswick church', *Transactions of the Cumberland and Westmorland Antiquarian and Archaeological Society* (2nd series), 11 (1911), pp. 462–8.

COLLINGWOOD, W. G., 'Anglian and Anglo-Danish sculpture in the West Riding', *Yorkshire Archaeological Journal*, 23 (1914–15), pp. 129–299.

COLLINGWOOD, W. G., 'The Brailsford Cross', *Derbyshire Archaeological Journal*, 45 (1923), pp. 1–13.

COLLINGWOOD, W. G., *Northumbrian Crosses of the Pre-Norman Age* (London, 1927).

COLLINGWOOD, W. G., ' A cross-fragment at Sutton-on-Derwent', *Yorkshire Archaeological Journal*, 29 (1927–9), pp. 238–40.

COLLINS, A. E. P. and COLLINS, F. J., 'Excavations on Blewburton Hill, 1953', *Berkshire Archaeological Journal*, 57 (1959), pp. 52–73.

COOK, A. M., 'The Evidence for the Reconstruction of Female Costume in the early Anglo-Saxon Period in the South of England', unpublished MA thesis (University of Birmingham, 1974).

COOK, A. M., *The Anglo-Saxon Cemetery at Fonaby, Lincolnshire*, Occasional Papers in Lincolnshire History and Archaeology, 6 (1981).

COOK, A. M. and DACRE, M. W., *Excavations at Portway, Andover, 1974–5*, Oxford University Committee for Medieval Archaeology Monograph, 4 (1985).

COXE, H. O. (ed.), *Rogeri de Wendover Chronica sive Flores Historiarum*, 4 vols (London, 1841–2).

CRAMP, R. J., 'An Anglo-Saxon pin from Birdoswald', *Transactions of the Cumberland and Westmorland Antiquarian and Archaeological Society*, 2nd series, 44 (1964), pp. 90–3.

CRAMP, R. J., *Early Northumbrian Sculpture* (Jarrow, 1965).

CRAMP, R. J., *Anglian and Viking York*, University of York Borthwick Papers, No. 33 (1967).

CRAMP, R. J., 'Tradition and innovation in English stone sculpture of the tenth to the eleventh centuries', in D. Milojĉić (ed.), *Kolloquium über spätantike und frümittelalterliche Skulptur*, 3 (Mainz, 1972), pp. 139–48.

CRAMP, R. J. (gen. ed.), *British Academy Corpus of Anglo-Saxon Stone Sculpture* (Oxford, 1984–).

CRAMP, R. J. (ed.), *British Academy Corpus of Anglo-Saxon Stone Sculpture*, 1, *County Durham and Northumberland* (Oxford, 1984).

CRAWFORD, S., 'Children, death and the afterlife in Anglo-Saxon England', *Anglo-Saxon Studies in Archaeology and History*, 6 (1993), pp. 83–91.

CRAWFORD, S. J. (ed.), *The Old English Version of the Heptateuch, Aelfric's Treatise on the Old and New Testament and his Preface to Genesis*, Early English Text Society, original series, 160 (1922).

CROWFOOT, E., Notes in S. E. Chadwick, 'The Anglo-Saxon cemetery at Finglesham, Kent, a reconsideration', *Medieval Archaeology*, 2 (1958), pp. 36–7.

CROWFOOT, E., 'The textile remains', in J. Musty and J. E. D. Stratton, 'A Saxon cemetery at Winterbourne Gunner, near Salisbury', *Wiltshire Archaeological Magazine*, 59 (1964), pp. 86–109, at p. 108.

CROWFOOT, E.,'The textiles', Appendix III in P. Hutchinson, 'The Anglo-Saxon cemetery at Little Eriswell, Suffolk', *Proceedings of the Cambridge Antiquarian Society*, 69 (1966), pp. 29–32.

CROWFOOT, E., 'Early Anglo-Saxon gold braids: addenda and corrigenda', *Medieval Archaeology*, 13 (1969), pp. 209–10.

CROWFOOT, E., 'Worthy Park, Kingsworthy, Hampshire, Textiles report', Unpublished Ancient Monuments Laboratory Report 1709 (1974).

CROWFOOT, E., 'The textiles', in B. Green and A. Rogerson, *The Anglo-Saxon Cemetery at Bergh Apton, Norfolk: Catalogue*, East Anglian Archaeology, 7 (1978), pp. 98–106.

CROWFOOT, E., 'The textiles', in A. M. Cook, *The Anglo-Saxon Cemetery at Fonaby, Lincolnshire*, Occasional Papers in Lincolnshire History and Archaeology, 6 (1981), pp. 89–100.

CROWFOOT, E., 'The Textiles', in R. L. S. Bruce-Mitford (ed.), *The Sutton Hoo Ship Burial*, 3, ed. A. Care Evans (London, 1983), i, pp. 409–79.

CROWFOOT, E. 'The textiles', in S. M. Hirst, *An Anglo-Saxon Inhumation Cemetery at Sewerby East Yorkshire*,York University Archaeological Publications 4 (1985), pp. 48–54.

CROWFOOT, E., 'Textiles', in A. M. Cook and M. W. Dacre, *Excavations at Portway, Andover, 1974–5*, Oxford University Committee for Medieval Archaeology Monograph, 4 (1985), pp. 99–102.

CROWFOOT, E., 'Textiles', Appendix VI in B. Green, A. Rogerson and S. G. White, *The Anglo-Saxon Cemetery at Morning Thorpe, Norfolk*, I: *Catalogue*, East Anglian Archaeology 36.1 (1987), pp. 171–88.

CROWFOOT, E., 'Textiles from Ardale Anglo-Saxon cemetery', in T. J. Wilkinson (ed.), *Archaeology and Environment in South Essex: rescue archaeology along the Grays by-pass, 1979–80*, East Anglian Archaeology, 42 (1988), pp. 54–5.

CROWFOOT, E., 'The textiles', in B. Adams and D. Jackson, D., ed. L. Badenoch,'The Anglo-Saxon Cemetery at Wakerley, Northamptonshire: excavations by Mr D. Jackson 1968–9', *Northamptonshire Archaeology*, 22 (1988–9), pp. 168–72.

CROWFOOT, E., 'The textiles', in G. Speake, *A Saxon Bed Burial on Swallowcliffe Down*, Historic Buildings and Monuments Commission Archaeological Report No. 10 (London, 1989), pp. 116–17.

CROWFOOT, E., 'Textiles', in M. Biddle (ed.), *Winchester Studies*, 7.ii: Artefacts from Medieval Winchester, ii: Object and Economy in Medieval Winchester (Oxford, 1990), pp. 468–88.

CROWFOOT, E., 'Textile fragments from "relic-boxes" in Anglo-Saxon graves', in P. Walton and J.-P Wild (ed.), *Textiles in Northern Archaeology*, *NESAT III*: Textile Symposium in York 6–9 May 1987, North European Symposium for Archaeological Textiles Monograph 3 (London, 1990), pp. 47–56.

CROWFOOT, E., 'Textiles associated with metalwork', in T. Malim and J. Hines (ed.), *Edix Hill (Barrington A), Cambridgeshire*, Council for British Archaeology Research Report, 112 (1998), pp. 235–46.

CROWFOOT, E., 'Textiles', in D. A. Hinton, *A Smith in Lindsey: the Anglo-Saxon grave at Tattersall Thorpe, Lincolnshire*, The Society for Medieval Archaeology Monograph Series, 16 (Leeds, 2000), pp. 94–6.

CROWFOOT, E. and EDWARDS, G., 'The textiles' and 'Fibre identification', in A. Hunn, J. Lawson and M. Farley, 'The Anglo-Saxon cemetery at Dinton, Buckinghamshire', in *Anglo-Saxon Studies in Archaeology and History*, 7 (1994), pp. 127–8.

CROWFOOT, E. and HAWKES, S. C., 'Early Anglo-Saxon gold braids', *Medieval Archaeology*, 11 (1967), pp. 42–86.

CROWFOOT, E., PRITCHARD, F. and STANILAND, K., *Textiles and Clothing c.1150–1458: medieval finds from excavations in London* (London, 1992).

CROWFOOT, G. M., 'Textiles of the Saxon period in the Museum of Archaeology and Ethnology', *Proceedings of the Cambridge Antiquarian Society*, 44 (1951), pp. 26–32.

CROWFOOT, G. M., ' Anglo-Saxon tablet weaving', *Antiquaries Journal*, 32 (1952), pp. 189–91.

CROWFOOT, G. M., 'The textile remains', Appendix II in E. T. Leeds and H. de S. Shortt, *An Anglo-Saxon Cemetery at Petersfinger, near Salisbury, Wilts* (Salisbury, 1953), p. 61.

CROWFOOT, G. M., Appendix to F. H. Thompson, 'Anglo-Saxon sites in Lincolnshire: Unpublished material and recent discoveries', *Antiquaries Journal*, 36 (1956), pp. 181–99, at pp. 188–9.

CROWFOOT, G. M., 'The Braids', in C. F. Battiscombe (ed.), *The Relics of St. Cuthbert* (Oxford, 1956), pp. 433–63.

CROWTHER-BEYNON, V. B., 'Notes on an Anglian cemetery at Market Overton, Rutland', *Archaeologia*, 62 (1911), pp. 481–6.

CUBBIN, G. P. (ed.), *MS D*, The Anglo-Saxon Chronicle, a collaborative edition, 6 (1996).

C[UMBERLAND], A., 'Saxon cemetery, "Riseley", Horton Kirby', *Transactions of the Dartford District Antiquarian Society*, 8 (1938), pp. 15–29.

DALE, M. K., 'The London silkwomen of the fifteenth century', *The Economic History Review*, 4 (1932–4), pp. 324–35.

DAMICO, H. and KARKOV, C. (ed.), *Aedificia Nova: papers in honour of Rosemary Cramp*, (Kalamazoo, MI, forthcoming, 2005).

DAMICO, H. and OLSEN, A. H. (ed.), *New Readings on Women in Old English Literature* (Bloomington and Indianapolis, IN, 1990).

DE CAMP, D., 'The genesis of the Old English dialects', *Language*, 34 (1958), pp. 232–44.

DEDEKAM, H.,'To tekstilfunde frå folkevandringstiden', *Bergen Museums Årbok* (1924–5), pp. 1–57.

DENNETT, I., 'Isle of Wight', *Transactions of the British Archaeological Association*, Winchester Congress (1845), pp. 148–60.

DESHMAN, R., 'Benedictus Monarcha et Monarchus: early medieval ruler theology and the Anglo-Saxon reform', *Frümittelalterliche Studien*, 22 (1988), pp. 204–40.

DESHMAN, R., *The Benedictional of Æthelwold*, Studies in Manuscript Illumination, 9 (Princeton, NJ, 1995).

DEWALD, E. T., *The Illustrations of the Utrecht Psalter* (Leipzig, 1933).

DEWING, H. B. (trans.), *Procopius*, 7 vols, Loeb Classical Library (London, 1914–40).

DI PAOLO HEALY, A. and VENEZKY, R., *A Microfiche Concordance to Old English*, Publications of the Dictionary of Old English, University of Delaware (Delaware, 1980).

DICKINSON, T. M., 'On the origin and chronology of the early Anglo-

Saxon disc brooch', in S. C. Hawkes, D. Brown and J. Campbell (ed.), *Anglo-Saxon Studies in Archaeology and History*, British Archaeology Reports, British Series, 1, 72 (1979), pp. 39–80.

DICKINSON, T. M., 'Fowler's Type G penannular brooches reconsidered', *Medieval Archaeology*, 26 (1982), pp. 41–68.

DICKINSON, T. M., 'An Anglo-Saxon "cunning woman" from Bidford-on-Avon', in M. Carver (ed.), *In Search of Cult: archaeological investigations in honour of Philip Rahtz*, University of York Archaeological Papers (Woodbridge, 1993), pp. 45–54.

DICTIONARY OF OLD ENGLISH PROJECT, *The Complete Corpus of Old English in Machine Readable Form*, Centre for Medieval Studies, University of Toronto (Toronto, 1994).

DOBBIE, E. V. K. (ed.), *The Anglo-Saxon Minor Poems*, The Anglo-Saxon Poetic Records, 6 (London and New York, 1942).

DOBBIE, E. V. K. (ed.), *Beowulf and Judith*, The Anglo-Saxon Poetic Records, 4 (London and New York, 1953).

DOCKRAY-MILLER, M., *Motherhood and Mothering in Anglo-Saxon England*, (Basingstoke and London, 2000).

DODWELL, C. R., 'L'Originalité icongraphique de plusieurs illustrations anglo-saxonnes de l'Ancien Testament', *Cahiers de civilisation médiévale*, 14 (1971), pp. 319–28.

DODWELL, C. R., *Anglo-Saxon Art: a new perspective* (Manchester, 1982).

DODWELL, C. R., *The Pictorial Arts of the West 800–1200* (New Haven, CT and London, 1993).

DODWELL, C. R. and CLEMOES, P., *The Old English Illustrated Hexateuch*, Early English Manuscripts in Facsimile, 18 (Copenhagen, 1974).

DOLLEY, M., 'The nummular brooch from Sulgrave', in P. Clemoes and K. Hughes (ed.), *England before the Conquest: studies in primary sources presented to Dorothy Whitelock* (Cambridge, 1971), pp. 333–49.

DOMMASNES, L. H., 'Male/female roles and ranks in late Iron Age Norway', in R. Bertelsen, A. Lillehammer and J.-R. Næss (ed.), *Were They All Men? An examination of sex roles in prehistoric society*, Acts from a workshop held at Utstein Kloster, Rogalan 2.–4. November 1979 (NAM Forskningsseminar nr. 1), (Stavanger, 1987), pp. 65–77.

DOUGLAS, J., *Nenia Britannica* (London, 1793).

DRINKALL, G. and FOREMAN, M., *The Anglo-Saxon Cemetery at Castledyke South, Barton-on-Humber*, Sheffield Excavation Reports 6 (Sheffield, 1998).

DRINKALL, G., FOREMAN, M. and WALTON ROGERS, P., 'Craft and weaving equipment', in G. Drinkall and M. Foreman, *The Anglo-Saxon Cemetery at Castledyke South, Barton-on-Humber*, Sheffield Excavation Reports 6 (Sheffield, 1998), pp. 292–4.

DRONKE, U. (ed. and trans.), *The Poetic Edda*, II, Mythological Poems (Oxford, 1997).

DU CANGE, C. D. F. (ed.), *Glossarium mediae et infimae Latinatis*, with supplements, edited and revised by L. Faure, 10 vols (Niort, 1882–7).

DÜMMLER, E. (ed.), 'S. Bonifatii et Lulli epistolae', *Monumenta Germaniae Historica Epistolae 3*, Merovingici et Karolini Aevi, I (Berlin, 1892).

DUMVILLE, D. and KEYNES, S. (ed.), *The Anglo-Saxon Chronicle: a collaborative edition* (Cambridge, 1983-).

DUNNING, R. C. and WHEELER, R. E. M., 'A barrow at Dunstable,

Beds', *Archaeological Journal*, 88 (1931), pp. 193–217.

EAST, K., 'The Shoes', in R. L. S. Bruce-Mitford (ed.), *The Sutton Hoo Ship Burial*, 3, ed. A. C. Evans, 2 vols (London, 1983), ii, pp. 788–812.

EDWARDS, G. and WATSON, J., 'Organic remains', in G. Drinkall and M. Foreman, *The Anglo-Saxon Cemetery at Castledyke South, Barton-on-Humber*, Sheffield Excavation Reports 6 (Sheffield, 1998), pp. 241–2, 283–4.

EDWARDS, H. J. (trans.), *Caesar The Gallic War*, Loeb Classical Library (London, 1917).

EHWALD, R. (ed.), *Aldhelmi Opera*, Monumenta Germaniae Historica, Auctores Antiquissimi, XV (Berlin, 1919).

EKWALL, E., *Dictionary of English Place-names* (Oxford, 4th ed., 1960).

ELLIS DAVIDSON, H. R., *Myths and Symbols in Pagan Europe* (Manchester, 1988).

EMERTON, E., *The Letters of Saint Boniface* (New York, 1940).

ENLART, C., *Manuel d'Archéologie française, depuis les temps mérovingiens jusqu'à la renaissance*, 3 vols (Paris, 1902–16).

EVANS, A. C. (ed.), *The Sutton Hoo Ship Burial*, 3, 2 vols (London, 1983).

EVISON, V. I., *The Fifth-century Invasions South of the Thames* (London, 1965).

EVISON, V. I., 'The Dover, Breach Downs and Birka men', *Antiquity*, 39 (1965), pp. 214–7.

EVISON, V. I., 'The Dover ring sword and other sword-rings and beads', *Archaeologia*, 51 (1967), pp. 63–118.

EVISON, V. I., 'Quoit brooch Style buckles', *Antiquaries Journal*, 48 (1968), pp. 231–46.

EVISON, V. I. (ed.), *Angles, Saxons and Jutes: essays presented to J. N. L. Myres* (Oxford, 1981).

EVISON, V. I., *Dover: The Buckland Anglo-Saxon Cemetery*, Historic Buildings and Monuments Commission for England, Archaeological Report No. 3 (1987).

FAIRHOLT, F. W., *Costume in England*, 4th ed. enlarged and revised by H. A. Dillon, 2 vols (London, 1896).

FAUSSETT, B., *Inventorium Sepulchrale*, ed. C. R. Smith (London, 1856).

FELL, C., *Women in Anglo-Saxon England; and the impact of 1066* by C. Clark and E. Williams (London, 1984).

FITCH, S. E., 'Discovery of Saxon remains at Kempston', *Reports of the Associated Architectural Societies*, 7 (1863–4), pp. 269–99.

FITZGERALD, M. A., 'Insular dress in early medieval Ireland', in G. R. Owen-Crocker (ed.), *Anglo-Saxon Texts and Contexts*, Bulletin of the John Rylands University Library of Manchester, 79.3 (1997), pp. 251–61.

FILMER-SANKEY, W. (ed.), *Anglo-Saxon Studies in Archaeology and History*, 6 (Oxford, 1993).

FLANAGAN, J. F., 'The Figured-Silks', in C. F. Battiscombe (ed.), *The Relics of St. Cuthbert* (Oxford, 1956), pp. 484–525.

FORBES, K. G., 'The Codford Saxon carving', *Wiltshire Archaeological Magazine*, 62 (1967), pp. 34–7.

FORD, W. J., *The Romano-British and Anglo-Saxon Settlement and Cemeteries at Stretton-on-Fosse, Warwickshire*, forthcoming.

FOSTER, W. K., 'Account of the excavation of an Anglo-Saxon cemetery at Barrington, Cambridgeshire', *Cambridge Antiquarian Society Communications*, 5 (1880–4), pp. 5–32.

FOWLER, E., 'Celtic metalwork of the fifth and sixth centuries A. D.', *Archaeological Journal*, 120 (1963), pp. 98–150.

FREMERSDORF, F., 'Zwei wichtige Frankengräber aus Köln', *Jahrbuch für Prähistorische und Ethnografische Kunst*, 15–16 [1941–2] (1943).

FREYHAN, R., 'The place of the stole and maniples in Anglo-Saxon art of the tenth century', in C. F. Battiscombe (ed.), *The Relics of St. Cuthbert* (Oxford, 1956), pp. 409–32.

FRITCHIE, C., 'Textile catalogue', in K. Parfitt and B. Brugmann, *The Anglo-Saxon Cemetery on Mill Hill, Deal, Kent*, The Society for Medieval Archaeology Monograph Series, No. 14 (1997), pp. 252–7.

FUCHS, S., *Die Langobardischen Goldblattkreuze aus der zone Südwärts der Alpen* (Berlin, 1938).

FYSON, D. R., 'Some late Anglian sculpture', *Archaeologia Aeliana*, 4th series, 38 (1960), pp. 149–52.

GABRA-SANDERS, T., 'A review of Viking-Age textiles and fibres from Scotland: an interim report', in L. Bender Jørgensen and C. Rinaldo (ed.), *Textiles in European Archaeology*, Report from the 6th NESAT Symposium, 7–11th May 1996 in Borås (*NESAT VI*) (Göteborg, 1998), pp. 177–85.

GARBSCH, J., *Die norisch-pannonische Frauentracht im 1 und 2 Jahrhundert* (Munich, 1965).

GARMONSWAY, G. N., *Aelfric's Colloquy* (London, 1939).

GEAKE, H., *The Use of Grave-Goods in Conversion-Period England, c.600-c. 850*, British Archaeological Reports, British Series, 261 (1997).

GEAKE, H., 'Invisible kingdoms: the use of grave-goods in seventh-century England,' *Anglo-Saxon Studies in Archaeology and History* 10 (1999), pp. 203–215.

GEARY, P. J., 'Ethnic identity as a situational construct in the Middle Ages', *Mitteilungen der Anthropologischen Gesellschaft in Wien*, 113 (1983), pp. 15–26.

GEIJER, A., *Birka, III: die Textilfunde aus den Gräbern* (Uppsala, 1938).

GEIJER, A., 'Var järnälderns "friska kläde" tillverkat i Syrien?', ['The *pallium fresonicum* of the Viking Age, was it manufactured in Syria?'], *Fornvannen*, 60 (1965), pp. 112–32 [English summary pp. 130–2].

GEIJER, A., 'The textile finds from Birka', in N. B. Harte and K. G. Ponting (ed.), *Cloth and Clothing in Medieval Europe: essays in memory of Professor E. M. Carus-Wilson* (London, 1983), pp. 80–99.

GERRITSEN, J., 'Þurh þreata geþræcu', *English Studies*, 35 (1954), pp. 259–62.

GILES, J. A. (ed.), *Complete Works of Alfred the Great*, 2 vols (1858, reprinted New York, 1969).

GILMOUR, B., Appendix II: 'X-Radiographs of two objects: the weaving batten (24/3) and sword (40/5)', in C. Hills, K. Penn and R. Rickett, *The Anglo-Saxon Cemetery at Spong Hill, North Elmham*, East Anglian Archaeology Report, 21 (Dereham, 1984), pp. 160–3.

GIRKE, G., *Die Tracht der Germanen in der vor- und fruhgeschichtlichen Zeit*, 2 vols (Leipzig, 1922).

GLOB, P. V., *The Bog People*, trans. R. L. S. Bruce-Mitford (London, 1969).

GLOB, P. V., *The Mound People*, trans. J. Bulman (New York, 1974).

GLOSECKI, S. O., *Shamanism and Old English Poetry* (New York and London, 1989).

GODDEN, M. (ed.), *Ælfric's Catholic Homilies: the second series. Text*, Early English Text Society, supplementary series, 5 (1979).

GODFREY-FAUSSETT, T., 'The Saxon cemetery at Bifrons', *Archaeologia Cantiana*, 10 (1876), pp. 298–315.

GODFREY-FAUSSETT, T., 'The Saxon cemetery at Bifrons', *Archaeologia Cantiana*, 13 (1880), pp. 552–6.

GOLDSMIDT, A., *Die deutsche Buchmalerei*, 2 vols (Florence and New York, 1928).

GOLLANCZ, I., *The Cædmon Manuscript of Anglo-Saxon Biblical Poetry, Junius XI in the Bodleian Library* (Oxford, 1927).

GOLLANCZ, I. (ed.), *Sir Gawain and the Green Knight*, Early English Text Society, original series, 210 (1940).

GOODWIN, C. W. (ed.), *The Anglo-Saxon Version of the Life of St Guthlac* (London, 1848).

GOOLDEN, P., *The Old English Appolonius of Tyre* (London, 1958).

GOOSSENS, L. (ed.), *The Old English Glosses of MS Brussels, Royal Library, 1650, Aldhelm's 'De laudibus virginitatis'* (Brussels, 1974).

GRAHAM-CAMPBELL, J., 'The Scandinavian Viking-Age burials of England – some problems of interpretation', in P. Rahtz, T. Dickinson and L. Watts (ed.), *Anglo-Saxon cemeteries 1979: the fourth Anglo-Saxon symposium at Oxford*, British Archaeological Reports, British Series, 82 (1980), pp. 379–82.

GRAHAM-CAMPBELL, J. and KIDD, D., *The Vikings* (London, 1980).

GRAHAM-CAMPBELL, J. and OKASHA, E., with an introductory note by METCALF, M., 'A pair of inscribed Anglo-Saxon hooked tags from the Rome (Forum) 1883 hoard', *Anglo-Saxon England*, 20 (1991), pp. 221–9.

GRANGER-TAYLOR, H., 'The weft-patterned silks and their braid: the remains of an Anglo-Saxon dalmatic of *c.* 800?', in G. Bonner, D. Rollason and C. Stancliffe (ed.), *St Cuthbert, his Cult and Community to 1200*, (Woodbridge. 1989), pp. 303–27.

GRANGER-TAYLOR, H., 'Byzantine textiles', in D. Buckton, *Byzantium: treasures of Byzantine art and culture* (London, 1994), pp. 16–17.

GRANGER-TAYLOR, H. and PRITCHARD, F., 'A fine quality Insular embroidery from Llan-gors Crannóg, near Brecon', in M. Redknap, N. Edwards, S. Youngs, A. Lane and J. Knight (ed.), *Pattern and Purpose in Insular Art*, (Oxford, 1991), pp. 91–9.

GREEN, B. and ROGERSON, A., *The Anglo-Saxon Cemetery at Bergh Apton, Norfolk: Catalogue*, East Anglian Archaeology, 7 (1978).

GREEN, B., ROGERSON, A. and WHITE, S. G., *The Anglo-Saxon Cemetery at Morning Thorpe, Norfolk*, I: *Catalogue*, East Anglian Archaeology 36.1 (1987).

GREIG, R. and HILL, D., 'The Bayeux Tapestry: a dramatic colour change', *Medieval Life*, 15 (2001), p. 15 and rear cover.

GREIN, C. M., WÜLCKER, W. R. P. and HECHT, H. (ed.), *Bibliothek der angelsächsischen Prosa*, 13 vols (Leipzig, 1872–1933).

GRIFFITH, A. F., and SALZMAN, L. F., 'An Anglo-Saxon cemetery at Alfriston, Sussex', *Sussex Archaeological Collections*, 56 (1914), pp. 16–53.

GUÐJONSSON, E. E., [GUÐJÓNSSON] 'On ancient and medieval pile weaving, with special reference to a recent find in Iceland' (English summary), *Árbók hins islenzka fornleifafélags* (1962), pp. 65–71.

GUÐJÓNSSON, E. E., 'Járnvarðr yllir. A fourth weapon of the Valkyries in Darraðarljóð?', Ancient and medieval textiles. Studies in honour of Donald King, *Textile History*, 20.2 (1989), pp. 185–97.

GUÐJÓNSSON, E. E., 'Some aspects of the Icelandic warp-weighted loom, vefstaður', *Textile History*, 21.2 (1990), pp. 165–79.

GUÐJÓNSSON, E. E., 'Warp-weighted looms in Iceland and Greenland: comparison of medieval loom parts excavated in Greenland in 1934 and 1990–2 to loom parts from eighteenth and nineteenth century warp-weighted looms in Iceland. Preliminary remarks', in G. Jaacks and K. Tidow (ed.), *Textilsymposium Neumünster: Archäologische textilfunde – Archaeological textiles: 4.–7.5. 1993 (NESAT V)* (Neumünster, 1994), pp. 178–95.

GUEST, E. M., 'A sculptured stone in Burford church', *Antiquaries Journal*, 10 (1930), pp. 159–60.

GUIDO, M., *The Glass Beads of Anglo-Saxon England c. AD 400–700*, ed. M. Welch (Woodbridge, 1999).

GURNEY, F. G., 'A pagan Saxon burial ground at Leighton Buzzard', *Bedfordshire Archaeologist*, 1 (1956), pp. 120–32.

GWARA, S. (ed.), *Aldhelmi Malmesbiriensis Prosa De Virginitate: cum glosa latina atque anglosaxonica*, 2 vols, Corpus Christianorum Series Latina, 124, 124A (Turnhout, 2001).

HADDAN, A. W. and STUBBS, W. (ed.), *Councils and Ecclesiastical Documents relating to Great Britain and Ireland*, 3 vols (Oxford, 1869–78).

HÄGG, I., 'Some notes on the origin of the peplos-type dress in Scandinavia', *Tor*, 1 (1967–8), pp. 81–127.

HÄGG, I., 'Viking women's dress at Birka: a reconstruction by archaeological methods', in N. B. Harte and K. G. Ponting (ed.), *Cloth and Clothing in Medieval Europe: essays in memory of Professor E. M. Carus-Wilson* (London, 1983), pp. 316–50.

HALD, M., *Jernalderens Dragt* (Copenhagen, 1962).

HALD, M., *Primitive Shoes*, trans. I. Nixon, Publications of the National Museum of Denmark, Archaeological-Historical Series, 1.13 (Copenhagen, 1972).

HALD, M., *Ancient Danish Textiles from Bogs and Burials*, trans. J. Olsen, English edition, Publications of the National Museum of Denmark, Archaeological-Historical Series, 21 (Copenhagen, 1980).

HALL, R. A., *Viking Age York* (London, 1994).

HAMEROW, H. and PICKIN, J. 'An early Anglo-Saxon Cemetery at Andrew's Hill, Easington, Co. Durham', *Durham Archaeological Journal*, 11 (1995), pp. 35–66.

HARDEN, D. B. (ed.), *Dark Age Britain* (London, 1956).

HARDEN, D. B. and TREWEEKS, R. C., 'Excavations at Stanton Harcourt, Oxon, 1949, II', *Oxoniensia*, 10 (1945), pp. 16–41.

HÄRKE, H., 'Knives in early Saxon burials: blade length and age at death', *Medieval Archaeology*, 33 (1989), pp. 144–8.

HÄRKE, H., 'Early Saxon weapon burials: frequencies, distributions and weapon combinations', in S. C. Hawkes (ed.), *Anglo-Saxon Weapons and Warfare*, Oxford University Committee for Archaeology Monograph 21 (1989), pp. 49–61.

HÄRKE, H., ' Changing symbols in a changing society: the Anglo-Saxon weapon burial rite in the seventh century', in M. Carver (ed.), *The Age of Sutton Hoo* (Woodbridge, 1992), pp.149–65.

HÄRKE, H., 'Early Anglo-Saxon social structure', in J. Hines (ed.), *The Anglo-Saxons from the Migration Period to the Eighth Century; an ethnographic perspective*, Studies in Historical Archaeoethnology, 2 (Woodbridge, 1997), pp. 125–60.

HARTE, N. B. and PONTING, K. G. (ed.), *Cloth and Clothing in Medieval Europe: essays in memory of Professor E. M. Carus-Wilson* (London, 1983).

HÄSSLER, H.-J. (ed.), *Studien zur Sachsenforschung (Festschrift A. Genrich)* (Hildesheim, 1977).

HAWKES, J., 'Sacraments in stone: the mysteries of Christ in Anglo-Saxon sculpture', in M. Carver (ed.), *The Cross goes North: processes of conversion in Northern Europe, AD 300–1300* (York/Woodbridge, 2003), pp. 351–370.

HAWKES, S. C. [see also Chadwick, S. E.]

HAWKES, S. C., 'Soldiers and settlers in Britain, fourth to fifth century' with Catalogue by S. C. Hawkes and G. C. Dunning, *Medieval Archaeology*, 5 (1961), pp. 1–70.

HAWKES, S. C., review of D. M. Wilson, *The Anglo-Saxons*, Ancient People and Places, 16 (London, 1960), in *Antiquaries Journal*, 41 (1961), pp. 106–8.

HAWKES, S. C., 'The dating and significance of the burials in the Polhill cemetery', in B. Philp, *Excavations in West Kent, 1960–70*, Kent Archaeological Rescue Unit (Dover Castle, 1973), pp. 186–201.

HAWKES, S. C., 'The archaeology of conversion: cemeteries', in J. Campbell (ed.), *The Anglo-Saxons* (Oxford, 1982), pp. 48–9.

HAWKES, S. C., 'Anglo-Saxon Kent *c*.425–725', in P. E. Leach (ed.), *Archaeology in Kent to AD 1500 in memory of Stuart Eborall Rigold*, Council for British Archaeology Research Report, No. 48 (London, 1982), pp. 64–78.

HAWKES, S. C. (ed.), *Anglo-Saxon Weapons and Warfare*, Oxford University Committee for Archaeology Monograph 21 (1989).

HAWKES, S. C., 'The Anglo-Saxon necklace from Lower Brook Street', in M. Biddle (ed.), *Winchester Studies*, 7.ii: Artefacts from Medieval Winchester, ii: Object and Economy in Medieval Winchester (Oxford, 1990), pp. 621–7.

HAWKES, S. C. and GROVE, L. R. A., 'Finds from a seventh-century cemetery at Milton Regis', *Archaeologia Cantiana*, 78 (1963), pp. 22–38.

HAWKES, S. C. and POLLARD, M., 'The gold bracteates from sixth-century Anglo-Saxon graves in Kent, in the light of a new find from Finglesham', *Frümittelalterliche Studien*, 15 (1981), pp. 316–70.

HAWKES, S. C., BROWN, D., and CAMPBELL, J. (ed.), *Anglo-Saxon Studies in Archaeology and History*, 1, British Archaeological Reports, British Series, 72 (1979).

HAWKES, S. C., ELLIS DAVIDSON, H. R. and HAWKES, C., 'The Finglesham Man', *Antiquity*, 39 (1965), pp. 17–32.

HAYMAN, G. N., ' Further excavations at the former Goblin Works, Ashtead (TQ 182 567), *Surrey Archaeological Collections*, 81 (1991–2), pp. 1–18.

HEATHER, P. J., 'Disappearing and reappearing tribes', in W. Pohl with H. Reimitz (ed.), *Strategies of Distinction: the construction of ethnic communities, 300–800*, The Transformation of the Roman World, 2 (Leiden, 1998), pp. 95–111.

HECHT, H. (ed.), *Bishofs Wærferth von Worcester Übersetzung der Dialoge Gregors des Grossen*, C. M. Grein, R. P. Wülcker and H. Hecht (ed.), Bibliothek der Angelsächsischen Prosa, 5 (1900).

HECKETT, E., 'Some Hiberno-Norse headcoverings from Fishamble

Street and St John's Lane, Dublin', *Textile History*, 18.2 (1989), pp. 159–74.

HECKETT, E., 'Some silk and wool head-coverings from Viking Dublin: uses and origins – an enquiry', in P. Walton and J.-P. Wild (ed.), *Textiles in Northern Archaeology*, *NESAT III*: Textile Symposium in York 6–9 May 1987, North European Symposium for Archaeological Textiles Monograph 3 (London, 1990), pp. 85–96.

HEDGES, J. H., 'Textiles and Textile Production in Dark Age Britain', unpublished M.Phil. thesis (University of Southampton, 1980).

HEDGES, J., 'Textiles', in A. MacGregor (ed.), *Anglo-Scandinavian finds from Lloyds Bank, Pavement and other sites*, *The Archaeology of York*, 17.3 (1982), pp. 102–27.

HENRY, F., *The Book of Kells* (London, 1974).

HENRY, P. A., 'An Analysis of Archaeological Textiles with Special Reference to the Scandinavian Period in Scotland', unpublished BA dissertation (University of Durham, 1992).

HENRY, P. [A.], 'The Textiles', in H. Hamerow and J. Pickin, 'An early Anglo-Saxon Cemetery at Andrew's Hill, Easington, Co. Durham', *Durham Archaeological Journal*, 11 (1995), pp. 59–63.

HENRY, P. A., 'Development and change in late Saxon textile production: an analysis of the evidence', *Durham Archaeological Journal*, 14–15 (1999), pp. 69–76.

HENSHALL, A. S., 'Early textiles found in Scotland', *Proceedings of the Society of Antiquaries of Scotland*, 86 (1951–2), pp. 1–20.

HENSHALL, A. S., Appendix to A. E. P. Collins and F. J. Collins, 'Excavations on Blewburton Hill, 1953', *Berkshire Archaeological Journal*, 57 (1959), pp. 68–71.

HERON, J., 'Report on the Stapenhill explorations', *Transactions of the Burton-on-Trent Natural History and Archaeological Society*, 1 (1889), pp. 156–93.

HERRTAGE, S. H. J., *Catholicon Anglicum*, Early English Text Society, original series, 75 (1881).

HERZFELD, G., *An Old English Martyrology*, Early English Text Society, original series, 116 (1900).

HIGHAM, N. J. and HILL, D. (ed.), *Edward the Elder 899–924* (London, 2001).

HILL, D., 'The Bayeux Tapestry and its commentators: the case of Scene 15', *Medieval Life*, 11 (1999), pp. 24–6.

HILLIER, C., *The History and Antiquities of The Isle of Wight* (London, 1855).

HILLS, C., 'The archaeology of Anglo-Saxon England in the pagan period', *Anglo-Saxon England*, 8 (1979), pp. 297–329.

HILLS, C., 'The Anglo-Saxon settlement of England', in D. M. Wilson (ed.), *The Northern World* (London, 1980), pp. 71–94.

HILLS, C., PENN, K. and RICKETT, R ., *The Anglo-Saxon Cemetery at Spong Hill, North Elmham*, East Anglian Archaeology Report, 21 (Dereham, 1984).

HILLS, C., PENN, K. and RICKETT, R., *The Anglo-Saxon Cemetery at Spong Hill, North Elmham: Part IV catalogue of cremations*, East Anglian Archaeology, 34 (1987).

HINES, J., *The Scandinavian Character of Anglian England in the Pre-Viking Period*, British Archaeological Reports, British Series, 124 (Oxford, 1984).

HINES, J., 'The seriation and chronology of Anglian English women's graves: a critical assessment', in L. Jørgensen (ed.) *Chronological Studies of Anglo-Saxon England, Lombard Italy and Vendel Period Sweden*, University of Copenhagen Institute of Prehistoric and Classical Archaeology, Arkæologiske Skrifter, 5 (1992), pp. 81–93.

HINES, J., *Clasps, Hektespenner, Agraffen. Anglo-Scandinavian clasps of classes A-C of the 3rd to 6th centuries A.D. Typology, diffusion and function* (Stockholm, 1993).

HINES, J., *A New Corpus of Anglo-Saxon Great Square-Headed Brooches* (Woodbridge, 1997).

HINES, J. (ed.), *The Anglo-Saxons from the Migration Period to the Eighth Century; an ethnographic perspective*, Studies in Historical Archaeoethnology, 2 (Woodbridge, 1997).

HINTON, D. A., *A Catalogue of the Ornamental Metalwork 700–1100 in the Department of Antiquities, Ashmolean Museum* (Oxford, 1974).

HINTON, D. A., 'Late Anglo-Saxon metal-work: an assessment', *Anglo-Saxon England*, 2 (1975), 171–80.

HINTON, D. A., 'Tag-ends', in M. Biddle (ed.), *Winchester Studies*, 7.ii: Artefacts from Medieval Winchester, ii: Object and Economy in Medieval Winchester (Oxford, 1990), pp. 547–52.

HINTON, D. A., 'Disc and rectangular brooches', in M. Biddle (ed.), *Winchester Studies*, 7.ii, ii, pp. 636–9.

HINTON, D. A., 'Metal finger-rings', in M. Biddle (ed.), *Winchester Studies*, 7.ii: Artefacts from Medieval Winchester, ii: Object and Economy in Medieval Winchester (Oxford, 1990), pp. 646–52.

HINTON, D. A., with a contribution by R. WHITE, ' A smith's hoard from Tattersall Thorpe, Lincolnshire: a synopsis', *Anglo-Saxon England*, 22 (1993), 147–66.

HINTON, D. A., 'The fifth and sixth centuries: reorganization among the ruins', in C. E. Karkov (ed.), *The Archaeology of Anglo-Saxon England: basic readings*, Basic Readings in Anglo-Saxon England, 7 (New York and London, 1999), pp. 423–85.

HINTON, D. A., *A Smith in Lindsey: the Anglo-Saxon grave at Tattersall Thorpe, Lincolnshire*, The Society for Medieval Archaeology Monograph Series, 16 (Leeds, 2000).

HINTON, D. A., KEENE, S. and QUALMANN, K. E., ' The Winchester reliquary', *Medieval Archaeology*, 25 (1981), pp. 45–77.

HINZ, H., 'Am langen Band getragene Bergkristallanhänger der Merowingerzeit', *Jahrbuch des Römisch-Germanischen Zentralmuseums Mainz*, 13 (1966), pp. 212–30.

HIRST, S. M., *An Anglo-Saxon Inhumation Cemetery at Sewerby East Yorkshire*, York University Archaeological Publications 4 (1985).

HODGES, C. C., 'Anglo-Saxon remains', in W. Page (ed.), *Victoria County History*, Durham, 1 (London, 1905).

HOFFMANN, M., *The Warp-weighted Loom: studies in the history and technology of an ancient implement*, Studia Norvegica 14 (Oslo, 1964).

HOGESTOL, M. (ed.), *Festskrift til Thorleif Sjovold på 70-årsdageni*, Universitets Oldsaksamlings Skrifter, Ny rekke, 5 (Oslo, 1984).

HOGG, R. M. (ed.), *The Cambridge History of the English Language I: the beginnings to 1066* (Cambridge, 1992).

HOHLER, C., 'The stole and maniples: the iconography', in C. F. Battiscombe (ed.), *The Relics of St. Cuthbert* (Oxford, 1956), pp. 396–408.

HOLTHAUSEN, F., 'Die Leidener Glossen', *Englische Studien*, 50 (1916–

17), pp. 327–40.

HOLTHAUSEN, F.,*Altenglisches etymologisches Wörterbuch* (Heidelburg, 1934).

HOUGEN, B., *Snartemofunnene*, Norske Oldfunn, 7 (Oslo, 1935).

HOWARD-JOHNSTON, J., 'Trading in fur, from classical antiquity to the Middle Ages', in E. Cameron (ed.), *Leather and Fur: aspects of early medieval trade and technology* (London, 1998), pp. 65–79.

HOWE, N., *Migration and Myth-Making in Anglo-Saxon England* (New Haven, CT, 1989).

HUGHES, T. McK., Untitled, *Proceedings of the Society of Antiquaries of London*, 2nd series, 18 (1899–1901), pp. 310–21.

HUNN, A., LAWSON, J. and FARLEY, M., 'The Anglo-Saxon cemetery at Dinton, Buckinghamshire', in *Anglo-Saxon Studies in Archaeology and History*, 7 (1994), pp. 85–148.

HURST, J. G., 'The pottery', in D. M. Wilson (ed.), *The Archaeology of Anglo-Saxon England* (London, 1976), pp. 290–2.

HUTCHINSON, P., 'The Anglo-Saxon cemetery at Little Eriswell, Suffolk', *Proceedings of the Cambridge Antiquarian Society*, 69 (1966), pp. 1–32.

HYSLOP, M., 'Two Anglo-Saxon cemeteries at Chamberlains Barn, Leighton Buzzard, Bedforshire', *Archaeological Journal*, 120 (1963), pp. 161–200.

INGSTAD, A. S., 'The functional textiles from the Oseberg ship', in L. Bender Jørgensen and K. Tidow (ed.), *Textilsymposium Neumünster:Archäologische textilfunde: 6.5–7.5. 1981 (NESAT I)* (Neumünster, 1982), pp. 85–96.

IVERSEN, M. (ed.), *Mammen: grav, kunst og samfund i vikingetid*, Jysk Arkæologisk Selskabs Skrifter 28 (Aarhus, 1991).

JAACKS, G. and TIDOW, K. (ed.), *Textilsymposium Neumünster: Archäologische textilfunde – Archaeological textiles: 4.–7.5. 1993 (NESAT V)* (Neumünster, 1994).

JACKSON, D. A., HARDING, D. W. and MYRES, J. N. L., 'The Iron Age and Anglo-Saxon site at Upton, Northants', *Antiquaries Journal*, 49 (1969), pp. 202–21.

JACKSON, K. H. (ed.), *The Gododdin: the oldest Scottish poem* (Edinburgh, 1969).

JACKSON, P., 'Footloose in Archaeology, *The Journal of British Podiatric Medicine*, 51.5 (1996), pp. 67–70.

JANAWAY, R. C., 'Corrosion preserved textile evidence: mechanism, bias and interpretation', *Evidence Preserved in Corrosion Products: new fields in artefact studies*, United Kingdom Institute for Conservation of Historic and Artistic Works, Occasional papers, 8 (1989), pp. 21–9.

JELLEMA, D., 'Frisian trade in the Dark Ages', *Speculum*, 30 (1955), pp. 15–36.

JENKINS, D. (ed.), *The Cambridge History of Western Textiles*, 2 vols (Cambridge, 2003).

JOCHENS, J., *Women in Old Norse Society* (Ithaca, NY and London, 1995).

JØRGENSEN, L. (ed.), *Chronological Studies of Anglo-Saxon England, Lombard Italy and Vendel Period Sweden*, University of Copenhagen Institute of Prehistoric and Classical Archaeology, Arkæologiske Skrifter, 5 (Copenhagen, 1992).

JØRGENSEN, L. B. *see* BENDER JØRGENSEN, L.

KANE, G. (ed.), *Piers Plowman, the A Version: Will's Vision of Piers Plowman and Do-well* (London, 1960).

KEENE, D., 'The textile industry', in M. Biddle, *Winchester Studies*, 7.ii (Oxford, 1990).

KEMBLE, J. M., *Codex Diplomaticus Ævi Saxonici*, 6 vols (London, 1839–48).

KENDRICK, T. D., *Anglo-Saxon Art to AD 900* (London, 1938).

KENDRICK, T. D., *et al.*, *The Lindisfarne Gospels (Codex Lindisfarnensis)*, 2 vols (London, 1956).

KENDRICK, T. D. and RADFORD, C. A. R., 'Recent discoveries at All Hallows, Barking', *Antiquaries Journal*, 13 (1938), pp. 14–18.

KENNEDY, A., 'Byrhtnoth's obits and twelfth-century accounts of the Battle of Maldon', in D. Scragg (ed.), *The Battle of Maldon AD 991* (Oxford, 1991), pp. 59–78.

KEYNES, S. (ed.), *The Liber Vitae of the New Minster and Hyde Abbey Winchester: British Library Stowe 944, together with leaves from British Library Cotton Vespasian A. VIII and British Library Titus D. XXVII*, Early English Manuscripts in Facsimile, 26, (Copenhagen, 1996).

KINDSCHI, L., 'The Latin-Old English Glosses in Plantin-Moretus MS 32 and BM MS Additional 32,246', unpublished PhD dissertation (Stanford University, 1955).

KING, D., *Opus Anglicanum: English medieval embroidery* (London, 1963).

KIRBY, T. A. and WOOLF, H. B. (ed.), *Malone Anniversary Studies, Philologica* (Baltimore, 1949).

KIRK, J. R., and LEEDS, E. T., 'Three early Saxon graves from Dorchester, Oxon.', *Oxoniensia*, 17–18 (1954), pp. 63–76.

KITSON CLARK, M., 'Late Saxon pin-heads from Roos, East Yorkshire, and South Ferriby, Lincolnshire, now in the collections at Hull', *Proceedings of the Leeds Philosophical and Literary Society*, 5 (1942), pp. 333–8.

KLAEBER, F. (ed.), *Beowulf and the Fight at Finnesburg* (Boston, MA, 3rd ed., 1950).

KLUGE, F., 'Angelsächsische Glossen', *Anglia*, 8 (1885), pp. 448–52.

KLUGE, F., 'Zur Geschichte der Zeichensprache angelsächsische Indicia Monasterialia', *Internationale Zeitschrift für Allgemeine Sprachwissenschaft*, 2 (1885), pp. 116–37.

KNOCKER, G. M., 'Early burials and an Anglo-Saxon cemetery at Snell's Corner, near Horndean, Hampshire', *Papers and Proceedings of the Hampshire Field Club and Archaeological Society*, 19 (1958), pp. 117–70.

KOSSAK, G. and ULBERT, G. (ed.), *Studien sur vor- und frühgeschichtlichen Archäeologie, Festschrift für Joachim Werner zum 65 Geburstag*, 2 vols (Munich, 1974).

KRAG, A. H., 'Dress and power in prehistoric Scandinavia c.550–1050 A.D.', in L. B. Jørgensen and C. Rinaldo (ed.), *Textiles in European Archaeology*, Report from the 6th NESAT Symposium, 7–11th May 1996 in Borås (*NESAT VI*) (Göteborg, 1998), pp. 125–30.

KRAPP, G. P. and DOBBIE, E. V. K. (ed.), *The Anglo-Saxon Poetic Records: a collective edition*, 6 vols (London and New York, 1931–42).

KRAPP, G. P. and DOBBIE, E. V. K. (ed.), *The Exeter Book*, The Anglo-Saxon Poetic Records, 3 (New York, 1936).

KRUSCH, B. (ed.), *De Vita Sanctae Radegundis libri II*, Monumenta Germaniae Historica, Script. rer. Merov., 2 (1888), pp. 358–95.

KUHN, S. M. (ed.), *The Vespasian Psalter* (Ann Arbor, 1965)

KURATH, H. and KUHN, S. M. (ed.), *Middle English Dictionary*, 118 fascicles (Ann Arbor, 1956–2001).

LAMM, J. P. and NORDSTRÖM, H.-Å. (ed.), *Vendel Period Studies*, The Museum of National Antiquities, Stockholm, Studies, 2 (Stockholm, 1983).

LANG, J. T., 'Some late pre-conquest crosses in Ryedale, Yorkshire: a re-appraisal', *Journal of the British Archaeological Association*, 3rd Series, 36 (1973), pp. 16–25.

LANG, J. T., *British Academy Corpus of Anglo-Saxon Stone Sculpture*, 3, *York and Eastern Yorkshire* (Oxford, 1991).

LAPIDGE, M. and HERREN, M. (trans.), *Aldhelm the Prose Works* (Ipswich and Cambridge, 1979).

LAPIDGE, M., BLAIR, J., KEYNES, S. and SCRAGG, D. (ed.), *The Blackwell Encyclopaedia of Anglo-Saxon England* (Oxford, 1999).

LASKO, P., 'The Bayeux Tapestry and the representation of space', in G. R. Owen-Crocker and T. Graham (ed.), *Medieval Art: recent perspectives. A memorial tribute to C. R. Dodwell* (Manchester, 1998), pp. 26–39.

LAVER, J., *Costume*, The Arts of Man (London, 1963).

LAYARD, N. F., 'An Anglo-Saxon cemetery in Ipswich', *Archaeologia*, 60 (1907), pp. 325–52.

LEACH, P. E. (ed.), *Archaeology in Kent to AD 1500 in memory of Stuart Eborall Rigold*, Council for British Archaeology Research Report, No. 48 (London, 1982).

LE BLANC SMITH, G., 'Some Norman and pre-Norman remains in the Dovedale district', *The Reliquary*, 3rd series, 10 (1904), pp. 232–47.

LEEDS, E. T., *The Archaeology of the Anglo-Saxon Settlements* (Oxford, 1913).

LEEDS, E. T., Untitled, *Proceedings of the Society of Antiquaries of London*, 2nd series, 29 (1916–17), pp. 48–63.

LEEDS, E. T., *Early Anglo-Saxon Art and Archaeology* (Oxford, 1936).

LEEDS, E. T., 'A Saxon village at Sutton Courtenay, Berkshire (third report)', *Archaeologia*, 92 (1947), pp. 79–94.

LEEDS, E. T. and ATKINSON, R. J. C., 'An Anglo-Saxon cemetery at Nassington, Northants', *Antiquaries Journal*, 24 (1944), pp. 100–28.

LEEDS, E. T. and HARDEN, D. B., *The Anglo-Saxon Cemetery at Abingdon, Berkshire* (Oxford, 1936).

LEEDS, E. T. and SHORTT, H. de S., *An Anglo-Saxon Cemetery at Petersfinger, near Salisbury, Wilts* (Salisbury, 1953).

LEIGH, A., 'Dialect dialling', *The Sunday Times* (Oct 20, 1974), p. 13.

LEIGH, D., 'Ambiguity in Anglo-Saxon Style I Art', *Antiquaries Journal*, 64 (1984), pp. 34–42.

LETHBRIDGE, T. C., *Recent Excavations in Anglo-Saxon Cemeteries in Cambridgeshire and Suffolk*, Cambridge Antiquarian Society Quarto Publications, 2nd series, 3 (1931).

LETHBRIDGE, T. C., 'Anglo-Saxon burials at Soham, Cambridgeshire', *Proceedings of the Cambridge Antiquarian Society*, 33 (1931–2), pp. 152–63.

LETHBRIDGE, T. C., *A Cemetery at Shudy Camps, Cambridgeshire*, Cambridge Antiquarian Society Quarto Publications, 2nd series, 5 (1936).

LEWIS, C. T. and SHORT, C. (ed.), *A Latin Dictionary* (Oxford, 1897, revised impression 1973).

LIEBERMANN, F. (ed.), *Die Gesetze der Angelsachsen*, 3 vols (Halle, 1898–1916).

LINDELÖF, U. (ed.), *Der Lambeth-Psalter*, 2 vols, Acta Societatis Scientiarum Fennicae, 35.1; 43.3 (Helsingfors, 1909–14).

LINDELÖF, U., *Rituale Ecclesiae Dunelmensis*, Surtees Society, 140 (1927).

LINDSAY, W. M. (ed.), *Isidori Hispalensis Episcopi Etymologiarum sive Originum*, 2 vols (Oxford, 1911).

LINDSAY, W. M. (ed.), *The Corpus Glossary* (Cambridge, 1921).

LIUZZA, R. M., *The Old English Version of the Gospels*, Early English Text Society, original series 314, 2 vols (Oxford, 1994–2000).

LOGEMAN, H. (ed.), *The Rule of St. Benet*, Early English Text Society, original series, 90 (1888).

LOGEMAN, W. S., 'De Consuetudine Monachorum', *Anglia*, 13 (1891), pp. 365–454.

LONGSTAFF, W. H., Untitled, *Archaeological Journal*, 5 (1848), pp. 220–1.

LOT, F., *The End of the Ancient World and the Beginning of the Middle Ages* (London and New York, 1931).

LUCY, S. J., 'Housewives, warriors and slaves? Sex and gender in Anglo-Saxon burials', in J. Moore and E. Scott (ed.), *Invisible People and Processes* (Leicester, 1997), pp. 150–68.

MACGREGOR, A. (ed.), *Anglo-Scandinavian finds from Lloyds Bank, Pavement and other sites*, The Archaeology of York, 17.3 (1982).

MACGREGOR, A., *Bone, Antler, Ivory and Horn. The technology of skeletal materials since the Roman period* (London, 1985).

MACGREGOR, A., 'Hides, horn and bones: animals and interdependent industries in the early urban context', in E. A. Cameron (ed.), *Leather and Fur: aspects of early medieval trade and technology* (London, 1998), pp. 11–26.

MACGREGOR, A., 'A seventh-century pectoral cross from Holderness, East Yorkshire', *Medieval Archaeology*, 44 (2000), pp. 217–22.

MACPHERSON, D., *Ðe Ogygynale Cronykil of Scotland be Androw of Wyntown*, 2 vols (London, 1795).

MADSEN, A. H., 'Women's dress in the Viking period in Denmark, based on the tortoise brooches and textile remains', in P. Walton and J.-P. Wild (ed.), *Textiles in Northern Archaeology, NESAT III*: Textile Symposium in York 6–9 May 1987, North European Symposium for Archaeological Textiles Monograph 3 (London, 1990), pp. 101–6.

MAGNUS, B., 'A chieftain's costume. New light on an old grave find from West Norway', in L. Bender Jørgensen and K. Tidow (ed.), *Textilsymposium Neumünster:Archäologische textilfunde: 6.5–7.5. 1981 (NESAT I)* (Neumünster, 1982), pp. 63–73.

MAINMAN, A. J. and ROGERS, N. S. H., *Craft, Industry and Everyday Life*, The Archaeology of York, 17.14 (2000).

MALIM, T. and HINES, J. with C. DUHIG, *The Anglo-Saxon Cemetery at Edix Hill (Barrington A), Cambridgeshire*, Council for British Archaeology Research Report, 112 (1998).

MATTHEWS, C. L., 'The Anglo-Saxon cemetery at Marina Drive, Dunstable', *Bedfordshire Archaeological Journal*, 1 (1962), pp. 25–47.

MAY, J., 'Romano-British and Saxon sites near Dorchester, Oxon.', *Oxoniensia*, 42 (1977). pp. 42–79.

MAYO, J., *A History of Ecclesiastical Dress* (London, 1984).

MCGURK, P., DUMVILLE, D. N., GODDEN, M. R. and KNOCK, A. (ed.), *An Eleventh-century Anglo-Saxon Illustrated Miscellany*, Early English Manuscripts in Facsimile, 21 (Copenhagen, 1983).

MCNULTY, J. B., 'The Lady Aelfgiva in the Bayeux Tapestry', *Speculum*, 55 (1980), pp. 659–68.

MCNULTY, J. B., *The Narrative Art of the Bayeux Tapestry* (New York, 1989).

MEADOWS, I., 'Wollaston: The "Pioneer" burial', *Current Archaeology*, 154 (1997), 391–5.

MEANEY, A. L., *A Gazetteer of Anglo-Saxon Burial Sites* (London, 1964).

MEANEY, A. L., *Anglo-Saxon Amulets and Curing Stones*, British Archaeological Reports, British Series, 96 (1981).

MEANEY, A. L., 'Girdle groups: reconstruction and comparative study', in T. Malim and J. Hines, *The Anglo-Saxon Cemetery at Edix Hill (Barrington A), Cambridgeshire*, Council for British Archaeology Research Report, 112 (1998), pp. 268–75.

MEANEY, A. L. and HAWKES, S. C., *Two Anglo-Saxon Cemeteries at Winnall, Winchester, Hampshire*, The Society for Medieval Archaeology Monograph Series, 4 (1970).

MERITT, H. D., *The Old English Prudentius Glosses at Boulogne-sur-Mer*, Stanford Studies in Language and Literature, 16 (Stanford, CA, 1959).

MEYR-HARTING, H., *Ottonian Illumination; an historical study* (London, revised one-volume edition, 1999).

MIGNE, J.-P. (ed.), *Sancti Isidori, Hispalensis Episcopi, Opera Omnia*, Patrologia Cursus Completus, Series Latina, 83 (Paris, 1862).

MILLARD, L. JARMAN, S. and HAWKES, S. C., 'Anglo-Saxon burials near the Lord of the Manor, Ramsgate', *Archaeologia Cantiana*, 84 (1969), pp. 9–30.

MILOJČIĆ, D. (ed.), *Kolloquium über spätantike und frümittelalterliche Skulptur*, 3 (Mainz, 1972), pp. 139–48.

MOORE, J. and SCOTT, E. (ed.), *Invisible People and Processes* (Leicester, 1997).

MORRIS, R. (ed.), *Old English Homilies*, Early English Text Society, original series, 34, 53 (1868–73).

MORRIS, R. (ed.), *The Blickling Homilies of the Tenth Century*, Early English Text Society, original series, 58. 63, 73 (1874–80).

MÜLLER, M., *Die Kleidung nach Quellen des frühen Mittelalters; Textilen und Mode von Karl dem Grossen bis Heinrich III*, Ergänzungsbände zum Reallexikon der Germanischen Altertumskunde, 33 (Berlin and New York, 2003).

MÜLLER-WILLE, M., 'Royal and aristocratic graves in central and western Europe in the Merovingian period', in J. P. Lamm and H.-Å. Nordström (ed.), *Vendel Period Studies*, The Museum of National Antiquities, Stockholm, Studies, 2 (Stockholm, 1982), pp. 109–16.

MUNKSGAARD, E., *Oldtidsdragter* (Copenhagen, 1974).

MUNKSGAARD, E., 'The Gallic coat from Rønbjerg', in L. Bender Jørgensen and K. Tidow (ed.), *Textilsymposium Neumünster: Archäologische textilfunde: 6.5–7.5. 1981 (NESAT I)* (Neumünster, 1982), pp. 41–43.

MUNKSGAARD, E., 'The embroideries from Bjerrinhøy, Mammen', in M. Hogestol (ed.), *Festskrift til Thorleif Sjovold på 70-årsdagen*, Universitets Oldsaksamlings Skrifter, Ny rekke, 5 (Oslo, 1984), pp. 159–71.

MUNKSGAARD, E., 'Kopien af dragten fra Mammengraven', in M. Iversen (ed.), *Mammen: grav, kunst og samfund i vikingetid*, Jysk Arkæologisk Selkskabs Skrifter 28 (Aarhus, 1991), pp. 151–54.

MUNRO, J. H., 'The medieval scarlet and the economics of sartorial splendour', in N. B. Harte and K. G. Ponting (ed.), *Cloth and Clothing in Medieval Europe: essays in memory of Professor E. M. Carus-Wilson* (London, 1983), pp. 13–70.

MURRAY, J. A. H., BRADLEY, H., CRAIGIE, W. A. and ONIONS, C. T. (ed.), *The Oxford English Dictionary*, 12 vols (Oxford, corrected edition with supplement, 1933); *Supplement* (1972).

MUSSET, L. (ed.), *Les Actes de Guillaume le conquérant et de la reine Mathilde pour les abbayes caennaises*, Mémoires de la Societé des Antiquaires de Normandie, 37.16 (Caen, 1967).

MUSTY, J. and STRATTON, J. E. D., 'A Saxon cemetery at Winterbourne Gunner, near Salisbury', *Wiltshire Archaeological Magazine*, 59 (1964), pp. 86–109.

MUTHESIUS, A., 'The silk fragment from 5 Coppergate', in A. MacGregor (ed.), *Anglo-Scandinavian finds from Lloyds Bank, Pavement and other sites*, The Archaeology of York, 17.3 (1982), pp. 132–6.

MUTHESIUS, A., *Eastern Silks in Western Shrines and Treasuries before 1200*, unpublished PhD thesis (University of London, Courtauld Institute, 1982).

MYRES, J. N. L., 'Romano-Saxon pottery', in D. B. Harden (ed.), *Dark Age Britain* (London, 1956), pp. 16–39.

MYRES, J. N. L., *A Corpus of Anglo-Saxon Pottery of the Pagan Period*, 2 vols (Cambridge, 1977).

MYRES, J. N. L., *The English Settlements*, The Oxford History of England, 1B (Oxford, 1986).

NAPIER, A. S. (ed.), *Old English Glosses*, Anecdota Oxoniensia, Medieval and Modern Series, 11 (Oxford, 1900).

NAPIER, A. S. and STEVENSON, W. H. (ed.), *The Crawford Collection of Early Charters and Documents* (Oxford, 1895).

NEUMAN DE VEGVAR, C. L., 'The origin of the Genoels-Elderen ivories', *Gesta*, 29 (1990), pp. 8–24.

NEVILLE, R. C., 'Anglo-Saxon cemetery excavated January 1853', *Archaeological Journal*, 11 (1854). pp. 95–115.

NEVINSON, J. L., 'The costumes', in F. M. Stenton (ed.), *The Bayeux Tapestry*, (London, 2nd ed., 1965), pp. 70–5.

NIELSEN, K. H., 'The Rønbjerg garment in tunic-form', in L. Bender Jørgensen and K. Tidow, (ed.), *Textilsymposium Neumünster:Archäologische textilfunde 6.5–7.5. 1981 (NESAT I)* (Neumünster, 1982), pp. 44–62.

NIELSEN, K.-H. S., 'The notorious Rønbjerg garment – once again', in G. Jaacks and K. Tidow (ed.), *Textilsymposium Neumünster: Archäologische textilfunde – Archaeological textiles: 4.–7.5. 1993 (NESAT V)* (Neumünster, 1994), pp. 236–52.

NOCKERT, M., 'Some new observations about the Boksten costume', in L. Bender Jørgensen and K. Tidow (ed.), *Textilsymposium Neumünster:Archäologische textilfunde: 6.5–7.5. 1981 (NESAT I)* (Neumünster, 1982), pp. 277–82.

NOCKERT, M., *The Högom Find and Other Migration Period Textiles and Costumes in Scandinavia*, Archaeology and Environment 9, Högom Find Part II (Umea, Sweden, 1991).

OHLGREN, T. H. (ed.), *Anglo-Saxon Textual Illustration: photographs of sixteen manuscripts with descriptions and index* (Kalamazoo, MI, 1992).

OKASHA, E., *Hand-list of Anglo-Saxon Non-runic Inscriptions* (Cambridge, 1971).

OLIPHANT, R. T., *The Harley Latin–Old English Glossary*, Janua Linguarum Series Practica, 20 (The Hague, 1966).

OLMSTED, G. S., *The Gundestrup Cauldron*, Collection Latomus, 162

(Brussels, 1979).

OMAM, C. C., 'Anglo-Saxon finger-rings', *Apollo*, 14 (1931), pp. 104–8.

ØSTERGÅRD, E., 'The medieval everyday costumes of the Norsemen in Greenland', in L. Bender Jørgensen and K. Tidow (ed.), *Textilsymposium Neumünster:Archäologische textilfunde: 6.5–7.5. 1981 (NESAT I)* (Neumünster, 1982), pp. 267–76.

OWEN, G. R. [later OWEN-CROCKER], 'Anglo-Saxon Costume', unpublished PhD thesis, 3 vols (University of Newcastle upon Tyne, 1976).

OWEN, G. R.,'Wynflæd's wardrobe', *Anglo-Saxon England*, 8 (1979), pp. 195–222.

OWEN, G. R., *Rites and Religions of the Anglo-Saxons* (Newton Abbot and Totowa, NJ , 1981).

OWEN, O., 'The carved whalebone plaque', in O. Owen and M. Dolland, *Scar: a Viking boat burial on Sanday, Orkney* (East Lothian, 1999), pp. 73–86.

OWEN, O. and DOLLAND, M., *Scar: a Viking boat burial on Sanday, Orkney* (East Lothian, 1999).

OWEN-CROCKER, G. R., *Dress in Anglo-Saxon England* (Manchester, 1986).

OWEN-CROCKER, G. R., 'Early Anglo-Saxon female dress – the gravegoods and the guesswork', *Textile History*, 18.2 (1987), pp. 147–158.

OWEN-CROCKER, G. R., 'Early Anglo-Saxon dress – remains and reconstructions', *Costume*, 26 (1992), pp. 1–20.

OWEN-CROCKER, G. R., 'The costume of the Bayeux "Tapestry": culottes, tunics, garters and the construction of the hanging', *Costume*, 28 (1994), pp. 1–9.

OWEN-CROCKER, G. R., 'Telling a tale: narrative techniques in the Bayeux Tapestry and the Old English epic *Beowulf*', in G. R. Owen-Crocker and T. Graham (ed.), *Medieval Art: recent perspectives. A memorial tribute to C. R. Dodwell* (Manchester, 1998), pp. 40–59.

OWEN-CROCKER, G. R., 'The search for Anglo-Saxon skin garments and the documentary evidence', in E. A. Cameron (ed.), *Leather and Fur: aspects of early medieval trade and technology* (London, 1998), pp. 27–43.

OWEN-CROCKER, G. R.,'Women's costume in the tenth and eleventh centuries and textile production in Anglo-Saxon England', in C. E. Karkov (ed.), *The Archaeology of Anglo-Saxon England: basic readings*, Basic Readings in Anglo-Saxon England, 7 (New York and London, 1999), pp. 423–85.

OWEN-CROCKER, G. R., *The Four Funerals in Beowulf: and the structure of the poem* (Manchester, 2000).

OWEN-CROCKER, G. R., 'Embroidered wood: animal-headed posts in The Bayeux "Tapestry"', in H. Damico and C. Karkov (ed.), *Aedificia Nova: papers in honour of Rosemary Cramp*, (Kalamazoo, MI, forthcoming, 2005).

OWEN-CROCKER, G. R., 'Gold in the ground or just rust in the dust: measuring wealth by metalwork in Anglo-Saxon graves' in R. Bork (ed.), *De Re Metallica: studies in medieval metals and metallurgy*, Avista Annual Series (forthcoming, 2004).

OWEN-CROCKER, G. R., 'Pomp, piety and keeping the woman in her place: the dress of Cnut and Ælfgifu/Emma', *Medieval Clothing and Textiles*, 1 (forthcoming, 2005).

OWEN-CROCKER, G. R. and GRAHAM, T. (ed.), *Medieval Art: recent perspectives. A memorial tribute to C. R. Dodwell* (Manchester, 1998).

OZANNE, A., 'The Peak Dwellers', *Medieval Archaeology*, 6–8 (1962–3), pp. 15–52.

PADER, E.-J., *Symbolism, Social Relations and the Interpretation of Mortuary Remains*, British Archaeological Reports, International Series, 130 (1982).

PAGE, R. I., Appendix A, in D. M. Wilson, *Anglo-Saxon Ornamental Metalwork 700–1000 in the British Museum* (London, 1964), pp. 67–90.

PAGE, W. (ed.), *Victoria County History*, Durham, 1 (London, 1905).

PALM, M. and PIND, J., 'Anglian English women's graves in the fifth to seventh centuries A.D. – a chronological analysis', in L. Jørgensen (ed.), *Chronological Studies of Anglo-Saxon England, Lombard Italy and Vendel Period Sweden*, University of Copenhagen Institute of Prehistoric and Classical Archaeology, Arkæologiske Skrifter, 5 (Copenhagem, 1992), pp. 50–80.

PARFITT, K. and BRUGMANN, B., *The Anglo-Saxon Cemetery on Mill Hill, Deal, Kent*, The Society for Medieval Archaeology Monograph Series, No. 14 (1997).

PATTERSON, R., 'Spinning and weaving', in C. Singer, E. J. Holmyard, A. R. Hall and T. F. Williams, *A History of Technology*, 7 vols (Oxford, 1956–78), 2 (1956), pp. 191–220.

PEDERSEN, I. R., 'The analyses of the textiles from Evebø-Eide, Gloppen, Norway', in L. Bender Jørgensen and K. Tidow (ed.), *Textilsymposium Neumünster: Archäologische textilfunde: 6.5–7.5. 1981 (NESAT I)* (Neumünster, 1982), pp. 74–84.

PEERS, C. R. and RADFORD, C. A. R., 'The Saxon monastery at Whitby', *Archaeologia*, 89 (1943), pp. 27–88.

PERTZ, G. H. (ed.), *Monumenta Germaniae Historica, Scriptores*, 7, 2 (Berlin, 1829).

PETERSON, W. and HUTTON, M., *Tacitus Dialogues, Agricola, Germania*, Loeb Classical Library (London, 1914).

PHILP, B., *Excavations in West Kent, 1960–70*, Kent Archaeological Rescue Unit (Dover Castle, 1973).

PHILP, B., 'Saxon gold ring found at Dover', *Kent Archaeological Review*, Spring 1973, p. 10.

PIRENNE, H., 'Draps de Frise ou draps de Flandre?', *Vierteljahrschrift für Social- und Wirtschaftgeschichte*, 7 (1909), pp. 308–15.

PIRLING, R., *Römer und Franken am Niederrhein, Katalog-Handbuch des Landschaftsmuseums Burg Linn in Krefeld* (Mainz, 1986).

PLANCHÉ, J. R., *History of British Costume* (London, 1847).

PLENDERLEITH, E., 'The stole and maniples: the technique', in C. F. Battiscombe (ed.), *The Relics of St. Cuthbert* (Oxford, 1956), pp. 375–96.

PLUNKETT, S. J. 'The Anglo-Saxon loom from Pakenham, Suffolk', *Proceedings of the Suffolk Institute of Archaeology and History*, 39 (1999), pp. 277–98.

POHL, W., 'Telling the difference: signs of ethnic identity', in W. Pohl with H. Reimitz (ed.)., *Strategies of Distinction: the construction of ethnic communities, 300–800*, The Transformation of the Roman World, 2 (Leiden, 1998), pp. 17–69.

POHL, W. with REIMITZ, H. (ed.)., *Strategies of Distinction: the construction of ethnic communities, 300–800*, The Transformation of the Roman World, 2 (Leiden, 1998).

POOLE, R. G., 'The textile inventory in the Old English *Gerefa*', *Review of English Studies*, 40 (1989), pp. 469–78.

PRIGG, H., 'The Anglo-Saxon graves, Warren Hill, Mildenhall', *Proceedings of the Suffolk Institute of Archaeology and Natural History*, 6 (1888), pp. 57–72.

PRITCHARD, F. A., 'Silk braids and textiles of the Viking Age from Dublin', in L. Bender Jørgensen, B. Magnus and E. Munksgaard (ed.), *Archaeological Textiles*, *(NESAT II)* (Copenhagen, 1988), pp. 149–61.

PRITCHARD, F., 'Textiles from recent excavations in the City of London', in L. Bender Jørgensen and K. Tidow (ed.), *Textilsymposium Neumünster:Archäologische textilfunde: 6.5–7.5. 1981 (NESAT I)* (Neumünster, 1982), pp. 193–203.

QUINN, J. J. (ed.), 'Minor Latin–Old English Glosses in MS Cotton Cleopatra Aiii', unpublished PhD dissertation (Stanford University, 1956).

RAHTZ, P., 'Buildings and rural settlement' and 'Gazetteer of Anglo-Saxon domestic settlement sites', in D. M. Wilson (ed.), *The Archaeology of Anglo-Saxon England* (London, 1976), pp. 49–98; 405–45.

RAHTZ, P., DICKINSON, T. and WATTS, L. (ed.), *Anglo-Saxon Cemeteries 1979: the fourth Anglo-Saxon symposium at Oxford*, British Archaeological Reports, British Series, 82 (1980).

RAINBIRD CLARKE, R., *see* CLARKE, R. R.

RAW, B. C., 'The archer, the eagle and the lamb', *Journal of the Warburg and Courtauld Institutes*, 30 (1967), pp. 391–4.

RAW, B. C., 'The probable derivation of most of the illustrations in Junius 11 from an illustrated Old Saxon *Genesis*', *Anglo-Saxon England*, 5 (1976), pp. 133–49.

RAW, B. C., *Anglo-Saxon Crucifixion Iconography and the Art of the Monastic Revival*, Cambridge Studies in Anglo-Saxon England, 1 (Cambridge, 1990).

READ, C. H., Untitled, *Proceedings of the Society of Antiquaries of London*, 2nd series, 15 (1893–5), pp. 250–5.

REDKNAP, M., EDWARDS, N.,YOUNGS, S., LANE, A. and KNIGHT, J. (ed.), *Pattern and Purpose in Insular Art*, (Oxford, 1991).

REES, W., 'Survivals of ancient Celtic custom in medieval England', *Angles and Britons*, O'Donnell Lectures (Cardiff, 1963).

RICHARDS, J. D., *The Significance of Form and Decoration of Anglo-Saxon Cremation Urns*, British Archaeological Reports, British Series, 166 (1987).

RICHARDS, J. D., *Viking Age England*, English Heritage (London, 1991).

RICHARDSON, K. M., 'Excavations in Hungate, York', *Archaeological Journal*, 116 (1959), pp. 51–114.

ROACH, M. E. and EICHER, J. B. (ed.), *Dress, Adornment and the Social Order* (New York, 1965).

ROBERTS, J. and KAY, C., with GRUNDY, L., *A Thesaurus of Old English*, King's College London Medieval Studies, 11, 2 vols (London, 1995).

ROBERTSON, A. J., *Anglo-Saxon Charters* (Cambridge, 1939).

ROBERTSON, A. S., *Roman Imperial Coins in the Hunter Coin Cabinet*, 5 vols (London, 1962–82).

ROESDAHL, E., GRAHAM-CAMPBELL, J., CONNOR, P. and PEARSON, K. (ed.), *The Vikings in England*, Catalogue of Exhibition held in Denmark in 1981 and at the Yorkshire Museum, York, in 1982 (London, 1981).

ROMILLY ALLEN, J. *see* ALLEN, J. R.

ROSS, S., 'Dress Pins from Anglo-Saxon England: their production and typo-chronological development', unpublished D.Phil thesis (University of Oxford, 1991).

ROSS, S., 'The pins', in G. Drinkall and M. Foreman, *The Anglo-Saxon Cemetery at Castledyke South, Barton-on-Humber*, Sheffield Excavation Reports 6 (Sheffield, 1998). pp. 267–70.

ROUTH, T. E., 'A corpus of pre-Conquest carved stones of Derbyshire', *Derbyshire Archaeological Journal*, 58 (new series 11) (1937), pp. 1–46.

RYDER, M. L., 'European wool types from the Iron Age to the Middle Ages', in L. Bender Jørgensen and K. Tidow (ed.), *Textilsymposium Neumünster:Archäologische textilfunde: 6.5–7.5. 1981 (NESAT I)* (Neumünster, 1982), pp. 224–38.

SAMUELS, M. L., 'Kent and the Low Countries: some linguistic evidence', in A. J. Aitken, A. McIntosh and H. Pálsson (ed.), *Edinburgh Studies in English and Scots* (London, 1971), pp. 3–19.

SCHIPPER, J. (ed.), *Konig Alfreds Übersetzung von Bedas Kirchengeschichte*, C. M. W. Grein, R. P. Wülcker and H. Hecht (ed.), Bibliothek der angelsächsischen Prosa, 4, 2 vols (Leipzig, 1898).

SCHRÖER, [M. M.] A. (ed.), *Die angelsächsischen Prosabearbeitungen der Benedictinerregel*, C. M. Grein, W. R. P. Wülcker and H. Hecht (ed.), Bibliothek der angelsächsischen Prosa, 2 (Leipzig, 1885–8).

SCHUMACHER, K., *Germanendarstellungen*, Katalogue des Römisch-Germanischen Zentralmuseums zu Mainz, I (Mainz, 1935).

SCOTT, J. G., ' A glass linen smoother of Viking type from Kirkudbright', *Proceedings of the Society of Antiquaries of Scotland*, 88 (1954–6), pp. 226–7.

SCULL, C., 'Excavation and survey at Watchfield, Oxfordshire, 1983–92, *Archaeological Journal*, 149 (1992), pp. 124–281.

SCULL, C., review of H. Geake, *The Use of Grave-goods in Conversion-Period England, c. 600-c. 850*, British Archaeological Reports, British Series 261 (1997) in *Archaeological Journal*, 156 (1999), pp. 432–3.

SERJEANTSON, M., *A History of Foreign Words in English* (London, 1935).

SHEPHARD, J., 'Anglo-Saxon Barrows of the Later Sixth and Seventh Centuries AD', unpublished PhD thesis (University of Cambridge,1979).

SHEPPARD, T., 'An Anglo-Saxon grave in East Yorkshire and its contents', *The Antiquary*, 42 (1906), pp. 333–8.

SHERLOCK, S. J. and WELCH, M. G., *An Anglo-Saxon Cemetery at Norton, Cleveland* (London, 1992).

SHETELIG, H., and FALK, H. S., *Scandinavian Archaeology*, trans. E. V. Gordon (Oxford, 1937).

SINGER, C., HOLMYARD, E. J., HALL, A. R. and WILLIAMS, T. F., *A History of Technology*, 7 vols (Oxford, 1956–78).

SKEAT, W. W. (ed.), *The Holy Gospels in Anglo-Saxon, Northumbrian and Old Mercian Versions* (Cambridge, 1871–87).

SKEAT, W. W., *Aelfric's Lives of Saints*, 3 vols, Early English Text Society, original series, 76, 82, 94, 114 (1881–1900, reprinted as two volumes, Oxford, 1966).

SKLUTE, L. J., '*Freoðuwebbe* in Old English poetry', in H. Damico and A. H. Olsen (ed.), *New Readings on Women in Old English Literature* (Bloomington and Indianapolis, IN, 1990), pp. 204–10.

SMALL, A., THOMAS, G. and WILSON, D. M., *St Ninian's Isle and its*

Treasure, Aberdeen University Studies No. 152 (Oxford, 1973).

SMEDLEY, N. and OWLES, E., ' Some Anglo-Saxon "animal" brooches, *Proceedings of the Suffolk Institute of Archaeology*, 30 (1965), pp.166–74.

SMITH, A. H. (ed.), *Three Northumbrian Poems*, (London, corrected edition, 1968).

SMITH, C. R., *Collectanea Antiqua*, 7 vols (London, 1848–80).

SMITH, R. A., 'Anglo-Saxon remains', *Victoria County History, Berkshire*, 1 (London, 1906), pp. 229–49.

SMYSER, H. M., 'Ibn Fadlan's account of the Rus with some commentary and some allusions to Beowulf', in J. B. Bessinger Jr. and R. P. Creed (ed.), *Medieval and Linguistic studies in honour of Francis Peabody Magoun, Jr* (London, 1965), pp. 92–119.

SOUTER, A., *A Glossary of Later Latin to 600 A. D.* (Oxford, 1949).

SOUTHWORTH, E. (ed.), *Anglo-Saxon Cemeteries: a reappraisal* (Stroud, 1990).

SPEAKE, G., *Anglo-Saxon Animal Art and its Germanic Background* (Oxford, 1980).

SPEAKE, G., *A Saxon Bed Burial on Swallowcliffe Down*, Historic Buildings and Monuments Commission Archaeological Report No. 10 (London, 1989).

SPIES, N., *Ecclesiastical Pomp and Aristocratic Circumstance: a thousand years of brocaded tabletwoven bands* (Jarettsville, MD, 2000).

SPELMAN, J. (ed.), *Psalterium Davidis Latino-saxonicum Vetus* (London, 1640).

STANILAND, K., *Medieval Craftsmen: embroiderers* (London, 1991).

STEAD, I. M., 'Excavations at the south corner tower of the Roman fortress at York, 1956', *Yorkshire Archaeological Journal*, 39 (1956–8), pp. 515–38.

STEINMAYER, E., 'Lateinische und altenenglische Glossen', *Zeitschrift für deutsches Alterthum*, 33 (1889), pp. 242–51.

STENTON, F. M. (ed.), *The Bayeux Tapestry*, (London, 2nd ed., 1965).

STENTON, F. M., *Anglo-Saxon England*, The Oxford History of England, 2 (Oxford, 3rd ed., 1971).

STILBORG, O., 'A chronological analysis of Anglo-Saxon men's graves in England', in L. Jørgensen (ed.), *Chronological Studies of Anglo-Saxon England, Lombard Italy and Vendel Period Sweden*, University of Copenhagen Institute of Prehistoric and Classical Archaeology, Arkæologiske Skrifter, 5 (1992), pp. 35–45.

STOODLEY, N., *The Spindle and the Spear: a critical enquiry into the construction and meaning of gender in the early Anglo-Saxon burial rite*, British Archaeological Reports, British Series, 288 (1999).

STROEBE, L. L., *Die altenglischen Kleidernamen – eine kulturgeschichtlich-etymologische Untersuchung* (Heidelberg, 1904).

STRUTT, J., *Horda Angelcynnan*, 3 vols (London, 1775–6).

STRUTT, J., *A Complete View of the Dress and Habits of the People of England*, 2 vols (London, 1796–9).

STUBBS, W. (ed.), *William of Malmesbury De Gestis Regum Anglorum*, Rolls Series, 40, 2 vols (London, 1887–9).

SUZUKI, S., *The Quoit Brooch Style and Anglo-Saxon Settlement: a casting and recasting of cultural identity symbols* (Woodbridge, 2000).

SWANTON, M. J., 'An Anglian cemetery at Londesborough in East Yorkshire', *Yorkshire Archaeological Journal*, 41 (1963–6), pp. 262–86.

SWANTON, M., 'The "Dancer" on the Codford Cross', in S. C. Hawkes,

D. Brown and J. Campbell (ed.), *Anglo-Saxon Studies in Archaeology and History*, 1, British Archaeological Reports, British Series, 72 (1979), pp. 139–48.

SWEET, H. (ed.), *King Alfred's Version of Gregory's Pastoral Care*, Early English Text Society, original series, 45, 50 (London, 1871–2).

SWEET, H. (ed.), *The Oldest English Texts*, Early English Text Society, original series, 83 (London, 1885).

TALBOT-RICE, D., *English Art 871–1100* (Oxford, 1952).

TALBOT-RICE, D., *Byzantine Art* (Harmonsworth, revised and expanded, 1968).

TANGL, M. (ed.), *S. Bonifatii et Lulli Epistolae*, Monumenta Germaniae Historica, Epistolae 4, Epistolae Selectae, 1 (Berlin, 1916).

TAYLOR, A., DUHIG, C. and HINES, J., 'An Anglo-Saxon cemetery at Oakington, Cambridgeshire', *Proceedings of the Cambridge Antiquarian Society*, 86 (1997), pp. 57–90.

TAYLOR, S. (ed.), *MS B*, The Anglo-Saxon Chronicle, a collaborative edition, 4 (1983).

TEMPLE, E., *Anglo-Saxon Manuscripts 900–1066*, A Survey of Manuscripts Illuminated in the British Isles, 2 (London, 1976).

THOMAS, G. W., 'On excavations in an Anglo-Saxon cemetery at Sleaford in Lincolnshire', *Archaeologia*, 50 (1887), pp. 383–406.

THOMPSON, F. H., 'Anglo-Saxon sites in Lincolnshire: unpublished material and recent discoveries', *Antiquaries Journal*, 36 (1956), pp. 181–99.

THOMSON, H. J. (trans.), *Prudentius*, Loeb Classical Library, 2 vols (London, 1949–53).

THORNTON, J. H., 'Shoes, boots and shoe repairs', in M. Biddle (ed.), *Winchester Studies*, 7.ii: Artefacts from Medieval Winchester, ii: Object and Economy in Medieval Winchester (Oxford, 1990), pp. 591–621.

THORNTON, J. H. and GOODFELLOW, A. V., 'Leather shoes', in I. M. Stead, 'Excavations at the south corner tower of the Roman fortress at York, 1956', *Yorkshire Archaeological Journal*, 39 (1956–8), pp. 525–30.

THORPE, B. (ed.), *Ancient Laws and Institutes of England* (London, 1840).

THORPE, B. (ed.), *The Homilies of the Anglo-Saxon Church*, 2 vols (London, 1844–6).

THORPE, L. (trans.), *Einhard and Notker the Stammerer Two Lives of Charlemagne* (Harmondsworth, 1969).

TIMBY, J. R., *The Anglo-Saxon Cemetery at Empingham II, Rutland: excavations carried out between 1974 and 1975*, Oxbow Monograph 70 (Oxford, 1996).

TOLKIEN, J. R. R. (ed.), *Ancrene Wisse*, Early English Text Society, original series, 249 (1962).

TREHARNE, E. M., 'A unique Old English formula for excommunication from Cambridge, Corpus Christi College 303', *Anglo-Saxon England*, 24 (1995), pp. 185–211.

TRUMAN, N., *Historic Costuming* (London, 1936).

TWEDDLE, D., *The Anglian Helmet from 16–22 Coppergate*, The Archaeology of York, 17.8 The Small Finds (1992).

TWEDDLE, D, BIDDLE, M. and KJØLBYE-BIDDLE, B., *Corpus of Anglo-Saxon Stone Sculpture*, 4, *South East England* (Oxford, 1995).

TYLER, E. M. (ed.), *Treasure in the Medieval West* (York, 2000).

TYLER, E. M., '"When wings incarnadine with gold are spread": The

Vita Ædwardi Regis and the display of treasure at the court of Edward the Confessor', in E. M. Tyler (ed.), *Treasure in the Medieval West* (York, 2000), pp. 83–107.

UNIVERSITY OF DELAWARE, *Old English Concordance* microfiche (Delaware, 1980).

VAN ES, W. A. and YPEY, J., 'Das Grab der "Prinzessin" von Zweeloo und seine Bedeutung im Rahmen des Gräberfeldes', in H.-J. Hässler (ed.), *Studien zur Sachsenforschung (Festschrift A. Genrich)* (Hildesheim, 1977), pp. 97–126.

VAN GIFFEN, A. E., 'Mededeeling omtrent her systematisch onderzoek, verricht in de jaren 1928, 1929 en 1930', *Jaarverslag van de Vereeniging voor Terpenonderzoek*, 13–15 (1929–31), pp. 16–46.

VIERCK, H., 'Trachtenkunde und trachtengeschichte in der Sachsen-Forschung, ihre Quellen, Ziele und Methoden'; 'Die anglische Frauentracht'; 'Zur angelsachsischen Frauentracht'; 'Zur seegermanischen Mannertracht'; 'Religion, Rang und Herrschaft im Spiegel der Tracht'; and 'Von der Trachtenprovinz zur bevolkerungs-geschichtlichen Ausage', in C. Ahrens (ed.) *Sachsen und Angelsachsen* (Hamburg, 1979), pp. 231–43; 245–53; 255–62; 263–70; 271–83; 285–93.

VIERCK, H., 'La "Chemise de Sainte-Bathilde" à Chelles et l'influence byzantine sur l'art de cour mérovingien au VIIe siècle', in É. Chirol (ed.), *Actes du colloque international d'archéologie, Rouen 3–4–5 Juillet 1975 (Centenaire de l'abbé Cochet)* (Rouen, 1978), pp. 521–64.

VON ERHARDT-SIEBOLD, E., 'The Old English "Loom Riddles"', in T. A. Kirby and H. B. Woolf (ed.), *Malone Anniversary Studies, Philologica* (Baltimore, 1949), pp. 9–17.

WAITZ, G. (ed.), *Pauli Historia Langobardorum*, Monumenta Germaniae Historica, Script. Rer. Germ., 48 (Hanover, 1878).

WALLACE-HADRILL, J. M., *The Long-haired Kings and Other Studies in Frankish History* (London, 1962).

WALTERS, H. B., *Catalogue of the Greek and Roman Lamps in the British Museum* (London, 1914).

WALTON, P. [later WALTON ROGERS, P.], 'A silk cap from Coppergate', *Interim [Bulletin of the York Archaeological Trust]*, 7.2 (1980), pp. 3–5.

WALTON, P., 'Old sock', *Interim [Bulletin of the York Archaeological Trust]*, 8.2 (1982), pp. 3–5.

WALTON, P. *Textiles, Cordage and Raw Fibre from 16–22 Coppergate*, The Archaeology of York, 17.5 (London, 1989).

WALTON, P., 'Textile production at Coppergate, York: Anglo-Saxon or Viking?', in P. Walton and J.-P. Wild (ed.), *Textiles in Northern Archae-ology, NESAT III*: Textile Symposium in York 6–9 May 1987, North European Symposium for Archaeological Textiles Monograph 3 (London, 1990), pp. 61–72.

WALTON, P., 'Dyes and wools in textiles from Mammen (Bjerringhøj), Denmark', in M. Iversen (ed.), *Mammen: grav, kunst og samfund i vikingetid*, Jysk Arkæologisk Selskabs Skrifter 28 (Aarhus, 1991), pp. 139–43.

WALTON, P. and WILD, J.-P. (ed.), *Textiles in Northern Archaeology, NESAT III*: Textile Symposium in York 6–9 May 1987, North European Symposium for Archaeological Textiles Monograph 3 (London, 1990).

WALTON ROGERS, P., 'Textile remains', in S. J. Sherlock and M. G. Welch, *An Anglo-Saxon Cemetery at Norton, Cleveland* (London, 1992), pp. 57–61.

WALTON ROGERS, P., *Textile Production at 16–22 Coppergate*, The Archaeology of York, 17.11 (1997).

WALTON ROGERS, P., 'Textiles and clothing', in G. Drinkall and M. Foreman, *The Anglo-Saxon Cemetery at Castledyke South, Barton-on-Humber*, Sheffield Excavation Reports 6 (Sheffield, 1998), pp. 274–9 and microfiche Mf. 2.B13-C12.

WALTON ROGERS, P., 'Identification of dye on Middle Saxon pottery from Christ Church College', *Canterbury's Archaeology 1996–7* (21st annual report) (1999), p. 36.

WALTON ROGERS, P., 'Stone spindle whorls', in A. J. Mainman and N. S. H. Rogers, *Craft, Industry and Everyday Life: finds from Anglo-Scandinavian York*, The Archaeology of York, 17.14 (2000), pp. 2530–1.

WALTON ROGERS, P., 'The re-appearance of an old Roman loom in medieval England', in P. Walton Rogers, L. Bender Jørgensen and A. Rast-Eicher (ed.), *The Roman Textile Industry and its Influence; a birthday tribute to John Peter Wild* (London, 2001), pp. 158–71.

WALTON ROGERS, P., BENDER JØRGENSEN, L. and RAST-EICHER, A. (ed.), *The Roman Textile Industry and its Influence; a birthday tribute to John Peter Wild* (London, 2001).

WARHURST, A., 'The Jutish cemetery at Lyminge', *Archaologia Cantiana*, 69 (1955), pp. 1–40.

WARREN, J., Untitled, *Journal of the British Archaeological Association*, 1st series, 27 (1871), pp. 258–9.

WATSON, J., 'Organic material associated with the metalwork', in T. Malim and J. Hines, *The Anglo-Saxon Cemetery at Edix Hill (Barrington A), Cambridgeshire*, Council for British Archaeology Research Report, 112 (1998) pp. 230–5.

WATSON, J. and EDWARDS, G., 'Conservation of material from Anglo-Saxon cemeteries', in E. Southworth (ed.), *Anglo-Saxon Cemeteries: a reappraisal* (Stroud, 1990), pp. 97–106.

WEBSTER, L. and BACKHOUSE, J. (ed.), *The Making of England: Anglo-Saxon Art and Culture AD 600–900*, British Museum Exhibition Catalogue (London, 1991).

WELCH, M. (ed.), Margaret Guido, *The Glass Beads of Anglo-Saxon England c.AD 400–700*, (Woodbridge, 1999).

WELLS, C., *Bones, Bodies and Disease* (London, 1964).

WELLS, C., 'Report on the human remains from Little Eriswell', Appendix II in P. Hutchinson, 'The Anglo-Saxon cemetery at Little Eriswell, Suffolk', *Proceedings of the Cambridge Antiquarian Society*, 49 (1966), p. 24.

WERNER, J., 'Frankish royal tombs in the Cathedrals of Cologne and Saint-Denis', *Antiquity*, 38 (1964), pp. 201–16.

WEST, S. E., 'The Anglo-Saxon village of West Stow', *Medieval Archaeology*, 13 (1969), pp. 1–20.

WHEELER, A. L., *Ovid in six volumes VI Tristia; Ex Ponto*, second ed., revised G. P. Goold, Loeb Classical Library (Cambridge MA and London, 1938).

WHITE, R., *Roman and Celtic Objects from Anglo-Saxon Graves*, British Archaeological Reports, British Series, 191 (Oxford, 1988).

WHITE, R., 'Scrap or substitute: Roman material in Anglo-Saxon graves', in E. Southworth (ed.), *Anglo-Saxon Cemeteries: a reappraisal* (Stroud, 1990), pp. 125–52.

WHITELOCK, D., *Anglo-Saxon Wills* (Cambridge, 1930).

WHITELOCK, D. (ed.), *English Historical Documents c. 500–1042* (London and Oxford, 1955, 2nd edition, 1979).

WHITELOCK, D., KER, N. and RENNELL, Lord, *The Will of Aethelgifu* (London, 1968).

WHITING, M. C., 'Dye analysis', Appendix 2 to E. Crowfoot, 'The Textiles', in R. L. S. Bruce-Mitford (ed.), *The Sutton Hoo Ship Burial*, 3, ed. A. Care Evans (London, 1983), i, p. 465.

WHITING, W. and STEBBING, W. P. D., 'Jutish cemetery near Finglesham, Kent', *Archaeologia Cantiana*, 41 (1929), pp. 113–25.

WICKHAM-CROWLEY, K. M., 'Looking forward, looking back: excavating the field of Anglo-Saxon archaeology', in C. E. Karkov (ed.), *The Archaeology of Anglo-Saxon England: basic readings*, Basic Readings in Anglo-Saxon England, 7 (New York and London, 1999), pp. 1–23.

WILD, J. P., 'Clothing in the north-west provinces of the Roman Empire', *Bonner Jahrbucher*, 158 (1968), pp. 166–240.

WILD, J. P., *Textile Manufacture in the Northern Roman Provinces* (Cambridge, 1970).

WILD, J. P., 'Some new light on Roman textiles', in L. Bender Jørgensen and K. Tidow (ed.), *Textilsymposium Neumünster:Archäologische textilfunde: 6.5–7.5. 1981 (NESAT I)* (Neumünster, 1982), pp. 10–24.

WILD, J. P., Introduction to Part I, 'General Introduction', in D. Jenkins (ed.), *The Cambridge History of Western Textiles*, 2 vols, (Cambridge, 2003), pp. 9–25.

WILKINSON, T. J. (ed.), *Archaeology and Environment in South Essex: rescue archaeology along the Grays by-pass, 1979–80*, East Anglian Archaeology, 42 (1988).

WILMART, A. (ed.), 'La Légende de Sta Édith en prose et vers par le moine Goscelin', *Analecta Bollandiana*, 56 (1938), pp. 4–101, 265–307.

WILSON, D. M., 'The initial excavation of an Anglo-Saxon cemetery at Melbourn, Cambridgeshire', *Proceedings of the Cambridge Antiquarian Society*, 49 (1956), pp. 29–41.

WILSON, D. M., *Anglo-Saxon Ornamental Metalwork 700–1000 in the British Museum* (London, 1964).

WILSON, D. M., 'A ring of Queen Arnegunde', *Germania*, 42 (1964), pp. 265–8.

WILSON, D. M., 'The Vikings' relationship with Christianity in Northern England', *Journal of the British Archaeological Association*, 3rd series, 30 (1967), pp. 37–46.

WILSON, D. M., *The Anglo-Saxons* (revised edition, Harmondsworth, 1971).

WILSON, D. M., 'The Bronze Ornament (Fig. 11 and Plate VI)', Appendix 3 to J. May, 'Romano-British and Saxon sites near Dorchester, Oxon.', *Oxoniensia*, 42 (1977). pp.73–5.

WILSON, D. M. (ed.), *The Archaeology of Anglo-Saxon England* (London, 1976).

WILSON, D. M. (ed.), *The Northern World: the history and heritage of northern Europe AD 400–1100* (London, 1980).

WILSON, D. M., *The Bayeux Tapestry* (London, 1985).

WILSON, P. R., CARDWELL, P., CRAMP, R. J. , EVANS, J., TAYLOR-WILSON, R. H., THOMPSON, A. and WACHER, J. S.,'Early Anglian Catterick and *Catraeth*', [including contributions from E.

Crowfoot] *Medieval Archaeology*, 40 (1996), pp. 1–61.

WINTERBOTTOM, M. (ed. and trans.), *Gildas The Ruin of Britain and Other Works* (London and Chichester, 1978).

WOBST, H. M., 'Stylistic behaviour and information exchange', *Anthropological Papers* (University of Michigan), 61, 1977, pp. 317–42.

WOOD, I., 'Before and after the migration to Britain', in J. Hines (ed.), *The Anglo-Saxons from the Migration Period to the Eighth Century; an ethnographic perspective*, Studies in Historical Archaeoethnology, 2 (Woodbridge, 1997), pp. 41–54.

WOOD, I., 'Conclusion: strategies of distinction' in W. Pohl with H. Reimitz (ed.), *Strategies of Distinction: the construction of ethnic communities, 300–800*, The Transformation of the Roman World, 2 (Leiden, 1998), pp. 297–303.

WOODRUFF, H., *The Illustrated Manuscripts of Prudentius* (Cambridge, MA, 1930).

WORMALD, F. 'Style and design', in F. M. Stenton (ed.), *The Bayeux Tapestry*, (London, 2nd ed. 1965), pp. 25–36.

WRIGHT, D. H. (ed.), *The Vespasian Psalter*, Early English Manuscripts in Facsimile, 14 (Copenhagen, 1967).

WRIGHT, J. (ed.), *The English Dialect Dictionary*, 6 vols (London, 1898–1905).

WRIGHT, T., 'Discoveries of Anglo-Saxon antiquities', *Journal of the British Archaeological Association*, 1st series, 2 (1847), pp. 50–9.

WRIGHT, T. (ed.), *Anglo-Saxon and Old English Vocabularies*, 2nd edition, ed. and collated by R. P. Wülcker, 2 vols (London, 1884, reprinted Darmstadt, 1968).

WYLIE, W. M., *Fairford Graves* (Oxford, 1852).

WYLIE, W. M., 'The graves of the Alemanni at Oberflacht in Suabia', *Archaeologia*, 36 (1855), 129–60.

YARWOOD, D., *English Costume* (London, 1952).

ZANDVOORT, R. W., 'The Leiden Riddle', *English and Germanic Studies*, 3 (1949–50), pp. 42–56.

ZELLER, G., 'Zum Wandel der Frauentracht vom 6. zum 7. Jahrhundert in Austrasien', in G. Kossak and G. Ulbert (ed.), *Studien zur vor- und frühgeschichtlichen Archäeologie, Festschrift für Joachim Werner zum 65 Geburtstag*, 2 vols (Munich, 1974), pp. 381–5.

ZUPITZA, J. (ed.), *Aelfrics Grammatik und Glossar* (Berlin, 1880).

ZUPITZA, J., 'Altenglische Glossen zu Abbos Clericorum decus', *Zeischrift für deutsches Alterthum*, 31 (1887), pp. 1–27.

Index

Names have been spelled according to F. M. Stenton, *Anglo-Saxon England*.

Names of countries and of English counties or unitary authorities are those currently in use. In some cases county names and boundaries have changed since sites were published and since the earlier edition of this book.

Bold type refers to figures *Bold italic type* refers to plates. Colour plates are identified by letter, black and white by numerals.